Human-Computer Interaction

Edited by

Iñaki Maurtua

Human-Computer Interaction,
Edited by Iñaki Maurtua

Published by InTech

Janeza Trdine 9, 51000 Rijeka, Croatia

2014 Edition

Additional hard copies can be obtained from orders@intechopen.com

Human-Computer Interaction,
Edited by Iñaki Maurtua
p. cm.
ISBN 978-953-307-022-3

Preface

In this book the reader will find a collection of 30 papers presenting different facets of Human Computer Interaction, the result of research projects and experiments as well as new approaches to design user interfaces. The book is organized according to the following main topics in a sequential order: new interaction paradigms, multimodality, usability studies on several interaction mechanisms, human factors, universal design and development methodologies and tools.

The editor would like to thank the authors the effort done in preparing this book, sharing with the research community their experience and expertise in this fascinating field.

Iñaki Maurtua

Contents

1

Context Awareness in Human-Computer Interaction

Jarmo Makkonen, Ivan Avdouevski, Riitta Kerminen and Ari Visa
Tampere University of Technology
Finland

1. Introduction

Since the development of the first computers in the middle of the twentieth century, their number and penetration into daily life has been increasing rapidly. However, not only has the number and computational power of computers been growing, but user - machine interaction paradigms have also developed and changed. From punch cards this evolution has slowly progressed to the third wave of computerization, ubiquitous computing.

The term *ubiquitous computing* was first used by Mark Weiser (1991) to describe the concept in which small cheap computers are integrated into most of the objects surrounding the user. The purpose of these devices is to assist users in their daily routines and perform automation of their environments. As examples, Weiser cites doors that open only to approved badge wearers, coffee machines that make coffee automatically when the user wakes up, and diaries that make notes on their own.

If users had to control all these devices using the traditional desktop human-machine interaction model, they would most probably find them annoying rather than helpful. This gives rise to the necessity for a completely new approach to the interaction. Weiser states that ubiquitous devices should provide their services semi-automatically, by sensing the environment, analyzing the situation and making a decision as to what functionalities should be offered to the user.

The surroundings of the device, relevant from the point of view of running an application, are often referred to by the term *context*. Devices able to adapt their functionality to changing surroundings are called context-aware devices. While few commercial applications exist to support the concept of context awareness, several prototypes have been introduced. However, more research is needed as the technology for recognizing context is not yet widely available, and many problems remain unsolved.

The purpose of this chapter is to provide an overview of the state-of-the-art in current context-awareness research and to argument for the increasing role of the concept in future human-computer interaction. Both applications and implementation issues are covered. In addition, the authors' findings and future research on the technology for context recognition are described. The authors of this chapter are researchers in the field, mainly studying activity recognition using wearable sensors. They address certain key problems associated with the use of the technology in mobile devices, such as power consumption and robustness.

The "Applications"-section provides a wide range of examples of applications that employ context-awareness. In the "Context recognition"-section, common approaches to the formulization of the context are described and techniques and devices used for recognition of the context are also presented. Finally, the "Main concerns"-section analyzes the concerns and major problems raised by new context-aware applications. The section also contains the description of the authors' work with information on future research.

2. Applications

2.1 Characteristics of context-aware applications

Early on, Schmidt et al. (1999) proposed three application domains that can benefit from context awareness: adaptive user interfaces that change according to the surrounding conditions, context-aware communication systems, and proactive application scheduling. Nowadays even more uses for the technology have been devised. This section discusses the use of the knowledge of context and the possible applications for the technologies that are used in context recognition. First, the characteristics of context-aware applications are described. Second, the major application fields are presented: home automation, work support systems for professional use, diary applications, mobile guides for free-time use, health care, abnormality detection, ubiquitous learning and advertising. Examples and the technologies used in each group of applications are given. Finally, there is a discussion of the use of the context recognition technology as an enhancer of HCI and as a new input modality is covered.

The need to determine the user's current context has emerged from the vision of ambient intelligence. Thus, the applications that use context information are mobile, ubiquitous services that offer the main benefits of context awareness: adaptation, personalization, and proactivity. Adaptation means that a system adjusts its behaviour according to the current context. A mobile phone can, for example, switch to silent mode when the user is at a meeting. Personalization means that a system adjusts its behaviour according to user preferences, habits, skills or tasks. For example, a shopping system can offer the user the products that are the most likely to be of interest. Proactivity means that the system can automatically act without user interaction and even anticipate future actions or contexts and act accordingly. (Pichler et al., 2004)

Dey and Abowd have another way of describing context aware applications: "A system is context-aware if it uses context to provide relevant information and/or services to the user, where relevancy depends on the user's task." They also state that the applications have three different main categories for the context-aware features. They are presentation of information and services to a user, automatic execution of a service, and tagging of context to information for later retrieval. This division is widely used in the literature for describing the functionalities of context-aware applications. The authors have also made an exhaustive survey of the different definitions related to context awareness. (Dey & Abowd, 2000b)

We have discussed user centric application design in our earlier work (Makkonen & Visa, 2007a). The idea was to make HCI more natural by considering the support of different human characteristics. Context awareness as such can enable this by increasing the amount of automation, memory support, and multimodality in the interaction.

Context-aware applications do not always contain all these characteristics. In fact, the utilization of all the possibilities that the concept enables is usually very limited. Many technical issues are yet to be solved before there is widespread adoption of context awareness, but eventually it will become more prevalent as cheaper and more energy-efficient sensors come to market.

2.2 Technology enhancing HCI

Enabling devices to act smartly and independently is possibly the most obvious use for context awareness. When a device or any smart object knows what is happening in its surroundings, it can make life easier for its user. Schmidt describes how context awareness can enhance HCI. Basic ways to help system output include finding a suitable time for user interruption, reducing the need for interruptions, and adjusting system output to match context. Conversely, the input can be helped by reducing the need for user input and making it easier by limiting input space, and adapting the input system to the context. (Schmidt, 2000)

An example of this kind of concept is a portable consumer device. A working example of a context aware mobile phone is SenSay, by Siewiorek et al. This uses light, motion and microphone sensors for determining the user context. Context in this case is restricted to determining if the user is engaged in physical activity, the level of the background noise and if the user is talking. Calendar entries of meetings etc. are also used. The phone has four states, according to which the ring sound volume and the vibration alarm are modified. For example, if the user is in a "do not disturb"-state, the phone sends an SMS to inform the caller. (Siewiorek et al., 2005)

Another growing field is home automation (also known as the "smart home") that increases automation of a normal home by using sensors and artificial intelligence. This attempts to make life easier for the residents, i.e. improve the usability of the home in various ways. This kind of system can control the heating or air conditioning, lights, curtains, audio and video devices, kitchen appliances, and even a sauna stove. Additionally, security related systems, like fire alarms and surveillance, can be linked to the system. The system detects the context of the home and the residents by using sensors, and then adapts itself accordingly. The system can also anticipate the future actions of the residents. The technology will become increasingly popular in the future. Its major drawback, however, is that the connected devices must utilize a common standard.

Moreover, context awareness can be thought of as an input modality when the system reacts to user actions on the basis of the context information. Salber et al. (2000) have addressed the topic. They state that multimodality refers to making explicit commands to a system and receiving output in multiple ways, whereas in context awareness the sensor input is done implicitly without explicit user commands. Feki et al. (2004) have also studied the issue and present a vision of how context awareness can be used along with multimodality to ensure more efficient update of functionality to user interface for people with disabilities.

An important point about context awareness is that it relates to many other technologies. The technology that enables us to recognize human physical activities and body movements, and thus enhances context recognition, can be used on its own to enhance HCI. Gesture recognition techniques often use data accelerometer sensors. Human hand gestures, for example, work as an effective input modality. Mäntylä et al. (2000) have tested an accelerometer-based system for hand gesture recognition for the use of a mobile device. The system can recognize some of the most common gestures that are made when using a mobile phone. For example, this enables automatic call reception when the phone is moved to the ear. Bui and Nguyen (2005) and Hernandez-Rebollar et al. (2002) have studied sign language recognition using accelerometer sensors placed on a special glove. Earlier, Lee and Xu (1996) have used HMMs for recognition of gestures of a sign language alphabet. Pylvänäinen (2005) has studied hand gesture recognition from accelerometer signals using a hidden Markov model (HMM). Mäntyjärvi et al. (2004) have designed a system for controlling a DVD-player using hand gestures. The system also uses accelerometers and a HMM. Darby et al. (2008) propose a HMM-based real-time activity recognition system for gaming using Vicon, an optical motion capture system, as the input sensor.

2.3 Healthcare

Healthcare systems that use context-aware computing are often used for ambulatory monitoring and remote-assisted rehabilitation. The health condition and physical activities of the patients can be monitored by using context recognition technology. By doing this, any alarming situations can be spotted. Preventive healthcare can also profit from the technology since tracking normal people's physical activities provides information on the amount of calories used and can act as a motivator for the user.

Tentori and Favela (2008) propose an activity-aware system for healthcare use. The system tracks the activities of hospital staff and assists their work by giving information on the status of the patient. The system also reports on other situations such as whether the patient has taken medication. Jovanov et al. (2005) introduce a wireless body area network (WBAN) based telemedicine system for ambulatory monitoring and remote-assisted rehabilitation. Many different sensors are used to monitor the patient's condition. Sherrill et al. (2005) have used activity recognition for monitoring motor activities of patients undergoing pulmonary rehabilitation. The authors state that the application would help clinicians and optimize the exercise capacity of patients.

Another type of applications that relates to activity monitoring and healthcare is abnormality detection. By tracking any activity over a prolonged period, it is possible to detect behavioral patterns and gain a good idea of what is normal. Thus, abnormal or undesirable can be detected or even anticipated and thus prevented. Industrial applications have used such monitoring for a long time in applications such as monitoring processes in a chemical plant. Yin et al. (2008) have studied abnormality detection using data from body-worn sensors. They state that the approach can be applied in security monitoring for identifying terrorist activities, and also in healthcare to detect signs of serious illness.

2.4 Diaries and memory support by tagging

Diary applications exploit tagging of context information to different time-related events. When a picture is taken with a camera, the device can get the context information automatically and store it as a tag for the picture. The information in this case can include who took the picture, and where was it taken. Mani and Sundaram (2006) use context awareness for media retrieval. They use context information for tagging and locating the most relevant photographs.

Such an approach can be useful in a wide variety of diary applications. Schweer and Hinze (2007) use context awareness this way for augmenting the user's memory. The idea is that human memory links the context of the situation to the memory, and thus the memories can be restored. In a similar manner, Dey and Abowd (2000a) propose a system that attaches context information to a reminder note in order to remind the user in an appropriate situation. It is useful if a reminder is activated just as it is needed such as, when you are leaving the house and you have to remember to take something with you. However, this kind of reminder and calendar would have to be created by hand. It would be useful if a system could learn the user's normal routines and act accordingly. TRAcME is an activity recognition system for a mobile phone by Choujaa and Dulay (2008). The system can recognize generic human activities, and learns the patterns of the user's habits.

2.5 Mobile guides

Mobile guidance systems and manuals are applications that offer the user information via a mobile device, normally a PDA or a mobile phone. Examples of such systems are mobile tourist guides. The guides can propose sights and services like restaurants based on the user context. They enable the user to get information on interesting sights and services easily, without the effort of searching.

It is important to consider user preferences and the history of previously visited sights and services to avoid repeatedly recommending the same ones. Moreover, the applications need to get the information somehow. It is obvious that this cannot be provided by the same provider as the application, but by the sights and services themselves. Another potential source of information are the experiences and suggestions of other travelers. This can be seen in several travel websites, like TripAdvisor.com, that is used by a great number of people. This kind of information is called consumer generated content (CGC). Overall, this kind of applications seems to a lot of potential for the application of context awareness.

Schwinger et al. have made a review of mobile tourist guides that utilize context recognition. Almost all applications presented in their paper use only user location and profile. The authors state that the main drawbacks of the systems are the lack of consideration of tourism as a social activity and time as context information. Moreover, only some applications use automatic context delivery. (Schwinger et al., 2008)

2.6 Advertising

A good advertisement is shown at the right time, to the right person, and in the right way. "Shown" in fact is not a good way to express this, because the advertisement can exploit several human senses by using multiple modalities. Using different smells is an example of this. Context awareness can address all these requirements, and it would be surprising if advertising companies did not show a keen interest in it. According to Neumann (2008), "Context awareness technology, based on the clues from a consumer's surroundings, can help you deliver your message to your target audience in a much more personalized and valuable way".

What would it be like if your mobile phone knew that you are hungry, or going to be hungry soon? The device could then suggest, for example a nearby restaurant suited to your personal taste and preferences. It could even show you the menu and possibly recommend some of your favorite dishes. This would be of great interest to advertisement companies. Today, of course, such information is not available as the mobile phone cannot read our minds. However, the device could learn the user's habits by registering how often and at what time the person eats. By using artificial intelligence methods, it is possible to gain clues about what is likely to happen next, and act accordingly.

Personalization and user profiles are commonly used means for doing this. Uhlmann and Lugmayr state that although numerous user profiling methods exist, they are mostly scattered among many different internet shops and services. Thus, each service has its own profile for the same user. The authors stress the need for a way to create a single mobile profile that does not depend on the internet, nor is limited to web-based services. Instead, the profile could be used in traditional shopping, too. As an example, they mention that several internet music stores gather users' musical tastes to profiles. This profile could well be used in traditional record stores, too, because the taste is the same and only the shop is different. (Uhlmann & Lugmayr, 2008)

Aalto et al. propose a location-aware system that delivers advertisements to a mobile device when the user location is near a shop. This is called proximity-triggered mobile advertising. The authors state that location information as such is not sufficient, but that personalization is necessary to be able to deliver the advertisements without causing annoyance (Aalto et al., 2004). Bluetooth is used for getting the location information. Rashid et al. (2008) propose a system with a similar approach. Mahmoud (2006) uses time, location, and user preferences as the context information for addressing advertisements to mobile devices. de Castro and Shimakawa (2006) use user location and interests as context information in a similar system.

2.7 Work assistance

Work assistance applications aim to support a worker to do a job better. They help by showing how the work is performed and by giving a reminder of the correct order of the working phases. They can also support learning. The applications can be, for example, workshop or maintenance assistance systems. In our previous work (Makkonen & Visa, 2007b) we have developed and tested a mobile assembly support application. The purpose of the application was to guide the worker through an assembly of a grid-anode for a corrosion prevention system. The application used a conventional hypertext-based user interface without any automatic functionality. The tests showed that due to awkward working conditions, the user interface was inconvenient. On the other hand, if context-awareness was used, it would be possible to determine which work phase is underway and to monitor the work quality. Quality-critical tasks in particular should profit from the approach.

Current applications in the field are specific for the task in hand and employ special techniques for determining the work context. This usually involves sound since different tools make distinct noises, and employ RFID tags mounted in parts in assembly tasks to recognize them. Therefore the solutions are usually not generalizable. Lukowicz et al. (2004) propose a system that attempts to segment and recognize user gestures in a workshop environment by using microphones and accelerometers. This could be used for reducing the cognitive load on the user and providing assistance. Stiefmeier et al. (2008) detect the steps in assembling a car part by using a finite state machine.

Tähti et al. (2004) have presented a context-aware mobile application for supporting work in an office-type environment. The application combines automation (by adjusting the device settings according to the context at hand) with tagging (reminders, documents related to meetings etc.) and service browsing (finds services that are available in the current context).

2.8 Ubiquitous context-aware learning

Ubiquitous learning tries to bring the learning environment to wherever the user may be and enables the learning to take place any time. Moreover, context awareness enables the learning to relate to the current situation or to nearby objects. Therefore, the learning can be more efficient than in a permanent classroom environment. The idea uses tagging - and, unlike in diary applications, time is not the main issue for the context, but rather the objects and the topics to be learnt.

According to Schmidt, context awareness can be utilized for deciding what, when, and how the learning resources are delivered to the learning user. The simplest way to do this is to select the most appropriate resources for the learner and the situation at hand. The challenges of such systems are that context is hard to identify, and that the time at which the resources are delivered has to be well-defined to avoid causing annoyance to the user. (Schmidt, 2005)

Ogata and Yano (2004) have tested a system for learning polite expressions in Japanese using a context aware system. They use the learner's profile (age, gender, occupation etc.), other people's profiles and the current environment as the context information, which determines the appropriate expressions to be used in each situation. According to the authors, the system proved to be very useful in tests. Similar approaches are proposed by Hsieh et al. (2007) and Chu and Liu (2007). Both use context-awareness for enhancing the learning of English. Jeong and Lee (2007) propose methodologies for implementing learning systems that use context awareness.

Context awareness is also used in less obvious fields. Doyle et al. (2002) propose a method for using context awareness for interactive story telling. The user is "in the story" and can interact with the story world by performing actions such as walking to affect the plot of the story.

3. Context recognition

Context recognition is a challenging task. The most problematic issue is the impossibility defining a fixed set of factors that should be determined to categorize the context. In the first work to introduce the term *context-awareness,* Schilit and Theimer (1994) use the term *context* to refer to the location of the entity. Later, however, Day and Abowd (2000b) extended the meaning to include any relevant information to characterize the situation of the entity. They proposed that a context can be seen as a combination of four context types: *Identity, Time, Location* and *Activity*. This context model was later enlarged by Zimmermann et al. (2007) to include an additional context type called *Relations.*

Identity specifies personal user information like contact list, age, phone numbers etc. *Time,* in addition to its intuitive meaning, can utilize overlay models to depict events like working hours, holidays, days of the week and so on. *Location* refers either to geographical location, like longitude and latitude or to symbolic location such as at home, in the shop or at work. *Activity* relates to what is occurring in the situation. It concerns both the activity of the entity itself as well as activities in the surroundings of the entity. Finally, *Relations* are used to define dependencies between different entities. *Relations* describe whether the entity is a part of a greater whole and how it can be used in the functionality of some other entities.

Acquisition of *Time* and *Identity* does not require any sophisticated techniques, but can be achieved using regular user profiles and hardware clock. Automatic methods for recognition of *Relations* have not so far been investigated. Therefore, this chapter concentrates on methods that can be used to determine *Activity* and *Location* context types. A range of established techniques based on machine learning and positioning is available for the recognition task.

3.1 Location recognition and positioning

GNSS-based methods

The most widely used methods for outdoor positioning are based on GNSS (Global Navigation Satellite Systems). Currently GPS (Global Positioning System) and DGPS (Differential Global Positioning System) are the predominant GNSS solutions. GPS provides accuracy of within a few meters depending on the number of visible satellites and their geometric orientation in relation to receiver.

GNSS positioning is based on the so called *trilateration* method. This method can determine the exact location of an unknown single point, when the locations of three known points and the distances between the known points and the unknown point are given. The distances between satellites and receiver are determined using the time difference between signal transmission and receive time. One additional satellite is required to overcome problems caused by unsynchronized satellite and receiver clocks. This means that GPS require at least four visible satellites to perform positioning. The positioning precision of GPS is about 20 meters.

GPS accuracy can be increased to a few centimeters using DGPS methods, but requires additional infrastructure. The drawback of the GPS - based positioning is a setting-up time of about half a minute when the receiver is turned on. However, this problem can be overcome using A-GPS (Assisted GPS) method. In A-GPS, a cellular network can be used to send initialization parameters to the GPS receiver to decrease the setting-up time and improve accuracy.

The major disadvantage of the GNSS based positioning systems is the requirement to have satellites in the line-of-sight of the receiver. This constraint means that utilization of GNSS receivers is impossible indoors or in narrow canyons.

Cellular network -based methods
Another approach is to obtain position from existing cellular networks. The fact that most of the currently used mobile computing devices are cellular mobile phones, make this concept particularly attractive. Consequently, positioning methods for the third generation of cellular networks (3G) are a research area receiving a lot of attention.

Four different positioning methods are included into 3GPP standard. The simplest method is to estimate the position of the mobile device relying on serving cell (the so called cell ID-based method). The wide variation in cell size (100m-35km) results in the poor positioning accuracy achieved using this method. The accuracy can be improved using other relevant information, like distance from the base station. The distance, in its turn, can be assessed using signal travelling time from mobile to base station and back to mobile (Round-Trip-Time).

Another method called OTDOA-IPDL (Observed Time Difference of Arrival - Idle Period Downlink) uses the geographical locations of several base stations serving adjacent cells. The relational distances to these base stations are determined using time of arrivals of special communication signals sent from base stations. Optionally, special communication signals can be sent from the mobile device to the base stations. In this case, position is calculated using the hardware installed in the network, which can determine position of any mobile phone irrespective of its type. This U-TDOA (Uplink - Time Difference of Arrival) method is highly attractive for positioning mobiles during emergency calls. Methods based on time difference of arrival provide accuracy of the order of few hundred meters.

Finally, A-GPS method already mentioned among the GNSS based methods is standardized to be used with UMTS. This method assumes that a GPS receiver is integrated into the user's mobile device and initialization parameters are sent through the UMTS network.

Methods based on signal strength or the travel times of the signal suffer from multipath effects. In urban areas signals hardly ever propagate from base station to mobile device along line-of-site route. This leads to poor positioning accuracy. To overcome this problem methods based on so-called *fingerprinting* have been introduced (Laitinen et al., 2001). First, the area, in which positioning is to occur, is divided into small sectors. In each sector a special information sample is taken and stored to a data base. The type of sample depends on the cellular system; for example, in UMTS the sample is a power delay profile of the sector (Ahonen & Laitinen, 2003). Later, when positioning takes place, the device performs similar measurements and seeks the data base from the most similar sample. The location, from which, the similar sample was taken is assumed to be the current position of the mobile device. The accuracy of this method is about 100 meters.

The benefit of cellular networks-based positioning methods is the possibility to use them in mobile phones without the need of additional hardware. However, their accuracy is significantly lower than that of GPS. Positioning methods based on cellular network can be used indoors, but problems of multipath-propagation decrease the accuracy there even further.

WLAN-based methods
The accuracy provided by cellular networks of 100 meters at best is usually not sufficient for indoor positioning. Therefore, use of Wireless Local Area Network (WLAN) networks, which usually have much smaller coverage, could be desirable. There are no positioning standards for WLAN technology, but some commercial realizations are available (e.g. Ekahau RTLS). Methods for WLAN positioning are very similar to those used in cellular networks. Positioning can be done either by using trilateration and received signal strength as a measure of relative distance between receiver and base station (Kotanen et al., 2003) or by using database correlation methods (Saha et al., 2003).

Proximity detection
Often information on proximately located resources is more important than exact geographical location. In such cases range of proximity detection solutions are available. Radio Frequency Identification (RFID) system consists of readers and tags. The reader device sends electromagnetic waves that are captured by a tag antenna. Transmitted electromagnetic radiation induces power into the tag microchip circuit and is used to send digital data stored in the tag back to the transmitter. In the case of passive RFID tags, only the reader energy is used to operate the tag. In the active RFID, the tag has its own energy source and electromagnetic radiation of the reader is used only to turn the tag into active mode.

Another approach for proximity detection is utilization of IR-beacons (Butz et al., 2000). The disadvantage of this technology is line-of-sight requirement, which means that the mobile device cannot be positioned if it is in the pocket or if the IR (Infra Red) receiver is not directed towards the light source. Other possibilities are utilization of Wireless PAN (Personal Area Network) communication equipment such as Bluetooth and ZigBee. These technologies are specified in IEEE 802.15 standard.

3.2 Activity Recognition Devices
According to the context definition of Dey and Abowd (2000b) activity context type is seen as referring to everything that answers the question of what is occurring in the situation. With regard to personal mobile computing devices such as mobile phones, this context type can be divided into two separate parts to simplify analysis: user activity and environmental activity. The present section demonstrates the measurement devices that can be used for monitoring these two context elements.

Environmental Activity Monitoring

Currently available mobile devices can already have several measurement devices capable of environmental monitoring like temperature sensor and photodiode. In this section these and some other sensors, introduced in the current research for environmental sensing related to context-awareness, will be described.

One device indispensible in any mobile phone is the microphone. Therefore, it received much attention from researchers in the field. In their work Korpipää et al. (2003) have used the microphone to recognize events such as speech, music, car and elevator. In another work Siewiorek et al. (2005) use the microphone as one of the context sources that can be used to update profiles of a mobile phone automatically.

In the two works mentioned above, the microphone was used in combination with other sensors to determine various environmental activities. In work by Clarkson et al. (1998) a microphone was used on its own in developing a Nomadic Radio application. In this work they introduce Auditory Scene Analysis (ASA) system, which divides an auditory scene into two layers. In the first layer single sound objects (speech, car, telephone ring) were detected and then, in the second layer of the ASA, the sequences and simultaneous occurrences of these objects were used to detect sound scenes (office, street, super market). Layered activity recognition architectures are discussed in greater detail later in this chapter in the section "Recognition Architectures".

Schmidt et al. (1999) have introduced integration of photodiode into PDA (Portable Digital Assistant) for automatic control of the backlight of the display. Currently, this technology is widely used in several smart phone devices. In addition to the light intensity, photo-diodes and other optical sensors (like IR and UV sensors) can be used to distinguish the quality of the light. Spectral properties of the illumination can be used to distinguish artificial light sources from daylight and possibly to make a distinction among different indoor spaces (Mäntyjärvi, 2003).

Multiple optical sensors can be combined to enrich the information acquired from the environmental lightning. Optical sensors on different sides of the device can be used to determine if the device is placed on a surface or held by the user. In addition, the difference between direct and indirect lighting can be detected (Schmidt, 2002).

The video camera is a standard device in mobile phones and thus should be considered within the scope of context recognition. The camera has all of the capabilities of an optical sensor described above. Additionally, it can be used to detect commonly used routs and places visited as Clarkson (2003) and Aoki et al. (1999) have shown. These research groups investigated sequences of pictures taken by camera. Repetitive patterns were used for indoor navigation or detection of places visited before. The drawback of the camera is significant computational power demand and therefore higher energy consumption, which is an important issue in the area of mobile computing.

Finally, sensors capable of monitoring humidity, temperature and air pressure can be integrated into mobile phone as well. Use of these sensors was discussed by Schmidt (2002).

Temperature can be used to determine if the mobile device is indoors. However, while low temperatures of -10^{0}C show that the device is most probably outdoors, high temperatures (e.g. +200C) do not rule out the possibility of it being indoors. In the same work Schmidt suggests that a humidity sensor can be used for weather monitoring and tracking of transitions from one space to another. Similarly, an air pressure sensor in can be used to detect the altitude of the device.

User Activity Monitoring

Accurate user activity recognition is as important as recognition of all the other context elements. In current research, wide range of different measurement devices has been introduced for user activity monitoring. However, it should be noted that in addition to the measurements provided by sensors, regular operations of the mobile device are an extensive source of user activity analysis. For example, calendar entries can be used to determine the availability of the user (Siewiorek et al., 2003).

An accelerometer is standard equipment in several mobile phone models (e.g. Nokia N95 and iPhone) and currently it is used for automatic picture rotation and as a control mechanism in certain games and interactive applications. Extensive research has been conducted into the capabilities of the accelerometer in the area of the user activity recognition.

Researchers have succeeded in determining a high number of different physical activities using accelerometers spread over the body of a user. Previous studies (Bao & Intille, 2004) have shown that two accelerometers mounted on the wrist and on the thigh are enough for accurate recognition of twenty different everyday activities like walking, sitting, working on computer, eating, watching TV, riding an elevator etc. In addition to dynamic motion measurements, three orthogonally mounted accelerometers are capable of determining the direction of the gravitation force and in this way estimate the orientation of the device (Bouten et al., 1997).

Detection of whether the device is held by the user is important information. It can be used to optimize the power consumption by turning the device to sleep mode when the user is not interacting with it. This information can be acquired using touch sensor. Realization of a touch sensor in practice has been achieved by Hinckley and Sinclair (1999). In this study the touch sensor was installed on a mouse and was used to improve the usability of an office application. Toolbars of the application were hidden when the user was not touching the mouse. This way, the part of the window reserved for text was increased and usability improved.

Physiological sensors are measurement devices capable of monitoring different mechanical, physical, and biochemical functions of living organisms. Several studies have examined the utilization of these sensors in the area of context recognition (Schmidt 2002, Krause et al. 2003, Pärkkä et al., 2006). The most popular physiological sensors are probably those capable of heart rate and pulse monitoring. These devices can be used to determine the physical and psychological load of the user. Another way of monitoring variations in the emotional state of the user is the measurement of the galvanic skin response. For instance, this technology is commonly used in lie detectors. Other sensor types used for monitoring physiological events include skin temperature and respiratory effort sensors.

There are numerous other sensors used in medicine for physiological monitoring tasks. However, they often require the insertion of the instruments into the human body. Currently, it is difficult to contemplate such devices as having context-awareness capabilities.

3.3 Architecture of Context Recognition Methods

Measurements obtained from the sensor devices described above are usually inadequate for recognizing an entity as complex as a context. Such complexity usually requires advanced processing techniques and the fusion of measurements from several sensing devices. This operation is performed using a combination of several machine learning techniques.

Context recognition methods proposed in previous research are very similar to the techniques used in the area of pattern recognition (Duda et al., 2001). The aim of the pattern recognition is to classify data on the basis of their properties and available a priori knowledge. In our case, the classification procedure involves associating different measurements with appropriate contexts.

Measurements are not usually processed by pattern recognition algorithms as such, but special analysis is required to extract more meaningful information from each sensor. For example, in sensors with rapidly varying output, like accelerometers, a single measurement value provides little information. Instead, measurements of such sensors should be analyzed in short bursts in order to determine properties related to variations and reduce noise. As a result, several descriptive measures, called features, are extracted from a windowed signal of each sensor. These features are then combined to numerical vectors and processed by a classification algorithm.

In several studies, the result of the classification algorithm is considered as a context (Bao & Intille, 2004; Bouten et al., 1997). The architecture described is commonly used for physical activity recognition (e.g. walking, running, sitting, etc.) (Ermes et al., 2008). In general this method is capable of recognizing events that can be characterized by the features extracted from a single signal window.

In some cases, a more accurate description of the context can be acquired, when a sequence of the classification results is analyzed. For example, a sequence of several sounds in the environment can be used to characterize more complex situations like supermarket, office and busy street (Clarkson et al., 1998). Detection of event sequences requires an additional layer in context recognition architecture.

The overall structure of the introduced architecture can be seen in Figure 1. The following sections describe in great detail the layers of this structure.

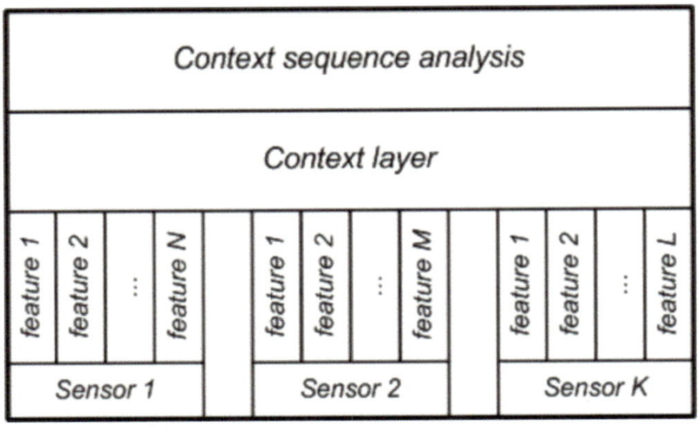

Fig. 1. Context recognition architecture

Feature extraction

While feature is a standard term in the area of the pattern recognition, studies in the area of context-awareness often refer to it as *cue* (Schmidt, 2002) or *context-atom* (Mäntyjärvi, 2003). The purpose of the feature extraction procedure is to convert rough sensor data into a more descriptive format for the given pattern recognition task.

Usually, features are extracted from longer measurement sequences, called windows. In the case of the periodical events, the duration of the window should be long enough to capture at least one period of the measured phenomena. In the case of monitoring non-periodic events, the window length can be chosen according to the amount of noise in the signal or other specific issues.

In general, there are two common types of features to be extracted: time domain features and frequency domain features. In the time domain, the windowed signal is analyzed as it is. In the frequency domain the window of signal is converted to Fourier-series using Fast Fourier Transform algorithm.

Common features extracted from the time domain representation of the signal include a mean value, standard deviation, median and quartiles. Another commonly used time domain feature is a count of zero-crossings in the signal window or differential of signal can be used to estimate the frequency of the signal.

More information on the spectral properties of the signal can be extracted from the frequency domain representation of the signal. Frequency of the spectral peak can be used to estimate period length of the periodic signal. Power of the spectral peak is proportional to the intensity of the periodic motion. Spectral entropy can be used to distinguish periodic signals from non-periodic ones.

Context Layer Algorithms

The purpose of the context layer algorithms is to match the derived feature vector to the best matching contexts. In other words, the goal is to find previously defined events that are most typical to the obtained measurements. This means that before the context can be recognized from measurements, recognition algorithms require some prerequisite knowledge about possible contexts and their characteristics. As a result, the context recognition process proceeds in two steps. The first step is learning. The prerequisite knowledge is obtained during this step. The second is classification, which matches unidentified features to one of the trained contexts.

In general, there are two learning strategies: supervised and unsupervised learning. The difference is that in the supervised learning, set of possible contexts is known during the training phase. An algorithm is trained using labeled feature vectors. A label is the name of the context that occurred at the time feature vector was recorded. The result is a trained algorithm capable of deciding on the most probable label for any given unlabeled feature vector.

In the unsupervised learning method, feature vectors used to train the algorithm do not have labels. Therefore, the purpose of the training is not to learn what the typical feature vectors are for each particular context, but to divide given feature vectors into groups based on their similarity. During the classification phase the trained algorithm is capable of deciding on which group any given feature vector belongs to, without giving any meaningful labels to the groups.

Patterns classification based on feature vectors is a widely studied subject in the field of pattern recognition. More detailed theoretical background on this topic can be found in the literature (Duda et al., 2001). Both of the training strategies are used as methods for context recognition and are briefly described below.

Supervised learning

The supervised learning strategy has the advantage of straight-forward applicability when the set of contexts to be recognized is known in advance. The disadvantage is the requirement for labeling feature vectors used for training. Usually this requirement involves a testee wearing measurement devices and performing different activities according to some predefined scenario. This scenario is then used to label the obtained measurements (Bao & Intille, 2004).

The supervised learning method is supported by algorithms such as classification trees, multilayer perceptron (MLP) and K-nearest neighbors –classifier (KNN). The classification tree represents the classification task as a sequence of questions. The answer to each question determines, which question will be asked next. At the end, each possible sequence of answers leads to some particular classification result. In the case of numerical feature vectors, questions usually attempt to clarify whether the value of a particular feature is greater than the threshold value obtained during training. Classification trees have been used in several studies (Bao & Intille, 2004; Ermes et al., 2008) and showed promising results.

Another widely used algorithm for user activity classification is the MLP, which belongs to a group of classification algorithms called artificial neural networks. Algorithms belonging to this group try to simulate behavior of biological neural networks in the decision making process. Multilayer perceptron consists of several interconnected layers of simple processing units called neurons. MLP is capable of obtaining accurate results in complex activity recognition tasks, though analysis why a particular classification result was suggested is problematic. Multilayer perceptron has been employed for user physical activity recognition in several works (Ermes et al., 2008; Aminian et al., 1999).

The third example of supervised learning methods is the KNN-classifier. In this algorithm during classification phase the measured feature vector is compared to all the feature vectors collected during the training phase. *K* most similar feature vectors are selected from the training set, where *K* is a predefined parameter. The classification result is chosen on basis of the majority of labels in the selected training set vectors. Examples of the use of KNN classifier for activity recognition can be found in several studies (Bao & Intille, 2004; Ravi et al., 1999).

Unsupervised learning

In the case of unsupervised learning, no scenarios are needed. The testee wearing sensor equipment does not even need to be aware of making measurements and this produces more realistic data. When it is important to maintain realistic sequences of the contexts, the unsupervised learning is a particularly suitable option. The disadvantage of unsupervised learning is a greater difficulty of interpreting the obtained data. It is possible to ascertain the time instances when the same context have occurred, but is impossible to know without additional knowledge which context it really was.

One commonly used algorithm based on unsupervised learning is the self-organizing map (SOM) by Kohonen (1998). This algorithm is a powerful tool for projecting high dimensional feature vectors to a lower dimensional (typically two dimensional) space. In the result of the projection, feature vectors that were similar in a high dimensional space, remain close to each other in the new lower dimensional space. The smaller number of dimensions makes the visualization of the measurements easier and the classification algorithms more powerful.

In the area of context recognition SOM is often used as a preprocessing method for other algorithms. This way, in (Van Laerhoven & Cakmakci, 2000) unlabeled measurements were processed by SOM algorithm to reduce the dimensionality of data to two dimensions and then several regions in the resulting map were labeled manually. During the classification phase the regular KNN algorithm was used for the context recognition. This helped reduce the time and computational effort expended on measurement annotations and computation.

In another study (Krause, 2003) measurements were preprocessed by SOM algorithm and then divided into several groups using K-means clustering. K-means clustering is an unsupervised learning based algorithm that divides given feature vectors into K distinct groups. No labels were assigned to the K extracted groups. The motivation of the authors was that context does not necessarily require any descriptive label to provide context aware functionality.

Context sequence analysis layer
Recognized context can be considered as a state of the system. In many cases this recognized state is overly fine-grained knowledge for context aware applications. Because of this, analysis of context sequences can be used to obtain more meaningful information. For example, Aoki et al. (1999) implemented an indoor positioning method based on sequence of video observations. In this work the authors used linear programming algorithm to recover the route taken by a person from individual pictures obtained from a video camera mounted on a rucksack strap.

Another benefit of context sequence analysis is the increased accuracy of the context recognition. For example, if we consider the case where the user is taking a bus and the output of the context recognition algorithm varies between riding a bus and driving a car, the sequence is clearly invalid. By performing sequence analysis, it is possible to check which context dominates the sequence and thereby resolve the problem. Of course, it is possible only in cases where the recognized context is correct most of the time.

Sequence analysis of the contexts has been used in several studies (Krause et al., 2003; Van Laerhoven & Cakmakci, 2000). In these research projects Markov Model was used to represent transition probabilities between various activities and thereby avoid invalid sequences of contexts. Markov Model is a common tool to represent the behavior of processes with discrete states and is commonly used in the area of speech recognition.

Sequence analysis is a desirable tool, when the events recognized on the context layer are expected to be rapidly changing over time. This is often the case for video and audio observation. When variations in the context are not particularly rapid, as in case of physical activity (walking, running, sitting, etc.), modeling of transition probabilities becomes more challenging. The measurements used for training should be recorded without any scenario, forcing the user to change activities in a particular order and at particular time instances. In general, it means that the unsupervised learning should be favored for the training of the transition probabilities in the case of slowly changing contexts.

4. Main concerns

4.1 Hardware

Context awareness is not a free lunch. There are several problems to be solved before a wide adoption of the technology is possible. First of all, the applications are supposed to run on portable devices that contain fragile sensors. Mobile phones are durable and do not usually break as a result of a minor fall, but a context-aware sensor system might suffer partial or total damage. (Schmidt, 2002)

Limited battery life, broken sensors, and faulty connections give rise to missing or defective sensor values. When sensor values are faulty the system might not be able to compensate for the information loss. Sensor loss could be compensated either by design with overlapping sensors or by signal processing algorithms. For example, in activity classification in case of missing or defective sensor values the classifier could be taught to compensate for information loss by using information from other sensors.

One way to overcome the problem of missing measurements is to use a classification tree supplemented with so-called surrogate splitters. We have proposed a novel classifier based on them (Avdouevski et al., 2008). A regular classification tree is an algorithm producing a sequence of questions. Each question analyzes if a particular feature value exceeds a predefined threshold. The following question is chosen based on the answer of the previous one. The resulting sequence of answers to these questions defines the final classification outcome. In a classification tree with surrogate splitters, instead of using just one set of features and thresholds for each question, multiple optional feature and threshold sets from several sensors are used. These are defined using statistical analysis of feature distributions. The supplemented tree is able to cope with missing sensor values, because a compensatory option is often available. In addition, the classifier uses the latest complete classification result as extra knowledge. We have shown that the method is able to compensate the loss of sensors for half a minute at a time without a significant reduction in classification accuracy compared to conventional methods.

Context aware devices are part of pervasive systems that strive for invisibility. Hence, the actual devices have to be small in size in order to be unobtrusive. This is especially true for portable devices such as mobile phones, which also have to be light in weight. These factors limit the possibilities to embed new functionality to any device. For example, a pocket-sized mobile phone cannot contain many sensors for context awareness. Similarly, battery and memory unit sizes are limited. Therefore, saving energy and efficient memory usage become critical.

4.2 Energy consumption

A context-aware system typically consists of a personal device, an external system and a connection between them. Portable devices, like mobile phones, are not connected to line current and so long battery life is an important part of usability. Energy consumption can be reduced with system design solutions, hardware selection and algorithms.

There is a tradeoff between the "always on"-demand of mobile applications and their energy consumption. If a device measured, for example, body movements of the user at a constant high sampling rate, the batteries would run out soon. For ideal use of resources, the device has to know when and what to measure. This is difficult because relevant information can be lost if the samples are taken too seldom.

There are several algorithms to minimize energy consumption. One way is to limit sampling frequency or instances at which the samples are taken. This also frees up processor time and reduces memory requirements and network usage. Moreover, in order to save memory, one might save preprocessed information, like features or statistics instead of raw signal. Heuristics related to the application field can also be used for the task, although generic solutions cannot be created this way. For example, in activity monitoring it is probable that the individual will continue the activity for prolonged period of time. Thus, in a week-long activity monitoring period, samples could be saved at intervals of only once a minute (Marschollec et al., 2007).

This idea can be extended so that sampling frequency is adapted to the current context. In our work (Makkonen et al., 2008) we considered the activity recognition problem by treating each activity as a state of a state machine. Each state defines how samples are measured and which features are calculated for the classification. Measurement parameters include the time interval between measurements blocks and the sampling rate of each block. Furthermore, after each measurement the stability of the state is determined based on feature values. In the case of stability, the algorithm skips samples as it is assumed that the state is not likely to change rapidly. Conversely, in the case of instability, the system measures more samples and performs a more thorough activity classification.

The approach reduces energy consumption by measuring and transmitting fewer samples, calculating fewer features, and performing the classification more seldom. We have shown that the recognition performance does not drop dramatically compared to the cases when all available samples are used. This enables the approach to be used in mobile applications. (Makkonen et al., 2008)

Processing capacity on small portable devices is limited. For the user, this usually means delays in functionality. Similarly, savings in processing time also have an effect on the power consumption. Again, processing complexity can be minimized by sensor selection, system design, and sampling schemes. Adaptive sampling or lowered sampling frequency minimized the amount of samples needed, and therefore processor time. Feature selection controls the amount of calculation needed. Usually, simple features like mean and variance are faster to calculate than, for example, Fourier transformation. Even classification algorithms can be selected to preserve processing time. For example, nearest neighbor classification can be done by calculating the distance to all previous samples, which is a heavy operation, or to the cluster centers, which is a significantly lighter task.

Despite network connection being a major energy drain, in some context aware applications mobile device needs to be in continuous communication with an external system. One of the ways to limit network power is timed functionality. If the system uptime is limited, energy drain is reduced. So instead of always on, there could be the following options: only on when selected on, on with limited functionality or on with timed functionality.

4.3 Interaction

Context awareness can enhance situation awareness and provide more services but it can also involve too much interaction so that using the system becomes burdensome. Conversely, if there is not enough interaction, the user can be denied important functionality. When users are subjected to barrage of enquiries, they are likely to give random responses in order to get rid of the query (Ackerman et al., 2001). In addition, some of the automatic actions taken by the applications can be even dangerous. These error situations can arise as a result of false recognition of the context.

For example, the autopilots of aircrafts and crash prevention systems of cars are critical applications. They use a sensor system for detecting abnormal situations. If they make false assumptions on the status of the environment, they might cause severe situations. Although these erroneous actions are unlikely, every now and then they happen and sometimes lives are lost.

Humans define context differently than computers and usually want devices to react in the same way in the same circumstances. However, when awaiting an important phone call, the user will probably willingly accept the call, even if it means interrupting a meeting or other such activity. Depending on the situation, context information might not be clear. The human aspect is hard to define and therefore a context aware system might not be able to differentiate between states. It is normal for a human to forget things, such as switching a mobile phone to off or to quiet and then back on. A context aware device might be able to compensate for much of this, but there are also situations when the user wants the system to act in the opposite way to previous situations.

4.4 Legislation and ethics

Apart of unintended fully automatic actions, a major concern is maintaining privacy. When a context aware system is in use, sensors continuously collect data that could be considered private. Since privacy is considered a human right, almost everything concerning personal information is regulated by laws: collecting, sharing, transferring, manipulating, storing, combining, using and so on. Some of the regulations can be by-passed with the users consent, but not all of them and not everywhere. Laws differ between information sources and regions and what may be legal in one country may be illegal in another.

Fair information practices are a group of commonly accepted principles in privacy protection. There are five principles involved: notice and awareness of collected information; choice and consent to give information; access to given information and participation; integrity and security of the information given; and enforcement and redress. The last item is included because without proper enforcement, the principles would be ineffective. (Federal Trade Commission, 2009)

Laws governing information privacy attempt to protect personal information from misuse and disclosure. Context awareness, and information technology overall, is still a new technology so the laws dealing with it are still changing in many regions. In the European Union the main guidelines are given by Directive 95/46/EC on the protection of individuals with regard to the processing of personal data and on the free movement of such data. However practices still vary within different countries in the area. Briefly, the Directive states that a reason must exist for the collection of such data, that the data is only used for that purpose and when the reason ceases to be valid the data is deleted. Collected data should not be shared without legal authorization or the consent of individuals concerned. Records must be kept up to date and be available for inspection. Data should be protected and should not be transferred to sources where it might be vulnerable. Finally data such as sexual orientation, religion and political beliefs must be considered too sensitive to be collected in all but extreme circumstances. (Wikipedia, 2009a; Wikipedia, 2009b; European Commission, 2009)

Although privacy is mainly a legal or ethical issue, the solution to privacy protection lies in technical details and design. There are several ways to maintain privacy in context aware systems. The system could either be designed to collect only information that is not considered private, or the information could be processed so that personal information is blurred or removed. Privacy protecting algorithms work at different levels. For example, sensors can remove some of the information and after that the processing unit that gathers data from several sensors can process it anonymously.

If the collected data is considered private, it is important that it is stored safely. Access to the information should be limited to authorized users. Interactive systems keep the user aware of the shared information, but more invisible technology, which is designed not to need interaction, can collect information that the user does not want to be collected. Information sharing is limited by laws that protect privacy, but ethics do not necessarily correspond to laws, and organizations may attempt to profit from such information.

Context awareness is a useful enhancement to many applications, but the ethics of the technology raise certain questions. From ecological perspective, the "always available" technology has implications for energy consumption and recyclability. Most context aware devices are designed to consume small amounts of energy. However, if every person were to have a device switched on mode, the energy drain would be significant. Recyclability in this context means the reusability of devices and sharing. If several devices can make use of the same sensors environmental and economical costs will be lower.

In a home monitoring system that records information on people inhabiting or visiting a house, ethical issues arise when individuals are unaware of being monitored or some of the information is made available to unknown people. For example, a doctor or other health care professional might check on the condition of the person using the monitoring system. The patient is aware of this and is aware of the sensors in use. There might be a camera in use, but the patient knows where it is and when it is on. However, this situation would be unethical, if the person was unaware of any monitoring activity or there was no privacy.

Kosta et al. (2008) have considered ethical and legal issues concerning user centric ambient intelligence services. These scenarios are comparable to other context-aware applications. For example, a home monitoring system enables the elderly to stay in their homes longer without the need for institutional care. Though this is beneficial, the system incurs costs which accrue from system parts and the monitoring personnel. Furthermore the person being monitored needs to know how to use the technology. This all indicates that the system is available to only privileged group, and thus could promote social inequality.

5. Conclusions

We have presented a wide variety of applications that use context-awareness and the technologies behind the concept. We have also discussed implementation issues and problems that are yet to be solved. Our own work in the field continues as we try to overcome these obstacles. Context awareness needs cheaper and lighter sensors, better ways to save energy, and novel ways of gathering knowledge about the surrounding world. In addition, the legislation has to be carefully considered when designing new applications that pose a threat to privacy.

Based on the evidence of the current state-of-the-art and our work, it can be said that the concept of context awareness is gaining more and more foothold in information technology. Thus, it is reasonable to assume that the concept will become widely used in future HCI, and many new application areas that use it will appear.

6. References

Ackerman, M.; Darrell, T. & Weitzner, D. (2001). Privacy in context, *Human Computer Interaction*, vol. 16, no. 2, pp. 167–176

Ahonen, S. & Laitinen, H. (2003). Database correlation method for UMTS location, *Proceedings of Vehicular Technology Conference*, pp. 2696-2700, ISBN 0-7803-7757-5, April 2003

Aminian, K.; Robert, P.; Buchser, E.; Rutschmann, B.; Hayoz, D. & Depairon, M. (1999). Physical activity monitoring based on accelerometry: validation and comparison with video observation, In: *Medical and Biological Engineering and Computing*, pp.304-308, Springer, ISBN 0140-0118

Aoki, H.; Schiele, B. & Pentland, A. (1999). Realtime Personal Positioning System for Wearable Computers, *Proceedings of 3rd International Symposium on Wearable Computers*, pp. 18-19, ISBN 0-7695-0428-0, 1999, IEEE Computer Society, Washington, DC, USA

Avdouevski, I.; Kerminen, R.; Makkonen, J. & Visa, A., Missing Values in the User Activity Classification Applications Utilizing Wireless Sensors, *Proceedings of MobiWac 2008*, pp.151-155

Bao, L. & Intille, S. (2004). Activity recognition from user-annotated acceleration data, *Proceedings of PERVASIVE 2004, vol. LNCS 3001*, pp. 1-17, ISBN 3-540-21835-1, Linz/Vienna, 18-23 April 2004

Bouten, C.; Koekkoek, K.; Verduin, M.; Kodde, R. & Janssen, J. (1997). A triaxial accelerometer and portable data processing unit for the assessment of daily physical activity. *Biomedical Engineering*, Vol. 44, No. 3, 1997 pp.136-147, ISSN 0018-9294

Bui, T. & Nguyen, L. (2005). Recognition of Vietnamese sign language using MEMS accelerometers, *Proceedings of 1st International Conference on Sensing Technology*, pp. 118-122, Palmerston North, New Zealand, November 21-23, 2005

Butz, A.; Baus, J. & Kruger, A. (2000). Augmenting buildings with infrared information, *Proceedings of Augmented Reality*, pp. 93-96, ISBN 0-7695-0846-4, Munich, Germany, 2000

Clarkson, B. (2003). Life patterns: structure from wearable sensors, Massachusetts Institute of Technology, USA, Ph.D. dissertation

Clarkson, B. ; Sawhney, N. & Pentland, A. (1998). Auditory Context Awareness via Wearable Computing, *Proceedings of Energy*, p. 600, 1998

Darby, J.; Li, B. & Costen, N. (2008). Activity classification for interactive game interfaces. *International Journal of Computer Games Technology*, Vol. 2008, No. 3, January 2008, Article No. 11, ISSN 1687-7047

de Castro, J. & Shimakawa, H. (2006). Mobile Advertisement System Utilizing User's Contextual Information, *Proceedings of 7th International Conference on Mobile Data Management (MDM2006)*, pp. 91-91, ISBN 0-7695-2526-1, 10-12 May 2006

Dey, A. & Abowd, G. (2000a). CybreMinder: A Context-Aware System for Supporting Reminders, *Proceedings of the 2nd international symposium on Handheld and Ubiquitous Computing, Lecture Notes In Computer Science; Vol. 1927*, pp. 172-186, ISBN 3-540-41093-7, Bristol, UK

Dey, A. & Abowd, G. (2000b). Towards a Better Understanding of Context and Context-Awareness, *Proceedings of the Workshop on The What, Who, Where, When, and How of Context-Awareness, as part of the 2000 Conference on Human Factors in Computing Systems (CHI 2000)*, the Hague, The Netherlands, April, 2000

Doyle, L.; Davenport, G. & O'Mahony, D. (2002). MOBILE CONTEXT-AWARE STORIES, *Proceedings of 2002 IEEE International Conference on Multimedia and Expo*, pp. 345-348, ISBN 0-7803-7304-9, Lausanne, Switzerland, August 2002

Duda, R.; Hart, P. & Stork, D. (2001). *Pattern classification*, Wiley New York, ISBN 978-0471056690

Ermes, M.; Pärkkä, J.; Mäntyjärvi, J. & Korhonen, I. (2008). Detection of Daily Activities and Sports With Wearable Sensors in Controlled and Uncontrolled Conditions. *IEEE Transactions on Information Technology in Biomedicine*, Vol. 12, No. 1, January 2008, pp. 20-26, ISSN 1089-7771

European Commission (2009) Directive 95/46/EC, viewed 17.4.2009. Available: <http://ec.europa.eu/justice_home/fsj/privacy/law/index_en.htm>

Federal Trade Commission (2009), Fair information practices, viewed 17.4.2009. Available: <http://www.ftc.gov/reports/privacy3/fairinfo.shtm>

Hinckley, K. & Sinclair, M. (1999). Touch-sensing input devices, *Proceedings of the SIGCHI conference on Human factors in computing systems: the CHI is the limit*, pp. 223-230, ISBN 0-201-48559-1, Pittsburgh, Pennsylvania, US, 1999, ACM, New York, NY, USA

Hsieh, H. ; Chen, C. & Hong, C. (2007). Context-Aware Ubiquitous English Learning in a Campus Environment., *Proceedings of Seventh IEEE International Conference on Advanced Learning Technologies (ICALT 2007)*, pp. 351-353, ISBN 978-0-7695-2916-5, Niigata, Japan, July, 2007

Jeong, C. & Lee, E. (2007). Context Aware Human Computer Interaction for Ubiquitous Learning, *Proceedings of HCI International (HCII 2007), Lecture Notes in Computer Science, Volume 4558/2007*, pp. 364-373, ISBN 978-3-540-73353-9, Beijing, China, July 2007

Jovanov, E. ; Milenkovic, A. ; Otto, C.; De Groen, P.; Johnson, B.; Warren, S. & Taibi, G. (2006). A WBAN System for Ambulatory Monitoring of Physical Activity and Health Status: Applications and Challenges, *Proceedings of 27th Annual International Conference of the Engineering in Medicine and Biology Society, IEEE-EMBS 2005*, pp. 3810-3813, ISBN 0-7803-8741-4, Shanghai, China, September 2005

Kohonen, T. (1998). The self-organizing map. *Neurocomputing*, Vol. 21, No.1-3, November 1998, pp. 1-6, ISSN 09252312

Korpipää, P; Koskinen, M.; Peltola, J.; Mäkelä, S.M. & Seppänen, T. (2001). Bayesian approach to sensor-based context awareness. *Personal and Ubiquitous Computing*, Vol. 7, No. 2, pp. 113-124, ISSN 1617-4909

Kosta, E.; Pitkanen, O.; Niemela, M. & Kaasinen, E. (2008). Ethical-Legal Challenges in User-Centric AmI Services, *Third International Conference on Internet and Web Applications and Services ICIW '08*, June 2008

Kotanen, A.; Hännikäinen, M.; Leppäkoski, H. & Hämäläinen, T. (2003). Positioning with IEEE 802.11 b wireless LAN, *Proceedings of Personal, Indoor and Mobile Radio Communications*, Vo. 3 pp. 2218-2222, ISBN 0-7803-7822-9, September 2003

Krause, A.; Siewiorek, D.; Smailagic, A. & Farringdon, J. (1996). Unsupervised, dynamic identification of physiological and activity context in wearable computing, *Proceedings of Seventh IEEE International Symposium on Wearable Computers*, pp. 88-97, ISBN 0-7695-2034-0, 2003, IEEE Computer Society, Washington, DC, USA

Laitinen, H.; Lähteenmäki, J. & Nordström, T. (2001). Database correlation method for GSM location, *Proceedings of Vehicular Technology Conference*, Vol. 4 pp. 2504-2508, ISBN 0-7803-6728-6, Greece, May 2001, Rhodes

Lukowicz, P. ; Ward, J. ; Junker, H. ; Stager, M. & Troster, G. (2004). Recognizing Workshop Activity Using Body Worn Microphones and Accelerometers, *Proceedings of the Second International Conference, PERVASIVE 2004, Lecture Notes in Computer Science, Volume 3001/2004*, pp. 18-32, ISBN 978-3-540-21835-7, Linz/Vienna, Austria, April 21-23, 2004

Mahmoud, Q. (2006). Provisioning Context-Aware Advertisements to Wireless Mobile Users, *Proceedings of IEEE International Conference on Multimedia and Expo*, pp. 669-672, ISBN 1-4244-0366-7, 9-12 July 2006

Makkonen, J.; Kerminen, R.; Avdouevski, I. & Visa, A. (2008). State Machine-Based Approach for Lightweight Online Activity Recognition in a Mobile Terminal, *International Conference on Digital Life ICDL 2008*, Guangzhou, China, November 2008

Makkonen, J. & Visa, A. (2007a). Interaction with Circles of Mind-Based Decision Support System, *Proceedings of the 8th European Conference on Knowledge Management*, pp. 601-606, September 2007, Barcelona, Spain

Makkonen, J. & Visa, A. (2007b). Some Empirical Results on a Multimedia Work Support System, *Proceedings of HCI International 2007*, pp. 654-662, ISBN 978-3-540-73109-2, July 2007, Beijing, China

Mani, A. & Sundaram, H. (2006). Context-Aware Media Retrieval, *Proceedings of 5th International Conference, CIVR 2006, Lecture Notes in Computer Science, Volume 4071/2006*, pp. 483-486, ISBN 978-3-540-36018-6, Tempe, AZ, USA, July 2006

Marschollec, M.; Ludwig, W.; Schapiewksi, I.; Schriever, E.; Schubert, R.; Dybowski, H.; Meyer zu Schwabedissen, H.; Howe, J. & Haux, R. (2007). Multimodal home monitoring of elderly people - first results from the LASS study, *Proceedings of the 21st International Conference on Advanced Information Networking and Applications Workshop (AINAW'07)*, IEEE, ISBN 0-7695-2847-3/07, 2007

Mäntyjärvi, J. (2003). Sensor-based context recognition for mobile applications, Ph.D. dissertation, University of Oulu, Finland.

Mäntyjärvi, J.; Kela, J. ; Korpipää, P. & Kallio, S. (2004). Enabling fast and effortless customization in accelerometer based gesture interaction, *Proceedings of the 3rd international conference on Mobile and ubiquitous multimedia*, pp. 25-31, ISBN 1-58113-981-0, College Park, Maryland

Mäntylä, V.; Mäntyjärvi, J.; Seppänen, T. & Tuulari, E. (2000). Hand gesture recognition of a mobile device user, *Proceedings of the IEEE International Conference on Multimedia and Expo (ICME 2000)*, pp. 281-284 vol. 1, ISBN 0-7803-6536-4, New York, NY, USA

Neumann, D. (2008). Context awareness -- the next step in mobile advertising. *Mobile Marketer*, December 2., 2008, viewed 23.03.2009.
Available: <http://www.mobilemarketer.com/cms/opinion/columns/2207.html>

Pichler, M.; Bodenhofer, U. & Schwinger, W. (2004). Context-awareness and artificial intelligence. *ÖGAI Journal*, Vol. 23, No. 1, pp. 4-11, ISSN 0254-4326.

Pylvänäinen, T. (2005). Accelerometer Based Gesture Recognition Using Continuous HMMs, *Proceedings of the Second Iberian Conference, IbPRIA 2005, Part I, Lecture Notes in Computer Science Volume 3522/2005*, pp. 639-646, ISBN 978-3-540-26153-7, Estoril, Portugal, June 2005

Pärkka, J.; Ermes, M.; Korpipää, P.; Mäntyjärvi, J.; Peltola, J. & Korhonen, I. (2006). Activity Classification Using Realistic Data from Wearable Sensors. *IEEE TRANSACTIONS ON INFORMATION TECHNOLOGY IN BIOMEDICINE*, Vol. 10, No. 1, 2006, pp. 119-120, ISSN 1089-7771

Ravi, N. ; Dandekar, N. ; Mysore, P. & Littman, M.L.. (1999). Activity Recognition from Accelerometer Data, *Proceedings of the national conference on artificial intelligence*, Vol. 20, No. 3 pp. 1541-1546, MIT Press, USA, 1999

Saha, S.; Chaudhuri, K.; Sanghi, D. & Bhagwat, P. (2003). Location determination of a mobile device using IEEE 802.11 b access point signals. *Wireless Communications and Networking*, Vol. 3, March 2003, pp.1987-1992, ISSN 1525-3511

Schilit, B. & Theimer, M. (1994). Disseminating active map information to mobile hosts. *Network IEEE*, Vol. 8, No. 5, pp.22-32, ISSN 0890-8044

Schmidt, A. (2005). Potentials and Challenges of Context-Awareness for Learning Solutions, *Proceedings of the 13th Annual Workshop of the SIG Adaptivity and User Modeling in Interactive Systems (ABIS 05)*, Saarbrücken, Germany, October 2005

Schmidt, A. (2002). Ubiquitous Computing -Computing in Context, Lancaster University, Ph.D. dissertation

Schmidt, A.; Beigl, M. & Gellersen, H. (1999). There is more to context than location. *Computers & Graphics*, Vol. 23, No. 6, December 1999, pp. 893-901

Schweer, A.; Hinze, A. (2008). Combining Context-Awareness and Semantics to Augment Memory, *Proceedings of the 6th New Zealand Computer Science Research Student Conference*, pp. 254-257, Christchurch, New Zealand, April 14-17, 2008.

Schwinger, W.; Grün, C.; Pröll, B. & Retschitzegger, W. (2008). A Survey on Mobile Tourism Guides, In: *HANDBOOK OF RESEARCH IN MOBILE MULTIMEDIA, 2nd edition*, Khalil-Ibrahim Ismail (ed.), IGI Global, ISBN 9781605660462, USA, 2008

Sherrill D.; Moy M.; Reilly J. & Bonato P. (2001). Using hierarchical clustering methods to classify motor activities of COPD patients from wearable sensor data. *Journal of NeuroEngineering and Rehabilitation*, Vol. 2, No. 1, Article 16, ISSN 1743-0003

Siewiorek, D.; Smailagic, A.; Furukawa, J.; Krause, A.; Moraveji, N.; Reiger, K. & Shaffer, J. (2005). SenSay: a context-aware mobile phone, *Proceedings of Wearable Computers*, pp. 248-249, ISBN 0-7695-2034-0, October 2005

Stiefmeier, T.; Roggen, D.; Troster, G.; Ogris, G. & Lukowicz, P (2008). Wearable Activity Tracking in Car Manufacturing, *IEEE Pervasive Computing*, Vol. 7, No. 2, pp. 42-50, ISSN 1536-1268

Tentori, M. & Favela, J. (2008). Monitoring behavioral patterns in hospitals through activity-aware computing, *Proceedings of the Second International Conference on Pervasive*

Computing Technologies for Healthcare, PervasiveHealth 2008, pp. 173-176, ISBN 978-963-9799-15-8, January, 2008, Tampere, Finland

Tähti, M., Rautio, V-M. & Arhippainen, L. (2004). Utilizing Context-Awareness in Office-Type Working Life, *Proceedings of the 3rd international conference on Mobile and ubiquitous multimedia*, pp. 79-84, ISBN 1-58113-981-0, October 27-29, 2004, College Park, Maryland

Van Laerhoven, K. & Cakmakci, O. (1996). What shall we teach our pants?, *Proceedings of The Fourth International Symposium on Wearable Computers*, pp. 77-83, ISBN 0-7695-0795-6, Washington, DC, USA, 2000

Weiser, M. (1991). The Computer for the 21st Century. *Scientific American*, Vol. 9, No. 3, July 1999, pp.3-11, ISSN 1559-1662

Wikipedia (2009a). Information privacy, viewed 17.4.2009, Available: <http://en.wikipedia.org/wiki/Information_privacy#legality>

Wikipedia (2009b). Information privacy law, viewed 17.4.2009, Available: <http://en.wikipedia.org/wiki/Information_Privacy_Laws>

Yin, J. & Yang, Q. (2008). Sensor-Based Abnormal Human-Activity Detection, *IEEE Transactions on Knowledge and Data Engineering*, Vol. 20, No. 8, (August 2008) pp. 1082-1090, ISSN 1041-4347

Zimmermann, A.; Lorenz, A. & Oppermann, R. (2007). An Operational Definition of Context. *Modeling and Using Context*, Vol. 4635, pp. 558-571, ISBN 978-3-540-74254-8

2

Attentive Computing

Ahmet Cengizhan Dirican and Mehmet Göktürk
Gebze Institute of Technology
Turkey

1. Introduction

Although the purpose of technological progress of humanity is open for debate, it can be concluded that the outcome of advancements should enhance the quality of life in general. This enhancement does not only depend on new functionalities provided by advancements but also depends on strategies to present these functionalities. Presentation strategies are particularly important for technologies that are used ubiquitously found in many modern digital computing systems.

One can observe that the functionality side of the enhancements provided by computing systems, parallel to the developments in electronics and communication technologies, has been under realization with a great success for years to come. The presentation side, on the other hand, although significant developments had been realized until the very beginnings of nineties, could not show the same advancement.

People live in a modern digital life surrounded by various digital computing systems. Such a life, as well as its numerous advantages, brings extra problems to cope with as discussed in Section 3.1. Due to their inattentive behavior described in Section 3.2, computing systems at hand both cause new problems and even worsen existing ones. This can be attributed to the over-visibility of current digital computing systems. They are too much visible to efficiently exploit. Yet, their visibility has been in constant increase parallel to their quantity and services (Weiser, 1991).

This might be attributed to the fact that traditional design approaches do not meet with the cravings of contemporary information hungry devices anymore. Managing the information conveyed through such systems has been gradually becoming heavier. The ubiquity of computing systems and the multiparty interaction leads to a breakdown in the existing channels of interaction (Vertegaal et al., 2006). Computing systems bombard their users with immediate attention requests by sending interruptions. The well known execution-evaluation cycle framework could not work properly due to the attention switching caused by these interruptions. Besides, computing systems fall behind to support their users compared to the increasing mental load of users. They still provide explicit and very limited interaction channels and methods to user for managing both the system and his or her information environment.

Since early 1980s, researchers have been emphasizing on above problems and seeking for new interaction methods and channels. Among these, Bolt's "Put-That-There: Voice and Gesture at the Graphics Interface" (Bolt, 1980), Jacobs' "What You Look is What You Get: Eye Movement-Based Interaction Techniques" (Jacob, 1990), Weiser's "Ubiquitous Computing" (Weiser, 1991), Nielsen's "Non-Command User Interfaces" (Nielsen, 1993) can be given as pioneering examples of early studies that shaped 21st Century computing paradigms. Consequently, several new computing paradigms emerged in the research scene such as Affective Computing, Context-aware Computing, Perceptual Computing and Attentive Computing, constituting the subject of this chapter.

The name of every suggested paradigm conveys details to readers about the kind of principal approach utilized. Affective Computing, for example, intend to improve the interaction between human and computing systems through sensing human emotions (Pickard, 1998). Context-aware computing is based on the situational awareness and contextual information of what and where the user task is located, what the user knows, and what the system capabilities are (Selker & Burlesson, 2000). Attentive Computing, on the other hand, aims to regulate the interaction through the observation of human attention.

Human attention is a crucial but limited and fragile cognitive resource that must be carefully exploited and even augmented if possible as described in detail in Section 2.3. The fundamental purpose of AC is to preserve and support human cognitive resources. By sensing humans' past, present and future attention, AC aims to specify user's ongoing tasks, interests, goals and priorities. Thus, it will be possible to provide the user with relevant information and necessary support. Consequently, AC aims to ensure a more natural, unobtrusive and efficient human computer interaction. This naturalness, unobtrusiveness and efficiency may well be turned into invisibility. This is because of that most of the "visible" things that are noticed by or attract attention of humans are things that are unnatural, obtrusive and hard-to-use.

The invisibility of computing system is also considered differently in the literature. Don Norman, for example, attribute the invisibility of computing system that the computing devices to become seriously task-specific and thus, the interfaces of the systems blend into the background and unnoticed by users (Borriello, 2000). This seems to be an important challenge for the future of computing systems. Nevertheless, even if we design task specific devices, the invisibility of their interface of these devices will probably depend on the behavior and user sensing and information presenting capabilities. From this point of view, AC is highly promising for both current multi-purpose computing systems and even next generation task specific devices.

The rest of the chapter is organized as follows. In section 2, we emphasize on a number of subjects for a good understanding of AC. In section 3, it's investigated the quest for AC. All aspects of this quest and the need for AC paradigm are discussed in detail. In Section 4, the attentiveness in the literature, the definition and the properties of AC and our PRO-D framework model for the implementation of Attentive Computing Systems (ACS) are highlighted. In Section 5, important examples of Attentive Computing Systems are given. The conclusions and future directions are in Section 6.

2. Background

In this section, we aim to provide the necessary background for a good understanding of Attentive Computing (AC). This requires detailed study on the following issues.

- Ubiquity of Computing Systems
- Multiparty Interaction
- Humans and Attention
- Multiparty Interruptions and the Broken Execution Evaluation Cycle

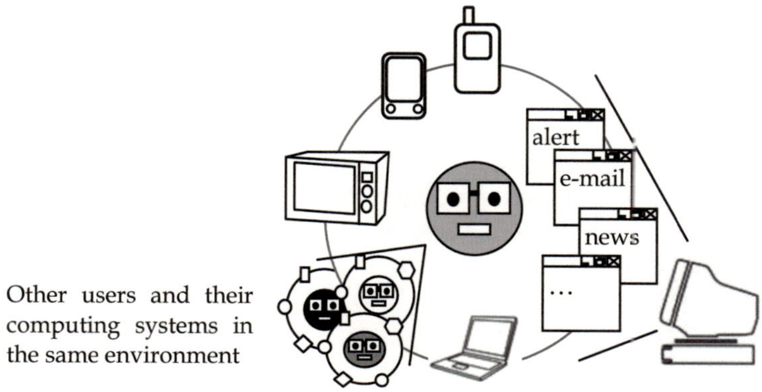

Fig. 1. Multiparty Interaction: A user (gray head) is surrounded by multiple digital computing systems.

2.1 Ubiquity of Computing Systems

At his first proposal "ubiquitous computing", Weiser envisioned the digital computing systems to be ubiquitous and become invisible like electric motors by interweaving themselves into the fabric of every day life until they are indistinguishable from it. They would be everywhere but people would not be aware of their existence (Weiser, 1991).

Today, one can observe that the predictions of Weiser about the ubiquity of computing technologies have substantially being implemented. Digital computing systems have become a part of everyday life. Although they still preserve their classic design and they are not as invisible as Weiser predicted, many are used ubiquitously in various kinds of devices and systems such that from a child's toy to the control system of a nuclear power plant.

2.2 Multiparty Interaction

People live a life surrounded by digital computing devices such as computers, PDAs, mobile phones, Blackberries, iPods or even infamous microwave ovens (Fig. 1. Multiparty Interaction). If there would be a Moore's Law equivalent for the number of various digital computing devices, it may well state that the numbers of types of computing devices per user would double every year. This would mean that the number of surrounding computing systems of a person has been gradually increasing for the last decades. Yet, in parallel to this increase, the interaction between humans and digital computing systems has also changed over time.

In earlier days of computing, computer users were sitting in a many-to-one interaction model against a mainframe computer through dummy terminals. With the introduction of personal computers, every user sooner or later possessed one or more standalone computers which are unarguably more powerful and capable than the early ones. This progress enabled one-to-one interaction model to come on scene. With the recent rise of mobile computing, and rapid decline in device costs, this model evolved as a one-to-many interaction. Today, a typical user attempts to use more than one device at a time: at least a desktop PC and possibly one or more cell phones loaded with running individual applications simultaneously.

Nevertheless, one-to-many interaction can not explain the whole picture efficiently. More complex situations can be observed with digital computing systems. Specifically in urban life, people share the same space most of the time such as offices, meeting rooms and public transportation vehicles. They are unable to avoid from being effected from other devices in the shared environment. The shared environments may belong to other people or may be embedded in within the environment such as air conditioners and coffee machines. As a result, people have developed a many-to-many or a multiparty interaction with surrounding digital systems (Vertegaal et al., 2006).

2.3 Humans and Attention

Shneiderman states that "Harnessing the computer's power is a task for designers who understand the technology and are sensitive to human capabilities and needs" (Shneiderman, 1998). Therefore, a good understanding of human capabilities, their limits or capacities, the underlying mechanisms and the cost of abusing and the gain supporting them are crucial for designing usable computing systems.

Humans are not machines. They get tired and forget easily. They are slow and not good at repetitive tasks like mathematical calculations and sorting, especially when tasks are too many and sequential. However, humans are distinct from computers and even other living things by their intelligence and their cognitive or mental capabilities like thinking, learning, problem solving, and decision making and remembering.

These crucial capabilities are basis on the cognitive mechanisms of humans to acquire, store and process the information. The information or stimulus coming from outside world through sensory organs exceeds what humans are actually capable of processing most of the time. Fortunately, humans have cognitive mechanisms called attentional mechanisms that enable them to filter and select the incoming sensory information (Roda & Thomas, 2006). These mechanisms or human attention specifies the selection of relevant information and the filtering of irrelevant information from incoming stimulus (Roda & Thomas, 2006). Later, this selected and filtered information carried in human working memory and become usable to realize the cognitive or mental capabilities. In other words, these capabilities depend on the health of human attentional mechanisms.

The underlying mechanisms of human attention have controversial issues. There are many questions ought to be answered scientifically such that "Are filtering and the selection cognition-driven or input driven?" or "Are they realized during perception or cognition?",

"How distracters effects the attention?,", "Do humans can attend many things at a time?" etc. There are many models and theories proposed for these and more questions in the literature. Discussion of the all these theories and models is beyond this chapter. Interested reader may find a comprehensive introduction of these theories and models from an Attentive Computing perspective in (Roda & Thomas, 2006). In this chapter, readers are provided with an introductory level of theories and findings about the subject.

Treisman's "Feature Integration Theory" states that the filtering and selection are guided by both input and cognition (Roda & Thomas, 2006). This means that the information is filtered before entering into brain during perception in a preattentive stage, and after entered the brain, during cognition in attentive stage. This is due to the fact that eye tracking alone is insufficient to indicate cognitive interest. When humans look at something, it's a good indication of physical observation but it is not clear whether the information has been mentally processed or not (Vertegaal, 2002).

Humans can only absorb and attend only one thing at a time. As user pay attention to something, any other stimulus that tries to use the single attentional channel may cause the user's attention to be distracted. According to "Modern theory of attention", irrelevant information will be excluded from processing only if the prioritized relevant processing exhausts all the available capacity (Roda & Thomas, 2006). Otherwise distracters will be processed. In this account the locus of selection depend on the load of incoming stimulus.

Although human attention is considered as an unlimited cognitive resource, it shows indeed a limited performance in reality. It is open to be easily broken by distracters (Vertegaal, 2002) and competing attention seekers. As a result, the increasing interest to the user attention is considered as a crucial usability problem (Vertegaal, 2003). Human attention or attentional capacities should not be wasted and even be supported if possible (Vertegaal, 2006).

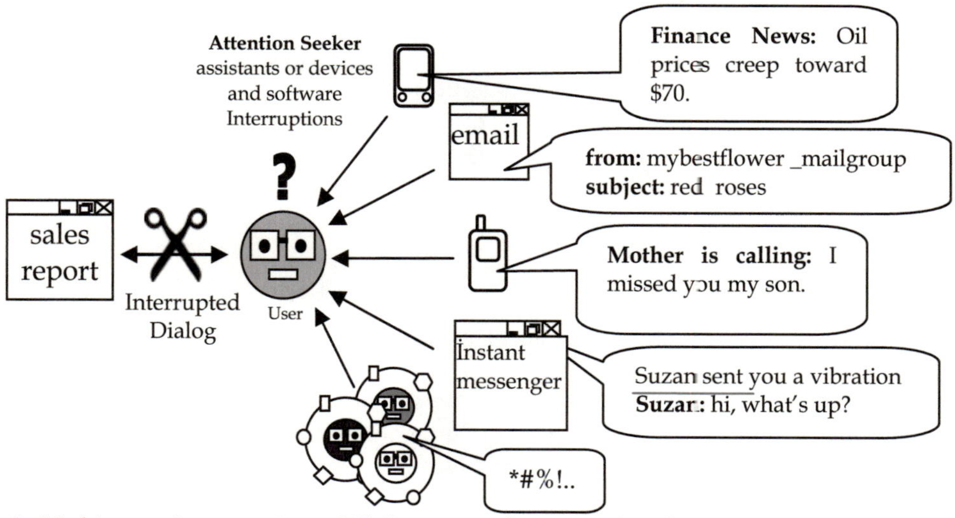

Fig. 2. Multiparty Interruptions: While a user (big gray head) tries to read a sales report other devices and software try to attract to user's attention by sending interruptions to present their information.

2.4 Multiparty Interruptions and Broken Execution-Evaluation Cycle

An interruption is an external stimulus that tries to attract the user's attention. It is sensed by users according to its incoming channel (visual, sight, touch, sound, smell), volume (weak or strong), relevance to the ongoing task and the user's concentration to the ongoing task (Roda & Thomas, 2006).

One can observe the interruptions come from multiple computing systems around a user in (Fig. 2. Multiparty interruptions). In this figure, it's seen a user (gray head) that is in a multiparty interaction with the computing systems around him. While the user tries to read a sales report document from a word processor, other software and computing devices try to roughly interfere and attract to person's attention by sending interruptions to convey their information. This cause the user to lost his focus of attention and the existing and primary interaction to be broken down. Thus, it will be inevitable a lost of motivation and performance for the person.

This is because of that humans are weak against interruption because of their cognitive limitations as discussed in Section 2.3 (McFarlane, 1999). Research suggests that a 15 seconds interruption may cause the user to drop some items from its short term to-do list (Gibbs, 2005). Bailey et al. indicates that a computer initiated interruption causes a significant increase in completion time for variety of web based tasks (Bailey, 2004). The study proposes that there is a positive relation between the task completion time and the memory load at the time interruption.

An interruption causes the alternation of the attentional channel of the user. This cause the well known execution-evaluation cycle to be broken. The framework of execution evaluation cycle has been suggested by Donald Norman and later revised by (Dix et al, 2004). It can be depicted as shown (Fig. 3. General Interaction Framework) below, where only one attentional and motor channel is reserved for a user:

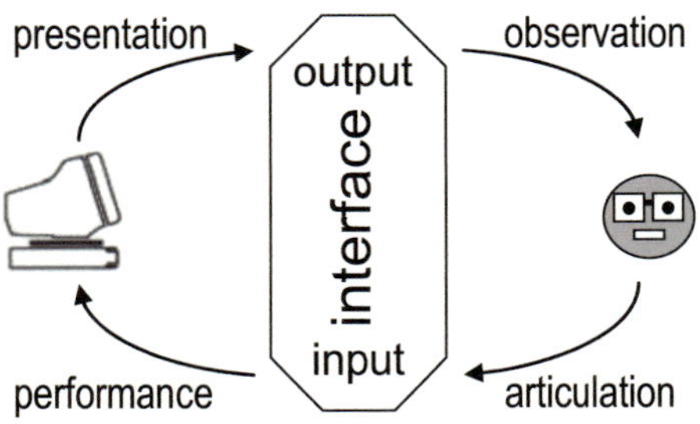

Fig. 3. General Interaction Framework (Dix et. al., 2004)

In a digital system scenario (Fig. 3. General Interaction Framework), reobservation of the system output becomes necessary due to the interrupted attention and the contention of presentations. Some of the presentations -including current one- might have reduced effect or get cut out completely from attentional channel of user.

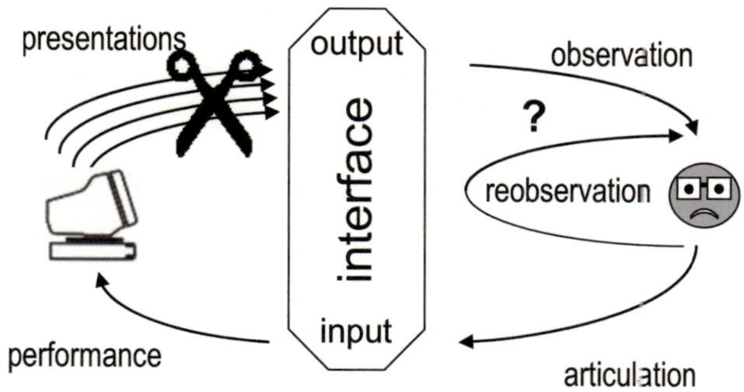

Fig. 4. Single System with multiple processes with individual attention demands

Since device interaction significantly utilizes short term memory, and factor with adverse effect on short term memory impairs the interaction. User frustration, reevaluation of screens and forgetting the temporary task list are typical results of such interruptions. When multiple digital systems are concerned, the situation becomes more complicated, yet exhibiting the same problem. Multiple digital systems with attentional demand are depicted in (Fig. 4. Multiple digital systems each demanding user attention):

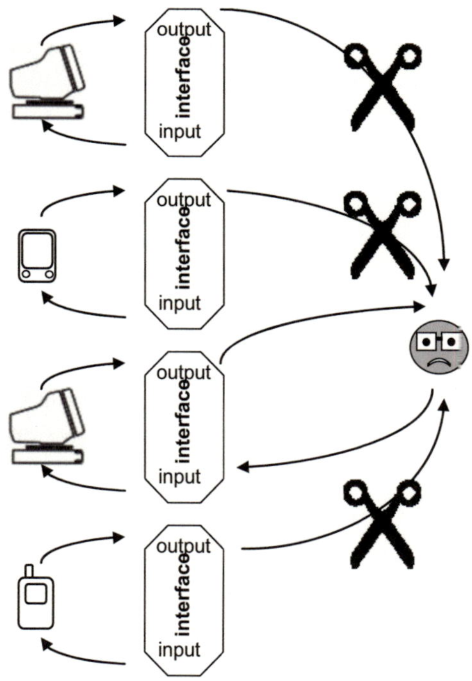

Fig. 5. Multiple digital systems: Each demanding user attention and send interruptions to the user.

Furthermore, when multiple digital systems are concerned, the problems of each single device with multiple processes are added automatically to the case above.

3. The Quest for Attentive Computing

In this section the quest for Attentive Computing (AC) is considered in detail. For that reason, following subjects are discussed by devising every subject a section.

- Problems Encountered in Modern Digital Life
- Behavior of Current Computing System
- Need for Attentive Computing

3.1 Problems Encountered in Modern Digital Life

An arrogant cell phone is heard during a meeting. The attendees hesitate a moment and control their phones whether the phone ringing is theirs or not. Then, the owner of the device is cleared because he or she has to turn it off immediately not to attract too much attention and anger. As the owner of the phone lives an unavoidable embarrassment, other people's attention is distracted and valuable meeting time might easily got spent for nothing.

Elsewhere, people may live the frustration of screen saver activations in the middle of presentations. In an office, while the head of sale department tries to focus on and finish an urgent report about the first quarter profit of the company, he or she may receive an obtrusive update warning from the operating system of the computer or the virus protection program. One can complaint about how problematic the management of multiple windows is, how much he or she face difficulties to find something on the computers desktop, how hard to use pointer & mouse in large screen displays etc..

It's possible to augment the number of above scenarios and one can surely say that these scenarios and similar situations are quite widespread all around the world. We live in a modern digital life that computing systems are ubiquitous (Section 2.1) and there is a multiparty interaction between users and computing systems (Section 2.2).

Lifestyle changes continuously as countries, companies and people act in a cruel competition. Latest innovations spread and affect the world in quite a short time. Whatever happens in the world is easily brought to the screens of people's digital computing devices although sometimes it is not quite desired. Managing information that is produced globally and conveyed through computing systems is becoming more difficult as the "information overload" has been getting heavier.

At a first glance, the ubiquity of computing systems and its natural result multiparty interaction may appear highly appealing and profitable to reader. Because, it may seem that having and using a number of computing systems with attractive properties and services is similar to have many ready to service and capable human assistants who never get tired at a low price. However, this is not the situation with computing systems at hand due to the isolated and inattentive behavior of current computing systems described in Section 3.2. They don't behave like human assistants.

While the price one pays to buy these systems decreases, the burden one has to carry to use increases contrarily. Vertegaal, the head of Human Media Laboratory of Queens University, explains this situation "Although the trend to use more computing devices may provide an opportunity for increased productivity, such benefit comes at a cost." He defines this cost as the requirement to be available, at any time or place, in order to swiftly adapt to changes in our information environment (Vertegaal, 2003).

Early computing systems, in a sense, were like powerful calculators, capable typewriters or fast electronic scriniaries with limited communication ability. After the rise of internet and other world wide mobile communication technologies such as GSM, computing systems have become humans' principal communication channels.

Most people use simultaneously at least email, instant messaging and cell phone technologies several times throughout the day. People are almost always connected and open to communication with the rest of the world most of the time. Additionally, computing systems are semi-autonomous and have multi tasking capabilities. Together with the operating system, all software in the device needs to communicate with the user without any care of his or her appropriateness to communication. Unfortunately, it's impossible to deny using or at least turning off computing systems due to economical and social demands of modern life in most cases (McCrickard & Chewar, 2005).

3.2 The Behavior of Current Digital Computing Devices

Today, a bathroom faucet or a hand dryer can recognize the physical status of their user and regulate their work accordingly, digital systems, that are more intelligent in a technical sense, do not exhibit such "attentive" user sensing and servicing abilities. Computing systems live in a world that is isolated from the outside world. They are unaware of the user's existence, proximity, context, actions, interests, goals, tasks and priorities. Strictly speaking, they are unaware of the physical, perceptual and cognitive state of the user.

They are designed in such a way that they only gives a response back if one explicitly indicates something by means of classical input devices a keyboard and mouse, otherwise they stay uninterested Worse, when they have something to tell, they do not hesitate to interrupt user without any care to current user context or current task. Systems and specifically computing devices still work as the user's single device, do not hesitate to confound the user's cognitive resources like attention and working memory through interrupts that they send (McCrickard & Chewar, 2003).

Additionally, computing systems at hand also fall behind to support their users. It's the responsibility of user to explicitly manage and control the screen real estate of the system and other resources. A large and complicated desktop, a pointer, tens of windows, lots of icons, many branching long menus, high resolution graphics etc. all wait for the "direct manipulation" of the user.

As it's thought the above attitudes of current computing systems, it can be said that they are "inattentive" or, by Gibbs's words, inconsiderate systems (Gibbs, 2005). Current computing systems are ill equipped to negotiate their communications with humans and bad in support (Vertegaal et al., 2006). This is because of that they still utilize traditional direct manipulation techniques based on traditional graphical user interfaces (GUIs), where standards are specified relatively early in 1983 (Nielsen, 1993). In traditional GUI principle, there is an explicit, object-driven and one-to-one interaction between the user and the system. The priority of interaction (locus of control) is given to device instead of user and his or her needs at this exclusive work style.

3.3 The Need for Attentive Computing

For a good understanding of the need for Attentive Computing (AC), it should first comprehend the following issues such that the cognitive limits and properties of humans (Section 2.3), the bad effects of interruptions on human performance (Section 2.4), the problems caused my modern digital life and the role of computing systems in these problems (Section 3.1), and the inattentive, arrogant and helpless behavior of digital computing systems (Section 3.2).

When it's considered together all above issues, it's obviously seen that current computing systems are insufficient to meet the increasing needs of users in today's modern digital life. However, these systems constitute an important part of users' life. They should no longer behave like passive ordinary tools like a typewriters, cupboards, pens and papers. Because, as it's considered the place of computing system in daily environment, the services provided and the time spending with them, they rather seems like partners or assistants.

Yet, attentive and helpful assistants or "good assistants" are needed with the words of "Maglio & Campbell. They describe a good assistant as an assistant that is actively filter incoming information, communicate in an appropriate manner and, aware of the supervisor's needs, goals and interest (Maglio & Campbell, 2003).

From a technical point of view, it is needed further development for interaction methods and new unobtrusive interaction channels between users and computing systems by considering social and individual behaviors. Direct manipulation, Graphical User Interfaces, WIMP (Windows, Icon, Menu and Pointer), classical input channels keyboards and mouse, even if they have served well so far, are showing their limits. They will off coarse continue to service but there is a need for computing systems that are:

1. Sensitive to the user: user's limits, natural communication styles and the environment user is in
2. Act according to user's interests, goals, priorities and tasks
3. Support the user attention by attenuating unnecessary details and augmenting it if possible.

4. Attentive Computing

4.1 Attentiveness in the Literature

Attentive Computing (AC) is a relatively new subject with respect to classical HCI computing paradigms. However, one can find variety of previous research work on AC in the literature in different names since the ends of nineties. The leading studies and subtopics can be named as Attentive User Interfaces, Attentive Information systems, Attentive Agents, Attention Aware Systems, Attention-Based User Interfaces, Attentional User Interfaces, Attention-Centric Notification Systems, Attentive Displays, Attentive Robots and Toys.

The name of the proposed systems under AC notion may exhibit some differences depending on the type of computing system and the point of view of the author to the problem. As some authors approach to the problem from a "system" perspective like Roda & Thomas's Attention-Aware Systems, others may consider it as user interface problem like Vertegaal and Attentive User Interfaces. In this chapter we have chosen to use the term AC as the basic computing paradigm that encompasses all the studies that are attentive and similarly, the term Attentive Computing System as an inclusive umbrella term for systems that have properties laid by AC.

An interesting study that handles the subject as a computing paradigm but in a less scientific manner is conducted by Gibbs (Gibbs, 2005). He throws the name "Considerate Computing" in article published in Scientific American. The article is referenced as a well organized study handling the subject from the popular point of view. Gibbs' article includes different researchers' opinions on the subject. It argues the reasons and problems of the current computing systems that are quite disrespectful and exhibit isolated behavior against their users. Consequently, it states that the computing systems to be considerate against their users.

Yet, readers may wonder why the term "attentive" has been selected in this chapter instead of the term "considerate". The answer lies on the fact that the term considerate is less formal than the term attentive whereas it points only to the behavior of computing systems. The term attentive, on the other hand, evokes the notion of attention which acts as a primary interaction channel of an ACS (Selker, 2004).

4.2 Definition and Properties

Selker defines an Attentive User Interface (AUI), being perhaps the most popular Attentive Computing System (ACS), as context-aware human-computer interfaces that rely on a person's attention as the primary input (Selker, 2004). Vertegaal defines it as "a user interface that is sensitive to user's attention" within in the introductory text of the special session that is dedicated to Attentive User Interfaces in CHI 2003 conference (Vertegaal, 2003).

In this chapter we propose to expand the notion of ACS to a degree, by the definition given for AUIs in (Dirican & Göktürk, 2008), and define an ACS as "A computing system that is sensitive to user's cognitive resources with attention being foremost". We believe that although AC propose to utilize the user's attention in optimizing the interaction, it address entire cognitive resources of user like perceptual mechanisms and working memory.

AC aims to create computing systems, called Attentive Computing Systems (ACSs), and behaves in harmony with their users. By preserving the user's attention and other cognitive resources, ACS tries protect users from today's ubiquitous pattern of interruptions (Vertegaal et al., 2006). It's done by unobtrusive negotiation and mediation, instead of imposing the messages. Besides, ACS tries to provide active support and assistance to their users by means of additional filtering and notification mechanisms relevant to user's needs, goals, tasks, ongoing activities and priorities.

4.3 Modified Interaction Framework

The general interaction Framework discussed in Section 2.4, can further be extended to include ACS (Fig. 7: Modified General Framework of Interaction for an ACS). Modified framework includes attentional monitor that watches user attention and context, filters and mediates necessary information to be presented to user and also capable of exchanging and declaring attention data to other digital devices.

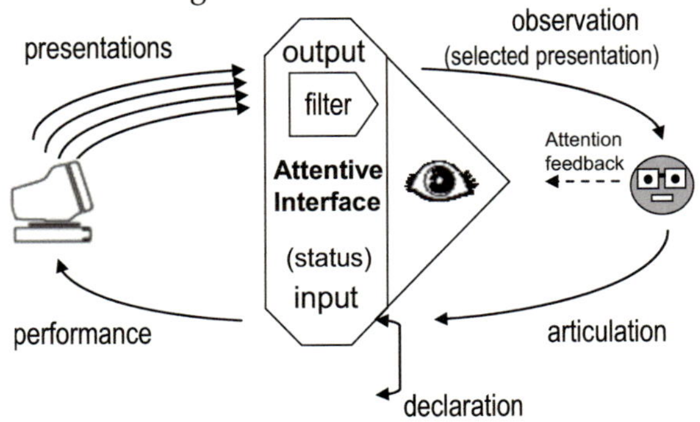

Fig. 6. Modified General Framework of Interaction for an ACS

When multiple digital systems are concerned, the case can be depicted as in (Fig. 8. Multiple digital systems with attentive user interfaces), where attention information is being exchanged between digital systems since some may lack required sensory capability to monitor user attention. Furthermore, exchange and fusion of attention data between digital systems would enable an even stronger mediation between the user and surrounding devices.

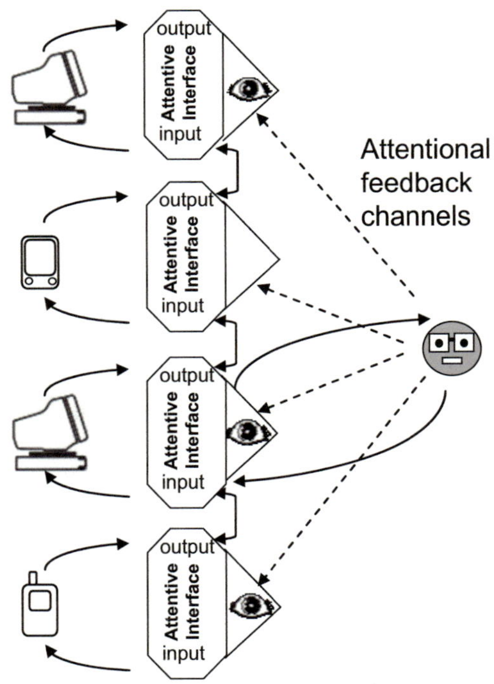

Fig. 7. Multiple digital systems with attentive user interfaces.

Through mediation of attention, execution evaluation cycles are delayed until proper candidate has been elected ACSs implement this mediation on the basis of measures and models of the past, present and future state of the user's attention (Maglio et. al, 2000). They need new communication channels to obtain and contract these measures and models and new interaction methods to maintain the above behavior. We combine these models, channels and methods within our suggested PRO-D framework model of ACS.

4.4 PRO-D Framework Model

PRO-D is a suggested framework model for ACSs based on the five key features proposed by Shell et al. such that sensing attention, reasoning about attention, gradual negotiation of turns and augmentation of attention, communication of attention (Shell et al., 2003).

By focusing on PRO-D, we aim to provide a generic framework model for attentive computing and other parallel computing paradigms. Our model has four key stages (Fig. 9. Framework model PRO-D for Attentive Computing), that are perception of attentional of cues, reasoning about the attention, optimization of attention and declaration of attention. Optimization stage has two sub stages: regulation of interaction and augmentation of attention. We think that if a computing system is attentive, it ought to have the first two stages exactly, and at least one of other two stages present. Otherwise, systems that do not preserve, support or declare the user's attention do not bring anything attentive.

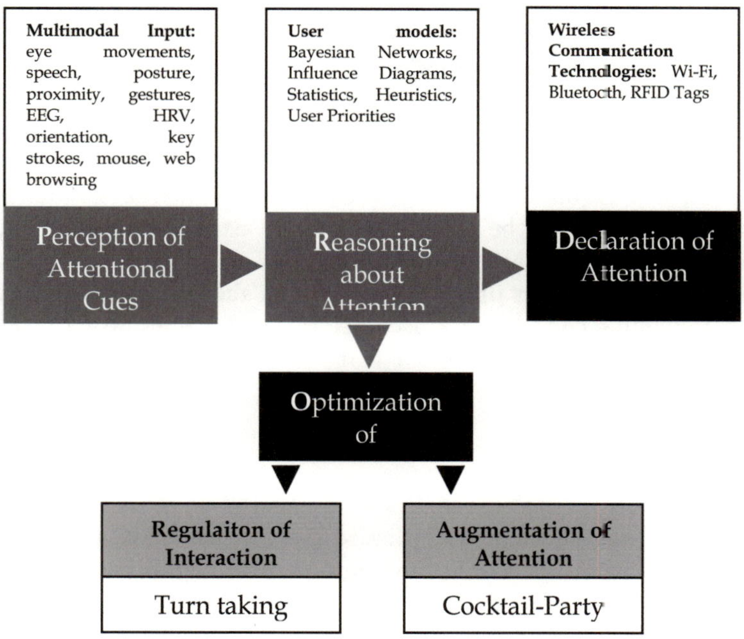

Fig. 8. Framework model PRO-D for Attentive Computing

4.4.1 Perception of Attentional Cues

In this stage, the user and the environment is monitored from several channels in order to obtain attentional cues about the user's current focus of attention. In other words, ACS tries to gather necessary information to be used in the next stage by monitoring the user.

Although, ACS take advantage of the classical explicit input channels mice, keyboard and joystick to track the user, they need richer input information. Enhanced multichannel or multimodal user information is required in order to implement an ACS that can determine the current status of the user, the place where user is in, focused human, device, object, etc. of attention.

Popular methods utilize gaze tracking where previous research suggest that people look at what they attend in most cases (Zhai, 2003). Maglio et al. did a study about how people point the computing devices during both verbal and non-verbal interaction. The results of their study suggest that, people use command phrases when they make do something the computing devices. They barely say the name of device. Instead, most of people look at the devices before or after giving the command. These findings confirm that eye tracking has a critical importance to understand the cognitive interests of users.

Other ways of collecting user information include speech recognition, presence detection, proximity detection, gesture detection and even posture detection. Heart rate variability (HRV), electroencephalography (EEG) and electrocardiography EOG studies in HCI also suggest that these can also convey user status and cognitive load data if processed correctly (Chen & Vertegaal, 2004 - Rowe et al., 1998).

ACSs and similar computing paradigms that collect multimodal information that sometimes include audio and facial video ultimately face a privacy protection problem. Since, any inference about the user requires various personal status information, evaluation of the data while keeping it private needs to be addressed carefully. Saving, protecting and gaining the user confidence is an important an open problem of AC (Shell, 2002). Few studies address privacy issues in AC where many others never mention about. On the contrary, addressing privacy is a key in gaining confidence of users. To this end, it's proposed to take advantage of the results of similar privacy done for computing paradigms and especially within ubiquitous computing.

4.4.2 Reasoning about Attention

Maglio et al. define ACS are systems that pay attention to what users do so that they can attend to what users need. In order to optimize the user attention, a system should first detect it. In this stage what the user is attending and his cognitive status are tried to be specified. By means of this information, users are provided more social interaction with computing devices, relevant information to their needs and goals, support with respect the his or her focus of attention.

AC uses models that incorporate users' past, present and future attention characteristics and specifies future interest and goals. Information gathered in perception stage is used as input to these models. Bayesian networks and influence diagrams are among the most popular methods for modeling in AC (Horvitz et al., 2003). Heuristic approaches, statistics and predefined user priorities are other methods used in the literature (Vertegaal et al., 2006).

Horvitz's Priorities is an attentional user interface that is a good example of reasoning about attention (Horvitz et al., 1999). The application decides on which received mails into a desktop computer of the user will be delivered to a mobile computing device. Priorities system makes this decision with respect to the user's mail replying frequency and main response time for the sender of interest. Thus, the system specifies the user's attention and interest to senders through the mail replying frequency and main response time.

Attentive Displays reason about what the user is looking at the display though the information gathered from eye gaze detection (Zhai, 2003). Maglio et al.'s SUITOR reason about their user attention and interests by means of eye gaze detection, application use, web browsing and user's email content. It supports users with suitable information that is related to their interests. Traffic lights, as an interesting example beyond personal computers and mobile computing devices, reason about the traffic density on the active information come from coils on the road and the statistics of normal traffic flow (Vertegaal, 2002).

Here the key word is user's interruptibility. Even if the user's focus of attention may not be specified exactly, whether the user is suitable for an interruption may be specified by different ways. Fogarty et al., for example, do this by using simple sensors and their success is %82.4 (Fogarty et al. 2005). Chen & Vertegaal do this by means of humans' physical properties EEG and HRV, and they specify four stages for a user (Chen & Vertegaal, 2003).

4.4.3 Optimization of Attention

The optimization of attention means effective and efficient use of user's valuable attention and other cognitive resources. This is done in two stages such that regulation of interaction where it's aimed to preserve the user cognitive resources and provide a natural mechanism to attention switching to user by means of turn-taking paradigm. The other stage is the augmentation of attention where it's generally aimed to support the user cognition by means of cocktail party effect.

4.4.3.1 Regulating of Interaction

Regulation of interaction is done on the information of user's current cognitive load, interests and goals specified in previous stages. AC implement turn taking paradigm, which coordinates the reaction timing of interfaces based on the attentional information. This process is also called as the gradual negotiation of turns in human group conversations (Vertegaal, 2003).

When multi person human group conversation takes place, people can easily specify the timing of speech, when to speak and when to be silent, usually by using their eyes, extracting contextual information and recognizing facial gestures. Turn taking process regulates the attentional demand of each interlocutor and enables smoother interaction between pairs.

AC tries to imitate turn taking process in computing systems in a similar manner. When an ACS decides to convey information to user, it first evaluates the importance and urgency of its own desire regarding user's focus of attention. Then with respect to the result of evaluation, the system signals its desire from a peripheral channel to user. AC waits for the user's approval before take essential information to foreground. SUITOR does it by using a one-line scrolling text display located at the bottom of the screen (Maglio et al., 2001).

4.4.3.2 Augmentation of Attention

AC tries to augment and support the user's attentional resources by imitating the Cocktail Party Effect phenomenon. This effect is the ability of focus on a particular conversation among many others in crowded places like parties. If we would not have such a capability, we would have serious difficulty in noisy places. ACS in an analogous fashion aims to let the user to focus his or her desires by attenuating peripheral details and highlighting the information to be focused. Bolt's Gaze Orchestrated Dynamic Windows (Section 5.2) and Attentive Displays (Zhai, 2003) are good examples to augmentation of attention.

4.4.4 Declaration of Attention

Notification of the specified user attention to other users and devices is considered as attention declaration. By means of this declaration, even if some of the devices can not monitor the user, they would be ensured that whether the user suitable for communication or not (Shell & Selker, 2003). Attentive Cell Phone application (Section 5.5) is an example to declaration of attention to other devices with eyeReason server (Vertegaal et al., 2002).

5. Attentive Computing Systems

5.1 Eye Contact Sensors: Eye-R & eyeConctact

Eye-R (Selker, 2001) and eyeContact (Vertegaal et al., 2002) are similar, low-cost, calibration free, wearable eye contact detection sensors. They are mainly indented to gather and deliver information about the person's visual attention.

Eye-R does this by sensing eye fixations. It use infrared red beams to detect eye movements when the eyes fixate on an object, it is usually considered good indication of intentional information. System also detects when a user orients his/her head toward to another person, device or appliances that wear Eye-R.

eyeContact uses infra red beams but in a different manner to detect the visual attention of users. It detect user's pupils in its filed of view. eyeContact is based on IBM's PupilCam. It has infrared LEDs on the camera that cause a bright pupil reflection and another set of LEDs cause the black pupils in eyes within range. By syncing the LEDs with the cameras clock a bright and black pupil effect is produced in the sequential video frames. Through a simple computer vision algorithm pupils are detected by subtracting odd and even frames. eyeContact sensor is said to have a 2 meters range. eyeContact sensor has the ability whether there is a person that looks at or maintain eye contact with the sensor by nature.

Both sensors are also able to deliver the obtained information about their user visual attention to a server over wireless TCP/IP connection.

5.2 Gaze-Orchestrated Windows

This application realized in 1985 by Rick Bolts is broadly accepted as the first serious Attentive User Interface (AUI) application (Bolt, 1980). This system is a good example to the augmentation of user attention by attenuating the unnecessary details. In this application, a user looks at a wide screen where 40 movie episodes were playing at the same time. Separate soundtracks from ever episode played simultaneously to form a cocktail-party effect. System understands where user looks on the screen by means of a couple of eye tracking glasses. As system detects which episode the user is looking at, the soundtrack of the intended episode is increased and other are decreased. Soon after, if the interest of user continues on this episode (continue to look at), it's ensured by the system the episode to cover the whole screen.

5.3 GAZE

GAZE is an Attentive Groupware system that aims to provide more efficient cooperative work by supporting gaze awareness in multiparty mediated communication and collaboration (Vertegaal, 1999). At the experimental study, four people were in a group conversation in a 3D virtual conference room. Every person is represented by their avatars to others. The difference of the system according to an ordinary one is that the information about that participant with the visual attention of group is displayed. Thus, it's aimed at the participant to do more natural group conversation remotely.

5.4 SUITOR

SUITOR is one of the first remarkable Attentive Information Systems (Maglio et al., 2001) and it is developed as an extensible framework for building Attentive Agents (Maglio & Campbell, 2003). The name SUITOR is the contraction of "Simple User Interest Tracker". The major objective of SUITOR is to inform its user according user's ongoing tasks, priorities and goals detected by the system without disturbing him or her. This detection is made means of eye-gaze tracking, application use, web browsing, email content, keyboard and mouse input. For that reason, the application is important with regard to monitor the user from many different channels. After SUITOR gathered necessary information about the user's interests, it looks for relevant information and provides this information to user in a unobtrusive manner by using a ticker tap display at the peripheral of the display. There are similar attentive information and notification systems in the literature such that Scope (Dantzich et al., 2002), Fred (Vertegaal et al., 2000) and Attention-Aware Peripheral Display (Park et al, 2009).

5.5 Attentive Cell Phones

Attentive Cell Phones are the phones that can understand whether their user is in a face-to-face conversation by eye sensor and voice analysis (Vertegaal et al., 2002). This study is a well organized example of declaration of attention. The attentive phone sends the attentional information to a eyeReason (Vertegaal et al., 2002) server. Server saves the information of all other people connected to the system. Thus, all users can obtain and use the information of whether a person is in a face-to-face conversation or not. By using this information in addition to the user's own phone other people can have the advantage of to regulate their communication more effectively.

5.6. MAGIC

MAGIC is the name developed for Manuel Gaze Input Cascade (Zhai et al., 1999). It is an Attentive Pointing System where it is ensured that the mouse pointer is sent automatically to the point where the user looks on the window. Thus, it's aimed at the user to be saved of the mouse eye coordination problem and to make faster selection. Experimental results showed that this method is faster than classical mouse approach. However, Midas Touch problem, inadvertent actions present challenges in these systems.

MAGIC is a system that eases the usage of graphical user interfaces by sensing the visual attention. Thus, it augments and supports the user's attention. A similar application in the literature is eyePoint (Kumar et al., 2007) with similar capabilities.

5.7 Pong

Pong is an Attentive Toy or Robot that pays attention to people so it can attend to people's needs using visual and audio sensors (Haritaoğlu et al., 2001). It is also considered as an Attentive Agent by (Maglio & Campbell, 2003). Pong is able to monitor user actions, react accordingly and convey attention and emotion. Pong can detect and track multiple people in a scene by means of real-time video and audio processing techniques, and speech recognition. It can maintain eye contact with people. Pong can express emotion through mimics or facial expressions like happiness, sadness, surprise and confusion etc.

PONG does these by means of its moving head, ping-pong eyes and artificial lips. Thus, PONG can develop a natural communication with people in a way that human uses. This means exactly to throw away the machine from their isolated autonomous worlds and to enable the machines and humans to work together more as partners (Haritaoğlu et al., 2001).

5.8. Gaze Contingent Display

A Gaze Contingent Display (Reingold, 2002) is an Attentive Display (Baudish et al., 2003) that dynamically adjusts their work according to the user's focus of attention. While these displays provide high resolution in the area of the screen at which the user looks, they provide lower resolution elsewhere. The measure of the area that will be shown in high resolution is specified by eye-gaze tracking and the user's perceptual span. Thus, both user's and computer's processing capacities are optimized over the most important information, that is the information that the user is interested in. Users are offered the high resolution information on the screen by filtering peripheral ones and the computer are free from to waste its processing power on peripheral information. These displays are used in many fields like simulators, virtual reality, remote piloting, and telemedicine (Baudish et Al., 2003). In the literature there are some other similar attentive display implementations such that Focus Plus Context Screens, Real-Time 3D Graphics, Easily Perceived Displays (Baudish et al., 2003)

5. Conclusion

In this chapter, interaction problems that are parallel to the increase in number and variety of digital computing systems are discussed in detail. In today's ubiquitous computing age, users are in a multiparty human computer interaction with computing devices. This renders the existing interaction channels and methods to be insufficient.

Users have many difficulties because of the modern lifestyle. The information that is needed to be processed by people is beyond the humans' mental or cognitive capacities most of the time. They are requested to be available and open to connection 7/24. Furthermore, current interaction design approaches and consequently computing systems designed accordingly augment these problems. They don't have individual or contextual sensitivity for user. They allow and redirect any incoming information towards their users without any filtering or mediation for unnecessary details according to the user's need, context and goals. They bombard their users by interruptions. One has to understand that every interruption is a cost to user. The work flow is broken up and user has to face a performance lost, frustration and reeveluation necessity of what has been going on for the past few seconds or more.

As a response to those problems, Attentive Computing (AC) proposes several solutions. AC promises a system that is sensitive to their users' needs and goals. It proposes a computing system that gracefully negotiates the volume and timing of user interruptions and messages instead of imposing them. It also proposes a system that helps and supports their users in their workplace by attenuating unnecessary and irrelevant information.

Strictly speaking, the well-known execution-evaluation cycle does not work properly anymore because of the ubiquitous pattern of interruption. Every interruption prevents the user from both observing the output of the computing system and articulating the input into the system. In case of interruption users have to start a new cycle in order to respond to the interruption. Then, after finishing the cycle caused by interruption, they have to turn back to the point that they leave the previous cycle. We have proposed an Attentive Computing Interaction Framework as a solution to this issue. An attentive system, while the user is in high attentive state, as he or she observes or articulates, may either delay a new interruption or show them from a peripheral channel or even highlight the current one.

AC paradigm is a relatively a new subject in Human Computer Interaction (HCI) field. Since the last 20 years, research done by a limited number of researchers on the subject. The problems of AC are still open problems to address. Yet, there are few valuable studies focusing on the classification, usability and frameworks of Attentive Computing Systems (ACS). Devising new user tracking methods and advancing the existing ones are also promising fields.

Maintaining the protection of privacy and user confidence to ACS is another significant research problem. There few studies on user privacy within AC. For this purpose, it is proposed to be benefited from the studies done within other computing paradigms. Studies and findings show that AC is important and has attractive properties for the future of invisible computing.

ACS have the potential of easing the computer usage. They save digital computing devices from their disruptive behaviors and enable them to behave more social. They support users in many different ways and allow them to focus their tasks instead of the interface itself. We therefore believe that the invisibility of any interaction artifact depends on the way that it is presented.

6. References

Bailey, B. P., Konstan, J. A., and Carlis, J. V. (2000) Measuring the effects of interruptions on task performance in the user interface, *IEEE International Conference on Systems, Man, and Cybernetics*, Vol. 2, , pp. 757—762, 2000

Bolt, R. A. (1980). Put that there: Voice and gesture at the graphics interface. *ACM Computer Graphics*, Vol. 14, No. 3, pp. 262-270

Bolt, R. A. (1981). Gaze-Orchestrated Dynamic Windows, *Computer Graphics*, Vol. 15, No. 3, pp. 109-119

Borriello, G. (2000). The Challenges to Invisible Computing, *Integrated Engineering*, November, 2000

Baudish, P.; DeCarlo, D., Duchowski, A, T. & Geiser, W., S. (2003). Focusing on the Essential: Considering Attention in Display Design, *Communications of ACM*, Vol. 46, No. 3, pp. 60-66, 2003

Buxton, W. (2001). Less is More (More or Less), The Invisible Future: The seamless integration of technology in everyday life., in P. Denning (Ed.), New York: McGraw Hill, pp. 145- 179.

Chen, D. & Vertegaal, R. (2004). Using Mental Load for Managing Interruptions in Physiologically Attentive User Interfaces, *Proceedings of the ACM CHI'04*, pp. 1513-1516, 2004

Dantzich, M.; Robbins, D., Horvitz, E., Czerwinski, M. (2002). Scope: Providing awareness of multiple notifications at a glance, *In Proceedings of Advanced Visual Interfaces*, 2002

Dirican, A., C. & Göktürk, M. (2008). Dikkatli Arayüzler, *ASYU:Akıllı Sistemlerde Yenilikler ve Uygulamaları Sempozyumu*, Haziran 2008

Dix, A.; Finley, A., Abowd, G. D., Beale, R. (2004), *Human Computer Interaciton*, 3rd Edition, Printicehall, 2004

Fogarty, J. (2004). Sensor-Based Statistical Models of Human Interruptibility, *IBM Research Human-Computer Interaction Symposium*, 2004

Fono D., & Vertegaal, R. (2005). EyeWindows: Evaluation of eye-controlled zooming windows for focus selection, *In Proceedings of CHI 2005*, 2005

Gibbs, W. (2005). Considerate computing, *Scientific American*, January, January 2005, pp. 54-61

Haritaoglu, I; Cozzi, A., Koons, D., Flickner, M., Zotkin, D., Duraiswami, R., Yacoob, Y.(2001), Attentive Toys, *IEEE International Conference on Multimedia and Expo*, pp. 917-920, August 2001

Horvitz, E.; Jacobs, A. & Hovel, D. (1999), Attention-sensitive alerting, *In Proceedings of UAI'99*, pp. 305–13, 1999, Stockholm

Horvitz, E.; Kadie, C,, Paek, T., Hovel, D. (2003). Models of attention in computing and communication: from principles to applications, *Communications of ACM*, Vol. 46, No. 3, pp. 52-59, 2003

Jacob, R. J. K. (1990). What You Look At is What You Get: Eye Movement-Based Interaction Techniques, *Proceedings of the ACM CHI'90*, 1990, Seattle, pp. 11-18., Washington, USA

Kumar, M.; Paepcke, A. & Winogard, T. (2007). eyePoint: Practical Pointing and Selection Using Gaze and Keyboard, *In Proceedings of CHI 2007*, San Jose, April 2007, California

Maglio, P.; Matlock, T., Campell, C. S., Zai S. & Smith, B. (2000). "Gaze and Speech in Attentive User Interfaces", *Lecture Notes in Computer Science*, 2000, Vol. 1948, pp. 1-7

Maglio, P. P.; Campbell, C. S., Barrett, R. & Selker, T. (2001), An architecture for developing attentive information systems, *Knowledge-Based Systems*, Vol. 14, 2001, pp. 103-110

Maglio, P.P. & Campell, C. S. (2003). Attentive Agents, *Communications of ACM*, 2003, Vol. 46, No. 3, pp. 47–51

McCrickard, D. S. & Chewar, C. M (2003). Attuning notification design to user goals and attention costs, *Communications of ACM*, Vol. 46, No. 3, 2003, pp. 67–72

McFarlane, D., C. (1999). Coordinating the Interruption of People in Human-Computer Interaction, *INTERACT'99*, 1999, pp. 295-303

Nielsen, J. (1993). Non-command User Interfaces, *Communications of the ACM*, 1993, Vol. 36, No. 4, pp. 82–99

Park, S.; Park, S., S., Lim, Y., Lee, G. & Hahn, M. (2009). Designing Attention-Aware Peripheral Displays with Gaze-Based Notification Control, *CHI 2009*, Boston, April 4-9, MA, USA

Perdikis, S.; Tzovaras, D. & Strintzis, G., M. (2008). Recognition Of Human Activities Using Layered Hidden Markov Models , *2008 IAPR Workshop on Cognitive Information Processing*, June 9-10, 2008, Santorini, Greece

Pickard, R. W. (1998). *Affective Computing*, MIT Press, ISBN-10: 0262661152

Reingold, E.; M., Loschky, L., C., McConkie, G., W. & Stampe, D., M. (2003). Gaze-Contingent Multiresolutional Displays: An Integrative Review, *Human Factors: The Journal of the Human Factors and Ergonomics Society*, Volume 45, Number 2 , pp. 307-328, Summer 2003

Roda, C., & Thomas, J. (2005). Attention Aware Systems, *Encyclopaedia of HCI*, IDEA Group

Roda, C. & Thomas, J. (2006). Attention Aware Systems: Theories, Applications, and Research Agenda, *Computers in Human Behavior*, 2006, Vol. 22, No. 4, pp. 557-587

Rowe D. W.; Sibert, J. & Irwin, D. (1998) Heart rate variability: indicator of user state as an aid to human-computer interaction, *Proceedings of the SIGCHI conference on Human factors in computing systems*, pp. 480-487, April 18-23, 1998, Los Angeles, California, United States

Selker, T & Burlesson, W. (2000), Context-aware design and interaction in computer Systems, *IBM Systems journal*, Vol. 39 , Issue 3-4 pp. 880 - 891, July, 2000,

Selker, T.; Lockerd, A., Martinez, J. & W. Burleson. (2001). Eye-R, a Glasses-mounted Eye Motion Detection Interface, *In Proceedings of ACM SIGCHI Conference on Computer Human Interaction*, 2001

Selker, T. (2004), Visual Attentive Interfaces, *BT Technology journal*, Vol. 22, No. 4, 2004

Shell, J. S. (2002). Taking Control of the Panopticon: Privacy Considerations in the Design of Attentive User Interfaces, *CSCW 2002 Conference on Computer Supported Collaborative Work*, 2002, New Orleans

Shell, J. S.; Vertegaal, R. & Skaburskis, A. (2003a). EyePliances: Attention-Seeking Devices that Respond to Visual Attention, *In Extended Abstracts of ACM CHI 2003 Conference on Human Factors in Computing Systems*, 2003

Shell, J. S.; Selker, T., Vertegaal, R. (2003b), Interacting with Group of Computers, *Communications of ACM*, Vol. 46, No. 3, pp. 40-46 , 2003

Shneiderman (1993), *Designing the Interface*, 3rd Edition, Addisson Wesley, 1993

Vertegaal, R. (1999), The GAZE groupware system: Mediating joint attention in multiparty communication and collaboration, *In Proceedings of CHI'99*, 1999, Pittsburg

Vertegaal, R.; Slagter, R., Van der Veer, G.C., and Nijholt, A. (2000). Why Conversational Agents Should Catch the Eye, *In Extended Abstracts of CHI'2000*, 2000, pp. 257-258, The Hague, Netherlands

Vertegaal, R. (2002). Designing Attentive Interfaces, *In Proceedings of ACM ETRA Symposium on Eye Tracking Research and Applications*, 2002, ACM Press, New Orleans

Vertegaal, R.; Dickie, C., Sohn, C. & Flickner, M. (2002), Designing attentive cell phone using wearable eyecontact sensors, *In Extended Abstracts of CHI'02*, 2002, pp. 646-647

Vertegaal, R. (2003). Introduction, *Communications of ACM*, Vol. 46, No. 3, pp. 30-33, 2003

Vertagaal, R.; Shell, J. S., Chen, D. & Mamuji A., (2006). Designing for augmented attention: Towards a framework for attentive user interfaces, *Computers in Human Behavior*, 2006, Vol. 22, pp. 771-789

Yamaoka, F; Takayuki Kanda, Hiroshi Ishiguro, Norihiro Hagita. (2009), Developing a model of robot behavior to identify and appropriately respond to implicit attention-shifting., *HRI 2009*, pp. 133-140, 2009

Weiser, M. (1991). The computer for the 21st century. *Scientific American*, pp. 94-100, 1991, September

Zhai, S. (2003). What's in the eyes for attentive input, *Communications of ACM*, Vol. 46, No. 3, pp. 34–39, 2003

Zhai, S.; Morimoto, C. & Ihde, S. (1999). Manual and gaze input cascaded (MAGIC) pointing, *In Proceedings of CHI'99*, pp. 246-253, 1999

3

Current Challenges and Applications for Adaptive User Interfaces

Victor Alvarez-Cortes, Víctor H. Zárate,
Jorge A. Ramírez Uresti and Benjamin E. Zayas
Instituto de Investigaciones Eléctricas; Tecnológico de Monterrey
México

1. Introduction

In this chapter we present the current advances in the field of adaptive user interfaces, analysing the different research efforts, the challenges involved as well as the more recent and promising directions in this field. Initially, we introduce the foundations of adaptive user interfaces, also referred in technical literature as Intelligent User Interfaces (IUIs), then we move to explore the motivation and rationale for their use, and finally we discuss the challenges they currently have to deal with. In this context, IUIs are presented as a multi-disciplinary field, with relevant research and cross-fertilized ideas derived from different areas, however special emphasis is put on the approaches taken by three core disciplines: Artificial Intelligence (AI), User Modelling (UM) and Human-Computer Interaction (HCI). After providing the foundations for IUIs, an in-depth revision for each approach is presented including the most recent findings in models, algorithms and architectures for adaptive user interfaces.

Although, adaptive user interfaces are considered a recent research field, this chapter is enriched with a state-of-the-art of IUIs applications. The material included presents the most relevant developed IUIs applied in different real domains either as a research prototype or as a complete system. A methodological analysis of these systems is presented, contrasting its advantages, limitations and domain-dependence for its success and acceptance by users. The analysis aims to uncover common principles for effective IUI design. Also, this chapter details our proposed taxonomy which is applied for the comparison of the different IUIs systems.

Finally, the chapter presents the gaps left by the approaches under analysis and concludes with a discussion of the challenges currently open, presenting a number of possible future research directions.

User interfaces (UI) for the computing systems have changed in the last 20 years. The first UIs based on text that used a command prompt to access the operating system resources, have been replaced for user graphics interfaces (GUIs) that are manipulated through entry devices like keyboard and mouse. At present, user interfaces attempt to be more intuitive to the user by presenting graphic elements visually associated with real elements by the use of metaphors (Dix et al, 2003.)

An interaction paradigm widely use in the current operating systems is the use of multiple windows to present information as well as the use of icons to represent environment elements such as folders, files, devices, etc, and the use of menus and buttons, that facilitate the interaction with the system. This paradigm known as WIMP (Windows, Icons, Menus, Pointers) was developed by Xerox PARC in the 80's, and was initially used by Apple Macintosh computers and currently present in others operating systems such as Microsoft Windows, OS/ Motif, Risc OS and X Window System (Shneiderman & Plaisant, 2004.) However, still with these advances and the functionality offered by current GUIs, most of current GUIs are still limited as to how to handle the differences existing between the different UI users, being clear that exists limitation in the development of systems that can be personalized and adapted to the user and to the environment.

Intelligent User Interfaces is a HCI sub-field and its goal is to improve the interaction human-computer by the use of new technologies and interaction devices, as well as through the use of artificial intelligence techniques that allow exhibiting some kind of adaptive or intelligent behavior.

2. Applications and usage for the IUIs

IUIs attempt to solve some of the problems that traditional user interfaces, known as direct manipulation cannot handle appropriately (Shneiderman, 1997).

- *Create personalized systems:* There are not two identical users and each one has different habits, preferences and ways of working. An intelligent user interface can take into consideration these differences and provide personalized interaction methods. Since a IUI might know each user preferences, it's feasible to use that knowledge to set the best communication channel with that particular user.

- *Filtering problems and information over-load:* Trying to find the required information in a computer or in the Internet can be a complicated task. Here an intelligent interface can reduce the quantity of relevant information to look at in a large database. Also, by filtering out irrelevant information, the interface can reduce the user's cognitive load. An IUI can suggest to the user new and useful sources of information been unknown at that moment.

- *Provide help for new programs:* The information systems can be very complicated to manage and user productivity cab be reduced at the beginning when user gets to know application features. Unfortunately, as the user begins to understand the program functionalities, new versions or upgrades appear including new functionality. In this situation an intelligent help system can detect and correct an inapropiate usages or sub optimal task accomplishments by explaining new concepts and providing information to simplify the tasks.

- *Take charge of tasks on behalf of the user:* An IUI can see what tasks the user is attempting to accomplish, understand the context and recognize his attempt, and finally deal with the execution of a complete set of certain task, allowing the user to focus its attention to others tasks.

- *Other interaction mechanisms:* Currently the most common interaction devices of a computer sytem are the keyboard and the mouse. An important and active IUI research area within HCI known as Multi-modals Interfaces aims to discover new ways of interaction. Multimodals user interfaces attempt to find new paradigms for input/output interaction between systems and users. It is believe that by providing multiple means of interaction, people with disabilities will be able to use complex computational systems.

3. Definition and Related Areas

Certainly through years numerous definitions of intelligence have been proposed in order to define systems and behaviors, however none consensus exist on what has to be considered an intelligent system or behavior. Nevertheless, most of proposed definitions associate the adaptation ability, ability to learn and handle new situations, ability to communicate and the ability to solve problems (Russell & Norvig, 2003)

A "normal" user interface is defined as a communication between a user (human) and a machine (Meyhew, 1999.) An extension of this definition for an intelligent interface is that computer uses some kind of human intelligence component to complete the human-computer communication. Likewise, they are also known as adaptive interfaces, since they have the ability to adapt to the user, communicate with him and solve its problems. A formal definition is as follow: *"Intelligent user interfaces (IUIs) are human-machine interfaces that aim to improve the efficiency, effectiveness, and naturalness of human-machine interaction by representing, reasoning, and acting on models of the user, domain, task, discourse, and media (e.g., graphics, natural language, gesture)"*. (Maybury, 1999).

Since adaptation and problem solving are core topics in the artificial intelligence research area, a lot of IUIs are orientated to the use of AI techniques, however not all IUIs have learning or problem solving capabilities. Many of the currently denominated intelligent interfaces are aimed to improve aspects related to the communication channel between the user and the system (machine) by applying novel interaction techniques such as Natural Language processing, *gaze tracking* and facial recognition. HCI literature reveals that a lot of research fields have influenced the IUIs development to its current state. Related areas to IUI includes disciplines such as psychology, ergonomics, human factors, cognitive sciences and others as shown in figure 1.

One of the most important properties for IUIs is that they are designed to improve the interaction and communication channel between the user and the machine.

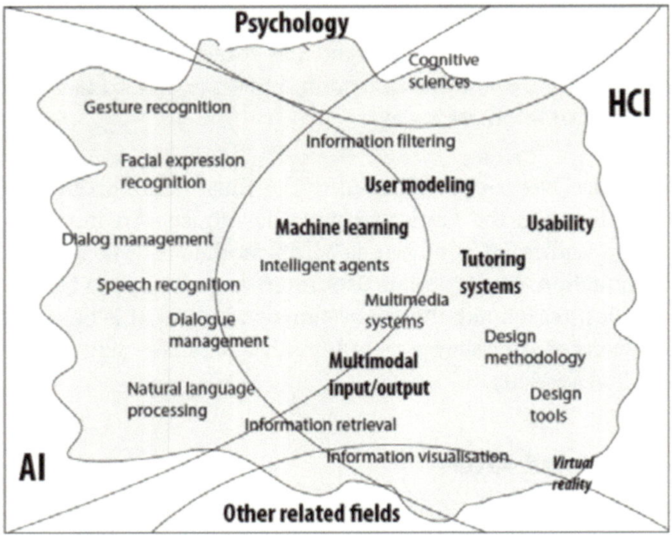

Fig. 1. Intelligent User Interfaces and its different disciplines involved

From an HCI point of view it is not so important what specific technique is used to get this improvement as long as the improvement is achieved. A number of techniques that are relevant are shown bellow:

- *Intelligent input technology:* It deals with the use of techniques to obtain user's input to the system. These techniques include natural language processing (speech recognition and dialog systems), gesture recognition, facial expressions recognition and lip reading.
- *User modeling:* This research area includes techniques that allow a system to keep or infer knowledge about a user based on the received information as input.
- *User adaptivity:* It includes all the techniques to allow that human-computer interaction to be adapted to different users and different usage situations.
- *Explanation generation:* It deals with techniques and mechanisms that aims to explain to the user in a logical and understandable form the underlaying reasoning in an intelligent user interface.
- *Personalization:* In order to be able to customize a user interface usually most current IUIs include some kind of user's representation. User's models logs data about users behavior, his knowledge and abilities. New discvored knowledge about user can infered based on new input data and user-system historical interaction loggins.
- *Usage flexibility:* In order to remain flexible, a number of IUIs integrates user adaptation and computational learning. Adaptation is accomplished by using the knowledge stored in the user model and inferring new knowledge using the current input. Computational learning is used when knowledge stored in the user model is changed to reflect new found situations or data.

4. Intelligent Interfaces and Intelligent Systems

It is common to assume that an IUI is also an intelligent system and confusion frequently arises. A system that exhibits some kind of intelligence not necessarily has an intelligent user interface. It is not rare for intelligent systems to have very simple user interfaces, even text-based user interface where no intelligence exist. Likewise, the fact that a system has an IUI does not reveal us anything about the system intelligence *per se*. See figure 2.

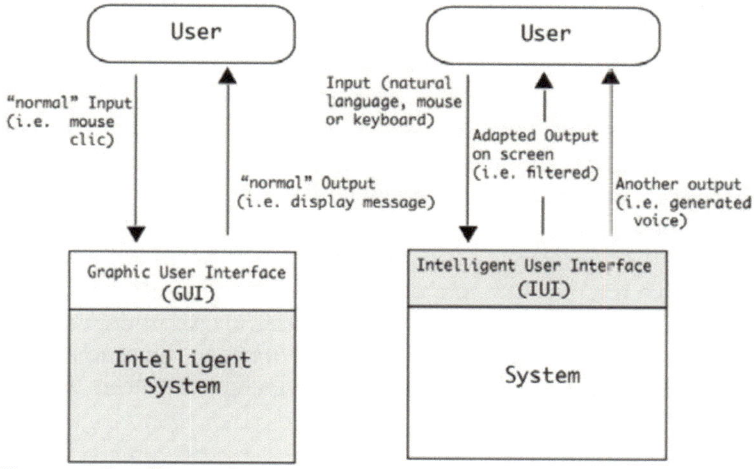

Fig. 2. The IUIs vs. an Intelligent System

Unfortunately the dividing border between a system and its user interface is not always clearly defined as it is shown in figure 2. Often times the technology the IUI is based on has an underlying connection with the core parts of the system, sometimes the IUI is actually the system itself. For practical purposes, in many applications for specific domains (i.e. power plants, utilities, etc.) usually not much attention is pay to the user interface side. An analysis, assessment and development assigned to an expert group in user interfaces and ergonomics is not always a reality. When developing an intelligent system the emphasis is put on the inner workings, algorithms and data manipulation, leaving out the user interface as another system component (Hook, 1999.)

5. Benefits and criticisms

IUIs research is a relatively new area, not yet unified and in constant evolution where a number of challenges remain open, still expecting a better approach or solution. Maybe the direct association between IUI and Artificial Intelligence has received skepticism from a part of HCI community. The central problem can be reduced to the fact that IUIs violate some of the long time established and accepted principles in the traditional (direct manipulation) user interfaces development. Maes's research work at the MIT Media Lab (Maes, 1994) and findings reported by Wernn (Wernn, 1997) present an extensive explanation of potential applications and domains for intelligent user interfaces, clearly establishing the points that have to be discussed and resolved before IUIs became widely accepted and used in commonplace.

A number of HCI researchers (Shneiderman, 1997) consider that an IUI or adaptive system is unpredictable and less transparent than a traditional user interface. If a system can adapt its response and cannot provide the same output twice for the same input, the system becomes unpredictable. A similar situation occurs regarding the control on the interface. Possible scenarios are that the user takes the control and decides the next action to accomplish. On the other hand the system could autonomously take control on the interface based on its partial knowledge and decides the next action. This situation has been confronted from different approaches resulting in specializing areas within the IUI discipline.

Adaptable interfaces grants the user full control over the interface by allowing him to manage and customize the adaptation through selections of available options to personalize and adapt the interface. On the other side we have the *Adaptive interfaces* where the system has sufficient intelligence and autonomy to evaluate the current state and make a decision to achieve some kind of adaptation without the user's intervention. A third interaction scheme that has been reported and received acceptance within the AI area is known a *mixed-initiative* or combined-initiative interfaces, where the interaction and control over the interfaces is share between the user and the system (Armentano, 2006). An in-depth discussion among user interface experts can be found in the reported work by Birnbaum (Birnbaum, 1997) where an analysis about the advantages and disadvantages between IUIs and traditional user interfaces is presented.

6. Machine Learning for the IUIs

The use of artificial intelligence techniques to design IUIs has been a widely accepted approach within the HCI interface community that has been applied to different applications and domains.

A wide spectrum of AI techniques have been applied for IUIs development, from traditional Production Systems (rule-based) to more sophisticated techniques such as planning and probabilistic graphic models (Horvitz, 1998) to recent techniques of IA such as autonomous agents (Rich & Sidner, 1996) (Eisenstein & Rich, 2002).

These AI techniques have been applied to generate different degree of intelligence (or adaptability) taking advantage of the knowledge the system has about the user and the tasks at hand to provide the best interaction experience using the system.

Machine Learning (ML) and related algorithms used to include the adaptibity component in IUI, have experience a fast growing development in the last ten years, gaining acceptance in AI community. Machine learning has been applied with relative success in several domains and applications, mainly in Web applications to collect information and mine data from user's interaction and of navigation logs (Fu, 2000). Likewise, machine learning has been used as a mean to infer user's models (Stumpf et al., 2007) based on past data (history logs) aiming to discover unknown patterns and adapting the IUI behavior accordingly.

In ML terms, an intelligent user interface can be conceptualized like "*a software component that improves its capacity to interact with the user by generating and maintaining a user model base on the partial experience with that user*" (Langley, 1999). This definition clearly state that an intelligent interface is designed to interact with real, human users. Even more, if a user interface is to be considered intelligent, then it must improve its interaction with the user as time passes by, considering that a simple memorization of those interactions is not sufficient, but the improvement must come as results of a generalization of past experiences in order to establish new interactions with the user.

It is possible to identify two intelligent user interfaces categories with a ML approach which are different in the kind of feedback the user must provide:

- *Informative:* This kind of interface attempts to select or modify information and present only those elements the user might find interesting or useful for the task at hand. The most common examples are the recommender systems (i.e online bookstore as Amazon.com) and news filters, where users attention is directed within a wide option space. In these systems the feedback provided by the user involves to mark recommendation options as desirable or not desirable and ranking them. However this type of interfaces is intrusive and distracts users attention from the central task, since the user must provide feedback. IUI literature (Sugiyama, 2004) reports a group of less intrusive methods to obtain feedback by observing the access process.

- *Generative:* These kind of interfaces are aimed mainly to the generation of some useful knowledge structure. This category includes programs for documents preparation, spreadsheets, as well as planning and configuration systems. These interfaces support an enhanced feedback because the user can ignore not only a recommendation, but simply replace it with another one. The feedback is linked to the kinds of interaction supported by the interface. A number of systems require the user to correct not desirable actions, which pose an interruption problem, however recent systems integrates less intrusive schemes by observing the user's actions. (Franklin et al., 2002.)

One feasible approach reported in HCI literature to generate adaptive interfaces is through mining Web usage loggings. The access Web logging constitutes an abundant source of information that allows to experiment with real datasets. Adaptive Web systems provide the user better user interface navigation by providing personalized direct links. During the adaptation process, the user's data access are the central source of information and is used to build the user's model, which reflex the pattern the system inferred for the users and describes several user characteristics. Data mining using Association Rules has been used to mine the navigation logs from web sites and also to suggest new links based on collaborative filtering. (Mobasher et al., 2001.)

7. User modeling of the user in the IUIs

User interface and User modeling (UM) can be seen as I two sides of a same component. User model consists of the algorithms that are implemented in the software level to show the personalization concept from the system's perspective. On the other hand, Graphic User Interfaces (GUI) display the content generated by the UM to the user, showing the personalization from the user's point of view as shown in figure 3.

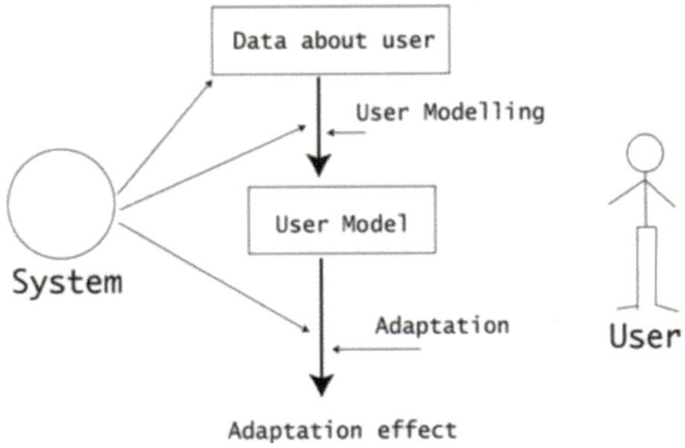

Fig. 3. Two perspectives for the User Model.

User modeling applications can be defined as applications where "*users with different objectives, interests, experience levels, abilities and preferences can adapt the program behavior to individual needs by using a user's profiles*" (Kobsa, 1994)

The UM purpose is collect, process and display adapted data to the interface level by a compilation of knowledge through two kinds of information:

- *Implicit:* This data compilation involves examining log files suchs as navigation history or the browser "cookies" (Fu, 2000). The discovery of patterns in data allows contents filtering and its addressing based on assumptions made on the user's behavior. For example, if a user regularly review certain particualr items, the UM will identify a pattern and can alter the user interface to unfold those elements and associate those elements in a web page accesible to the user. This is a UM automated technique that does not require a straight forward feedback from user in order to identify a behavior pattern and modifying the content according to it.

- *Explicit:* Explicit data gathering involves the data analysis entered by users, providing information about their preferences by filling out a user profile. For example: age, gender, city, shopping history, contents preferences and display data layout. This technique is known in the UM area as an informed technique and requires the user to enter data and a mechanism for recognizing patterns in the user preferences in order to modify the user interfaces based on those preferences.

User models can be used to create personalized services, adapting its elements to individual needs through information or collaborative filtering techniques (Carenini, 2003). Users can take control over the interaction by choosing explicitly based on user profiles through recommendation systems that establish associations between an individual purchase records or of navigation log with that similar users (Kirsh-Pinheiro et al., 2005.)

Adaptive user interfaces present users models at the user interface level by displaying personalized contents. (Eirinaki & Vazirgiannis, 2003). Likewise users also have the opportunity to interact directly with user model when creating and editing the profiles. User modeling and the adaptive user interface essentially both present personalized views for contents that can save time for locating information or guiding the users to available and unknown contents the user.

In summary, the UM is a solid alternative for presenting personalized content and it is considered a useful tool to the user that allows the use of Explicit data. On the other hand there is skepticism about the use of implicit data to create imprecise stereotypes based on complex inference algorithms (Peyton, 2003), since a large amount of literature reports few tests with real users. "*An UMUAI review in the last 9 first years reveals that a third part of the articles includes some kind of evaluation only. This is a very short percentage* (Chin, 2001.)

8. HCI in the IUIs

An HCI approach to solve the interaction problems has been centered on the use of different ways of interaction or means to communicate the user with the system. The central idea is to make this interaction in the most natural way, similar to that found between humans. If we take into account that we as humans perceive the world through our senses (touch; sight; hearing; smell and taste), then it seems logical the idea to unify this information in a computer capable to process it through different available devices (keyboard, microphone, camera; etc) in a multi-modal scheme, presenting what is known as multi-modal user interfaces. Multi-modal interfaces integrate two or more means of communication in order to improve the interaction channel between system and human.

Current state-of-the-art multi-modals interfaces can process two or more combined input modes based on recognition technologies, aiming to accurate identify and interpret the user communication intentions (Reeves et al., 2004). There are a number of multi-modals interfaces, including those that process voice and pencil input or through touch-sensitive screens and voice systems. Computational vision technologies and voice processing are fundamental to the development of this kind of interfaces and they are extensively reviewed in Oviatt's research (Oviatt et al., 2000.)

A novel approach in the multi-modals interfaces area is the integration of agent's technology, multimedia components and virtual reality with artificial intelligence techniques for the development of characters similar to humans who interact with the users in a more natural way. Throughout the use of computational vision and voice processing, these human-like characters or agents known as ECAS (*Embodied Conversational Agents)* represent a research line that integrates several areas (Cassell, 2000.) It has been revealed that in these ECAs virtual environments the user interfaces developed for interaction need to address new design challenges.

9. Related systems

A number of related systems reported in the user interface literature with relevant adaptivity features are presented in this section.

9.1 SurfLen System

One of the core elements in adaptive user interfaces is its capacity to anticipate the tasks the user will execute based on observing current actions, his behavior and the user model. A research line reported in IUI literature is based on setting future actions (tasks; navigation; plans; strategies, etc.) considering the analysis of history logging of the last actions of the user (or also of a group of users) by using AI techniques in order to complete some kind of reasoning on this information and deduce the action to do. Fu's work (Fu, 2000) is one of this kind, however it is focused on an on Web based information recommender system.

Author's hypothesis state that user's navigation logs contain sufficient information to discover knowledge about interesting pages for the user, without the need for a user to assigns a grade or input additional information, which is a disadvantage in current systems. Likewise authors express that it is possible keep track of what the user has read, in an active but silent way and collect the navigation logs in a centralized repository in order to apply AI techniques to discover knowledge. For example, if two users have read several similar pages, it's possible to infer that both users have similar interests. This knowledge about pattern navigation similarity is used to generate (infer) the recommendations.

To probe these positions, the authors developed a recommendation system prototype called *SurfLen* that suggests to users interesting pages on specific topics. Developed prototype uses Agrawal algorithm proposed by authors for generating a set of association rules with an *a-priori* optimization. The prototype evaluation reports that the number of correct suggestions by user increases as the navigation record becomes more representative of his interests.

A relevant part of this work is the use of the Agrawal *a priori* optimization algorithm applied to navigation logs but aimed at making recommendations. Likewise, suggested scheme with association rules offers advantages on similar systems since no intervention is required from the user. A weak part of its developed prototype and testing is that experiments were simulated and carried out in a well controlled environment. Prototype test results mentioned that it has advantages over other techniques; however no comparison with a similar system is mentioned. On the other hand, is not discussed either the fact that datasets creation as URL number increase (as well as the users) must be costly in terms of processing time, even with the optimization applied.

This prototype is relevant to HCI issues since it exhibits AI techniques that might be suitable and extensible to other domains such as those found in user interfaces for supervision and control, in power plants operation that aim to implement an adaptation mechanism. A possibility would be to analyze the navigation logs for operators (expert, beginner, medium) in different situations (normal, emergency) or in different stages (start; operation; shut down) to create a navigation pattern that allows to predict and recommend the next displayed screen (or action) based on the operators loggings (or loggings from a number of similar operators)

9.2 Adaptive Interfaces for Process Control

The reported system by Viano (Viano et al., 2000) is relevant because it deals with the adaptive user interfaces, particularly aimed at user interfaces for critical operations such as those used for process control. Additionally the presented prototype is designed to be used in two applications: systems for the power grids handling and a system for the supervision of a thermoelectric plant generation.

The authors argue that due to the increasing complexity in control systems, operators limitations to handle in real-time a large amount of information as well as in fault situations, along with the demands for keeping the operation continuity, allows a serious consideration for adaptive systems. These systems can alter its structure, functionality or interface in order to adjust its behavior to different individual requirements or groups of users. The adaptive approach proposed in this research, allows to assist the operator in acquiring the most relevant information in any particular context.

The central position of the article is that the operator's interface design is rigid; since it is established at design time, taking into account the best accepted practices or ergonomic guides recommended by HCI literature. However, once established this situation, it is kept immutable during the application execution. This mapping between the kind of information that is receiving from field and the way (and means) used to display it to the user, it is not unique, but the one the designer selects and considers more effective and efficient, however other possible mappings are discarded. So, no matter how good the initial design it is, it will be a static one from the design stage. This situation poses associated disadvantages since the user interface design is a rigid, not designed to fault or emergency situations, and so on. The adaptive user interface architecture proposed in this work considers the adaptation in the information presentation. Authors paper denominate their model as "Flexible Mapping" based on that current process state, environment and of human factors knowledge.

The paper proposes architecture based on multi-agents technology, where agents for the following functions are included: Process model, communication means, display resolution, presentation, human factor database and operator. Likewise two principles are considered to start the adaptation mechanism: When a deviation from normal process is detected and when there is an operator's deviation (not reacting accordingly to the expected procedure.)

Initially authors mention their suggested approach has benefits that are evaluated in two prototypes, however in the Prototypes section, it is stated that those prototypes are still in development. An important contribution from this research the hypothesis presented and the arguments presented for a description of the needs in the process control systems and why an adaptive approach is required and desirable.

Another relevant point fro this research is the architecture presented, still when the given explanation on the components and the interaction between them is scarce, since no other work in the electric area had reported this architecture based on multi-agents. On the other hand, a weak part of found is the fact that authors do not mention the coordination mechanisms, which represent an important aspect and a real challenge in the multi-agents systems. In general terms this work present at a high level overview but do not go deeper into details and the state of the art presented could include more related works in the area.

9.3 ADAPTS System

The ADAPTS system developed by Brusilovsky (Brusilovsky & Cooper, 2002) use the approach to include different models (tasks, users and environment) to adapt content and navigation in a hypermedia adaptable system. These features are relevant and open a possibility to extend research works in adaptive user interface models for other domains. E electrical and control processing domain are feasible domains for intelligent assistant system to aid in adapting the presented content, taking into account the user characteristic as well as the plant status.

ADAPTS system *(Technical Support Personalized And Diagnostics Adaptive)* is described as an electronic help system for maintenance that integrates an adaptive guide from a system of diagnosis system which has adaptive access to technical information covering both sides of the process: What to do and how to do it. ADAPTS is an extensive project, a result of the joint collaboration between the Naval Research Airs Warfare Center, Aircraft Division, Carnegie Mellon University researcher center, University of Connecticut and the Antech Systems Inc company.

A core component in ADAPTS architectures is the IETM (*Interactive Electronic Technical Manuals*) which provides a large amount of information about the system: how is built, its operation and what do in the event of specific problems, etc. ADAPTS is a complex adaptive system that adjust its diagnostic strategy according to who is the technician and what he is doing, dynamically adapting the configurations sequence, tests, repair or replacement procedures based on technician's answers. Likewise the system integrates domain knowledge of the control, maintenance tasks and users uniqueness.

User model proposed by authors determines which task must be accomplished, which technical information should be selected to describe the task and how to present it in the more adequate form for a particular technician. The problematic issue established in this research works has to do with the amount of potentially relevant information at a given moment in the process of repairing can become really large and is a challenge for a technician to find the more suitable information according to their experience level and work context. To accomplish this task it is necessary to find a way to permanently and dynamically evaluate the technician knowledge, his experience level, work preferences and context.

Also, the proposed model handles the experience level by calculating from several evidences of the technician's experience level. These evidences are silently collected by the system when interacting with the technician. Likewise ADAPTS uses Multi-Aspect Overlay Model that is a more expressive UM, but at the same time it is more complex to generate and maintain.

ADAPTS authors presents the developed system, its proposed models and how they can be used to build an adaptive system, however it is not clearly stated or justified why the 20 suggested aspects used to evaluate the user experience are sufficient or the adequate ones. An uncertain aspect in the proposed model is that it is assumed that if a user asks the IETM for a display, he necessarily reads it. It would be appropriate to include a certain level of probability uncertainty or time before assuming this situation, as it is done in other similar systems. It is relevant the fact that scarce data on validation experiments is presented. More information regarding ADAPTS evaluation, real utility, application in the field, users satisfaction, and so on, might require more details, however it is fair to acknowledge that ADAPTs is a complex, large and complete system.

9.4 A Decision Making Model

The suggested approach discussed in Stephanidis (Stephanidis et al., 1997) conceptualizes Intelligent User interfaces as components that are characterized by its adapting capacity at run time to make several relating communication decisions such as "what," "when," "why" and "how" for interacting with the user, all this accomplished by the use of an adaptation strategy.

The use of models as central part to broaden our understanding on the processes involved in the adaptation of user interfaces has been widely discussed in the HCI area (Puerta, 1998) and a clear difference is known between a model, architecture and the objectives pursue by them.

Stephanidis conceptualize the adaptation strategy as a decision making process, where different attributes that involve aspects of the user interface are subject to adaptation and they are denominated by the authors as "*adaptation constituents.*" Likewise, the adaptation at run time involve certain monitoring at the interface level in order to evaluate the critical element state of the interaction and they are denominated as "*adaptation determinants*" which impact and set conditions for the adaptation decisions. Another considered aspect deals with the adaptation goals of the adaptation process itself. In the proposed scheme, authors establish that the adaptations will be made by a group of rules, called "*adaptation rules*". Essentially the proposed scheme works this way: adaptation rules assign certain *"adaptation constituent"* to "*adaptation determinants*", given a group of "*adaptation goals.*"

A motivation for the proposed scheme is the fact the even though several approaches have been reported in the HCI literature, there is no consensus regarding to which features, behavior and essential components must comprise an intelligent user interface. The core problem discussed by Stephanidis is that the critical elements of the adaptation process (determinants, constituents, goals and rules) are substantially different in current systems. Existing systems adapt certain predefined constituents, based on a predetermined group of determinants, through the use of specific rules, in order to reach pre-specified objectives.

This situation is discussed by authors and concludes that the adaptation process is not flexible and that it can not be easily transferred between applications. To confront the previous limitations the authors propose:

1. A methodological approach which allows the personalization for the set of adaptation determinants and adaptation constituents.

2. Integrate the adaptation goals at a base level as a core and essential component in the adaptation process.

3. A flexible mechanism to modify the adaptation rules, taking into account the adaptability objectives.

The central idea of the proposed scheme is based on establishing a clear separation between the adaptations attributes from the adaptation process. It is also discussed the hypothesis that by establishing this separation, the adaptation strategy attributes can be personalized in a more flexible way to different application domains and user groups, and eventually could be reused with minor modifications in other applications.

Stephanidis present a generalized architecture for an intelligent user interface, describing the components, the interaction between them and its relation with the adaptation strategy. Additionally, a formal representation for the adaptation elements is presented. The proposed work conclude summarizing the benefits of the proposed approach, however no experimentation is presented. Also, some of the claimed benefits are questionable and the proposed scheme seems too general and probably more detail is required for a particular domain application.

9.5 Mixed-Initiative Systems

Mixed-Initiative systems (MI Systems) have emerged as an alternative to the existent interaction schemes that allows to handle the interaction initiative from a more flexible perspective, even though is indeed a more sophisticated and complex scheme.

Research work reported by Bunt (Bunt et al., 2004) discusses the relevance of the adaptive support, a central topic in the field of Mixed-initiative user interfaces (Horvitz, 1999) and emphasizes the necessity of the current adaptive systems to provide the user with an adaptive mechanism to assist them in the user interface personalization.

In MI systems is established that at certain moments the system makes the adaptations automatically, assuming the associated problems such as lack of control, transparency and predictability, and at other times, the system offer mechanisms so the same user can take control of the interaction and complete the adaptation himself. However there are evidences that the user usually does not uses this available mechanism to make this adaptation and when he finally decides to do it, is not clear if he makes it in an effective way (Jameson & Schwarzkopf, 2002).

Bunt proposes a Mixed- initiative solution, where the system observes if the user is able to personalize efficiently by himself, and if he does, then no system initiated adaptation is required. If that is not the case, then the system can intervene to provide assistance to the user. Likewise, the personalization value is analyzed and how to offer what they call *adaptive support* (i.e. help users to take advantage of an adaptable user interface). An experimental study is presented and it is also analyzed the required aspects for users to complete the personalization of a menu-based GUI based on menus.

It is presented a relevant analysis regarding task characteristic and personalization behaviors that affect the user performance. Additionally a study is presented with a simulation of the process model using GOMS (*Goals, Operators, Methods, and Selection rules*) based on a cognitive model that generates predictions of the user performance. Authors analyses with data test the personalization process and if it's worth it and if there are real tangible benefits.

This research presents 2 exploratory experiments using the GLEAN simulator (Baumeister et al., 2000.) In the first experiment author present a comparison of different strategies of personalization that differ from each other in the moment when they are applied, that is, when are made and analyze if the "*overhead*" of personalizing represents an advantage in some degree. In the second experiment they focus on comparing strategies that differ regarding which functionality the user chose to add to the personalize interface and its implications.

As a contribution of this research, could be considered the use of a GOMS model that allows simulating and evaluating the impact in the personalization taking into consideration the combined personalization strategy based on: the moment it is accomplished, the task execution frequency, its complexity and the user experience level.

The results from the experiments demonstrate the importance in performance terns derived from personalizing the user interface, and consequently strengthens the justification for this work of "*guiding*" the user to personalize the user interface, providing initial insights to consider the *adaptive support* as an important research line.

10. Discussion

Resulting from the revision of IUIs literature presented in this chapter, it is observed that most of the existing prototypes and experimental systems that integrates an intelligent user interfaces, are designed and applied to Web based systems and office applications. However, the system presented by Viano's research group (Viano et al., 2000) represents one of the few systems specifically targeted to critical applications for control and supervision such as that found in electric power plant.

Another model aimed at critical systems is found in MI-IAM (Alvarez, 2009), a model for adaptive user interfaces based on the integration of different sub-models using a mixed-initiative approach for supervision in electric power plants. MI-IAM model is aimed at critical and infrequent tasks, which is a specific area where more efforts are required and a reduced number of research work is reported in IUI literature.

ADAPTs system (Brusilovsky & Cooper, 2002) is similar in some aspects to the MI-IAM model, since it uses several models to achieve the adaptation, such as the user model, a control model and a task model similar to the MI-IAM approach. Likewise ADAPTs uses an intelligent system that reports faults diagnostic and uses an electronic manual to find the information that explains to the user how to accomplish a repairing. This situation seems to be similar to the MI-IAM which is also connected to a proprietary Operators Help System and makes the adaptation to navigation and contents.

An important difference between MI-IAM and ADAPTs is that the latter is an adaptive system, whereas the first is a Mixed-Initiative system scheme, offering more flexibility in the interaction with the user. Likewise, ADAPTs system emphasis is its complex and novel multi-aspects user model that allows in a dynamic way to set the user experience level at any given time. MI-IAM by having a comprehensive integration of different models, attempts to derive from them the key component to make a more accurate adaptation process, not by the amount of information collected but by presenting the more adequate information to the operator according to the power plant status. Other key difference is that ADAPTS is designed for maintenance purposes but not for critical or infrequent operational situations.

Since some IUIs build their models by observing their users behavior, a still open challenge is to generate useful models by using a small amount of datasets and efficient algorithms that make the pattern learning faster. The issue here in not related to CPU processing time, but to a reduce number of training datasets required to generate an accurate users preferences model. Most of data mining applications require a considerable amount of data, sufficient to infer and discover patterns and generate knowledge. In contrast, the adaptive interfaces depend on the user's time when using them and consequently require mechanisms for induction that can provide a high accuracy from a limited number of datasets.

An open challenge is the fact that currently exists a limited amount of empirical evaluation for the adaptive systems, and more research is necessary for setting measurable aspects to determine if an intelligent user interface is better in some measurable way compared to a non-intelligent user interface. A number of empirical usability evaluation methods have been used and extended to the adaptive user interface context, such as interviews, questionnaires, Think Aloud (Dix et al., 2003) and others that are essentially variations of the most traditional validations a evaluations methods, however its applicability to adaptive systems should be considered with limitations.

11. Conclusion

We have presented in this chapter the research in the area of IUIs, its challenges and approached solution with special emphasis on the fact that it is a multi- disciplinary field. It is observed in our discussion that the three approaches described are the ones currently used with superior success to confront the open challenges. At present it is our conclusion that there is still a lack of interchange in the findings between the involved areas in order to share conflicting problems, approaches and findings between experts.

Derived from the literature review it is detected in the area of IUI the necessity of a wider integration and interchange of ideas between the different disciplines that comprise this area. We foresee that the research aimed at the design of novel models for intelligent user interfaces that adapts and integrates components from several disciplines will help to find diverse and richer solutions. It is observed that in general terms the research currently in evolution tends to favors the use of the same knowledge, techniques and proven methodologies that are accepted within the same discipline, and the so called cross-fertilization is really necessary.

12. References

Armentano, M.; Godoy, M. and Amandi, A. (2006) Personal assistants: Direct manipulation vs. mixed initiative interfaces. *Int.J. Hum.-Comput. Stud.*, 64(1):27–35.

Alvarez, V.; (2009) MI-IAM: A Mixed-Initiative User Interface Model for Process Supervision in Power Plants. *Int. Conf. User Modeling, Adaptation and Personalization Adj. Proc. UMAP '09*, pages 97-102, Trento, Italia.

Baumeister, L.K.; John, B. E. and Byrne. M. D. (2000) A comparison of tools for building GOMs models. *In CHI '00: Proceedings of the SIGCHI Conference on Human Factors in Computing Systems*, ACM Press, pages 211–214, New York, NY, USA.

Birnbaum, L.; Horvitz, E.; Kurlander, D.; Lieberman, H. ; Marks, J. and Roth, S. (1997) Compelling intelligent user interfaces. How much AI? In *IUI '97: Proceedings of the 2nd international conference on Intelligent user interfaces*, pages 173–175, New York, NY, USA.

Brusilovsky, P. and Cooper, D. W. (2002) Domain, task, and user models for an adaptive hypermedia performance support system. *In IUI '02: Proceedings of the 7th international conference on Intelligent user interfaces*, ACM Press, pages 23–30, New York, NY, USA.

Bunt, A.; Conati, C. and McGrenere, J. (2004) What role can adaptive support play in an adaptable system? *In IUI '04: Proceedings of the 9th international conference on Intelligent user interfaces*, ACM Press, pages 117–124, New York, NY, USA.

Carenini, G,; Smith, J. and Poole D. (2003) Towards more conversational and collaborative recommender systems. *In IUI '03: Proceedings of the 8th international conference on Intelligent user interfaces*, ACM Press, pages 12–18, New York, NY, USA.

Cassell, J. (2000) Embodied conversational interface agents. *Commun. ACM*, 43(4):70–78, USA.

Chin, D. (2001) Empirical evaluation of user models and user-adapted systems. *UMUAI 01', User Modeling and User-Adapted Interaction*, 11(1-2):181–194, USA.

Dix, A.; Finlay J.; Abowd G.; and Beale R. (2003) *Human-computer interaction (3rd ed.)*. Prentice-Hall, Inc., Upper Saddle River, NJ, USA.

Eirinaki, M and Vazirgiannis, M. (2003) Web mining for web personalization. *ACM Trans. Inter. Tech.*, 3(1):1–27, USA.

Eisenstein, J. and Rich, C. (2002). Agents and GUIs from task models. *In IUI '02: Proceedings of the 7th international conference on Intelligent user interfaces,* ACM Press, pages 47–54, New York, NY, USA.

Franklin, D.; Budzik, J. and Hammond, K. (2002) Plan-based interfaces: keeping track of user tasks and acting to cooperate. *In Proceedings of the 7th international conference on Intelligent user interfaces,* ACM Press, pages 79–86, USA.

Fu, X.; Budzik, J. and Hammond, K. (2000) Mining navigation history for recommendation. *In IUI '00: Proceedings of the 5th international conference on Intelligent user interfaces,* ACM Press, pages 106–112, New York, NY, USA.

Hook, K. (1999) Designing and evaluating intelligent user interfaces. In *IUI '99: Proceedings of the 4th international conference on Intelligent user interfaces,* ACM Press,pages 5–6, New York, NY, USA.

Horvitz, E.; Breese, J.; Heckerman, D.; Hovel, D.; and Rommelse, K. (1998) The Lumiere project: Bayesian user modeling for inferring the goals and needs of software users. *In Proceedings of the Fourteenth Conference on Uncertainty in Artificial Intelligence,* pages 256–265, Madison, WI, USA.

Horvitz, E. (1999) Principles of mixed-initiative user interfaces. *In CHI '99: Proceedings of the SIGCHI conference on Human factors in computing systems,* ACM Press, pages 159–166, New York, NY, USA.

Jameson A. and Schwarzkopf, E. (2002) Pros and cons of controllability: An empirical study. *In AH '02: Proceedings of the Second International Conference on Adaptive Hypermedia and Adaptive Web-Based Systems,* Springer-Verlag, pages 193–202, London, UK.

Kirsch-Pinheiro, M.; Villanova-Oliver, M.; Gensel, J. and Martin H. (2005) Context-aware filtering for collaborative web systems: adapting the awareness information to the user's context. *In SAC '05: Proceedings of the 2005 ACM symposium on Applied computing,* ACM Press, pages 1668–1673, New York, NY, USA.

Kobsa, A. (1994) User modeling and user-adapted interaction. *In CHI '94: Conference companion on Human factors in computing systems,* ACM Press, pages 415–416, New York, NY, USA.

Langley, P. (1999) User modeling in adaptive interfaces. *In UM '99: Proceedings of the seventh international conference on User modeling,* Springer-Verlag New York, Inc., pages 357–370, Secaucus, NJ, USA.

Maes, P. (1994) Agents that reduce work and information overload. *Commun. ACM,* 37(7):30–40, USA.

Maybury, M. (1999) Intelligent user interfaces: an introduction. In *IUI '99: Proceedings of the 4th international conference on Intelligent user interfaces,* ACM Press, pages 3–4, New York, NY, USA.

Mayhew, D.J. (1999) *The usability engineering lifecycle: a practitioner's handbook for user interface design.* Morgan Kaufmann Publishers Inc., San Francisco, CA, USA.

Mobasher, B.; Dai, H.; Luo, T. and Nakagawa, M. (2001) Effective personalization based on association rule discovery from web usage data. *In WIDM '01: Proceedings of the 3rd international workshop on Web information and data management,* ACM Press, pages 9–15, New York, NY,USA.

Oviatt, S.; Cohen,P.; Wu, L.; Vergo, J.; Duncan, L.; Suhm, B.; Bers, J.; Holzman, T.; Winograd, T.; Landay,j.; Larson, J. and Ferro, D. (2000) Designing the user interface for multimodal speech and gesture applications: State-of-the-art systems and research directions for 2000 and beyond.

Peyton, L. (2003) Measuring and managing the effectiveness of personalization. *In ICEC '03: Proceedings of the 5th international conference on Electronic commerce,* ACM Press, pages 220–224, New York, NY, USA.

Puerta, A. R. (1998). Supporting user-centered design of adaptive user interfaces via interface models. *In Proceedings of the First Annual Workshop On Real-Time Intelligent User Interfaces For Decision Support And Information Visualization.*ACM. Press. USA.

Reeves, L.M.; Lai, J.; Larson, J. A.; Oviatt, S.; Balaji, T. S.; Buisine, S.; Collings, P.; Cohen, P.; Kraal, B.; Martin, J.; McTear, M.; Raman, T.V.; Stanney, K. M.; Su, H. and Ying Q. Guidelines for multimodal user interface design. *Commun. ACM,* 47(1):57–59. USA.

Rich, C. and Sidner, C.L. (1996). Adding a collaborative agent to graphical user interfaces. *In Proceedings of the 9th annual ACM symposium on User interface software and technology,* ACM Press, pages 21–30.

Russell S. and Norvig P. (2003) *Artificial Intelligence: A Modern Approach (2nd ed.).* Prentice-Hall, Englewood Cliffs, NJ, USA.

Shneiderman, B. and Plaisant, C. (2004) *Designing the User Interface : Strategies for Effective Human-Computer Interaction (4th ed.).* Addison-Wesley Publishing, Boston, USA.

Shneiderman, B. (1997) Direct manipulation for comprehensible, predictable and controllable user interfaces. In *IUI '97: Proceedings of the 2nd international conference on Intelligent user interfaces,* ACM Press, pages 33–39,New York, NY, USA.

Stephanidis, C.; Karagiannidis, C. and Koumpis, A. (1997) Decision making in intelligent user interfaces. *In IUI '97: Proceedings of the 2nd international conference on Intelligent user interfaces,* ACM Press, pages 195–202, New York, NY, USA.

Stumpf, S.; Rajaram, V.; Li, L.; Burnett, M.; Dietterich, T.; Sullivan, E.; Drummond, R. and Herlocker, J. (2007) Toward harnessing user feedback for machine learning. *In IUI '07: Proceedings of the 12th international conference on Intelligent user interfaces,* ACM Press, pages 82–91, New York, NY, USA.

Sugiyama, K.; Hatano, K. and Yoshikawa, M. (2004) Adaptive web search based on user profile constructed without any effort from users. *In WWW '04: Proceedings of the 13th international conference on World Wide Web,* ACM Press, pages 675–684, New York, NY, USA.

Viano, G.; Parodi, A.; Alty, J.; Khalil, C.; Angulo, I.; Biglino, D.; Crampes, M.; Vaudry, C.; Daurensan, V. and Lachaud, P. (2000) Adaptive user interface for process control based on multi-agent approach. *In AVI '00: Proceedings of the working conference on Advanced visual interfaces,* ACM Press, pages 201–204, New York, NY, USA.

Wernn, A. (1997) Local plan recognition in direct manipulation interfaces. In *Proceedings of the 2nd international conference on intelligent user interfaces,* ACM Press, pages 7–14. USA.

4

Wearable technology in automotive industry: from training to real production

Iñaki Maurtua
TEKNIKER Technology Centre
Spain

1. Introduction

This paper describes two different research activities carried out in the context of the wearIT@work project to analyse the benefits and drawbacks of using wearable technology to support blue-collar workers in real situations. To this aim we describe the UCD process followed, the tests performed and the results obtained in several experiments performed at the SKODA production facilities in Czech Republic.

User Centred Design approach has been followed in the two scenarios identified: training and quality control activities.

Compared to stationary computer systems, mobile- and wearable computing technology have seriously caught up in performance, functionality, scalability. This makes training solutions based on mobile- and wearable computing an attractive consideration for industrial organisations. In this sense, the objective was to supplement the training procedures at Skoda with a context-sensitive wearable computing solution. The idea was that the trainees gained mobile access to the information to carry out their assembly tasks. In fact, the wearable system was used to recognize the context of performed work, and as a result to provide the trainee with the required information to adequately perform individual assembly tasks. The wearable solution was able to track and analyse the trainee's actions, while providing the end-user with means for error handling. As a result, semi-autonomous training of trainees in automotive production was possible.

In the second scenario we moved to real production environment, specifically to the CP8: check point 8, the place where cars are visually and manually inspected before being delivered to customers. There, two worker teams work in parallel in inspection tasks: examining lights and bumpers misalignment, identifying dents and scratches, checking the spaces between doors and windows, and any other kind of faults.

Each time an error is found, the worker reports in one of the three check-list forms they handle. The sheets have a matrix structure identifying the different parts in the car and the possible types of faults.

The objectives of using wearable technology in this scenario are multiple, among others: making the worker activity easier and more efficient, allowing a paperless and hands-free inspection, to guarantee that all verifications have been performed (avoid oversights-mistakes), allow permanent documentation access and to facilitate workers interaction.

2. Summary of activities carried out

The *'wearit@work: empowering the Mobile Worker by wearable computing'* project aimed to study wearable technologies and their application in the workplace to improve the conditions in which workers carry out their activities.
To this end we created the multidisciplinary consortium with 35 partners from 15 countries that have worked together for the four and half years that the project was officially programmed for.
The technological developments have been based on User Centred Design (UCD) and have been developed in 4 different scenarios:

- Maintenance. Led by Giunti Labs and EADS. The target market was made up of workers carrying out maintenance tasks in the aeronautical sector.
- Emergencies. Led by the Paris fire service and Fraunhofer FIT. The study focused on fire-fighters in emergency situations.
- Health. Led by GESPAG and SAP. This study focused on health workers on their daily ward rounds in hospitals.
- Production. Led by TEKNIKER and SKODA. This is the scenario that Tekniker has been most involved in and which will be described in more detail below.

The following common viewpoint was reached after internal discussions about the wearable computing concept compared with mobile computing:

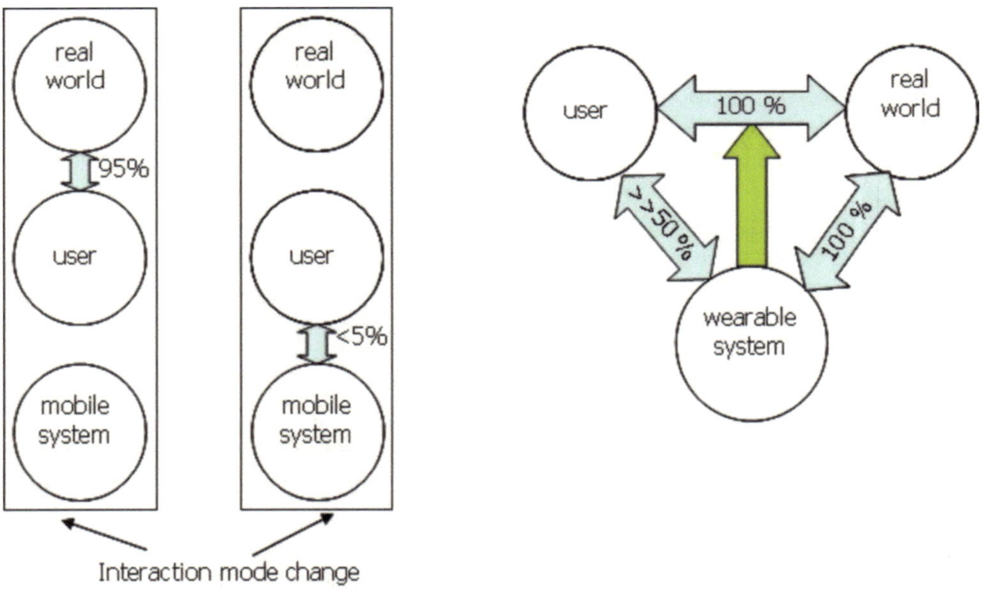

Fig. 1. Mobile vs Wearable

"Wearable computing is working with instead of on the computer, meaning: Using the computer is not the main activity but it is used while the activity is being carried out"

In the production scenario, TEKNIKER focused on designing prototypes and experimenting with end users in the two SKODA plants where the developments and pilot studies were validated.

- Pilot Case Study: Learning in the Vrchlabí plant
- Pilot Case Study: Quality Control in the Mladá Boleslav plant

3. Pilot Case Study: Learning

It took place at the SKODA plant in Vrchlabí. The facilities have what they call an 'E-factory', this being the certification process that must be passed by the workers before they start working on the production line. During this training period they are taught the basics of the work related to a particular task by means of a PowerPoint presentation and small questionnaires. After passing the test they then have a prototype car chassis on which they have to carry out the assembly task in question within a time limit while being supervised by an instructor. When they achieve the established production parameters they can join the assembly line.

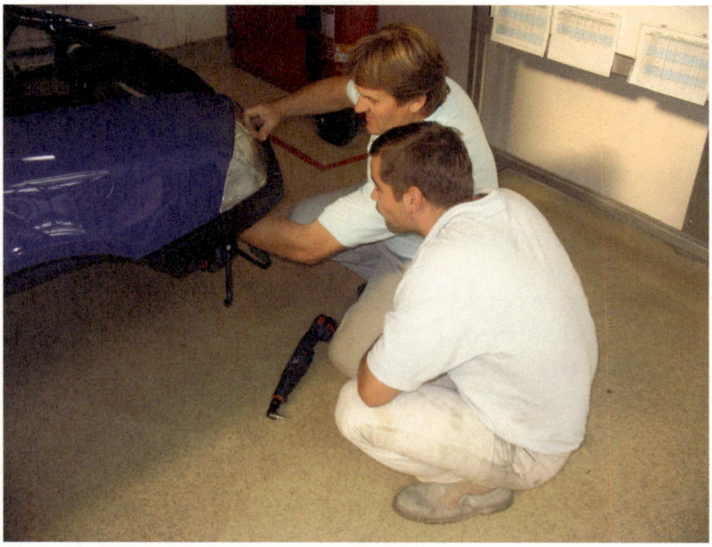

Fig. 2. The learning island, the foreman and the trainee

This pilot case study was designed to create an environment that facilitated the worker training programme so that:

- The training period could be shortened
- It could be carried out by the trainees alone, without needing to have an instructor

When designing the prototype, different factors were taken into consideration to ensure that the wearable system did not interfere with the assembly work and that it could be accessed as naturally as possible.
The development process involved working directly with the plant workers and carrying out a usability experiment in the plant.

The prototype consisted of the following components:

- Hardware: Xybernaut V computer, Microoptical SV6 Head Mounted Display and a standard headset.
- Software. A programme that presented the 14 steps needed to carry out the chosen task in the proper sequence and allowed different forms of interaction. Each of the tasks was documented with the use of text, photo and video resources that could be selected by users according to their preferences.

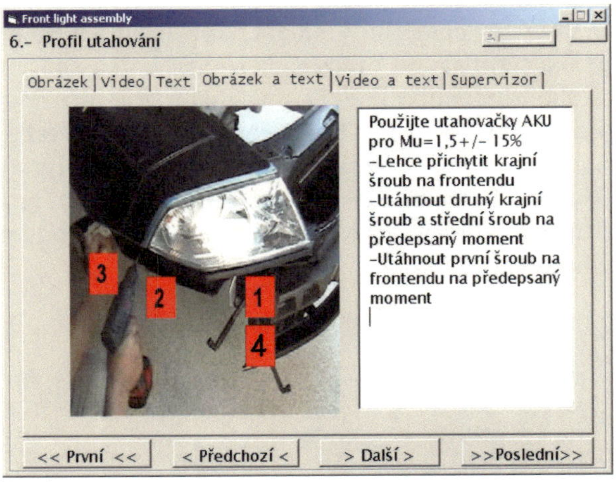

Fig. 3. UI of the application

The operators had to use the application to 'learn' and practice assembling the right-hand front headlight.
As certain functionalities were not yet implemented, the Wizard of Oz (Kelley J.F., 1983) technique was used to simulate them. For example:

- We did not have an Automatic Speech Recognizer (ASR) for voice-based interaction, so we used a Czech speaker who understood the user and 'simulated' the interaction using a remote control application.
- To simulate task recognition, the 'Wizard' pressed the 'Next' button every time the operator completed a task, so that the information about the following task was displayed on screen.
- We wanted to test the validity of a virtual keyboard, so we created keyboard strips that were attached to the operators. They pressed the simulated keys and the 'Wizard' interacted with the application.

Fig. 4. Virtual fabric keyboard layout

The system recorded the most important process information: time used and mistakes.
The operators had to complete an evaluation questionnaire after carrying out the process.

The analysis of the experiment results allowed us to conclude that the system was well accepted in general terms, highlighting the nil use of the videos and the difficulty of accessing the information using the HMD.
As a result of the experiment, we decided to carry out more intensive experiments at TEKNIKER, in which a large number of individuals could take part without the limitations found in the Czech Republic caused by the lack of a common language for the participants and the TEKNIKER researchers.

3.1 Experiment: Validation of Wearable Technology for Learning Tasks

In order to carry out the experiments, we built a metal structure on which those taking part in the tests had to carry out the allocated assembly tasks. The following was taken into account when designing the structure:

- It should allow different manual tasks to be carried out
- All tasks should be of similar difficulty

Fig. 5. Platform for experiments at Tekniker

The task to be carried out by the operators consisted of:

- Assembling a set of metal shapes (three shapes) on a metal plate with 100 holes with different size threads. The assembly had to be carried out using Allen head screws and an Allen key.
- Make 3 pairs of connections using three wires on a panel with 16 BNC connectors.

The experiment was designed to:

- To validate the initial results of the experiment at Vrchlabí
- To measure user acceptance
- To analyse the improvement in learning in terms of time

40 workers divided into two groups took part in the experiment:

- With the first group, the aim was to measure and compare their efficiency in assembling when they accessed to information on paper compared to using wearable technology. To this end, the participants in the experiment had to carry out a single assembly as quickly as possible.
- The second group had to learn (memorise) the whole assembly process as quickly as possible, this being the parameter to be measured. In this case, the operators had to carry out the assembly as many times as was needed with the support of information until they managed to learn it and carry it out with no help at all. The information could be accessed on paper or by using wearable technology. In order to take into account the short-term memory effect, the assembly had to be carried out once again the following day.

In both cases, the operators had to perform the experiment twice: once using information on paper and once using wearable technology. In the second case, each operator was allocated a different mode of interaction:

- Access always involved using an Head Mounted Display (HMD)
- Interaction was in one of the following modes: textile keyboard on the sleeve of the working clothes, by voice or implicit interaction, this involving simulating that the system had detected completion of a task to present the information about the following task automatically.

The following parameters were measured during the experiment:

- Time
- Mistakes made
- Users acceptance, measured through open and closed questionnaires
- Measurement of mental load. We used the NASA TLX test (Hart & Lowell,1988), a subjective tool for evaluating the mental load of the operators when they carry out activities using machines
- Influence of learning styles. We used the VARK questionnaire (Fleming, 2001) to provide a learning preferences profile in accordance with four categories: Visual (learn through seeing), audio (learn through listening), Reading/writing (learn through reading) and kinaesthetic (learn through doing)

The workers used the following infrastructure for the wearable technology test:

- Microoptical VI head mounted display
- OQO computer

As at Skoda, we used the Wizard of Oz technique to simulate the three types of interaction (textile keyboard, voice and automatic recognition of activities).
The following fundamental conclusions were drawn from the experiments:

- Users improved their efficiency when they used recognition of activities as their source of automatic interaction. The operations were performed faster and with fewer mistakes: using implicit interaction (automatic recognition of activities) they used an average of 67 seconds less than when accessing the information on paper, the second best option.

- Users did not learn faster using wearable technology. They only achieved similar learning times to learning using paper when they used implicit interaction.
- Curiously, during the test carried out the following day, learning using paper gave the best results and implicit interaction the worst.
- Interaction using the voice was the option preferred by the users.
- Information in images was better accepted than that presented as text.
- In general terms, the workers rated the wearable technology based system as very useful for carrying out complex tasks, allowing them to work with their hands free and avoiding movements to access information

3.2 Experiment: Usability of Visual Information Access Devices

The second experiment was designed to compare the benefits of using Head Mounted Displays (HMDs) with using a large monitor near the workstation to access the information. 20 workers took part in the experiments and they had to perform four complete assembly procedures using the above-described infrastructure.
The devices compared were:

- A large monitor near the workstation
- HMD Carl Zeiss look-around binocular
- HMD, Carl Zeiss see-through HMD
- Microoptical VI monocular look-around.

The time used by each operator for assembly was measured and a usability questionnaire was used to measure the satisfaction and subjective opinions of the participants.
The experiment allowed us to conclude that:

- The best response in terms of times was obtained when using the big monitor
- The worst response was obtained using the binocular model HMD. However, we should point out that this access model obtained the best ratings in the satisfaction survey.

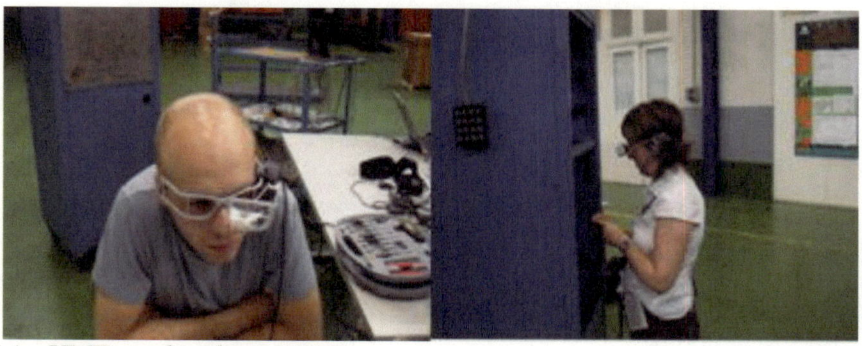

Fig. 6. Zeiss HMD used in the experiment

3.3 Wearable System Prototype

On the basis of the results obtained from the experiments and trials at the Skoda plant and at Tekniker, the first 'real' prototype was defined and built in collaboration with ETHZ, Univ. Passau and HP.

The prototype required the inclusion of different kinds of sensors:

- 5 FSR (force sensitive resistor) and 4 reed switches on the chassis of the car used for the learning process. These sensors detected the termination of certain assembly operations: screwing certain parts, fitting the headlight and checking its correct alignment with the bodywork.

The prototype also consisted of the following elements:

- An RFID reader on the back of the user's glove. This allowed the user to verify that the right tools are used for the fixing operations.
- The same glove was fitted with a triaxial accelerometer and a gyroscope to detect the movement caused when the preset torque was reached in certain fixing operations.
- All this information was sent via bluetooth to a central P.C. where the activity detection data was processed. Here we used the Context Recognition Toolbox, a Framework containing a set of frequently used data processing algorithms.

The wearable computing prototype used was that shown in the Figure and consisted of:

- For the wearable computer we used an OQO Model 01+ attached to the operator's belt.
- Microoptical VI monocular HMD
- A Bluetooth Sony Erickson HBH-300 headset
- A sensorised glove with the RFID reader, gyroscope, accelerometer and a set of FSR sensors to detect muscle activity

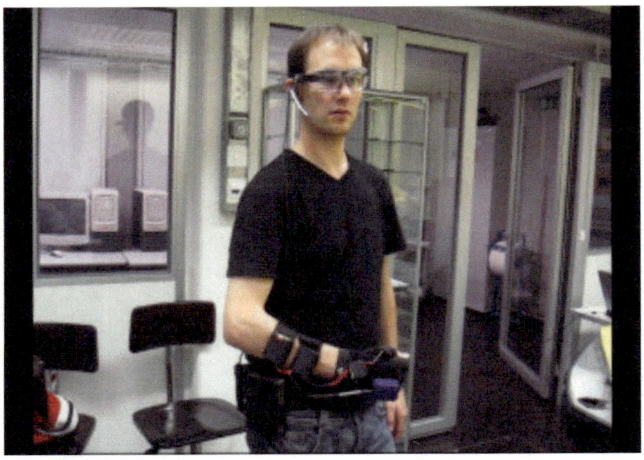

Fig. 7. Hardware prototype

The software architecture used is shown in the figure below:

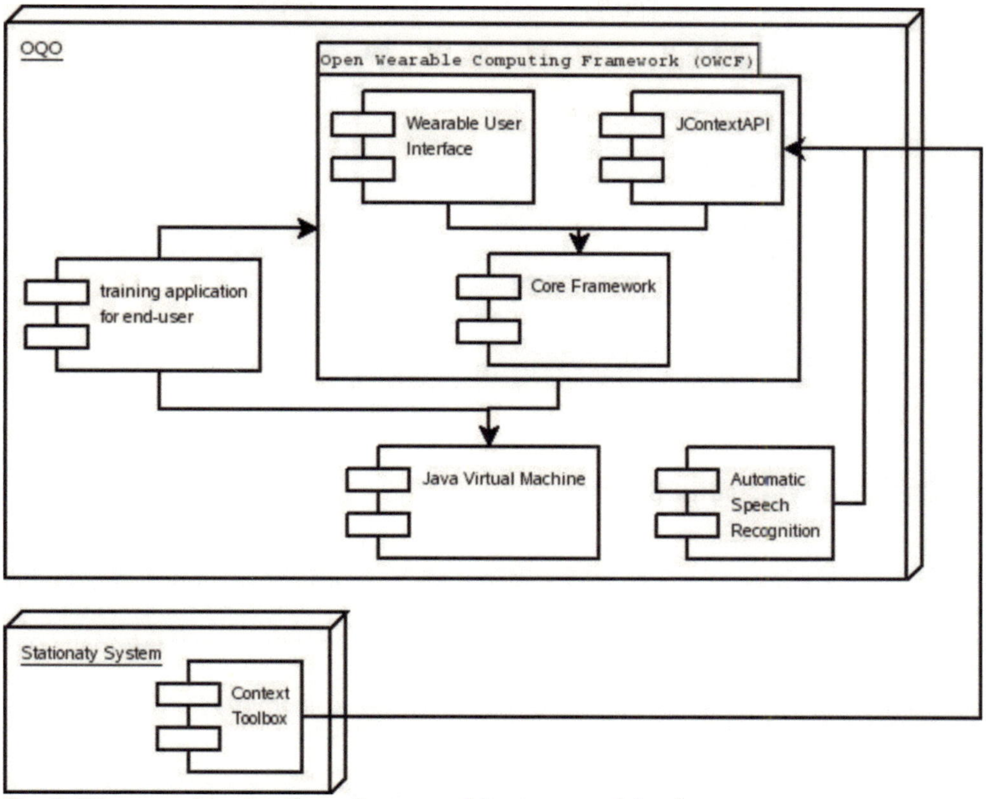

Fig. 8. Diagram showing the software architecture used for the protctype

The application was written in Java and used the Open Wearable Computing Framework (OWCF) developed in the project, more exactly the following components:

- Wearable User Interface (WUI)
- Context component (JContextAPI)

The application was modelled as a state machine in which each of the sub-tasks making up the assembly process were represented. The transitions were triggered by user actions, both explicit (e.g. by voice) and implicit (automatically detected by the system).
The application could monitor the actions of the user and inform him/her if there was a mistake detected.

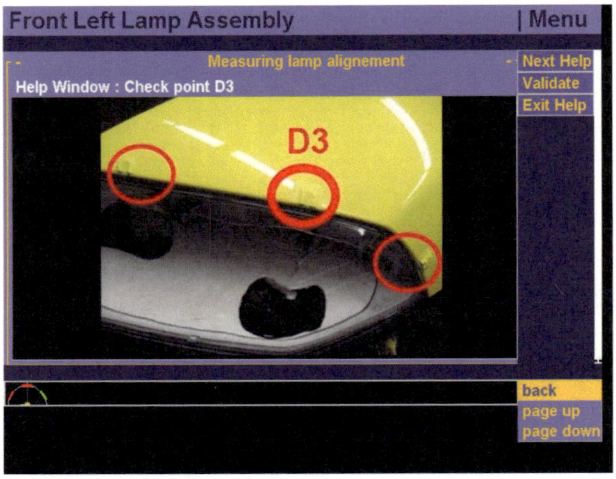

Fig. 9. Example of the UI, showing the verification positions

4. Pilot Case Study: Quality Control

After the initial phase, where we focused on the operator training process, we transferred our attention to the production line. After in-depth analysis of the possibilities of applying wearable technology, we opted to work on the last of the operations carried out on the cars just before they are sent to the dealers. Manual and visual inspection of the finish of the cars is carried out in this phase.

The process takes place on an inspection line, where a team of operators (two parallel lines of ten operators each) verifies different parts of the cars and, where necessary, repair small defects and misalignments. Basically, they detect impacts, marks on the paintwork, correct door opening and closing, headlight misalignment, etc. Hands and eyes are the tools used as inspection tools. During the inspection process they have to enter in the vehicle, stand, sit, crouch and walk around the cars.

During the process they carry a set of sheets with a matrix on them, on which they have to note down the errors detected. The procedure should not be regarded as a check-list. On the contrary, the operators use their own criteria to carry out the inspection and only mark the form when they find something wrong. This procedure can clearly lead to possible mistakes.

Once again, we followed the user-based design process to design the system aimed at helping operators to carry out their wok in a more usable fashion. To this end, we carried out two on-site studies that gave us an in-depth understanding of the process and gather the opinions of the potential users. This process took place in late 2006 and early 2007 and included video recordings and interviews with operators and line managers.

4.1 Social factors

Over the two days of our visit to the Mladá Boleslav plant, we used the following techniques to gain an understanding of the process from the social point of view:

- **Observation** – of the workers performing their normal tasks in the workplace, the interactions between them and the supervisors, time pressure, speed of the activity, rotations, atmosphere at work, etc.

- **Interviews** - semi-structured, based on a questionnaire and aimed at identifying the expectations of the workers as regards wearable computing, their attitude to new technologies and factors related to their normal activities in the plant. 8 people took part in the interviews (4 men and 4 women)

The study led to the following conclusions:

- The atmosphere at work was calm and relaxed. The environment was clean, tidy and well lit. There are common areas for relaxation and meetings. The staff is friendly and polite.
- The workers were continually interacting and helping each other. They rotated throughout every eight-hour shift to avoid the monotony of repetitive work. One person in each team acted as a "joker" to allow other members of the team to leave the line in case of need.
- At inspection point 8, the subject of the final pilot case study, the working atmosphere was even more relaxed.
- **Communication** – All the workers interviewed thought that wearable computing could be an interesting support tool. They didn't see it as a threat that would limit their capacity for interaction, but they didn't think it was either viable or desirable to use it permanently.
- **Privacy** – Although this was one of our major concerns, the interviewees didn't rate it negatively. In fact, they said that the presence of cameras in the plant was already more 'threatening' than the solution we were proposing.
- **Responsibility** – There were contradictory ratings regarding the possibility that wearable computing might affect the responsibilities assumed at the workstation.
- **Experience with the technologies** – except for one person, all the others were habitual users of computers. Obviously, none of them had experience with wearable computing.

In general terms, the workers were willing to use wearable computing because it could be of benefit to them in the following ways:

- To avoid errors and oversights
- To perform the work more quickly and efficiently
- To improve communication mechanisms

4.2 Activity recognition

During this stage of the study, we acquired data to create a prototype that would allow us to identify the activities performed by the workers.
The following sensors were used to capture the movements of the trunk and upper extremities:

- 7 **Xsens MTx** inertial sensors to detect body posture
- FSR (force sensing resistor) on the arms: 8 FSR of 4.7 x 4.7 cm. Fitted to each arm to detect gestures and activities
- A set of Ubisense sensors allowed us to locate the position of the operator of the car being inspected. In practice, they gave calibration problems

A worker was equipped with this equipment and the data was captured during an inspection process to allow later calibration of the algorithms for automatic recognition of activities.
Given the low quality and insufficient data obtained, the process was repeated in the laboratory with 8 individuals and 10 hours of data capture. See (Stiefmeier, 2008) for more details.

4.3 Prototype

The prototype for inspection post number 8 was designed to:

- Facilitate and make the activities of the operators efficient
- Allow paper-free inspection
- Guarantee verification of all points by avoiding oversights
- Provide permanent and easy access to the documentation
- Enhance interaction between the workers

On the basis of these goals, a prototype was created with the following functionalities:

- The worker and the car arriving at the inspection post are identified automatically
- Compliance with all programmed inspections is recorded
- Every time a worker is located in a different area around the car, he/she is presented with a list of possible tasks
- Voice is used as the interaction mechanism: using natural language or identifying the columns and rows that represent the verification document (check-list type)
- The OQO cursor is used for interaction whenever necessary
- The operator can consult the list of faults, related documents and establish a VoIP connection with other operators or the shift manager

Fig. 10. Inspection using the wearable prototype

The system consisted of the following Hardware:

- Zeiss HMD binoculars
- OQO
- Headset
- The above-mentioned system for recognising gestures and activities
- A specially-designed jacket to carry the hardware (Bo et al., 2006)

4.4 Test & Results

The prototype created was used with 8 Skoda workers to evaluate different factors:

- The validity of paper-free inspection
- Remote support
- Access to documentation
- Voice interaction
- Recognition of activities
- Usability of the HMD and the jacket

A document explaining the experiment was drafted and the workers were asked to collaborate voluntarily. Finally, 8 of them took part in the experiment.
The experiment took place without interrupting normal work processes. The process was as follows:

- They were told how the system worked (in Czech) and they were helped to adjust the hardware
- They carried out their work with the prototype as a support element
- They answered two questionnaires (open and closed questions with a 7 point Liekert scale)

The most significant results of the study were as follows (in brackets the mean value of their answers on a scale from 1 to 7, where 1 means completely disagree and 7 completely agree):

- The system is easy to use (3.7)
    - The users didn't have long to familiarise themselves with the system. A longer adaptation session would improve this perception
- I'll be able to carry out my work faster (4.8)
    - An interesting result that could be improved as they become more used to the system
- The system is comfortable (3.0)
    - Heat and the size of the jacket (one size only) could be the reason for this result
- The system is easy to learn (5.0)
    - It's clear that it's easy to learn, but they need to become more familiar with its use
- The information is effective for completing the work (4.8)
    - Positive response
- The font size is right (4.6)
    - A specific trial should be carried out to optimise this size

- I like the interface (5.5)
    - Positive response
- The system has the expected functionalities (5.3)
    - It responds to initial expectations. Continued use could lead to new expectations
- In general, I am satisfied with the system (4.4)
    - Positive response
- I can contact the supervisor easily (5.4)
    - Relevant
- I always knew where I was in the application (5.7)
    - Means that the UI was well designed to avoid operators getting lost between windows
- The commands are obvious (5.8)
    - They knew what the result of each command was going to be
- The system responds quickly to the commands (4.8)
    - This response is more positive than it may seem, as the Wizard of Oz was used for certain functionalities, something that creates an additional response delay
- I would recommend the system to my fellow workers (4.4)
    - Positive and could be improved by resolving certain aspects.
- The glasses are heavy (3.0)
    - The glasses used (Binocular HMD from Carl Zeiss) offer the best quality vision, but they are heavy and their use in longer sessions should be analysed
- The jacket makes my work more difficult (4.3)
    - Interesting, despite the problems inherent with using a single size for all
- The system is heavy (3.9)
    - Includes the weight of the complete unit: jacket + OQO + Cable + HMD battery
- I would use the current system if it were optional (2.7)
    - Very negative. Taking other answers into account, we believe that re-engineering the system would improve this rating.
- The on-screen image is large enough (6.8)
    - Corroborates the results of the experiment at Tekniker.
- I will make less mistakes in my work (4.0)
    - Positive but with room for improvement. The limited time of the experiment did not allow them to evaluate the benefits of the system when real oversights occurred.
- The voice interaction is simple (4.5)
    - Positive but with room for improvement through training
- The jacket is comfortable (3.3)
    - The size and stiffness of the OQO-HMD cable may lie behind this response.
- Paper-free inspection is easier than using paper (4.3)
    - Positive but with room for improvement through continued use of the system.
- The clothing is very hot (5.9)
    - This is the most critical factor. Most of the heat comes from the OQO and not from the clothing itself.

- It is easier to access the information on paper (5.0)
    - Negative response. The fact that we used a PDF document with no specific formatting may lie behind this.
- I prefer to access the information using the glasses than by using a large screen (3.8)
    - No clear conclusion, as they didn't evaluate access to such a screen from different positions in and around the car.
- I felt tense at times (5.3)
    - Not relevant. The presence in the surroundings of 5 members of the research team during the experiment may explain this response.
- The glasses made my work more difficult (4.7)
    - They sometimes forgot the fact that this model has an option allowing them to partially remove the glasses.
- I like the on-line supervisor option (5.9)
    - Positive.
- I felt controlled (3.8)
    - By the system or by the 5 members of the research team?
- I wouldn't like to use the system all day long (4.2)
    - Resolving certain aspects could improve this score.
- I felt that the system distracted me (4.9)
    - It was the first time and everything was new: from the hardware to the functionality
- The menus and the information were well organised (6.8)
    - This means that the UI was well designed.
- I felt stupid wearing the glasses (5.7)
    - Although negative, if everyone used the same system they wouldn't feel that way.
- It's easy to get used to the glasses (3.6)
    - They didn't have enough time to become familiar with them.
- The jacket made it difficult to get into the car (5.4)
    - The size and stiffness of the OQO-HMD cable may lie behind this response.
- I was afraid of breaking the system (3.3)
    - Positive, it was the first time and the system was not specifically designed not to be damaged or not to cause damage.
- I was afraid of damaging the car with the system (3.4)
    - Positive, it was the first time and the system was not specifically designed not to be damaged or not to cause damage.

To sum up, the evaluation was positive, although we detected certain aspects with room for improvement.

5. Final conclusions and acknowledgement

The wearIT project has highlighted the possibilities of wearable computing when it comes to improving the working conditions of certain groups of workers. It's obvious that there is no single valid option for all situations, but each case needs to be analysed with the help of the user groups to design a tailored solution.

In more general terms, we need to make more effort to design the hardware elements needed to exploit these benefits: lighter HMD (wireless where possible), more robust computing elements (the original QBIC solution continues to be an attractive option, due to its shape, although it has connection and computing power limitations), longer life batteries, more usable headphones, systems with better heat dissipation, etc.

We would like to thank the European Union for the funding that made it possible to carry out this research as part of the Sixth Framework Programme.

We would also like to thank all the Partners who collaborated on the project, especially Skoda, ETHZ, Univ. Passau, Univ. Cork, HP-Italy, Edna Pasher, Carl Zeiss, TZI-Univ. Bremen and BIBA

6. References

Fleming, ND (2001). *Teaching and Learning Styles: VARK Strategies,* Honolulu Community College, ISBN 0-473-07956-9, Place of Publication

Hart, S. ; Staveland LE. (1999). Development of NASA-TLX (Task load Index) : Results of Empirical and Theoretical Research, In: *Human Mental Workload,* Hancock & N. Meshkati, 239-250, North Holland Press, ISBN, Amsterdan

Stiefmeier, T. ; Roggen, D. ; Ogris, G. ; Lukowicz, P. & Tröster, G. (2008). Wearable Activity Tracking in Car Manufacturing, *IEEE Pervasive computing,* Vol. 7, No. 2 (April-June 2008), ISSN 1536-1268

Bo, G.; Lorenzon, A., Chevassus, N. & Blondie, V. (2006). Wearable Computing and Mobile Workers: The Aeronautic Maintenance Showcase in the WearIT@Work Project, *Proceedings of IFAWC 2006*,pp 33-44, ISBN 978-3-8007-2954-8 , Bremen, March 2006, Mobile Research Center, TZI Universität Bremen

Kelley, J.F. (1984). An iterative design methodology for user-friendly natural language office information applications, *ACM Transactions on Information Systems,* pp 26-41, ISSN 1046-8188, Boston, 1984, ACM, New York

An Empirical Investigation into the Use of Multimodal E-Learning Interfaces

Marwan Alseid and Dimitrios Rigas
University of Bradford
United Kingdom

1. Introduction

Recently, most of e-learning user interfaces mainly depend on text with graphics in the delivery of information, and frequently disregard other communication metaphors within the visual and auditory channels. The lack of multimodality results in overloading user' visual channel (Brewster 1997; Brewster 1998). Also, in some cases important information being communicated could be missed (Oakley, McGee et al. 2000). Including more than one communication metaphor or channel in the human-computer interaction process could improve the usability of interfaces. Multimodal interaction could reduce the amount of information communicated by one specific metaphor or channel (Brown, Newsome et al. 1989) and increase the volume of communicated information (Oviatt 2003). Also, it enables users to interact with an application using the most suitable type of interaction metaphor to their abilities (Dix, Abowd et al. 2004). Multimodality also often makes the user interface more natural (Dix 1993) and offers conveying multiplicity of information through different channels (Sarter 2006).

The reviewed previous work demonstrated that using speech sounds and earcons improved the usability of computer applications in many different domains including e-learning. Also, it showed the usefulness of avatars with facial expressions in e-learning interfaces. However, there is a need for additional research to integrate multimodal metaphors in e-learning applications. Multimodal metaphors may help to alleviate some of the difficulties that e-learning users often encounter. This empirical study represents the initial experiment of a research project that aimed at exploring the usability aspects of e-learning interfaces that incorporate a combination of typical text with graphics metaphors and multimodal metaphors such as speech sounds, non-speech sounds and avatar with simple facial expressions. The main question is whether the inclusion of these metaphors can increase the usability and learning. The secondary question is related to the contributing role that each of these metaphors could play in enhancing the usability and learning of e-learning tools. The third question is whether the use of an avatar with human- like facial expressions and body gestures could help in improving the usability and learning. Finally, does it make difference between one avatar and two in the interface of e-learning applications? The purpose of this experiment was to answer the first question. An e-learning experimental platform, with two interface versions (a text with graphics and a multimodal), was developed to serve as a basis for this study. The e-learning topic was class diagram notation that is often used in the design of software systems. The study involved two groups of users (one group for each interface version) in which the usability performance of the two groups in terms of efficiency, effectiveness, and user satisfaction was compared. The next two sections review the relevant literature in e-learning and multimodal interaction. Section 4 describes the experimental e-learning platform, and section 5 provides in detail the design of the experiment. The obtained results are presented and discussed in sections 6 and 7 respectively. Finally, section 8 concludes this chapter and indicates future work directions.

2. E-learning

In general, E-Learning could be defined as a term that describes the learning process in which information and communication technology could be utilized (Alexander 2001; Yu, Zhang et al. 2006) were computer machines and networks could be used to facilitate easier and faster access to a huge amount of educational content. Due to the continuous development of information and communication technology (ICT), research in e-learning and the technology employed in the development of e-learning applications have been increased (Hamilton, Richards et al. 2001). For example, Internet technology could be applied to manage the learning material and to store information about learners as well as to facilitate communication and cooperation between learners and to monitor their progress (Mikic and Anido 2006). Further technology used for e-learning include scheduled and on-demand delivery platforms (Hamilton, Richards et al. 2001). Scheduled delivery platforms were designed to simulate real learning environment but restricted by time and location constraints. Examples of this technology include video broadcasting, remote libraries and virtual classrooms. On the other hand, on-demand delivery platforms offer anytime and anywhere learning such as web based training and interactive training CD ROMs.

In comparison with traditional learning, e-learning offers better adaptation to individual needs and provides more flexible learning in terms of time and location, and ease monitoring student's knowledge and skills (Mikic and Anido 2006). Also, e-learning content could easily and quickly be updated and then redistributed again so that all users receive the same educational material in the same manner (Rosenberg 2001). Furthermore, it enables users to learn collaboratively (Correia and Dias 2001) and could enhance their motivation and interest in regard to the presented material (Theonas, Hobbs et al. 2008). Lastly, e-learning could be used to accommodate different teaching methods (Spalter, Simpson et al. 2000). However, e-learning environments also have challenges and difficulties. For example, users of e-learning are supervised only by parents or other adults not by a teacher. Also, teaching methods and computer technology must be combined appropriately (Russell and Holkner 2000) despite that this technology is not always available and accessible (Brady 2001). Furthermore, it was found that students, sometimes, are not satisfied with computer-based learning and experienced lack of traditional face-to-face contact with tutor. Hence, users' attitude towards e-learning should be enhanced and their accessibility to the needed technology should be facilitated (Shaw and Marlow 1999).

From pedagogical perspective, there are basic principles that must be considered to insure successful implementation of e-learning (Govindasamy 2001) . Govindasamy stated that development and evaluation of e-learning environments involves analysis of both learner and learning tasks, determination of instructional objectives and strategies, testing and

production of the initial version of the e-learning tool. It is not always the case that every e-learning system presents high quality learning. According to Henry (Henry 2001), a comprehensive e-learning solution consists of content, technology, and services. Also, the content of online courses as well as the tools used for producing this content should be carefully selected (Correia and Dias 2001). In addition to the ease of use, e-learning solutions should also be accessible without any hardware or software limitations (Kapp 2003). Moreover, the user interface of e-learning software should support independent learning, incorporate suitable communication metaphors, and provide a collection of pedagogical activities to suit the individual differences among users (Tabbers, Kester et al. 2005).
Human working memory is a short-term memory that plays an important role in the cognitive process for remembering and retaining the learning information that has been received (Graf, Lin et al. 2007). The capacity of this memory is limited and considered as one of the main cognitive features (Lin and Kinshuk 2003) therefore, when a large amount of information is presented via only one channel (i.e. visually), users will be cognitively overloaded (Low and Sweller 2005). It was found that the use of computers in learning could be advantageous over other media such as static and text-based material (Carswell and Benyon 1996). Also, involving other human senses than the visual one in e-learning interfaces will assist in extending the capacity of working memory and, as a result, users' ability to perceive and understand the presented information will be enhanced (Fletcher and Tobias 2005).

3. Multimodal Interaction

Multimodal interaction is a human-computer interaction in which more than one of human senses are involved through the incorporation of multimodal communication metaphors. These metaphors include text, graphics, speech sounds, non-speech sounds and avatars. Several studies have been carried out to examine how these metaphors could affect the interaction process. These studies showed that multimodal metaphors could be utilised to enhance the usability of many computer applications including e-learning.

3.1 Speech and Non-Speech Sounds

Sound is more flexible than visual output because it could be heard from all sides without paying visual attention to the output device. However, they are complement to each other and could be used simultaneously to transmit different types of information. Earcons are short musical sounds of non-speech nature (Blattner, Sumikawa et al. 1989) that has been used to involve the human auditory channel in the interaction with computer applications. It has been employed efficiently and effectively to improve the interaction with components frequently appeared in user interfaces such as scrollbar (Brewster, Wright et al. 1994) and progress bar (Crease and Brewster 1998). Also, it was successfully used to draw users' attention to events related to the development of program code (DiGiano, Baecker et al. 1993) and to communicate aspects of program execution (Rigas and Alty 1998). Other studies demonstrated that earcons could help in conveying auditory feedback to visually impaired users in order to communicate graphical information such as coordinate locations, simple geometrical shapes and their sizes (Alty and Rigas 2005; Rigas and Alty 2005). Moreover, it could be beneficial for sighted uses in accessing information represented in line graphs (Brown, Brewster et al. 2002), spreadsheets (Stockman 2004) and numerical data tables (Kildal and Brewster 2005). In education, it was found that earcons could improve students' understanding (Bonebright, Nees et al. 2001) as well as their satisfaction in regards to the learning material (Upson 2002). Furthermore, earcons were successfully integrated with speech sounds to convey information to users (Rigas, Memery et al. 2001) and were found to have a positive contribution when included with recorded speech in the interface of a multimedia on-line learning tool as it helped users to perform different learning tasks more successfully (Rigas and Hopwood 2003).

3.2 Avatars

An avatar is another multimodal interaction metaphor that involves both of visual and auditory human senses. It is a computer-based character that could be utilised to represent human-like or cartoon-like persona (Sheth 2003) with the ability to express feelings, emotions and other linguistic information through facial expressions and body gestures (Beskow 1997). The six universally recognisable categories of human expressions are happiness, surprise, fear, sadness, anger and disgust (Fabri, Moore et al. 2002). It was found that adding an avatar with these facial expressions in the interface of Instant Messaging tools improved the involvement of users and created a more enjoyable experience for them (Fabri and Moore 2005). Also, a study conducted by Gazepidis and Rigas demonstrated the importance of specific facial expressions and body gestures when it has been used by a virtual salesman in an interactive system (Gazepidis and Rigas 2008). The role of avatar as a pedagogical agent in e-learning virtual environments has been evaluated by a series of empirical studies. Results of these studies suggested that avatar could facilitate the learning process (Baylor 2003; Holmes 2007), and could provide students with a sense of presence and enhance their satisfaction with the online courses (Annetta and Holmes 2006). What is more, the inclusion of avatar as a facially expressive virtual lecturer could lead to a more interesting and motivating virtual educational experience, and that the use of specific expressions (i.e. smiling) could increase students' interest about the learning topic and therefore enhance their learning performance (Theonas, Hobbs et al. 2008).

4. Experimental Platform

An e-learning platform was developed from scratch to serve as a basis for this empirical study. The platform provided two different versions; a text with graphics interface version, and a multimodal interface version. Both interfaces were designed to deliver the same information about class diagram representation of a given problem statement. The material presented by both interfaces, in the form of three common examples, included explanations about classes, associations among classes and the multiplicity of a given class in the diagram. The complexity of these examples was gradually increased, and each of which given in a separate screen display. Also, the order in which these examples were presented was similar in both interfaces..

4.1 Text with Graphics Interface

Figure 1A shows an example screenshot of the text with graphics interface. In this version of the experimental platform, the required information was delivered in a textual approach and could be communicated only by the visual channel without making use of any other human senses in the interaction process. When the mouse cursor is placed over a given notation in the class diagram (denoted by 1), a textual description of that notation is displayed in the notes textbox (denoted by 2).

4.2 Multimodal Interface

Figure 1B shows an example screenshot of the multimodal e-learning interface. Guidelines for the design of multimodal metaphors (Sarter 2006) and multimodal user interface (Reeves, Martin et al. 2004) were followed. The same design of the text with graphics e-learning interface was used but the notes textbox was removed and replaced with a combination of recorded speech, earcons, and avatars with facial expressions. The life-like avatar with simple facial expressions (see figure 1C) was included to speak the explanations about classes with prosody. Multiplicity and notation of associations were communicated with earcons and recorded speech respectively. Two command buttons were also provided in both interfaces to allow users to select the three examples

Earcons employed in the multimodal interface were designed based on the suggested guidelines (Brewster, Wright et al. 1995; Rigas 1996). Musical notes (starting at middle C in the chromatic scale) were used to create six earcons each of which was utilized to communicate one of the six different types of multiplicity found in the three class diagram examples. Table 1 shows the design structure of these earcons. Each of the first four earcons were composed of two parts separated by a short pause (0.6 second) in between, and communicated one of the multiplicities: zero or 1 (0..1), one or more (1..*), two or more (2..*), and one or two (1..2). The remaining two earcons had only one part and used to represent the multiplicities: one (1) and many (*) which means zero or more. So, in order to create these six earcons, there was a need to musically illustrate the values 0, 1, 2, and *. For this purpose, different numbers of rising pitch piano notes were used as follows: one

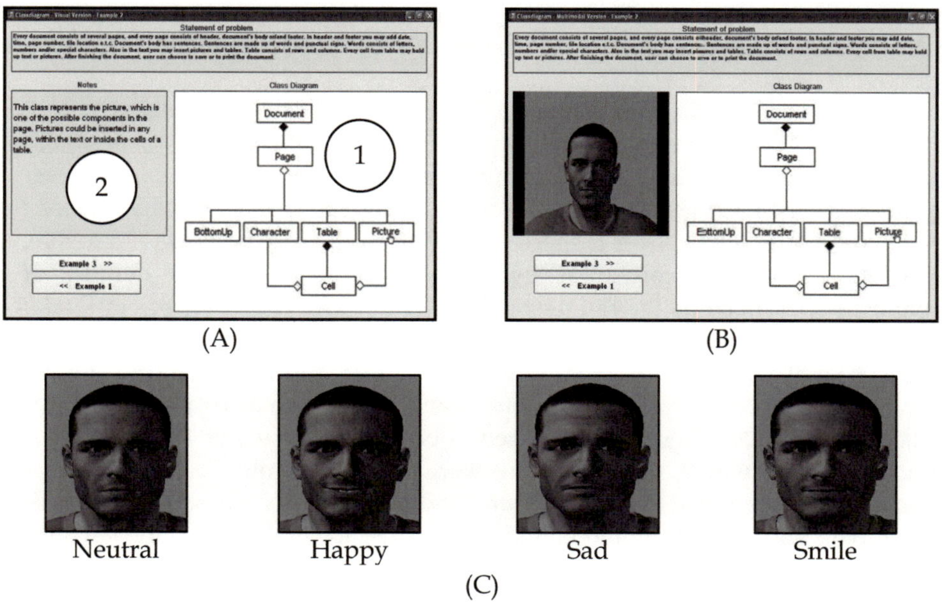

Fig. 1. A screenshot of text with graphics interface (A), multimodal interface (B) and the facial expressions used in the multimodal interface (C)

musical note to communicate 1, two rising notes to communicate 2 and four rising pitch notes to communicate many (*). In order to distinguish zero and to represent it in the multiplicity 0..1, only one note of seashore sound was used.

		Multiplicity					
		0..1	1..*	1..2	2..*	1	*
Duration (second)		1.8	2.2	1.9	2.4	1	1.2
Part 1	Sound	Seashore	Piano	Piano	Piano	Piano	Piano
	No. of tones	1	1	1	2	1	4
Part 2	Sound	Piano	Piano	Piano	Piano	-	-
	No. of tones	1	4	2	4	-	-

Table 1. The structure of earcons that communicated multiplicity in the multimodal interface

5. Design of The Two-Group Empirical Study

In order to explore the effect of multimodal metaphors and to find out which interface would be better in terms of efficiency, effectiveness, and user satisfaction for the e-learning process, the two e-learning interface versions were empirically evaluated by two independent groups each of which has fifteen users. One group used the text with graphics interface and served as a control and the other group used the multimodal interface in order to serve as experimental. Therefore, the main hypothesis stated that the multimodal e-learning interface would be more efficient, more effective and more satisfactory compared to a similar interface with only text with graphics metaphors.

Participants in the experiment were first-time users of the experimental platform. The majority of them in both groups were postgraduate students coming from a scientific background and had no or limited experience in class diagram notation. They were regarded as expert computer users because most of them use computer ten or more hours a week.

Both groups performed six common tasks. The tasks were designed to increase in difficulty and equally divided into easy, moderate and difficult. The tasks also covered all types of presented information such as class attributes and operations, associations between classes, and multiplicities. Each task comprised a set of requirements each of which asked the user to place the mouse cursor over a specific notation in the displayed class diagram, and to receive the delivered information related to that notation. The number of task's requirements depended on the complexity level of the task. Each task was evaluated with a memory recall and a recognition questions. To answer the recall question correctly, user had to retrieve part of the presented information from his/her memory. However, the recognition one offered a set of 2 to 4 options and user had to recognize the correct answer among it. In total, each user answered twelve questions consisted of 4 easy, 4 moderate and 4 difficult. In other words, these questions were categorised into 6 recall and 6 recognition questions. For the purpose of data collecting and analysis, each question was considered as a task. Table 2 shows the multimodal metaphors used to communicate the key information needed by users in the multimodal interface group to complete the tasks successfully.

	Tasks											
	Easy				Moderate				Difficult			
	Rl	Rn	Rl	Rn	Rl	Rn	Rl	Rn	Rl	Rn	Rl	Rn
	1.1	1.2	2.1	2.2	3.1	3.2	4.1	4.2	5.1	5.2	6.1	6.2
Speech		√		√		√		√				√
Earcons		√		√	√					√		√
Avatar	√		√				√		√		√	

Table 2. The multimodal metaphors used to communicate the key information needed by users in the multimodal interface group to complete the tasks successfully (Rl=Recall, Rn=Recognition)

The experiment was conducted individually for each user in both groups with an average duration of thirty five minutes. It started by filling the pre-experimental questionnaire for user profiling. Then, two tutorials were presented; the first tutorial demonstrated the class diagram notation for five minutes and was shown to each user in both groups. The second tutorial had two versions, one for each group. The aim of each of these tutorials was to provide an introduction to the e-learning interface version that the user was to use. Both of these tutorials run for two minutes. After completing all tasks, users were asked to give their satisfaction ratings about the different aspects of the tested interface version by answering the post-experimental questionnaire.

6. Results

The results of both groups were analysed in terms of efficiency (time users needed to accomplish the required tasks), effectiveness (percentage of correctly completed tasks) and user satisfaction (based on a rating scale). The mean completion time for all tasks (see figure 2B) in the experimental group was significantly lower than the control group ($t=1.74$, $cv=1.72$, $p<0.05$). Experimental observations revealed that users in the control group regularly divided their visual attention between the notes in the textbox and the class diagram representations in order to understand the presented information and in some cases a visual overload occurred. However, users in the experimental group maintained

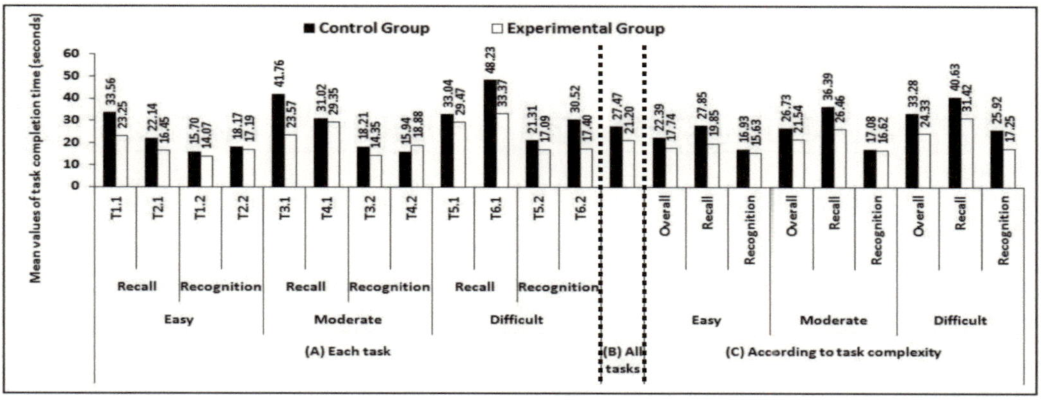

Fig. 2. Mean values of task completion time (A) for each task, (B) for all tasks, and (C) according to task complexity in both control and experimental groups

their visual attention to the class diagram representations while they were listening to the auditory messages.
A more detailed analysis of the mean completion time for each task in both groups is shown in figure 2A. The time users needed to complete the tasks in the experimental group was lower in 11 out of 12 tasks. It could be noticed that the difference between mean values of the two groups was varied over the twelve tasks. It was higher in four tasks (T1.1, T3.1, T6.1, and T6.2) which represent 33% of the tasks. However, it was lower in other four tasks (T2.1, T5.1, T3.2, and T5.2) and even more lower in the tasks T1.2, T2.2 and T4.1. Only task T4.2 recorded higher time when using multimodal interface without critically affecting the overall result. These variances in the difference between mean values of the two groups are attributed to the differences in the presented information and in the complexity of the required tasks. Furthermore, it was noticed that these difference did not clearly explained the role that each of speech, earcons and avatar played in enhancing the accomplishment time when used in the multimodal interface. The reason behind this could be returned to the design of the required tasks.
The tasks were designed to increase in difficulty and they were equally divided into easy, moderate and difficult. Figure 2C demonstrates that there is a relationship between the complexity of the tasks and the time required to complete the task. The completion time in the experimental group was lower for all tasks regardless the level of difficulty. However, the variance in completion time between the two groups increased as the task complexity increased. This demonstrates that the users in the experimental group were significantly aided by the multimodal metaphors. The t-test calculations were performed between the two groups to evaluate completion time for easy, moderate, difficult, recall and recognition tasks (see table 3). Values obtained in t-test calculations showed a statistical significant difference between the two groups in relation to the time users spent to complete recall tasks regardless of the tasks' complexity. The t values were 2.4 for easy recall, 2.25 for moderate recall, 1.93 for difficult recall and 3.94 for overall recall tasks. In recognition tasks, t values for easy (0.68) and moderate (0.17) tasks were not significant but significant was reached in the difficult tasks (3.40). Nevertheless, users in the experimental group spent significantly lower time than users in the control group to perform all recognition tasks.

	Easy			Moderate			Difficult			Rl	Rn
	Overall	Recall	Recognition	Overall	Recall	Recognition	Overall	Recall	Recognition	Overall	Overall
t value	**2.27**	**2.40**	0.68	**2.12**	**2.25**	0.17	**2.99**	**1.93**	**3.40**	**3.94**	**2.42**
Degree of freedom	118	58	58	118	58	58	118	58	58	178	178
Critical value	1.66	1.67	1.67	1.66	1.67	1.67	1.66	1.67	1.67	1.65	1.65

Table 3. Values obtained through t-test calculation when comparing the task completion time between the two groups. Statistically significant values are displayed in bold (Rl=Recall, Rn=Recognition)

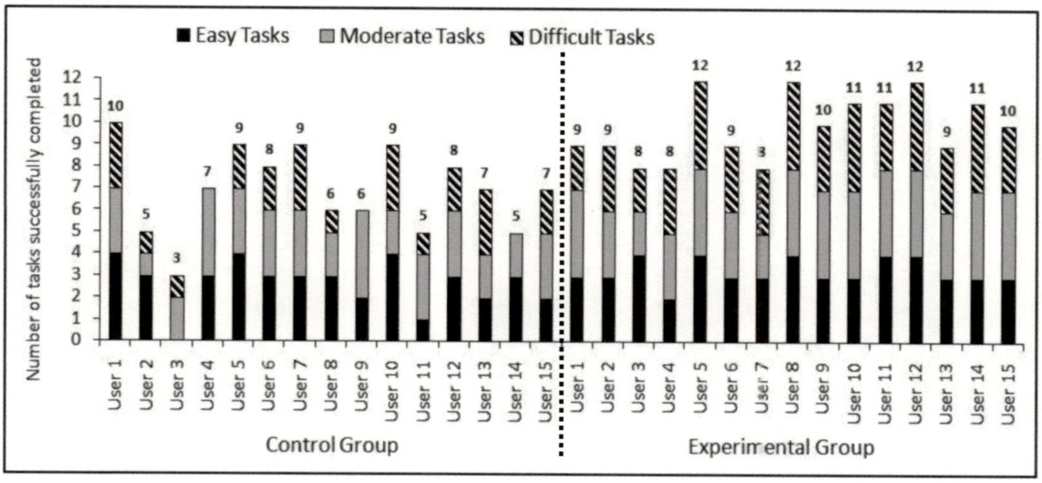

Fig. 3. The number of successfully completed tasks for each user in both groups: control and experimental

Figure 3 shows the number of correctly completed tasks (out of 12) for each user in both groups. The number of correctly completed tasks was higher in the experimental group as users successfully completed 149 (83%) out of 180 tasks. Users in the control group successfully completed 104 tasks (58%) out of 180 tasks. This difference was significant ($t=4.75$, $cv=1.70$, $p<0.05$).

Table 4 shows the mean values of successfully completed tasks for both groups and the t values obtained by t-test calculations (degree of freedom= 28, critical value= 1.70). The t values show that the successfully completed tasks in the experimental group are significantly higher regardless of the task complexity (easy, moderate, and difficult) or task type (recall and recognition). The only non significant difference was in the easy and moderate recognition tasks in which the multimodal metaphors used in the experimental interface did not contribute as much as in the other types of tasks.

			Easy			Moderate			Difficult			Rl	Rn
		All tasks	Overall	Recall	Recognition	Overall	Recall	Recognition	Overall	Recall	Recognition	Overall	Overall
Mean	C	6.9	2.7	1.1	1.5	2.7	1.2	1.5	1.6	0.7	0.9	3.0	3.9
	E	9.9	3.3	1.5	1.7	3.5	1.9	1.6	3.2	1.7	1.5	5.1	4.9
t value		**4.75**	**1.84**	**1.88**	0.81	**2.81**	**3.39**	0.57	**4.73**	**3.78**	**2.95**	**5.07**	**1.94**

Table 4. Mean values of successfully completed tasks in both control group (C) and experimental groups (E), and the t values obtained by t-test calculations (Rl=Recall, Rn=Recognition)

Figure 4 shows the percentage of tasks successfully completed in both groups. It can be noticed that the difference between the two groups in successfully completed tasks increased as the difficulty of the task increased (15% in easy tasks, 20% in moderate tasks

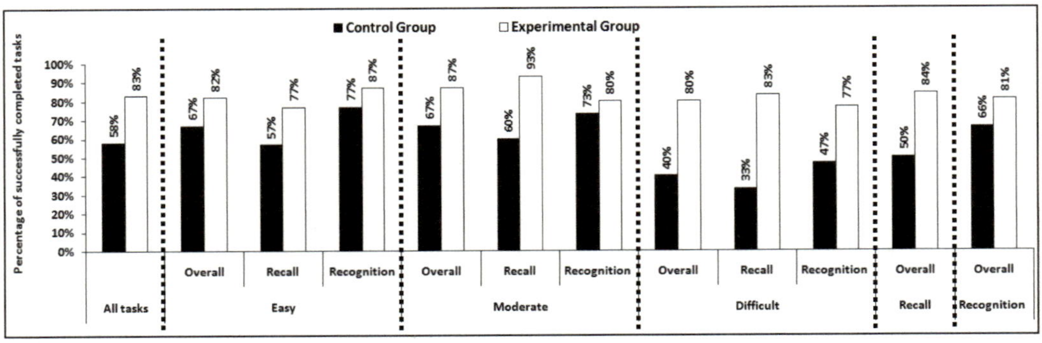

Fig. 4. Percentage of successfully completed tasks in control group and experimental group

and 40% in difficult tasks). Also, users of the multimodal interface performed better in both recall and recognition tasks but the difference between the two groups is smaller in the recognition tasks. Therefore, the contribution of multimodal metaphors, as used in the experimental interface, aided users to successfully complete more recall than recognition tasks.

User satisfaction in regards to different aspects of the applied interface was measured in both groups by users' responses to the post-experimental questionnaire. These aspects included ease of use, confusion, nervousness, ease of learning, identification and recognition of the learning material and overall satisfaction. A scale with six points was used for each statement in the questionnaire. This scale ranged from 1, the value of strongly disagree, to 6, the value of strongly agree. For the sake of data analysis, responses of each user were summated to obtain the satisfaction score for each user in each group. These total scores were then used in the statistical analysis and users in the experimental group were found to be significantly more satisfied ($t=2.76$, $cv=1.70$, $p<0.05$).

Figure 5A shows the overall mean values of user satisfaction score which was 4.4 in the control group and 5.2 in the experimental group. The multimodal e-learning interface was easier to use than the text with graphics one. It was observed that users in the experimental group were more relaxed, and less confused and nervous (see figure 5B).

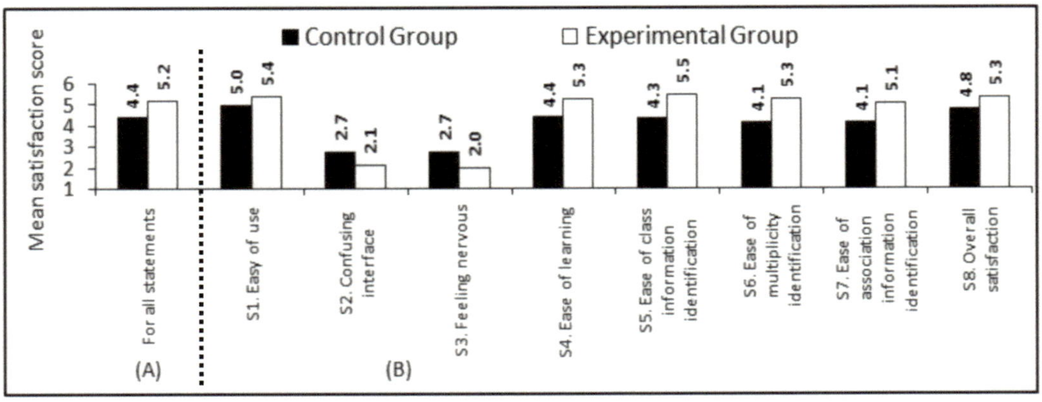

Fig. 5. Overall mean values of user satisfaction score for all statements (A) and for each statement (B) of the control and experimental groups

7. Discussion

The results of this two-group empirical study can be discussed in terms of the contribution of the multimodal metaphors to the usability and to the learning process of users. The analysis is presented from three angles:

1. Time taken to complete the various tasks in terms of type of tasks (recall and recognition) and in terms of the difficulty of the task.
2. Successful completion of tasks (again in terms of type and difficulty).
3. User satisfaction and experience in terms or ease of use, confusion of users, nervousness of users, ease of learning, identification and recognition of learning material, and overall satisfaction.

Although the text with graphics interface offered a simpler typical interaction, the results of the experiment showed that the use of multimodal metaphors (recorded speech, earcons, and avatars) was significantly more efficient and effective than using text with graphics to communicate information in an e-learning interface. Also, users who used the multimodal interface were significantly more satisfied than users who used the text with graphics interface.

7.1 Time Taken to Complete Tasks

During the experiment, it was noticed that users of the textual based interface switched their attention between the textual descriptions and the class diagram to understand the presented textual information, which may have overloaded their visual channel. On the other side, users of the multimodal interface were able to focus their attention on the class diagram while receiving information from the spoken messages and earcons. The inclusion of more than one communication metaphor in the multimodal interface helped users to concentrate better on the presented information through the auditory channel and at the same time use the visual channel to understand this information. The results of the study demonstrated that these metaphors assisted users to learn quicker especially as the required task became more difficult. The time spent on the completion of tasks increased as the task difficulty increased. However, the more important aspect is that the variance in completion time between the two groups increased as the task complexity increased. This demonstrates the contribution of speech, earcons, and avatar in users' efficiency of higher complexity tasks.

In recall tasks, users needed to retrieve the presented information from their memory and this may have taken time depending on the complexity of the task. Users in the experimental group used less time to complete easy, moderate and difficult recall tasks and difficult only recognition tasks. In other words, no significant difference between the two groups was observed for only easy and moderate recognition tasks. This means that the use of multi-modal metaphors as applied in the experimental interface particularly contributed to memory recall activities regardless of its complexity.

7.2 Successful Completion of Tasks

The use of more than one communication metaphor assisted users to distinguish among the different types of information provided by each of these metaphors and enabled them to remember this information for longer time. The fact that users in the multimodal group retained the communicated information for longer time (compared to the text with graphics group) enabled them to successfully complete more tasks

In order to successfully perform the recall tasks, users had to correctly retrieve from their memory the presented information. Information in the multimodal group was presented in a teacher like scenario in which the avatar simulated a teacher with natural head movement, facial expressions and natural speech while other aspects of the learning materials were presented using earcons. The results of the study demonstrated that the user experience as formed by combined multimodal metaphors enabled users to learn better. This is particularly demonstrated in the recall tasks which are more difficult to be completed than the recognition tasks (84% completion rate in the experimental group compared with 50% in the control group). The low completion rate of recall tasks in the text with graphics interface demonstrates that the users' memory was not aided as much as the multimodal interface. To perform recognition tasks successfully, users had to choose the correct answer among the given options. There is always a possibility that a correct answer could be chosen by the user due to chance (this is far more difficult to happen in a recall task). The successful completion was 66% in the text with graphics group and 81% in the multimodal group. The difference, although smaller than the one in the recall tasks, still indicates that users performed better when their e-leaning has taken place in the presence of multimodal metaphors.

In terms of task difficulty, the tasks were structured to gradually increase in complexity. Similarly to the results of time taken to complete the tasks, the results of the experimental study showed that the experimental group successfully completed more tasks as the level of difficulty increased. This is particularly noticeable in the difficult tasks were the difference was significant regardless of the tasks type (recall or recognition). In the moderate and the easy tasks, the difference was significant for recall and not for recognition.

7.3 User Satisfaction

The two interface versions (text with graphics and multimodal) did not demonstrate a significant difference for the ease of use, making users confused or nervous (see statements S1 to S3 in figure 5B). A larger difference however was observed on the specific statements relating to learning (see statements S4 to S7 in figure 5B). These results derived from two independent groups and users within those two groups were not presented with both interface versions in order to make an informed comparison. However, the users in the multimodal group may have had prior experience to typical learning interfaces and this probably served as a comparison point. Typically, users in the experimental group thought that their learning was better aided by the multimodal metaphors by one point more (in a 1 to 6 scale) than the users in the control group. Users easily identified learning information about classes, associations, and multiplicity, which communicated by avatar, speech, and earcons respectively. This result on its own is not conclusive as it is based on subjective rating of users and the typical mean difference is not large enough (although a statistical significance for the overall satisfaction results was reached). However, when the user satisfaction data is combined with the efficiency and effectiveness results, the argument that users in the experimental group were helped by the multimodal metaphors becomes much stronger. It can therefore be extrapolated that multimodal aided learning, particularly in recall situations and complex learning material, is more likely to result in an enjoyable and satisfying experience for the user. This experience is linked with the ability to complete learning tasks correctly and quickly.

8. Conclusion and Future Work

In this chapter, we investigated the employment of multimodal metaphors (speech sound, non-speech sounds, and avatars with simple facial expression) as communication means to present information in the interface of e-learning platforms, and explored its effect on the usability of such interfaces. An experimental two-group study was conducted in which usability parameters: efficiency, effectiveness, and satisfaction of two different versions of the experimental e-learning platform were compared. In the first version, only visual channel of the users were used in the interaction to get textually presented information about class diagram notation. The second version of the experimental e-learning platform provided a combination of speech sounds (recorded), non speech sounds (earcons) and avatar with simple facial expressions to deliver the same information. The chapter then concluded with a discussion of the obtained results and research directions for future work.

The results obtained from this empirical study confirmed that the multimodal interface could indeed help to spend lower time in performing the required tasks and was more effective in conveying information in an e-learning platform. Also, it was more satisfactory. Nevertheless, these results did not clearly clarify the contributing role of each of earcon, speech and avatar. So, the inclusion of multimodal metaphors is suggested and should be taken into consideration when designing the user interfaces of e-learning applications. This will enable the user to make use of more than one channel of communication and, hence, shorten the time needed to perform the required tasks with higher level of accuracy. As a result, aspects of the usability in these interfaces will be improved.

Based on the experimental results and users' feedback, further enhancements on both of the experimental platform and the required tasks were needed to be used later in the next experimental work which will aim at investigating the contribution of each of speech, earcons, and avatar when used in the interface of an e-learning platform. In addition to the use of more than one avatar in the same e-learning interface, specific facial expressions and body gestures of a teacher-like avatar will be also explored.

9. References

Alexander, S. (2001). "E-learning developments and experiences." Education and Training **43**(4-5): 240-248.

Alty, J. L. and D. Rigas (2005). "Exploring the use of structured musical stimuli to communicate simple diagrams: the role of context." International Journal of Human-Computer Studies **62**(1): 21-40.

Annetta, L. A. and S. Holmes (2006). "Creating Presence and Community in a Synchronous Virtual Learning Environment Using Avatars." International journal of instructional technology and distance learning **3**: 27-43.

Baylor, A. L. (2003). The impact of three pedagogical agent roles. Autonomous Agents & Multi-Agent Systems Conference, Melbourne, Australia, ACM New York, NY, USA.

Beskow, J. (1997). "Animation of Talking Agents." Proceedings of AVSP **97**: 149-152.

Blattner, M. M., D. A. Sumikawa, et al. (1989). "Earcons and Icons: Their Structure and Common Design Principles." Human-Computer Interaction **4**(1): 11-44.

Bonebright, T. L., M. A. Nees, et al. (2001). "Testing the effectiveness of sonified graphs for education: A programmatic research project." International Conference on Auditory Display, Espoo, Finland.

Brady, L. (2001). "Fault lines in the terrain of distance education." Computers and Composition **18**(4): 347-358.

Brewster, S. A. (1997). "Using non-speech sound to overcome information overload." Displays **17**(3-4): 179-189.

Brewster, S. A. (1998). "The design of sonically-enhanced widgets." Interacting with Computers **11**(2): 211-235.

Brewster, S. A., P. C. Wright, et al. (1994). "The design and evaluation of an auditory-enhanced scrollbar." Proceedings of the SIGCHI conference on Human factors in computing systems: celebrating interdependence: 173-179.

Brewster, S. A., P. C. Wright, et al. (1995). "Experimentally derived guidelines for the creation of earcons." Adjunct Proceedings of HCI **95**: 155-159.

Brown, L., S. Brewster, et al. (2002). "Browsing modes for exploring sonified line graphs." Proceedings of British HCI **2**: 2–5.

Brown, M. L., S. L. Newsome, et al. (1989). "An experiment into the use of auditory cues to reduce visual workload." Proceedings of the SIGCHI conference on Human factors in computing systems: Wings for the mind: 339-346.

Carswell, L. and D. Benyon (1996). "An adventure game approach to multimedia distance education." SIGCUE Outlook **24**(1-3): 122-124.

Correia, A. P. and P. Dias (2001). "Criteria for evaluating learning web sites: how does this impact the design of e-learning." Actas da II Conferência Internacional de Tecnologias da Informação e Comunicação na Educação: Desafios Challenges: 521-528.

Crease, M. and S. Brewster (1998). "Making Progress With Sounds-The Design and Evaluation Of An Audio Progress Bar." Proceedings of ICAD **98**.

DiGiano, C. J., R. M. Baecker, et al. (1993). "LogoMedia: a sound-enhanced programming environment for monitoring program behavior." Proceedings of the SIGCHI conference on Human factors in computing systems: 301-302.

Dix, A., G. Abowd, et al. (2004). Human-Computer Interaction (3rd Edition). Prentice Hall.

Dix, A. J. (1993). Human-computer interaction. New York; London, Prentice-Hall.

Fabri, M. and D. J. Moore (2005). "Is empathy the key? Effective communication via instant messaging." Proceedings of the 11th EATA International Conference on Networking Entities.

Fabri, M., D. J. Moore, et al. (2002). "Face Value: Towards Emotionally Expressive Avatars." In proceeding of AISB Convention on Animated Expressive Characters for Social Interaction, London, UK.

Fletcher, J. D. and S. Tobias (2005). "The multimedia principle." The Cambridge handbook of multimedia learning: 117–133.

Gazepidis, N. and D. Rigas (2008). "Evaluation of Facial Expressions and Body Gestures in Interactive Systems." International Journal of Computers, NAUN **2**(1): 92-97.

Govindasamy, T. (2001). "Successful implementation of e-Learning Pedagogical considerations." The Internet and Higher Education **4**(3-4): 287-299.

Graf, S., T. Lin, et al. (2007). "Analyzing the relationship between learning styles and cognitive traits." Seventh IEEE International Conference on Advanced Learning Technologies (ICALT 2007): 235-239.

Hamilton, R., C. Richards, et al. (2001). An examination of e-learning and e-books.

Henry, P. (2001). "E-learning technology, content and services." Education+ Training **43**(4): 249-255.

Holmes, J. (2007). "Designing agents to support learning by explaining." Computers & Education **48**(4): 523-547.

Kapp, K. M. (2003). "E-learning basics: essay: The e-learning market: it's about the learner, not the instructor!" eLearn **2003**(6).

Kildal, J. and S. A. Brewster (2005). "Explore the Matrix: Browsing Numerical Data Tables Using Sound." Proc. ICAD2005.

Lin, T. and P. A. Kinshuk (2003). "Cognitive Trait Model-A Supplement to Performance Based Student Models." Proceedings of International Conference on Computers in Education, Hong Kong: 629-632.

Low, R. and J. Sweller (2005). "The Modality Principle in Multimedia Learning." The Cambridge handbook of multimedia learning: 147–158.

Mikic, F. and L. Anido (2006). "Towards a Standard for Mobile E-Learning." International Conference on Systems and International Conference on Mobile Communications and Learning Technologies, 2006. ICN/ICONS/MCL 2006. International Conference on Networking: 217-222.

Oakley, I., M. R. McGee, et al. (2000). "Putting the feel in 'look and feel'." Proceedings of the SIGCHI conference on Human factors in computing systems: 415-422.

Oviatt, S. (2003). "MULTIMODAL INTERFACES." The Human-Computer Interaction Handbook: Fundamentals, Evolving Technologies, and Emerging Applications.

Reeves, L. M., J. C. Martin, et al. (2004). "Guidelines for multimodal user interface design." Communications of the ACM **47**(1): 57-59.

Rigas, D. and J. Alty (2005). "The rising pitch metaphor: An empirical study." International Journal of Human Computer Studies **62**(1): 1-20.

Rigas, D. and D. Hopwood (2003). "The Role of Multimedia in Interfaces for On-Line Learning." 9th Panhellenic Conference on Informatics (PCI'2003). , Thessaloniki, Greece.

Rigas, D., D. Memery, et al. (2001). "Experiments in using structured musical sound, synthesised speech and environmental stimuli to communicate information: is there a case for integration and synergy?" Proceedings of 2001 International Symposium on Intelligent Multimedia, Video and Speech Processing: 465-468.

Rigas, D. I. (1996). Guidelines for Auditory Interface Design: An Empirical Investigation, PhD thesis, Loughborough University of Technology.

Rigas, D. I. and J. L. Alty (1998). "Using sound to communicate program execution." Proceedings of the 24th EUROMICRO Conference **2**: 625–632.

Rosenberg, M. J. (2001). E-learning-strategies for delivering knowledge in the digital age, McGraw-Hill.

Russell, G. and B. Holkner (2000). "Virtual schools." Futures **32**(9-10): 887-897.

Sarter, N. B. (2006). "Multimodal information presentation: Design guidance and research challenges." International Journal of Industrial Ergonomics **36**(5): 439-445.

Shaw, G. and N. Marlow (1999). "The role of student learning styles, gender, attitudes and perceptions on information and communication technology assisted learning." Computers & Education **33**(4): 223-234.

Sheth, R. (2003). "Avatar Technology: Giving a Face to the e-Learning Interface." The eLearning Developers' Journal.

Spalter, A. M., R. M. Simpson, et al. (2000). "Considering a full range of teaching techniques for use in interactive educational software: a practical guide and brainstorming session." Frontiers in Education Conference, 2000. FIE 2000. 30th Annual **2**.

Stockman, T. (2004). "The Design and Evaluation of Auditory Access to Spreadsheets." Proceedings of ICAD.

Tabbers, H., L. Kester, et al. (2005). "Interface design for digital courses." In W. Jochems, J. van Merriënboer, & R. Koper (Eds). Integrated e-learning: implications for pedagogy, technology & organisation (pp. 100-111). London: Routledge Farmer.

Theonas, G., D. Hobbs, et al. (2008). "Employing Virtual Lecturers' Facial Expressions in Virtual Educational Environments." International Journal of Virtual Reality **7**(1): 31-44.

Upson, R. (2002). "Educational sonification exercises: Pathways for mathematics and musical achievement." International Conference on Auditory Display, Kyoto, Japan.

Yu, D., W. Zhang, et al. (2006). "New Generation of E-Learning Technologies." Proceedings of the First International Multi-Symposiums on Computer and Computational Sciences (IMSCCS'06).

6

The role of audio-visual metaphors to communicate customer knowledge

Mutlaq Alotaibi and Dimitrios Rigas
University of Bradford
United Kingdom

1. Introduction

The increasing complexity of organisations and volatility of markets led to a dramatic shift from information to knowledge societies (Thierauf 1999; Goh 2005). Although the volume of knowledge triples every eighteen months, its concept is still not completely well-defined (Becerra-Fernandez, Gonzalez et al. 2004). Knowledge elicitation can take place not only within the organisational boundary (Davenport and Prusak 1998), but also beyond, in which the active customer engagement is sough. Customer Knowledge (CK) is considered as the most valuable type of knowledge (Rowley, Kupiec-Teahan et al. 2007), due to its important role in the value creation and sustainability (Goh 2005). However, CK is not easy to gather, identify, interpret and integrate, due to the multiplicity of the customer's communication channels (Bueren, Schierholz et al. 2005). This called for the integration and management of CK elicited from different channels (Bueren, Schierholz et al. 2005), and hence to the synergy between Customer Relationship Management (CRM), and Knowledge Management (KM) in E-Business environments (Tiwana 2001; Bueren, Schierholz et al. 2005). The concept of CKM is widely used to refer to the synergy between two management tools, namely KM and CRM. In CKM contexts, it is important to consider that human experts, in general, tend to be reluctant to share knowledge, due to the fear of losing social power and intellectual rights (Davenport and Prusak 1998; Gibbert, Leibold et al. 2002). In deed, Dealing with customers exacerbates the problem, due to their position outside the organisational boundary and in a click away from competitors (Gibbert, Leibold et al. 2002). However, this demands higher levels of knowledge-based social interaction to take place in a platform supported by the organisation, especially on the web channel (García-Murillo and Annabi 2002). It is possible for the web channel to offer multimedia interactions to enable collaboration and self-services, and more importantly motivate further customer-web interactivity (Senger, Gronover et al. 2002). Although the potential of interactive multimedia interaction is well recognised to address lack of trust and information overload (Gibbert, Leibold et al. 2002), empirical studies that evaluate this role is generally lacking in the current literate to CKM. Therefore, this chapter describes an investigation into the use of multimodal metaphors to communicate CK, compared to text with graphics. This comparative evaluation measured traditional usability attributes, including effectiveness, efficiency, and user satisfaction.

	KM	CRM	CKM
Knowledge sought in	Employ, team, organisation	Customer database	Customer expectations, and innovation
Underlying principle	Employ knowledge integration	Customer knowledge discovery	Elicitation of customer experience and expansion of its sharing and use
Objectives	Cost and time saving, avoidance of re-inventing the wheel	Marinating customer base	Collaboration with customers to gain jointly created value
Measures	Performance against budget	Customer satisfaction and loyalty	Performance against rivals in terms of innovation and growth, and contribution to customer success
Advantage	Customer satisfaction	Customer retention	Customer success, innovation
Rewards recipient	Employee	Customer	Customer
Customer role	Passive consumer	Captive, tied by loyalty schemes	Active partner in value-creation process
Firm role	Motivate employees to share knowledge	Build long lasting relationships with customers	Transforming customer from passive to active role in co-creation of value

Table 1. Differences between CKM, CRM, and KM (adapted from (Gibbert, Leibold et al. 2002)).

2. Customer Knowledge Management (CKM)

The externalisation of KM constitutes CKM, due to the great similarities between them in terms of aims, objectives, techniques, and outcomes (Lopez-Nicolas and Molina-Castillo 2008). When considering the external perspective of KM, it is important to consider the application of its associated process of generation, storage, sharing, and utilisation of knowledge that resides in customers' heads. Another argument suggested that CKM is neither an evolution of CRM, nor application of KM in CRM; it is a combination of both (Feng and Tian 2005). CRM and KM have several differences and similarities (Gebert, Geib et al. 2002). KM and CRM have, to some extend, similar goals, as they help organisations to grow, innovate and compete against competitors (Gebert, Geib et al. 2002). Table 1 differentiates CKM from both KM and CRM. Generally speaking, CKM aims to support knowledge-based interaction, reduce customer waiting time, improve quality of services, increase transparency, increase customer satisfaction and loyalty, which eventually lead to increasing revenue and lower costs (Bueren, Schierholz et al. 2005). In brief, CKM is an external perspective of KM.

With this huge contribution, there are several CKM outstanding issues, including lack of trust, and information overload. Interactive multimodal is identified to have the potential to address these issues. For example, the lack of trust (Davenport and Prusak 1998; Gibbert, Leibold et al. 2002) can be tackled by optimising a customer-company dialogue (Interaction), and building an environment of care, trust and mutual empathy (Gurgul, Rumyantseva et al. 2002). More importantly, interactive multimedia systems are proposed to tackle trust and interactivity issues (Gibbert, Leibold et al. 2002). Another example is information overload (Bueren, Schierholz et al. 2005), which can be tackled by integrating the visual presentations of information with auditory ones (Brewster 1997). In summary, it can be said that CKM

encounters the lack of customer's trust, and information overload, which can be tackled by incorporating multimedia systems.
A great deal of emphasis is placed on rethinking the role customer can play in innovation through the five styles of CKM: *prosumersim (co-production), team-based co-learning, mutual innovation, communities of creation,* and *joint IP ownership* (Gibbert, Leibold et al. 2002). With focus on E-Business and software application suitability, two CKM styles were considered for further elaboration, namely *COC* and *co-production.*

2.1 Communities of Customers (COC)

COC constitute a group of users who share the same culture, value, interest, and objectives, and exchange product-related knowledge (Rowley, Kupiec-Teahan et al. 2007). When considering that customers share opinions about products and services (contributors), and evaluate opinions of peer customers (seekers) for their own benefits, it is important to consider that the organisation also reduces the overhead associated with handling customer enquiries, which leads to various organisational benefits, such as time saving and cost avoidance (Cheung, Shek et al. 2004). Furthermore, Amazon.com case study represents the typical example of COC, in which E-Business customers share experience about products (reviews), and knowledge about customers is discovered (recommendations) in this context (Gurgul, Rumyantseva et al. 2002). It is argued that 62% of the online purchases were driven be customer reviews and website recommendations (Cheung, Shek et al. 2004). Another argument presented in the case study of Flexifoil International (Rowley, Kupiec-Teahan et al. 2007) suggested that increasing interactivity of web-based systems has contributed substantially in the rising sales figures. With these two arguments in mind, it can be investigated whether an interactive COC platform would outperform interactive non-COC, or static COC platforms. In summary, fostering COC is linked to various personal positive gains, such as continuous access to knowledge and information, as well as organisational benefits, such as cost time saving, cost avoidance, and increasing sales.

2.2 Co-Production

The customer participation in product and service creation has shown to have a positive influence on the successfulness of New Product Development (NPD), and innovativeness of products and services (Salomo, Steinhoff et al. 2003). However, the choice between product innovativeness and speed to market involves trade-off. A study (Fang 2008) on addressing the trade-off between idea novelty and speed to market indicated that the customer's participation as co-developer has a considerable positive effect on product innovativeness, but it undermines speeds to markets, particularly in high process interdependences. In general, harnessing customer competencies has shown to be a major contributor towards various benefits, such as organisational growth, innovation and competition against aggressive rivals (Gebert, Geib et al. 2002; Gebert, Geib et al. 2002). In particular, an experimental study (Matthing, Sanden et al. 2004) on the originality and value of user ideas suggested that observing customer real actions during co-production improves the anticipation of customer future needs. It provides predictions, which are more accurate, than that provided by the traditional knowledge discovery techniques. This suggestion aligns with other proposals that customers can easily generate novel ideas more than developers can, whereas professionals create products that are more reliable (Kristensson,

Gustafsson et al. 2004). Also, a study (Bendapudi and Leone 2003) on the psychological implications of customer involvement in self-service co-production revealed that the participated customers expressed more positive feelings toward the experience, compared to those who did not participate in co-production. Another investigation (Auh, Bell et al. 2007) into the role of co-production to support competition in the financial services industry and its effect on customer loyalty revealed that co-production relates positively toward both attitudinal and behavioural customer loyalty. In summary, it is possible to say that the customer participation in co-production is linked to not only economic benefits, but also customer positive attitudes, such as satisfaction and loyalty.

3. Customer Interaction

Knowledge exchange between customers who share the same background and interest led to an increasing demand for direct interactions with customers and effective CK elicitation (García-Murillo and Annabi 2002). The customer's interaction needs to be managed and aided, especially in the web-based environments (Senger, Gronover et al. 2002). CKM facilitates instance delivery of knowledge and real-time offers to customers involved in the web-based interaction (Pan and Lee 2003). This argument is in agreement with other work in literature (Massey, Montoya-Weiss et al. 2001). Another argument suggests that real-time customer interaction and fostering COC contribute positively toward the improvement of CK elicitation (Gibbert, Leibold et al. 2002), and exploitation (Lesser, Mundel et al. 2000). Customer interaction (Dous, Salomann et al. 2005) can be whether face-to-face or Electronic (Gurgul, Rumyantseva et al. 2002). The former helps transferring tacit knowledge and the latter utilises the electronic means to deal with both explicit and tacit knowledge (Mertins, Heisig et al. 2003). Moreover, compared to human-to-human dialogues, it is argued that IT with the aid of multimedia can tackle knowledge hoarding by improving perception of trust (Senger, Gronover et al. 2002). In summary, the role customer interaction is identified to be contributing toward the improvement of CK elicitation, and hence organisational growth.

Typically, innovative interaction is curial to improve the user's performance, as opposed to the traditional interaction. In CKM, it is more suitable to gather CK directly from customers, compared to the sale representative approach (Gibbert, Leibold et al. 2002). Although, little effort has been devoted to examine the role of multimodal interaction in CKM, there is a general agreement that user interface can be enhanced by the introduction of auditory stimuli, including speech (Kehoe and Pitt 2006), earcons (Rigas, Memery et al. 2000; Alty and Rigas 2005; Rigas and Alty 2005), and auditory icons (Cohen 1993; Gaver 1997). In fact, previous work in multimodal interaction literature (Alty and Rigas 2005; Rigas and Alty 2005; Alsuraihi and Rigas 2007; Alsuraihi and Rigas 2007; Kieffer and Carbonell 2007; Rigas and Alsuraihi 2007) carried out traditional usability evaluation to measure effectiveness, efficiency and satisfaction. For example, an experimental work (Rigas and Ciuffreda 2007; Rigas and Ciuffreda 2007) was carried out to investigate the usability of using multimodal metaphors in browsing internet search results. The experiments aimed to address the identification of document relevancy, and found that the multimodal approach can improve presentation, and hence the browsing process. This view is supported by other work in literature (Rigas and Bahadur 2006). Therefore, it is important to examine the hypothesis that the use of multimodal interaction in the context of CKM can improve usability, compared to text with graphics.

Condition		Communities of Customers (COC)				Co-production CK		Product Information	
		Trends	Reviews	Ratings	Intelligent advices	Cost	Comparison	Price	Features
VCKMS	Text		√			√	√	√	√
	Graphics	√		√	√				√
MCKMS	Text		√				√	√	√
	Graphics	√		√	√	√			√
	Speech		√				√		√
	Earcons	√		√	√		√		
	Auditory icons		√		√		√		√

Table 2. Differences between the VCKMS and MCKMS experimental systems

4. Experimental Platform

The experimental platform provided typical functions of web-based mobile phones retailing systems, and included an additional function labelled as co-production. With focus on the use of multimodal interaction, prior experimental studies suggested comparative evaluation between various conditions of user interface, which mainly includes visual and multimodal conditions. This experiment applied the same concept to Electronic Customer Knowledge Management Systems (E-CKMS). This involved developing an experimental E-CKMS with two interfaces: text with graphics (VCKMS), and multimodal with speech, earcons, and auditory icons (MCKMS). In VCKMS, the communication of CK utilised the visual channel only, whereas in MCKMS it utilised both visual and auditory channels. This required categorisation of CK and auditory and visual metaphors, and utilisation of a wide range of technologies. It can be seen that there were several CK types organised into six categories: trends, customer reviews, customer ratings, intelligent advices, co-production CK, and product features. In addition, there were two visual-only metaphors employed: text and graphics, and three auditory ones: speech, earcons, and auditory icons. Table 2 illustrates the differences between the VCKMS and MCKMS experimental systems.

In order to include sounds into the E-CKMS interface, several technologies, tools and sounds has been used. This included a speech agent (Microsoft 2006), a text-to-speech engine, environmental sounds (Gaver 1986), multi-timbre synthesiser software (Shah 2006), musical notes, and a sound recoding software (KYDsoft 2006). In addition, the empirically derived guidelines provided by Brewster (Brewster, Wright et al. 1995) were followed in the creation of earcons. For example, families of earcons was differentiated by employing timbre, including *guitar, violin, trumpet, drum, organ,* and *piano* (Rigas and Alty 1998). Further differentiation was made by utilising rising pitch metaphors. For example, *guitar* and violin were mapped to trends category to convey the best and worst rated products respectively, and rising pitch to communicate the product position in both lists. Furthermore, to present each individual earcons in a rhythmic form, the first note was accented, and the last one was played for a longer period (Brewster, Wright et al. 1995). Earcons were played in sequence (serial compound earcons), with a 0.1 seconds gap, so the user can make a decision where one note finishes, and when the other starts. In addition, the environmental sounds used were sound of *typing, cheering, clapping, laughing, gasping, foghorn, side whistle,* and *camera shot*. In brief, the experimental E-CKMS was implemented with two interface conditions.

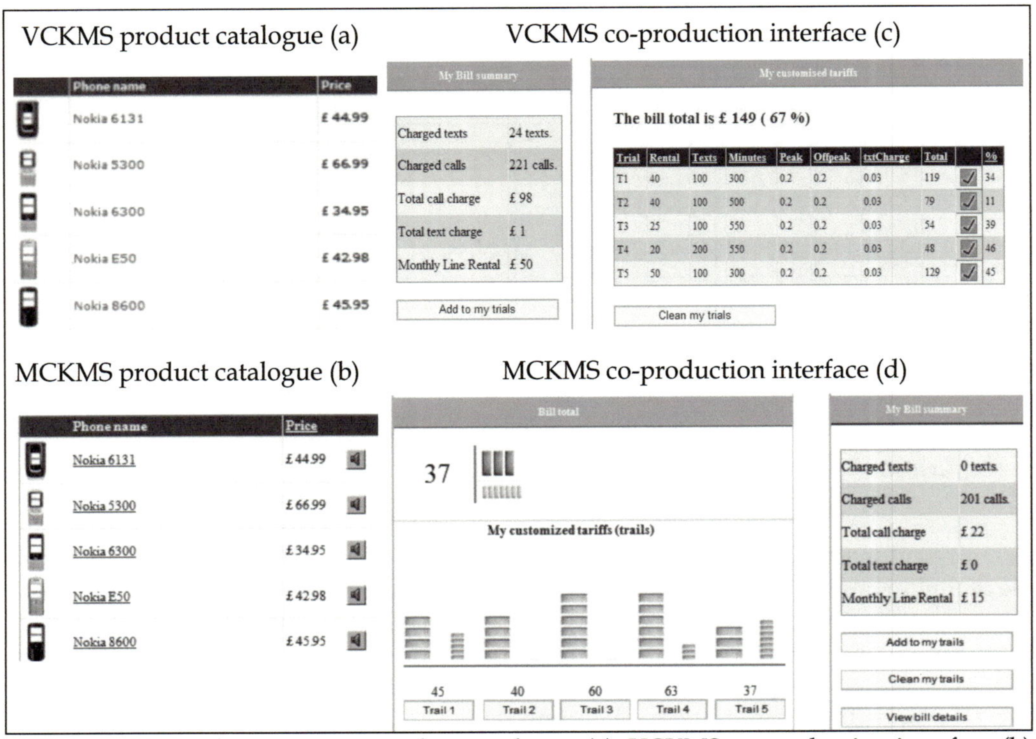

Fig. 1. Snapshots of the VCKMS product catalogue (a), VCKMS co-production interface (b), MCKMS product catalogue (c), and MCKMS co-production interface (c)

4.1 Implementation of Product Catalogue

The implementation of product catalogue in VCKMS and MCKMS was consistent with Amazon.com interface. Both used the typical tabular catalogue, and presented product image, name, rating, and price. However, MCKMS introduced an additional feature, which optionally allowed the user to assess other product related knowledge from the catalogue. In MCKMS, there was a button associated with each product to communicate CK and product features by a serial combination of speech, earcons, and auditory icons. Figure 1 (a) shows the VCKMS product catalogue with visual presentation of product image, name, and price. Similarly, Figure 1 (b) shows the MCKMS product catalogue that communicated the same information visually, and provided an additional communication method to convey further information using the auditory channel. In summary, the tabular product catalogue was implemented in VCKMS and MCKMS to communicate basic product information visually. In addition, MCKMS can convey other CK and product features aurally.

4.2 Implementation of Co-Production

The co-production of Electronic Products (E-Products) is more suitable for online customers, because it do not require a complete line of production, instead only software is needed.

E-Products requires only a software to be produced (Gurgul, Rumyantseva et al. 2002), such as the open source software and user innovation communities (Von Hippel 2001) presented in Microsoft case study (Rollins and Halinen 2005). This avoids the repeated shifts from production lines to customer care departments and visa-versa (von Hippel 2001). This study considered co-production of billing schemes, due to its electronic nature (E-Products), which enables E-CKMS to produce trail products in the absence of a complete line of production. Billing scheme parameters were manipulated to examine the effect of such manipulation on the bill total. This manipulation provided customised billing scheme through several trail-and-error productions. In each trail-and-error, the trial was stored in an array to facilitate trials comparison, and hence supported customer decision making. In VCKMS, the trial comparison feature was lacking, because trials were presented in a tabular form. Figure 1 (c) shows the VCKMS co-production interface that uses texts with graphics to communicate basic co-production information. In MCKMS, a graph aided by auditory stimuli (speech, earcons, and auditory icons) was used to communicate the same information, in addition to trail comparison knowledge. Figure 1 (d) shows the MCKMS co-production interface that uses interactive graph to present co-production and trial comparison knowledge. The user was required to click whether the left vertical bars to facilitate trail comparison by musical notes or the right vertical bars to compare more than one trial by synthesised speech. In summary, the MCKMS co-production interface was implemented differently, in which an interactive graph and multimodal metaphors were used.

Complexity	Task code and description		Task requirements	Available selections
Simple	T1	Product selection in the presence of COC contexts	6	18
	T2	Product selection in the absence of COC contexts	4	22
Moderate	T3	Product selection in the presence of COC contexts	7	8
	T4	Product selection in the absence of COC contexts	5	9
	T5	Co-production with two trials	3	N/A
Complex	T6	Product selection in the presence of COC contexts	7	2
	T7	Product selection in the absence of COC contexts	4	2
	T8	Co-production with five trials	6	N/A

Table 3. Review of the eight common tasks, and complexity levels

5. Design of Experimental Study

This study demonstrates usability aspects of multimodal interaction in three levels of task complexity levels: *simple, moderate,* and *complex*. To disseminate the three complexity levels, two influential factors were proposed: *number of task requirements*, and *number of available selections*. The former reflects how many task requirements required to be fulfilled in order to consider the task as successfully completed, while the latter refers to the number of available products that when selected by the user, the task is regarded as accomplished. Three were eight common tasks categorised into simple (T1 and T2), moderate (T3, T4 and

T5) and complex (T6, T7 and T8) tasks. Table 3 reviews the eight common tasks and the two complexity factors. When the task is designed as complex, the number of task requirements was increased, while the number of available selections was decreased. More information on task levels, types and workload is provided in (Burke, Prewett et al. 2006). In brief, this study identified three complexity levels, and proposed two factors to differentiate these levels.

The task was also organised into two types: *COC* and *co-production*. The COC tasks referred product selection in the present and absence of CoC contexts. Types of products were phones and tariffs. The eight common tasks were six product selection tasks in the presence (T1, T3 and T6) and absence (T2, T4 and T7) of COC contexts, and two co-production tasks (T5 and T8). In product selection tasks, the user was provided with a scenario, in which the presumed task requirements were presented as user preferences. In T3, for example, a user was provided with a scenario: say that your phone preferences are, the phone should be among the top10 or intelligent advice lists, the phone should be a camera phone with capacity between 0.5 and 3MP, a 3G phone, and the number of positive reviews should be greater than the negative ones. It was worth noting that scenarios of product selection tasks in the presence of COC included at least one requirement from the COC context (e.g. rating, trends, and website advice), whereas in the absence of COC lacked the COC requirements.

This study evaluated the difference between groups to explore the cause-effect relationship between factors. A selected sample was instructed to use the two conditions in order to observe and measure of a set of three variables. Forty participants were selected randomly from the population, based on the non-probability strategy and convenience-sampling method (Salkind 2006). Participants were assigned randomly to two groups (n=20 each), and offered a short training session. Each group was introduced to examine a platform that they had not used or experienced prior to the experiment, to control user familiarity with the system. The two groups were provided with the mapping between information represented and the metaphors used to communicate them. The ability of users to interpret such metaphors was tested prior to the experiment through specially design tasks, in which users provided with help needed until the full understanding of the perceptual context is demonstrated. Subsequently, participants were asked to perform the eight tasks and fill a questionnaire devised for this study. The task order was balanced as so to eliminate any possible task learning effect.

Upon the completion of the eight tasks, a set of factors were quantified and measured. These variables were task completion rate and time as objective factors, and user satisfaction as a subjective dimension. The task completion rate and time were observed during the task performance to reflect aspects of E-CKMS effectiveness and efficiency. User satisfaction was measured by a set of questionnaire statements, to which the user's agreement/disagreement was sought (Jordan 1998). A six-point Likert scale ranging from agree strongly (6) to disagree strongly (1) was used (Salkind 2006). The satisfaction items included *Ease of Use (EOU)*, *Extent of Confusion (EOC)*, *Extent of Frustration (EOF)*, *Ease of Navigation (EON)*, and *Convenience (CON)*. Based on the System Usability Scale (SUS) technique (Brooke 1996), user responses were summed up to generate an overall score for user satisfaction. In brief, E-CKMS interaction mode and task complexity denote the independent variables. In addition, E-CKMS effectiveness, efficiency, and user satisfaction represent the dependent variables.

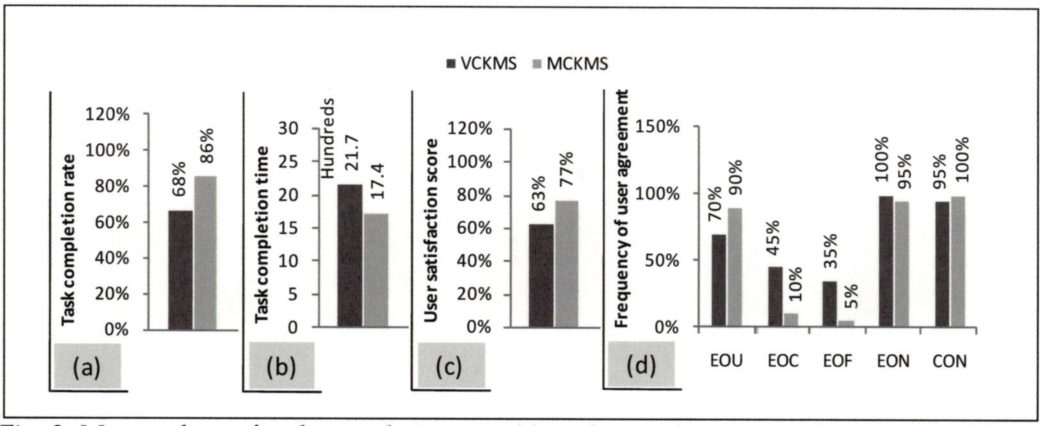

Fig. 2. Mean values of task completion rate (a), task completion time (b), user satisfaction score (c), and frequency of user agreement on the five satisfaction factors (c) using the VCKMS and MCKMS experimental systems

6. Analysis of Results

Figure 2 shows the mean values of task completion rate (a), task completion time (b), user satisfaction (c), and frequency of user agreement (d) on aspects of satisfaction for using the VCKMS and MCKMS experimental systems. At a glance, the multimodal E-CKMS platform (MCKMS) was more usable than the control condition (VCKMS) as regards effectiveness, efficiency, and user satisfaction. In Figure 2 (a), it can be noticed that the two groups differ considerably in favour of the multimodal E-CKMS platform (MCKMS) with E-CKMS effectiveness. The task completion rate for using MCKMS (141 tasks, 86%) was considerably higher than using VCKMS (102 tasks, 68%). Chi-square results showed significant different between the two interaction modes as regards task completion rate ($x^2=26$, df=1, $p<0.05$). In Figure 2 (b), it can be seen that MCKMS outperform VCKMS with regard to E-CKMS efficiency. The mean value of task completion time for MCKMS was 20% higher than that for VCKMS. The t-test results showed that there was a significant difference between the two E-CKMS experimental platforms with regard to task completion time ($t_{37}= 6.004$, cv=2.02, $p<0.05$). In Figure 2 (c), it can be noticed that there was a considerable improvement in user satisfaction in favour of MCKMS. The mean value of user satisfaction score for using MCKMS was 19% greater than that for VCKMS. In addition, the t-test results showed a significant difference between the two conditions regarding the satisfaction score (t38=4, cv=2.02, $p<0.05$). In Figure 2 (d), user responses suggested that the experimental condition (MCKMS) was easier to use, less confusing, and less frustrating. Actually, 90% of the users agreed that the MCKMS was easy to use, compared to 70% for VCKMS. In user confusion statement, 45% of the users agreed that VCKMS was confusing, whereas 90% disagree in MCKMS. In addition, 95% of MCKMS users felt frustrated, compared to 55% of VCKMS users. However, a 5% difference between the two conditions was found with regard to ease of navigation and convenience. 95% of MCKMS users agreed that it was easy to navigation, compared to all the VCKMS users. All the MCKMS users felt that it was convenient, compared to 95% of VCKMS users. In brief, the MCKMS has shown to be generally more usable than the VCKMS.

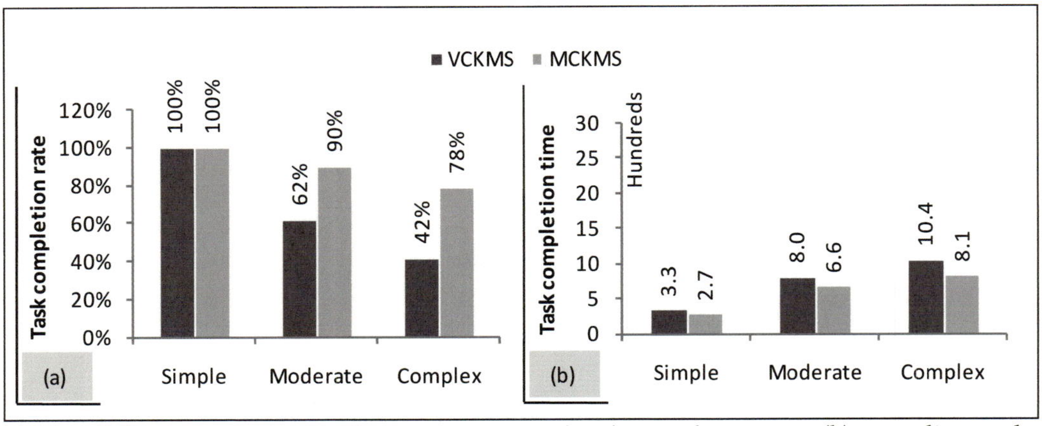

Fig. 3. Mean values of task completion rate (a) and task completion time (b) according to the three task complexity levels using the VCKMS and MCKMS experimental systems

6.1 Task Complexity

Figure 3 shows the mean values of task completion rate (a) and task completion time (b) according to the three task complexity levels using the VCKMS and MCKMS experimental systems. Overall, the effectiveness and efficiency of multimodal metaphors has shown to be influenced by the task complexity, as the more complex the task is, the more usable these metaphors become. In Figure 3 (a), it can be seen that the variance between VCKMS and MCKMS went hand in hand with the complexity level with regard to task completion rate. In the simple tasks, the completion rate was insensitive to the complexity levels. In contrast, the variance between the two conditions rose considerably in moderate and complex tasks. In moderate tasks, the completion rate for VCKMS was considerably lower than that for MCKMS. Chi-square results showed a significant difference between the two conditions with regard to moderate task completion rate (x^2= 13.1, df=1, $p<0.05$). In complex tasks, the completion rate for using MCKMS was considerably greater than that for VCKMS. Chi-square results also suggested that there was a significant difference between the two interfaces regarding the completion rate for complex tasks (x^2=16.8, df=1, $p<0.05$). In Figure 3 (b), the use of multimodal metaphors has shown to have a considerable effect on task completion time, particularly for complex tasks. It can be noticed that the completion of complex tasks were achieved significantly faster using MCKMS than VCKMS. Overall, the difference in task completion time between the two conditions went hand in hand with the task complexity, in favour of MCKMS. In the simple and moderate tasks, the mean value of task completion time for using VCKMS was slightly higher than that for MCKMS. In the complex tasks, the mean value for VCKMS was 22% higher than that for MCKMS. The difference in task completion time was found significant with regard to the performance of simple (t_{38}= 2.2, cv= 2.03, $p<0.05$), moderate (t_{33}= 6.3, cv= 2.03, $p<0.05$), and complex tasks (t_{35}= 5.7, cv= 2.03, $p<0.05$). In summary, the level of task complexity has been identified as a key factor that effects the contribution of multimodal metaphors to communicate CK. Using multimodal metaphors has shown to be more effective and efficient than the traditional visual information communication, especially for complex tasks.

Interface		Aspects of user satisfaction				
		EOU	EOF	EOC	EON	CON
VCKMS	Mode	4	3	3	5	5
	Frequency	16 (80%)	11 (55%)	13 (65%)	19 (95%)	20 (100%)
	Mean	3.85	3.45	3.10	4.95	4.45
MCKMS	Mode	5	2	2	5	5
	Frequency	18 (90%)	14 (70%)	14 (70%)	16 (80%)	17 (85%)
	Mean	4.80	2.20	2.20	5.00	4.95

Table 4. The mode, frequency of the mode, and mean values of the five aspects of users' satisfaction for using two interaction modes

6.2 User Satisfaction

Table 4 shows the mode, frequency of the mode, and mean values of user satisfaction factors for using the VCKMS and MCKMS experimental systems. In general, the use of multimodal metaphors led to greater user satisfaction, and hence participants responded highly favourably to MCKMS. It can be seen that 80% of VCKMS users agreed slightly that the system was easy to use (EOU), whereas 90% of MCKMS users agreed moderately. In addition, over half of the VCKMS sample disagreed slightly that the system was confusing, whereas 70% of MCKMS users disagree moderately. Furthermore, 56% of VCKMS users disagreed slightly that they have felt frustrated during the interaction, whereas 70% of MCKMS users disagree moderately. It can be seen from the table that the 95% of VCKMS users and 80% of MCKMS users agreed moderately that it was easy to navigating through. Similarly, all VCKMS users and 85% of MCKMS users felt comfortable during the interaction. The Mann-Whitney results indicated that the difference between VCKMS and MCKMS was insufficient in both EON ($U=183$, $cv=127$, $p>0.05$) and CON ($U=131$, $cv=127$, $p>0.05$). However, there was a statistical significance found between the two conditions as regards EOU ($U=79$, $cv=127$, $p<0.05$), EOC ($U=65$, $cv=127$, $p<0.05$), and EOF ($U=102$, $cv=127$, $p<0.05$). In summary, it can be said that the greater user satisfaction was found by using multimodal metaphors, because participants expressed interest to, and rated in favour of MCKMS over VCKMS.

7. Conclusion

There has been an increasing demand for modern organisations to have real-time interaction with consumers, because their views or perceptions are often used for innovation. Typically, interfaces are used to elicit customers' views within E-CKMS. Therefore, interface design and customer interaction are important to the organisation. There are few CKM empirical studies, which investigated whether or not these technologies can be put into practice. Therefore, this experiment tested the hypothesis that multimodal interaction can improve E-CKMS usability as opposed to text with graphics. This involved implementing control and experimental E-CKMS experimental platforms (text with graphics and multimodal), which were evaluated by two independent groups of users (n=20 for each group). Results showed that the use of multimodal metaphors in E-CKMS was more usable than text with graphics. Although this experiment has proven to be successful, it is essential to introduce multimodal metaphors of social presence, such as avatars with facial expressions. It is important to examine several combinations of multimodal metaphors and evaluate the social aspects of avatars in order to promote further understanding and identify sources of variance between text with graphics and multimodal E-CKMS.

8. References

Alsuraihi, M. and D. Rigas (2007). Efficiency on Speech Recognition for Using Interface Design Environments by Novel Designers. the 7th WSEAS International Conference on Applied Informatics and Communications. Athens, Greece.

Alsuraihi, M. and D. Rigas (2007). How effective is it to design by voice? the 21st British HCI Group Annual Conference. University of Lancaster, Lancaster, UK.

Alty, J. and D. Rigas (2005). "Exploring the use of structured musical stimuli to communicate simple diagrams: the role of context." International Journal of Human-Computer Studies **62**(1): 21-40.

Auh, S., S. Bell, et al. (2007). "Co-production and customer loyalty in financial services." Journal of Retailing **83**(3): 359-370.

Becerra-Fernandez, I., A. Gonzalez, et al. (2004). Knowledge management: challenges, solutions, and technologies. Upper Saddle River, N.J., Pearson/Prentice Hall.

Bendapudi, N. and R. Leone (2003). "Psychological Implications of Customer Participation in Co-Production." Journal of Marketing **67**(1): 14-28.

Brewster, S. (1997). "Using non-speech sound to overcome information overload." Displays **17**(3-4): 179-189.

Brewster, S., P. Wright, et al. (1995). "Experimentally derived guidelines for the creation of earcons." Adjunct Proceedings of HCI **95**: 155-159.

Brooke, J. (1996). "SUS: a quick and dirty usability scale." Usability Evaluation in Industry: 189-194.

Bueren, A., R. Schierholz, et al. (2005). "Improving performance of customer-processes with knowledge management." Business Process Management Journal **11**(5): 573-588.

Burke, J., M. Prewett, et al. (2006). "Comparing the effects of visual-auditory and visual-tactile feedback on user performance: a meta-analysis." Proceedings of the 8th international conference on Multimodal interfaces: 108-117.

Cheung, C., S. Shek, et al. (2004). Virtual Community of Consumers: Why People Are Willing to Contribute. the eight Pacific Asia Conference on Information Systems (PACIS'2004). Shanghai, China**:** 2100–2107.

Cohen, M. (1993). "Throwing, pitching and catching sound: audio windowing models and modes." International Journal of Man-Machine Studies **39**(2): 269-304.

Davenport, T. and L. Prusak (1998). Working knowledge: how organizations manage what they know. Boston, Mass., Harvard Business School Press.

Dous, M., H. Salomann, et al. (2005). Knowledge Management Capabilities in CRM: Making Knowledge For, From and About Customers Work. the Eleventh Americas Conference on Information Systems. Omaha, NE, USA**:** 167-178.

Fang, E. (2008). "Customer Participation and the Trade-Off Between New Product Innovativeness and Speed to Market." Journal of Marketing **72**(4): 90-104.

Feng, T. and J. Tian (2005). "Customer Knowledge Management and Condition Analysis of Successful CKM Implementation." Machine Learning and Cybernetics. **4**: 2239- 2244

García-Murillo, M. and H. Annabi (2002). "Customer knowledge management." Journal of the Operational Research Society **53**(8): 875-884.

Gaver, W. (1986). "Auditory Icons: Using Sound in Computer Interfaces." Human-Computer Interaction **2**(2): 167-177.

Gaver, W. (1997). "Auditory Interfaces." Handbook of Human-Computer Interaction **1**: 1003-1041.

Gebert, H., M. Geib, et al. (2002). "Towards Customer Knowledge Management." Proceedings of the 2nd International Conference on Electronic Business (ICEB 2002).

Gebert, H., M. Geib, et al. (2002). "Towards Customer Knowledge Management–Integrating Customer Relationship Management and Knowledge Management concepts." The Second International Conference on Electronic Business (ICEB 2002): 296-298.

Gibbert, M., M. Leibold, et al. (2002). "Five Styles of Customer Knowledge Management, and How Smart Companies Use Them To Create Value." European Management Journal **20**(5): 459-469.

Goh, A. (2005). "Harnessing knowledge for innovation: an integrated management framework." Journal of Knowledge Management **9**(4): 6-18.

Gurgul, G., M. Rumyantseva, et al. (2002). "Customer Integration–Establish a constant bilateral knowledge flow." Diskussionspapier des Research Centers Knowledge Source der Universität St. Gallen.

Jordan, P. W. (1998). Measures of usability. An introduction to usability. London, Taylor & Francis Ltd.: 18-23.

Kehoe, A. and I. Pitt (2006). "Designing help topics for use with text-to-speech." Proceedings of the 24th annual conference on Design of communication: 157-163.

Kieffer, S. and N. Carbonell (2007). "Computer Science> Human-Computer Interaction Title: How really effective are Multimodal Hints in enhancing Visual Target Spotting? Some evidence from a usability study." Journal reference: Journal on Multimodal Interfaces (JMUI) **1**(1): 1-9.

Kristensson, P., A. Gustafsson, et al. (2004). "Harnessing the Creative Potential among Users." Journal of Product Innovation Management **21**(1): 4-14.

KYDsoft (2006) "Easy MP3 Sound Recorder (Sound Recording Software)." www.softplatz.com/Soft/Audio-Multimedia/Audio-Encoders-Decoders/Easy-MP3-Sound-Recorder.html **Volume**, DOI:

Lesser, E., D. Mundel, et al. (2000). "Managing Customer Knowledge." Journal of Business Strategy **21**(6): 34-7.

Lopez-Nicolas, C. and F. Molina-Castillo (2008). "Customer Knowledge Management and E-commerce: The role of customer perceived risk." International Journal of Information Management **28**(2): 102-113.

Massey, A., M. Montoya-Weiss, et al. (2001). "Re-engineering the customer relationship: leveraging knowledge assets at IBM." Decision Support Systems **32**(2): 155-170.

Matthing, J., B. Sanden, et al. (2004). "New service development: learning from and with customers." International Journal of Service Industry Management **15**(5): 479-498.

Mertins, K., P. Heisig, et al. (2003). Knowledge Management: Concepts and Best Practices. Berlin, Springer.

Microsoft (2006) "Microsoft Software Agent." www.microsoft.com/Msagent/ **Volume**, DOI:

Pan, S. and J. Lee (2003). "Using e-CRM for a unified view of the customer." Communications of the ACM **46**(4): 95-99.

Rigas, D. and M. Alsuraihi (2007). A Toolkit for Multimodal Interface Design: an Empirical Investigation. 12th International Conference of HCI. Beijing, China.

Rigas, D. and J. Alty (1998). How Can Multimedia Designers Utilise Timbre? HCI-98, People and Computers XIII. Sheffield, UK, Springer, British Computer Society.

Rigas, D. and J. Alty (2005). "The rising pitch metaphor: an empirical study." International Journal of Human-Computer Studies **62**(1): 1-20.

Rigas, D. and I. Bahadur (2006). "A Two Platform Empirical Study to Investigate the Use of Audio in a Stock Control Application." WSEAS Transactions on Computers **5**(10): 21-40.

Rigas, D. and A. Ciuffreda (2007). An Empirical Investigation of Multimodal Interfaces for Browsing Internet Search Results. the 7th WSEAS International Conference on Applied Informatics and Communications. Athens, Greece.

Rigas, D. and A. Ciuffreda (2007). The Use of Multimodality in Delivering Web Results: an Empirical Investigation. IADIS International Conference in Computer Graphics and Visualisation. Lisbon, Portugal.

Rigas, D., D. Memery, et al. (2000). "Using non-speech sound to communicate information in user interfaces." Applied Informatics 2000: 357–362.

Rollins, M. and A. Halinen (2005). Customer Knowledge Management Competence: Towards a Theoretical Framework. the 38th Annual Hawaii International Conference on System Sciences (HICSS'05). Hawaii: 240a-240a.

Rowley, J., B. Kupiec-Teahan, et al. (2007). "Customer community and co-creation: a case study." Marketing Intelligence & Planning **25**(2): 136-146.

Salkind, N. J. (2006). "Methods of measuring behavior." Exploring research **Sixth edition**: 123-144.

Salkind, N. J. (2006). "Sampling and generalizability." Exploring research **Sixth edition**: 85-98.

Salomo, S., F. Steinhoff, et al. (2003). "Customer orientation in innovation projects and new product development success-the moderating effect of product innovativeness." International Journal of Technology Management **26**(5): 442-463.

Senger, E., S. Gronover, et al. (2002). Customer Web Interaction: Fundamentals and Decision Tree. the Eighth Americas Conference on Information Systems. Dallas: 1966-1976.

Shah, S. (2006) "Visual Music (Software Programme)." www.shitalshah.com/vmusic **Volume**, DOI:

Thierauf, R. (1999). Knowledge management systems for business. Westport, Conn.; London, Quorum.

Tiwana, A. (2001). The essential guide to knowledge management: e-business and CRM applications. Upper Saddle River, NJ. London, Prentice Hall PTR ; Prentice-Hall International.

Von Hippel, E. (2001). "Learning from Open Source Software." Sloan Management Review **42**(4): 82-86.

von Hippel, E. (2001). "User Toolkits for Innovation." Journal of Product Innovation Management **18**(4): 247-257.

7

Piloting tourist guides in a mobile context

Bente Evjemo, Sigmund Akselsen and Anders Schürmann
Telenor R&I
Norway

1. Introduction

The "self-made tourist" and the "active tourist" are trends within tourism today. He goes globally to see exotic sceneries and looks up small and less known attractions in his own neighbourhood - if they in some way stimulate his curiosity. He is skilled and demanding, and finds satisfaction in the process of composing the travelling route and program of events. Many decisions are made on the way – being the choice of visiting a museum or the time spent on specific items within the museum. The handy mobile phones seem promising as a tool mediating the dynamic updated information needed The mobile context is complex and holds qualities relevant to the ongoing search for factors decisive to form attractive tourist guides and good user experience. This context is here explored through the analyses of how two digital tourist guides were welcomed by real users.

1.1 Digital tourist guides

Travel guides are to a large extent launched as glossy brochures and most tourist attractions appear as fixed products regulated by opening hours and guided tours. This is about to change. Cultural institutions exceed their physical borders to face their audience by making parts of their collections available on the Internet, and most important – they look for new audiences. Alternative media channels and mobile guides are put to use and multimedia shows are available on location. The storytelling power of multimedia technology accompanied by digitalisation trends and diffusion of handy mobile devices, support these changes.

The great number of digital tourist guides tells about a strong belief in the potential of digital guiding. One of the earliest digital guides, the Cyberguide, provided a positioning component that enabled questions of the kind "What am I looking at" to be answered (Abowd et al., 1997). This system developed from being an indoor guide to an extended outdoor guide. Subsequent guides vary according to several dimensions. Some guides store the content locally on the device (Aoki et al., 2002), while others transfer information on demand through wireless networks (Cheverst et al., 2000) or Bluetooth (Luyten & Coninx, 2004). Some are closely tied to one tourist attraction (Aoki et al., 2002; Laurillau & Paternò, 2004; Föckler et al., 2005; O'Hara et al., 2007) while others cover several attractions or points of interest (POIs) within a geographical area where automatic positioning and map based user interfaces are essential components (Cheverst et al., 2000; Schilling et al., 2005). The so called route planners (e.g. Kray et al., 2003) and city visitor recommender systems (Modsching et al., 2007; Takeuchi & Sugimoto, 2009) benefit from automatic positioning as well.

A basic distinction is the use of stationary versus portable devices. The portable approach is regarded promising, but the procedures for lending out portable devices (e.g. PDAs) often turns out to be expensive. Thus the guide that runs on the visitor's own mobile phone becomes an interesting alternative. This approach is supported by the technological development that is about to transform the mobile phone into a multimedia device and also the overwhelming market penetration of mobile phones. Still mobile tourist guides are not widely used. The price structures of mobile Internet usage and/or the network coverage might hamper wide usage, but the explanation might as well be found in shortcomings of the understanding of the mobile phone context.

1.2 The mobile phone context

An attractive mobile guide is a mobile phone application with particular physical and networking capabilities. It is meant to be handled by a great variety of users. Further, the user and the device are parts of a changing and rather complex context that altogether decides the level of adoption and use, the user interaction style, and the overall user satisfaction. This mobile context can be specified as the physical context, the technological context, the mental context, and the social context (Kiljander, 2004; Biljon & Kotzé, 2007).

The physical context refers to the possibilities and constraints of the mobile phone device and the surrounding into which the use takes place. The possibilities refer to the multimodal aspects of the mobile phone and the dynamics that occur when digital content and guidance are received just-in-time, while the constraints refer to the specific and somewhat restricted user interaction mechanism of mobile phones (problems concerning small displays, keys, etc) and actual environmental factors like illumination, background noise, etc. Dim light or bright sun light might make the displays hard to read, and not all phones have the robustness needed for rain or snowy weather.

The technological context refers to the mobile infrastructure and the features and qualities of the mobile device utilising this infrastructure. Of course the network coverage and network bandwidth are salient factors as they put restrictions on service availability and quality. Most interesting are the location aware services that support discovery of POIs and also filter information based on the user's context to increase relevance and improve efficiency.

The mental context includes the user's understanding of how to use the mobile handset. The handset's multitasking or simultaneous interaction with the environment is part of the mental context. Obviously the user's technical skills and interests impact on the mental context.

The social context refers to the inter-human aspects of mobile phone use. Some might consider this approach as less relevant to this setting as tourist guides are made primarily for information retrieval. When recognising the tourist setting as a social setting (Brown & Chalmers, 2003) the importance of the social context is actualised.

1.3 Attractive services and user acceptance

Great effort has been invested to specify the factors that are decisive to service adoption and wide usage. The Technology Acceptance Model (TAM) was constructed to explain adoption of utilitarian office systems (Davis 1989). The model has been extended and revised to better explain the determinants of user behaviour and also to address a wider specter of technology, mobile phone applications included (Kwon & Chidambaram, 2000; Bergvik et al., 2006; Biljon & Kotzé, 2007). Utilitarian factors are of course important but recent studies suggest hedonic factors and social influence to have significant impact (Nysveen et al., 2005; Chtourou et al., 2007). One might ask if these aspects are of special importance to the emerging self-made tourism. Thus the questionnaires used to evaluate the tourist guides of this chapter address the pleasure aspect as well as utilitarian factors.

Another fundamental question is how to gain reliable knowledge on technology acceptance and the effect of various user interfaces. You might simply ask people, or even better, you can offer them hands-on experience and then ask. This was the chosen strategy for the evaluation of the two tourist guides in this study, one addressing attractions within a wide region and one addressing a particular attraction.

2. RegionGuide – the traveller's guide

The RegionGuide informed tourists about attractions, hotels, places to eat etc. within a region. Relevant multimedia information occurred on a map based user interface as POIs which was downloaded over the mobile phone network when needed. The following POI categories (based on a national classification scheme for tourist services) were used: accommodation, dining, attraction, activity, events, and tourist information. The overall design of RegionGuide reflected the results of a major tourist survey that was performed to better understand tourist behaviour, the tourist role, and the tourist's particular interests and tasks.

As maps are frequently used and constitute an important source of information for people on the move, the main user interface was based upon a scaleable map (see figure 1). It was implemented as a Java ME Midlet.

To avoid information overload and too many overlapping icons, *attraction* was selected initially as the preferred and only category, but all categories could be shown simultaneously. When clicking an icon, the map screen was replaced by a short description of the POI limited to 255 characters to reduce download time and scrolling. There were links to contact information enabling phone calling and messaging and also WAP pages with multimedia content.

Fig. 1. Initial map is shown with POIs, including star-like icons that hide several specific icons (left), a simple POI description page (mid), and a WAP site with multimedia information (right).

A key based or a stylus based user interface was automatically selected when device capabilities were detected during installation of the software. In the key based interface the panning operation moved the map half a screen width in the desired direction (see figure 2). In the stylus version panning was achieved by dragging the map in the desired position. Zooming was done by drawing a rectangle around the area of interest. Icons at the top left of the screen (figure 2) provided additional functions and toggled between zoom-mode and pan-mode for the stylus.

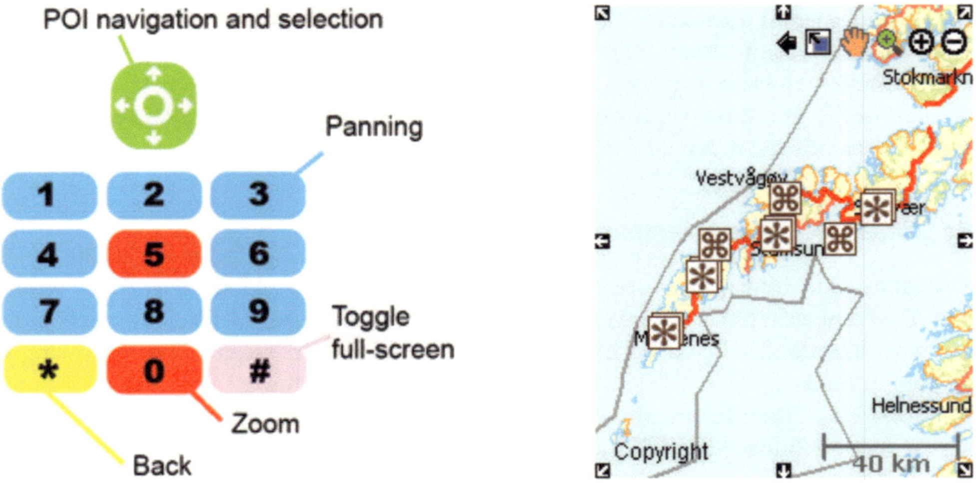

Fig. 2. Key based interface (left) and stylus based interface (right).

2.1 Survey and field trial

The trial was performed in the archipelago of Lofoten in Northern Norway. Tourists waiting for the ferry were invited to a short demonstration of the RegionGuide, including some minutes hands-on and then answered a questionnaire. Those with capable phones were asked to install and use RegionGuide during their stay in the archipelago. A similar recruitment process was performed at the region's main tourist office.

The survey included 107 respondents, most of them middle aged. Less than half of them had phones that handled the necessary Java software, and practical problems occurred during installation of RegionGuide. Thus the field trial included about 30 participants from whom 13 were contacted after the trial period for a semi-structured interview. The duration of usage corresponded to the duration of their stay in the region which was typically 2-3 days.

2.2 Results

Most of the respondents seemed impressed by the detailed map on the small display and the possibilities to navigate and zoom, and finally recognize the link between the map section on the display and their physical location. However, this link was not obvious to everybody as the automatic positioning was not part of the solution and consequently no icon signalling "You are here" was shown. Comments related to automatic positioning was probably actualised by their knowledge of satellite positioning systems in vehicles.

They were surprised to find the phone capable of anything else but calling and messaging: "*This is great! The mobile is always there – and that makes it a handy service!*". Doubtlessly they

found pleasure in using the guide, even though they moderated the suggested entertaining element: *"Well, not actual entertaining or fun, but nice"*.
More than two thirds agreed upon the statement: *"I think this guide will be useful to me"*, and even more respondents claimed that they would install and use the system if their mobile terminal allowed them to do so. Some respondents asked for more POIs and extended POI information, and they were concerned about the comprehensiveness and quality of the information available.
The majority stated that the RegionGuide was easy to use, and this attitude remained positive throughout the field trial. However, the informants reported problems related to accurate navigation and to find back to a recognisable location on the map. Also lack of smooth panning seemed to reduce the overall user experience.
Technical problems reported were mainly related to the configuration procedure and had presumably limited impact on the test users' assessment of ease of use. Configuration problems occurred because the devices had various implementations of Java ME specifications and WAP and Internet settings.

3. MuseumGuide – visit without entering

MuseumGuide was developed to vitalise a museum located next to a monumental cathedral providing vivid teasers and complementary information about the museum attractions. The museum consists of four separate buildings that enclose a square courtyard. The thick stone walls and the rooms and artefacts inside hold parts of the city history and anecdotes about its inhabitants.

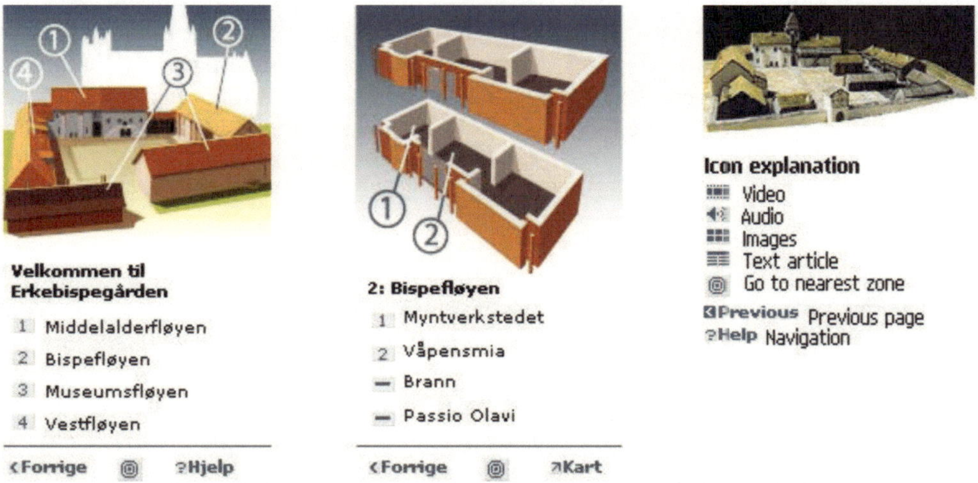

Fig. 3. User interface of the MuseumGuide. The silhouette of the cathedral was meant to support the user's orientation and identification of buildings (left), and the numbers on the building correspond to the entry options (left and mid). Different icons denote the type of media (right).

The design of the MuseumGuide reflected a pedagogical storytelling ambition, which is recommended within tourism and acculturation (Luyten & Coninx, 2004). The content was

held on hierarchical structured WAP pages on three levels. The welcome page directed the user towards historical events related to the buildings or alternatively to particular rooms and items within the buildings. The users were presented to a mix of short texts, images and graphical sketches, as well as video clips and audio tracks, both in Norwegian and English. Some of the audio tracks were supposed to be played close to statues of historical persons - placed outside - to support an intended conception of "talking heads". They varied from 30 to 180 seconds in length, and the video clips from 24 to 150 seconds. Images with calm transitions were used throughout the videos to improve the viewability of the video on small screens, and the WAP pages were relatively short to minimize the need for scrolling.
The MuseumGuide was implemented as a so-called location based service, utilizing advanced antenna technology[1] and WLAN for positioning. The 3G mobile phones[2] in use were equipped with WLANSIM[3] cards. The system utilized WAP Push[4] to load WAP pages related to the user's current location.

3.1 The field trial

The guide was tested by 90 persons during three October days in 2005. The majority was college students, aged 17-18 years, and their attendance was arranged in advance. Additionally the museum staff and people crossing the yard during the day were asked to participate.
The test users were given mobile phones and a short introduction to the MuseumGuide. This briefing included an explanation of main features and navigation capabilities. They used the service for approximately half an hour. In case of technical problems, members of the project staff were present at the courtyard. When returning the handset they were asked to fill in a questionnaire. They received two lottery tickets with an approximate value of 6 € for the participation.
The 3G coverage happened to be weak during the pilot period. Consequently the handsets frequently switched between the 3G and 2G networks. This situation caused software deadlocks and reduced the user experience of video clips considerably. To avoid additional frustration it was decided to reduce complexity by deactivating the location aware functions of the guide.

3.2 Results

The MuseumGuide was welcomed by the test users and most of them supported the following expressions: *"If I get a chance, I will use a guide like this again"* and *"I will recommend others to use this kind of guide"*.
The aspect of usefulness was measured through several items, amongst them a rather provocative one: *"To what degree is MuseumGuide a substitute to entering the museum and visit it traditionally?"* Not surprisingly only a third agreed upon this latter statement (when considering those who had few technical problems the share rose to 50%), but their overall

---

[1] Cordis RadioEye

[2] 6630 and Sony Ericsson K600i

[3] Wireless Local Area Network, Subscriber Identification Module

[4] WAP Push Service Load (SL) was used

curiosity about this ancient palace was strengthened. This effect was not dependent of gender, age, profession or general historical or cultural interests.
However, more than half of the test users reported difficulties in linking the information given by the MuseumGuide to the actual buildings. One test user formulated his frustration like this: *"I'm here to see the court yard, not to watch a display"*. The leads given by the graphical design were obviously not good enough.
In periods of few network problems, the test users found the guide easy to use. The user interface was considered intuitive, and not surprisingly, those who had prior knowledge to the phone found the use of the keys more intuitive than others. The older informants seemed to be distracted by technical problems whereas the younger ones were thrilled by the multimedia approach and the guide's innovativeness.
Most informants preferred audio over video even if some of the audio clips lasted for nearly three minutes. In particular the "talking heads" were appreciated. A young boy exclaimed: *"I don't like reading – I feel good about the story being told to me"*.
Nearly half of the test users would like to see co-visiting or content sharing facilities added to the guide, and among the museum staff these facilities were regarded most important.

4. Discussion

The discussion addresses tourist guide success criteria categorised according to the different qualities of the mobile context. Finally some considerations about piloting new services are given.

4.1 Physical context

A mobile phone is often described by a list of shortcomings. The display is small, the keys are hard to hit and the network bandwidth and battery capacity are among other resources denoted as limited. In other words; a mobile phone is a bad copy of another and more useful device, namely the personal computer. The assessment of ease of use is therefore influenced by expectations relevant to the computer or also other tools. Thus the map as it is displayed on a mobile screen is compared with a map on a computer or a paper based map, and likewise the navigational possibilities.
In both systems the users reported difficulties in navigating the map. They found it rather cumbersome to use keys and joystick (see figure 2) and it did not offer the qualities experienced when looking at an ordinary paper based map. This is in line with findings from other studies (Kjeldskov et al. (2005). Improvements might be gained through minimising navigation by adding automatic positioning and context based adaptation. The map displayed by RegionGuide should for instance be equipped with contour lines whenever the user is hiking off road, larger fonts when moving fast, and brighter display colours in dimmed environments.
Both services utilised the mobile phone's multimedia and visualisation features. When audio and video clips are produced by talented expertise, the results are appreciated by the users. However, the production is resource and time demanding. These conditions prevent large scale production of high quality multimedia content, which is probably a major reason why such guides are still not widely used.

4.2 Technological context

The mobile network infrastructure and the basic network services available constitute the so called technological aspects of the mobile context. In contrast to the fixed network and ditto services the mobile network is associated with scarce resources (e.g. bandwidth and coverage) as well as opportunities or strengths that make particular sense when the users stay elsewhere than their normal location or they are travelling. The positioning facilities and the camera and multimedia handling mechanisms are among these opportunities (c.f. the comments on multimedia content in chapter 4.1).

Multimedia content might as well be key elements in the request for information. The most obvious approach is to include images, taken by the phone's camera, directly into an information retrieval request. The success of such applications depends on the qualities of the image recognition module and also on the matching images available. So far these systems have achieved some success when usage presupposes a limited scope of possible outcomes (Föckler et al., 2005). It is obviously challenging to come up with a general image recognition module that meets the expected demands for precision.

Considering the positioning abilities we find systems that show promising results. Modsching and colleagues (2007) claim for instance that the use of tourist recommender systems implies an increased number of discovered attractions and prolonged stay at the attractions. They emphasize, however, that these impacts would not be achieved unless the system succeeded in choosing relevant information to push. Unfortunately the mobile network available when the MuseumGuide was tested turned out to be unstable. Hence the trial failed to test the solution's possible advantages with respect to push of information based on positioning.

Positioning is one among several possible context sources. According to Grün et al. (2008) a combined usage of many context factors might improve the perceived relevance of the retrieved information. Systems that utilise location combined with time, weekday or season might be appealing to tourists as this group is particular responsive to such parameters. Pushing information about a local guided sea safari tour in frozen winter hours will probably attract few tourists while the same information given in summer season is more likely to hit the target, in particular if also the weather conditions are taken into consideration.

The main concern of context aware systems is the inclination of being intrusive (Ramaprasad & Harmon, 2007). This threat might be counteracted by user consent requirements and user control (Tsang et al., 2004). Still some users want to remain anonymous while at the same time having the context sensitive information available. This contradiction is referred to as a "location paradox" (Bruner & Kumar, 2007). Future success depends on the ability to dynamically identify the user's intentions and balance the system's supportive and intrusive effects.

A more generic problem is the systems' lack of portability which is often linked to the use of proprietary interfaces to other systems, e.g. GPS, and the use of non-public content repositories (Grün, 2005). In addition there is an overall challenge related to production and maintenance of high quality content: it is time and resource demanding and presupposes skills related to the subject of interest as well as to the multimedia and content production for small displays. Recent automatic generation of narrative audio tracks based on public information sources is suggested as one mean to counteract this problem (Schöning et al., 2008).

4.3 Mental context

The mental dimension of mobile phone context deals with the user's understanding and actual use of the handset and service at hand. It is likely that technological skills and general attitudes towards technology impact considerably on the user's mental models and further on how the service is utilised. This is most important when the actual service is seldom used and within non-familiar environments as is the typical tourist guide usage situation. Thus, the requirements regarding ease of use and ease of learning should be strengthened compared to applications used regularly.

The informants using RegionGuide were mainly middle-aged. They found the content interesting but were not familiar with advanced mobile phones and mobile services. This finding indicates a mismatch between the target group and the technological platform used. This is further illustrated by an informant's utterance: *"This is great - this is the future, but perhaps it suits the younger ones even better."*

In the RegionGuide case the installation of Java-based software and configuration of communication settings were problematic and cumbersome. As you never get a second chance to make a first impression, the first try should be a positive experience. Consequently access and eventual installation of software should be flexible and free from hassle (Grün, 2005; Kaasinen, 2005). The maturing field of automatic detection and configuration (ADD/ADC) of mobile device and installation of software over the air (OTA) will probably reduce these problems.

Later on a WAP based version of RegionGuide was developed which reduced the problems related to installing Java programs. There is a risk however, that technical simplifications imply a less appealing service to be launched.

The shifting of attention between the physical surroundings, the content presented by the digital guide, and finally, the social context including other persons, is another problem, also suggested by others (Brown & Chalmers, 2003). Aoki et al. (2002) claim that in particular the visual user interfaces take attention away from the physical object, whilst listening to audio clips seem to balance the attention much better. One might further speculate in the impact of authenticity: an image is dramatically reduced in size compared to the real world, while a voice from an audio device is rather equal to a voice from a person next to you. This might make the audio approach preferable.

Those who tested the MuseumGuide reported that the link between the stone walls located in front of them and the information given by the MuseumGuide was not clearly depicted. Similar problems were raised by Kjeldskov et al. (2005) when the influence of location according to perceived relevance was evaluated. These problems might have been reduced by some kind of linkage between the relative direction of the user and the actual content provided by the guide. Tourist navigational guides utilise automatic positioning to assure the user of his/her immediate position. Services that combine the use of position, direction and images have recently been demonstrated by Google[5] and by Nokia[6].

Some years ago Kray et al. (2003) provided 2D maps to show the user's location and destination, and also a 3D navigational aid. The users found the 3D model amusing and attractive even if it did not add significant value. To gain overview of the situation a flying perspective was preferred to a pedestrian view.

---

[5] HTC G1 Android phone and Google Mobile Maps with StreetViews

[6] Image Space service

Another less hardware demanding approach to the recognition problem is to identify what's in front of the user by image recognition. Such a system should utilise standard features of the mobile phone like the mobile phone's camera and multimedia messaging abilities. Here the main problem is to achieve image recognition of needed precision within reasonable time, - a claim that encourages client based image computation solutions to occur (Föckler et al., 2005). Capturing 2D bar codes by the camera (see for instance O'Hara et al. (2007)) or utilising NFC technologies reduce the impact of imperfect image recognition, but on the other hand, presuppose physical tags to be placed on every item of interest.
Cheverst et al. (2008) combine the photo and 2D map approaches when they suggest a system providing navigational aids upon physical public maps which are found on location. They are supposed to have the wanted detail level and an appealing design.

4.4 Social context

A mobile phone is made for connecting people, but when the phone is used for information retrieval the support for social connections might be reduced. To understand this apparent built-in conflict, let us have a closer look on the tourist role and the tourist setting. Tourists interact and collaborate with fellow travellers, personnel in shops, local residents and other tourists, and the barriers to get new acquaintances seem to be lower than usual (Brown & Chalmers, 2003). The sharing of events seems essential, not least when visiting a museum. From this point of view an attention demanding tourist guide might cause a kind of social isolation (Woodruff et al., 2001). Not surprisingly this aspect was pinpointed by those who used the MuseumGuide. They should like to co-listen and simultaneously follow the same path through the digital content. These challenges have been recognized and partly met in other projects (Aoki et al., 2002; Laurillau & Paternò, 2004). In a study of visitors using the Collect system at London Zoo, O'Hara and his colleagues (2007) give examples of selective sharing of content snippets for particular social effects, such as humour. They also found that visitors created shared experiences by watching content together but on separate phones in approximately synch, and that audio content sharing to a small group was achieved by simply turning the mobile phone speaker volume up. Another issue, raised by the same study, was the interesting tension between cooperative and sharing attitudes on one side and competitive attitudes on the other, as both moods were encouraged by the application.
Dealing with social needs might create other challenges, for instance privacy and discretion concerns which are non-ignorable parts of a mobile social context. The co-located other person, not included in the actual social context, might feel embarrassed and disrupted. Häkkilä (2007) argues that designers of mobile context-aware applications should consider possible effects of social context in relation to the application. In some social context, certain device or user behaviour may be considered awkward or even unacceptable. Social context has also an effect on interruptability. For example, a volume alert may be considered as inappropriate. In a tourist setting the problem of social disturbance is a combined result of individual, situational, and technological factors (Bergvik, 2004), and thus no straight forward solving procedure is given.
The RegionGuide was built to support tour planning - another communication aspect of tourism. The results indicate that the guide supported and even encouraged the social aspects of planning and coordination amongst fellow travellers.

Interacting with other people is found to be a source for tourists to seek information. People tend in general to rely more on informal sources such as family and friends and general "word of mouth" than on official channels. Recently mobile services are developed to seek travel related information through social interaction with other people and to share experiences with each other anytime and anywhere (Carlsson et al., 2008) and a variety of social web services are suggested to enhance the experience of tourists (Coppola et al., 2008).

4.5 Field trials

The need of field trials is an ongoing discussion (Kjeldskov et al., 2004; Nielsen et al., 2006). Our claim is that challenges related to supportive links between physical objects and digital content, demand for co-visiting mechanisms and configuration problems would not have been uncovered without studies in the field. Field studies involving avant-garde technologies are highly desirable but also risky as new technology is more unstable and unpredictable than mature technological platforms. The RegionGuide was adapted to the GSM network only, which has sufficient capacity to transmit text and images. To download videos was time consuming, but did not provoke technical problems. The problems occurred however in the software installation phase, as the devices vary according to implementation of Java ME specifications and WAP and Internet settings. Presumable ongoing efforts related to mobile device management might reduce these problems.

5. Conclusion

There were great differences between the tourist guide services, the devices involved, the measuring instruments, and the degree of hands-on experience that the users actually were offered. Still the piloting enlightened aspects related to user acceptance of mobile services and the multi-faceted mobile context, not easily uncovered in laboratories.

Both the MuseumGuide and the RegionGuide were welcomed by the test users, and the multimedia and storytelling approach seemed appealing to groups beyond the traditional museum visitors. The appearance of multimedia content was considered a surprising and positive add-on to a mobile phone still recognised as a talking and messaging device.

The possibility of establishing an immediate and accurate link between physical objects and digital information is fascinating. However, small screens and bandwidth limitations accentuated the competition of the user's attention. These studies prove that it is challenging to design a service that enriches the experience without introducing a filter that actually reduces the experience in situ. Perhaps the coming generations of multimedia consumers will more easily benefit from the alternating real and virtual impressions and also better cope with installation and configuration procedures needed to use such services.

The social dimension of tourist guides has so far been underestimated. There is an obvious demand for co-visiting mechanisms addressing the interaction between co-visitors, and the rapid developing mobile infrastructure, handsets included, calls for exploration of mechanisms that support interaction between the tourist and people located elsewhere.

The technological dimension of the mobile context is not fully explored and the time and resource demanding content production seem to decelerate the diffusion of high quality and attractive tourist guides. However, as the demand for dynamic content and multimodal links between the real world and digital content is generally growing, the efforts invested will indirectly be increased and eventually fed back to the benefit of the active information seeking tourist.

6. References

Aoki, P M., Grinter, R E., Hurst, A., Szymanski, M H., Thornton, J.D. & Woodruff, A. (2002). Sotto Voce: Exploring the Interplay of Conversation and Mobile Audio Spaces. Proceedings of Human Factors in Computing Systems. Minneapolis 2002, 431-438

Abowd, G D., Atkeson, C G., Hong, J., Long, S., Kooper, R. & Pinkerton, M. (1997). Cyberguide: A mobile context-aware tour guide. *Wireless Networks*, 3, 421-433

Bergvik, S. (2004). *Disturbing cell phone behaviour – a psychological perspective. Implications for mobile technology in tourism.* Telenor R&D, Report 29/2004.

Bergvik, S., Svendsen, G B. & Evjemo, B. (2006). Beyond Utility. Modelling User Acceptance of Mobile Devices. Workshop User Experience, *NordiCHI'06*, Oslo, 14-18th October

Biljon, J. & Kotzé, P. Modelling the Factors that Influence Mobile Phone Adoption. *Proceedings of SAICSIT 2007*, 2-3th October 2007

Brown, B. and Chalmers, M. (2003). Tourism and mobile technology. In proceedings of ECSCW 2003, 335-354

Bruner, G. & Kumar, A. (2007). Attitude toward Location-Based Advertising. *Journal of Interactive Advertising*, 7 (2)

Carlsson, C, Walden, P and Yang, F. (2008). Travel MoCo- A Mobile Community Service for Tourists. *Proceedings of the 2008 7th International Conference on Mobile Business*, 49-58

Cheverst, K., Davies, N., Mitchell, K, Friday A. & Efstratiou, C. (2000). Developing a context-aware electronic tourist guide: Some issues and experiences. *Proceedings of CHI 2000*, 17-24

Cheverst, K, Schöning, J, Krüger, A, Rohs, M. (2008). Photomap: Snap, Grab and Walk away with a "YOU ARE HERE" map. *Proceedings of Mobile CHI 2008*, 73-82

Chtourou, M S., Souiden, N. & Sellami, A. (2007). Factors affecting consumers' adoption of new wireless Internet peripherals. *Proceedings of the Academy of Marketing Studies*, volue 12, no1, 11-16

Coppola, P., Lomuscio, R., Mizzaro, S. and Nazzi E. (2008). m-Dvara 2.0: Mobile & Web 2.0 Services Integration for Cultural Heritage. Presented at SWKM'2008: Workshop on Social Web and Knowledge Management

Davis, F D. (1989). Perceived Usefulness, Perceived Ease of Use, and User Acceptance of Information Technology. *MIS Quarterly*, 13, 319-340

Föckler, P., Zeidler, T., Brombach, B., Bruns, E. Bimber, O. (2005). PhoneGuide: Museum Guidance Supported by On-Device Object Recognition on Mobile Phones. *Proceedings of International Conference of Mobile and Ubiquitous Computing*, 2-10

Grün, C. (2005). Evaluation of the state of the art and development of a light-weight framework for location-based services. Diplomarbeit, Johannes Kepler Universität Linz.

Grün, C., Pröll, B., Werthner, H., Retschitzegger, W. & Schwinger, W. (2008). Assisting tourists on the move – an evaluation of mobile tourist guides. *Proceedings of IEEE International Conference on Mobile Business*, 171-180

Häkkilä, J. (2007). *Usability with context-aware mobile applications. Case studies and design guidelines.* Ph.D. dissertation. Oulo University Press, Oulo, Finland.

Kaasinen, E. (2005). User acceptance of location-aware mobile guides based on seven field studies. *Behaviour & Information Technology*, Vol. 24, 1, (2005) 37 – 49

Kiljander, H. (2004). *Evolution and Usability of mobile Phone Interaction Style*. Ph.D Thesis, Department of Computer Science and Engineering, Helsinki University of Technology

Kjeldskov, J, Skov, M B, Als, B S, Høegh, R T. (2004). Is it worth the hassle? Value of evaluating the usability of context-aware mobile systems in the field. *Proceedings of Mobile HCI '04*, 61-73

Kjeldskov, J., Graham, C., Pedell, S., Vetere, F., Howard, S., Balbo, S. & Davies, J. (2005): Evaluating the Usability of a Mobile Guide: The influence of Location, Participants and Resources. *Journal of Behaviour and Information Technology* 24, 1, 51-65

Kray, C, Laakso, K, Elting, C, Coors, V. (2003). Presenting Route Instructions on Mobile Devices. *Proceedings of IVI 2003*, 117-124

Kwon, H S. & Chidambaram, L. (2000). A test of the Technology Acceptance Model. The case of cellular Telephone Adoption. *Proceedings of HICSS 2000*

Laurillau, Y. & Paternò, F. (2004). Supporting Museum Co-visits Using Mobile Devices. *Mobile CHI'04*, 451-455

Leiner, U. (2008). How to offer excellent user experience to billions of different end users? *Proceedings of HFT 2008*, 113-120

Luyten, K. & Coninx, K. (2004). Imogl: Take Control over a Context-Aware Electronic Mobile Guide for Museums. *Workshop on HCI in Mobile Guides*, 6th International Conference on Human Computer Interaction with Mobile Devices and Services

Modsching, M., Kramer, R., ten Hagen, K. & Gretzel, U. (2007). Effectiveness of Mobile Recommender Systems for Tourist Destination: A User Evaluation. *Proceedings of IEEE International workshop on Intelligent Data Aquision and Advanced Computing Systems: Technology and Applications*, 663-668

Nielsen, C M, Overgaard, M, Pedersen, M B, Stage, J, Stenild, S. (2006). It's worth the Hassle! The added Value of Evaluating the usability of Mobile Systems in the Field. *Proceedings of NordiCHI 2006*, 272-280

Nysveen, H., Pedersen, P E. & Thorbjørnsen, H. (2005). Intentions to use mobile services: Antecedents and cross-service comparisons. *Journal of the Academy of Marketing Science*, 33(3), 330-346

O'Hara, K, Kindberg, T, Glancy, M, Baptista, L, Sukumaran, B, Kahana, G, Rowbotham, J. (2007). Collecting and sharing location-based content on mobile phones in a zoo visitor experience. *Computer Supported Cooperative Work*, 16, 11-44.

Ramaprasad, U. & Harmon, R. (2007). Perceived Effectiveness of Push vs. Pull Mobile Location-Based Advertising. *Journal of Interactive Advertising*, 7 (2)

Schilling, A., Coors, V. & Laakso, K. (2005). Dynamic 3D Maps for Tourism Applications. In Zipf, A. et al. *Design of map-based mobile services*. Springer, Heidelberg

Schöning, J., Hecht, B. & Starosielski, N. (2008). Evaluating Automatically Generated Location-Based Stories for Tourists. *Proceedings of CHI 2008*, 2937-2942.

Takeuchi, Y. & Sugimoto, M. (2009). A user –adaptive city guide system with an unobtrusive navigation interface. *Personal and Ubiquitous Computing*, 13, 119-132

Tsang, M M., Ho, S-C. & Liang, T-P. (2004). Consumer Attitudes towards Mobile advertising: An empirical study. *International Journal of Electronic Commerce*, 8, 2, 65-78

Venkatesh, V., Morris, M G., Davis, G B. & Davis, F D. (2003). User acceptance of information technology: Toward a unified view. *MIS Quarterly*, 27, 425-478

Wang, A I., Sørensen, C-F., Brede, S., Servold, H. & Gimre, S. (2005). Development of a location-aware application. The Nidaros framework. *IFIP TC8, MOBIS*. Leeds, UK.

Woodruff, A., Aoki, P M., Hurst, A. & Szymanski, M H. (2001). Electronic Guidebooks and Visitor Attention. *Proceedings of the 6th International Cultural Heritage Informatics Meeting*, 437-454

8

Supporting new ways of interaction in cultural environments

Ricardo Tesoriero, José A. Gallud, María D. Lozano
and Víctor M. R. Penichet
University of Castilla-La Mancha
Spain

1. Introduction

Cultural environment guides are evolving. Some years ago, these guides were audio devices where visitors had to introduce a code to get information about an art piece. Nowadays these devices are being replaced by PDAs or SmartPhones where multimedia information (audio, video, photos and audio text) is acquired from a server that is part of the cultural environment management system. Thus, through this architecture the information is easily updated on the server providing visitors with latest information about the expositions. Besides, mobile devices provide visitors with new possibilities of interaction through different communication technologies such as Bluetooth, Wi-Fi, IrDA, RFID and so on that can be applied to provide location awareness.

Some of the reasons this type of systems are difficult to develop are: the distributed nature of the system considering the development of both the client and the server applications. As this is an this information based application, the internationalization process may not be trivial because information is not limited to just to text (multimedia information should be localized, too). Location aware information should be attached to art pieces, rooms, showcases and so on in order to gather information from the system. Although localization in outdoor environments is almost solved with GPS technology; there is not a definitive solution for indoor environments, even more, combination of technologies should be taken into account to succeed. Finally, the system integration with legacy software is one of the most important issues to take into account because these systems are mainly intended to exposition designers, so the implementation of the system should only affect them and not the whole personnel.

The starting point of every project is the definition of a conceptual model that should be able to represent the information contained in this type of scenarios. As a consequence, a conceptual model for Cultural environments is exposed, where information is clearly divided into two well defined domains: the environmental and the catalogue information ones.

While catalogue information contains technical information that is not relevant to cultural environment visitors, but very important to museum stuff (i.e. arrival and maintenance dates, owner, and so on); the environmental information provides cultural environment

exposition designers with the ability to adapt this information to visitors. Besides, environmental information provides the system with the ability to indentify objects and use this information to provide visitors with context aware information.
Once the conceptual model is defined, the software system architecture is defined by five components: the Client (visitor device), the Server (information repository), Space Administrator (the ex location designer interface to locate art pieces), the External Database (containing legacy information) and the Synchronizer (that keeps information repository up to date with external database data).
The software architecture supports the location aware system that provides visitors with new ways of interaction according not only to the user position but to the user gestures. This is possible thanks to the multi-technology position support that offers the system. Thus, different ways of interaction according to space granularity and user attention are provided to visitors.

2. Related Work

Studies performed by (Barber, C. et al., 2001) revealed that PDAs are the most suitable device to be used for augmenting museums and art galleries. The study includes prototypes of a guide using HMD (Head Mounted Displays), PDA and Tablet PCs and is focused on efficiency, effectiveness and overall preference. Results showed that the most effective device was the PDA. The first place on efficiency, conducted by an ANOVA, was shared by a PDA and a HMD. And, in the overall selection of devices, the first place was for the PDA.
There are several projects that have tried to use wearable computers in museums. One of the most important references in this subject is the work developed by (Ciavarella, C. & Paternò, F., 2003); (Ciavarella, C. & Paternò, F., 2004) in the Marble Museum of Carrara (Italy). This project is currently running at the museum and it offers a PDA to the visitors with all the information pre-loaded in memory cards. The PDA is able to detect when a visitor is entering in a new room using infrared devices located at the entrance of each room.
Other Museums have already developed projects based on handled devices (Steele B., 2002), as the Field Museum in Chicago[1], Herbert F. Johnson Museum of Art of New York[2] or Kew Gardens outside London[3]. Most of them use handled devices as a useful tool in the inventory process. All these projects are prototypes, and ordinary visitors do not have access to this information by PDA.
Exhibitions are ideal scenarios for applying augmented reality or mixed reality. There are many HCI groups working in this area. In (Ciolfi, L & Bannon, L., 2002) an interactive museum exhibit is designed using mobile devices or the work performed by (Schiele, B. et al., 2001) where a wearable computer is developed as an alternative to the traditional guides.
A system that is currently being exploited, and turns this vision into reality on art museums is exposed in (Gallud J. et al., 2005) at The Cutlery Museum in Albacete, known as MCA in Spain.

---

[1] Field Museum in Chicago, http://www.fmnh.org/
[2] Herbert F. Johnson Museum of Art of New York, http://www.museum.cornell.edu/
[3] Kew Gardens outside London, http://www.rbgkew.org.uk

This work has been evaluated by final users. These user evaluations were performed according to the CIF (Common Industry Format for Usability Reports) standard defined by the ISO/IEC DTR 9126-4 (Tesoriero, R. et al., 2007).
According to the evaluation results we have improved both the system model and architecture (Lozano, M., et al., 2007) and the user interface (Gallud, J., et al., 2007).
The final version of the system including all features we describe in this book chapter were published in (Tesoriero, R. et al., 2008).

3. A Conceptual Model for Cultural Environments

One of the first tasks related to the design of mobile software for museums is the definition of the conceptual model.
We think a museum entity is conceptually composed by, at least, two types of information, the *Catalogue information* and the *Environmental information.*
Catalogue information is related to museum registry and it is stored according to defined structures and procedures that museums should follow to accomplish international standards (Carretero et al., 1996) (ICOM-CIDOC, 1995). Usually, this information is available in electronic format and is described in technical language. On the other hand, *environmental information* represents information surrounding a piece instead of the piece itself.

3.1 Catalogue Information

Although environmental information is provided to visitors in general; technical information may be extremely useful for users that are related or simply require more information about pieces in the museum.
The person in charge of managing the art exhibition uses the *Space Manager* application to define spaces which will host art objects. The concrete art object is managed by means of a legacy software. This software is supposed to be in the museum before introducing the mobile solution based on PDA.
The existence of legacy software introduces the need of a Synchronizer that will maintain the coherence between the external database and the internal one.
The *Catalog component* is responsible of managing the technical information for an art object with the information provided by the legacy database.
The *Contents Provider* provides the Client with the information to be shown and all the information needed to keep user the state.
Figure 1 shows the class diagram modelling the entities we have in our system. As we can see, the key entity is the piece. This model has been defined according to national and international recommendations (Carretero et al., 1996) (ICOM-CIDOC, 1995) allowing us to easily deploy the system in different museums.

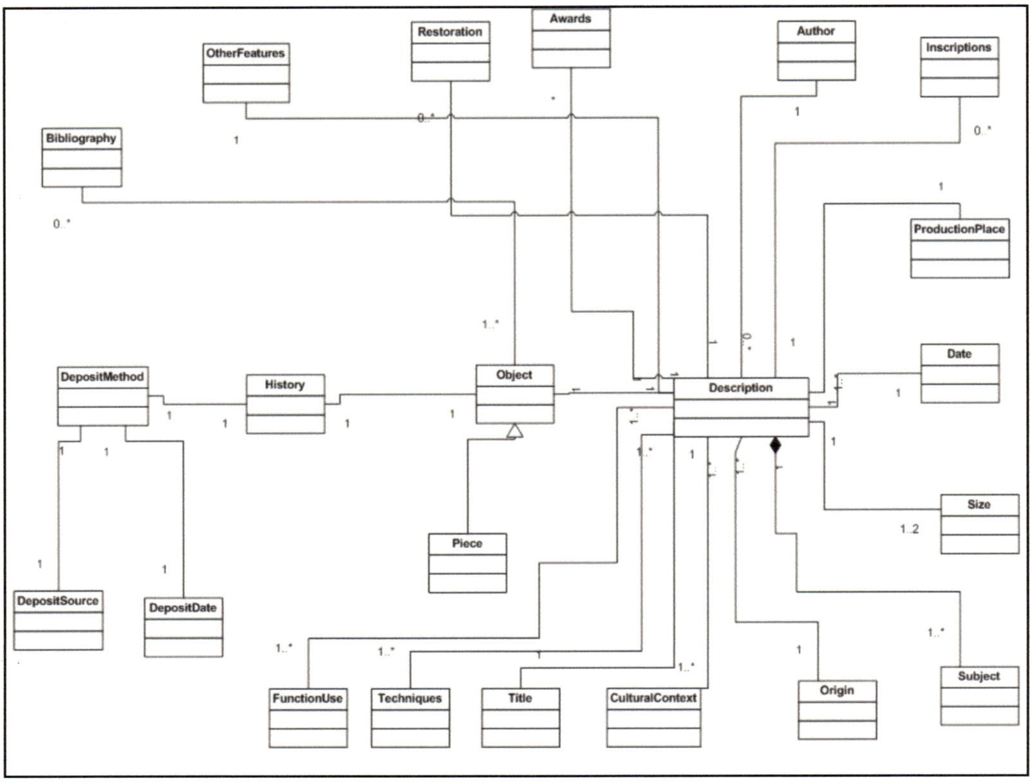

Fig. 1. Catalogue Model

3.2 Environmental Information

An art object or piece being exposed is wrapped by extra information that depends on the exposition environment; for example the physical place of a piece. Thus, a central item of our model is the Space. A piece must be exposed into a Space and this piece has a Space associated to itself.

Pieces are usually exposed within a container, for instance a show. A show may represent a showcase or a frame, in the case of a painting, or anything that is able to contain a piece (or a set of them). A Space has a graphical representation, an associated resource and an identifier.

An overview of the conceptual model is depicted in Figure 2.

An interesting thing to point out is the fact that the *Identifier* entity allows the system to be isolated from the specific technology used to locate the object in the real world (RFID, WI-FI, etc). Besides, an object may be identified by one or more Identifiers. Thus it is possible to use different position and location technologies at the same time to improve the system precision. For instance, you can use RFID to identify a showcase and a barcode to identify a piece into the identified showcase.

Although a museum may have a media repository associated to its catalogue, extra information about pieces should be provided in order to present or adapt the information to visitors.

Media and content exposed to visitors may differ from the museum technical information. This information should be related to museum pieces. Pieces are not the only spaces that may have related information. Often, spaces provide contextual information about the pieces they contain.

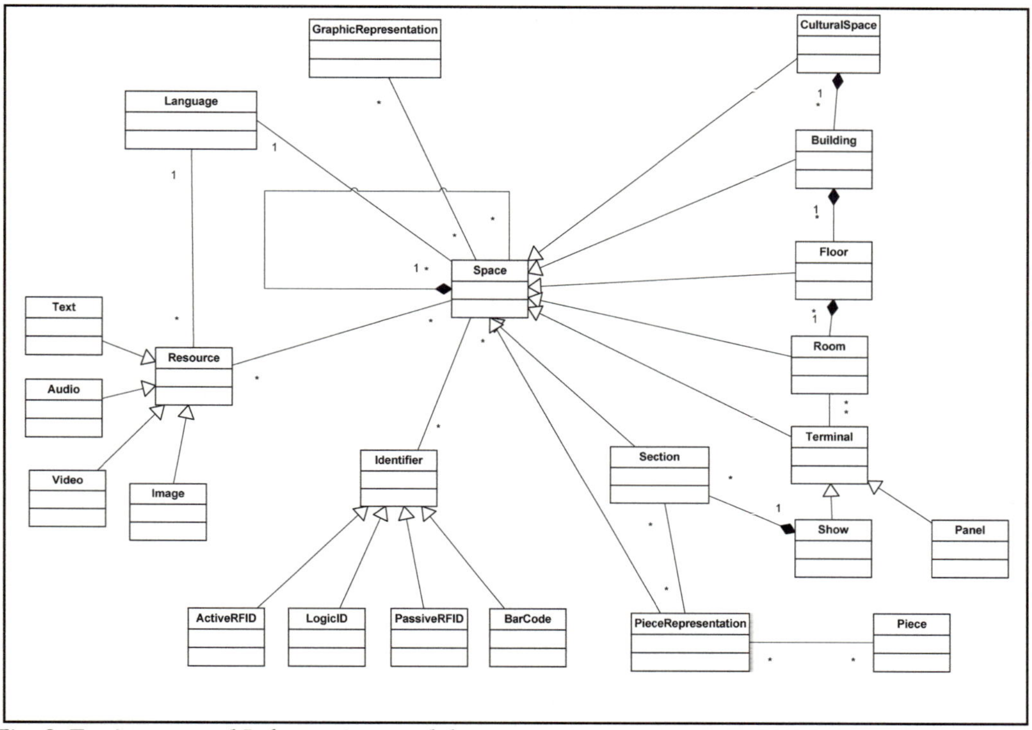

Fig. 2. Environmental Information model

The information described on the previous paragraph is represented by resources. Art objects may be associated to different media resources, for instance; images, audios, videos or texts. Media should be also customized in different languages.

A museum is a cultural environment which may be physically organized in one or more buildings. A building is divided into floors and a floor is divided into rooms. In a room we can find terminals. A terminal represents a device that can be placed into a room. It can be a show or a panel.

Museums usually have information about catalogued pieces. These pieces are exhibited in shows. However, there is some information that is not catalogued; this information is provided to visitors through panels.

Sometimes large shows are divided into regions to organize pieces in groups in order to improve information understanding. Each region is represented by a section that groups pieces that are related in some way. In consequence, pieces may be contextualized according to some defined criteria, providing a context for each group of pieces.

Pieces are physically represented by a physical representation (PieceRepresentation) that relates the physical place of the piece to the piece information itself.

The only linking point between catalogue information and environmental information is established by *PieceRepresentation* and *Piece*. Thus, we decouple the piece physical representation (*PieceRepresentation*) from the piece technical information (*Piece*). *PieceRepresentation* acts as an Adapter (Gamma et al., 1993) between a concrete piece and the place it takes in the real world, providing additional information about the environment. This characteristic provides us with the ability to adapt the model to any kind of pieces.
The *GraphicRepresentation* is the graphical representation of a space. Each space is represented in two ways: Internally and Externally.
The Internal representation is used to show the space itself while the external representation represents the space from the container space point of view.
GraphicRepresentation is a way to decouple the space graphical representation.

4. Software Architecture

In this section we will focus on the definition of the architecture that is based on these elements: positioning, client, server, DB Server and space manager (see Figure 3 on the left). They lead to the definition subsystems and components shown on Figure 3 (on the left) and discussed in the following subsections.

4.1 The Client System

The positioning subsystem is responsible for giving the PDA a specific location according to a reference system. The client is composed by two components: the client GUI and the positioning system.

The Positioning System allows the system to provide users with an unknown experience when they are visiting an art museum. From a technological point of view, we consider the most relevant techniques to solve the automatic positioning system, and up to now, we have not closed the topic with a definitive decision. We have considered using infrared, RFID, WI-FI and mixed approaches.
The variety of positioning systems forced us to define the system separately from the hardware employed. Figure 3 shows how the client is able to interact with the environment in order to know its position in the real building. The client program running on the PDA can receive information from the environment in different ways: infrared sensors, RFID tags, Bluetooth or WI-FI devices or any other system available now or to appear in the future. Then, it sends this information to the server and receives the requested information back from the server.

4.2 The External Database System (External DB)

This database contains legacy information that is loaded through legacy systems (Enterprise Information Systems). This point is really important to take into account when you are deploying the system in existing museums with previous software applications.
Personnel in charge of loading information (mainly catalogue information) are not usually the same in charge of designing the cultural environment exposition; thus, user profiles are not the same.

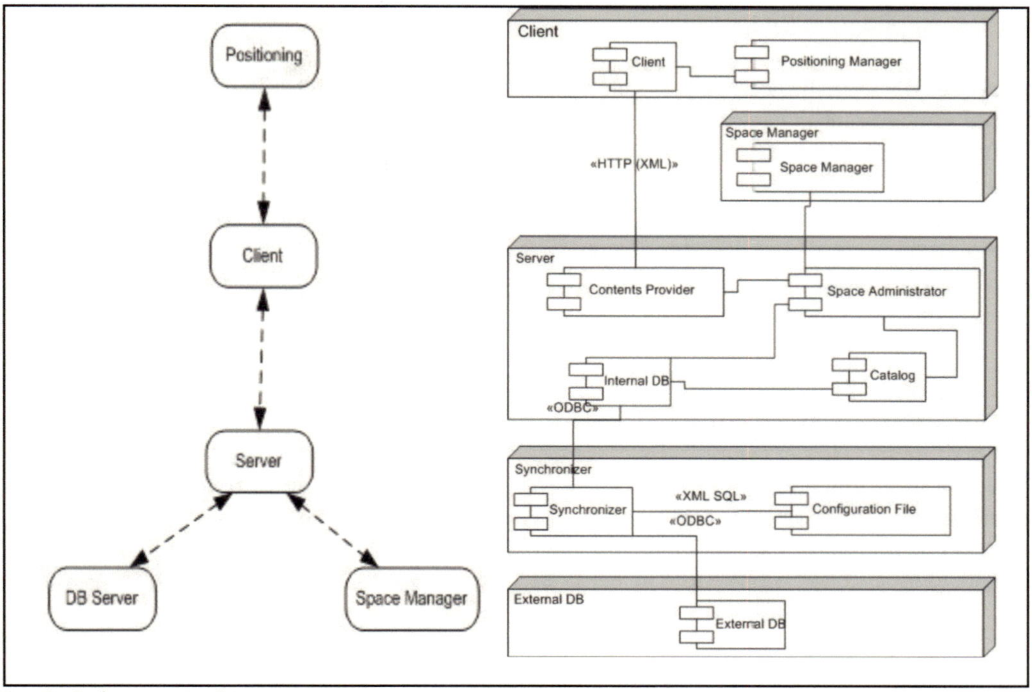

Fig. 3. Software Architecture

As the system is designed for exposition designers and visitors instead of cataloguing personnel, the idea of rebuilding the whole information system, for both designers and catalogue personnel, is not welcomed by cataloguing personnel because they have to learn how to interact with a new system without getting any benefit.
The alternative is the integration of the system into an existing architecture that is the responsibility of the *Synchronizer*, as shown in figure 3.

4.3 The Database Synchronization System (Synchronizer)

The automatic database synchronization subsystem is responsible for maintaining the coherence between both the internal and external databases. The internal database refers to the database that may be previously installed in the museum containing piece catalogue information and eventually a media repository. The external database refers to our specific database to support the positioning subsystem and other requirements.

4.4 The Space Manager

The person in charge of managing the art exhibition uses the *Space Manager* program to define spaces which will host art objects. The concrete art object is managed by means of legacy software. This software is supposed to reuse the information the museum had before the introduction of the new mobile solution based on PDA.
To cope with information reuse, the system integrates with any legacy software introducing the need of a *Synchronizer*. The *Synchronizer* keeps the coherence between the External and Internal databases.

4.5 The Application Server

The *Catalogue* component is responsible for accessing information stored in the internal database. Relationships among art object information that is not related to environment is solved by this component. The *Space* administrator relates the museum catalogue information to the environment information. This information is usually structured and organized by the *SpaceManager*.

The *Contents Provider* provides the client with the information to be showed. This information is client independent because it is represented in XML format and it can be easily read by most devices. All the information translation and communication is managed by this component too.

5. Location aware information

The positioning element is responsible for giving the PDA a specific location according to a coordinate system allowing visitors to experience location aware information gathering.

From the visitors' point of view, this new way of interaction has the following advantages against traditional interaction methods:

1. No specific interaction is explicitly required to access information that can be deduced from the user position;
2. The information provided to users may be filtered according to user interests avoiding information overload (profiling).
3. From the museum exhibitor point of view, this system may provide information about visitor's interests and their personal opinion piece interest.

5.1 Granularity Levels

We have conceptually modelled physical spaces as a hierarchy of virtual spaces in order to consider all approaches and even the mixed ones. A space is composed by spaces; consequently a tree of spaces is created. The root node represents the Cultural Space and the leaves represent Pieces.

As mentioned before, a Cultural Space is composed by Buildings, and each Building is composed by floors, floors contain rooms and rooms may contain Panels, Showcases, Frames, etc. Panels contain information that is not directly related to a piece, a Frame contains a painting and showcases are composed by sections. A section groups a set of pieces that are related among them. This kind of spaces allows expositors to manage big sets of pieces according to the PDA screen size. Finally, *PieceRepresentation* entities are contained in sections. They represent the physical information about concrete pieces from the Catalogue.

Based on this hierarchy, we faced two problems in order to get location aware information from users. The first one is the user position within indoor spaces. The second one is how to provide the user with a way to identify objects that are not identified by his / her position, for instance a piece. The user position may identify a showcase or a frame; however, it is not possible to identify a piece within a showcase using the same data.

Thus, two granularity levels have been defined: coarse grained and fine grained spaces. Coarse grained spaces are spaces that may be implicitly identified by the user position. On the other hand, fine grained spaces need an explicit action performed by the user to be identified.

Coarse grained spaces may be identified using positioning systems. For example, GPS is a good solution for outdoor location; however it is proved that it is not a good one for indoor location. There are lots of alternatives to achieve indoor position of users, Wi-Fi, IrDA, Active RFID, etc. Each alternative has advantages and disadvantages and provide better or worst solutions according to a specific situation.
On the other hand, fine grained spaces may be identified by other mechanisms, such us barcodes, IrDA, passive RFID, graphical marks, and so on. Figure 4 shows this situation.
As the model supports multiple ways of identifying spaces, it is possible to use different position and location technologies at the same time to improve the system precision. For instance, we could use active RFID tags to identify a showcase and barcodes to identify pieces into showcases.

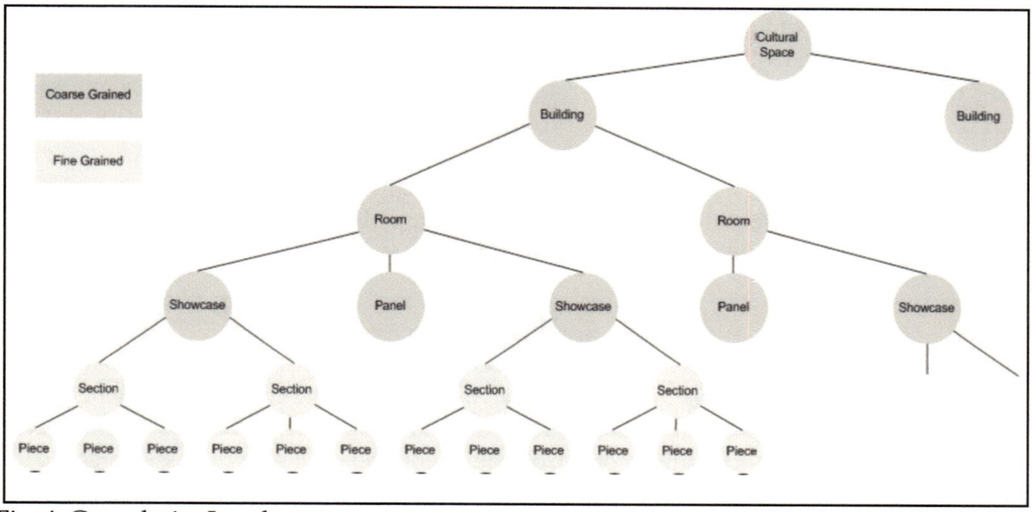

Fig. 4. Granularity Levels

5.2 Attention Levels

The concept of Granularity allows the definition of a system that may be used with different levels of attention. Coarse grained spaces will remain on the user periphery and will not take his/her attention until necessary. Based on Calm Technology (Weisser M. & Brown, J. S., 1997) characteristics, the system is able to warn user, without taking his/her whole attention, using a beep for instance; when he/she is near to a coarse grained space of interest. Thus, users can easily perform other activities as talking while they are visiting the museum. If the user is interested in the information the system is warning about, he/she can focus on it. On the other hand, as users can explicitly perform an action, for instance by a gesture, to retrieve information in fine grained spaces.
It is important to note that although some pieces, as sculptures and paintings, can be treated as coarse grained spaces; usually fine grained spaces are accessed through coarse grained spaces.
As a result of this Analysis, three levels of attention have been defined (low, medium and high) according to the degree of attention is required by the user to interact with the application.

The lower level of attention allows us to perceive the periphery without requiring attention from the user. So the user can perform other activities without being interrupted; but, he or she can be aware of other interesting events when they occur. For instance, if we are visiting a gallery and we are talking while walking across a corridor. We may come across an important masterpiece without noticing and we would miss it. However, if we were notified on time, we would not have missed it. To implement the solution, we used active RFID tags to perform this task. When the PDA is near to an interesting point, the user is notified about it and related information is retrieved.

The medium level requires more attention from the user because he or she has to perform an explicit action to retrieve information about a piece or space. For instance, if we are watching a showcase and we want to get some information about a specific piece, then we can put the device near the piece label and retrieve extra information about it. This technique uses passive RFID tags that are detected by the reader at 5 - 8 cm from the tag.

The higher level requires even more attention than its predecessors, and the user should point to an object or label in order to retrieve information about it. Interaction is not as natural as the other alternatives, but it provides a good method when information is not easily reachable because of the distance. Suppose that we would like to retrieve information about an artefact that hangs from the roof. The user may point to the object and retrieve information. To implement this alternative, IR technology is used and the user has to point the mobile device to the object to get the information.

5.3 The Location-Based Positioning and Suggestion Systems

The positioning system used in this project is a centralized relative position system. It means that each device can get its position relative to an object based on server information.

To determine a device position, an identifier is read by the device and is sent to the server. The server looks for the identifier posted by the client and retrieves the associated space. The required space information is retrieved and sent back to the client. This information contains the space associated to the object identifier among other useful information.

As we have mentioned before, a space may be identified by several identifiers, so many positioning systems can be used simultaneously.

Barcodes, passive RFID, active RFID, IrDA, etc., can generate an identifier, so coarse and fine grained spaces can be referenced by the system in order to get the user location.

The positioning system is closely related to maps, thus, in order to add a space into the system using the Space Manager Tool, internal and external representations should be defined.

The internal representation is defined as an image. This image defines the map of the space; it contains information about image resolution and physical size of the space. This data can be used to define the physical / virtual size relation (centimetres by pixel) to define distances between objects. Distances will be used by the suggestion system to get information about near objects. As the PDA screen resolution is not high, long rooms with lots of terminals on them can be difficult to see. A solution to this problem may be a virtual room; a physical room may be divided into several virtual rooms. The representation of virtual rooms may be represented by images of a lower resolution keeping the physical / virtual size relation.

On the other hand, the external representation is defined by a polygon into the internal representation of the parent space, that is to say the space that contains the space from which we want to define the external representation.
The Space Manager Tool also manages the information related to the space description, associated resources and identifiers, and internationalization issues
The system prototype uses an active RFID reader (shown at the bottom right of Figure 5) to read active RFID tags (shown at top right of Figure 5) for coarse grained space identification. On the other hand, it uses a passive RFID reader (at the bottom left of Figure 5) to read passive RFID tags (at the top left of Figure 5) for fine grained space identification.

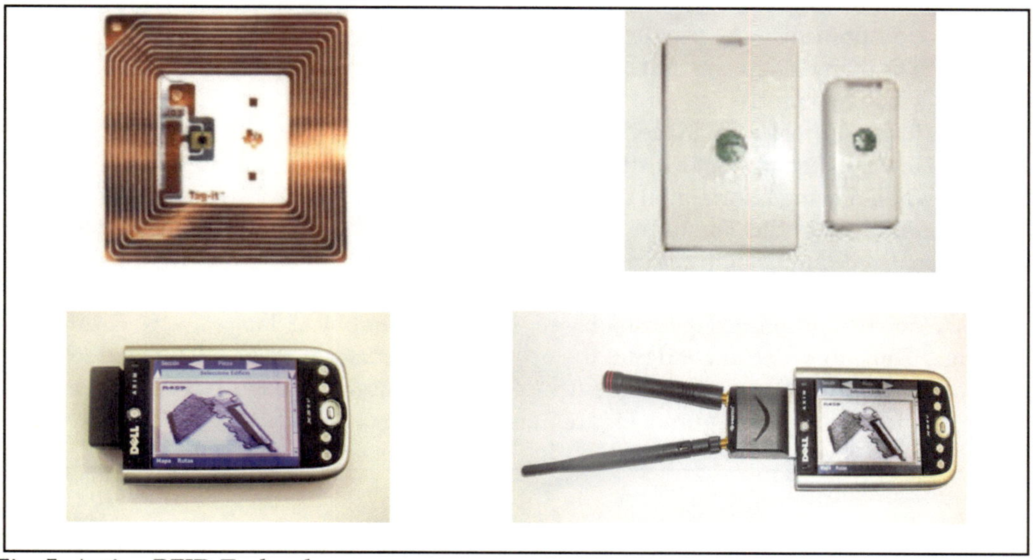

Fig. 5. Active RFID Technology

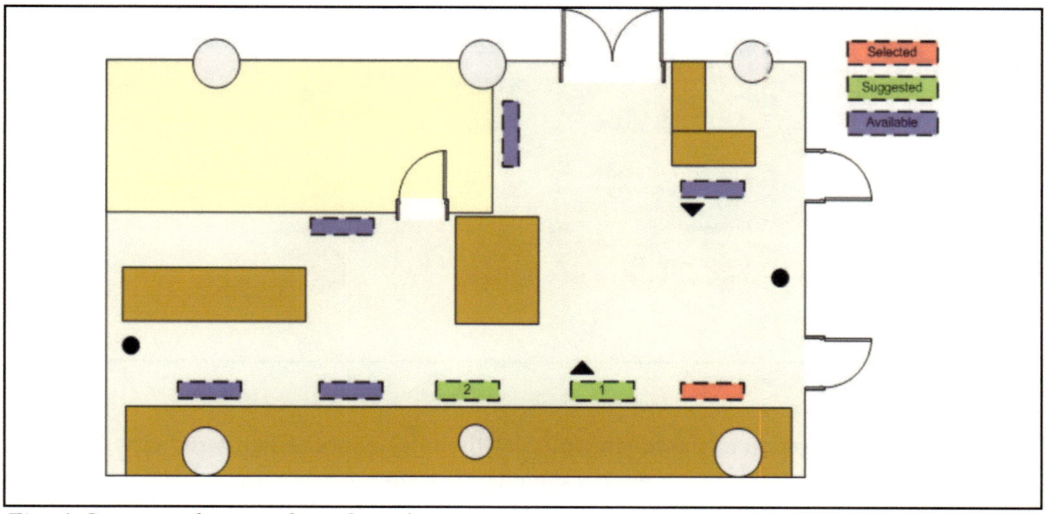

Fig. 6. Suggested routes based on distances

Although both systems can be used simultaneously, they cannot work together because of hardware restrictions (only one compact flash port is available on PDAs commercially available up to now).
Finally, a suggestion system based on the user location is provided by the system (see Figure 6). Thus, the system is able to point out in the map of the client pieces that may be interesting for the user to visit based on the physical / virtual relationship established in the space definition.

6. Internationalization

Cultural environments are usually visited by people from all around the world and supporting as many languages and cultures as possible, is a must.
We mainly face two problems:

1. How to choose a language?
2. How to organize information and resources in different languages and cultures, while reusing information of a legacy catalogue database?

The first problem is the language selection. This is a very common problem regarding internationalized applications. It is a "base case"like problem, how to interact with something that I cannot understand or communicate?
In this case, we propose a gesture based interface. Graphical language is a universal language. Thus, in order to configure the application the user goes to a language selection panel and brings the device near a flag (that defines the user language and culture) and the device is automatically configured. Figure 7 shows the language selection panel.

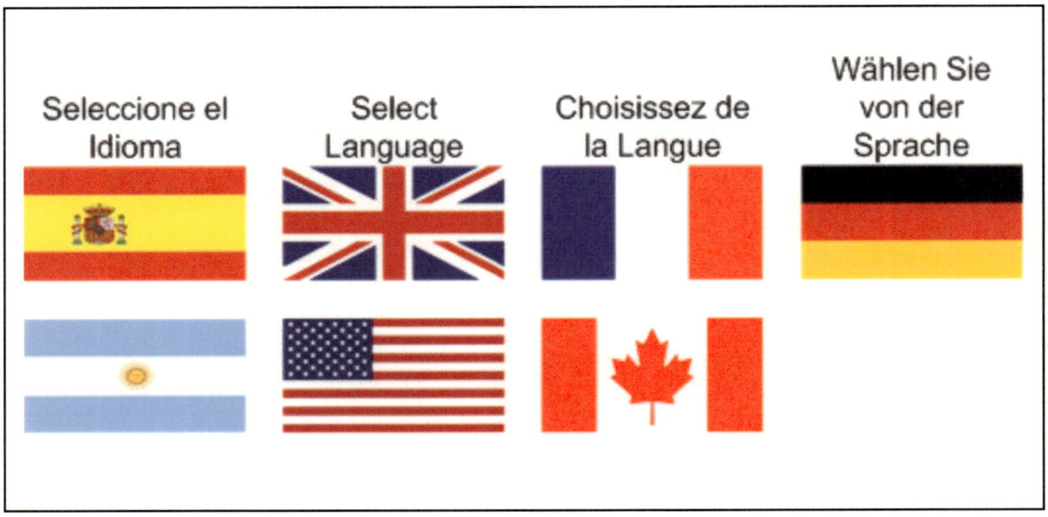

Fig. 7. Language selection panel

The second problem refers to the organization of the information. There are many issues to take into account when organizing related data that is represented in many languages.
Our approach is based on separating textual from media information.

Textual information as a piece description and names are stored in a collection of databases. Each database contains information related to a culture, thus in order to access this information related to a specific language or culture, the right database should be accessed (Figure 8 on the left).
Media information cannot be stored in the same way as textual information due to the following reasons. Media information is usually specific to each particular language (i.e., audio files). However, there are some resources (photos, original audios or some video clips) that are common to all languages.
The replication of resources is not an option because of space and maintenance reasons. Thus, resources are hierarchically organized according to language and culture. For instance, a picture or photo that is common to all languages, and subsequently, to all cultures is placed on the root of the hierarchy. On the other hand, a resource common to all cultures belonging to a language is placed on the first level of the tree, in a language node, being common to all cultures of this specific language. Finally, there are resources that are specific to a culture (for instance, audios); so they are placed on the lower level of the hierarchy (right hand side of Figure 8).

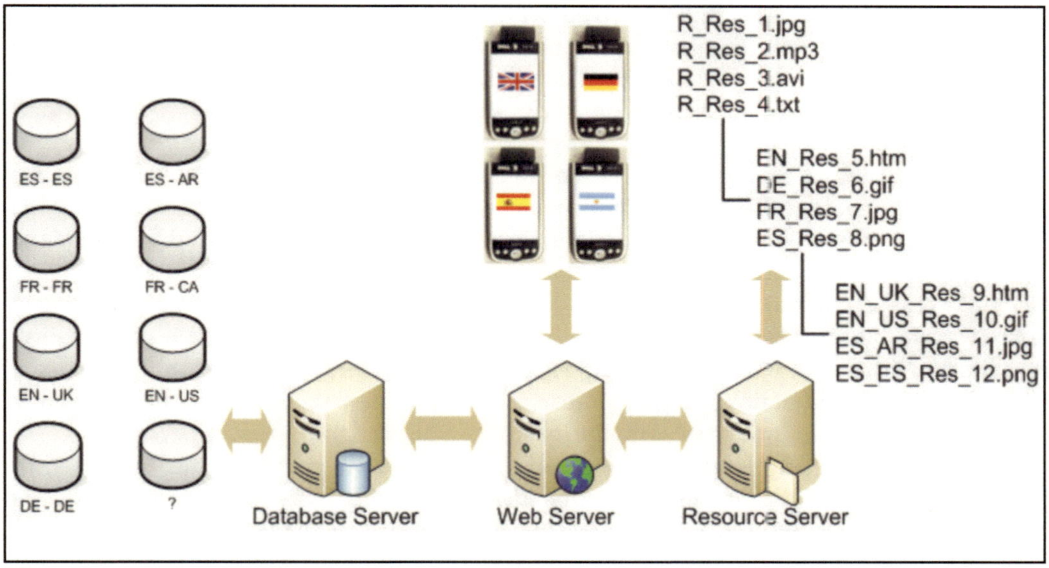

Fig. 8. Internationalization scheme

The implementation is based on resource naming conventions. Prefixes for resource file names are added according to the language and culture. Resources on the root starts with R_, resources for all cultures in a language LANG starts with LANG_ and finally resources for culture CUL in a language LANG starts with LANG_CUL_. For example, a resource for a specific culture, Spanish for Spain is named ES_ES_xx.
A search order is established in order to have default resources for missing files. If a resource for a specific culture (LANG_CUL_) is not found, then a search for resource language is performed on the parent node (on files LANG_xx) and if it is not found then the default resource (on root, R_xx) is retrieved.

7. Conclusions

This chapter presents a novel approach to improve and enrich the users experience when visiting any kind of cultural environments such as museums or art galleries.
The use of audio guides is widely used in these environments to assist visitors along their visit. In this context, we define a system architecture which includes the use of mobile devices to provide visitors with new possibilities of interaction through different communication technologies such as Bluetooth, Wi-Fi, IrDA, RFID and so on that can be applied to implement location systems.
This type of systems are difficult to develop due to its distributed nature considering the client and server applications involved in the development and the communication mechanisms needed for gathering the correct information and offering it accurately to the user.
Besides, as this is an information based application, the internationalization process is not trivial as the information managed is not limited just to text, but multimedia information is also very important. Location aware information need to be attached to art pieces, rooms, showcases and so on in order to gather information from the system. Although localization in outdoor environments is almost solved with GPS technology; there is not a definitive solution for indoor environments, even more, a combination of technologies have be considered. Another important issue to take into account in the development of this kind of interactive systems is the integration with legacy software which stores important information.
The starting point of this approach is the definition of a conceptual model for cultural environments that represents the information contained in this type of scenarios. The information is divided into two well defined domains: the environmental and the catalogue information ones.
Once the conceptual model is defined, the software system architecture is described defining five components: the Client (visitor's device -PDA-), the Server (information repository), Space Administrator (the exposition designer interface to locate art pieces), the External Database (containing legacy information) and the Synchronizer (that keeps the information repository up to date with the external database data).
The software architecture supports the location aware system that provides visitors with new ways of interaction according not only to the user position but to the user gestures. This is possible thanks to the multi-technology position support that offers the system. Thus, different ways of interaction according to space granularity and user attention are provided to visitors, improving considerably their experience along their visit.

8. References

Barber, C., Bristow, H., Cheng, S., Hedley, A., Kuriyama, Y., Lien, M., Pollard, J., Sorrell, P. (2001). Augmenting Museums and Art Galleries. *Human-Computer Interaction - INTERACT '01*, pp. 439-447, Tokyo, Japan, 2001, IOS.

Carretero A., Chinchilla M., Barraca de Ramos, P., Adellac M. D., Pesquera I., Alquézar E. (1996). *Normalización documental de museos: Elementos para una aplicación informática de gestión museográfica*. Ministerio de educación y cultura. Dirección general de Bellas Artes y Bienes Culturales. ISBN: 84-818-148-3. Spain.

Ciavarella, C., Paternò, F. (2003). Design Criteria for Location-aware, Indoor, PDA Applications. *Proceedings Mobile HCI 2003*, Lecture Notes in Computer Science 2795, pp. 131-144, Springer Verlag.

Ciavarella, C., Paternò, F. (2004). The design of a handheld, location-aware guide for indoor environments. *Personal and Ubiquitous Computing*, Vol.8 No. 2, Springer Verlag, pp. 82-91.

Ciolfi, L., Bannon, L. J. (2002). Designing Interactive Museum Exhibits: Enhancing visitor curiosity through augmented artifacts. *Proceedings Eleventh European Conference on Cognitive Ergonomics*.

Gallud, J. A., Penichet, V. M. R., Argandoña, L. González, P., García J.A. 2005. Digital Museums: a multi-technological approach. *Proceedings of HCI-International Conference*. Las Vegas (USA). Lawrence Erlbaum Associates. ISBN 0-8058-5807-5.

Gallud, J. A., Tesoriero, R., Lozano, M. D. y Penichet, V. M. R.: Using mobile devices to improve the interactive experience of visitors in art museums. *Proceedings of 12th International Conference on Human-Computer Interaction (HCII 2007)*. Beijing, China July 22 - 27, 2007. Springer Lectures Notes on Computer Science (ISBN 978-3-540-73106-1). ISSN 0302-9743 (Printed) 1611-3349 (Online). Vol. 4551. Pages: 280-287. Publisher: Springer. Berlín, Germany (2007).

Gamma E. and Helm R. and Johnson R. and Vlissides J. (1993). Design Patterns: Abstraction and Reuse in Object-Oriented Designs. *Proceedings of ECOOP'93*. Springer-Verlag. Berlin.

ICOM-CIDOC (1995). *International Guidelines for Museum Object Information: The CIDOC Information Categories*. International Committee for Documentation of the International Council of Museums. ISBN 92-9012-124-6.

Lozano, M. D.; Tesoriero, R.; Gallud, J. A.; Penichet, V.M.R.: A Mobile Software Developed for Art Museums: Conceptual Model and Architecture. *Proceedings of 3rd International Conference on Web Information Systems and Technologies - WEBIST 2007.* Special Session "Science Art and Internet Technology". Barcelona, Spain. March, 2007. ISBN: 978-972-8865-77-1. Vol. IT, pp 469-474. Editors Joaquim Filipe, José Cordeiro, Bruno Encarnação and Vitor Pedrosa. Publisher INSTICC.

Schiele, B., Jebara, T. and Oliver, N. (2001). Sensory Augmented Computing: Wearing the Museum's Guide. IEEE Micro 21 (3).

Steele B. (2002). Human-Computer Interaction Group tests systems for electronic guides. *Computer Science, Cornell University*. November 2005. ISBN-13: 9780596008031.

Tesoriero, R.; Lozano, M.D.; Gallud, J. A.; Penichet, V. M. R. (2007). Evaluating the Users' Experience of a PDA-Based Software Applied in Art Museums. *Proceedings of 3rd International Conference on Web Information Systems and Technologies - WEBIST 2007.* Barcelona, Spain. March, 2007. Vol. Web Interfaces and Applications. pp 351-358. ISBN: 978-972-8865-78-8. Editors Joaquim Filipe, José Cordeiro, Bruno Encarnação and Vitor Pedrosa. Publisher INSTICC.

Tesoriero, R.; Gallud, J. A.;Lozano, M. D.; Penichet, V. M .R.: A Location-Aware System Using RFID and Mobile Devices for Art Museums. The Fourth International Conference on Autonomic and Autonomous Systems: IARIA-ICAS 2008. IEEE Computer Society Press; ISBN: 0-7695-3093-1. Gosier, Guadeloupe; March 16-21, 2008.

Weiser,M and Brown, J. S. (1997). The coming age of calm technology. Beyond Calculation: The Next Fifty Years of Computing, Copernicus. p.p. 75-85.

9

Establishing the Hallmarks of a Convincing Chatbot-Human Dialogue

Jurek Kirakowski, Patrick O'Donnell and Anthony Yiu
Human Factor Research Group, UCC, Cork Enterprise Centre
Cork, Ireland.

Introduction

Intelligent agents are systems that are capable of performing actions on behalf of computer users; in essence, reducing the cognitive workload on users who are engaging with computer systems. There is a potentially diverse range of applications for such agents in software use. These types of agents have a part to play in domains such as user interfaces, the negotiation of information retrieval and organization, and electronic purchasing. Intelligent agents represent the active use of weak Artificial Intelligence units in computer use in general. The search engine "Encarta", devised by Microsoft, is a good example which demonstrates some of the applications associated with these kinds of agents. The software uses Natural Language Processing (NLP) in order to give the program ability to carry out sophisticated information retrieval tasks. This stems from the capacity of sophisticated NLP programs to parse the typed requests of human users and approach an "understanding" of these requests in terms of keywords which can then be used to search the web for relevant information and parse the resulting text in order to construct a response to a request.

"Encarta" offers an attractive user interface because it can parse, analyse and produce natural language utterances. This allows the program to produce relevant responses to human utterances in natural language form. As such, it represents a particular style of intelligent agent, most commonly known as a Chatbot (or Chatterbot). It is this aspect of NLP agents as Chatbots that is the concern of this paper. In theory, a powerful enough Chatbot could offer a hugely attractive form of Human Computer Interaction in that computer use could be mediated by an agent that behaves as though it can understand instructions that are typed in by human users and respond in kind with natural-seeming utterances. The point has been raised that in order to communicate with computers, humans must learn the language of computers and that computers are, at present, incapable of communicating by using human languages (Pinker: 2004). The prospect of an Chatbot that is powerful enough to deal with human languages would radically change this state of affairs.

There are several ways of approaching the problem of building a software engine that has to deal with human language utterances. Since an agent that is successful in this task is essentially a form of Artificial Intelligence, it seems fitting to begin by describing the traditional approach to AI and how it relates to this problem. Traditional AI approaches rely on a Strong Physical Symbols System approach (SPSS), whereby a series of symbols is given to the engine in question, the symbols are manipulated in some logical manner within the engine and a series of symbols is given as output (Newell and Simon; 1976). For language systems such as Chatbots, this would involve arming the program with certain rules about grammar and word meanings. The system relies on manipulating these rules to derive meaning from incoming information and to then construct responses. If for example, a Chatbot built using the SPSS approach were given an input such as "The dog was big", it would decompose the sentence into its component parts; 'The' (determiner) 'dog' (noun) 'was' (verb) 'big' (adjective) and then ascribe a meaning to each component of the sentence, perhaps from a database of related concepts ('big' being an adjective related to size). The advantage of this approach to language processing is that, once a sentence such as 'The dog was big' can be analysed, any sentence employing a similar structure ('A girl will arrive') can be similarly interpreted, since the same grammar rules are involved in examining this sentence structure.

There are however several problems attendant on these approaches, both in general and in the specific case of language processing. A general criticism of SPSS approaches is that of symbol grounding (Harnad; 1990). The problem is essentially that of how a system that depends on the manipulation of virtual symbols can ever ascribe any kind of meaning to those symbols, except in terms of other arbitrary symbols thus defined themselves. So, even though a Chatbot system is able to deduce that 'big' is an adjective related to 'size', it will have no essential understanding of the concept 'big' since it has no essential understanding of a concept like 'size'. There is no way in which a system can arrive at an understanding of concepts by simply relating them to other concepts.

Another problem that is of particular interest with regards SPSS-style Chatbots in as far as they approach language processing is the problem of emergent problem spaces, effectively, the tendency of such systems to generate all possible meanings and interpretations of a sentence that are allowed by the grammar of a language, without being able to settle on one appropriate interpretation. This problem is endemic of all SPSS systems, but is especially relevant to language processing as it is a task that must occur in real time, and any attempt by a language engine to test each individual solution before choosing the correct one will be time consuming. Indeed, even if the time taken to process all possible variations in the meaning of a sentence were not an issue, it is likely that SPSS style Chatbots would never be able to settle on a suitable meaning for a sentence since, as discussed, they have no essential understanding of the various concepts that might be represented in the sentence and thus cannot relate those concepts to non-verbal, contextual cues. The classic example of this type of problem in language processing comes from early attempts to build sentence parsers along this line. The engine, when tested, generated five possible meanings for the sentence "Time flies like an arrow." (Bobrow: 1963). These alternate interpretations of the sentence involved the system ascribing different meanings to concepts like 'time' and 'arrow'. Thus, while the most obvious way of interpreting this sentence for most people would be that 'time moves quickly, like an arrow', the Chatbot engine also generated interpretations such as 'a species of fly, known as the "time fly" enjoys arrows'.

The second prominent approach in contemporary Artificial Intelligence is the connectionist approach (also referred to as parallel distributed processing or the neural net approach). This approach operates in a fundamentally different way to SPSS style processing. Connectionist approaches eschew strong, inviolable rules in favour of a network of concepts that are related to one another to greater or lesser extents. The degree of relatedness between two concepts is flexible. There are at least three unique features that make a connectionist network a powerful system for handling human conversation: namely superpositioning, intrinsic context sensitivity, and strong representational change. (Clark 1993)

Firstly, two representations are said to be fully superposed when the resources used to represent item 1 are co-extensive with those used to represent item 2. The natural mechanism of connectionist learning and superpositioning-storage yield a system that will extract the statistical central tendency of an exemplar. This is usefully seen as embodying prototype-style knowledge representation.. The network extracts various feature complexes and thus comes to encode information not just about specific exemplars but also about the stereotypical features set displayed in the training data. In other words, a number of concepts are related to one another in the connectionist system in order to yield the prototypical example of a class or category. For a concept like 'dog', sub-concepts like 'four-legged', 'hairy' and 'animal' would be related to each other to produce an archetypal example of 'dog' The network can generalise novel cases sensibly by dint of its past training.

Secondly, the connectionist network concept can also display intrinsic context sensitivity. The most radical description of this would be that connectionist system does not involve computations defined over symbols. Instead, any accurate picture of the system's processing will have to be given at the numerical level of unites, weights and activation-evolution equations, while the symbolic-manipulating computational description will at most provide a rough guide to the main trends in the global behaviour of the system (Clark, 1993). The network can then learn to treat several inputs, which result in subtly different representational states, as prompting outputs which have much in common. So, many inputs may have features in common with a prototypical representation of a concept, but also have distinct differences (a three-legged dog, for example). In these cases, the network is capable of adjusting to the fact that slight differences in input do not necessitate a radically new concept (a whole new category for 'dog' that deals only with three-legged dogs, say).

Thirdly, a connectionist network can show strong representational change. Fodor (1981) suggested concept learning can only consist in the triggering of innate representational atoms or the deployment of such atoms in a "generate and test" learning style. According to Clark (1993) this is weak representational change as the product necessarily falls within the expressive scope of the original representational base. The connectionist network on the other hand, can acquire knowledge without the benefit of any such resource. For example the NETtalk (Sejnowski and Rosenberg 1986) and the past-tense learning network (Rumelhart and McClelland 1986) both begin with a set of random connection weights and learn about a domain "from scratch". Such adaptiveness is a vital feature of any system that must engage in processing language, since language is, by its nature, a fluid and changing system of rules and related meanings.

Thus, Connectionism has much to recommend it; its sensitivity to contextual change makes Chatbot-systems based on connectionist models extremely adept at picking up on fine shades of meaning. A connectionist-style Chatbot would be much less likely to be caught between five alternative meanings of a sentence like 'time flies like an arrow' than would an SPSS-style system.

Connectionist models however have a similar symbol-grounding problem as the SPSS approach does. Connectionist models explain symbols by a series of context-sensitive connections. The process itself does not 'bottom-out' or come to a definition that is not prone to context infection. In other words, even if a connectionist system is capable of dealing in finer shades of meaning than an SPSS-style system, there is no point at which the small, atomic concepts that go into building up bigger concepts are related to the world at large in any essential way. In additional, there is a problem involving systematicity (Hadley, 1994) in that a connectionist network can fail to process sentences with constituents in novel syntactic position and at a novel level of embedding when processing includes determining the word's semantic role.

The symbol grounding problem is the problem of representing meaning in a system of purely arbitrary symbols. One approach to robotics and AI in general that may be able to address this problem involves dodging the question of representation altogether. Wallis (2004) discusses the possibility of producing systems that can exhibit all the characteristics of an intelligent agent (intention, planning etc.) without using any more representation "than a microwave oven would." Wallis' stance is informed by Brooks' (1991) approach to robotics, wherein robots can be developed that behave in an autonomous, intelligent fashion without any bona fide "understanding" of their own behaviours or why they are performing them. The essential tenet that underlies this approach is that an agent's intelligent behaviour arises out of an interaction between the agent and its environment, in the service of achieving some goal. Reflective reasoning about the environment, the goal or the behaviour by the agent is not necessary for the behaviour to be described as intelligent. The agents that exhibit this type of architecture can perform behaviours that can be described as intelligent without possessing any capacities that we would describe as "intelligence" because their actions make sense within their environment with regards to the satisfaction of some goal. Thus, if it is possible to produce a chatbot that has no representation of meaning but can behave as though it did (i.e. seem to understand utterances and interact with users), then users would be forced to conclude that its conduct within a dialogue was "intelligent". The earliest types of chatbot programs, that scan for keywords and match responses, can be seen as non-representational chatbot agents. The archetypal example of this type of Chatbot is 'Eliza', a system that consists of a database of phrases to be matched to keywords. The Chatbot itself does not contain anything that we might label as an 'understanding' of the concepts that it is discussing or the process by which it operates, but users can be gulled into believing (if only for a short period of time) that the Chatbot with whom they are communicating is in fact a person. Essentially, if the ability of non-representational Chatbots like these ones can be extended, to have users fully or partially convinced that they are conversing with another human being, then to all intents and purposes we can say that we have an 'intelligent language-processing system'. It is intended to specifically examine the way in which one of these non-representational Chatbot agents will interact with users, and how it might be possible to improve on its ability to be regarded as an agent that produces intelligent language behaviour. What is interesting is whether a non-representational approach such as this can be brought to bear in an arena such as language, a system of representational symbols.

It is not appropriate in this paper to attempt to select between these three approaches to the architecture of a natural language machine. No doubt in the end the "best" approach will be a hybrid of some kind and there are problems of principle as well as of implementation. We note that in the past research has taken a particular technology as a given and focussed on the application. We propose to turn the problem round.

That is, it is intended to do a much more "requirements" orientated survey, to identify what aspects of language comprehension and production by software agents characterise them as being "inhuman" in the eyes of computer users and which aspects are characteristic of human language behaviour. It may later be appropriate to discuss which types of programs and architectures are best equipped to support the type of behaviours seen as quintessentially "human". In other words, the research question addressed in this paper is: when users interact with an agent that is equipped to process human language and respond with utterances of its own, what kind of mistakes can the program make that a human wouldn't and that make the dialogue between user and agent seem unnatural. At that point, it will perhaps be more appropriate to return to questions of which approach to Artificial Intelligence is best equipped to deal with the various problems involved in language processing.

Method

In the experiment fourteen participants were asked to interact with an Eliza-style computer program (chatbot) for three minutes and then to participate in the elicitation of critical incidents with a transcript of their session. The program was based on the classic Eliza design with two important differences. Firstly, there was no mechanism that retained previous phrases entered by the user which could be used to re-start a stalled conversation (eg: "Tell more more about [a previous utterance]".) This was for theoretical reasons as will be discussed later. Secondly, there was a mechanism which enabled the chatbot to switch contexts on detecting particular words. Thus if the chatbot detected the word "music" the whole list of trigger phrases and responses changed to a music-orientated set.

A qualitative approach incorporating the Critical Incidents Technique (CIT) and content analysis of responses is involved in this study. At the end of this interaction, the participants were presented with a printed transcript of the dialogue and asked to highlight instances of the conversation that seemed particularly unnatural (up to three examples) and then to report why this was so. The same was done for up to three examples of speech that did seem convincing. The data produced by the critical incident technique were content analysed, with user responses being sorted by theme. The data coding was cross-checked independently by another individual. Inter-rater reliability of approx. 0.53 was obtained in the first pass. Items on which there was disagreement were discussed and placed in mutually agreeable categories with the assistance of a third independent rater. We are reasonably sure that the categories that have emerged represent reproducible aspects of the data set.

Results

The various themes that were produced during the content analysis were as follows. Firstly, under the heading of unconvincing characteristics-

- Fails to maintain a theme once initiated. In that, once a theme emerged in the dialogue, the chatbot failed to produce statements relevant to that theme in the following section of the dialogue.
- Formal or unusual treatment of language. Some statements in the chatbots database seemed overly stiff and formal or used unusual words and language.
- Failure to respond to a specific question. Users would ask for a specific piece of information, such as asking the chatbot what its favourite film might be, and receiving no answer.
- Fails to respond to a general question or implicit cue. Users offer the chatbot a cue (in the form of a general question, like "How are you?", or offer a cue in the form of a statement, like "Tell me about yourself." Or "Let's talk about films then.") and receive an irrelevant response.
- Time delay. A fairly cosmetic fault, users felt that the chatbot responded too quickly to a detailed question or too slowly to a courtesy.
- Phrases delivered at inappropriate times, with no reference to preceding dialogue. Where generic type phrases did not fit into the conversation in a natural way, or the chatbot responds to an inappropriate key phrase, with a resulting nonsequitur.

Under the heading of convincing aspects of the conversation-

- Greetings. Several participants identified the greeting as a human-seeming characteristic.
- Maintains a theme. When the chatbot introduced a theme and was successful at producing a few statements that were relevant to that theme, users found this convincing.
- Damage control. When the chatbot produced a breakdown in communication (for any of the reasons mentioned earlier) and then produced a statement that seemed to apologise for the breakdown or seemed to redirect the conversation in a more fruitful direction, users found this a convincingly human trait.
- Reacts appropriately to cue. Users found it convincing when the chatbot responded appropriately to a cue such as "How are you?" or "Tell me about yourself."
- Offers a cue. Users found it convincing when the chatbot offered a cue for further discussion, such as "What do you want to talk about?" or offered a range of topics for discussion.
- Language style. Users found conversational or colloquial English to be convincing.
- Personality. The fact that the chatbot was given a name (in fact, even users who did not report the inclusion of a name as convincing referred to it as a "Sam" or a "he") suggests that users wish to assign a personal agency to the chatbot even in the teeth of discrepant knowledge.

Discussion

This research focuses on requirement and not any kind of implementation. For now it is enough to identify what traits in the bot-human interaction make it different to human-human interaction and how best these shortcomings might be addressed. Indeed, a reassuring symmetry emerges in the themes identified by users as being convincing or not: maintaining a theme is convincing, while failure to do so is unconvincing, formal or unusual language is unconvincing while colloquial or conversational English is the opposite. Reacting appropriately to a cue is human while failing to a react to one isn't. Delivering an unexpected phrase at an inappropriate time does not impress, but damage control statements can rectify the situation. It is time to address each feature of the bot-human dialogue in a little more detail.

Maintenance of themes

One of the factors, upon which the success or failure of the program to appear human seems to depend, is its ability (or lack thereof) to maintain a conversational theme once introduced. The Eliza-style chatbot used in this trial has no memory of a conversation as such (it operates on a first order Markov process, whereby each token is generated in response to the token immediately preceding, with no reference to the accumulated tokens, in this case token = utterance and accumulated tokens = the whole dialogue). This does not preclude it from maintaining a theme however; indeed several participants reported its ability to do so as a convincing feature of its dialogue. The means by which this is accomplished (given that the program has no "memory" of the conversation) is now described.

The chatbot used was unlike the classic Eliza program in that as well as having specific phrases activated by the presence of a keyword, the program could activate a whole database of phrases in response to a key phrase that are specifically related to that phrase (for example, an inventory of keyword-response pairs that are related to music can be prompted by the word "music").

Thus, the program has access to a database of phrases that are most likely to be relevant to the theme raised. At present, failure to maintain a theme that has activated one of these databases may be due to the fact that these databases contain all the same generic response phrases and keyword-response pairs as the general text database that serves as the default set of responses. This makes the likelihood that a theme-relevant phrase is activated lower than if the specialised databases were to contain theme-relevant phrases only. Thus, a means of improving the ability of this program to maintain a theme in conversation might be to enlarge the number of theme relevant keyword-response pairs in these databases and remove most of the generic keyword-response pairs from these "themed" databases.

Failure to respond to a specific question

This problem, essentially, is a question of how much information is contained in the program's memory and whether or not it can be accessed. Thus, if a person were to ask the program "What is the capital of France?" and the program did not have the information required, the program seems less human. There is no easy way to solve this problem. The solutions are to give the program a large enough database of information to be able to cope with most information requests of this kind (this approach suffers from the fact that the database is still a finite resource and almost certainly contains less information than a human would be expected to) or to grant the program access to the internet and equip it with a more powerful means of parsing information requests so that it can then establish the exact nature of a request and search for the relevant data on the internet. This first solution is brute force and is probably most relevant to a personal-use "humanised" AI, with a role as a user-interface for small-scale personal computer use, while the second is the type of approach that might be associated with a general information retrieval agent such as Microsoft's "Encarta".

Responding to social cues

This category covers the failure or success of the program to react appropriately to a social cue such as "How are you?" or "Tell me about yourself." Some of these cues can be treated in a similar way to the information requests dealt with above, in that an appropriate response can be matched, from a database, to a specific cue.

Formal and colloquial language

In general, formal language was regarded as being an unconvincing trait of the program's, with casual or colloquial language being preferred. Replacing formal phrasings with casual equivalents is a relatively minor adjustment that can be made to improve the program's performance. It is worth bearing in mind however that this trial involved a chatbot that was geared towards free conversation as opposed to being a helper agent in a structured task. In other circumstances, language style might not be a consideration for users at all, or perhaps even more formal and precise language might be preferred (eg in making a financial transaction.)

Greetings and personality

Some users reported that certain surface details involved in the chatbot's dialogue made it seem more human by their very presence. The fact that the bot "introduced itself" at the beginning of the dialogue and was given a human name for the trial influenced people into regarding it as slightly more human. This is separate from the functional issues involved in recognizing conversational breakdown and issuing damage repair, and is probably more related to personal preferences.

Offers a cue

The chatbot was deemed to be very "humanlike" when it offered cues on which users could elaborate. The possibility has already been raised of including more cues which are designed to elicit clarification in situations where the chatbot does not have enough information to respond appropriately to a cue. This promotes information exchange between the user and the chatbot and is likely to reduce ambiguity and allow the chatbot to react more reliably to user-statements.

Phrases delivered at inappropriate times

This is an enduring problem of the Eliza style keyword-response chatbot, generic phrases are produced which do not fit well into the conversation, or a keyword prompts a response that is inappropriate in the context it is used. The first problem can be caused when the generic "placeholder" phrase is a poor one. In the case of the second problem, the chatbot might produce an inappropriate phrase due to the fact that it is insensitive to context. A word which means one thing in a certain context, and which prompts an appropriate response, might mean something completely different in a different context and the same response, when prompted, will no longer be appropriate. Some suggestions for remedying this problem are to equip the program with statements that ask for clarification and to refine the types of keywords that prompt particular responses. In addition, a chatbot that relies on a connectionist architecture may well be more sensitive to context than the model described here and may thus be able to select appropriate responses with a high degree of accuracy.

Damage Control

In certain situations, the chatbot seemed to be offering to change the topic of conversation after a particular line of conversation broke down, or to try and clarify previous statements. This is a further example of the kind of information-exchange that can occur between users and agents. Not only does this ability seem to make the chatbot appear more human, it would be a valuable ability to develop in any of the major potential applications of chatbots as helpful agents. This type of capability would allow for a more refined search when using information-retrieval agents. In personal computer user-interfaces, this kind of information-exchange opens up the possibility for the agent to make suggestions as regards computer-use.

Comments on method of analysis

With regards to the method of analysis employed in this study, it is intended to discuss the level to which the Critical Incident Technique was an appropriate tool of assessment in this trial. The benefits of the Critical Incident Technique as regards this study were as follows:

- Rare events were noted as well as common events, thus the situation in which bot-human interaction could break down and then be retrieved by the bot in a damage control exercise did not occur in all or most of the dialogues but it was identified alongside more common shortcomings of the bot nonetheless.
- Users were asked to focus on specific instances of communication breakdown (as opposed to being allowed to offer the vague opinion that the dialogue "felt wrong") and this allows for a more precise focus on individual problem areas (such as being able to treat "failure to answer a specific question" as a separate problem to "failure to respond to a general question or cue").

However, some shortcomings of the Critical Incident Technique as used in this trial were as follows:

- There is no indication as to the relative severity of failures by the bot to appear human. In other words, it is difficult to tell if users found the agent's inability to maintain a conversational theme a more serious problem than the delivery of unexpected and inappropriate phrases during the dialogue, or even if there is a degree of individual difference involved in which characteristics of the bot's conversation-style are pertinent to its seeming human.

- This method of analysis requires a focus on specific incidents of success or failure and is not particularly sensitive to context. This trial involved a simulated conversation, in which context would be important in establishing whether or not the dialogue seemed natural and though participants are asked to describe the events that lead up to a critical incident as part of their report, some information regarding the context of the conversation as a whole is probably missed.

References

Bobrow, D: Syntactic Analysis of English by Computer - A Survey, tech report 1055, BBN 1963

Brooks, R.A.: Intelligence without representation, Artificial Intelligence 47 (1991), 139–159.

Clark, A.: Associative Engine: Connectionism, Concepts, and Representational change. Bradford Book; London, England (1993)

Fodor, J: Representations: Philosophical Essays on the Foundations of Cognitive Science. MIT Press. (1981)

Hadley, R. F: Systematicity in connectionist language learning. Mind and Language, Vol. 9 P.247-272. (1994)

Harnad, S: The Symbol Grounding Problem. Physica D 42: 335-346. (1990)

Newell, A., and H. A. Simon: Computer science as empirical inquiry: Symbols and search. Commun. Assoc. Comput. Machinery 19: (1976) 111-26.

Pinker, S: The Language Instinct. Penguin. London (1994) p193

Rumelhart, D. and McClelland, J:'On learning the past tense of English verbs' in Parallel Distributed Processing: Exploration in the Microstructure of Cognition, Vol. 2, ed. Rumehart et al. MIT Press (1986)

Sejnowski, T., and Rosenberg, C: NETtalk: A Parallel Network That Learns to Read Aloud. Technical report JHU/ECC-86/01, John Hopkins University. (1986)

Wallis P., Intention without representation, Philosophical Psychologyy, vol. 17, no. 2 (2004)

10

Immersive Interaction

Gerold Wesche, Maxim Foursa and Manfred Bogen
Fraunhofer Institute Intelligent Analysis and Information Systems (IAIS)
Germany

1. Introduction

Virtual reality (VR) is a technology that allows users to interact with computer-simulated environments. Virtual reality applications are normally displayed either on a computer screen or in a stereoscopic display system. The latter is also referred to as an immersive display system. In this chapter we discuss immersive interactive real-time VR systems, related devices, interaction techniques, and applications in the context of numerous industrial and research projects of the Virtual Environments department of the Fraunhofer Institute of Intelligent Analysis and Information Systems (IAIS)[1].

Applications running in immersive virtual reality display systems are nowadays widely used in industry and in research laboratories. Design, engineering, and simulation are the most prominent application areas. However, the maturity of the corresponding 3D user interfaces (UI) is far from being able to cope with the functional abilities desired by users. This leads to restricted usability, comfort and efficiency, particularly for highly interactive applications, counterbalancing the benefits that the use of virtual environments (VE) can offer. There are many reasons for this situation: missing standards for immersive interaction, limited resources for development, and a focus on the engineering functionality, neglecting the importance of usability issues. Simple transformation of desktop user interaction concepts to immersive VR for the sake of simplicity and reduced development time fails.

In recent years, many novel concepts for immersive interaction have been developed and published. Most emerged in research laboratories; and some have been developed in close cooperation with industrial partners who are the potential users. This method ensures that industrial end user requirements are considered. Our department has successfully applied this concept in the VRGeo Consortium, which studies the usability of VR for the Geosciences[2]. However, not all developed immersive interaction concepts have been successfully transformed into productive tools for a broader audience or even a mass market.

In the next sections, we want to contribute to the advancement of immersive interaction, concentrating on large-scale VR installations. We also offer an overview of existing technology and its trends. The text can serve as a guide for application developers that need to consider 3D input. It aims at encouraging them to put enough effort on the design of 3D interaction techniques, including customer requirements, and not to neglect these aspects in

---

[1] http://www.iais.fraunhofer.de

[2] http://www.vrgeo.org

favour of pure application functionality. Nowadays, it is by far not sufficient to impress potential customers or users with pure 3D. They need to be convinced that the investment into this technology leads to a substantial benefit - which can only be achieved if the user interface is elaborated enough so that a user recognizes the whole system as an effective tool.
So what are the key benefits of VR that can be of interest for industry? First of all, VR systems can help decreasing design costs by allowing designers to work with virtual models. Second, VR systems can facilitate decision-making by providing integrated views demonstrating different alternatives with additional information. Third, VR systems can be used as demonstration and training environments because of their high-impact visualization possibilities and the ability to reproduce situations that could be dangerous or difficult to observe in the real world. Developing successful VR applications requires a deep understanding of the key features of VR, namely 1) immersion, the ability to of a system to immerse a user into the world of a virtual model and facilitate its spatial perception 2) interaction, the possibility to control virtual objects and get feedback 3) collaboration, support for simultaneous work of two or more users.
Immersive or 3D interaction is human computer interaction in which a user's tasks are performed in a 3D spatial context. Before considering the 3D interaction techniques and their implementation, we briefly survey modern 3D input and output devices. Another important topic that will be considered in this chapter is the evaluation of 3D applications. Several application examples will be presented in the last part of the chapter. For further reading please refer to (Bowman, 2005).

2. 3D Display Systems

Various application fields that already use immersive interaction have different display system requirements. Different screen sizes, resolutions, and 3D viewing technologies exist. For example, a presentation environment for groups of people needs to satisfy different demands as opposed to an interactive training environment designed for a specific scenario. The result is a relatively large number of available display system configurations that are all based on the same principle: projection of a stereo image pair onto a large screen. The following components are common to most 3D projection-based display systems: 1) a rendering system - a powerful computer with respective graphics hardware and software, 2) a projection system and corresponding glasses, 3) additional output devices, such as auditory and olfactory displays, 4) a tracking system, 5) interaction devices. The most important characteristic of a display system is the used technology to generate a 3D impression. In most cases, stereo image pairs are rendered, so that a user perceives a 3D virtual model using stereo glasses. The most common systems are:

- ***Passive stereo systems.*** Images rendered by the computer are projected for the left and right eye in perpendicular polarization and respective polarization glasses are required to get the 3D effect. For each eye, a separate projector is needed.
- ***Active stereo systems.*** The rendered images are projected in sequence for left and right eye and special shutter glasses are used to get the 3D effect. The glasses are see-through so that a user could perceive the virtual environment as being integrated in his or her normal environment; the glasses are synchronized with the projectors on infrared channel. Only one active-stereo-capable projector is needed per screen.

- ***The Infitec (color separation) system***[3] separates the stereo image pair by using different, complementary spectra of lights for both eyes. The crosstalk is very small. However, because of the different wavelength triples used for both eyes, slight deviations of colors are noticeable.
- ***Autostereoscopic displays.*** Such systems do not require stereo glasses, since they separate the images for both eyes on the display surface using layers of masks and lenticular optics, see (Börner et al., 2000). This causes different images to be seen from different viewing angles, and consequently, the user can perceive a 3D effect when viewing from the corresponding sweet spot. Some displays of this kind support several sweet spots, which allow multiple viewers to see 3D, or to see the effect from different angles. Furthermore, some displays support correct 3D effect even for a moving head, using eye tracking methods. Noticeably, most autostereoscopic displays still have normal desktop monitor s sizes and therefore they are not suited for most of the immersive interaction techniques discussed here. However, some manufacturers have started recently to offer large autostereoscopic displays with up to 57" diagonal[4].
- ***Quasi-holographic displays.*** Consisting of optical modules, like projectors and mirrors, and a holographic screen, this innovative kind of display system (Balogh, 2006) is capable of generating a true 3D effect without using auxiliary means, such as glasses. The holographic screen emits light beams received from the optical modules under different angles as if they were emitted from real artifacts. Note that, in contrast to all other display systems mentioned so far, there is no static flat image (or image pair). Instead, at a certain position on the screen, subtle image changes occur when observed from different positions in front of it. Unlimited number of viewers can walk in front of the screen and see 3D objects with just the naked eye. The inventors of this technology[5] describe the underlying principle as a digital window through which virtual objects can be seen as real objects are seen through a normal window. The display has suitable size for the support of immersive interaction and could also be used for co-located multi-user interaction.
- ***Light-field displays.*** A true 3D display that does not require stereo glasses has been proposed by (Jones et al., 2007). It is constructed using a high-speed projector and a spinning reflective device that is synchronized with the projected image sequence. In this way it is possible to project multiple center-of-projection images. The reflecting device behaves like a mirror horizontally, allowing a 360° field of view and scatters vertically. Head tracking can be used to display the correct images for different observer heights. This display type is not suited for direct interaction with virtual objects, simply because their location coincides with rotating mechanical parts of the display.

For immersive interaction, currently large projection-based systems for the display of stereo image pairs, requiring the use of stereo glasses, are predominantly used. Many types of such systems have been developed and presented since over more than one decade. Most of them were originally developed in research labs and emerged from prototypes as commercially available products. They are available from projector manufacturers[6] or special

---

[3] http://www.infitec.net
[4] http://www.tridelity.de
[5] http://www.holografika.com
[6] http://www.barco.com

VR hardware suppliers[7]. However, tiled, large-scale autostereoscopic displays have already been proposed, see e.g. (Sanding et al., 2005). A rough system classification is presented below.

- ***Projection screen.*** The simplest VR display consists of just one vertical projection screen, with e.g. one projector for active stereo, and one graphics computer. A reasonable investment into a robust tracking system that supports both hand and head tracking benefits spatial interaction and therefore highly interactive applications are perfectly possible in these relatively simple settings.
- ***Desk and workbench systems.*** Turning the screen by 90 degrees results in a table-like projection. One of the first systems of this kind was the Responsive Workbench™ (RWB) (Krüger et al., 1995), which was developed by our department (being a part of German National Research Center for Information Technology (GMD) at that time). The RWB consists of a horizontal projection plane, onto which active stereo images are projected via a mirror. The utilized interaction metaphor resembles a working desk: users directly grasp 3D objects located on the table top, and also use interaction widgets placed within the work space. The fact that these objects seem to be placed on the surface, particularly enhances spatial impression and makes the RWB suited for applications like landscape planning, architecture, or surgery simulation and training. Later, a vertical projection plane was added so that objects that have a high extend can be displayed completely.
- ***Projection walls.*** Vertical projection walls are often composed of an array of projection areas, projectors, and graphics computers in order to increase size and resolution of the image. Such systems are not easy to calibrate and maintain and need a lot of space. Projection needs edge blending in order to achieve seamless image borders. In case of active stereo, the shuttering of all image channels need to be synchronized. This is achieved using a dedicated sync signal, produced by one of the graphics cards and fed into all other graphics cards. Note that multiple graphics cards can be driven either by a PC cluster or by dedicated hardware capable of combining several graphics cards connected to one computer, e.g. the NVIDIA QuadroPlex[8]. These systems are often used for marketing and presentation purposes and they have limited interaction capabilities.
- ***Surround-screen projection systems.*** These systems resemble a room and consist of up to six planar, back-projected screens. Back projection is needed because the interior space must be kept free for the users, and in order to avoid shadow casting. This increases space requirements because of the needed exterior positioning of projectors and mirrors. Normally, only four or five screens are used in order to reduce needed space and costs, and to keep an open entrance area. The degree of immersion is very high in these systems and consequently they are very well suited for walkthrough scenarios in which users are immersed within virtual spaces and rooms, e.g. architecture and interior design. The first such system was the CAVE™ (Cruz-Neira et al., 1993), which has been a success worldwide. The CyberStage (Tramberend et al.; 1997) was the first European CAVE-like display system and was developed by our department (being with GMD at that time). The CyberStage is a 3m x 2.4m room with stereoscopic projections on three walls and onto the floor as well. It allows a user to move freely around and feel immersed in an unbounded space. It is an immersive room with 8-channel sound and vibrating floor. Surround-screen projections are widely used in the industry, especially

[7] http://www.viscon.de, http://www.valleyviewtech.com
[8] http://www.nvidia.com

in the automotive sector; and they are still being further developed. Recently, (DeFanti et al., 2009) proposed a six-sided system, each side consisting of a tiled screen. The ground forming a pentagon, each side has three screens, with the top and bottom screens tilted inwards. In order to get inside, one of the sides can be moved like a door. There is no top screen. Front projection is used for the ground, whereas the sides are back-projected. Since stereo viewing is based on circular polarization, screen material had to be chosen carefully. This setup has several advantages over standard four-sided CAVE-like displays: increased resolution, reduced visibility of interreflections due to increased 108° angle between screens, and less off-axis viewing angles since the screens are facing the viewer position.

- ***Cylindrical, curved screen systems.*** Surrounding screens can enhance the degree of immersion, compared to flat screens. They are curved to create a seamless transition of the projection field (no visible edges), and to reduce the visibility of perspective errors resulting from observer positions away from the centre of projection (the main view point). These errors are easier noticeable at transitions between flat screens (like in the CAVE™), particularly for straight lines. The projectors must be calibrated to pre-distort the image so that from the main view point, a rectilinear image can be observed, which is checked by projecting a suitable test grid.

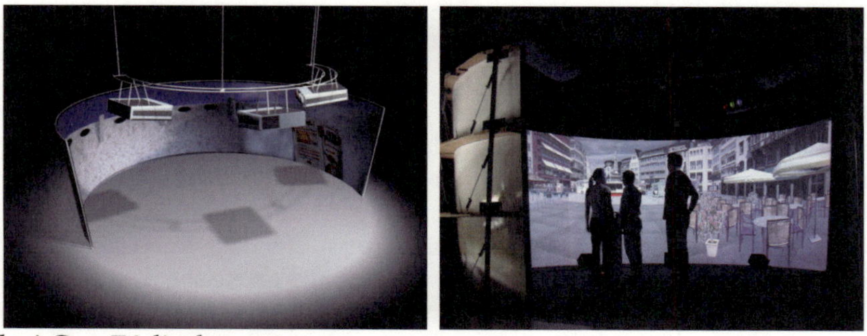

Fig. 2.1 The i-Cone™ display system

- The i-Cone™ (Simon & Göbel, 2002) display developed by our department has a slightly slanted projection area, forming a cone-shaped display, in order to minimize disturbing echoes perceivable at the centre of the system. Another positive effect of the slanting is that front projection can be used in a way that shadow casting by viewers is reduced (see Figure 2.1). Notice that, compared to the CAVE™, space requirements are significantly reduced taking into account the higher number of viewers that can reside in the i-Cone™. The Varrier™ display developed by (Sandin et al., 2005) is making innovative use of 35 autostereoscopic display panels arranged in a tiled array, forming a cylindrical immersive VR display. The work demonstrates how standard autostereoscopic panels should be modified for use in a VR display system. For example, the image slices forming the interleaved left and right eye perspectives are generated according to world coordinates, taking into account the viewer position in the display area, contrary to standard autostereoscopic displays that use integer device coordinates and compress the depth of the scene.
- ***The TwoView display system.*** Normally, in projection based VEs, only one user is head-tracked and can see perspectively correct. All other users wearing stereo glasses see a

stereo image computed for a different centre of projection, which is distorted. The TwoView display developed by our department removes this limitation and supports two head tracked users. Because of correct perspective, the virtual and physical spaces are correctly aligned for both users allowing true co-located collaborative work with 3D objects. The image pairs of the two users are separated using polarization, whereas stereo is achieved by shuttering (active stereo). This means that polarization filters need to be mounted to the shutter glasses, and two active-stereo capable projectors are needed, see Figure 2.2. Other display systems (Froehlich et al., 2004) support even more viewers, based on shuttered LCD projectors.

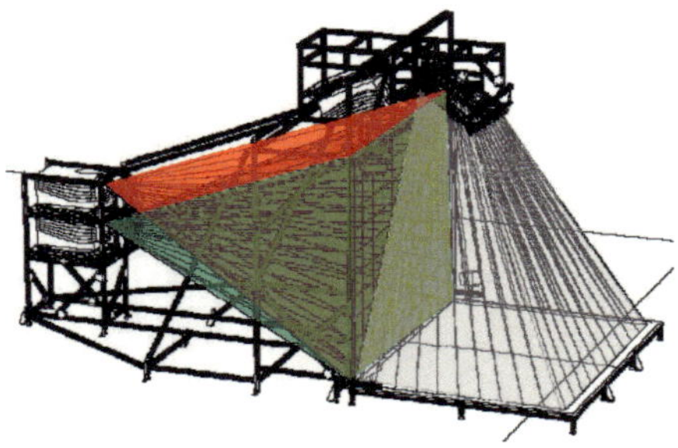

Fig. 2.2 The TwoView display system.
Note that the ground projection is inactive in TwoView mode.

- ***Augmented Reality (AR) displays.*** These displays combines virtual 3D object with the physical world seen by the user. This can be achieved using cameras or semi-transparent mirrors. There are mobile displays such as head mounted displays and also projection-based systems. As an example, consider the Spinnstube display system (Wind et al., 2007) also developed in our department. It uses a small, lightweight active stereo projector to project stereo images onto a screen located above the user (see Figure 2.3). A user is seated and is looking onto a semi-transparent mirror, which reflects the screen. In addition, a user can observe physical artefacts underneath the mirror, which are placed on a working desk. This technique is used in school environments and supports all kinds of training applications, since it can overlay physical objects with additional, helpful information. Furthermore, a unified collaborative manipulation space can be formed for up to four users by aligning several displays as shown in Figure 2.3. A new version of the Spinnstube® is expected in 2009.

Fig. 2.3 The Spinnstube® AR display system: design (left) and use (right).

3. Tracking Systems

Tracking systems (or trackers) provide information about position and orientation of real physical objects for the use in VR applications. Trackers can measure the motion of interaction devices, as well as user's head, hands, and sometimes the whole body or just eyes. This information is then used to calculate the correct perspective projection and auditory inputs accordingly to the position of a user and react on his/her actions. Hence, together with signalling functions of interaction devices, trackers are the primary means of input into VR applications. Trackers can be described by a set of key characteristics, which can be used for a system evaluation and comparison (Meyer et al., 1992):

- Resolution. Measures the exactness with which a system can locate a reported position. Resolution shows the smallest change a system can detect.
- Accuracy. The range within which a reported position is correct. This is a function of the error involved in making measurements and often it is expressed in statistical error.
- System responsiveness comprising sample rate (the rate at which sensors are checked for data, usually expressed as frequency), data rate (the number of computed positions per second, usually expressed as frequency, update rate (the rate at which the system reports new position coordinates to the host computer, also usually given as frequency), and latency (the delay between the movement of the remotely sensed object and the report of the new position).

Different technologies have been used in the development of tracking devices: there exist optical, magnetic, mechanical, acoustic, inertial and hybrid trackers. Many tracking systems consist of a signal emitter and a signal receiver. For example, in the case of magnetic sensors, an emitter can be connected to the stereoscopic glasses, so that when a user moves his/her head, so does the position of the emitter. A receiver senses the signals from the emitter and an algorithm determines the position and orientation of the receiver in relation to the emitter. Each tracking technology has its own advantages and disadvantages (Welch & Foxlin, 2002). The most widely used systems in VR today are based on the optical technology, although some systems based on other technologies are also quite popular (such as the products of Polhemus[9], Intersense[10], Ascension[11] and XSens[12]). Companies such as A.R.T.[13], Vicon[14] and NaturalPoint[15] provide a wide range of hardware and software solutions for video-based infrared tracking of configurations of passive markers, which can be attached to different devices. Normally, the hardware in their systems employs infrared emitters integrated with synchronised high-resolution cameras, which have built-in image processing possibilities, and their software is able to track multiple targets (reflective spheres) in the tracking volume defined by the number and configuration of cameras.

In our projects we have not only used numerous commercial systems, but also developed our own prototypes and evaluated innovative systems developed by other research

[9] http://www.polhemus.com
[10] http://www.intersense.com
[11] http://www.ascension-tech.com
[12] http://www.xsens.com
[13] http://www.ar-tracking.de
[14] http://www.vicon.com
[15] http://ww.naturalpoint.com

institutions. For example, the system developed by (Foursa, 2004) employed three infrared cameras and was able to track active markers (light-emission diodes - LEDs), which were mounted on the glasses and on a stylus. The system has been used to study reconstruction from multiple cameras (a metric that took into account local errors of reconstruction has been developed), to develop methods of system performance analysis (including reliability analysis), to design new interaction devices (a stylus with 2 LEDs has been used to control 6 degrees-of-freedom) and to study movement-based interaction with markers in different VR applications (Foursa & Wesche, 2007). In the HUMODAN project (Perales et al., 2004) we have integrated a markerless tracking system with our VR installations and evaluated its usability. The system employed two color cameras and required a uniform background; the segmentation, matching and reconstruction algorithms of the system allowed to track several reference points of human body (such as hands, head and shoulders) and to provide biomechanically corrected positions of up to 20 points of a human model.. However, since the tracked persons had to be visible on the cameras, additional light sources had to be placed in front of the users, distracting their attention from the VR display. Furthermore, since the accuracy of segmentation of the system was worse than one in marker-based systems, it led to position reconstruction errors of the feature points. Nevertheless, we could use the system for application control and simple interaction tasks (Foursa & Wesche, 2007). Although some companies[16] offer commercial markerless tracking solutions for motion capturing today, they are normally not used with virtual environments and their accuracy evaluation results are not easily available.

Current trends in tracking systems include the development of affordable, but high-performance hardware and software systems, which are wireless, scalable, support multiple targets and employ flexible calibration techniques, such as the prototype developed by (Pintaric & Kaufmann, 2007). New opportunities are opened by the so-called depth-sensing cameras (for example, the ZCam[17]), which provide depth information for each pixel and do not require any additional background. Commercial applications using this technology for 3D control have been already developed[18].

4. Interaction Devices

Interaction devices are physical tools that are used for different interaction purposes in VR, such as view control, navigation, object selection and manipulation, and system control. Sometimes the devices are integrated and supported by tracking systems. Normally they are equipped with buttons and controls; in addition, they may support force and audio feedback. Any input device may be used for various interaction techniques. The goal of a developer is to select the most appropriate technique for a device or vice versa, aiming at natural and efficient interaction. An interaction device may be discrete (generating events on user's request, e.g. a button), continuous (continuously generating events, e.g. a tracker) or hybrid (combining both controls). Most interaction devices belong to one of the following categories: 1) gloves/hand masters 2) mice and joysticks 3) remote controls/wands 4) force/space balls. Input devices may be described by the follows characteristics:

---

16 http://www.organicmotion.com
17 http://www.3dvsystems.com
18 http://www.gesturetek.com

- Degrees-of-freedom (DOF) of an input device. Many devices supported by tracking systems have 6 DOFs (3 for position and 3 for orientation).
- Number and type of buttons and controls.
- Compatibility with interaction tasks.
- Presence of feedback channels (sound, vibration etc).
- Other specific characteristics: it may be one- or two-handed device, wireless or wired device and so on.

Below we describe several interaction devices developed in our department (see Figure 4.1):

- ***YoYo*** (Simon & Fröhlich, 2003) is an input device for controlling 3D graphics applications. The device consists of three elastically connected rings in a row, which can be moved relative to each other. The centre ring holds a tracking sensor and a few application programmable buttons. The left and the right ring are elastic 6DOF controllers. The device is designed for two-handed interaction and combines elastic force input and isotonic input in a single device. Compact size, symmetric shape, and the elastic properties result in a "soft" and responsive feel of this device. YoYo can be used for navigation and manipulation in three-dimensional graphics applications in the area of data exploration and scientific visualization. An informal user study and user observations have shown that novice users are quite confident with the device after a short introduction, and that most users alternate between using elastic rate control and isotonic control for navigation.
- ***NoYo*** (Simon & Doulis, 2004) is a joystick-like handheld input device for travel and rate-controlled object manipulation. NoYo combines a 6DOF elastic force sensor with a 3DOF source-less isotonic orientation tracker. This combination allows consistent mapping of input forces from local device coordinates to absolute world coordinates, effectively making NoYo a "SpaceMouse to go". The device is designed to allow one-handed as well as two-handed operation, depending on the task and the skill level of a user. A quantitative usability study shows the handheld NoYo to be up to 20% faster, easier to learn, and significantly more efficient than the SpaceMouse desktop device.
- ***CubicMouse™*** (Fröhlich & Plate, 2000) is an input device that allows users to intuitively specify 3D coordinates in graphics applications. The CubicMouse™ consists of a box with three perpendicular rods passing through the centre and buttons for additional input. The rods represent the X-, Y-, and Z-axes of a given coordinate system. Pushing and pulling the rods specifies constrained motion along the corresponding axes. Embedded within the device is a 6DOF tracking sensor, which allows the rods to be continually aligned with a coordinate system located in a virtual world.
- ***PioDA*** is a combined 3D interaction device for virtual environments. It was particularly developed for the A.R.T. tracking system, but it can also work with any optical tracking system able to track passive markers. PioDA is PDA-based. It is used as a 6DOF interaction device with portable graphical user interface for application/system control in virtual environments. It integrates wireless optical tracking (room-size) and is useful for most projection based virtual environments. Having only one handy device for both interaction and application/system control is the major advantage of this device. The GUI of the device can display interactive content, which can be synchronized with the context of a VR application.

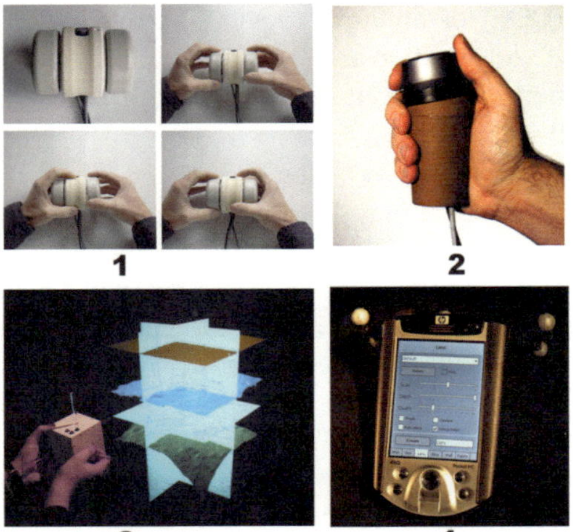

Fig. 4.1. Selected interaction devices developed in the Virtual Environments department of Fraunhofer IAIS (1 - YoYo, 2 - NoYo, 3 - CubicMouse, 4 - PioDA)

Current trends in interaction devices include the development of wireless lightweight devices with multiple sensors feedback. For example, Nintendo's Wii Remote[19], the primary controller for Nintendo's Wii console, has motion sensing capability through the use of accelerometer and optical sensor technology, provides basic audio and rumble functionality, and supports Bluetooth. Such functionalities allow developing simple but effective interactive applications[20]. Another interesting direction is the integration of haptic devices with virtual environments (for example, the Inca 6D device[21]). One should also be aware that there exist other input channels, such as speech input, brain input[22] and gestures, and sometime the combination of different input channels can significantly increase the usability of applications.

5. Interaction Techniques

3D interaction techniques are methods for performing certain interaction tasks within a 3D environment. Typically, a user is partly or fully immersed in the 3D environment and can access its objects to control the application via 3D input devices. 3D interaction techniques are not device-centric in the first place; instead a number of design decisions are needed to achieve usability performance and comfort, particularly considering highly interactive 3D applications. Designing a 3D interaction technique needs to take into account the following aspects:

- Spatial relationship of users and virtual objects in the environment
- Number and type of available input devices (special purpose vs. general purpose, many controls vs. few basic controls, spatially tracked vs. non-tracked)
- Single-user vs. collaborative applications

---

[19] http://www.nintendo.com/wii

[20] http://johnnylee.net/projects/wii

[21] http://www.haption.com

[22] http://bci2000.org

Consequently, the following basic interaction techniques can be distinguished:

- Direct interaction (the control of nearby objects in reach for being grabbed by hand) vs. indirect interaction (the control of distant objects, or transition between nearby and distant objects)
- Two-handed vs. traditional, one-handed input methods
- Application control using many control channels (buttons, sliders, touch-screen, etc), or utilizing pure hand movement in space
- Traditional single user interaction vs. co-located multi-user interaction that supports multiple users working together at the same location and sharing the same virtual manipulation space

Interaction tasks of complex applications in 3D environments can be categorized into *selection, manipulation, navigation, creation, system control,* and *collaboration*.

5.1 Selection

Selection refers to the process of selecting a 3D object for further interaction. This can be further subdivided into indicating the desired object, confirming the selection, and receiving a feedback (Bowman et al., 2005). It can be quite complex to select the right object due to inappropriate size, large distance to the user, occlusion, or even movement. The basic selection techniques are direct grabbing and ray casting. These basic techniques have been further developed to solve the mentioned selection problems. E.g. the *flexible pointer* technique (Olwal & Feiner, 2003) allows selecting partially obscured objects. The *aperture selection technique* (Forsberg et al., 1996) replaces the pick ray by a conic volume. It is even possible to control the opening angle of the cone dynamically, depending on requirements.

5.2 Manipulation

Manipulation means changing the state of a previously selected 3D object, including its geometry. It normally immediately follows the selection of an object; consequently in the literature selection and manipulation sometimes are considered together. The multitude of object properties requiring especial treatment cannot be considered in summary. However, the most basic task, moving objects in space, is so common that several techniques for it have been presented.

Direct manipulation. The direct, isomorphic method is used to attach the 3D object to the hand. Situations in which this can be applied in a comfortable way are nonetheless very rare. As soon as the object is not in reach for direct grasping with the hand, a technique for distant interaction is needed. Consider e.g. pointing at a distant object using a pick ray and rotating it. In this situation, rotation can in fact only be applied in a reasonable way around the axis of the pick ray (Bowman et al., 2005). Imagine also how tedious it would be to change the distance of the object to the user: a user would have to grab and push or pull the object several times, by clutching to it repeatedly.

Distant interaction. Some techniques have been proposed to improve the comfort and performance of direct distant manipulation. The virtual hand can be placed at the object's location after object selection, using a scaled selection technique based on ray casting (Bowman & Hodges, 1997), which effectively increases the reaching distance of the hand. A similar effect can be accomplished by applying a non-linear growth of the (virtual) arm length of the user (Poupyrev et al., 1996). Alternatively, the whole virtual environment can be scaled down so that the selected object is brought in reach close to a user, allowing direct, isomorphic manipulation (Mine et al., 1997).

3D widgets. Instead of selecting and dragging a 3D object of the scene, manipulation can also be accomplished indirectly, by using 3D widgets. They are commonly used in 2D environments as a means for mouse-based object movement, in particular, for rotation, as the well-known trackball. This technique is applicable also in 3D environments to support rotation control for distant objects. An advantage of using 3D widgets is that object manipulation can be constrained, assigning different handles to the coordinate axes. Regarding object geometry, the applicability of these standard manipulation techniques is restricted to rigid-body transformations and scalings. Manipulations of parametric objects can be much more involved, e.g. imaging the task of smoothing or dragging a free form curve.

Manipulation of complex objects. Manipulation of complex, parametric objects is still not very common in 3D virtual environments, although the design of suitable methods is possible. However, inventing deformation tools for certain parametric objects is a challenge on its own, like for free form curves and surfaces, as used in Computer-Aided Geometric Design (CAGD). We have developed deformation tools for this class of objects to be used in environments that support direct interaction. A user can smooth, sharpen, and warp curves and surfaces in an intuitive way, and does not need to interact with the low-level mathematical parameters. Curves can be smoothed and sharpened locally by pointing at the corresponding locations at the curve, which causes the shape continuously changing close to the input device, whereas the farther curve segments are almost unchanged. Similarly, curve segments can be warped. The details of these tools are described in (Wesche, 2004) and are based on the idea of variational modeling (Wesselink & Veltcamp, 1995). The mode of operation of the smoother and sharpener is shown in Figure 5.1. Notice the rather indirect but still intuitive way of how hand movement is mapped to the shape deformation: the hand just points to the involved locations instead of performing a direct push or pull; therefore we can argue that the installation of a force feedback device is not necessary since the interaction mode does not imply it.

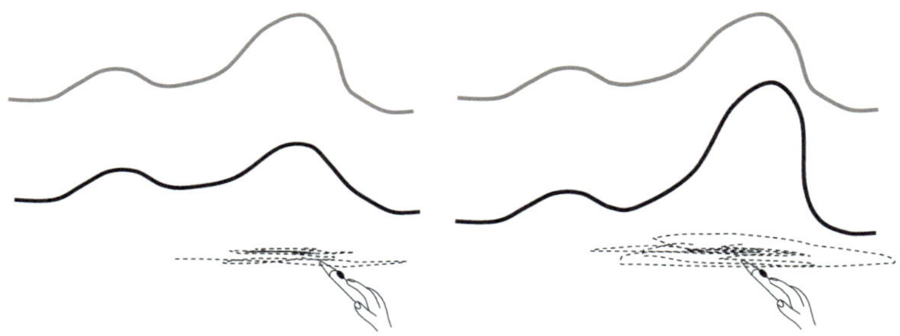

Fig. 5.1. Curve smoother and sharpener

5.3 Navigation

Need for navigation. Navigation is the process of setting the user's position and orientation relative to a 3D environment. In many cases the whole VE can be overlooked and is in reach and there is no direct need for navigation, since the relative alignment of user and scene is accomplished by manipulation such as orienting the scene with the hand. Therefore, navigation often implies that the VE or the scale of the VE is very large compared to the user's size or area of arm reach. In these cases, particular techniques are needed for traveling around in the VE (strictly, navigation should be divided into way finding, which is a cognitive process needed acquire knowledge of the 3D surroundings, and travel, the process to change position (Bowman et al., 2005)).

Walking. Most naturally, a user can travel by walking. Since the available space of display systems is limited, walking simulators that support walking in place are needed. The disadvantage is that the technological effort is high. 3D input devices are more convenient to control a user's locomotion. They can also be combined with head tracking. The NOYO input device (see section 5) is such a device operated by both hands. The disadvantage is that hands are not free to perform selection and manipulation task simultaneously. It is also possible to evaluate tracked body parts for deriving the travel direction, e.g. the gaze vector. Notice that the direction of view should normally be independent from the walking direction.

Movement platforms represent an elegant method for controlling locomotion. The "Virtual balance" (Fleischmann et al., 1997), is a disk placed on three pressure sensors on which a user is standing and, by changing his/her weight on the platform, can travel in the virtual space, see Figure 5.2.

Fig. 5.2. Virtual balance

Notice that this is based on only two degrees of freedom supported by the device. The chairIO device, proposed by (Beckhaus et al., 2007), is used in a similar way. The person sits on a rotatable seat that can be tilted in any direction. Shifting the body weight is mapped to the direction of movement in the virtual environment. The travel speed is calculated from the degree of displacement. Compared to the Virtual Balance, the movement direction can be controlled more easily because of the additional rotational degree of freedom. Other interesting moving platforms are the sphere-based systems (such as a system developed by (Fernandes et al., 2003)), which are already available commercially[23], and a tile-based system developed by (Iwata et al., 2005). However, such systems are normally used with head-mounted displays.

[23] http://www.virtusphere.com

5.4 Creation

We see *creation* as a separate, new interaction task in order to distinguish it from manipulation. Creation is the task of instantiating or constructing a new 3D virtual object from scratch and adding it to the environment. Instantiating can be simple in case the object class only has a few parameters, e.g. consider the creation of primitive geometric objects like spheres, cylinders, or boxes. On the other hand, construction of objects can involve complex interaction needed to specify a high number of object parameters and properties. To cope with this, creation techniques can be designed that support the successive input of the various parameters and of the needed topological connection information, which could result in techniques that are not intuitive. Alternatively, an intuitive shape creation technique that extracts all properties from hand input may result in unpleasing or undesired results. In addition, complex algorithms for the connection of objects created in that way may be required. As an example, consider the task of free-from shape creation. A number of different techniques have been proposed for shape input in 3D virtual environments. The surface drawing technique (Schkolne et al., 2001) extracts polygonal surfaces out of intuitive free-hand drawing strokes at the Responsive Workbench™. The surfaces of (Kuriyama, 1994) are based on the input of parametric boundary curves and result in pleasant shapes with well-defined geometric continuity properties across the boundaries. However, they are not supported by standard computer aided geometric design (CAGD) systems. The free-form sketching system of (Wesche, 2004), which runs at the Responsive Workbench™, supports these surfaces, and Spline-based surfaces as well; see also section 9. In addition, this application allows a user to specify the topology (i.e. the connectivity) of curves forming surface boundaries. This is achieved by pointing at the surface or curve locations directly in 3D space. In summary, the creation of complex objects may involve multiple successive interaction tasks. Furthermore, the pure geometry is not sufficient to fully specify a 3D object; in most cases the topology needs to be defined explicitly by suitable 3D input methods.

5.5 System control

Up to now, all 3D interaction techniques were related to spatial control of objects or of the whole scene. However, no application can exist without means to issue certain commands to control mode or state changes. These activities are referred to as system control, and they exist in a Virtual Environment as well. However, system control is often simply neglected in a 3D application. Normally, poor UI performance and high user frustration is the result. Although there is no standard for system control in a 3D environment, research in recent years has produced a variety of techniques. The 2D counterpart of 3D system control is the well-established WIMP (windows, icons, menus, pointer) standard. Compared to that, a much richer set of possibilities and techniques are available for 3D. These include

- Adaptation of menu techniques
- Posture and gesture based input
- Speech control
- 3D widgets
- GUI of integrated standard input devices, like personal digital assistants (PDA)

From this it can be seen that there are two principal approaches (possible to use in combination): the 3D UI elements are an integral part of a 3D scene, or the GUI of standard devices, which can be instrumented with 6DOF tracking targets, is used for system control.

We provide two examples in which the 3D widgets are rendered as part of the scene graph, general-purpose and a special purpose 3D widget.

General-purpose 3D widgets. 3D menus are widely used in VR applications since the menu concept is well-known from the WIMP interface. In 3D, a variety of different menu approaches exist. They make use of the third dimension in different ways: in the worst case a user needs to hit a 2D region in space using a pick ray, thus he/she needs to solve a task that is conceptually 1D (select an item from a list) in three dimensions.

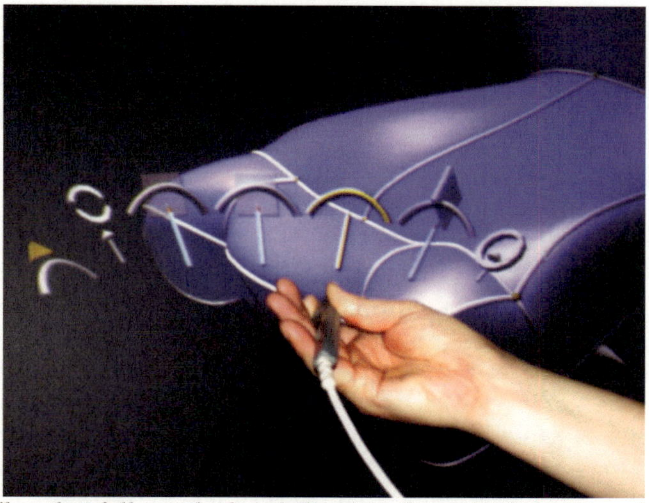

Fig. 5.3. hand toolbar that follows the hand. Turning the wrist is used to select a tool.

This demonstrates why the straightforward transformation of concepts initially developed for the desktop to a 3D environment fails. 3D menu solutions not only need to utilize the third dimension in a useful way, they also should take into account the spatial relationships between menu widget, user hands and arms, view direction, manipulation space, and size of virtual objects. In some cases the 3D manipulation space is relatively large so that fixed menu locations are not the optimal solutions. We have developed a hand-oriented toolbar (Wesche, 2004) that follows hand movement; but at the same time it evaluates how a user turns his/her wrist to select an item (see Figure 5.3). However, notice that the toolbar size should be limited to allow a comfortable use.

Special-purpose 3D widgets. The design of system control for special applications can benefit from approaches that intentionally deviate from physical world situations. The *ToolFinger* (Wesche, 2003) is such as technique, since it supports providing several *virtual* tools held in one hand at the same time; an idea that would sound completely impracticable in the real world. In contrast to this, in a virtual environment a user can quickly transition between several tools that need to be applied to an object in order to change its properties. Applications like 3D shape design can benefit from this technique (Figure 5.4). A designer can iteratively elaborate the shape of an object in 3D using several tools in quick succession. Thus the system control subtask that is optimized using this approach is tool selection. An advantage of integrated UIs like 3D widgets is that they can be placed and configured within the manipulation space, i.e. within the scene the user looks at.

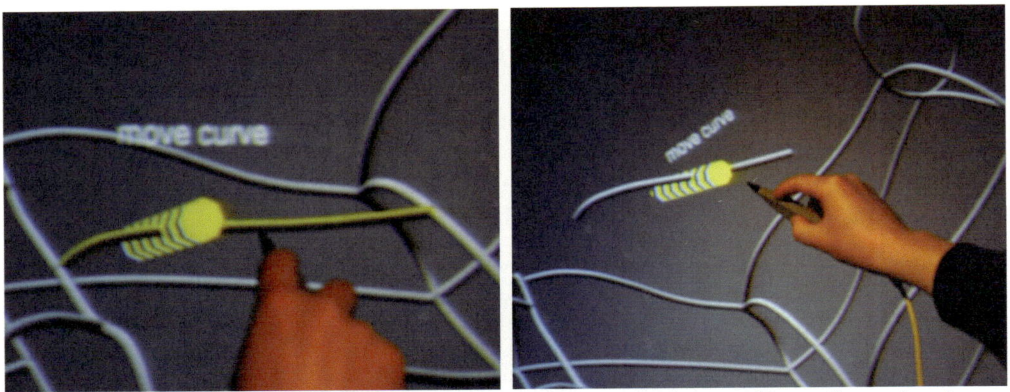

Fig. 5.4. Using the ToolFinger: selecting and applying the tool is one fluent flow of actions. Tools are represented as colored sections.

Multi-frame rate rendering. The problem with virtual UI elements is that they are rendered and updated with the same frame rate as the normal 3D scene. This means that in case the scene is complex and the frame rate drops, no reasonable user interaction is possible any more. The decoupling of rendering performance of the UI from the actual scene was topic of the research of (Springer et al., 2007), who introduced multi frame rate rendering. By optically or digitally composing interactive and less interactive parts of a scene, the interactive performance of users can be significantly increased. The use of standard input devices like PDAs for system control avoids the frame rate problem, but requires a user to shift his/her point of focus repeatedly from the 3D scene to the screen of the input device and back that breaks any immersive experience.
Current trends in developing UIs include the research in post-WIMP, non-command driven interfaces, which could be used also in 3D VEs. The translation of the intent of a user into a sequence of commands is replaced by much more fluent user input, based on so-called freeform UIs. This is expected to lead to new ways of system control for VEs as well. E.g. (Igarashi, 2003) utilizes free form drawing strokes to overcome the limitations of the WIMP interface.

5.6 Collaboration

In projection-based environments, several users can work together interacting with the same application. In most display systems, this kind of interaction is not supported since only one user can be head-tracked and sees the correct perspective space. In the TwoView display system, developed at Fraunhofer IAIS, this restriction is removed and two users each receive their own perspectively correct stereo image pair. Therefore they can manipulate the same virtual scene collaboratively. A basic collaborative selection and manipulation technique is the *bent pick ray* (Riege et al., 2006), The normally straight pick ray of two users interacting together in one place, when selecting the same object, is bent to provide visual feedback of the fact that a part has been grabbed by both users (see Figure 5.5).

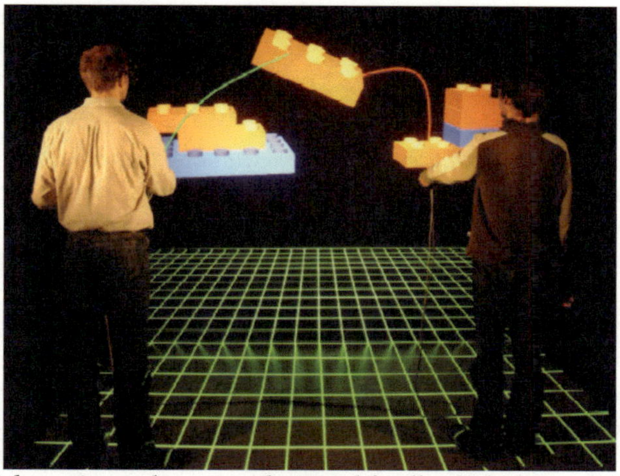

Fig. 5.5. The bent pick ray is used to provide visual feedback during collaboration

6. Design and Evaluation of 3D Applications

6.1 Developing 3D user interfaces

How to select the appropriate 3D user interface for a particular application? Since standards are rare or do not exist at all (especially for system control), design considerations should be based on similar application settings *in 3D environments* (not on the same application on the desktop) that have proven successful. Many such applications have been published, however not all put the needed attention towards usability in 3D. In general, a selection depends on the answer to questions like:

- How easy is it to extend the given VE system by new input devices?
- What kind of input devices is available? How many control channels (i.e. buttons, wheels) do they offer?
- How can the users be characterized that will use the application? Are they domain experts? Are they (additionally) VR experts? Is quick learning of UI techniques a must? Are users already accustomed to other 3D user interfaces? Is it a public installation?
- What are the properties of the 3D scene and the VE? What are the relationships between a user's height, the size of the 3D scene and the distance to the scene? Is it an immersive setting or a semi- or non-immersive environment? Are the objects in reach i.e. can you apply direct interaction? Are resting positions of input devices or for a user's arm available? Should co-located collaboration in groups be supported?

The following basic approaches can be followed when designing 3D UIs:

- *Adapting from 2D environments*: this in many cases leads to crude solutions in which the same GUI as in the 2D counterpart application needs to be operated in a 3D environment, using a pick ray. However, there are notable exceptions of this approach leading to usable 3D graphical menu systems especially tailored to 3D. As an example, consider the work of (Dressler, 2007), who developed a 3D menu system for immersive environments. The optimized layout of menus improves performance and error rate for pick ray based interaction, compared to the use of PDAs and tablet-PCs. Moreover, positioning and scaling of the menu are rule-based, enhancing reachability and readability of text, and reducing occlusion.

- *Imitating the reality*: this is appropriate for simple direct interaction tasks for objects in reach; however, it fails for more complicated tasks. One reason for this is the missing tactile and force feedback channels. Moreover, this approach does not exploit possibilities only available in a *virtual* world.
- *Inventing 3D behaviour deviating from the physical world*: this approach can lead to interesting new techniques and it seems to be the most promising one. This is because certain constraints and certain feedback cannot easily be established or are not available in VEs.

The design guidelines for 3D user interfaces are manifold; the most important ones are:

- *Support fluent flow of actions.* This is particularly important if the application is characterized by many successive changes of tools, or modes, as e.g. in a 3D computer aided styling application.
- *Spatially organize the 3D scene and interaction objects.* This can be done in such a way that the focus of attention does not need to change often. Consider e.g. the benefit of a hand-mounted virtual 3D menu, compared to a menu positioned at a fixed location on the screen.

A more detailed discussion on such and more guidelines can be found in (Bowman et al., 2005). Another guideline is based on the human capabilities, i.e. based on the interplay of the use of both hands. The corresponding analysis of (Guiard, 1987) is often cited in work about interaction, and has proven to be a good principle. Guiard distinguishes among the following ways of using both hands: asymmetric bimanual (e.g. playing a violin, writing on a piece of paper), more or less symmetric bimanual (e.g. indicating the width of some object), or one-handed. In asymmetric bimanual tasks, the non-dominant hand usually forms a reference frame for the finer and more accurate movement of the dominant hand. These observations can be used for the design of powerful manipulation techniques in 3D. This has been achieved e.g. in the work of (Cutler et al., 1997). For example, consider their two-handed rotation tool, where one hand specifies the axis of rotation, and the other hand is rotating the selected object around it.

6.2 Evaluating applications

Similar to evaluating any other artefacts, an evaluation of 3D user interfaces involves assessing their strengths and weaknesses in order to improve their effectiveness. The main purpose of 3D user interfaces evaluation is the analysis of their usability and generation of recommendations on how they could be improved. Evaluation should always follow significant design changes and it may be necessary to perform evaluation several times during an interface development. Evaluation performed at an early stage may be dedicated more to the study of importance of different features and functionalities, while evaluation performed at a later stage may be dedicated to their effectiveness. The most widely used evaluation techniques are the following (Bowman et al., 2005):

- Formative evaluation is an observational user study in which users try out the proposed interface. They may be asked to simply explore the interface or to perform some specific tasks.
- Summative evaluation compares various techniques in one experiment. Users may be given a specific task that they perform both in the proposed system and in another one or in a different configuration of the proposed system.

During an evaluation one could assess functionality, performance, and ergonomics of an interface. Evaluation may be done in a formal or informal manner. The results of the evaluation may be obtained in the form of a questionnaire, an expert interview or automatic registration of some events. They may be qualitative and quantitative. The latter requires a metric, such as time, number of tasks performed, accuracy of actions etc.

Assessment techniques may include the evaluation of the following parameters:

- Evaluation of systems performance, which may be used in case the analysis of a computer or graphics system is necessary, for example to calculate frame rate or latency.
- Task performance. It is the main focus of many evaluations. The quality of a task performance may be analyzed in terms of the time needed to perform it, number of errors a user makes, accuracy of the performance, quantity of the information learnt and other entities.
- User performance. It refers to the subjective perception of the interface by a user. Here one should analyze if the interface has any barriers to a task completion, if the interface is comfortable and if the interface is intuitive and may be used without specific knowledge.

A thorough evaluation approach should contain application-specific experiments, use a wide range of metrics and engage sufficient amount of users. Statistical methods should be applied to calculate average values and their confidence intervals, understand, if the results are statistically significant and, finally, understand, if the number of the test participants was big enough. Some web-resources on usability and statistical analysis[24] have online calculators and brief explanations of procedures and could be recommended as a starting point for researchers, who do not have expertise in usability analysis.

6.3 An example of application evaluation

In order to identify the influence of immersion and collaboration on the performance in assembly and manipulation tasks in a virtual environment, we performed a quantitative assessment of user performance in an assembly modeling application on the basis of our framework described in section 7.3 (D'Angelo et al., 2008). We asked each of the twenty participants to perform a specific task ten times in four modes: in single and collaborative two-user modes with stereoscopic and monoscopic vision for each mode. The participants had to assemble a table out of a table plate and four table legs and place it at a specific position on a floor plate. In each assembly task, the modeling parts were randomly positioned in space, while the sum of the inter-object distances was kept constant for all initial configurations. An automatic timer clock measured and logged the task completion times, starting with first and stopping with last assembly operations. The results showed average speed-up factors of 1.6 and 1.4 for collaborative interaction and stereoscopic vision respectively. With both collaboration and stereo vision the performance of users could be increased by a factor of 2.2.

7. Application Examples

7.1 Interactive Visualization of geo-seismic data for the oil and gas industry

The huge amount of geo-seismic data acquired for searching oil reservoirs is one of the greatest challenges for information analysis. The approach is to use interactive 3D visualization in a Virtual Environment, from which geophysicists and geologists expect the

---

[24] http://www.measuringusability.com, http://www.quantitativeskills.com/sisa/

best achievements. A lot of visualization algorithms and user interface technologies have been developed in recent years in order to offer these users a benefit.

Fig. 7.1. Interacting with seismic data, using the CubicMouse

Important features of the framework developed at Fraunhofer IAIS are the visualization of multiple data types, support for well planning (i.e. paths for drilling after oil), combined visualization and sonification of well log data, and multi-resolution techniques for volume visualization. For navigation and interaction new input devices tailored to geo-seismic data interpretation were engineered. This allows users to focus on their exploration tasks rather than on operating a computer.

The most important aspect is the combination of algorithms that enable browsing through gigabytes of 3D seismic data volumes at interactive frame rates directly in 3D (Plate et al., 2002, 2007), with particularly suited interaction techniques and input devices. Figure 7.1 presents the VRGeo demonstrator at the Responsive Workbench™.

7.2 Sketching free-form shapes

Shape design is one of the most important activities in design and product development. It is well known that buyers base their decisions of what product to choose on the shape appearance and, if applicable, on the ergonomics of a product. The main decisions about the shape of a new product take place in the conceptual design phase, which benefits from rapid prototyping and 3D printing technologies in order to cope with the high number of variants to be built and with the iterative nature of that process. For this to work, a digital model even in the beginning of shape conceptualization is a must. However, most design processes are still dominated by hand-crafted models made out of deformable or workable material, like clay, or wood, which are difficult or impossible to change. On the other hand, designers like to use hands and tools in a natural way, and not to operate a computer system, which hinders their creative thinking.

Tools for sketching free-form shapes have been developed for Virtual Environments, because these environments are very well suited to offer designers the tools adapted to their specific needs. At the same time, a digital model can be obtained and can be used for rapid prototyping.

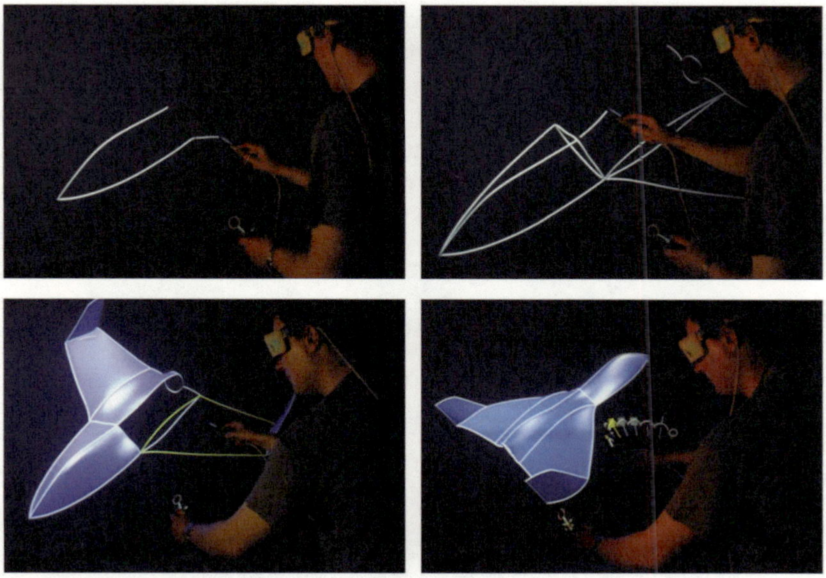

Fig. 7.2. Conceptual styling of free form shapes

The work shown in Figure 7.2 is an example of such an approach; see also (Wesche, 2004). The user draws curves and constructs a curve network that forms the skeleton of the surface he/she has in mind. Automatic surfacing methods generate shapes that correspond to the outlined boundary, thus freeing a designer from specifying all surface parameters by hand. The designer draws and alters shapes directly in space, using the hands. Since the size and the location of the virtual model corresponds to the region easily in reach by a user's hands, direct hand-based interaction at the location of focus is very natural and intuitive. On the other hand, controlling all available degrees of freedom when hand-drawing a shape requires elevated concentration from designer.

Results and user tests (Deisinger, 2000) have shown that designers were indeed able to use these tools, however have also shown the fact that the underlying technology is still too immature and not robust enough to replace traditional procedures. This is by all means true for tools that require drawing in 3D. More specialized approaches computerize a certain subtask of shape design, and these have proven more successful, e.g. digital tape drawing (Balakrishnan, 2002).

The styling application has even been tested using markerless tracking (see section 3), and it was usable for interactive surface deformations using the naked hand. Drawing curves, however, representing a complex constructive task could not easily be accomplished with this technique.

7.3 Virtual Environment for Product Customization

The TwoView display system is used to support flexible and quick customization of products from a great number of parts. The application developed by (Foursa et al., 2007) is an effective instrument that can be simultaneously used by two users for rapid assembly tasks, allowing engineers and designers to work collaboratively (see Figure 7.3). Furthermore, it is directly connected to a manufacturing environment, which is able to produce the product right after customization. An XML-based language is used for the specification of all possible configurations based on a set of predefined parts. Using the VE modeler, a user effectively adds connection information by constructing a virtual product out of these parts. This is stored and, together with the part description, it forms a complete product configuration for use in successive steps of the process chain. Two users can work collaboratively together, which is more effective compared to a single user environment (see section 6.3).

Fig. 7.3. Collaborative assembly environment.

7.4 Augmented Reality in School Environments

Technological advances in the field of information and communication technologies enable innovative ways to mediate knowledge. Among them, Augmented Reality becomes increasingly a field of interest. Integrated in e-learning systems, AR provides innovative ways to transfer knowledge in education. This was the purpose of the project Augmented Reality in School Environments[25] we had in our department (Wind et al., 2007). The aim was to create an innovative teaching aid, enabling teachers to develop, with a moderate effort, new teaching practices for teaching scientific and cultural content to school classes in a comprehensive way. 3D presentations and user-friendly interaction techniques lead to a better understanding of scientific and cultural content coupled with high student motivation. The students had the possibility to interact together with the virtual objects in a virtual shared space provided by the Spinnstube® display system and thereby performed learning by doing instead of learning by reading or listening. Furthermore, the new technology promoted team work and collaboration between classes in the same school or even remotely between schools in different countries. A co-located learning environment with four pupils sharing a common work space is shown in Fig 2.3. The pupils can hand over real objects among each other on a table. The objects are augmented with 3D information using the Spinnstube® display system.

---

[25] http://www.arise-project.org; funded by the European Commission between 2006 and 2008, contract No. IST-027039

8. Conclusion

The development of the VR technology is driven by two main factors: technological advancements and end-user requirements, the latter one being more important. The appearance of new products on the one hand and new industrial requirements emerging as a result of continuously growing information flows on the other hand, require the development of new interaction techniques. Although there are no universal techniques that can be applied in any case, the experience collected by the academic community in the recent years allows developers to find appropriate solutions quickly and should always be taken into consideration before designing new 3D applications. However, more efforts are required in order to increase the maturity of 3D interfaces and to continuously update this area of knowledge taking into account the advancements of adjacent areas. This includes the achievements both in technical areas, such as tracking technologies and input device engineering, and in human factors science. Combining these areas, suitable immersive interaction methods could be developed based on thorough usability studies. Furthermore, it could be useful to evaluate the usability of interaction techniques initially designed for immersive applications in semi- or non-immersive environments, bringing it closer to our everyday life. This approach could particularly benefit desktop-based environments using large displays that not necessarily offer stereoscopic viewing. In summary, increasing technical maturity and a lot of already existing immersive interaction concepts now allow the productive use of spatial interfaces, including the extension of standard desktop systems. However, the existing concepts are still mostly isolated from each other, and the current state of the art has not yet reached the level to provide a common standard for immersive interaction.

9. References

Balakrishnan, R.; Fitzmaurice, G.; Kurtenbach, G.; Buxton, B. (2002). Creating principal 3D curves with digital tape drawing, *Proc. of the SIGCHI conf. on Human factors in computing systems: Changing our world, changing ourselves*, ACM New York, pp. 121-128. ISBN 1-58113-453-3

Balogh, T. (2006). The HoloVizio system. *Proc. of SPIE*, Vol. 6055, pp. 279-290. San Jose, CA, USA, January 2006, ISSN 0277-786X

Beckhaus, S.; Blom, K.; Haringer, M. (2007). ChairIO - the Chair-Based Interface, *In: Concepts and Technologies for Pervasive Games: A Reader for Pervasive Gaming Research*, Magerkurth, Rötzler (Ed.), Shaker Verlag, pp. 231-264, ISBN 978-3-8322-6223-5

Börner, R.; Duckstein, B.; Machui, O.; Röder, H.; Sinnig, T.; Sikora, T. (2000). A Family of Single-User Autostereoscopic Displays with Head-Tracking Capabilities. *IEEE Trans. on Circuits and Systems for Video Technology*, Vol. 10, No. 2, pp. 234-243, ISSN: 1051-8215

Bowman, D. A.; Kruijff, E.; LaViola J.J.; Poupyrev I. (2005). *3D User Interfaces: Theory and Practice*, Addison-Wesley Professional, ISBN 978-0-2017-5867-2

Bowman, D.; Hodges, L. (1997) An Evaluation of Techniques for Grabbing and Manipulating Remote Objects in Immersive Virtual Environments. *Proc. of the 1997 symposium on Interactive 3D graphics*. pp. 35-38. Providence, Rhode Island. ISBN:0-89791-884-3

Cruz-Neira, C.; Sandin, D. J.; DeFanti, T. A. (1993). Surround-screen projection-based virtual reality: the design and implementation of the CAVE. *Proc. of the 20th Annual Conf. on Computer Graphics and interactive Techniques (SIGGRAPH '93),* pp. 135-142, Anaheim, CA, USA. ISBN:0-89791-601-8

Cutler, L.D.; Fröhlich, B.; Hanrahan, P. (1997) Two-Handed Direct Manipulation on the Responsive Workbench, *Proc. of Symposium on Interactive 3D Graphics*, pp. 107-114, Providence, Rhode Island. ISBN 0-89791-884-3

D'Angelo, D.; Wesche, G.; Foursa, M.; Bogen, M. (2008). The benefits of co-located collaboration and immersion on assembly modeling in virtual environments. *Proc. of the 4th International Symposium on Advances in Visual Computing*, pp. 478-487. ISBN 978-3-540-89638-8

DeFanti T. A.; Dawe, G.; Sandin, D. J.; Schulze, J. P.; Otto, P.; Girado, J.; Küster, F.; Smarra, L.; Rao, R. (2009). The StarCAVE, a third-generation CAVE and virtual reality OptIPortal. *Future Generation Computer Systems,* Vol. 25, Issue 2, pp. 169-178. ISSN 0167-739X

Deisinger, J.; Blach, R.; Wesche, G.; Breining, R.; Simon, A. (2000). Towards immersive modeling - challenges and recommendations: A workshop analysing the needs of designers. *In Eurographics Workshop on Virtual environments,* pp. 145-156. Amsterdam. June 2000.

Dressler, A. (2007) Benutzergerechte Menügestaltung für Virtuelle Umgebungen im Expertenkontext. Diploma thesis. Technical University of Ilmenau, Germany.

Fernandes, K.J.; Raja, V.; Eyre, J. (2003) Cybersphere: the fully immersive spherical projection system. *Communications of the ACM*. Vol.46, Issue 9, pp. 141-146. ISSN 0001-0782

Fleischmann, M.; Sikora, T.; Heiden, W.; Strauss, W.; Sikora, K.; Speier, J. (1997) Virtual balance: An input device for VR environments. *Proc. of 6th Int. Conf. on Man-Machine Interactions and Intelligent Systems in Business*, pp. 20-23, Montpellier, May 1997

Forsberg, A.; Herndon, K.; Zeleznik, R. (1996). Aperture Based Selection for Immersive Virtual Environments, *Proc. of the 9th annual ACM symposium on User interface software and technology*, ACM New York, pp. 95-96. ISBN:0-89791-798-7

Foursa, M. (2004). Real-time infrared tracking system for Virtual Environments. *Proc. of the 2004 ACM SIGGRAPH int. conf. on Virtual Reality continuum and its applications in industry*. ACM New York, pp. 427-430. ISBN:1-58113-884-9

Foursa, M.; Wesche, G.; D'Angelo, D.; Bogen, M.; Herpers, R. (2008). A Two-User Virtual Environment for Rapid Assembly of Product Models within an Integrated Process Chain. *Proc. of the X Symposium on Virtual and Augmented Reality*. May 2008, Joao Pessoa, Brazil. pp. 143-150. ISBN 857669167-1

Foursa, M.; Wesche G. (2007). Movement-based interaction and event management in virtual environments with optical tracking systems. *Proc. of the 12th Int. Conf. on Human-Computer Interaction. Lecture Notes in Computer Science.* Springer Berlin/Heidelberg. Vol.4552/2007, pp. 615-624. ISBN 978-3-540-73108-5

Fröhlich, B.; Blach, R.; Stefani, O.; Hochstrate, J.; Hoffmann, J.; Kluger, K.; Bues M. (2005) Implementing Multi-Viewer Stereo Displays. *Proc. of 13th Int. Conf. in Central Europe on Computer Graphics, Visualization and Computer Vision*, pp.139-146. ISBN 80-903100-7-9

Fröhlich, B.; Plate, J. (2000). The cubic mouse: a new device for three-dimensional input. *Proc. of the SIGCHI Conf. on Human Factors in Computing Systems.* ACM New York. pp. 526-531. ISBN:1-58113-216-6

Guiard, Y. (1987) Asymmetric division of labor in human skilled bimanual action: The kinematic chain as a model, *Journal of Motor Behaviour.* Vol. 19, No.4, pp. 486-517. ISSN 0022-2895

Igarashi, T. (2003) Freeform User Interfaces for Graphical Computing, *Proc. of the 3rd International Symposium on Smart Graphics, Lecture Notes in Computer Science,* Springer Berlin/Heidelberg, Vol. 2733, pp. 15-43, ISSN 0302-9743

Iwata, H.; Yano, H.; Fukushima, H.; Noma, H. (2005) CirculaFloor [locomotion interface]. *IEEE Computer Graphics and Applications,* Vol.25, Issue: 1, pp. 64-67. ISSN: 0272-1716

Jones, A.; McDowall, I.; Yamada, H.; Bolas, M. & Debevec, P. (2007). An interactive 360° light field display. *Int. Conf. on Computer Graphics and Interactive Techniques, ACM SIGGRAPH 2007 emerging technologies,* San Diego, CA, USA. Art. No.13

Krüger, W.; Bohn, C. A.; Fröhlich, B.; Schüth, H.; Strauss, W. & Wesche, G. (1995). The Responsive Workbench: A virtual work environment. *IEEE Computer,* Vol. 28, No. 7. pp. 42-48. ISSN: 0018-9162

Kuriyama, S. (1994). Surface modelling with an irregular network of curves via sweeping and blending. *Computer-Aided Design,* Vol. 26, No. 8, pp. 597-606, ISSN 0010-4485

Meyer, K.; Applewhite H. L.; Biocca F. A. (1992). A Survey of Position Trackers. *Presence: Teleoperators and Virtual Environments,* Vol. 1, No. 2, pp. 173-200. ISSN 1054-7460

Mine, M.; Brooks, F.; Sequin, C. (1997) Moving Objects in Space: Exploiting Proprioception in Virtual Environment Interaction, *Proc. of the 24th annual conf. on Computer graphics and interactive techniques.* ACM Press/Addison-Wesley Publishing. pp. 19-26. ISBN 0-89791-896-7

Olwal, A.; Feiner, S. (2003). The Flexible Pointer: An Interaction Technique for Augmented and Virtual Reality, *In Conf. Supplement of ACM UIST 2003,* Vancouver, BC, November 2-5, pp. 81-82.

Perales F.; Buades J.; Mas R.; Varona X.; Gonzalez M.; Suescun A.; Aguinaga I.; Foursa M.; Zissis G.; Touman M.; Mendoza R. (2004) A New Human Motion Analysis System Using Biomechanics 3D models. *Int. Conf. on Computer Graphics and Interactive Techniques. ACM SIGGRAPH 2004 Posters.* ACM New York, p. 83. ISBN 1-58113-896-2

Pintaric T. & Kaufmann H. (2007) Affordable Infrared-Optical Pose Tracking for Virtual and Augmented Reality. *Proc. of IEEE VR Workshop on Trends and Issues in Tracking for Virtual Environments.* Shaker Verlag. pp. 44 – 51. ISBN: 978-3-8322-5967-9

Plate, J.; Tirtasana, M.; Carmona, R.; Fröhlich, B. (2002). Octreemizer: a hierarchical approach for interactive roaming through very large volumes. *Proc. of the ACM symposium on Data Visualisation,* pp. 53-60. ISBN:1-58113-536-X

Plate, J.; Holtkämper, T.; Fröhlich, B. (2007). A Flexible Multi-Volume Shader Framework for Arbitrarily Intersecting Multi-Resolution Datasets. *IEEE Trans. on Visualization and Computer Graphics,* Vol. 13, No. 6, pp. 1584-1591. ISSN:1077-2626

Poupyrev, I.; Billinghurst, M.; Weghorst, S.; Ichikawa, T. (1996) The Go-Go Interaction Technique: Non-linear Mapping for Direct Manipulation in VR. *Proc. of the 9th annual ACM symposium on User interface software and technology,* pp. 79-80, Seattle, Washington, ISBN:0-89791-798-7

Riege, K.; Holtkämper, T.; Wesche, G.; Fröhlich, B. (2006). The Bent Pick Ray: An Extended Pointing Technique for Multi-User Interaction. *Proc. of 3D User Interfaces,* pp. 62-65, Alexandria, VA, USA. ISBN: 1-4244-0225-5

Sandin, D. J.; Margolis, T.; Ge, J.; Girado, J.; Peterka, T.; DeFanti, T. A. (2005). The Varrier™ autostereoscopic virtual reality display. *ACM Trans. on Graphics, Proc. of ACM SIGGRAPH 2005*, Vol.24, Issue 3, pp. 894-903, ACM New York, ISSN:0730-0301

Schkolne, S.; Prütt, M.; Schröder, P. (2002). Surface drawing: Creating Organic 3D Shapes with the Hand and Tangible Tools. *Proc. of the SIGCHI conf. on Human factors in computing systems*, pp. 261-268. ACM New York. ISBN 1-58113-327-8

Simon, A.; Göbel, M. (2002). The i-Cone - A Panoramic Display System for Virtual Environments, *Proc. of the 10th Pacific Conf. on Computer Graphics and Applications.* pp. 3-7, ISBN 0-7695-1784-6

Simon, A.; Fröhlich, B. (2003). The YoYo: A Handheld Device Combining Elastic and Isotonic Input. *Proc. of IFIP TC13 Int. Conf. on Human-Computer Interaction*, pp. 303-310, Zurich, September 2003. IOS Press. ISBN 1586033638

Simon, A.; Doulis, M. (2004). NOYO: 6DOF elastic rate control for virtual environments. *Proc. of the ACM Symposium on Virtual Reality Software and Technology*, pp. 178-181, Hong Kong, November 2004. ACM New York. ISBN:1-58113-907-1

Springer, J.; Beck, S.; Weiszig, F.; Reiners, D.; Fröhlich, B. (2007) Multi-Frame Rate Rendering and Display, *Proc. of IEEE Virtual Reality Conf.*, Charlotte, NC, pp. 195-202. ISBN: 1-4244-0906-3

Tramberend, H.; Hasenbrink, F.; Eckel, G.; Lechner, U.; Göbel, M. (1997). CyberStage - an advanced virtual environment. *ERCIM News No. 31*, pp. 22-23. ISSN: 0926-4981

Welch G.; Foxlin, E. (2002) Motion Tracking: No Silver Bullet, but a Respectable Arsenal. *IEEE Computer Graphics and Applications*. Vol.22, Issue 6, pp. 24-38. ISSN: 0272-1716

Wesche, G. (2003). The ToolFinger: supporting complex direct manipulation in virtual environments, *Proc. of the Eurographics workshop on virtual environments 2003*, pp. 39-45, Zurich, Switzerland. ISBN 1-58113-686-2

Wesche, G. (2004). A User Interface for Free-Form Shape Design at the Responsive Workbench. *Trans. of the ASME, Journal of Computing and Information Science in Engineering*, Vol. 4, No. 3, pp. 178-185. ISSN 1530-9827

Wesselink, W.; Veltkamp, R. C. (1995). Interactive design of constrained variational curves. *Computer-Aided Geometric Design*, Vol. 12, No. 5, pp. 533-546, ISSN 0167-8396

Wind, J.; Riege, K.; Bogen, M. (2007). Spinnstube: A seated augmented reality display system, *Proc. of immersive projection technology workshop of Eurographics symposium on virtual environments*, pp. 17-23. Weimar, Germany. ISBN: 978-3-905674-02-6

11

Integration of Speech Recognition-based Caption Editing System with Presentation Software

Kohtaroh Miyamoto, Masakazu Takizawa and Takashi Saito
Accessibility Center, Tokyo Research Laboratory, IBM Japan
Japan

1. Introduction

1.1 Background

Recently an increasing amount of e-Learning material including audio and presentation slides is being provided through the Internet or private networks referred to as intranets. Many hearing impaired people and senior citizens require captioning to understand such content. Captioning is a vital part of accessibility and there are national standards such as "WCAG 2.0" [1], "JIS X8341-3 5-4-d" and also laws such as "Section 508 of the Disabilities Act" [2] to assure accessibility to publicly available contents.
There are much on-going efforts for automated speech recognition enhancement, but here we will focus on the post editing to assure accurate captioning for digital archives. We introduce the method of "IBM Caption Editing System with Presentation Integration (hereafter CESPI)" which is an extension to IBM Caption Editing System (hereafter CES) [3]. CESPI completely includes all the functions within CES, but is further extended to include the presentation integration functions.
CES encapsulates the speech recognition engine for transcribing audio into text (CES Recorder) and also allows various editing features for error correction (CES Master and CES Client). As shown in Figure 1, CESPI integrates presentation software in various ways for both the CES Recorder and the CES Master System. Figure 2 shows a sample output of CESPI which composes of video, captioning and presentation image slide show.

[1] See http://www.w3.org/TR/WCAG20/.
[2] See http://www.section508.gov/.
[3] See http://www.alphaworks.ibm.com/tech/ces/.

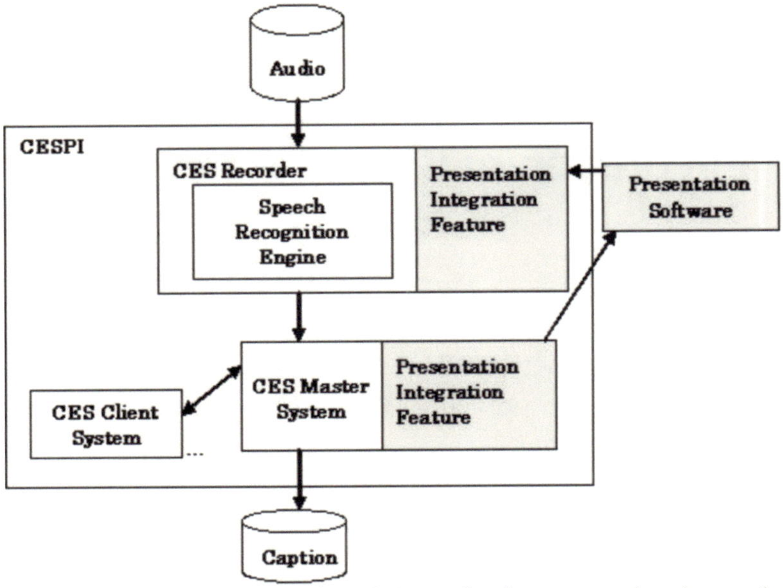

Fig. 1. CESPI receives audio input and CES Recorder by encapsulated speech recognition engine, transcribes the audio into text. CES Master System and CES Client System allows collaborative editing. CESPI adds a presentation integration feature to both CES Recorder and CES Master System.

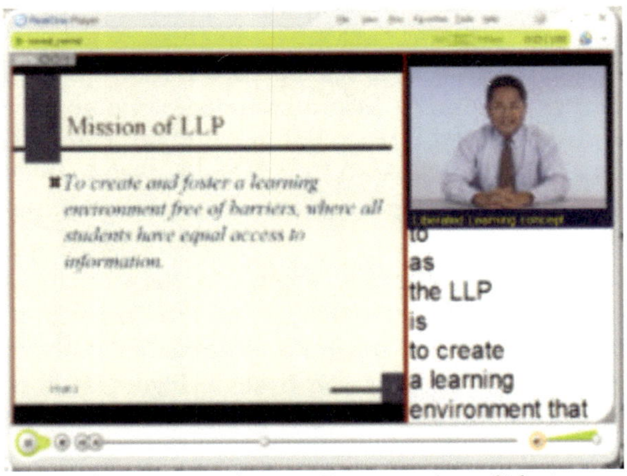

Fig. 2. The sample output of CESPI is shown. Presentation slide image is on the left hand side, video image is on the upper right hand and the caption is on the lower right hand side.

1.2 Previous Methods

Automatic Speech Recognition (ASR) engines have improved its accuracy[4] over time. And there are many ASR related programs being introduced. Most noticeable is to use the ASR

[4] McCowan et. al. (2004) discusses in detail how error rates should be handled for speech recognition results.

for University lecture transcription. Bain et. al. (2005) introduces the ASR technology and how they are being adopted to Universities. Wald & Bain (2008) introduces the Liberated Learning Project, Kheir & Way (2007) introduces the VUST project, Hewitt et. al. (2008) introduces the SpeakView project. Itoh et. al. (2008) introduces the Join Project which is based on CES.

Also there are some limited efforts to use ASR for transcribing television broadcasting. Lambourne et. al. (2004) and Imai et. al. (2005) discusses the difficulties in adapting ASR to broadcasting since captioning must be completely accurate. Making corrections to the ASR transcriptions in near real-time introduces many challenges.

While most of these programs focus on the real-time transcription, there is also a strong request to transcribe the digital archives for lecturers, videos, etc. In order to create such content, it is necessary to correct the transcribed errors. Making corrections to edit these errors is a very labor intensive task (hereafter we call this task caption editing, and the system to perform the caption editing as caption editing system). Therefore our primary focus is to provide a caption editing system which is highly efficient to the user.

Goto et. al. (2007) introduces PodCastle [5] which is a service available on the Internet to transcribe podcast content by ASR. And users can make corrections to erroneous words basically by selecting from ASR candidates. Also Munteanu et. al. (2008) introduces a wiki-like caption editing feature to enhance the Webcast system.

1.3 Our Prior Work

We have introduced (Arakawa et. al. 2006) our CES technology and how it has been adopted in Universities. We previously introduced (Miyamoto 2005, Miyamoto & Takizawa 2009) how the system can help collaborate between different roles of editors. Specifically, the master editor who is responsible for the final output uses CES Master Editing System while the client who may be any novice user uses the CES Client Editing System and both are connected by network. We also showed how the caption editing steps can be improved using three major concepts. The three concepts were "complete audio synchronization", "completely automatic audio control", and "status marking". As a result, we showed 30.7% improvement in caption editing cost.

In CES, the output phrases (as candidate caption lines) from the voice recognition engine are laid out vertically as individual lines along with timestamps. "Complete audio synchronization" means that the keyboard focus always matches the audio replay position. For example, if the audio is playing the time position of one position (e.g. 5 seconds) while the keyboard input focus is on a different position (e.g. 10 seconds), it is quite obvious that it would make it extremely difficult to make corrections to the erroneous words while listening to the audio. CES plays the audio in synchronization with the associated caption lines. This means the audio focus always matches the caption line focus.

The second concept of "completely automatic audio control", means that the audio is fully controlled automatically by the system. Users are not required to "replay" and "stop" the audio manually (usually a huge number of times). As the editing begins, the focus is set on the initial series of words, and the audio which is associated to that portion is replayed automatically. By comparing the audio with the transcribed words, user needs to determine if the words are correct. If it is, the user can press the enter key to move focus to the next

[5] See http://podcastle.jp/

series of words, but if not the user needs to make the correction. The audio will be repeatedly replayed over again to urge the user for action. The replay stops automatically when the user types any key since it is usually annoying to hear the audio during typing. A long pause in typing will automatically restart the audio again. As a result the user does not need to operate the audio replay at all and he/she can solely concentrate on making corrections. In writing it may seem quite obvious, currently we identify that CES is the only system which has this feature.

The last concept is "status marking". The unverified lines are automatically distinguished from the corrected lines as shown in Figure 3, in CES, each caption line includes a button which is used to mark the status of each caption line. The mark also corresponds to the color of the font. The marks have several useful meanings, but basically these marks make it easier to keep track of how far the caption editing has progressed. This is very important in many cases because it is required to keep track of the caption editing work progress. And then estimate the projected finishing time and also it is needed to take appropriate action in cases such that the target deadline may be missed.

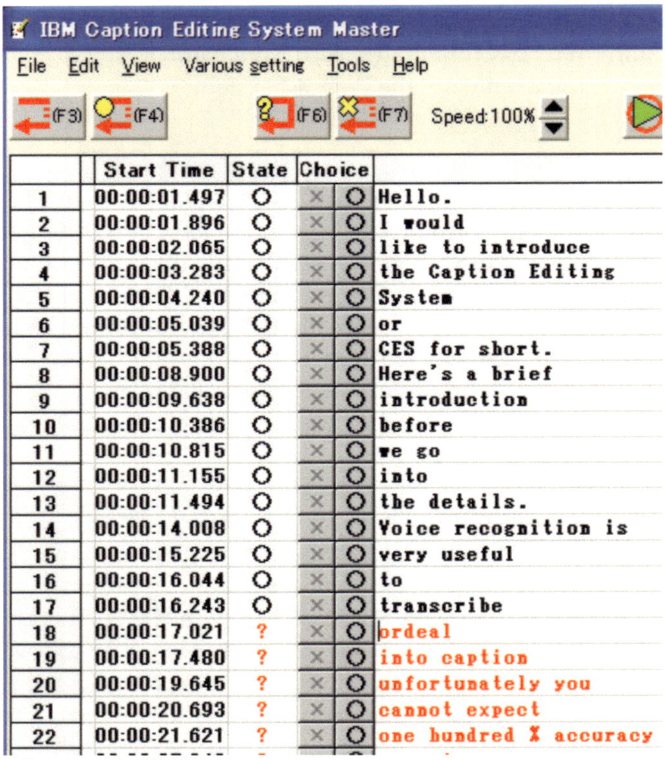

Fig. 3. The sample image of CES is shown.

Here in this example, all of the caption lines are initially marked as "unverified" (question mark "?"). As the corrections proceed the flags are automatically converted to "determined" (circles). Here, caption lines 1 to 17 are correct since they were either correctly transcribed by the voice recognition engine or they were corrected using the editing feature in CES. Caption lines 18 and later are still unverified.

Figure 4 illustrates how the system works from the (caption) editor's perspective. The audio is played automatically, and so the editor focuses on the audio. As soon as the editor begins to type the audio stops automatically. But when the editor is not sure and pauses the typing, the audio automatically starts to play again. The editor makes the necessary changes (and hits the enter key) then the keyboard and audio focus automatically moves to the next target line.

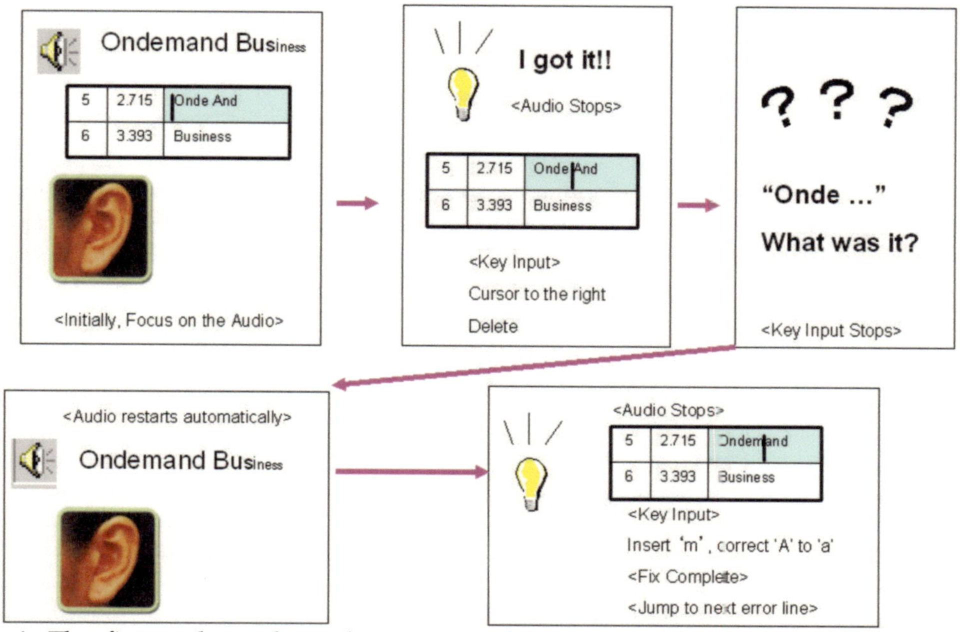

Fig. 4. The figure shows how the caption editing task using the CES. All the audio processing is automatic and user merely needs to focus on making the necessary correction.

We also showed how external scripts can help reduce the caption editing work. The experimentation results show that for example, when the recognition rate is 60.9%, editing total hours decreased by 35% (Miyamoto 2006) and the method of matching the script with the erroneous transcription results are introduced (Miyamoto 2008) as well. Furthermore, we introduced a hybrid caption editing system (Miyamoto et. al. 2007) which integrates "line unit type" (which is efficient in editing in relatively high speech recognition rate situations) with "word processor type" (which is efficient in editing in relatively low recognition rate situations). The input strings to the "word processor type" subsystem is matched to the "line unit type" subsystem. As a result of experimentation in a various speech recognition rate conditions for caption editing efficiency against previous caption editing methods, the hybrid system shows significant advantage in number of interaction and editing time. Another technique we introduced (Arakawa, et. al. 2008) the technique to make real-time automated error corrections by using confidence scores of speech recognition and automated matching algorithms of sources such as text in presentation software or scripts.

Our work goes beyond the efficiency of caption editing and also discloses the method (Miyamoto & Ikawa 2008) to safely eliminate and dynamically distribute confidential

information from multimedia content with audio, caption, video and presentation materials. In this chapter, we focus on the integration of Presentation software with the CES to increate the efficiency of caption editing. Presentation software provides many useful features to easily create effective e-Learning contents by the following 2 steps.
1) Prepare presentation file by combination of text, pictures, visual layout, and any other provided feature.
2) Make oral presentation using the slide show feature of the presentation software. At the same time record the movie by any video camera and/or oral presentation audio.

2. Preliminary Survey and Investigation

We conducted a survey to see whether the combination of video with audio, captions, and presentation slides (hereafter "multimedia composite") is helpful in understanding the content. We created 4 multimedia composites, and then allowed a total of 80 senior citizens and people with disabilities to view any content of interest freely. After viewing, we administered a survey, and asked whether the multimedia composite is useful. The results as shown in Table 1, showed that 66.3% found the multimedia composite either "Strongly Agree" or "Agree", irrelevant of age group. So we concluded that a multimedia composite is very useful for better understanding in e-Learning.

Age Group	Strongly Agree	Agree	Disagree	Strongly Disagree
20s	0	4	0	0
30s	0	1	1	0
40s	0	3	2	0
50s	0	6	6	0
60s	2	9	6	0
70s	3	21	10	0
80 and higher	2	2	2	0
Total	7	46	27	0

Table 1. Usefulness of Multimedia Composite

Next, we conducted an investigation to see whether multimedia composites are captioned. We searched through the internet for multimedia composites, and found that out of 100 composites, only 21 were adequately captioned, 1 merely provided transcript text. (Conditions were web sites free of charge, max of 5 composites per domain.) It seems that the main reason for this low rate of captioning is due to the high labor costs. There are several approaches for captioning, but here we focus on using speech recognition technology. Unfortunately the voice recognition accuracy rate is still not 100%, and therefore there is still a need for an effective caption editing system to correct the errors.
The conclusion of our preliminary survey and investigation is that in order to reduce the costs of captioning content with audio and presentation slides, there is a strong need for an effective caption editing tool. The presentation slides are mostly created by commercial presentation software. In this paper, we focus on a speech recognition error correction system which integrates a caption editing system with presentation software.

3. Problems and Apparatus

Based on the preliminary survey and investigation, we investigated the available caption editing tools that generate captions from audio, and identified 3 major problems. The three major problems between CES and presentation software were identified as "Content Layout Definitions", "Editing Focus Linkage", and "Exporting to Speaker Notes". To address these problems, we extended our Caption Editing System (CES) to integrate it with Microsoft PowerPoint, creating our new Caption Editing System with Presentation Integration (CESPI). The architecture in terms of code interface is shown in Figure 5.

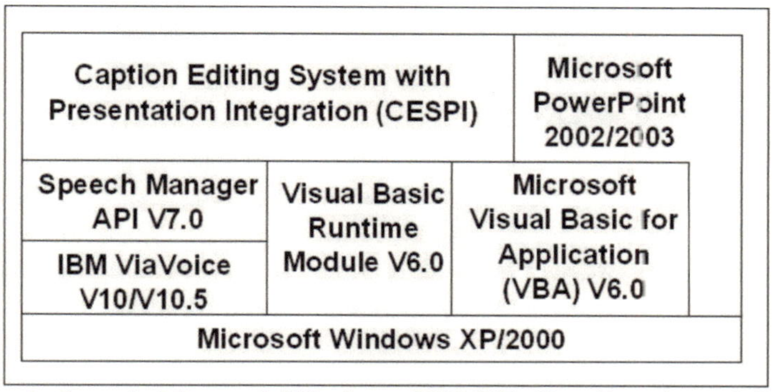

Fig. 5. The base platform is Microsoft Windows 2000/XP. User Interface of CESPI is built on Visual Basic V6.0. IBM ViaVoice engine control is implemented by Microsoft Visual C++ 6.0. The interface between ViaVoice and CESPI is Speech Manager API (SMAPI) V7.0. Also, the interface between CESPI and Microsoft PowerPoint is Visual Basic for Application (VBA) V6.0.

Finally we conducted a field test to see if the real-time transcription accuracy of state-of-the-art speech recognition can show satisfactory results. We transcribed 11 University lectures in real-time and as a result obtained 81.8% accuracy. Unfortunately we have found that the speech recognition accuracy does not necessary reach the satisfaction level. There are many observations but we received many comments which required the speech recognition rate to be 85% at the least and preferably 90% for satisfactory level. So we conclude that it is required to seek a human computer transcription method to raise the accuracy (obviously without raising the cost by relying on many human resources).

3.1 Content Layout Definition

A multimedia composite consists of several visual components such as video, presentation images, and captions. These components needs to be laid out effectively in position and size according to such parameters as font face, font size, number of maximum characters per line, presentation image size, vice image size, resolution, overall size, and overlapping options. (Figure 6 shows a bad example of by excessive space, overlap, cut off.) CES (and CESPI) supports the RealOne Player by SMIL[6] format and also Windows Media Player by SAMI format.

---

6 See http://www.w3.org/AudioVideo/.

The task of effectively laying out these components manually can be quite time consuming. CESPI solves this problem by automatically laying out these components based on each parameter. As shown in Figure 7, CESPI also provides a layout customization feature which allows the user to easily change the details of the layout.

Fig. 6. The figure shows a sample of ill defined layout, where presentation image is surrounded by excessive empty space. Video and caption overlap with the presentation image. The caption is being cut off by the window boundary.

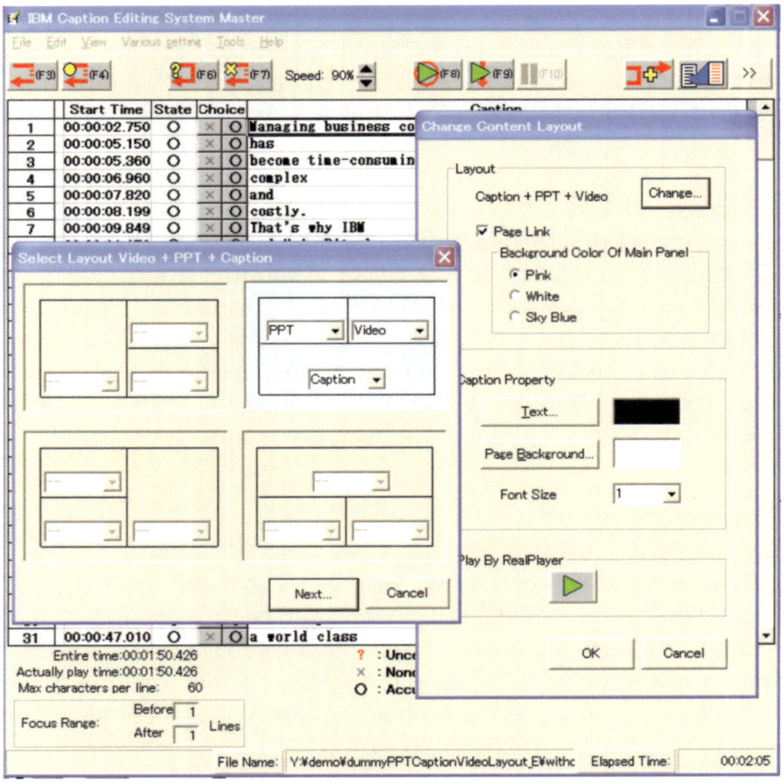

Fig. 7. The figure shows the Change Content Layout dialog on the left hand side and the Select Layout Video + PPT + Caption dialog with the focus on the right hand side

3.2 Editing Focus Linkage

While editing the captions of certain multimedia composites, it is useful to reference special terminology used in the presentation slides. Because caption editing tools and presentation software were separate applications, the operating system only allows one application to have the focus at one time. Therefore it was necessary to frequently switch the focus between these two applications. Also, the user had to change to the corresponding slide pages manually. CESPI solves this problem by automatically laying out the captions, page images, and page text in a single application window, which makes it easier to view and edit the captions. CESPI also automatically interlinks between the caption timestamps and the presentation page. In other words, the presentation page always corresponds to the focused caption. (Figure 8 shows the actual user interface of the CESPI Master Editing Subsystem.)

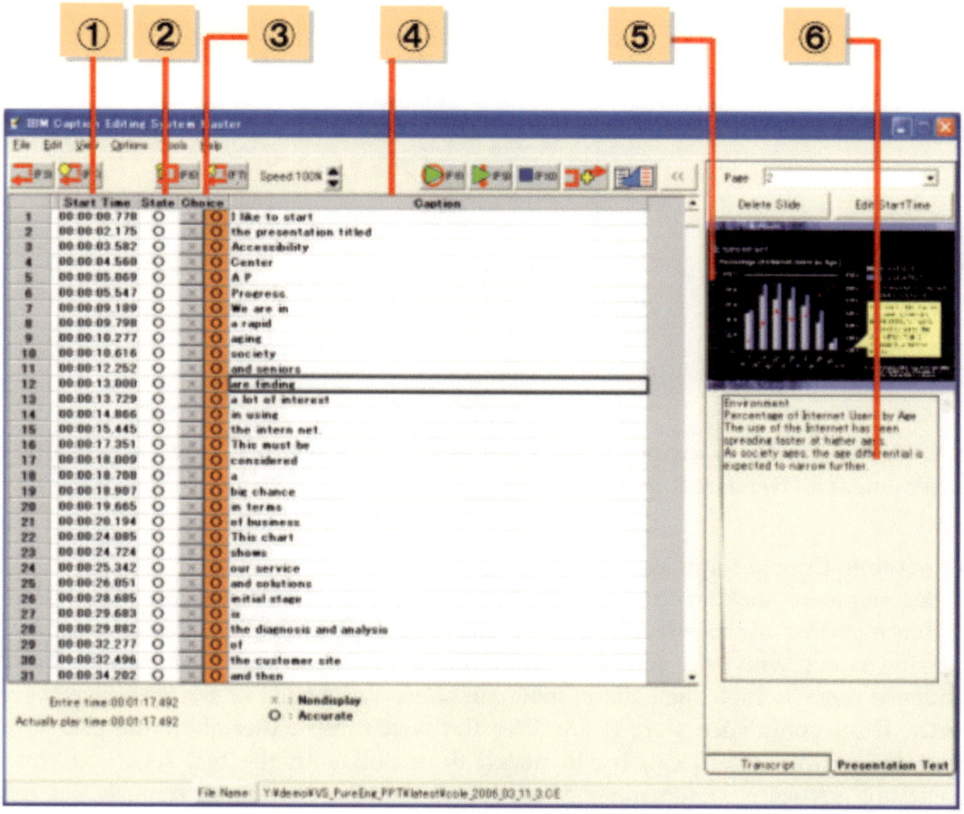

Fig. 8. On the left hand side basically shows the "Caption Line Text" (start time, state, choice, and caption). "Start Time" pointed to by the "1" represents the 0 based timestamp which to display the caption. "State" pointed to by the "2". "Choice" is pointed to by the "3". "Caption" is pointed to by the "4".On the right hand side basically shows the "Presentation Page". "Presentation Image" is pointed to by the "5" and retrieved text is pointed to by the "6".

3.3 Speaker Notes Export

Using presentation software, a speaker may define narrative notes for each presentation page (the "speaker notes"). In many cases, a single presentation package used by one presenter will be later reused by another presenter. In such cases, since the captions and speaker notes are similar, it is efficient to use the initial caption. Previously, in order to export captions to speaker notes, manual operations such as moving to the proper page and then performing copy and paste operations were required. Therefore as illustrated in Figure 9, CESPI has a capability for automatically exporting the corresponding page of the caption into the speaker notes of the presentation package.

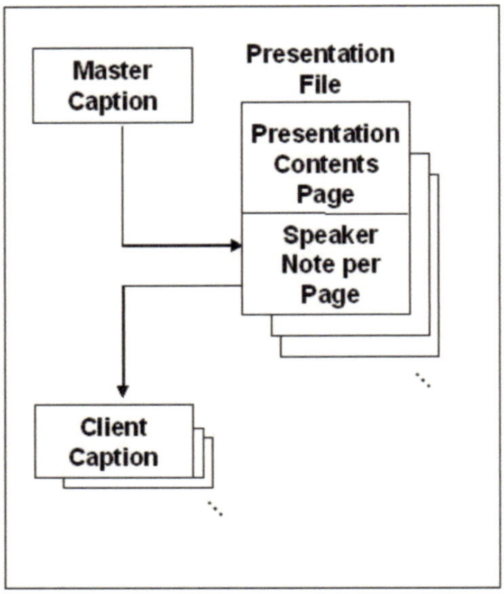

Fig. 9. Master caption is exported into the speaker notes portion of the presentation. The speaker notes can be referenced to the client caption.

3.4 Real-time Checker and Matching

Our technique to make automated error corrections (Arakawa, et. al. 2008) is to use confidence scores of speech recognition and also matching algorithms (to match the transcribe result with text retrieved from presentation software). Theoretically if the confidence score is high then the system can show the results of the speech recognition directly. If the confidence score is low then the system can either allow the user to make corrections or the system can try to match the result with the text retrieved from the presentation software. Unfortunately we found that the confidence score is not reliable enough to be able to detect each word's correctness by high accuracy. So here we would like to propose making use of a human resource checker. The human resource checker merely flags the transcribed result as correct or incorrect. It needs to be noted that human resource (unlike computer systems) can sometimes be very slow in processing their assigned job (which can result in a long delay). Therefore the system assures real-time captioning presence by routing the words to the matching subsystem by a higher degree as the captioning presence starts to delay. Finally, when the captioning is presented the words which were automatically corrected by the matching will be shown in blue colour and italic.

4. Results

An experiment was performed to measure the editing time under the following conditions.
1. Editors are to use CES and CESPI for an approximately 30 minutes of content each.
2. It is known that as you get used to 5 editors who already have enough experience with CES and CESPI were chosen to eliminate any inconsistencies due to the learning curve effect(Barloff 1971).
3. Each editor was also assigned different portions of the content for CES and CESPI so that memory from the previous content will not take effect.
4. Task consists of correcting all the speech recognition errors, laying out the multimedia composite without each overlapping or excessive blank space, and exporting the speaker notes to the appropriate page. (Conditions are shown in Table 2.)

Category	Conditions
Window Size	800x460
Component Layout Position (Video)	Right Upper Position
Component Layout Position (Presentation Image)	Left Upper Position
Component Layout Position (Caption)	Bottom
Caption Font Charset	x-sjis
Caption Font Face	osaka
Caption Font Color	black
Caption Font Size	+3
Other Conditions-1	No Excessive Empty Space
Other Conditions-2	No Overlap
Other Conditions-3	No Cutoff

Table 2. Various Conditions for the Experiment

As shown in Table 3, the results showed that CESPI provided a 37.6% improvement in total editing time.

	CESPI	CES
Speech Recognition Rate	81.4%	80.8%
Average Content Time	28min 24sec	27min 58 sec
Number of Characters[7]	9240	9221
Total Average Editing Time[8]	93min 46sec	127 min 2 sec
Editing Time Average per Content Time	3.30	4.54
Total Efficiency in Percentage	37.6%	(N/A)

Table 3. Result of the Experiment

Figure 10 shows the ratio of time which accounted for the saved time by "Content Layout Definition", "Editing Focus Linkage", and "Speaker Notes Export". It can be seen that

[7] Mainly Japanese characters, number includes punctuation marks.
[8] Does not include the common initial time required to listen to the whole content.

Content Layout Definition accounted for approximately half of the time, while Editing Focus Linkage follows and then Speaker Notes Export made the slightest difference.

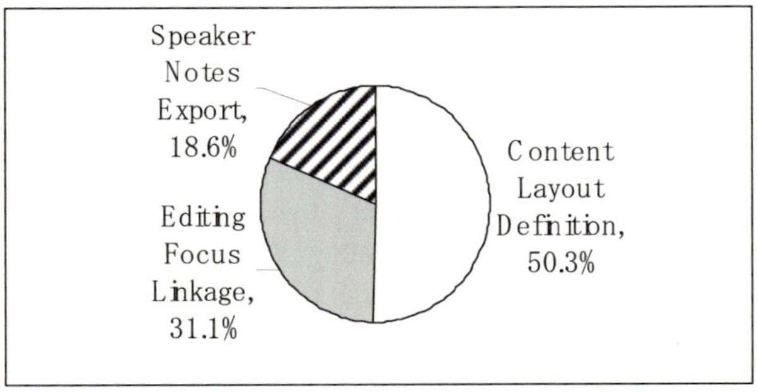

Fig. 10. Figure shows that out of the improvement of editing time shown in Table 2, 50.3% accounted for Content Layout Definition, 31.1% accounted for Editing Focus Linkage, 18.6% for Speaker Notes Export.

Content Layout Definition saved much time for CESPI since content layout required much trial and error type of editing for CES. CESPI practically required almost no time since layout can be done automatically.

5. Summary

The three major problems between CES and presentation software were identified as "Content Layout Definitions", "Editing Focus Linkage", and "Exporting to Speaker Notes". This paper has shown how CESPI solves each of these problems. And experiment showed a 37.6% efficiency improvement compared with the previous method. Among the 3 items "Content Layout Definition" accounted for the most improvement in time, followed by "Editing Focus Linkage" and "Speaker Notes Export" came last.
Currently CESPI only supports Microsoft PowerPoint as the choice of presentation software. Future work item will be to support other presentation software.

6. Acknowledgements

Many people have participated in preliminary survey, so we would like to thank all those people for sparing their time.

7. References

Arakawa, K.; Miyamoto, K.& Negishi, K.(2006). Caption Editing System for University-Level Students with Hearing Disabilities, Closing the Gap 2006 Conference

Arakawa, K.; Miyamoto, K.& Ohgane, T.(2008). Caption Correction Device, United States Patent Application 20080040111, International Business Machines Corporation

Bain, K.; Basson, S.; Faisman, A.& Kanevsky, D.(2005). Accessibility, Transcription, and Access Everywhere, IBM Systems Journal: Accessibility Vol. 44 No. 3

Baloff, N.(1971). Extensions of the Learning Curve-Some Empirical Results. Operations Research Quarterly, pp.22-44

Goto, M.; Ogata, J.& Eto, K.(2007). PodCastle: A Web 2.0 Approach to Speech Recognition Research. in: Proceedings of the 8th Annual Conference of the International Speech Communication Association, Interspeech 2007, pp.2397-2400

Harvey, A.(2004). Nevada Legislature Develops Web Captioning System for the Hearing Impaired While technology can provide some elegant solutions, cost is still a major factor, National Association of Legislative Information Technology Newsletter

Hewitt, J.; Lyon, J.; Britton, C.& Mellor, B.(2005). SpeakView: Live Captioning of Lectures, in: Proceedings of Universal Access in Human Computer Interaction Vol. 8, HCI International 2005

Imai, T.; Sato, S.; Homma, S.; Onoe, K.& Kobayashi, A.(2007). Online Speech Detection and Dual-Gender Speech Recognition for Captioning Broadcast News, IEICE Trans. Inf. & Syst., Vol. E90-D, No. 8, pp.1286-1291

Itoh, E.; Asahi, Y.& Aoki, T.(2008). Lecture Assisting Used by Speech Recognition for the University Students with Disabilities - JOIN Project, Trace of 3 years, in :Proceedings of Rehabilitation Engineering Society of Japan, RESJA 2008, pp.241-242

Kheir, R.& Way, T.(2007). Inclusion of deaf students in computer science classes using real-time speech transcription, in: Proceedings of the 12th annual SIGCSE conference on Innovation and technology in computer science education ITiCSE '07, Volume 39 Issue 3, pp.261-265

Lambourne, A.; Hewitt, J.; Lyon, C.& Warren S.(2004). Speech-Based Real-Time Subtitling Services, International Journal of Speech Technology, Volume 7, Number 4, pp.269 - 279

McCowan, I.; Moore, D.; Dines J.; Gatica-Perez D.; Flynn M.; Wellner M.& Boulard H.(2004). On the Use of Information Retrieval Measures for Speech Recognition Evaluation, Institut Dalle Molle d'Intelligence Artificielle Perceptive IDIAP Research Report 04-73, pp.1-13

Miyamoto, K.(2005). Effective Master Client Closed Caption Editing System for Wide Range Workforce, in: Proceedings of the Universal Access in Human Computer Interaction Vol. 7, HCI International 2005

Miyamoto, K.(2006). Reduction of Caption Editing Using Supplemental Text Information, Technology & Persons with Disabilities Conference CSUN 2006

Miyamoto, K.; Arakawa, K.& Saito, T.(2007). Hybrid Caption Editing System by Integrating Line Unit Type and Word Processor Type. IEICE Transactions on Information and Systems, Vol. J90-D No. 3, pp.673-682

Miyamoto, K.& Ikawa, Y.(2008). Apparatus and method for rendering contents, containing sound data, moving image data and static image data, harmless, USPTO Application #: 20080262841, International Business Machines Corporation

Miyamoto, K.& Shoji, M.(2008). Displaying text of speech in synchronization with the speech, United States Patent 20050203750, International Business Machines Corporation

Miyamoto, K.& Takizawa, M.(2009). User Efficient Speech Recognition-based Caption Editing System Technology & Persons with Disabilities Conference CSUN 2009

Munteanu, C.; Baecker, R.& Penn, G.(2008). Collaborative Editing for Improved Usefulness and Usability of Transcript-Enhanced Webcasts. in: Proceedings of CHI 2008, ACM Press, pp.373-382

Wald, M.& Bain, K.(2008). Universal access to communication and learning: the role of automatic speech recognition, in: Universal Access in the Information Society, Vol. 6, No4, pp.435-447

Interaction Paradigms for Bare-Hand Interaction with Large Displays at a Distance

Kelvin Cheng and Masahiro Takatsuka
HxI Initiative, NICTA & ViSLAB, The University of Sydney
Australia

1. Introduction

Large displays are now more widely used than ever before, yet the computer mouse remains the most common pointing tool for large displays users. The main drawback of the mouse is that it is only a tool for mapping hand movements to on-screen cursor movements, for the manipulation of on-screen objects. Such an indirect mapping is due to differences between input space (usually a horizontal table used by the mouse) and output space (display) (Hinckley, 2003). This indirectness enlarges the Gulf of Execution and the Gulf of Evaluation (Norman, 1986), and thus reduces users' freedom and efficiency.

Much effort has been made on making this interaction more natural and more intuitive for users. One common approach is to use our own hand as the input method, making pointing as easy as pointing to real world objects. Computer vision can be used to detect and track user's pointing gesture and is an active area of research. Computer vision based systems have the advantages of being a non-invasive input technique and do not require a physically touchable surface, which is highly suitable for interaction at a distance or hygienically demanding environments such as public spaces. However, while previous works seemingly employ a similar interaction model, the actual model itself has not been well researched.

This chapter examine the underlying interaction models for bare-hand interaction with large display systems from a distance. Theories and techniques that make interaction with computer display as easy as pointing to real world objects are also explored. We will also investigate the feasibility of using low-cost monocular computer vision to implement such a system.

2. Background & Previous Work

We start off by reviewing important work historically and investigate significant related research in this area and take a close look at the current trend in immersive interaction and the state of the art techniques that researchers around the world have proposed to improve interactions with large surfaces. We focus on non-intrusive techniques where users do not need to wear or hold any special devices, nor will there be wires attached. Users only need to approach the surface and use their bare hand. Most of these use some kind of sensors or computer vision to detect the hand. We will also present literature that has adopted hand pointing as one of the main approaches to selection.

2.1 Sensitive Surfaces

DiamondTouch (Dietz & Leigh, 2001) is a touch sensitive table from Mitsubishi Electric Research Laboratories (MERL) that can detect and identify multiple and simultaneous users' touches. Antennas are place under the surface of the table each with a different electrical signal. When the user touches the table, a small electrical circuit is completed, by going from a transmitter to the table surface to the user's finger touching the surface, through the user's body and onto a receiver on the users' chair. Users must be seated to operate this device.

SmartSkin (Rekimoto, 2002) is a similar technique proposed by Rekimoto. Instead than using electricity, it relies on capacitive sensing by laying a mash of transmitter and receiver electrodes on the surface. When a conductive object (such as the human hand) comes near the surface, the signal at the crossing point is decreased. This also enables the detection of the multiple hand position. They are also able to detect the hand even when it is not actually touching the surface.

More recently, multi-touch techniques have been widely researched. One example is the use of frustrated total internal reflection (FTIR) to detect multiple fingers on a tabletop display (Han, 2005). This technique makes use of the fact that when light is travelling inside a medium (e.g. acrylic pane), while undergoing total internal reflection, an external material (e.g. human finger) is encountered causing light to escape from the medium. An external camera can capture exactly where the light escapes, thereby detecting position of the fingertip. Multiple fingertips can thus be detected at the same time

2.2 Tracking hands above surfaces

Computer vision can also be used to track different parts of the human user. The most notable is the implementation of DigitalDesk (Wellner, 1993) by Wellner in 1993 who used a projector and a camera looking down from above a normal desk. It allows users to use their finger, detected by using finger motion tracking, and a digitizing pen. It supports computer based interaction with paper documents allowing such tasks as copying numbers from paper to the digital calculator, copying part of a sketch into digital form and moving digitals objects around the table.

In a similar research, rather than aiming a camera at a desk, the camera is directed to a vertical whiteboard. Magic Board (Crowley et al., 2000) used a steerable camera so that screens can be larger than the field of view of the camera. Rather than using motion detection, cross-correlation is used instead, which extracts small regions from an image (e.g. image of a pointing finger) as template for searching in later images.

The SMART board (SMART, 2003) fixes 4 tiny cameras on four corners of its display which can detect any objects that come into contact with the surface or when it hovers above it.

The Everywhere Displays Project uses a "multi-surface interactive display projector" so that it can make any surface in the room interactive (Pinhanez, 2001). It is done by attaching a rotating mirror so that any surface in the room can be projected onto and captured by the camera. Finger detection is performed on the same surface that is being projected generating a "click" event as if it is a computer mouse.

The use of infrared has been used to remove the need for color hand segmentation and background subtraction due to fact that they sometimes fail when scene has a complicated background and dynamic lighting (Oka et al., 2002). Diffused illumination (DI) is another common technique used in HoloWall (Matsushita & Rekimoto, 1997) and Barehands (Ringel & Henry Berg, 2001), where infrared LEDs are emitted from behind the wall as well as a back projected display. An infrared filtered camera is positioned behind as well to detect the presence of hand or finger when it comes near the wall (within 30 cm) which reflects additional infrared light. The Microsoft Surface (Microsoft) is a tabletop display that also uses this technique, in addition, the camera can also recognize tagged physical objects placed on the surface.
EnhancedDesk (Oka et al., 2002) used hand and fingertip tracking on an augmented desk interface (horizontal). An infrared camera is used to detect areas close to the human body temperature. Selection is based on where the fingertip is.
The Perceptive Workbench (Leibe et al., 2000) uses infrared illuminated from the ceiling and a camera under a table. When the user extends their arm over the desk, it casts a shadow which can be picked up by the camera. A second camera fitted on the right side of the table captures a side view of the hand. Combining together, the location and the orientation of the user's deictic (pointing) gesture can be computed. The approach assumes that the user's arm is not overly bent. It fails when shadow from the user's body is casted, as well as when two arm are extended at the same time.
All of these techniques require the user to be at the location they want to point at. This also requires large movements of the arm, as well as pacing across surfaces. They do not work well when surfaces are hard to reach.

2.3 Free Hand Pointing

Perhaps the most direct form of selection at a distance is being able to point at something with your hand without any restrictions. The current trend is to make pointing as easy as pointing to real world objects. Taylor and McCloskey identified that "to indicate accurately the position of an object that is beyond arm's reach we commonly point towards it with an extended arm and index finger" (Taylor & McCloskey, 1988). The pointing gesture belongs to a class of gesture called "deictics". Studies have shown that the pointing gesture is often used to indicate a direction as well as to identify nearby objects (McNeill, 1992). This is an interesting concept because the pointing gesture is natural, intuitive, and easy to use and understand. Indeed, children can use body postures and gestures such as reaching and pointing by about nine months (Lock, 1980).
Here, we will review some of the literature, approaches to pointing and the varied implementations where hand pointing was used for interactive systems. In general these systems have the advantages of having no physically touchable surfaces thereby highly suitable for hygienic demanding environment such as factories or public spaces. Depending on the system setup, this usually allows users to interact with the display wherever they are standing.

2.3.1 Stereoscopic Systems

The pointing finger has been used in many existing systems. A pair of uncalibrated stereo cameras can be used with active contours to track and detect the position and direction of the index finger in a 40cm workspace (Cipolla & Hollinghurst, 1998).

The Hand Pointing System (Takenaka, 1998) developed by Takenaka Corporation uses two cameras attached to the ceiling to recognize the three-dimension position of user's finger. A mouse click is mimicked by using a forward and backward movement of the finger.

The Free-Hand Pointing (Hung et al., 1998) is a similar system that also uses stereo camera to track the user's finger. They first detect and segment the finger with a global search, then the fingertip and finger orientation is determined in a local search, and finally the line from finger to display is extracted.

The PointAt System (Colombo et al., 2003) allows users to walk around freely in a room within a museum while pointing to specific parts of a painting with their hand. Two cameras are setup to detect the presence of a person by using modified background subtraction algorithm as well as skin color detection. The tip of the pointing hand and the head centroid is then extracted. By using visual geometry and stereo triangulation, a pointing line is then deduced. This method can be applied to more than 2 cameras as well, and do not require manual calibration. Dwell clicking is used in this implementation.

Similarly, Nickel and Stiefelhagen (Nickel & Stiefelhagen, 2003) also used a set of stereo cameras to track the user's hand and head to estimate the pointing direction in 3D. Pointing gesture is recognised by using a three-phase model: *Begin* (hand moves from arbitrary position towards pointing position), *Hold* (hand remains motionless while pointing) and *End* (hand moves away from pointing position). They found that adding head orientation detection increases their gesture detection and precision rate. Comparing three approaches to estimate pointing direction, they found that the hand-head line method was the most reliable in estimating the pointing direction (90%). The others were forearm direction and head orientation.

In most case studies above, the design choice for the interaction technique, such as the different hand signal or hand gestures used, was not based on observation from prior user study. These are frequently based solely on the authors' intuition. These are inconsistent across different experiments.

There are a number of problems associated with using two cameras (Takatsuka et al., 2003). One is the reduced acquisition speed as there is a need to process two images entirely to locate the same point. With stereoscopic view, it is not difficult to find out the exact location of a certain object in the scene and is the reason many gesture based computer vision research has been based on stereo cameras. However, there are few studies in literatures that use monocular vision to allow the use of remote hand pointing gesture as well as being non-intrusive.

2.3.2 Monocular Systems

A single camera makes it much easier and simpler to allow real-time computation. Nowadays, most computer users have one web-camera at home, but possessing two or more is less likely.

In the EyeToy game for PlayStation2 (SONY), a motion recognition camera can be placed on top of a large display. A mirror image from the camera is presented on the display, as well

as additional game play information. A selection is made when users place their hands at specific location so that it's on-screen image coincided spatially with on-screen targets.
In the Ishindenshin system (Lertrusdachakul et al., 2005) a small video camera is placed near the center of a large vertical display directly in front of the user. The user is able to keep eye-contact and use the pointing gesture to interact with another user in a video conference. The fingertip location is detected by the camera and its location in x and y coordinates are determined.
A similar method is also used in another study (Eisenstein & Mackay, 2006) to compare the accuracy using two computer-vision based selection techniques (motion sensing and object tracking). They found that both techniques were 100% accurate and that the object tracking technique was significantly fewer errors and took less time.
The Virtual Keypad implementation (Tosas & Li, 2004) detects the user's fingertips position in both the x and y directions for interacting with targets on-screen. It is used much closer to the camera. Note that in all of these systems, the fingertip or hand can only be tracked in 2D, depth is not registered.
In the computer vision community, various researchers have investigated the use of monocular vision to estimate depth (Torralba & Oliva, 2002, Saxena et al., 2007). It has even been suggested that monocular vision is superior in detecting depth than stereo vision due to the fact that "small errors in measuring the direction each camera is pointing have large effect on the calculation (Biever, 2005)". On the other hand, very few examples in the HCI literature have been found using monocular vision to allow the use of remote hand pointing gesture whilst being non-intrusive.
Compared with monocular vision techniques, it is easier to find the exact location of a certain object in the scene using stereoscopic view. The need for a pair of stereo cameras would be eliminated if depth recovery is achievable with a single camera. This in turn transfers the problem from one that involves the hardware to one of software. However, few researchers have investigated interaction methods that rely on monocular computer vision, and where depth information recovery is required.
3DV Systems developed the "ZCam" to detect depth information based on the Time-Of-Flight principle (3DV, 2008). Infrared light are emitted into the environment and a camera captures the depth by sensing the intensity of the reflected infrared light reaching back to the camera. The major drawback of this setup is that it requires potential users to purchase this special camera.
The above mentioned systems used monocular vision to detect the users hand only. However, in order to provide a truly non-intrusive and natural pointing system, the system should also take into account the user's standing position.
The "Peek Thru" implementation does exactly this (Lee et al., 2001). A single camera is used to detect the user's pointing finger and the eye position. However, the detection of the fingertip was deemed too difficult to identify due to the observed occlusion by the user's torso. Users were asked to wear an easy to detect thimble on their fingertip. We feel that this violates the notion of using nothing but our own hand for interaction. Even if the fingertip position was detected using computer vision, this setup only differential between different angels from the camera's view, rather than the exact x and y coordinates.
As can be seen, we can observe numerous attempts to further the current keyboard and mouse interface for the large display.

At this point in time, we are starting the transition from the mouse based UI to that of surface based hand tracking era. They currently exist commercially in the form of public directory touch screen and multi-touch interfaces such as iPhone and Microsoft Surface. We believe that camera based hand pointing is the next frontier in the future of HCI, as users do not even require to touch the display, they are able to interact from a distance. It is time for the computer system to finally adapt to humans, rather than humans adapting to technologies. This research is invaluable for us in developing more natural interaction methods that are easy to setup and use.

3. Pointing Strategies

We begin our investigation by focusing on the use of natural pointing for interacting with the computer.
Although many interactive systems have focused on improving the detection of the users' pointing direction, few have considered the kinds of pointing strategy that is natural to the users and analyzed the accuracy of these strategies provided by the users themselves.

3.1 Background and Related Work

Let's look at the pointing strategies used in recent literature.
The MobiVR system (Rakkolainen, 2003) captures and detects a pointing finger behind a handheld micro display - a non-see-through binocular near-eye microdisplay (taken from a Head Mounted Display) attached to a reconfigured SmartNav infrared camera aiming forward. By attaching an infrared reflector ring on the finger, the user can perform a pointing gesture in front of the device to control a mouse cursor. This makes use of the eye-fingertip strategy, where the pointing direction is extracted from a line starting at the eye and continues to the fingertip. An interesting point here is that the fingertip is behind the near-eye display.
Various researchers have investigated the use of the head-hand line (similar to the eye-fingertip strategy but detecting the whole head and hand rather than specifically the eye or fingertip) for interacting with their systems (Colombo et al., 2003, Nickel & Stiefelhagen, 2003). All of these systems used a set of stereo cameras to track the user's head-hand line to estimate the pointing direction in 3D at a distance of around 2 meters. However, Nickel and Stiefelhagen (Nickel & Stiefelhagen, 2003) also found that adding head orientation detection increases their gesture detection and precision rate. Comparing three approaches to estimate pointing direction, they found that the head-hand line method was the most reliable in estimating the pointing direction (90%). The others were forearm direction (73%) and head orientation (75%). However, their result is based on whether 8 targets in the environment were correctly identified, rather than accurately measuring the accuracy from a specific target. The forearm orientation and head-hand line were extracted through stereo image processing while the head orientation was measured by means of an attached sensor.
There is evidence to suggest that the natural pointing gesture may be estimated to be somewhere between the head-hand line and the arm pointing strategy. Mase (Mase, 1998) used a pair of stereo cameras to determine the fingertip position. In order to extract a virtual line between the finger and a target, the location of the "Virtual Project Origin (VPO)" must be calculated. The VPO varies according to the pointing style of each individual. They made

used of a pre-session calibration and experimental results suggested "the VPO is mostly distributed along the line of the eye on the pointing hand's side and the shoulder".
In an experiment to investigate the effect of vision and proprioception in pointing ("the ability to sense the position, location, orientation, and movement of the body and its parts" (The Gale Group, 2005)), it has been reported that users tend to point (with an extended arm) to the target (about a meter away) by placing their fingertip just lateral to the eye-target line (Taylor & McCloskey, 1988). However, a line extended from the direction of the pointing arm would miss the target. They explained that this may be used to avoid the fingertip occluding the target or, alternatively, influenced by proprioception (which usually results in using the whole arm as a pointer). Their result suggests that the eye-target line is a good predictor of the pointing direction.
It is interesting to note that Olympic pistol marksmen and archers aim their targets by extending their arm and standing side-on to the target, so that the line running from the eye to the target coincide with the line running from the shoulder to the target (Taylor & McCloskey, 1988)
The accuracy estimated by vision systems is only as good as the pointing accuracy provided by the user, and in practice this can be even worse. To make any system more reliable and accurate, one should begin by understanding the pointing strategies adopted by users when pointing, and methods in which they can adopt to point to the best of their ability. Only then should we focus on detecting the hand accurately. It is observed that different systems require different strategies for targeting. There is currently a gap in the literature on systematically describing how and why natural interaction methods work and classifying them based on their accuracy, naturality and how well they capture the exact intention of the user. The above mentioned literature has mainly focused on extracting or detecting different pointing gestures through image processing or by different sensors. However, no known strategies for pointing were recommended which allow users to point naturally and accurately (to best represent their aim). In this context, we investigate how people point naturally and better understand the mechanism and the strategy behind targeting.

3.2 Style of Pointing Gesture

A preliminary experiment was conducted to investigate how people naturally point at objects on a vertical wall in a normal environment and to investigate the style of gestures people adopt when pointing. We hypothesized that there are three main pointing strategies: (1) using a straight arm, (2) using only the forearm and extended fingertip, and (3) placing their fingertip in between the eye and target (line-up).
Nineteen volunteers were recruited for the study but were not told the main objective at the beginning, only that they are required to point at a target using their arm. Subjects were asked to stand at three distances (1.2m, 3m and 5m) away from a wall and point to a target object, 5mm by 5mm, was marked on the wall, 155 cm from the ground (around eye level for most participants). The study was a within-subject study so that each of the subjects had to complete all tasks for each distance. The order of distances was counter-balanced with approximately one third starting at each distance.
In the first task, subjects were asked to point at the target using their preferred hand. They were free to use any strategies they wanted and were not told specifically how they should point. This allows us to observe the kind of strategy used naturally by each subject to point at objects from a distance. In the second task, subjects were specifically asked to point using

their forearm and their fingertip only, limiting the movement of their upper arm. This allows us to observe different variations of the forearm pointing method.
In the final task, subjects were specifically asked to use their whole arm to point while keeping it straight.

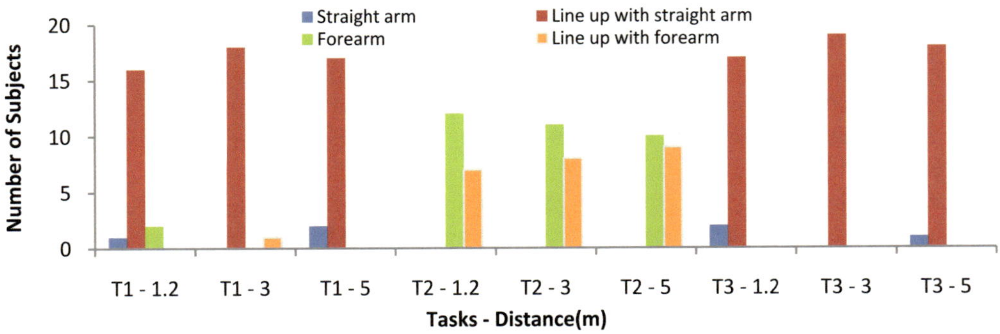

Fig. 1. The number of subjects using different pointing styles for each task/distance combination.

The main observation for task 1 was that almost all subjects used a full arm stretch to point regardless of distance. This may be due to the fact that during full arm pointing, they can see their arm in front of them, which provides a better visual approximation than the limited view of the arm provided with just the forearm.
Except as required in task 2, almost no subject used the forearm pointing method. While this method was praised for the minimal effort required to point, subjects felt that this method was unnatural and awkward.
In task 3, even though users were specifically asked to use full arm pointing, we observed two main strategies used to point at the target. Three subjects used their arm as a pointing instrument where the pointing direction is estimated from the shoulder to their fingertip (Figure 2b), while most users tried to align their fingertip in between the eye and target (Figure 2c) as hypothesized. This observation can also been seen in task 1.

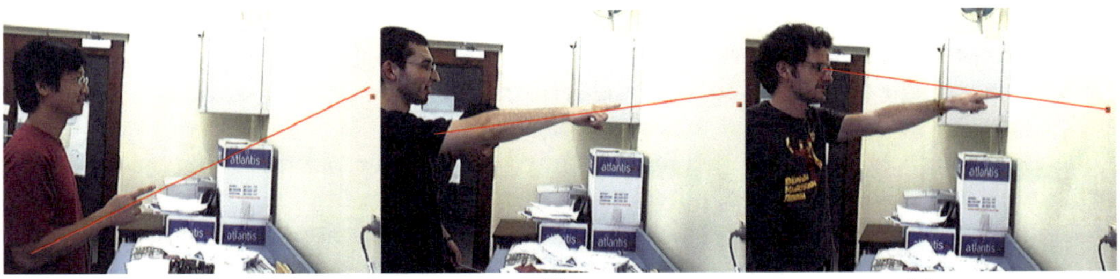

(*a*) (*b*) (*c*)

Fig. 2. (a) Forearm pointing: only using the forearm and fingertip to point, while keeping their upper-arm as close to the body as possible (b) Full arm pointing 1: using the arm as a pointing instrument while keeping the arm as straight as possible (c) Full arm pointing 2: the fingertip is placed between the eye and the target.

Overall, we observed a clear preference for the line-up method when pointing with a straight arm, while the two different forearm pointing methods are roughly equally used. Agreeing with our hypothesis, we did observe three different methods of pointing. The results from this study suggested that the line up pointing method is shown to be the most natural way of pointing to targets. Qualitative measures also suggest that users prefer to use a full arm stretch to point at targets.

Given the small scope, this experiment should only be treated as a preliminary work on this subject. However, this may serve as a basis for further analysis and experimentation with different size of targets.

Having studied the styles of pointing that are natural to the users, we observed informally that the forearm pointing method may be less accurate than both form of full arm pointing. However, further investigation would be required to justify this.

3.3 Pointing Accuracy

In most vision-based interactive system the accuracy of the estimated pointing direction is an essential element to their success. The focus is usually in finding new ways of improving the detection, estimation and tracking the pointing hand or finger, and deduce the pointing direction (Cipolla & Hollinghurst, 1998, Nickel & Stiefelhagen, 2003). However, it is assumed implicitly that the user is always pointing to their desired location all the time, and the systems do not take into account inaccuracies made by the user. A study was, therefore, conducted to investigate the accuracy provided by three common pointing strategies used in previous interactive systems (without the presence of feedback to the user): Forearm, Straight-arm, Line-up methods.

Despite advances in computer vision, there is still no consistent method to segment and extract the pointing direction of the arm. To minimize error introduced by a computer vision system, we detect the pointing direction of the arm by asking subjects to hold a laser pointer in their hand in a way that best represent the extension of their arm direction and which was consistent in all three methods (Figure 3).

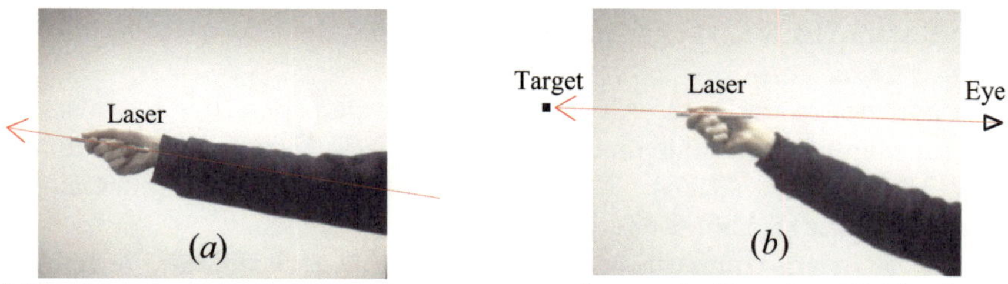

Fig. 3. (*a*) The laser pointer was used to represent the arm's direction (*b*) The laser pointer used with the line-up method, where the target, two ends of the laser pointer and eye are collinear.

Laser dot gave us a way to quantitatively compare the different targeting strategies. Although physically pointing with hand or arm compared to holding the laser in the palm are slightly different, we believe that this difference would be consistent enough so that it would still be comparable relatively between the strategies. In addition, users were not provided feedback from the laser pointer to adjust their accuracy. The effect of distance on the accuracy of pointing - whether pointing deteriorates as user moves away from the target - was also investigated in this experiment.

Fifteen volunteers participated in this study. A webcam was used to detect a 5x5mm target on a wall and the laser dot produced by the laser pointer. The study was a within-subject study, where each subject performed pointing tasks with all three pointing styles from the three distances: 1, 2 and 3 metres from the target. Three blocks of trails were completed for each of the 9 combinations and the mean position for each combination was determined. The order of pointing styles and distances were counter-balanced. Without turning on the laser, subjects were asked to aim as accurately as possible, and hold the laser pointer in their hand in a way that best represents the direction of their pointing arm (for straight arm and forearm pointing, Figure 3a). For the line-up method, users were asked to place the laser pointer so that both ends of the laser pointer are collinear with the target and the eye (Figure 3b). To prevent subjects receiving feedback from the laser dot, the laser was only turned on after they have taken aim.

Accuracy was measured in terms of the distance between the target and the laser dot produced on the wall. In summary, the experimental design was: 15 subjects x 3 pointing techniques x 3 distances x 3 blocks = 405 pointing trials.

Figure 4 illustrates the mean distance from target for each pointing method at three distances and their interactions for all trials.

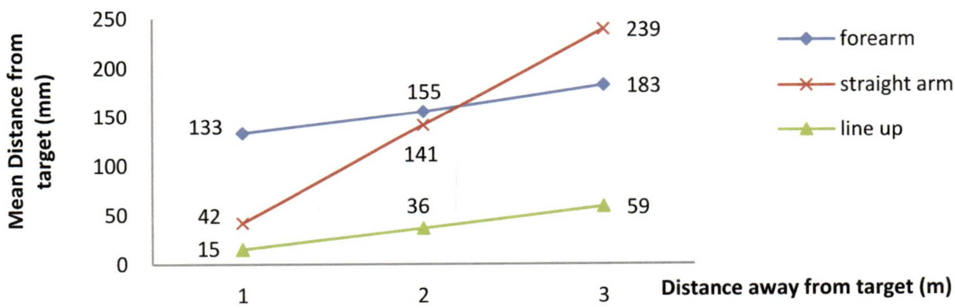

Fig. 4. Mean distance between target and the laser dot position.

A two-way analysis of variance (ANOVA) with repeated measures reveals a significant main effect for pointing technique on accuracy ($F[2,28]=37.97$, $p<0.001$), and for distance on accuracy ($F[2,28]=47.20$, $p<0.001$). We also observed a significant interaction between technique and distance ($F[4,56]=9.879$, $p<0.001$).

Multiple pairwise means comparisons were tested within each pointing technique (table 1) with Bonferroni correction. Trend analyses were also performed on each of the technique. Significance in the linear component signifies a linear increase in accuracy with increasing distance within that particular technique.

Technique	1m vs 2m	2m vs 3m	1m vs 3m	Linear component
Forearm	1.000	0.378	0.055	0.018*
Straight arm	<0.001*	0.002*	<0.001*	<0.001*
Line up	0.003*	0.116	0.014*	0.005*

*Denotes significance at the 0.05 level

Table 1. The significance of multiple pairwise means comparisons within each pointing technique.

Multiple pairwise means comparisons were also performed within each distance to investigate possible differences between each technique (table 2).

Distance	Forearm vs straight arm	Straight arm vs line up	Forearm vs line up
1m	0.001*	<0.001*	<0.001*
2m	1.000	<0.001*	<0.001*
3m	0.182	<0.001*	<0.001*

*Denotes significance at the 0.05 level

Table 2. The significance of multiple pairwise means comparisons within each distance.

The results suggest that the line-up method is the most accurate at all distances. We can also observe a linear increase throughout at a rate of 14.7mm per meter. The forearm pointing technique was consistently less accurate than the line-up method. It is interesting to note the insignificance between the three distances within the forearm pointing method. This may suggest that the pointing method has a high tolerance with increasing distance from target. On the other hand, straight arm pointing method is highly affected by the increase in distance from target. This is illustrated by the significant difference across all distances as well as the high linear increase (65.7mm per meter). Compared to forearm pointing, the accuracy at 2m and 3m is not significant. The only difference between forearm and straight arm pointing is at 1m. This may be due to the higher level of feedback given from the longer arm extension, and that the straight arm pointing resembles the line-up method at close proximity to the target.

From this experiment, we have identified inaccuracies in users pointing performance, which varies depending on the strategy used. We observed that the line-up method is the most accurate pointing method, and that the straight arm method is more accurate than the forearm method only at a distance of one metre. Understanding the natural pointing accuracy can assist future vision-based hand pointing interaction researchers and practitioners to decide the input strategy that best suit their users in completing the required tasks.

From the literature review, we observed that different interactive systems use different strategies for pointing. However, the pointing strategies used have not been systematically studied. Here, we attempt to characterize the mechanism of pointing in terms of their geometric models used in these systems, and in the process, we use the results from our experiments to gain a better understanding of how and why the line-up method is a more accurate pointing method.

3.4 Models for Targeting

We hypothesized that there is a difference between the two strategies of targeting using full arm stretch. To investigate the reason for this difference, we begin by formalizing the concept of targeting from a geometrical perspective based on our observations and from previous work. We then introduce three models for targeting - the Point, Touch and the dTouch model. It should be noted that the word "pointing" and "targeting" can be used interchangeably to mean the act of aiming (at some target).

3.4.1 Geometrical Configuration

We now define the geometrical configuration in which our models for targeting from a distance will be based. These are the building blocks for the models of targeting.
From a point at the eye, P_e, a line of gaze, l_g, is directed towards a point on a target object, P_o. While a point provided by a pointing mechanism, P_p, guides a line of ray, l_r, to the same target P_o. Figure 5a illustrates this geometrical arrangement.

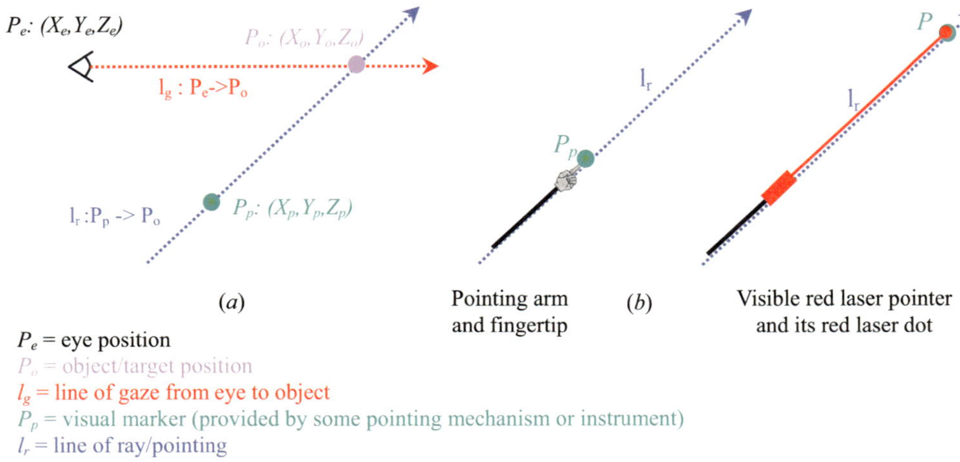

Fig. 5. (a) The general configuration for targeting (b) Examples of visual markers.

The task of targeting is therefore to intersect l_g with l_r at object P_o. A pointing mechanism or visual marker (P_p) may include a variety of pointers that the user holds or use to point. The fingertip (when user is using their arm) and the laser dot produced by a laser pointer are examples of such (Fig. 5b). On the other hand, the arm direction is an example of line of pointing (l_r).
We now distinguish three models that can explain most of the common strategies used in the real environment and in many previous interactive systems.

3.4.2 The Point Model

The Point model describes the occasion when users' point at a target from a distance using their arm or a presentation pointer as the pointing instrument. Targeting is characterized by having the eye gaze, l_g, intersects with the pointing direction provided by the arm, l_r, at the target object, P_o, such that the pointing marker, P_p, doesn't meet at the target object P_o (i.e. $P_o \neq P_p$). Figure 6a illustrates this geometrical arrangement. The task for the user is to use their pointing instrument to approximate a pointing direction that meets the target object.

However, it is only an approximation, rather than precise targeting, since the visual marker is not on the surface of the target to assist the targeting process.
This can be used to model the cases when the arm is fully stretched, when only the forearm is used to point to the target (Nickel & Stiefelhagen, 2003) or when only the fingertips are used, in the case of (Cipolla & Hollinghurst, 1998). This technique is known as *ray casting* for interacting with virtual environments (Bowman & Hodges, 1997). It can also be used to model the straight-arm method and the forearm method that were observed and used in our experiments in this section 3.2 and 3.3. In these cases, the length of the whole arm, forearm or fingertip is used as a pointing instrument P_p to infer a line of pointing l_r towards a target P_o (Figure 6b). This model can also be used to explain the use of an infrared laser pointer (Cheng & Pulo, 2003). In that work, the infrared laser pointer is used to point at an on-screen target (similar to a regular red laser pointer). However, the laser dot is not visible to the user. Cameras are used to capture the infrared laser dot on the display to determine the on-screen target selected. The only visual marker to guide the user to point to the target is the laser pointer itself (and not the laser beam). In this case, the infrared laser pointer is represented by P_p and its inferred pointing direction l_r.

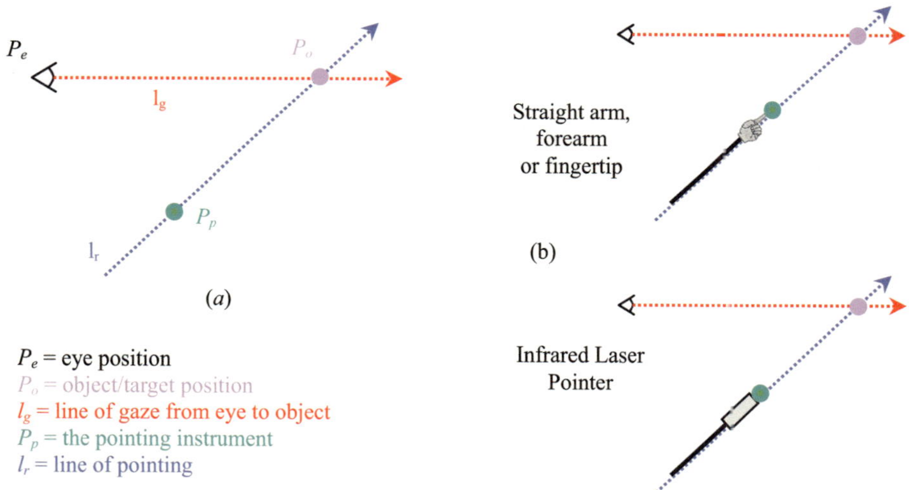

Fig. 6. (a) The Point Model for targeting (b) Examples of techniques that use the Point model.

Pointing using this Point model may be inaccurate, due mainly to the distance between P_p and P_o. Consistent with the results of our accuracy experiment in 3.3, the straight arm pointing method was observed to be more accurate when the subject, and hence the arm and hand (P_p), is close to the target, is at a distance of 1 meter from the target (mean error of 42mm). However, as the user moves further away from the target, the inaccuracy increased dramatically (mean error of 141mm at a distance of 2m). Therefore, it can be seen that accuracy is not guaranteed when pointing techniques which make use of the Point model are used.

3.4.3 The Touch Model

The Touch model describes the occasion when the fingertip is used to physically touch a target object or when a pointing instrument is used and a visual marker is seen on the surface of the object. Targeting is characterized by having the eye gaze, l_g, intersects with the pointing direction provided by the arm, l_r, at the target object, P_o, such that the pointing marker, P_p, meets at the target object P_o (i.e. $P_o = P_p$).

Figure 7 illustrates this geometrical arrangement. With this model, the task for the user is to use a visual marker (e.g. their fingertip or a pointing instrument) to physically makes contact with a target object (more specifically on the surface of the object). This is a form of precise targeting as the visual marker assists the targeting process.

This can be used to model any kinds of touch based interaction including DiamondTouch (Dietz & Leigh, 2001) and SmartSkin (Rekimoto, 2002). The fingertip acts as a pointing instrument P_p and is used to make physical contact with the target P_o (Figure 7b). Other input methods may be used in place of the fingertip, such as a stylus (a pen like object with a tip), to act as the pointing instrument.

This model can also be used to explain the use of a red laser pointer, for example in (Olsen & Nielsen, 2001). The red laser dot produced by the pointer is represented by P_p and its pointing direction l_r. The red laser can be thought of as an extended arm, and the laser dot, the index finger.

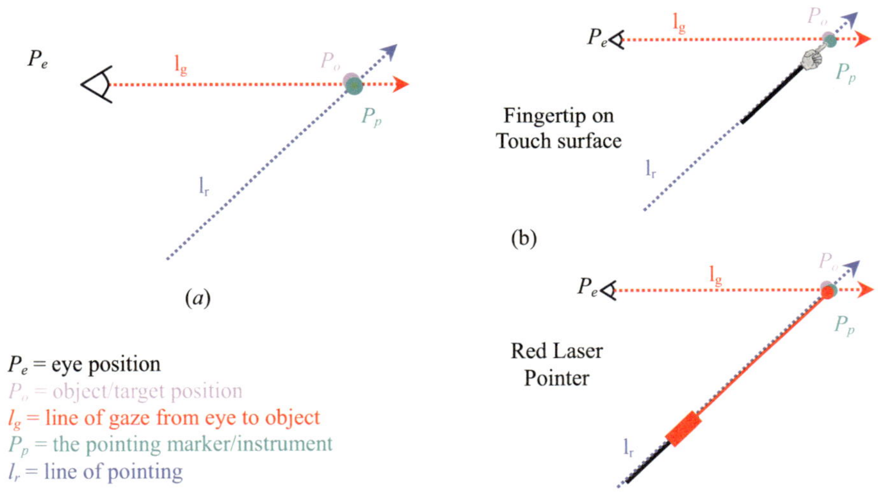

Fig. 7. (a) The Touch Model for targeting (b) Examples of techniques that use the Point model.

Targeting using the Touch model is accurate. This is because the distance between P_p and P_o is zero and they overlap at the same position, which makes targeting a precise task. Unlike the Point model, estimating the direction of pointing, l_r, is not required. Even when users misalign their pointing instrument and the target, the misalignment can be easily observed by the user, allowing readjustment of the position of the pointing instrument. Therefore, it can be seen that accuracy is guaranteed when pointing techniques which make use of the Touch model are used.

3.4.4 The dTouch (distant-Touch) Model

The dTouch model describes the occasion when the fingertip or a visual marker is used to overlap the target object in the user's view, from a distance. It may also be describes as using the fingertip to touch the target object from a distance (from the user's point of view).
Targeting using the dTouch model is characterized by having the eye gaze, l_g, intersects with the pointing direction provided by the arm, l_r, at the pointing marker, P_p, such that the eye, P_e, the pointing maker, P_p, and the target object, P_o, are collinear. P_p may or may not coincide with P_o. Figure 8 illustrates this geometrical arrangement.
With this model, the task for the user is to align a visual marker, P_p, anywhere along the gaze from eye to target, l_g, so that it aligns with the object (as seen from the user's eye). It is not a requirement that the user is located close to the target object. The target may even be unreachable to the user (Figure 8a). In such case, the dTouch model can be considered a remote touch, a touch that occurs from afar (touch interaction without physically touching).
In the case when P_p coincides with P_o (i.e. the fingertip touches the target, Figure 8b), it fits both the Touch model and the dTouch model. The dTouch model can be considered a generalization of the Touch model since the dTouch model can be used to encompass the case when P_p coincide with P_o (defined by the Touch model), as well as other cases where P_p and P_o do not coincide. In other words, the Touch model is a specific case of the dTouch model. The main difference between the Touch model and the dTouch model is the position of the pointing marker, P_p. Even though both models restrict the marker to lie on the line of gaze, l_g, it must be coincident to the target object with the touch model, while it is unrestricted with the dTouch model. The dTouch model can therefore represent a wider selection of pointing techniques than the Touch model.

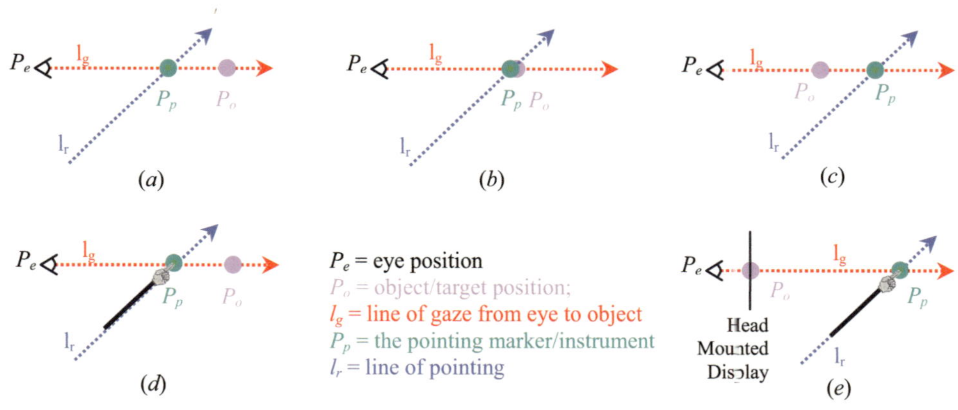

Fig. 8. (a-c) The dTouch model for targeting (d) An example using the eye-fingertip line (e) An example using a head mounted display and finger to interact with virtual object.

The generalized dTouch model can be used to model previous works that uses the eye-fingertip line (Lee et al., 2001) or the head-hand line (Colombo et al., 2003) and the line-up method that were observed and used in our experiments in this section, 3.2 and 3.3. The fingertip or hand act as a pointing instrument, P_p, and is aligned with the target P_o, on the line of gaze. When the user interacts with an object using the dTouch model, the user's intention is realized on the screen target.

This model can also be used to explain the interactions in previous works on head mounted virtual displays (Rakkolainen, 2003, Pierce et al., 1997). In these works, a head mounted display is worn in front of user's eye, and the fingertip is used to interact with the virtual objects. However, the virtual target, P_o, is located between the eye, P_e, and the fingertip, P_p, on the line of gaze, l_r (Figure 8c).
The accuracy of targeting using the dTouch model depends on the distance between P_p and P_o. Due to hand instability by users, the further away the two points are from each other, the larger the amount of hand jitter. However, unlike the Point model, estimating the direction of pointing, l_r, is not required. Users can readjust their position of the pointing instrument when misalignment of the two points is observed by the user.
This is consistent with the results observed from our accuracy experiment in 3.3, at a distance of 1 meter the line-up method (mean error of 15 mm) is more accurate than the other two methods based on the Point model (means of 42 and 133mm). This is also consistent with the results from Nickel and Stiefelhagen (Nickel & Stiefelhagen, 2003), where the percentage of targets identified with the head-hand line using our dTouch model (90%) is higher than the forearm line using our Point model (73%). As can be seen, the accuracy of the dTouch model is better than the Point model.
When the distance between the two points is reduced to zero, we can expect a guaranteed accuracy, as with the Touch model.

3.4.5 Indirect Interaction

Even though our Touch model is only relevant when the interaction is direct, the model can actually be used to represent indirect interactions, with only minor modifications. The interaction is indirect when the input space is no longer the same as the output space. The computer mouse is a good example of this. In such cases, the line of ray is no longer a straight line. The input and the output space may certainly have some form of correlation; however, a direct relationship (in terms of physical space) is no longer necessary. The ray of pointing is therefore no longer relevant. Here are some examples:

1) The mouse cursor appearing on the screen can be represented as P_p. When the cursor moves onto an on-screen UI widget, and the mouse is clicked, P_o and P_p coincides. The task for the user here is to align a mouse cursor to the target (indirectly through a mouse) (Figure 9a).

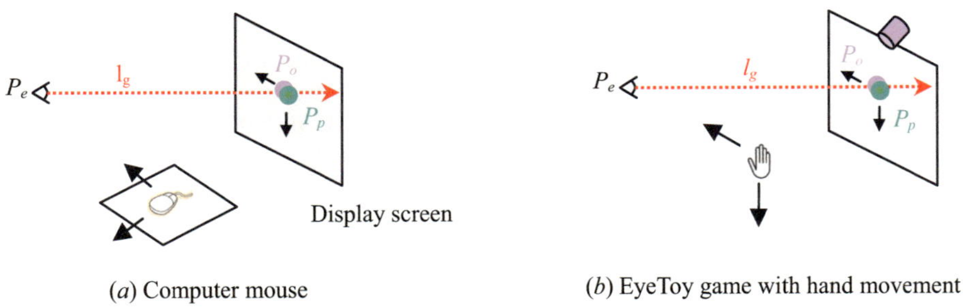

Fig. 9. Examples of indirect techniques that use the Touch model.

2) Even though remote controllers are discrete input device, they can be thought of in terms of this model as well. The directional keys on the remote controller may be mapped to the physical grid-like space on the display screen. When a directional key is pressed, the on-screen selection indicator (P_p) is moved closer to its intended target (P_o).
3) Yet another example of the use of this model is the EyeToy camera (SONY). The user's hand image displayed on the screen is represented by P_p. The task for the user is to shift their on-screen hand image as close to the target (P_o) as possible (Figure 9b).

Therefore, the Touch model can also be used to model any interactive system that relies on visual feedback, either direct or indirect. However, in our work, we are mainly interested in direct interaction. Interactions where users are not required to hold on to any devices (i.e. no intermediary devices), they are able to perform from a distance. Interaction techniques that use this model do not require the user to touch the screen or be within reach of the output display. They are able to interact remotely.

However, we should still recognize the benefits exhibited when the Touch model is adapted to indirect devices. For example, the computer mouse can provide users with stability, as hand jitter and fatigue will no longer be concerns. It also provides users with a higher degree of accuracy.

In summary, from these models, we have deduced that the Point model does allow direct interaction from a distance but can be highly inaccurate. The Touch model provides high accuracy but does not allow bare-hand interaction from a distance. While the dTouch model provides good accuracy and allows direct hand pointing strategy that we observed to be most natural to the users (eye-fingertip).

Understanding the mechanism of targeting can assist future human-computer interaction researchers and practitioners to decide the input strategy that best suit their users in completing the required tasks. When designing an interactive system that is natural, unintrusive and direct, we recommend that the dTouch model be used as the underlying strategy.

4. dTouch Pointing System - Conceptual Design

To demonstrate the use of the dTouch method, we proposed an example interactive system using the eye-fingertip method that allows direct and non-invasive interaction with a large display at a distance with a single camera. We call this the "dTouch pointing system".

Our goal is to design a natural interactive system for large screen displays that uses only a single camera, which relies on monocular computer vision techniques.

A single camera setup has only gained popularity in recent years in the form of webcam for personal computing and for console gaming (SONY). The main advantage of using a single camera as a basis for designing a new interactive system is the availability of the webcam. Most PC owners will already have one, and they are commonly included in laptop computers. This reduces the need for users to purchase expensive specialized hardware (in the case for a new input device), or the need for a second webcam (in the case for a stereo camera setup) which may otherwise be unnecessary. By using computer vision, users are able to use their natural ability to interact with the computer thus allowing a more enjoyable experience. Such an approach may also allow a wider adoption of new interactive technologies in daily life.

Current monocular systems often use a single camera to detect the position of the user's hand. The x and y coordinates in 2D space are determined. This is used to determine an intended target position on the screen. Interaction, then relies on visual feedback, usually in the form of an on-screen cursor. Although demonstrated to be accurate due to the feedback, this provides only an indirect interaction. The major drawback of this type of interaction is the fixed interaction space in a 2D area. The user is not able to move around freely as they must stay within the same area to interact with the system. To provide a more natural interactive system, we attempt to extract 3D information from the environment and the user.

4.1 Design Overview

We envision that our pointing system would be used in situations where occasional, quick, and convenient interaction is required, such as in a presentation setting or information kiosk, as opposed to highly accurate and continuous mouse movement such as those required for typical personal computing usage.

To provide natural interaction, the system must allow users to point at the display directly using their bare hand. A web-camera is placed above the screen and angled downwards in order to determine the location of the user. To estimate the user's pointing direction, a vector is approximated from the user's eye through the pointing finger to a point of intersection on the display screen. The resulting position on the display would be the user's intended on-screen object. This makes use of the eye-fingertip method in the dTouch model (Figure 10).

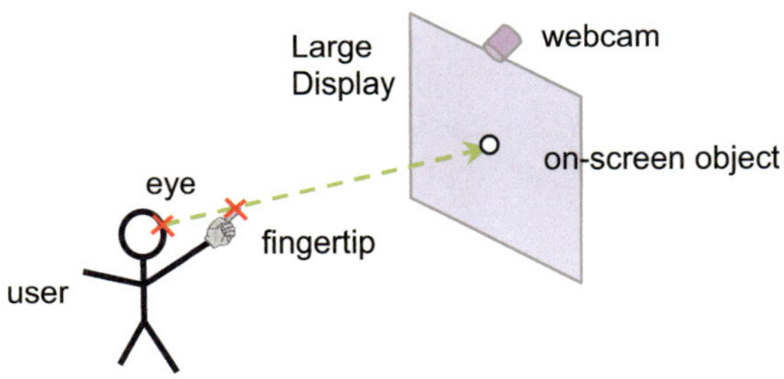

Fig. 10. Overview of the dTouch Interactive Pointing System.

To determine the pointing direction, image processing must be performed to track the eye and fingertip. In effect, we wish to construct a straight line in 3D space which can be used to give us a 2D coordinate on the display screen.

The specific concepts used in this setup are examined.

4.2 The View Frustum

A view frustum is used in computer graphics to define the field of view of a camera, or a region of space which may appear on a computer screen (Figure 11a). The view frustum is the area within a rectangular pyramid intersected by a near plane (for example a computer screen) and a far plane (Wikipedia, 2008). It defines how much of the virtual world the user will see (Sun, 2004). All objects within the view frustum will be captured and displayed on the screen, while objects outside the view frustum are not drawn to improve performance.

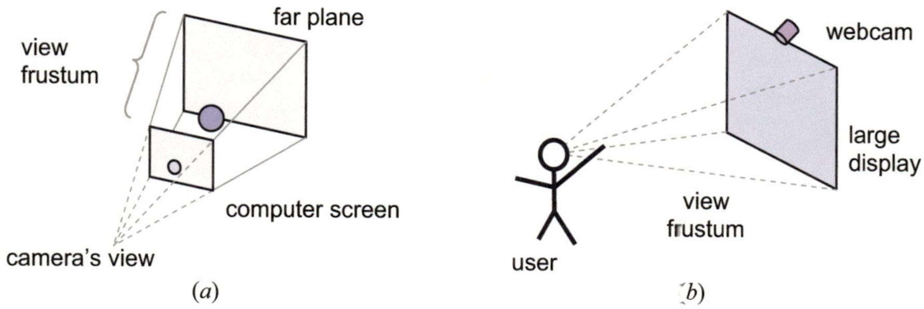

Fig. 11. (a) View frustum in computer graphics. (b) The view frustum.

An interaction volume is an area where the interaction occurs between the user and the system (the display, in our case). In computer vision based interactive systems this area must be within the camera's field of view. Users can use their hand within this area to interact with objects displayed on the screen.

In interactive systems that do not require explicit knowledge of the user's location, the interaction volume is static. To adequately interact with the system, the user must adjust themselves to the volume's location by pacing or reaching out. In addition, because the interaction volume is not visible, users must discover it by trial and error. On the other hand, when the user's location is known, the interaction volume adjusts to the user, and is always in front of the user.

To achieve the latter, as is the case of our method, a camera can be used to detect the face of the user. A view frustum can then be constructed between the origin (at the eye position) and the large display (Figure 11b). The view frustum can therefore be used as a model for approximating the interaction volume. The user can use their hand and fingers within this volume to interact with the display. The view frustum thus defines the interaction area available to the user.

4.3 Virtual Touchscreen

To investigate the integration of the benefits afforded by large displays and the interaction space afforded by the user, we proposed improving interaction with large displays by leveraging the benefits provided by touch screens.

Our idea is to imagine bringing the large display close enough to the user so that it is within arm's length from the user (thereby reachable), and users can imagine a touchscreen right in front of them (Cheng & Takatsuka, 2006). The distance between the user and the virtual objects remains unchanged. This "virtual" touchscreen and the original large display share the same viewing angle within the confines of the view frustum (Figure 12).

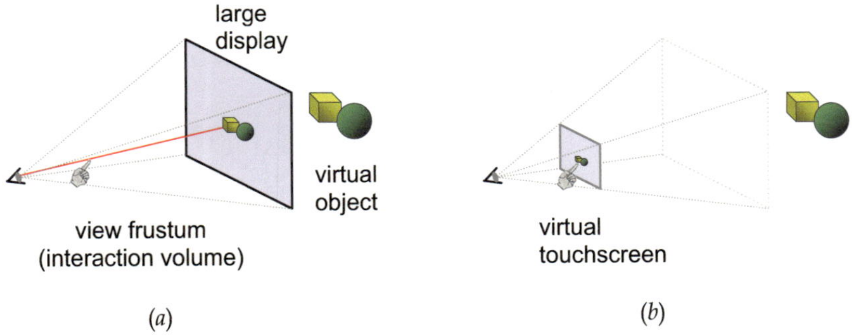

Fig. 12. (a) Pointing at the large display. (b) Pointing at the virtual touchscreen

With this approach, users can use their finger to interact with the virtual touchscreen as if it was a real touchscreen (Figure 13).

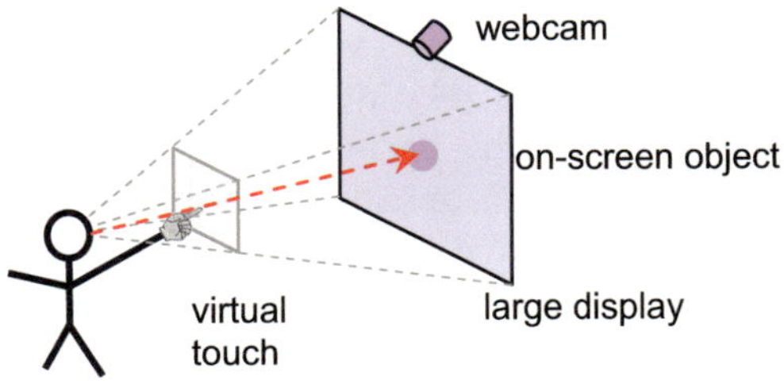

Fig. 13. A user interacting with the large display using their fingertip through a virtual touchscreen at arms' length

The user is therefore restricted to using their fully stretched arm, so that a virtual touchscreen can always be approximated at the end of their fingertip, eliminating the guess-work for the user to find the touchscreen. From the experiment in section 3.3, the majority of subjects were observed to use the full arm stretch and the eye-fingertip method to point at the target. Therefore, rather than feeling constrained, it should be natural for the user to point in our system.

An advantage of this approach is that it provides a more accurate estimation of the fingertip position, as the distance between finger and display can now be estimated from the position of the user. The other advantage is that the virtual touchscreen is re-adjusted as the user moves. In previous interactive systems, the interaction volume, and therefore the virtual touchscreen, is static. To interact with such systems, the user must determine the interaction area by initially guessing and/or through a feedback loop. While the user moves around, the interaction area does not move correspondingly, it is therefore necessary to re-adjust their hand position in order to point to the same target. Conversely, in our approach, as the user's location is known, the virtual screen adjusts to the user accordingly, while staying in front of the user. The user will always be able to "find" the virtual touchscreen as it is always within their view frustum (where the origin is at the user's eye position). As long as the user extends their hand within the bounds of the view frustum (or visibly the large display) they can always interact with the system. By taking into account the users' location, the dynamic virtual touchscreen enables users to roam around the room and still be able to interact with the display.

4.4 Interaction Model

The moment the user touches a virtual object on the virtual touchscreen, the dTouch model can be used to define this targeting action, as illustrated in Figure 14.

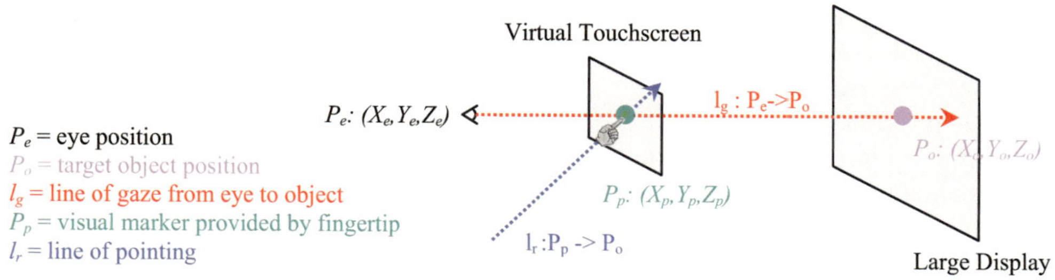

Fig. 14. The dTouch model for targeting with the virtual touchscreen.

In our system, the task for the user is to move their fingertip (P_p) to the line of gaze from eye to target (l_g) so that it aligns with the object (as seen from the user's eye). P_p is also the location of the virtual touchscreen. The object on the large display is indicated by, P_o, which is unreachable to the user, when used at a distance. When the eye, fingertip and on-screen object coincide, the dTouch model is in action and the virtual touchscreen is automatically present. The use of dTouch in this case can be considered a distant touch, a touch that occurs from afar. When the user walks towards the large display and is able to touch it physically, P_p and P_o coincides. The fingertip touches the target. The virtual touchscreen coincides with the large display, making up a large touchscreen. In this case, the Touch model applies. In practice, due to the placement and angle of the camera, the user may not be able to interact with the display at such close proximity, as the fingertip may be out of the camera's view.

4.5 Fingertip Interaction

To select an on-screen object, it is expected that users will use the virtual touchscreen as a normal touch screen where they select objects by using a forward and backward motion. However, it may be difficult for the user to know how far they have to push forward before the system will recognize the selection. Furthermore, since we are only using a single web-camera, it may be difficult to capture small changes in the distance of the fingertip from the image. One possible solution is to use dwell selection, where the user has to stay motionless at a particular position (with a given tolerance) for a specified time (typically around one second).

5. Monocular Positions Estimation

To demonstrate the feasibility of our system design using the dTouch model, a prototype was implemented. In this section, we present the method used for this implementation.

The aim is to produce a method for finding the head and fingertip position in 3D space, as well as the resultant position, all from a 2D camera image. It should be noted that cameras will become cheaper and better with time, however, the contributions here can be used as a basis for further advancement in this field for the years to come.
Our proposed interactive system is designed to be used for large displays together with the use of a webcam. The webcam is positioned on top of the display to detect the users pointing direction. The pointing direction is estimated by two 3D positions in space the eye and the fingertip. As users will be using the dTouch model of pointing with the use of a virtual touchscreen, the first position is the eye position and the second is the fingertip position from the user. To estimate the pointing direction and the final resulting point, we divide the process into three steps:

1) eye position (E) estimation
2) fingertip position (F) estimation
3) resultant point (P) estimation

The first two steps both involve finding two points in 3D space given a single 2D image. In our system, the z-coordinate is the missing information. To acquire extra information, constraints from the environment are often exploited. It is possible to use known size of familiar objects in the scene within an unknown environment (Torralba & Oliva, 2002). We proposed that it is also possible to use the kinematic constraints provided naturally by the human body (Zatsiorsky, 1998). This has the advantage of being more robust to different users and is indifferent to the environment. This is the main approach that we will use in this work.
Face detection is used to detect the position at the dominant eye, while depth (from the camera) is determined from the width of the face (Cheng & Takatsuka, 2005). The fingertip is detected as the lowest skin colour pixel from the view of the camera (Figure 15a). The depth of the fingertip is calculated by intersecting a sphere (where the center is at the user's shoulder, using arm's length as the radius) and a line vector from the center of camera through the detected fingertip in the camera's image plane, and towards the user's fingertip (Figure 15b).

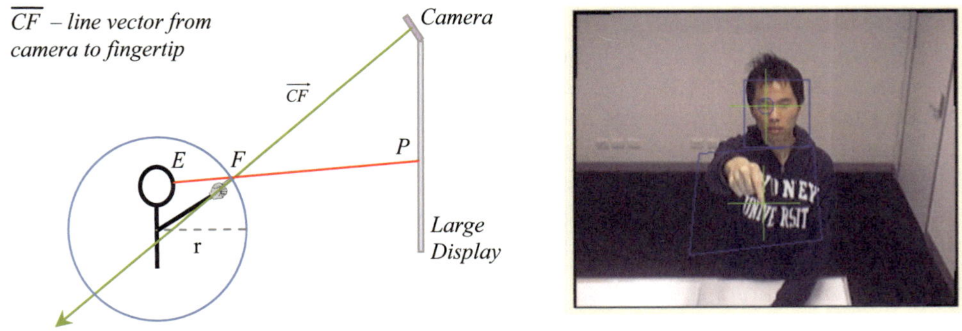

(a) (b)

Fig. 15. (a) The fingertip position is estimated by the intersection of the line vector and the arm's sphere (b) The webcam's view highlighting the estimated positions of the eye and fingertip, and the size and position of the virtual touchscreen.

We have also introduced the use of Kalman filtering on the detected eye positions as well as the final estimation to increase stability.

6. Usability Evaluation

A usability experiment was conducted to evaluate this proof-of-concept prototype. We investigated the minimum target size that can be selected using our system with twenty-two volunteers. The body measurements of these subjects were collected and adjusted for their hand preference and eye dominance. They were then asked to stand at a distance of 160cm from the display and performed the calibration process by pointing to the four corners of the display. The display was 81.5cm x 61.5cm with a resolution of 1024x768. The webcam used was Logitech QuickCam Pro 4000 at a resolution of 320x240. A circular target was placed at the center of the display. The user was asked to point to the target for 5 seconds keeping their hand steady. This was done directly after the calibration process so that factors such as change in user's posture were reduced to a minimum. Circular targets were chosen as it provides a uniform acceptable distance from the center of target, compared to square targets. We selected six target size, the smallest being 50 pixels, while the largest 175 pixels in diameter. The effective accuracy required to select the target is half the target size.

Target Size (diameter in px)	50	75	100	125	150	175
Effective pointing accuracy required (distance from target in px)	25	37.5	50	62.5	75	87.5

Table 3. Target size and their corresponding effecting pointing accuracy required

This study was a within-subjects study, where each subject performed the six conditions. Subjects were asked to perform 3 blocks of these trials. The order of the targets was randomized to avoid ordering effects. A time limit of five seconds was imposed on each selection task. Unsuccessful selection occurs at two occasions: 1) when the user had not selected the target after the time limit and 2) when the user was pointing inside the target but had not stabilized enough to activate a dwell.

In summary, the experimental design was: 22 subjects x 6 targets x 3 blocks of trials = 396 pointing trials

The number of successful selection for each target size was added up, giving a total of 66 trials for each target size. We classified the trials into three categories:

In target & within time limit	-	Successful selection
In target but over time limit	-	Borderline
Out of target & over time limit	-	Unsuccessful selection

The case when the trials are in target but went over the time limit was classified as borderline because strictly speaking, they would have selected the target if more time was given. The delay in selection may have been due to a number of reasons:

- hand jitter causing unstable pointing position, thereby increasing time required to dwell
- pointing position may have been inside the target in one frame and outside in the next frame due to hand jitter
- slow hand movement from the subject to begin with

Because of all these uncertainties, we listed these as borderline. Figure 16 shows the percentage of successful and unsuccessful trails for each target size. As can be seen, the number of successful trials increases as the target size increase, while at the same time the number of unsuccessful trials decreases at a similar rate. A peak of 72.7% success was observed at the largest target size. An increase of 19.7% for successful selection was observed from size 50 to size 62.5px, while only a modest increase of 6.1% was observed from size 62.5 to 75px.

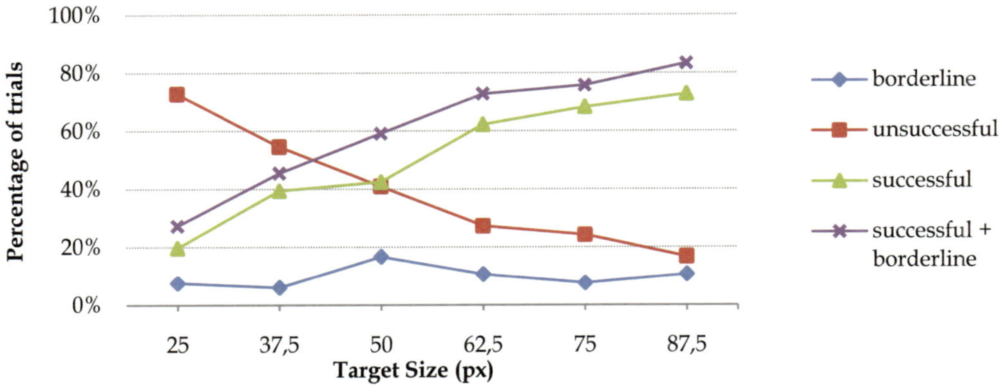

Fig. 16. Percentage of successful and unsuccessful trials for each target

Borderline cases are overall quite low in numbers, on average around 10% of all trials. If borderline cases are included as successful selection, we can observe a peak of 83.3% success rate. With the combined success rate, a slowing down in improvement can again been seen from size 62.5 to 75px (3.1% increase compared to an increases of 13.6% from 50 to 62.5px). This may suggest a target size of 62.5 as an optimal size, as further increase in size does not result in a consistent gain.

We can conclude that a target size of 62.5px (125px diameter) is the most suitable choice for system such as ours. On a 1024x768 screen, one can fit around 8 targets horizontally, and 6 targets vertically, a total of 48 targets. In terms of physical dimensions in our setup, this translates to around 99.5mm for each target both vertically and horizontally. Further investigation may be under taken to refine the target resolution than those used in this evaluation.

6.1 Limitations

With current segmentation techniques, it is still difficult to detect the fingertip from a frontal view. Subjects were asked to lower their fingertip so that it would appear as the lowest skin colour pixel. Many subjects felt that this was awkward and uncomfortable after prolonged use. However, as this style of pointing was used in all conditions, users' ability to use a particular style of pointing for target selection was not impaired.

Users' body postures were restricted as slight deviation would increase system estimation error. This was seen by the user during the calibration phase of the system. These estimation errors were found to have stemmed from the inaccuracy of the face detector used. Improving the face detection algorithm would minimize such errors.

In light of these limitations and constraints, it was felt that the results were not significantly distorted and are sufficient for testing on our prototype.

7. Summary

In this chapter, we have investigated the interaction paradigms for bare-hand interaction at a distance. Through the initial studies, we found that full arm stretch was the most common pointing strategy, while the most accurate strategy was when users line up the target with their eye and fingertip. From the observations, we systematically analysed the various natural pointing strategies and formalized geometric models to explain their differences. The dTouch model was found to give the most accurate strategy and we recommend the use of this model for designing future interactive systems that requires interaction at a distance. The dTouch interactive system was designed and implemented as an example that uses the dTouch pointing strategy. We exploited geometric constraints in the environment, and from this we were able to use monocular computer vision to allow bare-hand interaction with large displays. The result of the experimental evaluation confirmed that using the dTouch technique and a webcam to recover 3D information for interaction with large display is feasible. Models developed and lessons learnt can assist designers to develop more accurate and natural interactive systems that make use of human's natural pointing behaviours.

8. Acknowledgement

NICTA is funded by the Australian Government as represented by the Department of Broadband, Communications and the Digital Economy and the Australian Research Council through the ICT Centre of Excellence program.

9. References

3DV Systems, ZCam http://www.3dvsystems.com/

Biever, C. (2005) Why a robot is better with one eye than two *New Scientist.* Reed Business Information Ltd.

Bowman, D. A. & Hodges, L. F. (1997), 'An Evaluation of Techniques for Grabbing and Manipulating Remote Objects in Immersive Virtual Environments', *in Symposium on Interactive 3D Graphics*, pp 35-38.

Cheng, K. & Pulo, K. (2003), 'Direct Interaction with large-scale display systems using infrared laser tracking devices', *in Proceedings of the Australian Symposium on Information Visualisation (invis '03)*, ACS Inc., Adelaide, pp 67-74.

Cheng, K. & Takatsuka, M. (2005), 'Real-time Monocular Tracking of View Frustum for Large Screen Human-Computer Interaction', *in Proceedings of the 28th Australasian Computer Science Conference*, Estivill-Castro, V., Newcastle, Australia, pp 125-134.

Cheng, K. & Takatsuka, M. (2006), 'Estimating Virtual Touchscreen for Fingertip Interaction with Large Displays', *in Proc. OZCHI 2006*, ACM Press., pp 397-400.

Cipolla, R. & Hollinghurst, N. J. (1998) In *Computer Vision for Human-Machine Interaction*(Eds, Cipolla, R. and Pentland, A.) Cambridge University Press, pp. 97-110.

Colombo, C., Bimbo, A. D. & Valli, A. (2003) Visual Capture and Understanding of Hand Pointing Actions in a 3-D Environment, *IEEE Transactions on Systems, Man, and Cybernetics,* **33(4),** pp 677-686.

Crowley, J. L., Coutaz, J. & Berard, F. (2000) Things that See, *Communications of the ACM,* **43(3),** pp 54-64.

Dietz, P. & Leigh, D. (2001), 'DiamondTouch: A Multi-User Touch Technology', *in Proc. UIST '01,* ACM Press, pp 219-226.

Eisenstein, J. & Mackay, W. (2006), 'Interacting with Communication Appliances: An evaluation of two computer visionbased selection techniques', *in CHI,* ACM Press., Montreal, Quebec, Canada, pp 1111-1114.

Han, J. (2005), 'Low-Cost Multi-Touch Sensing through Fustrated Total Internal Reflection', *in UIST '05,* ACM Press., Seattle, Washington, pp 115-118.

Hinckley, K. (2003) In *The Human-Computer Interaction Handbook*(Eds, Jacko, J. A. and Sears, A.) Lawrence Erlbaum Associates, Inc, pp. 151-168.

Hung, Y.-P., Yang, Y.-S., Chen, Y.-S., Hsieh, I.-B. & Fuh, C.-S. (1998), 'Free-Hand Pointer by Use of an Active Stereo Vision System', *in Proceedings of 14th International Conference on Pattern Recognition (ICPR),* Brisbane, pp 1244-1246.

Lee, M. S., Weinshall, D., Cohen-Solal, E., Colmenarez, A. & Lyons, D. (2001), 'A computer vision system for on-screen item selection by finger pointing', *in Proceedings of the 2001 IEEE Computer Society Conference on Computer Vision and Pattern Recognition,* pp 1026-1033.

Leibe, B., Starner, T., Ribarsky, W., Wartell, Z., Krum, D., Weeks, J., Singletary, B. & Hodges, L. (2000) Towards Spontaneous Interaction with the Perceptive Workbench, a Semi-Immersive Virtual Environment, *IEEE Computer Graphics and Applications,* **20(6),** pp 54-65.

Lertrusdachakul, T., Taguchi, A., Aoki, T. & Yasuda, H. (2005) Transparent eye contact and gesture videoconference, *International Journal of Wireless and Mobile Computing,* **1(1),** pp 29-37.

Lock, A. (1980), 'Language Development: past, present and future.', *in Bulletin of British Psychological Society 33,* pp 5-8.

Mase, K. (1998) In *Computer Vision for Human-Machine Interaction*(Eds, Cipolla, R. and Pentland, A.) Cambridge University Press, pp. 53-81.

Matsushita, N. & Rekimoto, J. (1997), 'HoloWall: Designing a Finger, Hand, Body, and Object Sensitive Wall', *in Proc. UIST '97,* ACM Press, pp 209-210.

McNeill, D. (1992) *Hand and mind: what gestures reveal about thought,* University of Chicago Press.

Microsoft Surface http://www.microsoft.com/surface/index.html

Nickel, K. & Stiefelhagen, R. (2003), 'Pointing Gesture Recognition based on 3D-Tracking of Face, Hands and Head-Orientation', *in Proceedings of ICMI '03 International Conference on Multimodal Interfaces,* ACM Press, Vancouver, pp 140-146.

Norman, D. A. (1986) *Cognitive Engineering,* Lawrence Erlbaum Associates, Inc., New Jersey.

Oka, K., Sato, Y. & Koike, H. (2002) Real-Time Fingertip Tracking and Gesture Recognition, *IEEE Computer Graphics and Applications,* **22(6),** pp 64-71.

Olsen, D. R. & Nielsen, T. (2001), 'Laser Pointer Interaction', *in Proceedings of ACM Conference on Human Factors in Computing Systems (CHI'01),* ACM Press., Seattle, WA, pp 17-22.

Pierce, J., Forsberg, A., Conway, M., Hong, S. & Zeleznik, R. (1997), 'Image Plane Interaction Techniques In 3D Immersive Environments', *in Symposium on Interactive 3D Graphics*, pp 39-43.

Pinhanez, C. (2001), 'Using a Steerable Projector and a Camera to Transform Surfaces Into Interactive Displays', *in CHI 2001*, IBM T J Watson Research Center, pp 369-370.

Rakkolainen, I. (2003), 'MobiVR - A Novel User Interface Concept for Mobile Computing', *in Proceedings of the 4th International Workshop on Mobile Computing*, Rostock, Germany, pp 107-112.

Rekimoto, J. (2002), 'SmartSkin: An Infrastructure for Freehand Manipulation on Interactive Surfaces', *in Proc. CHI '02*, ACM Press, pp 113-120.

Ringel, M. & Henry Berg, Y. J., Terry Winograd (2001), 'Barehands: Implement-Free Interaction with a Wall-Mounted Display', *in Proc. of CHI 2001*, ACM Press, pp 367-368.

Saxena, A., Chung, S. H. & Ng, A. Y. (2007) 3-D Depth Reconstruction from a Single Still Image, *International Journal of Computer Vision,* **76(1),** pp 53-69.

DViT: Digital Vision Touch Technology, White Paper, SMART Technologies Inc, 2003 http://www.smarttech.com/dvit/DViT_white_paper.pdf

SONY EyeToy http://www.eyetoy.com

Sun Microsystems Inc., definition of View Frustum, http://java.sun.com/products/java-media/3D/forDevelopers/j3dguide/glossary.doc.html#47353

Takatsuka, M., West, G. A. W., Venkatesh, S. & Caelli, T. M. (2003) Low-cost interactive active range finder, *Machine Vision and Application,* **14(**pp 139-144.

Takenaka Corporation, Input System Which can Remotely Click the Screen Without hand Contact Developed http://www.takenaka.co.jp/takenaka_e/news_e/pr9806/m9806_02_e.htm

Taylor, J. & McCloskey, D. I. (1988) Pointing, *Behavioural Brain Research,* **29(**pp 1-5.

Gale Encyclopedia of Neurological Disorders, The Gale Group, Inc. http://www.answers.com/topic/proprioception

Torralba, A. & Oliva, A. (2002) Depth Estimation from Image Structure, *IEEE Transactions on Pattern Analysis and Machine Intelligence,* **24(9),** pp 1226-1238.

Tosas, M. & Li, B. (2004), 'Virtual Touch Screen for Mixed Reality ', *in European Conference on Computer Vision*, Springer Berlin, Prague, pp 72-82.

Wellner, P. (1993) Interacting with Paper on the DigitalDesk, *Communications of the ACM,* **36(7),** pp 87-96.

Wikipedia, the free encyclopedia, definition of View Frustum http://en.wikipedia.org/wiki/View_frustum

Zatsiorsky, V. M. (1998) *Kinematics of Human Motion,* Human Kinetics Publishers.

The Role of Facial Expressions and Body Gestures in Avatars for e-Commerce Interfaces

Dimitrios Rigas and Nikolaos Gazepidis
University of Bradford
United Kingdom

1. Introduction

As e-commerce user interfaces continue to expand, the need for interaction with multimodal content becomes noticeable (Böszörményi et al., 2001; Jalali-Sohi & Baskaya, 2001). User interfaces for e-Commerce (EC) applications occasionally use speaking avatars with facial expressions and body gestures to deliver information. The challenge is to provide a series of guidelines for e-commerce interfaces that attract the users' interest (Nemetz, 2000) and usable. Facial expressions and body gestures, as part of an expressive avatar may play an important role in interfaces. This paper describes three experiments that investigated the role of expressive avatars with facial expressions and body gestures in e-Commerce interfaces in terms of effectiveness, efficiency and user satisfaction.

2. Multimedia metaphors

2.1 Avatars

Avatars are interactive characters in real time virtual environments (VEs) (Dix et al., 2003; Sengers et al., 1999; Benyon et al., 2005; Bartneck et al., 2004). They are often depicted as three-dimensional (3D) animated human-like models (Theonas et al., 2008a). Users from any physical location can interact, communicate and cooperate with each other (Burford & Blake, 1999; Prasolova-Førland & Monica Divitini, 2002; Krenn et al., 2003) in Collaborative Virtual Environments or CVEs (Fabri et al., 1999). Other researchers (Hobbs et al., 1999; Thalmann, 1997) remark that VEs cover a wide range of applications such as educational, edutainment, e-commerce and simulation.

Fabri and Moore argue that when CVEs incorporate facial expressive avatars, they can be beneficial for people with special needs (e.g. autism) in terms of achievement and performance (Fabri & Moore, 2005). Emotional expressive avatars can also help with the interaction process of communicating information (Fabri et al., 1999). Fabri et al. experimented in a two-person messaging application that aimed to measure "richness of experience" (Fabri & Moore, 2005; Fabri et al., 2007). Their results indicated that users who interacted with the expressive avatars were more active, provided positive feedback, and enjoyed the experience. On the other hand, users who did not come into contact with

expressive avatars were less active and they did not appear to be more intensive in completing their tasks.
The reason for experimenting with these human-like characters in EC websites is mainly commercial; to see how much they attract individuals and encourage them to visit the site again in the future (Krenn et al., 2003).

In commercial web sites, there is a lack of a face to face communication between the customer and the seller. In addition, referring to a website that sells for example, electronic products are not tangible. Hence, it is necessary to experiment and evaluate some multimedia aspects that can be embedded in the designing of an EC site. It will measure the effect of audio-visual stimuli and multimodal interactions by introducing other modes of communication (see multimedia metaphors) between the user and the EC application. These metaphors will be used either separately or simultaneously, or with some combinations so as to have precise results (Ostermann & Millen, 2000).

It has been speculated, that human-like interface agents with a combination of facial expressions like moving eyebrows, head movement, smiling, quiver of the eyelids, opening and closing eyes, or lip movement synchronised with a text-to-speech generation system (Krenn et al., 2003; Cassell et al., 2001; Nijholt et al., 2000) will have a positive effect on consumers' decisions (Paradiso & L'Abbate, 2005) as they simulate a real-life character interacting in a realistic way with them. Several projects have been developed such as the BEAT (Cassell et al., 2001), the COGITO (Paradiso & L'Abbate, 2005), and the SoNG (Guerin et al., 2000).

Facial expressions give a more realistic interaction in human computer interfaces. The face is a means of expressing emotions, feelings, and linguistic information and due to the improvement of computer hardware (high performance graphics and processing speed) instances of cartoon-like and human-like synthesized faces have been investigated and developed for use in computer applications (Beskow, 1996a).

Animated or realistic characters are used in spoken dialogue interfaces, conveying information for verbal and non-verbal communication by several means of facial modalities e.g. lip-synchronization, eyes gazing and blinking, turn taking and further advanced modelling capabilities such as the use of gestures and motion (Beskow, 1996b). Beskow (Beskow, 1996a) developed a three-dimensional human face model complimented by a rule-based audio-visual text-to-speech synthesis system. The benefit of such an auditory-visual (bimodal) system as far as speech perception is concerned is that it could have a better success in an environment with a reduced level of acoustics and could be significantly used in applications for hearing impaired people (Cohen & Massaro, 1993).

Theonas et al. (Theonas et al., 2008a; Theonas et al., 2008b), conducted an experiment in a real academic lecture environment to study the relation of the facial expressions of three lecturers with the way students react based on lecturers' expressions. An observer attended all the lectures to study the role of lecturers' expressions and whether their expressions motivate students and increase their interest during the lecture. He also experimented in a virtual classroom aiming to study virtual lecturers' expressions to evaluate students' performance. His experimental study indicated that being more expressive (smiling) can increase students' motivation and interest and can also make them more enthusiastic towards the lecturer. As a result, it positively affects the students' learning and performance.

Li Gong (Gong, 2006) from Ohio State University conducted a research on digital characters to measure the effect of whether a happy expression is better than a sad one when being used from talking-head interface agents. He states that "…emotion is an essential factor in human psychology for it conveys feelings and attitudes, regulates motivation colours cognition and affects performance" (Gong, 2006). According to Massaro as well (Massaro, 1998) when synthetic faces are combined with speech to generate an animated–talking face in order to convey information or emotion, the results are more effective.

Human communications often involve the use of verbal communication (speech, writing) (Wiki, 2005; Hartley, 2003) that means direct or indirect contact with a person or a number of people, and in some other circumstances it involves non-verbal signals (eye contact, facial expressions, hand, arm, and leg gestures, body postures) where several times could be more expressive and meaningful in a conversation than the use of words or talks. The study of the body language and its non-verbal parameters is widely used in our everyday communication or business life and whoever knows how to use it, realises what a fascinating skill it is, enhancing his communication in every bit of life (Kyle, 2001).

Beskow (Beskow, 1996b) talked for a set of parameters in communication, the verbal and the non-verbal. The verbal refers to the control of speech articulation and the morphing and shaping of lips and mouth during a speech process whereas the non-verbal communication refers to facial expressions and gestures.

In order to give emphasis to our speech or to point at an object the movement of the body, of hands and head, play a major role. Gestures are used widely in our everyday life and they are also known as 'body language" communication (Cohen & Massaro, 1993).

McBreen (McBreen, 2001) with the ANOVA taking agent gender test experiments found that human-like gestures complement the agent's human-like appearance and she states that "gestures promote friendliness, politeness and lifelikeness" and that subjects significantly preferred female gestures than male ones. Cassell (Cassell, 2001) states that hands rather than eyes and speech are an excellent representation tool of events or objects and more specifically on describing ambiguous contexts. Pease (Pease, 1981) states that "many researchers rely on the idea that verbal communication is primarily used for conveying information where as the non-verbal aspect is for negotiating interpersonal attitude and sometimes they can substitute some verbal meanings". Regardless the culture, geographical parts, traditions and folkways there are some common gestures that people use. For instance people are showing that they are happy with a smile on their face, mad by frown their eyebrows, or a negation by shaking the head from side to side. On the other hand, there are some non-verbal gestures that differ from country to country or it is possible the same gesture to have a different meaning. The O.K. gesture for instance, in the USA it has the meaning that everything is fine, in France it has the meaning of zero notation or nothing, in

Japan means money and in Brazil has the meaning of insulting someone. Pease also states that "When in Rome do as the Romans do" (Pease, 1981).

2.2 Multimodal metaphors

Speech metaphor is often used in multimodal user interfaces so as to provide users with feedback along with the graphical environment about system's current state (Preece et al., 1994) and it is a very useful tool especially for visually impaired users (Lines & Home, 2002). We distinguish two types of speech; natural and synthesised. Natural speech output is a digitally recorded message of a male or female spoken word. It is often useful for applications that require short sentences to be spoken but a dynamic use of recorded speech by incorporating short recorded messages (as building blocks) is a complex process given the need for grammatical structure, context, tone changes and phonemes. Large storage capacity is also required due to the vast vocabulary. Synthetic speech output is produced using a speech synthesizer. It can be generated mainly by two methods: Concatenation or Synthesis by Rule (also referred to as formant synthesis) (Preece et al., 1994; Lines & Home, 2002). Using the concatenation method, digital recordings conducted by real human speech are stored and later on controlled as single words or sentences in a computer (Preece et al., 1994). An example based on concatenation is when someone uses a phone card and a recorded voice informs the user how many minutes left in the card. The audio message is digitally recordings of each digit separately, controlled by the computer system generating the spoken message. Synthesis by rule, involves the combination of synthesised words generated by rules of phoneme. It is useful for large vocabularies and as a result the quality of speech produced is poorer compared to the concatenation method (Lines & Home, 2002). Janse (Janse, 2002) had studied the perception of natural speech compared to a synthetic speech and derived that although synthetic speech is becoming more and more intelligent, natural speech still more comprehensible for listeners. A numerous of studies on synthesised speech have shown that natural speech still more intelligible and comprehensible than the synthetic. Voltrax, Echo, DECTalk, Voder, are some good examples of speech synthesizers developed in the past but with poor quality (Reynolds et al., 2002; Lemmetty & Karjalainen, 1999).

Computer-based systems offer a speech technology, known as Text-to-Speech (TTS) synthesis technology (Dutoit, 1999). TTS systems have the ability to read any arbitrary text, they analyze it and after converting it, they output it as a synthesised spoken message comprehensible by the user (Schroeter et al., 2000; Wouters et al., 1999). TTS technology is widely used in software applications, and many corporations are taking into account the benefits of involving this technology in EC websites (Kouroupetroglou & Mitsopoulos, 2000). TTS brings out new issues for the development of EC systems (Xydas & Kouroupetroglou, 2001) and provides the scope for new innovative applications.

2.2.1 Facial expressions and body gestures in avatars

This experiment aimed to investigate usability (effectiveness and user satisfaction) of avatars with facial expressions only or avatars with facial expressions and body gestures, and compare the use of expressive avatars with a typical textual and graphical metaphors in an e-commerce interface. The experiment was performed with 42 users in a specially developed experimental platform. This platform presented three products using three different conditions. The first two conditions involved avatars with facial expressions and the same facial expressions but with the addition of body gestures. The third condition provided typical textual and graphical representations. During the experiment, three products were presented randomly to the users using, again randomly, the three different conditions of presentation.

Figure 1 shows users' preferences for each presentation method used in the experiment and their preferences for the multi-modal metaphors. Almost 50% of the users described the text and graphic presentations of the products as poor. Another 33% and 12% described that particular presentation as good and very good respectively. The avatar with the facial expressions was chosen and ranked positively almost by every user. The total of good and very good ranking for the avatar with the facial expressions almost reached the ultimate acceptance level of 90% satisfaction and only a 10% described it as poor but none of the users judged it as very poor. Similarly to the avatar with the facial expressions, the avatar with the facial expressions and body gestures had 89% of positive views.

As far as the multimedia metaphors' ability to play an important role when shopping online, users decided that Speech output could be considered very important getting the majority of the users' preference with an 87%. Moreover, graphics are the most essential part in a website and play an important role for all the 42 users that participated in the experiment. Furthermore, avatars with facial expressions is viewed as positive with an 80% and it is believed that it could help users when shopping online whilst avatar with facial expressions and body gestures comes with a 67% of positive views and a 33% of negative ones.

Figure 1 also shows the percentages of the way that users selected a presentation method for each of the three products presented in random order. It also presents the figures for the way users selected or rejected a presentation method, regardless of the product. Initially, users selected product 1 mostly with the avatar with facial expressions (78.57%) and as a second preference the avatar with facial expressions and body gestures (50%); in the third place comes the text and graphics way with only 28%. Here it is necessary to mention that the avatar with facial expressions and body gestures was not well manipulated it could be compared with the avatar with facial expressions and body gestures of the other two products. Product 2 and product 3 were chosen by almost every user with avatar with facial expressions and body gestures getting over 85%-90% of their preference, while text and graphics was chosen by a 40% or less. Figure 3 also shows that regardless of the product, about 64% of the users in total did not choose the text and graphics presentation, 88% chose the avatar with facial expressions and only a 12% rejected it. Lastly, the avatar with facial expressions and body gestures presentation was selected by more than 75%.

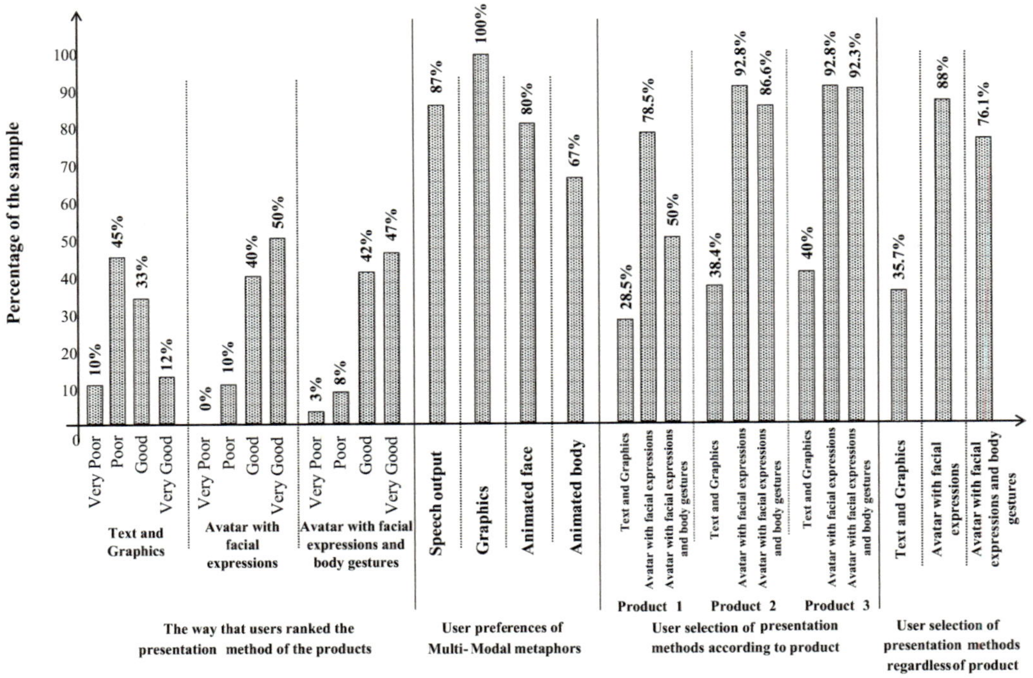

Fig. 1. Users' preferences and views regarding the presentation methods and multimodal metaphors as well as the results in percentages of the way users selected the presentation according to product and regardless of it.

These results were significant for both facial expressions (χ^2 = 24.38) and body gestures (χ^2 = 11.52), but not significant for the textual with graphics presentation (χ^2 = 3.42) at p-value 0.05 and critical value at 3.84.

Table 1 shows the percentages and the details related to three products. When P1 was selected with the text and graphics, it achieved 100% of correct answers by the users. However, there was only a small number of users that selected that way of presentation minimising error-making (distinctly 4 out of 14). For the successful non-selected answers for the text and graphics way the average dropped to 80%.When the avatar with facial expressions was chosen, the corresponding success for the selected way was over 80% almost 10% more than the avatar with facial expressions and body gestures. When users did not select these two ways of presentation the success rate of answering the product's question was about 65% for the avatar with facial expressions and about 94% on average for the avatar with facial expressions and body gestures. On the other hand, for the successful non-selected answers the percentages are about 65% for the avatar with facial expressions and quite higher for the avatar with facial expressions and body gestures reaching almost 95%.

As far as product 2 (P2) is concerned, there are some fluctuations regarding the successful answers within the 3 methods. Based on average correct answers it can be seen that the text and graphics reached high as 80%, the avatar with facial expressions a bit above 81% and the avatar with facial expressions and body gestures presentation is at 76.92%, almost 77% for the selected questions. When the corresponding presentation methods were not selected the correct answers for text and graphics were 81.25%, for the avatar with facial expressions 50% due to the very small number of users that did not select that method, and for the avatar with facial expressions and body gestures 75% for the same reason as the avatar with facial expressions.

Product 3 (P3) illustrates absolute success (100%) for the text and graphics when selected, again due to the small number of users who chose it, and at the same time almost total success for the avatar with facial expressions with 96.15%. The average slightly dropped for those users who chose the avatar with facial expressions and body gestures that is 79.16%. For the non-selected ways of presentations the mistaken answers for all of the presentation methods are null for avatar with facial expressions and body gestures and nominal for the text and graphics method.

			Product 1	**Product 2**	**Product 3**	**All Products**
Text and Graphics	Question 1	Selected	100%	100%	100%	100%
		Not Selected	70%	87.5%	88.8%	81.4%
	Question 2	Selected	100%	60%	100%	86.3%
		Not Selected	90%	75%	100%	88.8%
	Mean	Selected	100%	80%	100%	93.3%
		Not Selected	80%	81.2%	94.4%	85.1%
Avatar with facial expressions	Question 1	Selected	81.8%	69.2%	92.3%	81%
		Not Selected	66.6%	100%	100%	80%
	Question 2	Selected	90.9%	84.6%	100%	91.8%
		Not Selected	66.6%	0%	100%	60%
	Mean	Selected	86.3%	76.9%	96.1%	86.4%
		Not Selected	66.6%	50%	100%	70%
Avatar with facial expressions and body gestures	Question 1	Selected	71.4%	46.1%	66.6%	59.3%
		Not Selected	100%	50%	100%	92.3%
	Question 2	Selected	71.4%	92.3%	91.6%	87.5%
		Not Selected	85.7%	100%	100%	80%
	Mean	Selected	71.4%	69.2%	100%	73.4%
		Not Selected	94.11%	75%	100%	86.9%

Table 1. Results in percentages for successful answers for selected and non-selected ways of presentations for each product & all products.

Table 1 also shows the total results of all products for both selected and non-selected presentations. It can be observed that in total the text and graphics reached 93% of successful answers from the users, 86.48% for the avatar with facial expressions and lastly for the avatar with facial expressions and body gestures users reached a score of 73.48% when selecting that presentation. On the other hand, the non-selected answers range as follows: about 85% for the text and graphics, 70% for the avatar with facial expressions and 86% for the avatar with facial expressions and body gestures.

During the experiment two main observations were made. First, when the avatar with facial expressions and body gestures was demonstrated to the users with speech metaphor, they focused more on the speech rather than the text description of the products. Second, many users were pleasantly surprised when they were shown the avatar with facial expressions and body gestures concentrating more on the animation (facial expressions, lips synchronisation, body and hand gestures, and body postures) rather than the specifications of the products.

2.2.2 User preference of specific facial expressions and body gestures

(a) Experiment with Interactive Context

This experiment measured effectiveness user satisfaction in realistic interface circumstances of an avatar with 13 facial expressions and 9 body gestures that demonstrated two products. The first product (Windows Vista) was presented with facial expressions and the second product (Nintendo Wii) with full body gestures. Users (n=42) were asked to indicate their perception (positive or negative) after each random presentation that used a specific facial expression and body gesture.

Figure 2 shows that all positive facial expressions obtained high results in positive views by users (i.e. over 85%). On the other hand, the negative facial expressions had only 5% of positive views by users. Lastly, according to the users' ratings for the neutral expressions, the neutral expression had 83% (35 out of 42 users) of a positive view and two thirds (67% or 28 out of 42) of the users rated the thinking expression positively.

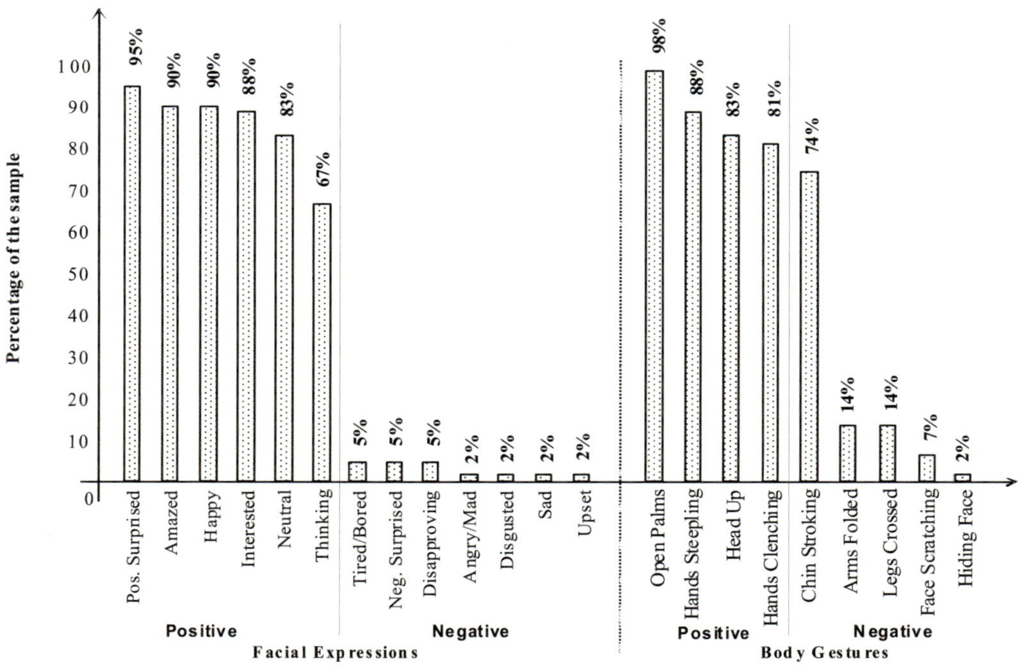

Fig. 2. Users' positive views on facial expressions and body gestures.

Figure 2 also shows that the positive body gestures were viewed positively by the users with some fluctuations in the percentages. The open palms obtained a positive score of 98% (41 out of 42) of users' answers, followed by an 88% (37 out of 42 users) for the hands steepling. An approximately 80% of the users viewed the hands clenching (34 out of 42 users) positively and the head up (35 out of 42 users) and another 74% of users found the chin stroking positive (31 out of 42 users).
According to the results for the negative body gestures, the majority of the users (i.e. over 85%) expressed a negative impression during their demonstration, especially for the face scratching (93% or 39 out of 42 users) and hiding face (98% or 41 out of 42 users).

2.2.3 Comparing facial expressions, body gestures and textual presentations

Lastly, the second section compared three interfaces (text and graphics, avatar with facial expressions and avatar with facial expressions and body gestures), where users had to select 2 our of 3 high-tech products according to the presentation method and regardless of the product information and then answer a number of questions upon each presentation of a product. The brand names of the products were not presented to avoid any influence on users' opinion. The description of each product was taken from CNET website. Each user was presented these products in a different order (GPS Navigator, Multimedia Player and PDA Phone) by using these methods of presentation, which followed 42 different combinations. Each product was presented twice. Product descriptions were categorised into short, medium and long in terms of text in order to investigate the error rating on users' answers. The effectiveness of communication metaphor, recall of information by users and learnability by users of each product according to interface were measured. This section discusses the users' views on the presentation method and the multimodal metaphors, the selection of users according to the presentation of products and the successful answers for the three product descriptions used in the experiment.

Figure 3 shows users' preferences for each presentation method used in the experiment and users' general viewpoint of multimodal metaphors. More than 60% (26 out of 42) of the users described the text and graphics method of presentation as very poor or poor expressions and about 1/3 of them as good. The presentation method with the avatar with facial expressions reached a level of acceptance of 96% (40 out of 42 users). The avatar with facial expressions and body gestures achieved a 46% of good, 40% as a very good and 14% poor.

Concerning the role of the multimodal metaphors could play an important role, the Speech output was chosen by a 90% (38 out of 42) of the users. At the same level was the preference for the Graphics with a 98% (41 out of 42 users), making it the most important metaphor when browsing a website. Moreover, avatar with facial expressions is being viewed by 83% (35 out of 42 users) of the sample positively, whilst avatar with facial expressions and body gestures is ranked at similar levels with an 81% (34 out of 42) of positive views from the users.

Figure 3 also depicts the percentages of the way users selected a presentation method among the three products presented in a random order as well as the percentages of the presentation method regardless of the products. The text presented was 112 words for product 3, 207 for product 1, and 289 for product 2.

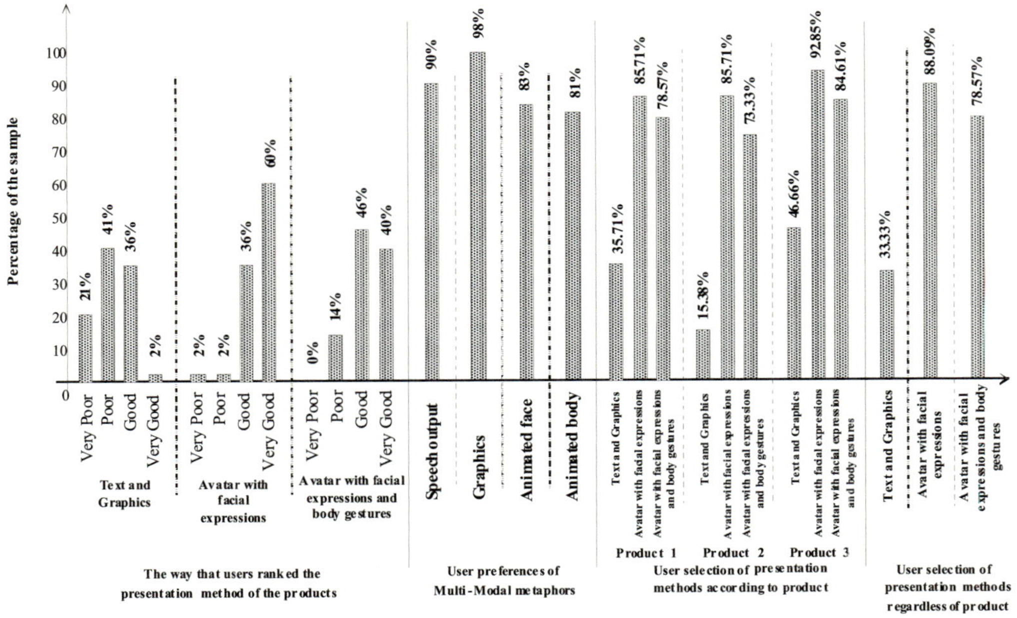

Fig. 3. Preferences and views of users regarding the presentation methods and multimodal metaphors, as well as the results in percentages of the way users selected the presentation method according to the product and regardless of it.

Results show that P1, P2, and P3 were mostly selected when an avatar with facial expressions was used, with percentages over 85%. The percentage was also large for all products when the avatar with facial expressions and body gestures was chosen by users, with an average score of 78%. As far as the text and graphics presentation is concerned, the highest score was achieved for P3 (i.e. the shortest length) with a 46%. P1 has a percentage of 35.71% and P2 was chosen by the smallest number of users compared to any other product with the low score of 15%. Figure 3 also shows the percentages of users that chose a presentation method regardless of the product. The avatar with the facial expressions was chosen by the majority of the users, nearly 90% followed by the 78% of the avatar with facial expressions and body gestures and only a 33% of the users selected the textual method of presentation. These results were significant for both facial expressions (χ^2 = 24.38) and body gestures (χ^2 = 13.71), but not significant for the textual with graphics presentation (χ^2 = 1.52) at p-value 0.05 and critical value at 3.84.

Table 2 shows the percentages and the details derived for P1 upon the selection of a presentation method. When P1 was selected with the text and graphics, the mean value of correct answers from the users was approximately 65%. Compared to the other presentation methods, only 5 users out of 14 selected this method. However, for the non-selected presentation method results, the score was approximately at 63%. When the avatar with the facial expressions was selected, the successful rate was relatively high at about 83%. A similar percentage was achieved when the avatar with the facial expressions was not selected which occurred with a small number of users (2 out of 14). When the avatar with facial expressions and body gestures was selected, the corresponding success was slightly lower than the avatar with facial expressions at about 79%. Likewise the percentage is high at 78% but the number of users (3 out of 14) and the result obtained is not representative.

Product 2 shows some fluctuations regarding the successful answers of the presentation methods chosen that were selected by users due to the long length of text. The method that achieved the highest score was the avatar with facial expressions and body gestures with 63.88%, followed by the avatar with facial expressions and body gestures with a 60.60%, and lastly the text and graphics with the lowest percentage of 33%. Approximately 50% of the users failed to answer correctly when the text and graphics was not selected (11 out of 13). Equal percentage applies for the avatar with facial expressions when it was not selected. Only 2 users though did not select it, therefore the error rates are not representative. For the not-selected answers given with the avatar with facial expressions and body gestures the mean rate of success was 66%.

			Text and Graphics		**Avatar with facial expressions**		**Avatar with facial expressions and body gestures**	
			Correct answers	mean	Correct answers	mean	Correct answers	mean
Product 1 (medium)	Selected	Q1:	4/5=80%	66.6%	9/12=75%	83.3%	7/11=63.6%	78.7%
		Q2:	2/5=40%		11/12=91.6%		9/11=81.8%	
		Q3:	4/5=80%		10/12=83.3%		10/11=90.9%	
	Not Selected	Q1:	4/9=44.4%	62.9%	1/2=50%	83.3%	2/3=66.6%	77.7%
		Q2:	6/9=66.6%		2/2=100%		2/3=66.6%	
		Q3:	7/9=77.7%		2/2=100%		3/3=100%	
Product 2 (long)	Selected	Q1:	0/2=0%	33.3%	7/12=58.3%	63.8%	5/11=45.4%	60.6%
		Q2:	2/2=100%		10/12=83.3%		8/11=72.7%	
		Q3:	0/2=0%		6/12=50%		7/11=63.6%	
	Not Selected	Q1:	4/11=36.3%	48.4%	2/2=100%	50%	3/4=75%	66.6%
		Q2:	7/11=63.6%		0/2=100%		3/4=75%	
		Q3:	5/11=45.4%		1/2=50%		2/4=50%	
Product 3 (short)	Selected	Q1:	4/7=57.1%	80.9%	11/13=84.6%	92.3%	10/11=90.9%	87.8%
		Q2:	6/7=85.7%		12/13=92.3%		8/11=72.7%	
		Q3:	7/7=100%		13/13=100%		11/11=100%	
	Not Selected	Q1:	5/8=62.5%	70.8%	1/1=100%	100%	1/2=50%	50%
		Q2:	4/8=50%		1/1=100%		1/2=50%	
		Q3:	8/8=100%		1/1=100%		1/2=50%	

Table 2. Results in percentages for correct answers for selected (A) and non-selected (B) ways of presentation for all products.

When P3 was selected due to its short length of text, there were no major statistical differences across the three presentation methods. Correct answers were higher than any other product. A remarkable high rate of successful answers was observed in the text and graphics when selected, approaching the 81%. Taking into account the other two methods, avatar with facial expressions and body gestures was around 88% and avatar with facial expressions was as high as 92%. For the text and graphics results were quite successful for the non-selected answers with a 70%. The avatar with facial expressions and body gestures, due to the small number of users that had not selected them cannot be fully judged.

2.2.4 Combining facial expressions and body gestures

This experiment aimed to verify the positive, negative, and combined effect and to measure effectiveness (i.e. correct answers), efficiency (i.e. time taken to answer with 60 sec being the maximum), and user satisfaction of expressive avatars with the best and least suitable facial expressions and body gestures to e-commerce interfaces. Table 3 shows the 13 facial expressions and 9 gestures used in the four experimental conditions. These were the best rated facial expressions (BRFE), the best rated body gestures (BRBG), the least rated facial expressions (LRFE) and the least rated body gestures (LRBG).

Conditions Expressive Avatars	Facial Expressions													Body Gestures								
	Positive						Negative							Positive					Negative			
	Amazed	Happy	Interested	Pos. Surprised	Neutral	Thinking	Angry/Mad	Disapproving	Sad	Upset	Neg. Surprised	Disgusted	Tired/Bored	Head Up	Open Palms	Chin Stroking	Hands steepling	Hands Clenching	Arms Folded	Face Scratching	Hiding Face	Legs Crossed
BRFE	√	√	√	√	√	√																
BRBG	√	√	√	√	√	√								√	√	√	√	√				
LRFE							√	√	√	√	√	√	√									
LRBG							√	√	√	√	√	√	√						√	√	√	√

Table 3. List of the facial expressions and body gestures consist each interface.

For the statistical analysis, the normal distribution of the continuous variables (e.g. time) was assessed by the nonparametric Kolmogorov-Smirnov test. The non-parametric Friedman test was applied as the time taken by users to answer each question in all conditions was not normally distributed. Furthermore, paired comparisons between experimental conditions (BRFE vs. BRBG, BRFE vs. LRFE, BRFE vs. LRBG, BRBG vs. LRFE, BRBG vs. LRBG and LRFE vs. LRBG) were performed by the non-parametric Wilcoxon test. Dichotomous variables (e.g. percentage of correct or incorrect answers for each question) were compared between interfaces by the McNemar test. The significance level was set at 0.05 with p-values < 0.05 indicating statistically significant differences.

Figure 4 shows the percentages of the users that correctly answered questions within the criterion time (60 sec) in each task for each experimental condition. The BRFE was the best performing condition with correct answers that reached, 96% of the users for task 4, approximately 91% for tasks 1 and 3, and 86% for task 2. The second best performing condition was the BRBG with percentages of correct answers that varied between 85% and 90%. In the LRFE and LRBG conditions, percentages dropped and ranged between 72% to 63% with the exception of 75% in task 2 in the LRBG. Similar performance of four conditions can also be observed using the mean values which are 91.3%, 87.82%, 70%, and 68.26% for BRFE, BRBG, LRFE, and LRBG respectively. Results indicated that 85% to 96% of the sample taken up to 60 seconds to answer all questions in the conditions in the BRFE and BRBG conditions respectively. These figures drop to approximately 65% to 75% in the LRFE and LRBG conditions.

Table 4 shows a comparison of the correct answers of the recall and recognition questions between the experimental conditions. The McNemar test was used to calculate the p-values obtained and determine the significance. The BRFE and BRBG conditions were significant when compared with the LRFE and LRBG. There was no significance difference between BRFE and BRBG as well as between the LRFE and LRBG conditions.
In the BRFE condition, 45 out of 46 (97.8%) users answered correctly questions 1 (recall) and 3 (recognition) and 40 out of 46 (87%) users questions 2 (recall), 4 (recognition) and 5 (yes/no). On overall, users performed well in all tasks in this condition. The results for the BRBG are similar to the BRFE. Users achieved the highest score in question 3 (recognition), as well as question 1 (recall) with correct answers being 97.8% and 91.3% respectively. Question 2 (recall) was answered by 40 out of 46 users (87%) and the rest of the results for BRBG condition ranged between 80% to 82%

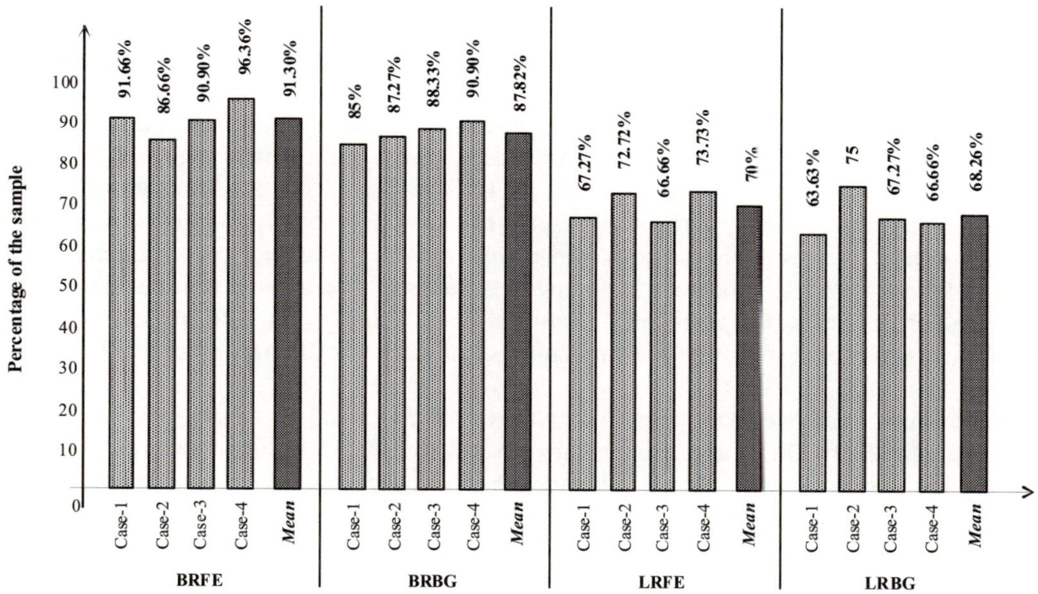

Fig. 4. Correct answers and mean values for each experimental interface and for each case used (n=46).

	All		Recall				Recognition				Yes/No	
	Questions		Question 1		Question 2		Question 3		Question 4		Question 5	
Conditions	%	p	%	p	%	p	%	p	%	p	%	p
BRFE *vs.* BRBG	91.3 *vs.* 87.8	0.280	97.8 *vs.* 91.3	0.375	87 *vs.* 87	1.000	97.8 *vs.* 97.8	1.000	87 *vs.* 82.6	0.774	87 *vs.* 80.4	0.581
BRFE *vs.* LRFE	91.3 *vs.* 70	**<0.001**	97.8 *vs.* 78.3	**0.012**	87 *vs.* 71.7	0.092	97.8 *vs.* 95.7	1.000	87 *vs.* 54.3	**0.003**	87 *vs.* 50	**0.001**
BRFE *vs.* LRBG	91.3 *vs.* 68.3	**<0.001**	97.8 *vs.* 71.7	**0.001**	87 *vs.* 69.6	0.077	97.8 *vs.* 95.7	1.000	87 *vs.* 58.7	**0.004**	87 *vs.* 45.7	**0.001**
BRBG *vs.* LRFE	87.8 *vs.* 70	**<0.001**	91.3 *vs.* 78.3	0.146	87 *vs.* 71.7	0.143	97.8 *vs.* 95.7	1.000	82.6 *vs.* 54.3	**0.007**	80.4 *vs.* 50	**0.003**
BRBG *vs.* LRBG	87.8 *vs.* 68.3	**<0.001**	91.3 *vs.* 71.7	**0.035**	87 *vs.* 69.6	0.115	97.8 *vs.* 95.7	1.000	82.6 *vs.* 58.7	**0.043**	80.4 *vs.* 45.7	**0.002**
LRFE *vs.* LRBG	70 *vs.* 68.3	0.752	78.3 *vs.* 71.7	0.648	71.7 *vs.* 69.6	1.000	95.7 *vs.* 95.7	1.000	54.3 *vs.* 58.7	0.845	50 *vs.* 45.7	0.839

Table 4. P-values among interfaces for all questions. (for p-values with many decimals close to 0 "<" used).

The results of the LRFE condition are considerably lower. It can be seen that users achieved a 78% for the first question and approximately 72% for the second question of the recall tasks. For the recognition tasks, users performed well in Question 3 with 44 out of 46 users (95.7%) answered correctly. However, the correct answers in the remaining questions were equally distributed and percentages range up to 50%. The LRBG condition was the least performing. Approximately 70% of the users answered the recall questions correctly. The third question (recognition) was answered correctly, as in the other three conditions by 44 out of 46 users (95.7%). However, the number of users who answered the fourth question (recognition) correctly dropped to 27 users out of 46 (58.7%). The fifth question (yes/no choice) was answered correctly by a small number of users (i.e. 21 out of 46 or 45.7%).

Table 5 shows that over 89% of the users answered the recall and recognition questions under the BRFE and BRBG and a range between 70% to 77% for the other two conditions. As for the last yes/no question, the BRFE experimental interface comes first on users' correct answers with an 87%, followed by the BRBG, with a slightly lower percentage of around 80%. Lastly, the percentages of the correct answers for the yes/no question have noticeably dropped for the other two conditions as half the number of the users answered correctly when the presentations were made using the LRFE, whereas the percentage was below 50% for LRBG, at 45.65%.

	Recall	Recognition	Yes/No
BRFE	92.39%	92.39%	87%
BRBG	89.13%	90.22%	80.43%
LRFE	75%	75%	50%
LRBG	70.65%	77.17%	45.65%

Table 5. Users' correct answers (n=46) shown in percentages for recall, recognition and yes/no question for each experimental interface (i.e. BRFE, BRBG, LRFE and LRBG)..

Figure 5 shows the results of user satisfaction for each experimental interface as well as the importance of the multimedia metaphors in e-Commerce applications. The most popular condition was the BRFE with the majority of users (93.48%) being satisfied with the facial expressions used. The second most preferred condition by users was the BRBG with approximately 85% of user preference. The level of user satisfaction in LRFE and LRBG was approximately 30.43% and 18%. Figure 5 also shows user satisfaction of other multimodal metaphors used in the interface. The use of speech output (recorded) was considered to be a good feature by 93.5% and graphics by 96% of the users. The use of avatars that incorporated facial expressions was considered by approximately 80% of the users as an essential metaphor for an e-Commerce interface. Finally, about 70% of the users preferred the full animated body that incorporated gestures with facial expressions. All these results are in agreement with the empirical data.

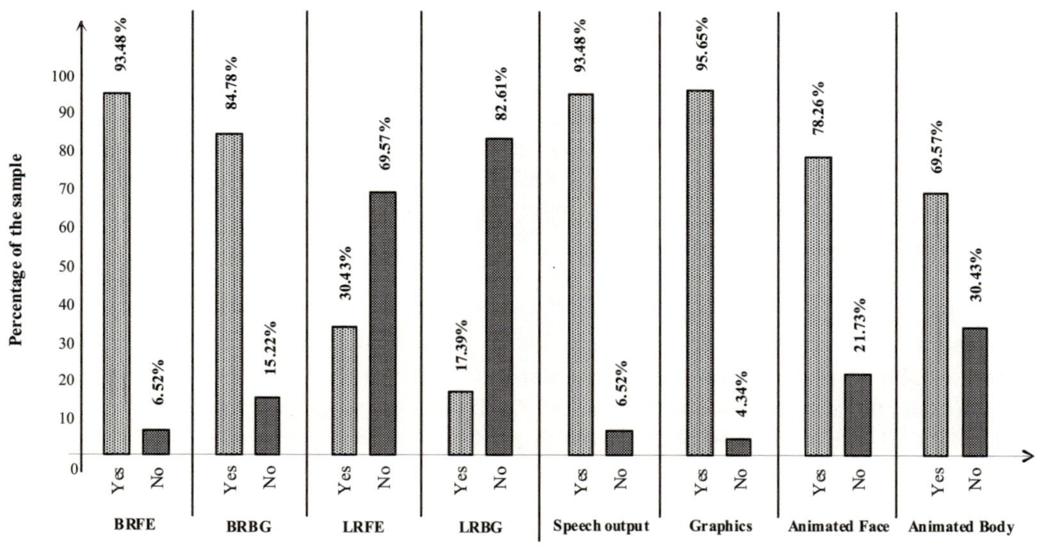

Fig. 5. User satisfaction for each experimental interface and specific multimodal metaphors.

3. Discussion

The first experiment showed that users preferred the avatar with facial expressions (88% or 37 out of 42 users) followed by the avatar with facial expressions and body gestures (76.1% or 32 out of 42 users). The text and graphics presentation was the least preferred method (35.7% or 15 out of 42 users). These findings were demonstrated consistently for all three products or presentation methods used in the experiments. One can therefore assume that this type of simulated face-to-face communication would positively contribute to an e-Business system.

Users were observed to focus more on the products themselves when these products were presented by using the avatar with facial expressions and body gestures. Post-experimental interviews suggested that users thought that the avatar with facial expressions and body gestures was amusing and entertaining and their attention was directed more towards the technical aspects of the presentation than towards the specifications of the products presented. This result is therefore confirmed by empirical observations as well as by user views. Users demonstrated the ability to remember the information communicated by using the avatar with facial expressions and body gestures could better than when the information was communicated with text and graphics.

The experiment with an interactive context indicated the users' views on avatar with facial expressions and body gestures with the presentation of two products. Results showed that positive expressions generally got over 85% of positive views; distinguishably the positively surprised expression (95%) was followed by the amazed and the happy expressions (90%). The negative expressions got high percentages of negative impressions from the users. Namely, the angry/mad, disgusted, sad and upset got 98% of negative users' views, whereas the remaining negative expressions got 95%. Neutral and thinking got 83% and 67% of positive views respectively.

As for the positive gestures the open palms once again got a high percentage with 98% of positive views followed by the hands steepling with 88%. The rest of the positive gestures reached approximately 88%. The negative gestures confirmed the initial hypothesis and results showed negative views by users for all of them. However, the most negatively rated body gestures were the hiding face with 98%, the face scratching and the legs crossed with 93% and lastly the arms folded with 86%.

The third experiment investigated the "best rated" and "least rated" by users facial expressions and body gestures in a human-like expressive avatar in a simulated e-commerce interface. The results indicated that on overall the percentage of correct answers in BRFE and BRBG conditions ranged from 85% to 96%, but dropped to 65% and 75% for the LRFE and LRBG. The mean values of the users' correct answers ranged between 87% to 91% for the BRFE and the BRBG and 68% to 70% for the LRFE and the LRBG conditions. The correct answers per interface per question showed an exceptional performance of the users for BRFE and BRBG. The BRFE results ranged from 87% to almost 98%, and the BRBG results ranged from 80% to approximately 98% for correct answers. On the other hand, correct answers are lower for the other two interfaces with results ranging from approximately 45% to 71%. However, 95% of the users managed to answer correctly the third question (recognition) using the LRFE and LRBG experimental interfaces. The level of user acceptance and satisfaction was also high for the BRFE and BRBG conditions (93.48% and 84.78% respectively) but low for the LRFE and the LRBG (less than 31%) conditions.

The results also showed that users prioritise metaphors in the order of speech output (93%) and graphics (95%), avatars with facial expressions (78%), and avatars with facial expressions and body gestures (69%). Users' correct answers of the recall, recognition and yes/no answers for the BRFE and the BRBG differed significantly from the LRFE and the LRBG. Avatars with a combination of positive facial expressions or facial expressions with body gestures contribute positively to the interaction process between the user and the interface and can successfully communicate product information in an e-commerce interface. On the other hand, a combination of negative facial expressions or facial expressions with body gestures could distract the user from perceiving the information.

4. Conclusion

The results obtained from this experimental study were interpreted and concluded with some key points on usability aspects of B2C interfaces. These empirical findings can be interpreted into a set of usability guidelines that would effectively enhance the usability of B2C interfaces. The guidelines derived are structured into length of text, speech metaphor, use of facial expressions, use of body gestures and combination of facial expressions and body gestures.

4.1 Length of text

When short text descriptions needed to be communicated, expressive avatars did not effectively enhance the usability of an interface. When short text descriptions needed to be communicated, expressive avatars did not effectively enhance the usability of an interface. User error ratings did not significantly differ among presentation methods (i.e. text with graphics, avatar with facial expressions, avatar with facial expressions and body gestures). In cases where the text was longer, results obtained indicated that facial expressions and body gestures effectively and efficiently contributed to the interface becoming more usable. However, a designer of a B2C platform should always have an option of textual method of presentation no matter what the length of the text is, as there are some users who find animated avatars annoying and do not want to familiarise themselves with the multimedia methods of presentation to communicate information.

4.2 Speech metaphor

Recorded speech enhanced the usability of the interface and kept the attention of the user to the presentation when being used efficiently. A clear, "crisp" speech articulation pattern maintained the interest of the user throughout the presentation. When speech tone was used with positive facial expressions, users showed more interest and they paid more attention to the text description. Results obtained indicate a significant increase in the efficiency and effectiveness of the users' interaction with the interface. This, however, did not happen with the negative facial expressions. In addition to the text, speech also enhanced the usability of the interface.

4.3 Use of facial expressions

Expressive avatars give a sense of presence in an interface and 'engage' users in the interface as users were often observed to mimic the avatars' expressions. The 13 facial expressions investigated in the experiments, in both the absence and presence of an interactive context, demonstrated that only the positive facial expressions contributed positively to the interaction process between the user and the interface. Expressions that are advised to be used with an avatar are the happy (not too excessively), interested, positive surprised or amazed. Users also thought that these expressions were suitable metaphors to communicate information. The results obtained indicate a significant increase in the efficiency and effectiveness for users in their interface tasks. Users were also more motivated and focused on product presentations when positive facial expressions were used. The same was not observed with negatively rated by users facial expressions. Negative facial expressions should not be used by an avatar. Users showed an antipathy for all the negative expressions and they were distracted from the communication of information. As a result, the use of negative expressions would only negatively influence users' decision when an avatar with negative facial expressions is used. These negative facial expressions are the angry or mad, disapproving, sad, upset, negatively surprised, disgusted and tired or bored. The results derived from the neutral facial expressions showed that users like the neutral expression, but not the thinking expression and in all cases (experiment with interactive context. When the thinking expression was used, it did not effectively persuade a user (prospective buyer) when shopping online, as a feeling of uncertainty was portrayed. Therefore, the thinking facial expression should not be used in B2C interfaces.

4.4 Use of body gestures

The experiments investigated 9 body gestures in an interface in both the absence and presence of an interactive context. It can be suggested that positive body gestures such as open palms, head up, or hands clenching could only improve and enhance the usability of an interface and can be used extensively by an avatar. Also experimental results indicate that hands steepling efficiently contributed to a presentation, although the exact use of this gesture has not been fully specified in literature. These gestures express openness and honesty, influencing positively users' decisions. Lastly, chin stroking should be carefully used as it often communicates a feeling of uncertainty by an avatar. Experimental results obtained about the use of negative body gestures indicate that negative gestures should not be used by an avatar. Body gestures such as the arms folded, face scratching, hiding face and legs crossed only convey a defensive and dishonest message when used by avatars. Body gestures however, may distract the attention of the user if they are used extensively, failing as a result, to achieve their main goal to successfully communicate information and persuade users to purchase specific products in an e-Commerce interface.

5. References

Böszörményi, L.; Hellwagner, H. & Kosch, H. (2001). Multimedia Technologies for E-Business Systems and Processes, Institut für Informationstechnologie, Universität Klagenfurt.

Jalali-Sohi, M. & Baskaya, F. (2001). A Multimodal Shopping Assistant for Home E-Commerce, Fraunhofer Institute for Computer Graphics.

Nemetz, F. (2000). The Missing Link: Multimedia and E-Commerce, Department of Mathematical Sciences, University of Bath.

Dix, A.; Finlay, J.; Abowd, G. D. & Beale, R. (2003). Human-Computer Interacrtion 3rd Edition, Prentice Hall, (379-381).

Sengers, P.; Penny, S. & Smith, J. (1999). Traces: Semi-Autonomous Avatars.

Benyon, D.; Turner, P. & Turner, S. (2005). Designing Interactive Systems - People, Activities, Contexts, Technologies, Addison-Wesley.

Bartneck, C.; Takahashi, T. & Katagiri, Y. (2004). Cross-Cultural Study of Expressive Avatars.

Theonas, G.; Hobbs D. & Rigas, D. (2008a). Employing Virtual Lecturers' Facial Expressions in Virtual Educational Environments, The International Journal of Virtual Reality, (31-44).

Burford, D. & Blake, E. (1999). Real-Time Facial Animation for Avatars in Collaborative Virtual Environments, Collaborative Visual Computing, Department of Computer Science, University of Cape Town.

Prasolova-Førland, E. & Divitini, M. (2002). Supporting learning communities with collaborative virtual environments: Different spatial metaphors, IDI, Norwegian University of Science and Technology.

Krenn, B.; Neumayr, B.; Gstrein, E. & Grice, M. (2003). Life-like Agents for the Internet: A Cross-Cultural Case Study.

Fabri, M.; Gerhard, M.; Moore, D.J. & Hobbs, D.J. (1999). Perceiving the Others: Cognitive Processes in Collaborative Virtual Environments, Virtual Learning Environment Research Group, School of Computing, Leeds Metropolitan University.

Hobbs, D.; Perera S. & Moore, D. (1999). The use of Metaphors to enhance Educational Hypermedia, Proceedings of the 7th International Conference on Computers in Education, Tokyo, Japan.

Thalmann, D. (1997). Virtual Humans in Virtual Environments: A New View of Multimedia Applications, Computer Graphics Lab (LIG), Swiss Federal Institute of Technology (EPFL), Lausanne, Switzerland.

Fabri, M. & Moore, D. (2005a). The use of emotionally expressive avatars in Collaborative Virtual Environments, ISLE Research Group, School of Computing, Leeds Metropolitan University.

Fabri, M.; Moore, D.J. & Hobbs, D.J. (1999). The Emotional Avatar: Nonverbal Communication between Inhabitants of Collaborative Virtual Environments, in Braffort et al (eds.) Gesture-Based Communication in Human-Computer Interaction, Springer Lecture Notes in Artificial Intelligence 1739, pp. 245-248.

Fabri, M. & Moore, D.J. (2005b). Is Empathy the Key? Effective Communication via Instant Messaging, in Proceedings of 11th EATA International Conference on Networking Entities, St. Pölten, Austria.

Fabri, M.; Elzouki, S. Y. & Moore, D. (2007) Emotionally Expressive Avatars for Chatting, Learning and Therapeutic Intervention, Human-Computer Interaction, Part III, HCII 2007, (275-285), Springer-Verlag Berlin Heidelberg.

Ostermann, J. & Millen, D. (2000). Talking Heads and Synthetic Speech: An Architecture for Supporting Electronic Commerce, AT&T Labs - Research, New Jersey, USA.

Cassell, J.; 0Vilhjálmsson, H. H. & Bickmore, T. (2001). BEAT: the Behavior Expression Animation Toolkit, MIT Media Laboratory.

Nijholt, A.; Heylen, D. & Vertegaal, R. (2000). Inhabited interfaces: attentative conversational agents that help, Deprtment of Computer Science, University of Twente, The Netherlands.

Paradiso, A. & L'Abbate, M. (2005). A Model for the Generation and Combination of Emotional Expressions, GMD - German National Research Center for Information Technology Institute (IPSI), Darmstadt, Germany.

Guerin, F.; Kamyab, K.; Arafa, Y. & Mamdani, E. (2000). Conversational Sales Assistants, Intelligent and Interactive Systems, Department of EEE, Imperial College of Science.

Beskow, J. (1996a). Talking heads - communication, articulation and animation, Department of Speech, Music and Hearing, KTH.

Beskow, J. (1996b). Animation of Talking Agents", Centre for Speech Technology, KTH, Stockholm, Sweden.

Cohen, M. M. & Massaro, D. W. (1993). Modeling Coarticulation in Synthetic Visual Speech.

Theonas, G.; Hobbs D. & Rigas, D. (2008b). The Effect of Facial Expressions on Students in Virtual Educational Environments, International Journal of Social Sciences, Volume 2, (42-49).

Gong, L. (2006). Is Happy better than sad even if they are both non-adaptive? Effects of emotional expressions of talking-head interface agents, School of Communication, Ohio State University, USA.

Massaro, D. W. (1998). Perceiving Talking Faces: From Speech Perception to a Behavioral Principle, MIT Press, Cambridge, MA.

Wiki, (2005). http://en.wikipedia.org/wiki/Talk:Nonverbal_communication.

Hartley, M. (2003). Body Language At Work, Sheldon Press.

Kyle, D. R. (2001). Reading Body Language for the Sales Professional.

McBreen, H. M. & Jack, M. A. (2001). Evaluating Humanoid Synthetic Agents in E-Retail Applications.

Cassell, J. (2001). Embodied Conversational Agents - Representations and Intelligence in User Interfaces.

Pease, A. (1981). Body Language - How to read others' thoughts by their gestures", Sheldon Press.

Preece, J,; Rogers, Y.; Sharp, H.; Benyon, D.; Holland, S. & Carrey, T. (1994). Human-Computer Interaction. Addison-Wesley, (252-253).

Lines, L. & Home, K. (2002). Older Adults' Evaluations of Speech Output. Department of Information Systems & Computing, Brunel University, Uxbridge, Middlesex, U.K.

Janse, E. (2002). Time-Compressing Natural and Synthetic Speech, University of Utrecht, The Netherlands.

Reynolds, M. E.; Isaacs-Duvall, C. & Haddox, M. L. (2002). A Comparison of Learning Curves in Natural and Synthesized Speech Comprehension, Marshall University, Huntington, West Virginia.

Lemmetty, S. & Karjalainen, M. (1999). Review of Speech Synthesis Technology, Department of Electrical and Communications Engineering, Helsinki University of Technology.

Dutoit, T. (1999). A Short Introduction to Text-to-Speech Synthesis, TTS research team, TCTS Lab.

Schroeter, J.; Ostermann, J.; Graf, H.P.; Beutnagel, M.; Cosatto, E.; Syrdal, A.; Conkie, A. & Stylianou, A. (2000). Multimodal Speech Synthesis, AT&T Labs - Research, New Jersey, USA.

Wouters, J.; Rundle, B. & Macon, M W. (1999). Authoring Tools for Speech Synthesis Using the Sable Markup Standard.

Kouroupetroglou, G. & Mitsopoulos, E. (2000). Speech-enabled e-Commerce for Disabled and Elderly Persons, University of Athens, Greece.

Xydas, G. & Kouroupetroglou, G. (2001). Text-to-Speech Scripting Interface for Appropriate Vocalisation of e-Texts, University of Athens, Greece.

Sharing and Composing Video Viewing Experience

Akio Takashima[1] and Yuzuru Tanaka[2]
[1]*Tokyo University of Technology*, [2]*Hokkaido University*
Japan

1. Introduction

People often take their similar action if they were in a similar situation. Most of these actions are selected based on the individual's empirical knowledge. In this study, we have focused on such actions; we call it habitual behaviours, encountered during the video viewing process. Video viewing is increasing in popularity for novices and the relationship between videos and the users who watch these videos has been gradually changing. We used to watch TV programs passively (Figure 1. (1)), then select videos on demand (Figure 2. (2)). Now, with the advancement in technology, we can watch videos more actively by skipping commercials, zooming into an important object in a certain video frame, examining a particular scene at various playing speeds, and so on (Figure 1. (3)). This notion, which is called "active watching," allows users to experience videos from numerous viewpoints [Takashima04]. Many researches on video viewing have aimed toward summarizing the videos such that they can be watched briefly; however, it is just one type of video viewing style. This study focuses on a method to utilize these video viewing styles to share video viewing experience, and compose styles for creating novel viewing experience (Figure 1.(4)).

2. Related Work

This work is illustrated by three research field, information recommendation, video viewing experience, and knowledge media technology.

Information Recommendation

The method for information recommendation is roughly divided into explicit way and implicit way. In the explicit way, a user input her/his preferences to a system directory. On the other hand, in the implicit way, which is also the method employed in this study, a system will recommend what the user wants based on her/his action history that is not related to their preference directory. As for implicit way, several researches have been reported for the web browsing process. Seo et al. described a method for an information filtering agent to understand the users' preferences by analyzing their web browsing behaviours such as time taken for reading, book marking, scrolling, and so on [Seo00]. Sakagami et al. developed a system that extracts the user preferences during the reading of

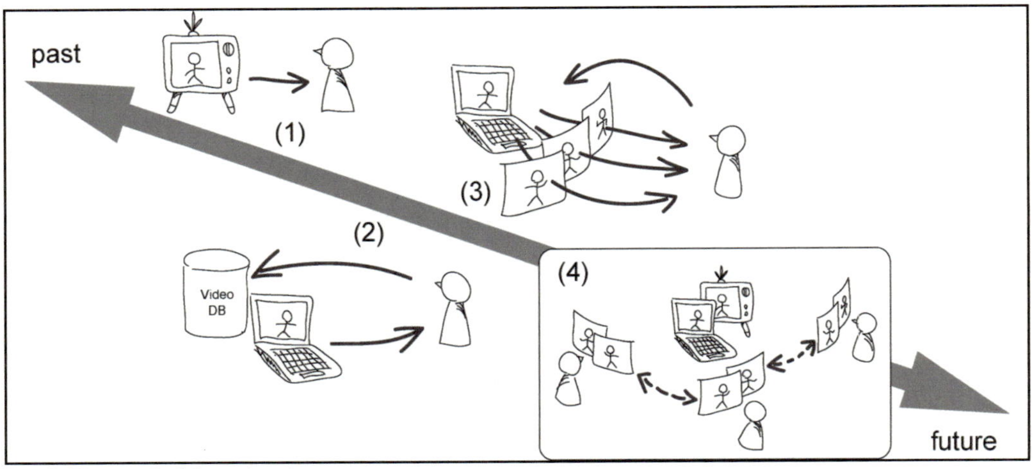

Fig. 1. Type of video viewing

online news by monitoring ordinary user operations such as scrolling and enlarging articles in an Internet browser [Sakagami97]. In the field of video viewing, a few studies have been reported. Yu et al. proposed an algorithm named ShotRank, which is similar to the PageRank system developed by Google [Brin98]; ShotRank is used to measure the interestingness and importance of segmented video scenes by using the data of how many times the users selected and watched each video shot [Yu03]. Mahmood et al. modeled the users' viewing behaviours using the hidden Markov model (HMM) and developed a system that generates video previews without any prior knowledge of the video content [Mahmood01]. Although both these studies employ the implicit method, they investigate only the summarizing of a particular video; no study has attempted to combine the user preferences encountered during the video viewing process.

In this study, we employ the user's behaviour analysis (and not semantic content analysis) and the implicit method for extracting the user's preferences (and not the explicit method); we then assist the users in reusing their habitual behaviours and combine them.

Video Viewing Experience

Many researches on video viewing have aimed toward summarizing the videos such that they can be watched briefly. However, the way to watch videos is gradually changing: summarization is just one type of video viewing style. The manner in which people interact with videos during their everyday lives involves complex knowledge-construction processes and not simple naïve information-receiving processes. Further, we have a large number of opportunities to use videos in increasing our knowledge, such as monitoring events, reflection on physical performances, learning subject matter, or analyzing scientific experimental phenomena. In such ill-defined situations, the domain knowledge about such contents is insufficient; hence, the users interact with videos according to their viewing styles [Yamamoto05]. However, such type of tacit knowledge, which is acquired through user experiences [Polany99], has not been effectively managed.

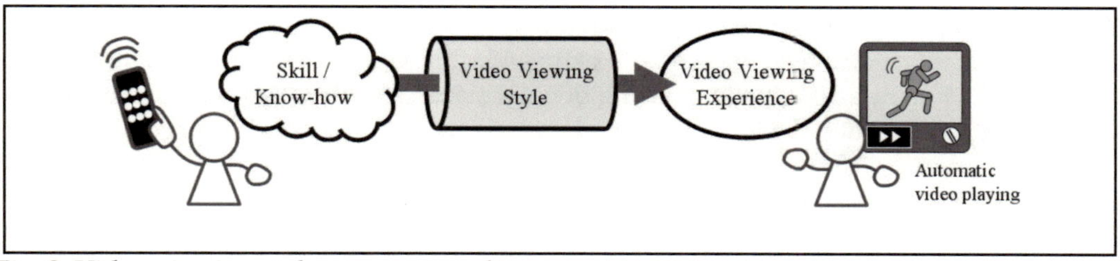

Fig. 2. Video viewing style as meme medium

Knowledge Media Technology

Many studies have been reported in the area of knowledge management systems [Alavi99]. As media for editing, distributing, and managing knowledge (called knowledge media), Tanaka introduced the meme media architecture and framework for reusing and combining such knowledge media by means of direct manipulation [Tanaka03]. In this framework, however, the target objects for reusing or sharing have been limited to the resources that are easily describable such as functions used in software [Fujima07] or services provided by web applications [Sugibuchi04]. In this study, this approach has been extended to be more user-friendly, which considers indescribable resources such as know-how or skills of human behaviour (i.e., tacit knowledge).

In this study, we consider video viewing styles as a type of knowledge media. Video viewing styles, which are considered as habitual behaviours in video viewing, are used to externalize one's viewing skills or know-how of video viewing; it allows the users to experience videos in various viewing styles. "To experience videos in various viewing styles" stands for to watch video which are automatically played based on the viewing skill (Figure 2.). In this case, experience is re-produced by watching automatically playing videos.

3. Reproducing Video Viewing Experience

3.1 Extracting video viewing style

To allow users to experience videos through video viewing styles, our approach employs extraction of relationship between video and human. From this point of view, we assume the following characteristics during video viewing:

- People often browse through videos in consistent and specific patterns
- User interaction with videos can be associated with the low-level features of such videos

While the user's manipulation of a particular video depends on the meaning of the content and the thought process of the user, it is difficult to observe these aspects. In this study, we attempted to estimate these associations between the video features and user manipulations. The low-level features (e.g., color distribution, optical flow, and sound level) have been associated with user manipulations, which reveal the changing speeds (e.g., fast-forwarding, rewinding, and slow playing). The identification of the associations from these aspects, which can be easily observed, implies that the user can possess a video viewing style even without the domain knowledge of the video content.

3.2 Scenario

In this section, we illustrate several examples for reusing and composing various video viewing styles.

3.2.1 Scenarios for reusing viewing style

Once a particular video viewing style is extracted, this video viewing experience can be reproduced. Here, we describe the reusing of scenarios that utilize the user's video viewing style as well as those of others.

Reusing the user's video viewing style

By using the user's video viewing style, the user can experience unknown videos through personalized efficient playback.

If the user is the coach of a particular football team, the video viewing style of the coach for the videos of football games may be distinguishable from the styles of novices. When a coach analyzes a particular game video of an opponent team, the coach may try to determine the weaknesses of the team by judging the positioning of the players or the formation shift of the entire team. In order to achieve this, if the coach repeatedly watches zoomed-out scenes, this habitual behaviour will be included in the video viewing style. For a diligent football player, the video viewing style might include behaviours that explore scenes, including tricky techniques, at a slower speed. On the other hand, novices tend to skip to scenes that excite them, such as goal scenes, to save time. This is also a type of video viewing style.

Several sports (e.g., American football, golf, Japanese sumo wrestling, and so on) include frequent interval scenes (out-of-play scenes). Skipping such scenes is a practical video viewing style that ensures efficiency in time spending.

For checking the weather report just before leaving one's home, weather forecasts from other areas might be a waste of time. If the weather report for a particular town is frequently watched (and the other areas are skipped), the weather information related to that particular town is included in the video viewing style.

Reusing others' video viewing styles

In addition to reusing one's own video viewing style, videos can be experienced through various types of video viewing styles produced by others.

The video viewing style of a particular famous head coach of a football team may have some special characteristics and a film reviewer may have a different video viewing style. By using such types of specialized video viewing styles, a particular video can be experienced in an unusual manner, leading to some serendipitous findings about the video.

3.2.2 Scenarios for composing viewing styles

One of the features of this study is the introduction of the notion of the composition of video viewing styles. These compositions will be utilized for experiencing both general and personal video viewing.

Composition for experiencing general video viewing

As described in the section on reusing scenarios, novices may tend to skip to the scenes that excite them, such as goal scenes, to save time. If most people skipped the same scenes based on their own respective video viewing style, these habitual skipping behaviours can be composed (i.e., pick up the same behaviours) and the scenes that are generally assumed to be attractive can be experienced. That is, making a digest video or summarizing the video is one of the practical applications of the composition of video viewing styles. Further, this

composition can achieve social filtering without any domain knowledge about the video content.
Similarly, people can re-edit some lengthy home video with the recording of a playing child. After the video has been played by skipping unwanted scenes, the video would transform into a digest version of the original video. If the video is viewed by many people, another viewer will find the clue to view a video effectively. This resembles a book that has been read repeatedly and has dog's-ears, finger marks, and stains left by the readers.

Composition for comparing personal video viewing experiences

One practical application obtained by comparing a particular video viewing experience with others is collaborative filtering. People with similar video viewing styles can experience video viewing through the others' video viewing styles, which may lead to a serendipitous way to watch the video. Collaborative filtering indicates, for instance, that "the viewers who have replayed this scene also replayed another particular scene," which is similar to Amazon.com's recommendation system in which "customers who bought this item also bought..." is mentioned.
Further, the user's video viewing style can be compared with a particular person's style, such as a famous head coach of a football team or a film reviewer, for learning their strategies in video viewing. These compositions help in the sophistication of the user's video viewing style.

4. System

In this section, we describe a system that extracts the user's video viewing style and allows the users to reuse and compose these styles.

System overview

To extract the associations between users' manipulations and low-level video features and then reproduce the viewing styles for other videos, we have developed a system called the video viewing experience reproducer (VVER). The VVER consists of the "association extractor" and "behaviour applier" blocks (Figure 3.).
The association extractor block identifies the relationships between the low-level features of videos and the user manipulation of these videos. This block requires several training videos and viewing logs of a particular user as input for these videos. In order to record the viewing logs, a user views the training videos using a simple video browser, which enables the user to control the playing speed. We categorized the patterns of changing the playing speeds into three types based on the patterns frequently used during an informal user observation [Takashima04]. The three types are (1) skip, (2) re-examine (rewind and then play at a speed less than the normal speed), and (3) others. The viewing logs possess pairs of the video frame numbers and the pattern for changing playing speed at which the user actually played the video. As low-level features, the system analyzes more than eighty properties of each frame. These features are categorized into five aspects, (1) statistical data of colour values in a frame, (2) representative colour data, (3) optical flow data, (4) number

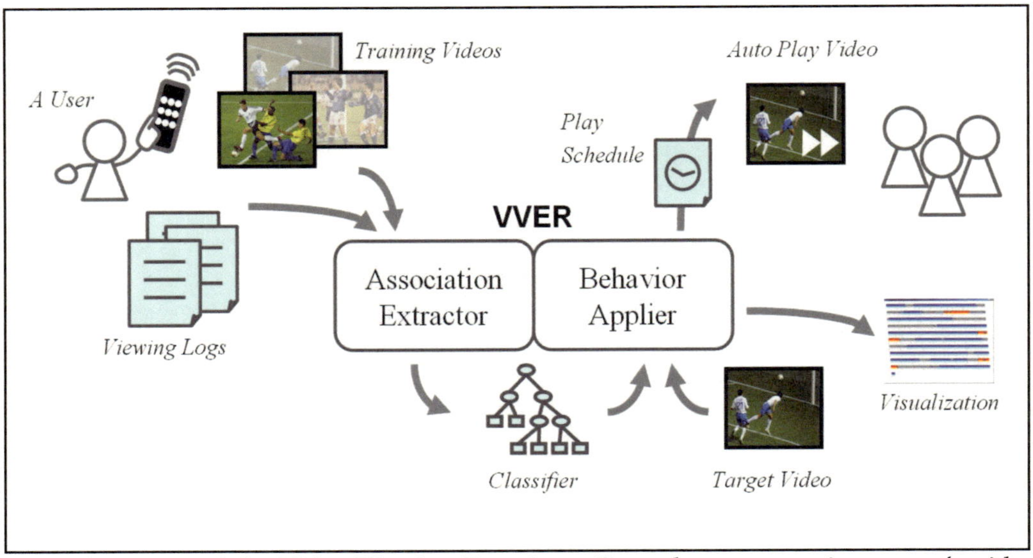

Fig. 3. Overview of the Video Viewing Experience Reproducer on reusing a user's video viewing style.

of moving objects, and (5) sound levels. Then, the association extractor generates a classifier that determines the patterns that associated with low-level features. In generating the classifier, we use the WEKA engine—a data mining software [WEKA].

The behaviour applier block creates a play schedule which plays the frames of the target video automatically at each speed in accordance with the pattern for changing playing speed that is produced by the classifier. We designed the mapping from the three types of patterns into specific speeds. The skipping behaviour is reproduced by playing at a faster speed (5.0x). The other behaviour is reproduced by playing at normal speed. The re-examining behaviour is reproduced by playing at a slower speed (0.5x). This play schedule possesses the pairs of the video frame number and estimated speed for the frame. The behaviour applier can remove the outliers from the sequence of frames, which should be played at the same speed, and it can visualize all the behaviours applied to each frame of the video. In addition, the behaviour applier allows the users to compose several play schedules.As described before, user manipulation was associated with the video features; in other words, the video viewing style was decomposed into rules. Then, each rule was composed so that other video viewing styles could be created. The timing when a particular composition is executed is after the generation of the play schedules (Figure 4.). As described earlier, a play schedule is a list of associations between each video frame in a video and the user's behaviour. A single play schedule is generated by a classifier of the behaviour applier; therefore, for Figure 4, two classifiers are formulated in order to generate two play schedules.
One play schedule is generated by one classifier of the behaviour applier; therefore, in this case, two classifiers are formulated in order to generate two play schedules. A composition is executed after the generation of the play schedules for composition purposes.

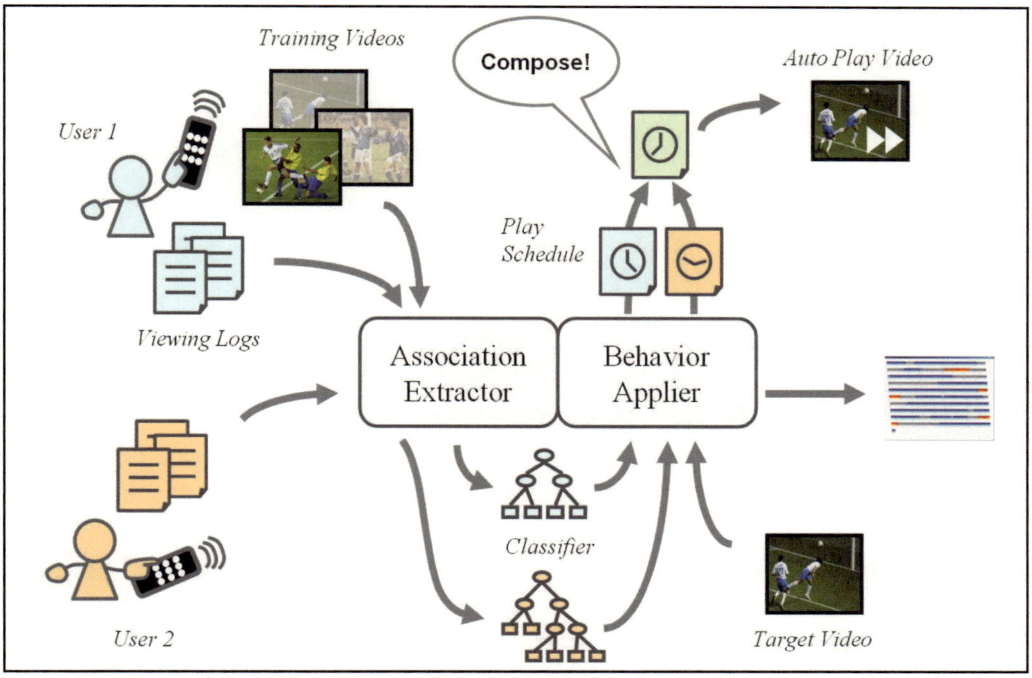

Fig. 4. Overview of the Video Viewing Experience Reproducer on composing two users' video viewing styles

To compose the video viewing styles, the system composes the play schedules via several operations. We defined a few simple operations, such as intersection $A \cap B := \{x \mid x \in A \text{ and } x \in B\}$, difference $A \setminus B := \{x \mid x \in A \text{ and } x \notin B\}$, and union $A \cup B := \{x \mid x \in A \text{ or } x \in B\}$, where A and B are sets of video frames that are associated with specific behaviours such as fast-forwarding or re-examining and x is a specific video frame. Some examples made by using these operations are as follows:

$$S_{USER1} \cap S_{USER2} \cap S_{YOU} \qquad \text{(ex.1)}$$
$$(S_{USER1} \cap S_{USER2}) \setminus S_{YOU} \qquad \text{(ex.2)}$$
$$(S_{USER1} \cap S_{USER2}) \cup S_{YOU} \qquad \text{(ex.3)}$$

Figure 5 illustrates these examples. The upper three belts in this figure indicate the estimated behavior of the video through the VVER based on the video viewing styles of three persons. For instance, the first belt shows that User1 may initially browse through the video at normal speed and later skip (fast-forward) the second part, re-examine the subsequent scenes, skip the fourth part, and then normally browse through the last part. The second and third belts can be described in a similar manner. The lower three belts correspond to three examples of composed behaviour (i.e., composed play schedules). The details are as follows:

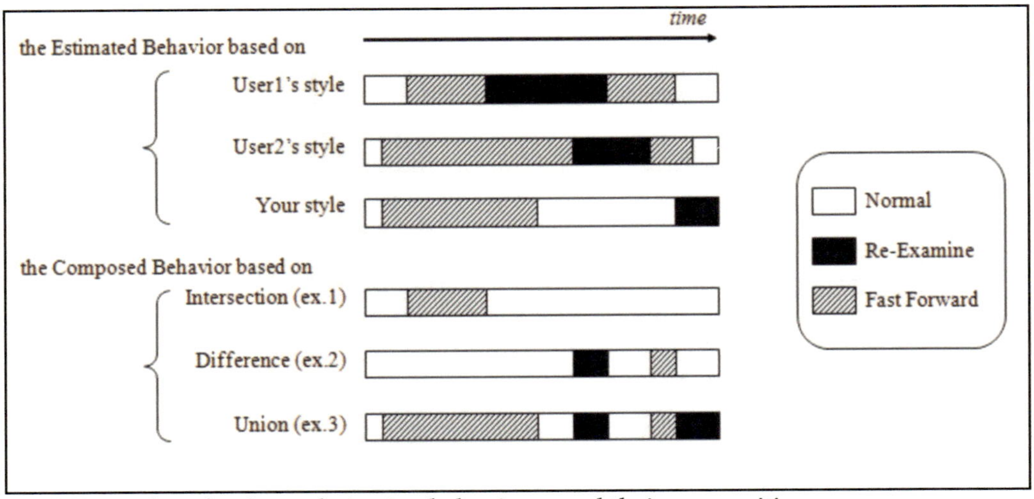

Fig. 5. Examples of estimated viewing behaviours and their composition.

Ex.1 describes the intersection of the three video viewing styles. In this case, the system estimates that these three persons will skip the earlier scenes. This operation detects meaningful manipulations for all the users. In other words, the operation functions as a social filtering system if the number of users is sufficiently large.
Ex.2 shows the difference between S_{YOU} and the intersection of S_{USER1} and S_{USER2}. This operation determines the habitual behaviour of other users that do not tend to be selected by a particular user. This operation can be regarded as an active help system [Fischer85].
Ex.3 describes the union of S_{YOU} and the intersection of S_{USER1} and S_{USER2}. The user can experience his/her habitual behaviour while taking into account the habitual behaviours of other users. (It should be noted that this union operation needs to determine the priority in order to avoid conflicts between the behaviours.)
These examples show that the simple compositions of the associations between a video frame and the viewing behaviour can create other meaningful viewing styles.

5. User study

We conducted two user studies concerning the reusing and composing the video viewing styles.

5.1 Setting

In both studies, we used three types of video content, broadcasted football game, broadcasted Japanese sumo wrestling match, and recording from a surveillance camera installed at the entrance of a building. Five 5-min videos for each type of video content were used as training videos for training each classifier respectively. And three 5-min videos were used as target video for applying the viewing style and automatic playing. The target videos are not included in the training videos. Four subjects were being observed. Each subject is a typical computer user.

	Football	Sumo	Surveillance Camera
SubA	OP: skipped RP: played at normal IP (center area): skipped IP (shoot scene): Re-examined	OP: skipped RP: played at normal	OP(person not exist): skipped IP(person exist): played at normal speed
SubB	OP: skipped RP: skipped (low frequency)	OP: skipped RP: played at normal	OP(person not exist): skipped IP(person exist): played at normal speed
SubC	OP: skipped RP: played at normal IP (center area): skipped IP (goal scene): Re-examined IP (faul scene): Re-examined	OP: skipped RP: played at normal	OP(person not exist): skipped IP(person exist): played at normal speed, or Re-examined
SubD	OP: skipped RP: played at normal IP (goal scene): Re-examined (low frequency)	OP: skipped RP: played at normal OP (commentator): played at normal	OP(person not exist): skipped IP(person exist): played at normal speed, or Re-examined

OP: Out of play scene, IP: In-play scene, RP: Replay scene

Table 1. The video viewing style of each user

5.2 Generating classifiers

In order to generate each subject's classifiers for each type of video content respectively, at first, subjects were asked to explore the five training videos and find interesting scenes. Table 1. shows the characteristics of subjects' video viewing style. "In-play scene" indicates the scenes that players are moving and the game is active for sports video. As for surveillance video, this means the scenes that include person in the frame. "Out of play scene" indicates the opposite. In viewing sports video, all subjects tended to skip the out-of-play scenes and play replay scenes at a normal speed. In surveillance video, all subjects tended to skip the frames that have no person in the frames.

VVER generated their classifiers by using their video viewing logs and low-level features of the videos.

5.3 Reusing video viewing styles

The first study involved observing the users' impression when they reuse their video viewing styles.

A few days after from the day that the subjects viewed the training videos, they viewed the target videos which are played automatically based on their own classifier (i.e. video viewing style) through the VVER. The result of interview asking them their impression shows that all subjects recognize the automatic plays were similar to their own viewing style. In addition this interview, we evaluated the performance of the VVER quantitatively. This evaluation investigated how the automatic play result through the VVER resembles to the result produced by human using "intentional viewing style". An intentional viewing style here means the style that consists of some predefined viewing rules, for instance, skipping out of play scene of football game and re-examining goal scenes and so on. In order to

		subA	subB	subC	subD	VVER
Football	video01	0.397	0.519	0.050	0.057	0.119
	video02	0.332	0.445	0.005	0.032	0.116
	video03	0.154	0.482	0.023	0.050	0.200
	Avr.	0.294	0.482	0.026	0.046	0.145
Sumo	video01	0.033	0.028	0.020	0.036	0.240
	video02	0.026	0.022	0.026	0.042	0.172
	video03	0.037	0.061	0.029	0.030	0.189
	Avr.	0.032	0.037	0.025	0.036	0.200
Surveillance camera	video01	0.045	0.151	0.055	0.073	0.103
	video02	0.012	0.018	0.018	0.109	0.023
	video03	0.025	0.031	0.030	0.033	0.020
	Avr.	0.027	0.067	0.034	0.072	0.049

Table 2. The gaps from *AnswerSet* to *ClassifierSet (VVER)* and *HumanSet (SubA,B,C,D)*

generate an intentional classifier, we first decided the predefined rules, and then check the whole frames of target videos manually, then created viewing logs. The VVER generated an intentional classifier by using the viewing logs. We call a play schedule for a target video that created with the intentional classifier *ClassifierSet*. As the same manner, we constrained subjects to view training video with the intentional viewing style. The VVER generated an intentional classifier based on a subject's viewing logs. A play schedule for the target video that created with the intentional classifier called *HumanSet*. To compare the similarity of *ClassifierSet* and *HumanSet*, we defined *AnswerSet* which is a play schedule that produced manually by checking whole frame of a target video. Ideally, both *ClassifierSet* and *HumanSet* should be same as *AnswerSet*. To calculate the gap between *AnswerSet* and the other sets, we introduce specific value for user manipulations; Re-examine=1, Normal=0, Skip=-1. The gap from *AnswerSet* to *ClassifierSet* and *HumanSet* is defined by following expressions respectively as error where A, C, and H indicate *AnswerSet, ClassifierSet,* and *HumanSet*. n indicates the number of target video, and m is the number of frame that each video possesses.

$$error_{classifier} = \frac{1}{nm}\sum_{i=1}^{n}\sum_{j=1}^{m}(A_{ij} - C_{ij})^2$$

$$error_{human} = \frac{1}{nm}\sum_{i=1}^{n}\sum_{j=1}^{m}(A_{ij} - H_{ij})^2$$

Table 2 shows the evaluation result which is calculated with three target videos for three type of video content. When a number is 0, there is no gap between *AnswerSet* and others. As the result on Table 2, the gap between A and C is almost same level as the one between A and H. This result brings us to the fact that when a user has a consistent viewing style, the VVER can reproduce viewing experiences as similar as the user does. In addition this, human views videos with understanding their content, however, the VVER reproduce such viewing experience only with the low-level video features (i.e. without the domain knowledge of the video content).

5.4 Composing video viewing styles

The second study involves the composition of these several viewing styles by the users. The purpose of this study is to investigate what kind of impression the composition gave to users. We interviewed the four subjects about their impression after viewing automatically playing nine target videos based on three compositions described below.

$$S_{SubA} \cap S_{SubB} \cap S_{SubC} \cap S_{SubD} \quad \text{(cmp.1)}$$

$$(S_{SubA} \cap S_{SubB} \cap S_{SubC}) \setminus S_{SubD} \quad \text{(cmp.2)}$$

$$S_{SubA} \cup S_{SubB} \cup S_{SubC} \cup S_{SubD} \quad \text{(cmp.3)}$$

Subscripts in cmp.2 assumes the user is SubD. The four subjects and nine target videos are the same as the study for reusing.

If the predicted automatic playing speed is the common for all users, Cmp.1 plays the frame at the speed. If not, Cmp.1 plays the frame at the normal speed. As shown in Table 1, the skipping behaviour in viewing sports videos were common. As a result, all subject recognize the automatic play through cmp.1 is almost the same as their own viewing style.

Cmp.2 produce an viewing experience that is generally common but not for SubD. SubB who does not re-examine video usually were interested in the scene played at a slower speed because other three subjects did. On the other hand, all subjects complained about not skipping the scenes that they wanted to skip. It is because, in the current setting, cmp.2 plays frames at a normal speed if all predicted speed were the same.

If even one subject take abnormal behaviour, Cmp.3 tries to reproduce the behaviour. Hence, this composition plays the videos with varied speed. As a result, SubB and SubC said that the football game videos were played like digest versions of the games. SubA found that there is characteristic walking of one person and gazed it.

6. Discussion / Future work

Reusing video viewing styles

Through the user study for reusing video viewing style, we found that the VVER allow users to experience the target videos in the same viewing style of them. In order to satisfy users, it is necessary for a genre of a video to be specified, and behaviours of a user must be consistent. As an additional user study, we applied classifiers to the target videos which are not the same genre of the training videos. The video viewing style that is produced with football game videos influenced to the target videos of sumo and vice versa. However they were not produce meaningful experience to users. Moreover, the video viewing style with surveillance camera skipped almost whole frames of the target videos of the other two sports game. In order to let a classifier learn user's viewing style, it might be necessary for the genre of videos to be specified by using meta-data information etc.

Composing video viewing styles

Through the user study for composing video viewing style, several subjects had unexpected experiences serendipitously. On the other hand, especially in the result through cmp.2, all subjects had negative impression when the scene did not played at the speed they wanted. It is not so easy to understand user's desire, however, a mechanism that allow users to understand the situation is needed. The visuallization of predicted speed for the video might be one solution.

7. Conclusion

In this chapter, we describe the notion of reusing the video viewing style, and present examples of composition using these styles to create new video viewing styles.

Contrary to researches that employ content-based domain knowledge, little has been reported about the composition of tacit knowledge such as video viewing styles in knowledge studies. It is well known that video data essentially have temporal aspects that might make users view the videos passively than other media such as text or images. On the other hand, the fact that we have increasingly more opportunities to use videos for our knowledge might facilitate the active browsing of videos. We believe that novices might be able to operate videos more freely and develop their own video viewing styles. To support these users, we need to clarify not only the semantic understanding of the video content but also the habitual behaviour of each user.

It is suggested that the social navigation technique for supporting the user's activity by using past information is useful [Dieberger00]. The contributions of our study are the provision of not only the notion of reusing past information but also the creation of new video viewing styles. In this study, we present three types of composition manipulations; composition manipulations have a greater possibility of generating new and meaningful video viewing styles. Refining composition manipulations can be considered as a future work.

8. References

Alavi, M. & Leidner, D. E. (1999). Knowledge management systems: issues, challenges, and benefits, Journal of Commun. AIS, Vol. 1, No. 2es, AIS, Atlanta, GA.

Brin, S. & Page, L. (1998). The Anatomy of a Large-Scale Hypertextual Web Search Engine, in Proc. of 7th International WWW Conference, Australia.

Dieberger, A.; Dourish, P.; H¨o¨ok, K.; Resnick, p. & Wexelblat, A. (2000). Social navigation: Techniques for building more usable systems. interactions, Vol. 7, No. 6, pp. 36–45

Fischer, G.; Lemke, A. C., & Schwab, T. (1985). Knowledge-Based Help Systems, In L. Borman & B. Curtis (Eds.), Proceedings of CHI'85 Conference on Human Factors in Computing Systems, ACM, New York, pp. 161-167.

Fujima, J. & Tanaka, Y. (2007). Web-application composition through direct editing of Web documents and multiplexing of information access scenarios. Systems and Computers in Japan 38(12): 1-13.

Polanyi, M. (1983). Tacit Dimension, Peter Smith Pub Inc.

Sakagami, H. & Kamba, T. (1997). Learning Personal Preferences on Online Newspaper Articles from User Behaviours, Proc. of the Sixth International World Wide Web Conference, In Computer Networks and ISDN Systems, Vol. 29, pp.1447-1456.
Seo, Y. & Zhang, B. (2000). Learning user's preferences by analyzing web-browsing behaviors, Proceedings of International Conference on Autonomous Agents, pp.381-387.
Sugibuchi, T. & Tanaka, Y. (2004). Integrated Framework for the Visualization of Relational Databases and RelatedWeb Content. In Proc. CDROM of Fourth IEEE Pacific-Rim Conference On Multimedia.
Syeda-Mahmood, S. & Ponceleon, D. (2001). Learning video browsing behavior and its application in the generation of video previews, Proceedings of the ninth ACM international conference on Multimedia, pp.119-128.
Takashima, A.; Yamamoto, Y. & Nakakoji, K. (2004). A Model and a Tool for Active Watching: Knowledge Construction through Interacting with Video, Proceedings of INTERACTION: Systems, Practice and Theory, Sydney, Australia, pp.331-358.
Tanaka, Y. (2003). Meme Media and Meme Market Architectures: Knowledge Media for Editing, Distributing, and Managing Intellectual Resources, IEEE Press.
WEKA: http://www.cs.waikato.ac.nz/ml/weka/
Yamamoto, Y.; Nakakoji, K. & Takashima, A. (2005). The Landscape of Time-based Visual Presentation Primitives for Richer Video Experience, Human-Computer Interaction: INTERACT 2005, M.F. Costabile, F. Paterno (Eds.), Rome, Italy, Springer, pp.795-808.
Yu, B.; Ma, W.Y.; Nahrstedt, K.; & Zhang, H.J. (2003). Video Summarization Based on User Log Enhanced Link Analysis. ACM MM 03, pp. 382-391, 2003.

Adaptive Evaluation Strategy Based on Surrogate Models

Yi-nan Guo and Jian Cheng
China University of Mining and Technology
China

1. Introduction

Interactive genetic algorithm(IGA) is a kind of genetic algorithms in which individuals' fitness values are evaluated by human subjectively. They combine canonical genetic algorithms with human intelligent evaluations. Now they have been applied to optimization problems whose objectives can not be expressed by explicit fitness functions, such as music composition(Biles,1996), production design(Takagi,1998), image retrieval(Takagi,1999) and so on. However there exits human fatigue in evaluation, which limits population size and the number of evolution generations. Moreover, subjective fitness values given by human mainly reflect human cognition and preference, which is related to domain knowledge. So IGAs need more knowledge than other genetic algorithms for explicit optimization functions.

In IGAs, human fatigue is a key problem which limits the application of the algorithm. According to physiological characters of human, if human are absorbed in one work for a long time, they are easy to feel tired. However, human need to evaluate each individual in each generation. More individuals human evaluate, they feel more tired. If cognition knowledge about human preference to optimization problems can be extracted from the evolution and utilized to evaluate individuals instead of human, the number of individuals evaluated by human shall decrease which will alleviate human fatigue. This cognition knowledge is generally described by surrogate models.

Surrogate models are trained by samples which consist of human evaluated individuals and their fitness values. Hence, they approximatively reflect human preference. When human feel tired, surrogate models can replace human to evaluate all individuals or part of individuals in each generation so as to reduce the number of individuals evaluated by human. This can reduce human burden and alleviate human fatigue.

Here, four key issues about surrogate models which influenc the performances of the algorithm are taken into account. Firstly, surrogate models must exactly keep consistency with human cognition and preference in order to ensure the convergence of the algorithms. So how to obtain the models with good prediction precision and generalization is the base. The second issue is when to use surrogate models instead of human in evaluation. The last two problems are how many and which individuals are selected to calculate fitness values by surrogate models in each generation.

Up to now, many researches on surrogate models have been done. But most of them focus on the structure of surrogate models. Different models adopting artificial neural networks(Zhou,2005) or support vector machines(Wang,2003) are proposed. However, how to rationally utilize surrogate models are not taken into account enough. Firstly, in existing researches, no matter whether surrogate models exactly reflect human real preference, the models are used to evaluate individuals when human feel tired. Secondly, population size is small and fixed all the time. And the number of individuals evaluated by the models in each generation is also fixed. These make IGAs alleviating human fatigue limitedly. Thirdly, few of researches concern which individuals are selected to be evaluated by models. To solve above problems, latter three issues are mainly studied, including when the models are used in evaluation, how many and which individuals are evaluated by the models in each generation.

In the chapter, assume that human preference to optimization problems is stable. A novel interactive genetic algorithms adopting adaptive evaluation strategy based on surrogate models(AES-IGAs) is proposed. Firstly, two measures reflecting the models' precision and human fatigue are given. Based on them, evaluation process is divided into three phases. In different phase, human participate in evaluation to different extent. Secondly, the number of individuals evaluated by surrogate models is adaptively tuned in evolution according to above two measures so as to alleviate human fatigue at most. Because surrogate models calculate individuals' fitness values by computers which do not need human participation, population size is enlarged when only surrogate models are adopted in evaluation so as to improve convergence speed. Thirdly, how to select rational individuals evaluated by the models from population is studied. Fuzzy c-means clustering algorithm is adopted And three kinds of approximate distance is put forward as measures. To validate the rationality of AES-IGAs, experiments based on fashion evolutionary design system are done. And testing results are analyzed at last.

2. Startup Mechanism about Surrogate Model

Startup mechanism offers some conditions which decide when to use surrogate model in evaluation process. That is, in which generation these conditions are satisfied, population can be evaluated by surrogate models in proper proportion. In general, when human feel tired or surrogate models have learned human preference exactly, the models are adopted to calculate the individuals' fitness values. So startup mechanism about surrogate models normally includes two conditions. They are the condition of human fatigue and the condition of models' precision. When any of conditions is satisfied, surrogate models are start up to evaluate.

Suppose F_M is the fitness value calculated by surrogate models. F_U is the fitness value given by human. x_M and x_U respectively denote individuals evaluated by the models and human. X(t) expresses the population in t-th generation. Adaptive evaluation strategy is shown as follows(Guo,2007).

$$\begin{aligned} &F(X(t)) = \{F_{\mathrm{M}}(x_{\mathrm{M}},t), F_{\mathrm{U}}(x_{\mathrm{U}},t)\}, x_{\mathrm{M}} \neq x_{\mathrm{U}}, x_{\mathrm{M}}, x_{\mathrm{U}} \in X(t) \\ &s.t. \qquad F_{\mathrm{M}} \neq \varnothing, \forall((Fa(t) \geq \varepsilon) \vee (Pr(t) \leq \Psi)) \end{aligned} \tag{1}$$

Here, $Fa(t)\geq\varepsilon$ describes the condition of human fatigue where $Fa(t)$ expresses the degree of human fatigue and ε is the threshold of $Fa(t)$.

Definition 1: the degree of human fatigue

The degree of human fatigue reflects how tired human are. In general, human will spend more time evaluating individuals when there are more similar individuals in the population. Therefore, human feel more tired when the total number of individuals evaluated by human is more and time for evaluation in each generation is more.

Letting $v(t)$ denotes how long human spend evaluating. $\beta(t)$ is the proportion of human evaluated individuals to population. The degree of human fatigue is defined as follows(Guo, 2007).

$$Fa(t) = 1 - e^{-tv(t)\beta(t)S(t)} \tag{2}$$

In formula(2), $S(t)$ denotes the similarity of population, which describes average similarity of individuals in population, shown as follows.

$$S(t) = \frac{2\sum_{i=1}^{|P-1|}\sum_{j=i+1}^{|P|}\sum_{l=1}^{n}\sigma_l\left(x_i(t), x_j(t)\right)}{|P||P-1|} \tag{3}$$

where $|P|$ is population size and n is the length of individuals. $\sigma_l(x_i(t),x_j(t))$ expresses the similarity of l-th bit between two individuals. $\sigma_l(x_i(t),x_j(t))=1$ if l-th bit of $x_j(t)$ is same as it of $x_j(t)$, otherwise $\sigma_l(x_i(t),x_j(t))=0$.

In formula(1), $Pr(t)\leq\Psi$ describes the condition of models' precision where $Pr(t)$ expresses the reliability of surrogate models and Ψ is the threshold of $Pr(t)$.

Definition 2: the reliability of surrogate models

The reliability of surrogate models reflect the consistency between surrogate models and human preference. It is measured by average Euclid distance between individuals' fitness values calculated by the models and them given by human, shown as follows.

$$Pr(t) = \sqrt{\frac{1}{|P|}\sum_{i=1}^{|P|}\left(F_U(x_i,t) - F_M(x_i,t)\right)^2} \tag{4}$$

Obviously Pr(t) also describes the generalization of surrogate models.

In a word, whether surrogate models are utilized lies on two conditions: whether or not the degree of human fatigue exceed the threshold; whether or not reliability of surrogate models exceed the threshold.

3. The Number of Substituted Individuals Evaluated by Surrogate Models

In AES-IGAs, some individuals are evaluated by human, whereas others' fitness values are calculated by surrogate models. Here, individuals evaluated by the models in each generation are called substituted individuals. How many substituted individuals are there is a key problem, which influences the performance of AES-IGAs. Up to now, in most of IGAs

adopting surrogate models based evaluation strategy, the number of substituted individuals is fixed and equal to fifty percent of population size. This limits the effect of surrogate models on performances. Aiming at this problem, the number of substituted individuals adaptively varies in AES-IGAs.
In general, one hopes to evaluate less individuals in IGAs when he feels tired. And when surrogate models can reflect human preference better, it shall be used to evaluated more individuals instead of human so as to reduce human burden. Therefore, two factors including human fatigue and models' precision are considered to decide the number of substituted individuals. When human feel more tired or models' precision is better, less individuals are evaluated by themselves. So the number of substituted individuals in t-th generation is defined as

$$N_{\mathrm{M}}(t) = \lfloor |P| \rho(t) \rfloor \tag{5}$$

Here, $\rho(t)$ is the proportion of substituted individuals to population, called the substituted proportion, shown as follows.

$$\rho(t) = e^{-(Pr(t)/\overline{f})(\varepsilon - Fa(t))} \tag{6}$$

Here, $\overline{f}$ denotes the upper bound of the fitness values. Obviously the substituted proportion also satisfies $\rho(t)+\beta(t)=1$.

4. Substitution Mechanism about Surrogate Model

In existing researches, the substituted proportion in evolution is normally fixed after surrogate models are used. Corresponding evaluation process in IGAs can be divided into two phases: human-evaluation phases and models-evaluation phases. According to the substituted proportion, two kinds of dual-phase evaluation strategies with different $\rho(t)$ are analyzed as follows.
(1) While the conditions of startup mechanism are satisfied, $\rho(t)=1$. That is, the evaluation process is divided into two phases. When surrogate models are not used, population is evaluated by human only. Otherwise, all individuals are evaluated by surrogate models.
(2) While the conditions of startup mechanism are satisfied, $\rho(t)=C(0<C<1)$. Here C is a constant(Zhou,2005). That is, when surrogate models are adopted, population is not evaluated by surrogate models only. Some of individuals are evaluated by human, others are evaluated by surrogate models. And the number of substituted individuals is $\lfloor |P| \rho(t) \rfloor$.

In above two evaluation strategies, fixed substituted proportion does not make surrogate models used enough. Therefore, variable substituted proportion is adopted in this chapter. Corresponding evaluation process is different from above two instances. It contains three phases.
Phase I: Population is evaluated by human only
In this phase, the models are not used and all of individuals are evaluated by human. The evaluation mode is defined as follows.

$$F(X(t)) = \{F_{\mathrm{U}}(x_{\mathrm{U}},t)\}, x_{\mathrm{U}} \in X(t) \\ s.t. \forall((Fa(t) < \varepsilon) \wedge (Pr(t) > \Psi)) \tag{7}$$

And the number of substituted individuals is

$$N_{\mathrm{M}}(t) = 0 \tag{8}$$

It is obvious that in this phase, human do not feel tired and surrogate models can not exactly reflect human preference. Above phenomena possibly appear at the beginning of evolution. So this evaluation mode is usually adopted in the former evolution. Note that surrogate models shall be continually update according to evaluated individuals in this phase.

Phase II: Population is mixed evaluated by human and surrogate models

In this phase, surrogate models are startup because they learn human preference approximatively. However, the degree of human fatigue does not exceed the threshold. That means human still participate in the evaluation process. And human evaluated individuals are used as samples to improve models' precision further. Obviously some of individuals are evaluated by human and others' fitness values are calculated by the models. So the evaluation mode are shown as follows.

$$F(X(t)) = \{F_{\mathrm{M}}(x_{\mathrm{M}},t), F_{\mathrm{U}}(x_{\mathrm{U}},t)\}, x_{\mathrm{M}} \neq x_{\mathrm{U}}, x_{\mathrm{M}}, x_{\mathrm{U}} \in X(t) \\ s.t. \forall((Fa(t) < \varepsilon) \wedge (Pr(t) \leq \Psi)) \tag{9}$$

In order to reduce human burden gradually, the number of substituted individuals in phase II is increasing along with the degree of human fatigue.

$$N_{\mathrm{M}}(t) = \left\lfloor |P| e^{-(Pr(t)/\bar{f})(\varepsilon - Fa(t))} \right\rfloor \tag{10}$$

In above two phases, population size is fixed and small because human participate in the evaluation process. In general, population size in IGAs is less than ten so as to alleviate human visual fatigue.

Phase III: Population is evaluated by surrogate models only

In this phase, all of individuals are evaluated by surrogate models. So the evaluation mode is described as follows.

$$F(X(t)) = \{F_{\mathrm{M}}(x_{\mathrm{M}},t)\}, x_{\mathrm{M}} \in X(t) \\ s.t. \forall((Fa(t) \geq \varepsilon) \wedge (Pr(t) \leq \Psi)) \tag{11}$$

In phase III, human often feel very tired. Individuals' fitness values given by human may differ from their real preference. So these individuals can not be used to train surrogate models. And the models are not updated any more. This evaluation mode is normally adopted in the latter evolution. Because the evaluation process based on surrogate models is done by computers, there does not exit human fatigue in phase III. That means the evolution

of AES-IGAs is the same as traditional genetic algorithms. So population size can be enlarged. But how to increase population size is a key problem.
Higher the models' precision is, the generalization of the model is better. So enlarged population size is defined as follows.

$$N_p(t) = |P|^{\left\lfloor \frac{\bar{f}}{Pr(\tau k)} + 0.5 \right\rfloor} \tag{12}$$

Here, $Pr(\tau k)$ expresses the reliability of surrogate models in Phase III. It is obvious that the exponent in formula(12) may be 1, 2 or 3. So population size may be enlarged to corresponding multiple of $|P|$.

5. Surrogate Model-based Evaluation Strategy with Oriented Selection of Substituted Individuals

In existing researches on surrogate model-based IGAs, substituted individuals are often randomly selected from population after the evaluation mode is decided. But if selected substituted individuals are far away from existing training samples, their fitness values calculated by surrogate models may differ from human cognition. This will misguide the evolution away from human real preference. Aiming at above problem, an oriented selection method of substituted individuals is proposed. Here, substituted individuals are selected in terms of the distance between individuals and samples so as to improve the evaluation precision to the utmost extent.
Taken oriented selection process in t-th generation as example, algorithm steps are shown as follows(Guo,2007).
Step1: The number of substituted individuals $N_M(t)$ is decided in terms of human fatigue.
Step2: Samples are composed of evaluated individuals and their fitness values given by human. They are grouped into sub-sample sets adopting Fuzzy-C mean algorithm.
Step3: Aiming at each sub-sample set, a surrogate model described by artificial neural networks is trained.
Step4: The distance between each individual in population and each samples or each sub-sample sets are calculated.
Step5: Individuals are sorted according to above distance. Then individuals with less distance are regarded as substituted individuals.
Step6: The fitness values of substituted individuals are calculated by their affiliated clusters' surrogate model.
Obviously how to group samples, train surrogate models and select substituted individuals are three main issues. Here, former two problems are mainly discussed.

5.1 Sample clustering

How to construct sample set and decide the cluster number are two key problems in sample clustering.
Sample set are composed of evaluated individuals and their fitness values given by human. They are expressed by $x_U(t)$ and $f(x_U(t))$. Because human cognition may vary in evolution, the fitness value of same individual may be variant in different generation. In order to track

human preference, latest fitness values of any individuals are reserved. Therefore, sample set are described as follows.

$$Q(t) = \{(x_U, f(x_U)) \mid x_U^l \neq x_U^k, l, k = 1, 2, \cdots Q(t) \mid\} \tag{13}$$

Sample set are grouped into clusters by fuzzy c-means clustering algorithm (Karayiannis, 1997). Suppose L=2,3,…,K(K<$|Q(t)|$) is the cluster number, which is normally decided according to domain knowledge. Improper K will lead to wrong clustering result. Aiming at this problem, comparison method(Cheng,2006) is adopted to obtain suitable cluster number. Assume that $Q_i(t)$(i=1,2, …,L) is sub-sample set. And each cluster center is

$$c_i(t) = \frac{\sum_{l=1}^{|Q(t)|} u_{il}^m(t) x_U^l(t)}{\sum_{l=1}^{|Q(t)|} u_{il}^m(t)}, i = 1, 2, \cdots L \tag{14}$$

Here, $m \in [1, \infty)$ is the weighing index. $u_{il} \in [0,1]$ denotes the subjection degree of $x_U^l(t)$ to $Qi(t)$, which satisfies $\sum_{i=1}^{L} u_{il} = 1, \forall l = 1, 2, \cdots, |Q(t)|$.

5.2 Selection of substituted individuals

How many substituted individuals are there in each generation is the principal issue, which is decided by $\rho(t)$. However, which individuals are selected as substituted individuals depends on their approximate distances. Here, the distances between an individual and each sample or each sub-sample set are called approximate distances.

Suppose $x_j(t)$ is an individual. Three kinds of approximate distances are defined as follows(Cheng,2009).

(1) Center approximate distance

The clustering center of each sub-sample set is used to judge which cluster does an individual belong to. Suppose $c_i(t)$ is clustering center of i-th cluster. The minimum distance between $x_j(t)$ and $c_i(t)$ is defined as center approximate distance, expressed by D1.

$$D1^j = \min_{i \in \{1, 2, \cdots L\}} d1(x_j(t), c_i(t)) \tag{15}$$

If individuals are encoded by real number, d1 is described as

$$d1(x_j(t), c_i(t)) = \sqrt{\sum_{h=1}^{n} (x_j^h(t) - c_i^h(t))^2} \tag{16}$$

If individuals are encoded by binary number, d1 is described as

$$d1(x_j(t), c_i(t)) = \bigcup_{h=1}^{n} (x_j^h(t) \oplus c_i^h(t)) \tag{17}$$

Because only clustering centers of sub-sample sets are taken into account, the computation complexity of center approximate distance is $O(|P|L)$.

(2) Cluster approximate distance

All of samples in each sub-sample set are used to judge which cluster does an individual belong to. The minimum distance beween $x_j(t)$ and samples in $Q_i(t)$ is defined as cluster approximate distance, expressed by D2.

$$D2^j = \min_{i\in\{1,2,\cdots L\}} d2(x_j(t), Q_i(t)) \tag{18}$$

Suppose $x_{\mathrm{U}}^i(t)$ is a sample in *i*-th cluster. If individuals are encoded by real number, *d2* is described as

$$d2(x_j(t), Q_i(t)) = \frac{1}{|Q_i(t)|}\sum_{l=1}^{|Q_i(t)|}\sqrt{\sum_{h=1}^{n}(x_j^h(t) - x_{\mathrm{U}}^{i,lh}(t))^2} \tag{19}$$

If individuals are encoded by binary number, *d2* is described as

$$d2(x_j(t), Q_i(t)) = \frac{1}{|Q_i(t)|}\sum_{l=1}^{|Q_i(t)|}\left[\bigcup_{h=1}^{n}(x_j^h(t)\oplus x_{\mathrm{U}}^{i,lh}(t))\right] \tag{20}$$

Here, $|Q(t)| = \sum_{i=1}^{L}|Q_i(t)|$. So the computation complexity of cluster approximate distance is $O(|P||Q(t)|)$.

(3) Generalized approximate distance

All of samples in sample set are used to judge which cluster does an individual belong to. The minimum distance between $x_j(t)$ and $x_{\mathrm{U}}(t)$ is defined as generalized approximate distance, expressed by D3.

$$D3^j = \min_{l\in\{1,2,\cdots|Q(t)|\}} d3(x_j(t), x_{\mathrm{U}}^l(t)) \tag{21}$$

If individuals are encoded by real number, *d3* is described as

$$d3(x_j(t), x_{\mathrm{U}}^l(t)) = \sqrt{\sum_{h=1}^{n}(x_j^h(t) - x_{\mathrm{U}}^{lh}(t))^2} \tag{22}$$

If individuals are encoded by binary number, *d3* is described as

$$d3(x_j(t), x_{\mathrm{U}}^l(t)) = \bigcup_{h=1}^{n}(x_j^h(t)\oplus x_{\mathrm{U}}^{lh}(t)) \tag{23}$$

Obviously the computation complexity of generalized approximate distance is $O(|P||Q(t)|)$.

Through comparison of the computation complexity of above three approximate distances, we know that the computation complexity of generalized approximate distance is the same as it of cluster approximate distance. In addition, population size is normally more than the cluster number, namely $|Q(t)|\geq L$. So the computation complexity of center approximate distance is least.

6. Analysis of Convergence

In genetic algorithms, whether and how fast they converge are used to measure the algorithm's performances. And many researches have discussed genetic algorithms' convergence. However, IGAs' convergence is seldom taken into account. In this chapter, AES-IGAs' convergence is analyzed in terms of drift analysis and the first hitting time condition proposed by Jun He(He, 2001).

Definition 3: critical generation

In AES-IGAs, when $t>\tau k$, surrogate models are used to calculate all individuals' fitness values. If the algorithms can converge to optimal solution under above condition, τk is called critical generation as shown in follows(Guo,2007). Whether τk exists is a key problem which influences AES-IGAs' convergence.

$$\tau k = \min\{t \mid (\rho(t+1)=1) \wedge D(X(t+\zeta))=0, \zeta \in [0,T-t), t \in (0,T]\} \tag{24}$$

Where

$$D(X(t+\zeta)) = \min\{i \mid D(x_i(t+\zeta)), x_i(t+\zeta) \in X(t+\zeta)\} \tag{25}$$

Here, $D(x_i(t+\zeta))$ is simplified description of $D(x_i(t+\zeta), x^*), x^* \in S^*$. S^* is the optimal variable space. D() denotes the distance between two individuals. If individuals are encoded by binary number, D() is calculated by Hamming distance. Otherwise, if individuals are encoded by real number, D() is calculated by Euclidean distance.

Theorem 1: For any generation satisfied $t>\tau k$, all individuals are evaluated by surrogate models. During this phase, the evolution of AES-IGAs is the same as genetic algorithms. Based on the first hitting time drift condition with exponential form(He,2001), there exists $\bar{\zeta}=\min\{\zeta \mid D(X(t+\zeta))=0\}$, which satisfies drift condition $E[\bar{\zeta} \mid d(X(\tau k))>0] < h(|P|)$. Here, $h(|P|)$ is a polynomial function of $|P|$.

Proof: Assume that individuals are encoded by binary number. So the distance between an individual and optimal solution is

$$D(x_i(t)) = \sum_{l=1}^{n} \sigma_l(x_i(t), x^*) \tag{26}$$

Given a random sequence $\{D(X(\tau k+j)), j=0,1,\cdots\}$, $\forall X(\tau k+j), D(X(\tau k+j)) \leq |P|$ is obviously satisfied. If the algorithms adopt one-point crossover, bit mutation and roulette selection, following inequation is obtained in terms of drift condition.

$$E[D(X(\tau k+j+1))-D(X(\tau k+j))\mid D(X(\tau k+j))>0]\geq h_1(|P|) \tag{27}$$

Here, $h_1(|P|)>0$.From Theorem.1 in reference(He,2001), we know $E\left[\zeta \mid d(X(\tau k))>0\right]\leqslant |P| h_1(|P|)$. Let $h(|P|)=|P|h_1(|P|)$. Then $E\left[\zeta \mid d(X(\tau k))>0\right]\leqslant h(|P|)$ is satisfied.
Theorem 2: When $t>\tau k$, the substituted proportion $\rho(t)$ converges to 1.
Proof: Suppose $\{\cdots\rho(t),\rho(t+1)\cdots \mid \forall\rho(t)>0\}$ is a random sequence. The gradient of $\rho(t)$ is

$$\frac{\rho(t+1)}{\rho(t)}=\frac{e^{-[(Pr(t+1)/\bar{f})(\varepsilon-Fa(t+1))]}}{e^{-[(Pr(t)/\bar{f})(\varepsilon-Fa(t))]}}=e^{-[(Pr(t+1)/\bar{f})(\varepsilon-Fa(t+1))]+[(Pr(t)/\bar{f})(\varepsilon-Fa(t))]} \tag{28}$$

Considering $\varepsilon-Fa(t)>0 \ \ and \ \ Fa(t+1)>Fa(t) \ \Rightarrow \varepsilon-Fa(t+1)<\varepsilon-Fa(t)$, then

$$\begin{aligned}&Pr(t+1)<Pr(t) \quad \Rightarrow Pr(t+1)(\varepsilon-Fa(t+1))<Pr(t)(\varepsilon-Fa(t))\\&Pr(t)(\varepsilon-Fa(t))-Pr(t+1)(\varepsilon-Fa(t+1))>0\\&\Rightarrow e^{-[(Pr(t+1)/\bar{f})(\varepsilon-Fa(t+1))]+[(Pr(t)/\bar{f})(\varepsilon-Fa(t))]}>1\end{aligned}$$

Therefore, $\frac{\rho(t+1)}{\rho(t)}>1$. This shows that random sequence $\{\cdots\rho(t),\rho(t+1)\cdots \mid \forall\rho(t)>0\}$ increases by degrees. And $\rho(t)$ continuously varies along with t. When $t\geq\tau k,\ Fa\geq\varepsilon$. So

$$\rho(t)=e^{-[(Pr(t)/\bar{f})(\varepsilon-Fa(t))]}\geq 1 \tag{29}$$

This makes $\lim_{t\to\tau k}\rho(t)=1$ while $\exists\, \tau k\leq T$. Therefore, total number of individuals evaluated by human in evolution is

$$N_{sum}=\sum_{t=1}^{\tau k}\lfloor |P|(1-\rho(t))\rfloor \tag{30}$$

7. Experiments and Analysis

7.1 Background for experiments

Here, fashion evolutionary design system is adopted as a typical background to validate the rationality of IGAs with adaptive evaluation strategy (AES-IGAs). The goal of the system is to find a dress which wins human favor (Kim,2000). Visual Basic 6.0 as programming tool for human-machine interface and Microsoft Access as database are utilized. Matlab 6.5 is adopted to train surrogate models based on artificial neural networks. System's human-computer interface is shown as follows.

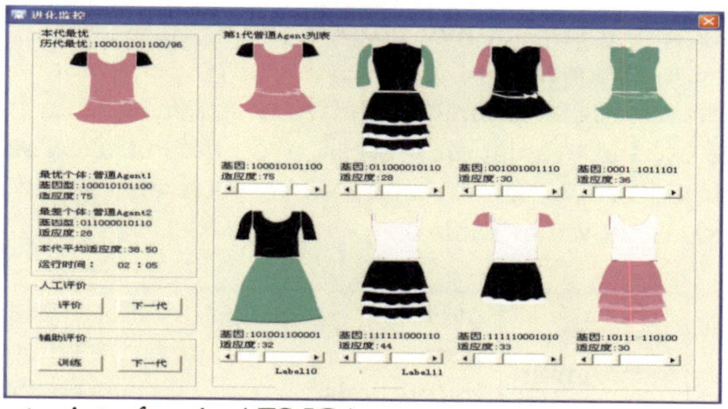

Fig. 1. Human-computer interface in AES-IGAs

In fashion evolutionary design system, each dress is composed of collar, skirt and sleeve. Each part has two factors including pattern and color which described by two bits. So each dress is expressed by twelve bits, which act as six gene-meaning-units (GM-units) (Guo,2007). Each gene-meaning-unit has four alleles. The meanings of each allele in gene-meaning-unit are shown in Table 1.

GM-unit	allele							
	meaning	code	meaning	code	meaning	code	meaning	code
collar's pattern	medium collar	00	high collar	01	wide collar	10	gallus	11
sleeve's pattern	long sleeve	00	medium sleeve	01	short sleeve	10	non-sleeve	11
skirt's pattern	long skirt	00	formal skirt	01	medium skirt	10	short skirt	11
color	pink	00	green	01	black	10	white	11

Table 1. The meanings of each allele in gene-meaning-unit

7.2 Desired objectives and parameters in experiments

In order to validate the rationality of adaptive evaluation strategy and the influence on performance of IGAs, two groups of experiments are designed. They have different desired objectives which reflect different psychological requirements of human. Desired objectives of experiments are shown as follows.

Experiment I: To find a favorite dress fitting for summer without the limit of color.

Experiment II: To find a favorite dress fitting for summer and the color is pink.

In both experiments, artificial neural network is adopted as surrogate model. The values of parameters about the model and the evolution process are shown in Table 2.

parameters about the evolution	crossover probability	mutation probability	population size	generation	ε	ψ
	0.6	0.01	8	40	0.8	0.9
parameters about the model	input neurons	hidden neurons	output neurons	learning rate	epochs	error
	6	15	1	0.09	15000	10^{-2}

Table 2. The values of parameters

7.3 Comparison of different substituted proportion

In order to validate the rationality of AES-IGAs, thirty persons are gathered to do two groups of experiments aiming at desired objective of experiment II. In experiments, when surrogate models are used in evaluation process, two kinds of fixed substituted proportion and adaptive substituted proportion are adopted respectively. Testing results done by all persons are integrated, as shown in Table 3.

the substituted proportion	average generation	average number of human evaluated individuals	average generation when the models are adopted
$\rho(t)$=0.5	15	104	11
$\rho(t)$=1	14	88	11
$\rho(t)=e^{-(Pr(t)/\bar{f})(\varepsilon-Fa(t))}$	12	55	8

Table 3. Comparison of the performance by different substituted proportion

Obviously when different $\rho(t)$ are adopted, convergence speed of the algorithms are similar. But total number of individuals evaluated by human varies. The reason for this is that surrogate models are adopted in evaluation only when formula(1) is satisfied. Firstly, if $\rho(t)$=0.5, half of population is evaluated by human when surrogate models are adopted. However, human shall evaluate individuals all along. So total number of individuals evaluated by human is more and human will feel more tired. Secondly, if $\rho(t)$=1, all individuals are evaluated by surrogate models when human feel tired and the models can reflect human preference exactly. Although human evaluate fewer individuals than first strategy, the models are used later than adaptive evaluation strategy. That is, less individuals are evaluated by human in AES-IGAs. Therefore, IGAs adopting adaptive evaluation strategy can effectively alleviate human fatigue more.

7.4 Comparison of different population size in Phase III

When population is evaluated by surrogate models only, fixed population size $|P|$ and population size N_P are adopted in experiments respectively. Testing results are shown in Table 4.

population size	average generation	average number of human evaluated individuals
$\vert P \vert$	12	55
N_P	10	55

Table 4. Comparison of different population size in Phase III

It is obvious that different population size in Phase III do not influence the degree of human fatigue in evolution because average number of individuals evaluated by human is same. As we know, no matter how many individuals are there in Phase IIL human do not participate in evaluation any more. That is, total number of human evaluated individuals in evolution only depends on the evaluation in Phase I and Phase II. However, convergence speed is faster while population size in Phase III is enlarged. The reason for this is that exploration of the algorithm with larger population size is better.

7.5 Critical generation when Phase III is started

Thirty persons are gathered to do two groups of experiments aiming at above two desired objectives. Results in experiments are shown in Figure 2.

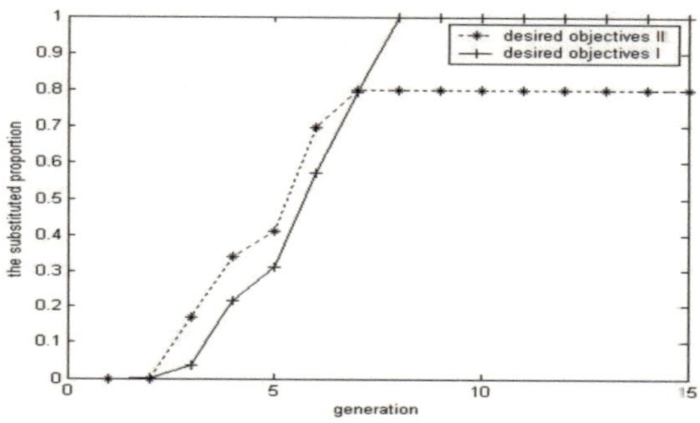

Fig. 2. $\rho(t)$ in experiments

From Figure 2, we know AES-IGAs converges. This matches Theorem.2. In addition, the substituted proportion is increasing along with the evolution. Aiming at desired objective of experiment II, all individuals are evaluated by the models when $t \geq 8$. That is, critical generation is 8. Obviously desired objective of experiment I include more detail requirements. So human need to pay attention to more GM-units, which make human feel more tired. This leads to larger critical generation. However, aiming at desired objective of experiment I, AES-IGAs converge when $t=7$. At this time, the degree of human fatigue do not exceed the threshold. So surrogate models are not completely used to replace human in evaluation process. That means critical generation do not exist in experiment I.

7.6 Comparison of different selection methods of substituted individuals

In order to analyze the performance of oriented selection methods, following three measures are given.

(1) Generation when stop rules are satisfied or human find the satisfied individuals reflects convergence speed, as shown in follows.

$$T = \arg\min_{t} | f(x(t)) - f^* | \leqslant \delta \tag{31}$$

(2) Total number of individuals evaluated by human in evolution influences the degree of human fatigue. Obviously T or N_U is larger, human feel more tired.

$$N_{\mathrm{U}} = \sum_{t=1}^{T} (|P| - N_{\mathrm{M}}(t)) \tag{32}$$

(3) Evaluation error of surrogate model describes square root error of the fitness values given by human human $f_{\mathrm{U}}(x_{\mathrm{M}}(t))$ and the models $f_{\mathrm{M}}(x_{\mathrm{M}}(t))$. Note that $f_{\mathrm{U}}(x_{\mathrm{M}}(t))$ is only used as reference and not utilized in evolution. Obviously this measure reflects generalization of the models.

$$E_{\mathrm{F}}(t) = \sqrt{\frac{1}{N_{\mathrm{M}}(t)\bar{f}} \sum_{k=1}^{N_{\mathrm{M}}(t)} (f_{\mathrm{M}}(x_{\mathrm{M}}{}^{k}(t)) - f_{\mathrm{U}}(x_{\mathrm{M}}{}^{k}(t))^{2}} \tag{33}$$

Sixteen persons are divided into four groups. Aiming at desired objective of experiment II, each group does experiments adopting random selection method and three kinds of oriented selection methods respectively. Here, cluster number L=3. This means human preference is divided into three ranks, including favor, normal, dislike. Testing results done by each group are integrated, as shown in Table 5.

measures		T	N_{U}
random selection		18	112
oriented selection (D1)	value	14	92
	comparison with random selection	↓22.2%	↓17.9%
oriented selection (D2)	value	12	76
	comparison with random selection	↓33.3%	↓32.1%
oriented selection (D3)	value	12	80
	comparison with random selection	↓33.3%	↓28.6%

Table 5. Comparison of different selection methods

From Table5, we know that: (I) Because the number of samples is small in AES-IGAs, generalization of surrogate models are bad. If substituted individuals are randomly selected, they may be far from samples, which may lead to large evaluation error of surrogate model. So convergence of IGAs adopting random selection method is worse. (II) Human may favor more than one satisfied dress. Hence desired objectives of both experiments in fact are implicit multi-mode functions. Because oriented selection methods adopting D2 or D3 all consider the distances between all samples and individuals, useful information embodied in evolution are utilized enough. So their performance are better. However, oriented selection methods adopting D1 only takes the distribution of cluster center into account. Incomplete information of individuals may result in larger evaluation error so as to make the performance worse.

In above experiments, evaluation error of surrogate models varies during the evolution, as shown in Figure 3. Obviously no matter which selection method is adopted, E_F increases in former evolution. During this stage, human do not feel tired and can not exactly decide which one is he most like. Surrogate models are trained based on samples and do not participate in evolution. Along with the evolution, human gradually know what they favor. Surrogate models are close to human preference. So evaluation error decrease in latter evolution. In addition, oriented selection methods adopting D2 or D3 reserve samples' information to largest degree. Hence AES-IGAs using these selection methods have less evaluation error. This can effectively avoid misguiding evolution.

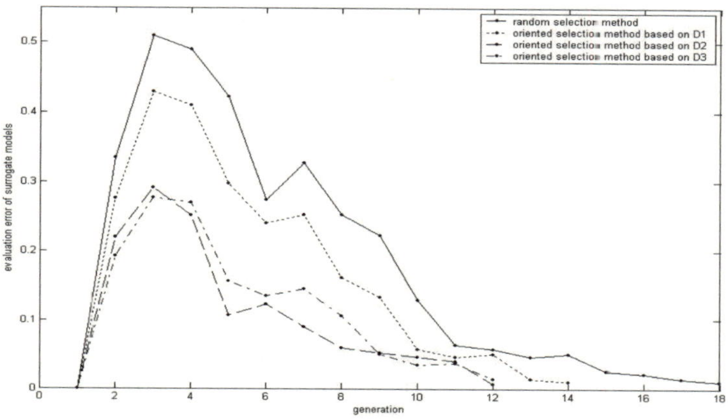

Fig. 3. Evaluation error of surrogate models

In each generation, different substituted individuals are selected when above four selection methods are respectively adopted. In order to compare the difference among random selection method and oriented selection methods, the number of dissimilar substituted individuals in each generation are noted, as shown in Table 6. Here, $N_{MD}(t)$ denotes the number of dissimilar substituted individuals.

generation		6	7	8	10	11	12	15	18
random selection	$N_M(t)$	0	0	0	0	4	4	4	4
oriented selection (D1)	$N_M(t)$	0	0	0	4	4	4	4	-
	$N_{MD}(t)$	0	0	0	4	3	2	2	-
oriented selection (D2)	$N_M(t)$	0	4	4	4	4	-	-	-
	$N_{MD}(t)$	0	4	4	4	3	-	-	-
oriented selection (D3)	$N_M(t)$	0	0	4	4	4	4	-	-
	$N_{MD}(t)$	0	0	4	4	3	3	-	-

Table 6. Comparison of dissimilar substituted individuals selected by different methods

In a word, the performances of oriented selection methods are better than random selection method. Through comparison of three kinds of oriented selection methods, oriented selection methods using D2 or D3 has better performance and stability, yet larger computation complexity. On the contrary, computation complexity of oriented selection methods using D1 is less, whereas the algorithm's performance is worse. Considering multi-mode property of human preference and small population size in IGAs, oriented selection methods using D2 is more fit for IGAs than others.

7.7 Comparison of selection methods with different cluster number

Experiments adopting AES-IGAs with different cluster number are done. Here, two fixed cluster number including 3 or 6 and adaptive cluster number are adopted. Testing results are shown in Table 7.

L		3		6		adaptive	
measures		T	N_U	T	N_U	T	N_U
random selection		18	112	17	108	15	100
oriented selection (D1)	value	14	92	12	80	11	72
	comparison with random selection	↓22.2%	↓17.9%	↓29.4%	↓25.9%	↓26.7%	↓28.0%
oriented selection (D2)	value	12	76	11	76	12	76
	comparison with random selection	↓33.3%	↓32.1%	↓29.4%	↓29.6%	↓20.0%	↓24.0%
oriented selection (D3)	value	12	80	12	84	11	76
	comparison with random selection	↓33.3%	↓28.6%	↓35.3%	↓22.2%	↓26.7%	↓24.0%

Table 7. Comparison of selection methods with different cluster number

By compare the results, we know that: (I) AES-IGAs using adaptive cluster number have best performance. Because cluster number is more reasonable, the clustering precision of individuals is better. This will speed up convergence. (II) No matter which kind of approximate distance is adopted, oriented selection methods converge faster than random selection method. And oriented selection method adopting D2 has better stability. The reason for this is individuals in each cluster contains more information than cluster center, which makes evaluation error less. Hence, surrogate model can participate in evaluation earlier so as to alleviate human fatigue at most.

In order to analyze the influence of selection methods and cluster number on human fatigue, the curves describing the degree of human fatigue are shown in Figure 4. Note that the threshold of human fatigue is 0.95 in these experiments.

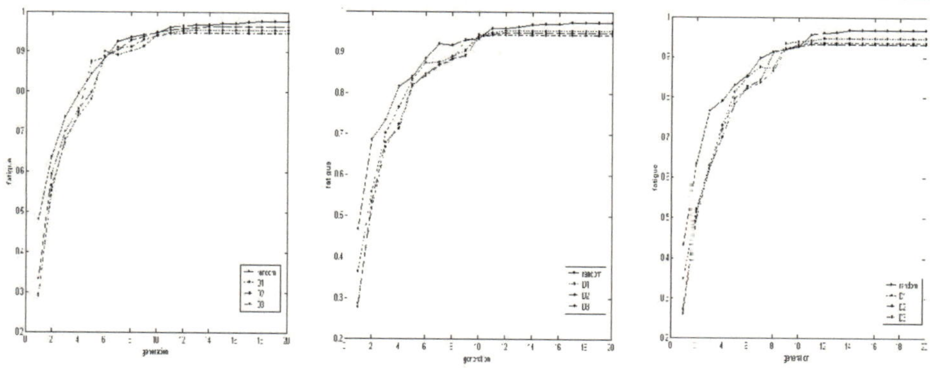

(a) L=3 (b) L =6 (c) adaptive L

Fig. 4. The trend of human fatigue

Obviously no matter which kind of selection methods are used, human fatigue all can be alleviated as long as cluster number is reasonable. Especially the degree of human fatigue is less if oriented selection methods using D2 or D3 are adopted.

7.8 Comparison of performance about IGAs

In order to validate the improvement in performance of IGAs with adaptive evaluation strategy, thirty persons are gathered. Everyone do experiments aiming at both desired objectives adopting conventional IGA and AES-IGA respectively. Testing results for above four experiments done by all persons are integrated, as shown in Table 8.

experiments	I		II	
algorithms	IGA	AES-IGA	IGA	AES-IGA
average generation	14	7	31	12
average number of individuals evaluated by human	112	38	248	55
average number of individuals evaluated by human in each generation	8	5	8	5
generations when $Fa(t)\geq\varepsilon$	-	-	-	8

Table 8. Comparison of the performance between IGAs and AES-IGAs

Through comparison of testing results in experiment I, generation adopting AES-IGA averagely reduces 52.1% than IGA. And total number of individuals evaluated by human adopting AES-IGA averagely reduces 71.5%. These indicate adaptive evaluation strategy can effectively alleviate human fatigue and speed up convergence.

8. Conclusion

In order to further alleviate human fatigue in interactive genetic algorithms, surrogate models are used to evaluate individuals instead of human. When to utilize surrogate models, how many and which individuals are calculate fitness values adopting the models are studied. Startup mechanism about surrogate models considering the degree of human fatigue and the models' precision is given. Variable proportion of population evaluated by surrogate models is proposed. Three phases including evaluated by human only, mixed evaluated by human and the models, evaluated by the models only, are discussed according to the number of substitution individuals. Especially, population size is enlarged in third phase. Surrogate model-based evaluation strategy with oriented selection of substituted individuals is proposed. Three kinds of approximate distance are presented so as to judge which cluster individuals belongs to. At last, convergence of AES-IGAs is proved.
Taking fashion evolutionary design system as a testing platform, the rationality of adaptive evolution strategy is validated aiming at different psychological requirements of human. Testing results indicate AES-IGAs converge faster than canonical IGAs and human feel less tired. Therefore, AES-IGAs can effectively alleviate human fatigue and improve the convergence speed so as to reduce human burden for evaluation which makes human absorbed in more creative design work.

9. Acknowledgements

This work was supported by National Natural Science Foundation of China (Grant No. 60805025) and the 863 Project of China (Grant No. 2007AA12Z162).

10. References

Biles J A.;Anderson P G; Loggi L W. (1996). Neural network fitness functions for a musical IGA, *Proceedings of the International ICSC Symposium on Intelligent Industrial Automation and Soft Computing*, pp. 39-44

H.Takagi. (1998). Interactive evolutionary computation: system optimization based on human subjective evolution. *Proceedings of IEEE Conference on Intelligent Engineering System*, pp. 1-6

H.Takagi.; Sung-Bae Cho; Toshihiko Koda. (1999). Evaluation of an IGA-based Image Retrieval System Using Wavelet Coefficients. *IEEE International Fuzzy Systems Conference Proceedings*, pp. 1775-1780

Zhou Yong; Gong Dun-wei; Hao Guo-sheng; et al. (2005). Neural network based phase estimation of individual fitness in interactive genetic algorithm. *Control and Decision*, Vol.20, pp. 234-236

Wang S F; Wang S H; Wang X F. (2003). Improved interactive genetic algorithm incorporating with SVM and its application. *Journal of Data Acquisition & Processing*,Vol.18, pp.429-433

Yi-nan Guo; Dun-wei Gong; Wang Hui. (2007). Adaptive evaluation strategy based on surrogate model. *Lecture Notes in Computer Science*. Vol.4550, pp. 472-481

Guo Yi-nan; Gong Dun-wei. (2007). Extraction and utilization about knowledge in hierarchical interactive genetic algorithms. *Control and Decision*, Vol.12, pp. 1329-1335

Karayiannis, N. B.; Bezdek, J. C. (1997). Integrated approach to fuzzy learning vector quantization and fuzzy c-means clustering. *IEEE Transactions on Fuzzy Systems*, Vol.5, No.4, pp. 622-630

Cheng Jian; Guo Yi-nan; Qian Jian-sheng. (2006). A multiple neural network architecture based on fuzzy c-means clustering algorithm. *Proceedings of 6th World Congress on Intelligent Control and Automation*, pp. 1875-1878

Cheng Jian; Guo Yi-nan; Gong Dun-wei; et al. (2009). Surrogate model-based evaluation strategy with non-random selection of substituted individuals. *Chinese Journal of Electronics*, No.1, pp. 190-195

He Jun; Yao Xin. (2001). Drift analysis and average time complexity of evolutionary algorithms. *Artificial Intelligence*.

Kim H.; Cho S.B. (2000). Application of interactive genetic algorithm to fashion design. *Engineering Applications of Artificial Intelligence*, Vol.13, pp. 635-644

16

Modelling and Evaluation of Emotional Interfaces

Sylvia Tzvetanova Yung, Ming-Xi Tang and Lorraine Justice
School of Design, The Hong Kong Polytechnic University
Hong Kong SAR, China

1. Introduction

Studies in psychology have acknowledged the importance of emotions for human cognition, motivation, learning, decision-making, and intelligence (Darwin, 1965; Goleman, 1995; Davidson et al., 2003). In particular positive emotions can increase the motivation and attachment of people (Isen, 1992) and facilitate constructive learning processes (Kort et al., 2000). Therefore emotions can be considered in the field of HCI as the factors for building affective, efficient and satisfying interfaces.

In HCI, however, "thinking" was still separated from "feeling" ignoring the role emotions play in human cognition. In a large part the design research focused on usability issues in HCI, with the role of emotions in interactions largely being ignored or simplified. Because of the above described important properties of emotion, and due to the fact that interfaces become more and more involved in the everyday life of people, to date interface designers attempted to model more user-friendly applications using emotional interaction. In the chapter we argue that the users' emotional responses to an interface performance, ways of interaction and content can be modelled, evaluated and supported. We look into the technological foundation of affective computing for the development of emotional interface design applications with the adoption of Artificial Intelligence and cognitive science researches. The goal of this research is to develop a framework for adaptive interface, which supports the users with positive emotion eliciting elements. Our research is based on the context of a computational and symbolic framework, which considers the general issues related to the theories of emotional appraisal in graphic interfaces, as well as specific issues concerning computational representation and the implementation of a design system.

In the chapter we present a methodology and a demonstration for the evaluation of an emotional interface with the experiment results of the implementation of several scenarios involving web based interface design. The evaluation results showed that our proposed model is able to recognize user's emotions and respond with changes in its interface design to encourage a positive emotional state or to improve a negative emotional state of a user. Finally we present the conclusions of this research and outline the issues for further research relating to the improvement of the current model with a particular focus on how to model and represent possible emotional transitions inside the system that provides the knowledge and factors supporting emotional user interaction in web based design systems. The research is addressed to HCI specialists and aims to benefit studies in applying cognitive studies in HCI and in particular cognitive appraisals of emotions.

2. Scope of research

Research in emotion design is concerned with giving machines the ability of emotional intelligence such as recognizing and modelling human emotions, to appropriately communicate emotion, and respond to it affectively. According to Picard (1997) affective systems should possess the abilities to: recognize, express and manage emotions. Recognition is the ability to detect the user's emotion, or make a belief about the user's emotional state. Expressing emotions is about affective communication, where the machine is able to "express" emotions about its state, for instance when a machine runs out of power or when a machine demonstrates understanding of the user's affect. Machines can appear to have emotions by "expressing" emotions. Managing emotions is concerned about the ability to respond to the user's recognized emotional state in a way that the machine supports emotionally the user. Previously there are several attempts to model emotions in HCI. Laboratories in Europe and USA, as well as in Asia, have focused their research on improving emotional reactions between users and computers. The existing research on design and emotion in HCI can be divided by: systems expressing emotion and systems recognizing and reacting according to the understanding of other's affect. Presently there exists a body of research literature on emotion design, which provides a basis for emotion-oriented computers from a technical perspective. The academics and industry developed emotion recognition tools and techniques using different sensing channels: physical sensing, (e.g. heart rate, galvanic skin response) self-reports, facial expressions, knowledge-based methods to derive likely affective state based on factors from current task context (e.g. type, complexity, time of day, length of task), personality and individual history (past failures and successes, affective state associated with current task) (Picard & Healey 1997, Burleson & Picard 2004, Hudlicka, 2003). Among this existing research, however, very few attempts really addressed exiting interaction issues and/or provided solutions for improving people's performance with interfaces in the application areas such as Social Systems, Collaboration, Intelligent Tutoring Systems (ITS), Robots and others. Applications of emotions in interfaces can be endless. Here we provide a few examples that demonstrate the use of emotions to improve HCI.

The MIT's huggable robot was developed to give emotional feedback to affective touch (Stiehl & Breazeal, 2005). The robot was designed for affective therapy with an emphasis on relational, affective touch interactions. When it is held, the robotic animal called Huggable would give a verbal and nonverbal feedback. In terms of technology, the Huggable has built in "sensitive skin" consisting of temperature, force, and electric field sensors, underneath a soft layer of silicone skin to promote a pleasant tactile interaction. Huggable is equipped with small video cameras in the eyes and microphones in the ears that provide visual and auditory input to the sensors of the robot. Huggable possesses an inertial measurement unit that senses the body movement as it is held in someone's arms. Huggable provides audio output with a speaker in its mouth and has seven actuators that provide motion for the neck, coupled eyebrow, coupled ear, and coupled shoulder mechanism. Equipped with simple technology, the robot is able to provide valuable help in treating children that have been violence victims for instance, where the machine is showing them the desirable behaviour.

Recently many of the studies addressed the efficiency of ITS and turned to emotions as a tool for enhancing user's performance with ITS. As mentioned earlier, emotions help memorizing while the person attaches emotions to the material learned. In particular positive emotions are involved in the constructive learning process (Kort et al., 2001). Positive emotions also increase the learner's motivation, and the learner is more focused on the material (Isen, 1992). Some of the ITS models had the goal to soften negative emotions and increase the positive ones, and to preserve the learner's positive experiences in order to facilitate the constructive learning process. One of the first attempts to improve user's learning performance was proposed by Burleson & Picard (2004). They built an affective companion that allowed the user to have optimal experiences and to sustain their motivation during studying by using verbal encouragement. Benchetrit & Frasson (2004)'s research focused on previous psychology knowledge in the pedagogical filed and proposed an agent that was based on the teaching method of the Bulgarian doctor and psychotherapist Lozanov (1978). However, the methods of the doctor were not confirmed and weren't practiced widely. Motivation has been important for ITS as well. Vicente & Pain (2002) developed an ITS system with features that supported user's motivation and reposted that the users had better performance when using such a system. Their model, based on affective theory that supports the user's motivation demonstrated better results than other existing systems that motivate the student by using conventional motivation tools such as games, multimedia, etc.

Other applications try to adapt their interfaces to model the expression of user's affective experience (Bianchi-Berthouze & Lisetti, 2002). Two example systems for kansei communication are MOUE (Model of User's Emotions) that adaptively builds semantic definitions of emotion and MIKE (Multimedia Interactive Environment for Kansei Communication) that along with the user co-evolves a language for communicating over subjective impressions. On those systems, the user is teaching and/or showing with their interaction styles emotional patterns to the system. The two systems attempt to make possible for computers to track and understand human emotion by building databases of emotion definitions.

Since affect is a critical component of effective social interaction, some of the work concerning emotions in HCI focused on developing agents capable of socially effective interaction, and on embodied agents. Implemented in a computational model this can be achieved by using agents reasoning on goals, situations, and preferences (Carofiglio et al. 2006, Conati 2002). Carofiglio et al. (2006) observed the problem of overlapped emotions representing the complexity of human emotions in real social life (for instance the phenomenon to feel happy for somebody else) and proposed a computational model for making an artificial triggering of emotions over time and represent to an educational agent by using Dynamic Belief Networks (DBSs). Events occurred during a time interval (T,T+1) are observed to make a belief of the new state and reason about emotions that might be triggered by these events. The calculation of the intensity of emotions made by the uncertainty in the agent's beliefs about the emotional state and the weight assigned to this emotion. The variation of intensity in the emotion is assigned by the probability that certain factor will take place, times the weight of this factor. de Rosis et al. (2003) also developed an animated agent with a 3-D human-like face that address the elements of social interaction.

The agent is build upon a cognitive theory of emotions and generates its own affective state as a function of the situation and its current goals and expresses this state via speech tone, word choice, facial expressions, and head movement and gaze direction.

3. Design Methodology

While the technology has made attempts to implement emotion recognition and processing in interfaces, there is still need for defining & modelling emotional appraisal to support the user emotionally. The examples above demonstrated that emotions can provide better solutions for various machine interfaces for improvement of the existing systems not only in terms of pleasure, but also in terms of user performance. The technological foundation of affective computing, such as the different tools and databases, makes it possible to develop applications in this field. In a large part design research has focused on usability issues in HCI, and emotions can contribute to addressing these issues. The approaches to implementing emotions in interfaces are largely computational and there is need for more detailed research on the emotions aroused in the interaction process between machine and user. The hypothesis of this research is that user might have emotion toward an interface in terms of ways of interaction, colours, images, or content. Furthermore, as a natural shift in focus from usability to emotions in interfaces, the HCI approach can be taken to create models of emotional interfaces that operate to improve user performance.

Here we propose our formulation of an emotional interface design in the field of HCI. For this purpose the objectives of the research are to develop a methodology and a demonstration of an emotional interface. There are three main questions in relation to the goals of the research on emotional interface:

- Which cognitive mechanisms studied in previous research on emotion are relevant to emotional appraisal in interfaces?
- What are the factors in interfaces that influence user's emotions?
- How can emotion be modelled in online graphic interfaces?

To address the questions the research methodology undertaken for the formulation of the emotional interface consisted of literature review on the theoretical basis, qualitative and quantitative research and prototyping. In our work we have proposed a model for emotional interface, where the interface adapts its elements based on user's emotion. A symbolic model was adopted from the cognitive psychology. In particular we selected the Ortony, Clore and Collince (1988) (OCC) cognitive model of emotions that was built with a computational application in mind. In short, to read cues, the OCC theory suggests that the emotions people experience depend on what they focus on in a situation. Emotions are categorized as positive or negative reactions to certain events, agents, or objects. When one is focusing on an event, it is interpreted as when one is interested in the consequences of the experienced past events with wondering of what is to follow on. When a person is focusing on agents one is attracted to actions, i.e., the functions of animate beings, inanimate objects or abstractions, such as institutions, and other contextual situations. When one is focusing on objects, one is interested in the properties of the object - such as aesthetics and surfaces. The model is represented as an if-then mechanism, which models the emotional interactions. Based on the recognized emotion of users the system responds with changes in its interface in order to stimulate the user towards a positive emotional state. The OCC model was used

as a theoretical basis for the emotional interface and the mechanism was further explored with qualitative research to customise it for a computer interface.
A qualitative research was conducted to further explore the factors in interfaces that influence the user's emotions. A group of experts on design research were asked to comment on the existing interfaces and the elements influencing user's emotions. The outcomes of the qualitative research were summarised in a branching hierarchy, which served as a foundation of the emotional interface symbolic model. Finally to test the hypothesis and to answer the research questions, a prototype of the interface was built to explore the validity of the models proposed. The interface was evaluated with users in an online survey, which is summarised below.

4. Evaluation

The emotional interface was evaluated with users by applying a usability approach in order to explore the functionality of the interface, as well as the hypothesis that emotional interface improves the performance of users. Comparison with the values inferred by the modelled emotional interface gave the researcher a chance to evaluate users' preferences. The personal characteristics and their relation to user's emotion, and the performance with adapted vs. plain interface are evaluated.
In an evaluation of emotions involved in an interaction process, subjects have to describe objects with words of an emotional nature. For the evaluation purposes in this work emotion sets are identified and these sets are used in the questionnaire for users to compare the existing interfaces with an emotional interface. It can be assumed that the users may have any kind of emotion, however how to identify from the long list of existing emotion words, is a question. In psychology researchers suggest about the existence of a basic set of small number of emotions that mixed can compose the entire rich spectrum of emotions. The set of basic emotions is largely discussed and it is not precisely defined for the reasons that different schools of thought believe in different sets of emotions are the basic. Theorists such as Oatley & Johanson-Laird (1987) used the concept of basic emotions in their psychology theories. Oatley & Johnson-Laird cited four basic emotions with evolutionary origins: happiness, sadness, fear, and anger. There are many more opinions on the basic set of emotions, the most popular which are those of: the psycho-evolutionary theory of Plutchik (e.g., acceptance, anger, anticipation, disgust, joy, fear, sadness, and surprise); Ekman, Friesen, and Ellsworth (e.g., anger, disgust, fear, joy, sadness, and surprise); and Aristotle (e.g., anger, mindless love, enmity, fear, confidence, shame, shamelessness, benevolence, pity, indignation, envy, emulation, and contempt). Here we adopt a list intended for interfaces, in particular for evaluation of ITS. Kort et al. (2001) constructed a scale of emotions related to learning ranging from negative to positive states. The set suggested by Kort et al. has the attribute of anxiety-confidence, boredom-fascination, frustration-euphoria, dispirited-encouraged, and terror-enchantment and the values assigned to the emotional words range from negative to positive (-1 to +1, and centred at 0). Here we adapted the list for the needs of the research and updated the emotional scale ranging from 0 to 4 for the evaluation. Based on this basic set an assumption was made about the possible emotions involved in interacting with web-based systems, see Table 1. The emotions are rated between 0 and 4 and centred at 2. Negative emotions are taken in the

range between 0 and 2 and the positive emotions are assigned between 2 and 4. The emotions are grouped according to the system specifications that we observed in the survey.

	RATING				
TYPE	0	1	2	3	4
Content	Enthusiastic	Excellent	Satisfactory	Not Satisfactory	Disappointment
Educational	Fascination	Captivation	Interest	No Interest	Boredom
Appearance	Joy	Enjoinment	Indifference	Repulse	Distress
Organization	Confident	Hope	Comfort	Uncomforted	Fear

Table 1. Rated emotion sets for evaluation purposes

An online questionnaire was distributed to the targeted users of Asia Pacific origin. No payment was offered to the subjects. A lucky draw for a small award was announced. At the end of the survey a small award could be drawn by one of the participants. The targeted users were young people aged 20 to 30 years old mainly from Hong Kong. Asian users were selected because different cultures may respond to interfaces with different emotions. Attitudes can influence cognition, in particular emotional appraisal, which depends on one's perception of the outside world in relation to one's goals and preferences. The cultural dependence of emotional appraisal has not been widely discussed. However, there is evidence of differences between cultures in relation to affect eliciting conditions (Markus & Kitayama 1991). In this research, differences are not sought. Rather in order to avoid confusion in the results the research is applied to an Asian context.

In the survey two online storytelling interfaces were compared. The stories originated from ethnic minorities in China and they are of similar length. The first interface was a plain user-friendly interface, which had no images (see Figure 1), with a white background and black typeface. Nevertheless it was easy to navigate. Furthermore this interface was designed according to the usability rules suggested by Nielsen (1999). The second interface evaluated in the online survey was an emotionally adapted interface (see Figure 2). The adapted interface differed from the plain one by having images and animations. These images and animations were activated automatically if the user showed negative emotion. The users were asked to read through the both stories to compare the two interfaces.

Two different stories were chosen so that each user would evaluate the two different interfaces, and the personality factor would not impact on the comparison. The hypothesis was that the users would engage more actively with the adapted interface and respond to it with positive emotion. For this purpose the participants were asked to report on their emotion toward the two interfaces in order to find out whether the adaptive mechanism was able to trigger positive emotion.

Fig. 1. Visual of the screenshots' flow of plain interface. The user browse trough the text content pages

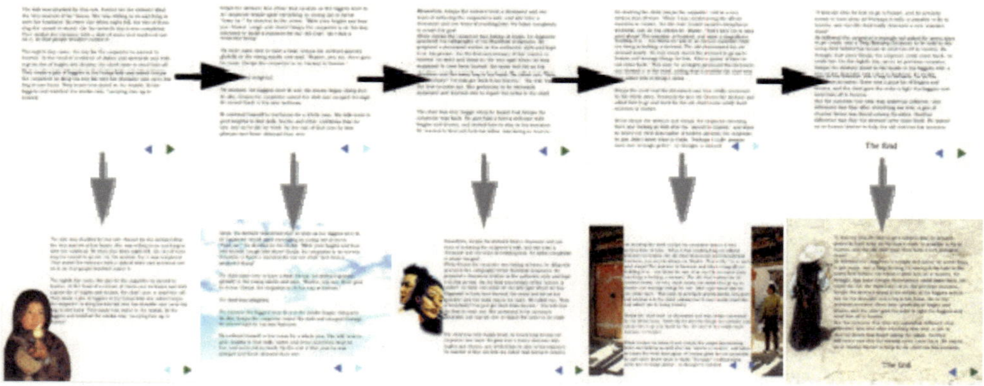

Fig. 2. Visual of the screenshots' flow of the adapted interface. The user browse trough the text content pages (on the top) and if the user shows dissatisfaction the systems switches to the images mode (on the bottom).

4.1 Online questionnaire setting

The survey consisted of 23 questions, with 5 general questions about the personal details of the participants and 9 questions about their emotional response to each story. This first group of questions from collected information about the personality and preferences of the participants, was included in order to identify the personal reasons of the users for their emotion. According to the OCC model (Ortony, Clore and Collince 1988), emotional appraisal depends on people's personal characteristics and concerns. The variables chosen for observation in this introductory group of questions of the survey were:
- gender – it aimed to explore if the subject's gender have any relation to their emotional response,
- motivation - this variable was chosen for observation in order to verify the importance of motivation in emotional appraisal of interfaces,
- personality - this variable was chosen in order to identify the relation of the subject's personality in general to the emotional appraisal of interfaces.

The second and third groups of questions were respectively about the first and the second interfaces. The same 9 questions were asked about each of the two stories. These questions were for identifying the emotional responses of the users to the two stories in order to compare the factors within the interfaces related to them. The variables observed were appearance and organization. Additionally, the users were asked to report on their feelings in general toward the two interfaces using the graded scale of emotions (see Table 1). The rated emotion set included:

- Enthusiastic,
- Disappointing,
- Fascinating,
- Boring,
- Happy,
- Distressing,
- Confident,
- Scary.

The question set was a comprehensive scale of graded emotions. The users could easily understand that each of the emotion factors varied from positive toward negative. The questionnaire also requested the subjects to comment on their emotional impressions in their own words.

4.2 Time recorder

Additionally, the time spent on each page of the two stories was recorded. A timer was set on each page to return the user's time spent on the page, the time of the day, and the total time needed to read through each story. As described in an earlier paper about the modelling of an emotional interface (Tzvetanova, 2007), some of the emotion mechanisms were based on the research findings of Beck (2005) on time response and its relation to emotion. The timer used in the survey was set to identify whether the implemented model of timing in the emotional interface tested showed a relationship to the user's emotion, and whether the timer had a positive influence on the user's emotions. The values of the time were returned on each subject for comparison with their emotional responses in the survey questionnaire. The time recorder used an action script communicating with a PHP script to return the values of the time and send them to an e-mail address for data recording.

5. Results

A total of 63 people took part in the survey, including 32 males, 28 females and 3 people whose genders were not returned. Most of these people were from Hong Kong. In general the participants reported that they were interested to read the two stories. A small number were not interested in the stories themselves, but were intrigued by the questionnaires.

In the survey several variables related to user factors were observed to see to what extent these variables influence the emotional appraisal. These included the influence of gender on the emotional preferences of the participants, and the influence of their personality on their emotional responses. The other variable observed was the factor of motivation, i.e., whether the participant found the online stories useful or not before reading the two stories and what their emotional responses were after they have read the two stories. The results were evaluated with an analysis of variance (ANOVA) statistical approach. Most researchers, in particular in the field of HCI, choose the ANOVA approach to their usability evaluation of multiple mixed variables (Park 2006).

5.1 User related factors

It was found that in general gender is not related to any significant difference in affective responses in the survey. However, the females responded with slightly more positive emotion on design, overall impression, and interface categories compared to the males, who responded more positively than the females on organization, presentation, and usability. The difference in responses between the two genders is shown in Figure 3. The results showed that the men were more likely to grade the two stories around neutral emotion compared to the women who were more likely to show higher arousal of emotion. In discussion about these results with Asian people, they commented: "Men will let women choose regarding aesthetics because men do not have an opinion". As far as the experiment indicates, in an Asian context, women express higher arousal and have more emotional concerns than men.

About motivation among the respondents to the survey, 53.7% thought that the online stories were useful, 25% thought that they were not and 12.3% did not have an opinion. Those who reported to have more motivation to read the stories also responded with slightly more positive emotions to most of the observed categories of the interfaces. See Figure 4.

The personality variable did not show any significant relation to the emotional responses to the two interfaces tested. For some of the observed elements of the two interfaces, the unhappy group reported more positive emotions than the group that was happy with the organization, presentation, and usability factors. The responses are shown in Figure 5.

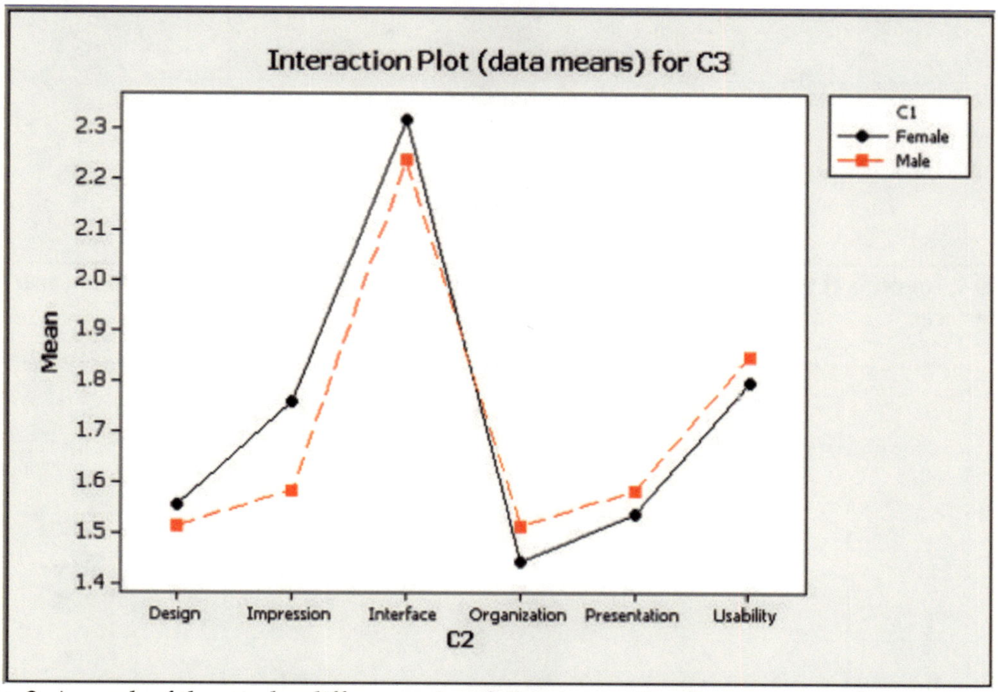

Fig. 3. A graph of the gender differences in relation to emotional responses to the two interfaces

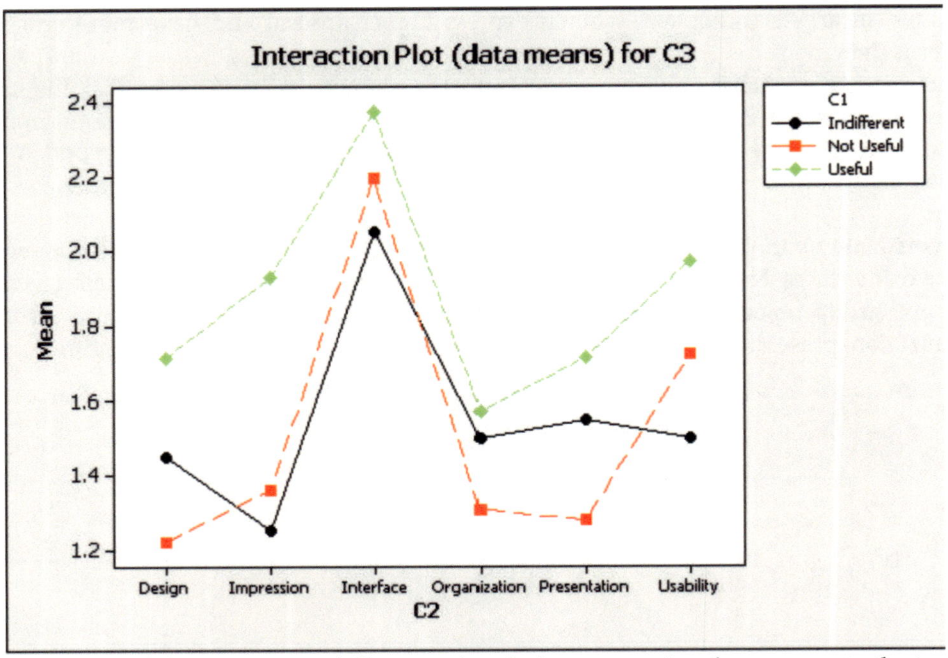

Fig. 4. A graph of the motivation differences in relation to emotional responses to the two interfaces

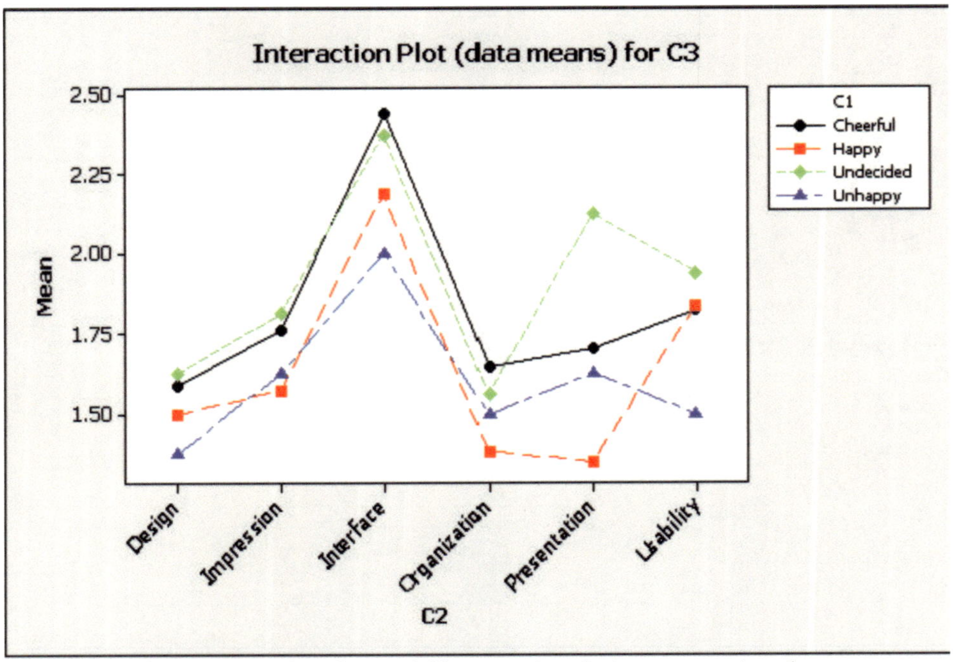

Fig. 5. A graph of the personality factor differences in relation to emotional responses to the two interfaces

5.2 Design factors

The survey showed both stories were easy to use. Reportedly there were no usability issues or unclear functions. The participants were driven by curiosity to fill in the questionnaires. 'First of all, I had not intended to read the story and I actually did not read it. But I would like to know what will happen to each paper. They seem more interesting than the story!' – one of them responded. The participants were asked to read through the two stories, which are very similar, coming from ethnic minorities in China. However, on the question about the content nearly one quarter of the people responded that the second interface was fascinating and captivating. The adapted interface evoked more positive emotion than the non-adapted one. Most of the users reported that the adapted interface was more interesting than the other, even though the emotional loading of the two stories was similar. Some of the people gave their personal impressions in their own words. Some people commented that the animation of the user-friendly plain interface was boring. Four people reported that they liked it because 'The animation of the word can make the description of the story more active'. Three people referred the animation as boring. Another function of the animation was that it drove the attention on a particular part of the story. Six people in their comments mentioned the relationship between the animated parts of the first interface and attention, and at the same time they did not find the interface's elements emotionally positive (in their words, it doesn't affect so much, the story was boring when reading in a text form...nothing can help). The typeface of the plain interface got slightly more positive feedback than the animated elements. It was described by the subjects as 'elegant', 'elegant modern and fashion', 'light, go upward'. It was also described as 'it seems to let me feel peace', 'It is easy to read, but it is boring', 'It is black and white, comfortable to read'. On overall it was reported positive emotional response to the ease of use, even thou the interface was not designed with emotional appearance in mind.

The images from the second interface were commented on as well. Thirty-four people commented on the love story image of two famous actors in a love scene. The most common association, made by 5 people, was that this was a sad image of love. Others replied positively, with desire about the image content: 'the image could be more animated, show how they hug, and kiss, would be even more emotional', 'I get emotion for these actors, celebrities make me interested, and they are beautiful to look at'. The other images in the adapted interface in the survey received comments such as, "peaceful", 'good, it makes me feel peace, refresh'.

On the whole, the second adapted interface got more positive evaluation in emotional appearance than the first one. The people were more likely to comment in one way or another that the adapted interface was emotionally arousing, compared to the plain user-friendly one, which was reported as good in terms of its usability factors (See Figure 6). In addition the second interface on overall got more positive emotions responses than the user-friendly plain interface averaging above the value of 2 (Satisfactory, Interest, Indifference, Comfort). The second interface's usability was graded with a more positive emotion by the users compare to the first interface. Among the design elements of the first interface however usability feature was highest emotional response (between 1.5: uncomfortable and 2: comfortable).

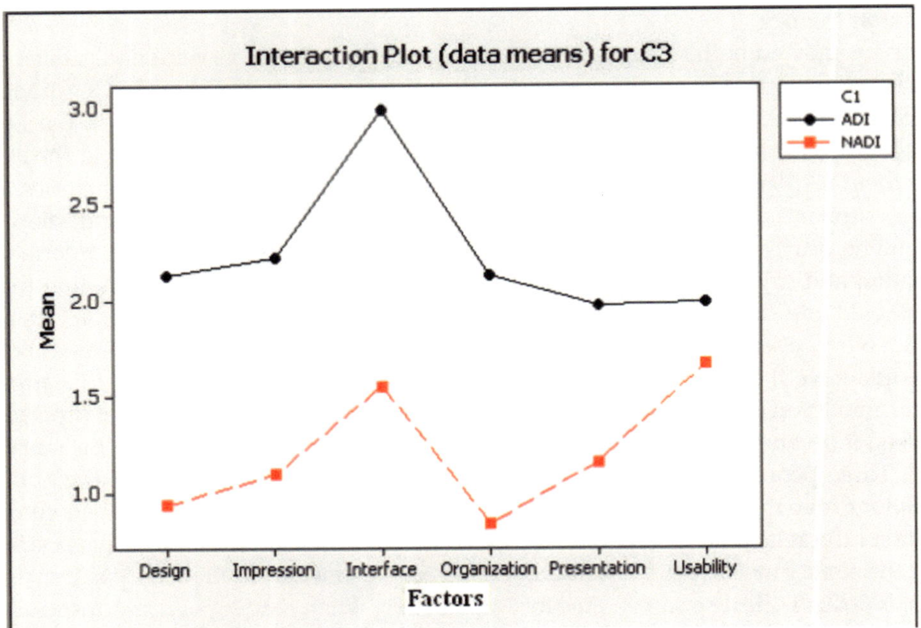

Fig. 6. Overall graph showing the differences in the responses between two interfaces. The graph of the first interface is marked with square pointers and the graph of the second is marked with round pointers.

The results show that the presentation of the evaluated interfaces was graded with a big difference in emotional response between the two stories (see Figures 7 and 8). The second interface presentation was more positively rated as satisfactory to excellent compared to the first, which was reported to be satisfactory to unsatisfactory. The participants' first impression of the adapted interface was more positive than that of the plain user-friendly one, with 39.6% of the participants rating it as not interesting compared to the 37.3% who answered the same question on the adapted interface rating it as interesting (see Figures 9 and 10). The participants had almost the same emotional response to the two interfaces overall. 50.9% of the participants rated the first interface as satisfactorily presented and 47.1% rated the second and considered the story satisfactorily presented (see Figures 11 and 12). However, comparing the means of the results, the second story had the positive value of emotion of 0.8 compared to the negative value of emotion of - 0.3 for the first. It was expected that the users would rate the first interface as more user friendly, because it is straight forward and based on usability rules with, in particular, easy navigation and readable black text on white background, as previously suggested (Dix 1998, Nielsen 1999). However, the participants rated the usability of the first interface as comfortable to uncomfortable compared to the second interface, which was rated more towards comfortable (see Figures 13 and 14).

The participants had more positive emotional response to the second interface design than the first (see Figures 15 and 16). Overall, the adapted interface was rated as interesting to captivating on the emotional scale compared to the plain user-friendly interface, which was rated as not interesting. It was pointed out that the content itself arouses emotion and it is more important than the appearance. Some commented that 'my emotion comes from the story, the meaning of the words, not the graphic or animation, because the association between the visual and the story is not strong enough'. On average the people reported that they preferred the second interface because of the images and the dynamics. They commented: 'With more images, the second story is more attractive to me'. However, some other users expressed preferences for the simplified version and they said 'The first story was easy and simple and easy to read and the second story was complicated and difficult to relate and comprehend easily'. The participants had more positive emotional response to the adapted interface organization than the plain user-friendly interface organization (see Figures 17 and 18).

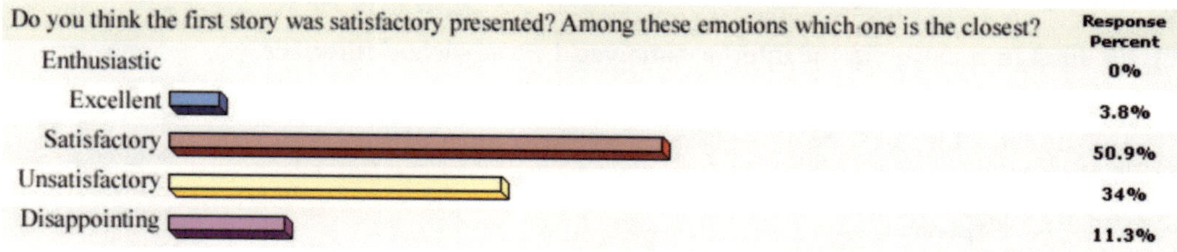

SumOfSquares	Min	Max	Mean	Standard deviation
44	-2	1	-0.5	0.7

Fig. 7. Presentation of the interface responses analysis for the first interface

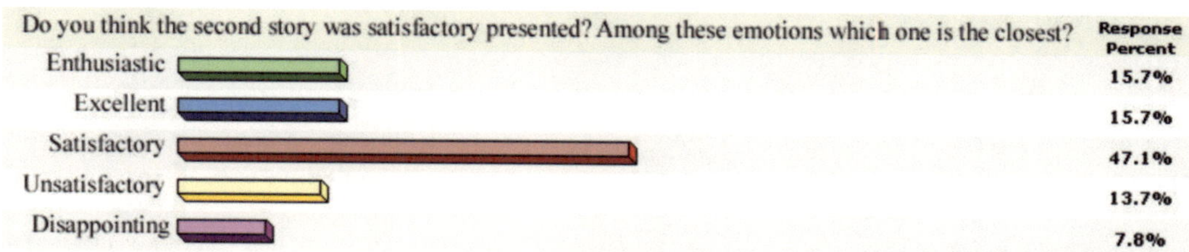

SumOfSquares	Min	Max	Mean	Standard deviation
63	-2	2	0.2	1.1

Fig. 8. Presentation of the interface responses analysis for the second interface

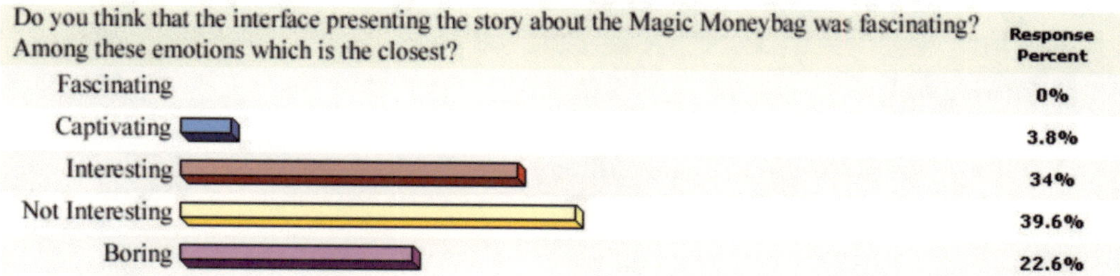

SumOfSquares	Min	Max	Mean	Standard deviation
71	-2	1	-0.8	0.8

Fig. 9. First impression of the interface analysis for the first interface

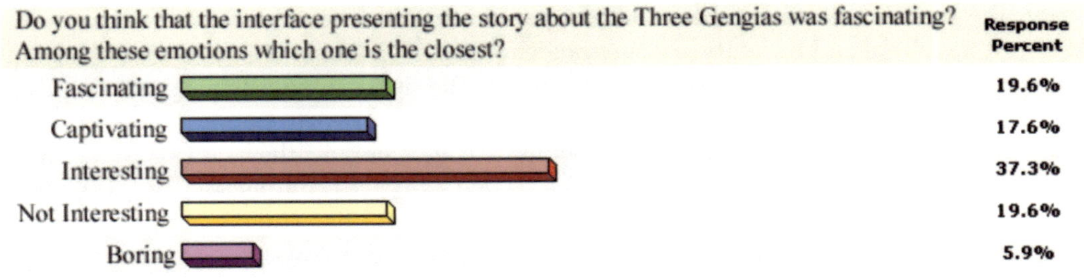

SumOfSquares	Min	Max	Mean	Standard deviation
71	-2	2	0.3	1.2

Fig. 10. First impression of the interface analysis for the second interface

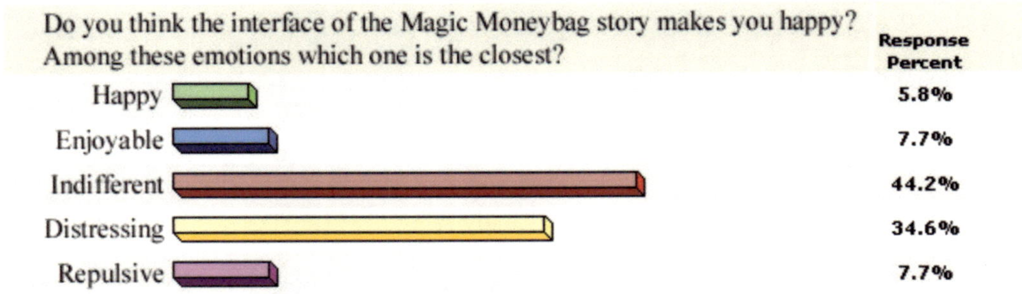

SumOfSquares	Min	Max	Mean	Standard deviation
50	-2	2	-0.3	0.9

Fig. 11. Overall happy vs. unhappy interface analysis for the first interface

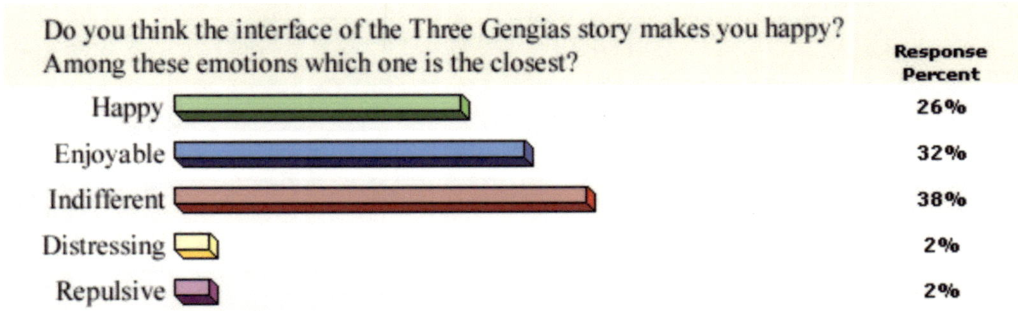

SumOfSquares	Min	Max	Mean	Standard deviation
73	-2	2	0.8	0.9

Fig. 12. Overall happy vs. unhappy interface analysis for the second interface

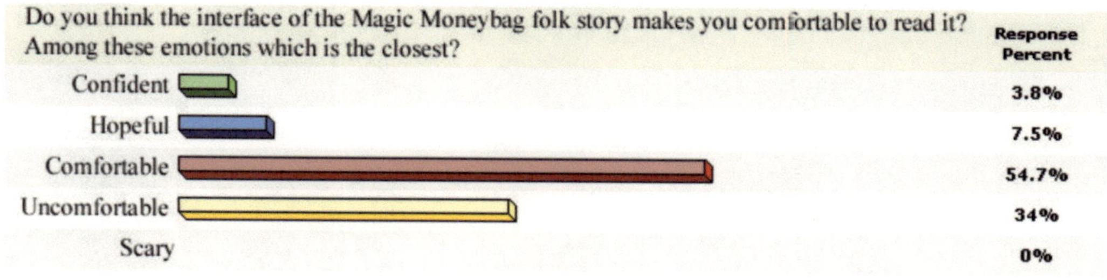

SumOfSquares	Min	Max	Mean	Standard deviation
30	-1	2	-0.2	0.7

Fig. 13. Usability of the interface analysis for the first interface

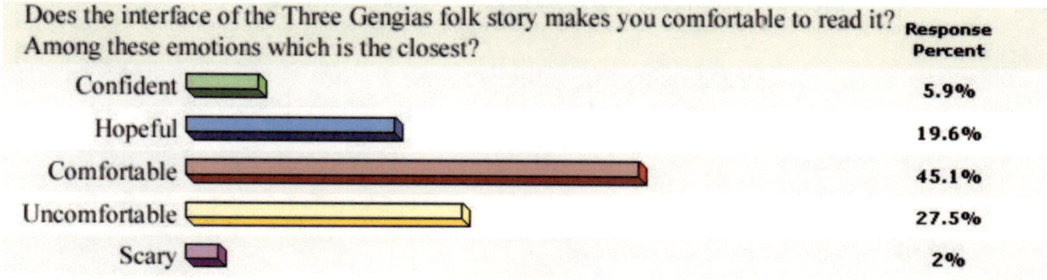

SumOfSquares	Min	Max	Mean	Standard deviation
40	-2	2	0	0.9

Fig. 14. Usability of the interface analysis for the second interface

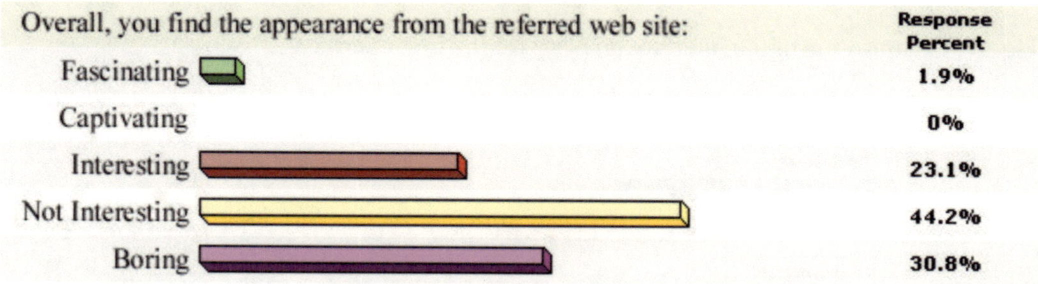

SumOfSquares	Min	Max	Mean	Standard deviation
91	-2	2	-1	0.9

Fig. 15. Design of the interface analysis for the first interface

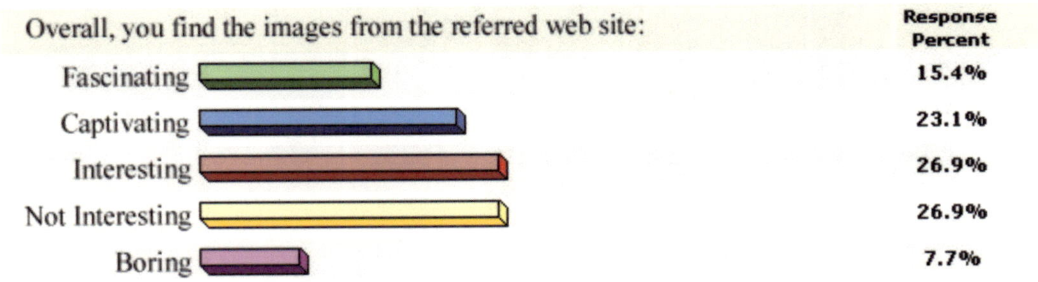

SumOfSquares	Min	Max	Mean	Standard deviation
74	-2	2	0.1	1.2

Fig. 16. Design of the interface factor analysis for the second interface

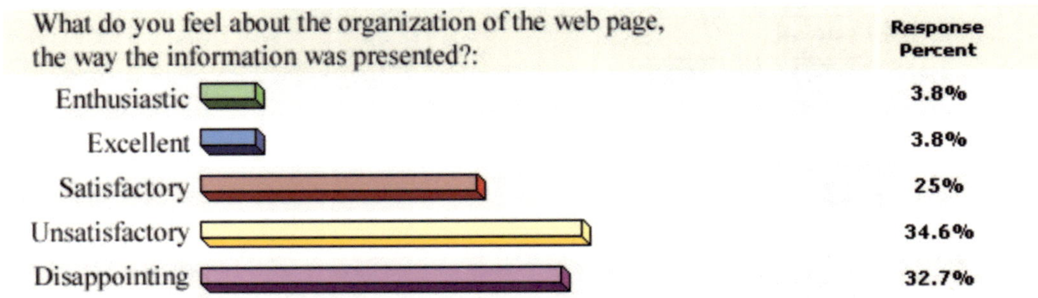

SumOfSquares	Min	Max	Mean	Standard deviation
96	-2	2	-0.9	1

Fig. 17. Organization of the interface analysis for the first interface.

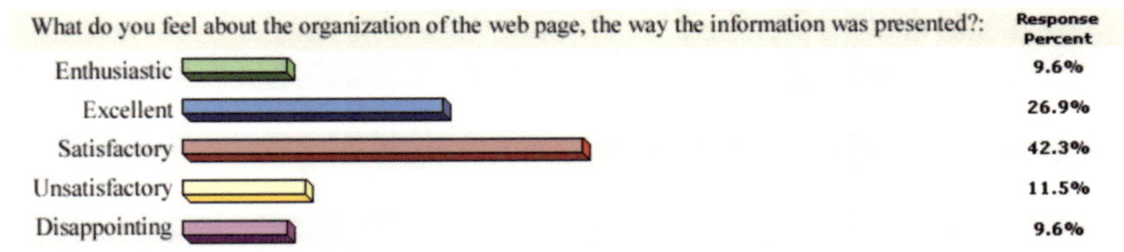

SumOfSquares	Min	Max	Mean	Standard deviation
60	-2	2	0.2	1.1

Fig. 18. Organization of the interface analysis for the second interface

5.3 Timer

The timer showed that the majority of the people read the two stories carefully in the average time frame. Short periods of time measured on a page showed that some of the participants browsed first the two interfaces to see what would be next, and then went back to read the story. The majority of the instances of short time in the sequential browsing of a page were with the second interface. It is possible that the subjects got curious about the images rather than the story, as the images helped them understand the content or increased their curiosity.

6. Conclusions

This chapter presented a research methodology for and an evaluation of the design of an emotional interface. The evaluation showed that people do have emotional responses towards design elements in interfaces. The research has also shown that the Asian people prefer more colourful interfaces with images rather than plain interfaces. The main contribution of this research however, is the research methodology for modelling and evaluating emotions in interfaces. This work presents an approach that can be used for exploring the emotional responses towards interaction systems, as well as adapting interfaces according to user's emotions.

Opposing previous research (Dix 1998, Nielsen 1999) users reported that they were better supported with an "emotional interface" than with a plain user-friendly interface. Despite that the adapted interface had more elements and was not as simplified as the plain interface the users rated the emotionally adapted interface as more user friendly. Emotional interface can be more efficient as previous research on psychology indicated (Darwin, 1965; Goleman, 1995; Davidson et al., 2003). Human emotions play an important role in our lives when we communicate with each other. Computers are an important everyday tool for communication, work, and learning and so on. Therefore user interfaces need to be more carefully planned based on the human cognition, rather than on machine reasoning. Emotions are essential for human cognition and consequently need to be appropriately addressed in HCI. Here we stressed the importance of emotions for user interfaces by evaluating the responses of the users to emotional interface. It was shown that such an interface has improved usability functions.

7. References

Beck, J.E. (2005). Engagement tracing: using response times to model student disengagement, *Artificial intelligence in education*, pp. 88-95, Amsterdam, Netherlands

Benchetrit, O. & Frasson, C. (2004). Controlling emotional conditions for learning. *Workshop on social and emotional intelligence in learning environments, In conjunction with the 7th International conference on intelligent tutoring systems*, Maceio - Alagoas, Brazil

Bianchi-Berthouze, N. & Lisetti, C. L. (2002). Modeling multimodal expression of user's affective subjective experience. *User modeling and user-adapted interaction*, Vol. 12, pp. 49 – 84, February 2002

Burleson, W. & Picard, R. W. (2004). Affective agents: sustaining motivation to learn through failure and a state of stuck, Workshop on Social and Emotional Intelligence in Learning Environments, In conjunction with the 7th International Conference on Intelligent Tutoring Systems, Maceio Alagoas, B. (Ed.)

Carofiglio, V., de Rosis, F. & Grassano, R. (in press) Animating Expressive Characters for Social Interactions, Canamero, L. & Aylett, R. (ed.) Dynamic models of mixed emotion activation, Amsterdam: John Benjamins

Conati, C. (2002) Probabilistic Assessment of User's Emotions in Educational Games, Journal of Applied Artificial Intelligence, 16(7-8), 555-575

Darwin, C. (1872/1965). The expression of emotions in man and animals. The university of Chicago press

Davidson, R. J., Scherer, K. & Goldsmith, H. (2003). Handbook of affective sciences. Oxford University Press

de Rosis, F., Pelachaud, C., Poggi, I., Carofiglio, V., & Carolis, B. D. (2003) From greta's mind to her face: modelling the dynamics of affective states in a conversational embodied agent. *International Journal of Human-Computer Studies - Special Issue on "Applications of Affective Computing in HCI"*, pp. 81–118

Goleman, D. (1995). Emotional intelligence: why it can matter more than IQ. New York: Bantam

Isen, A. M. (1992). Positive Affect and Decision Making, Handbook of Emotions, Lewis, M. & Haviland, J. M. (Ed.), pp. 261-277, Guilford Press, New York

Hudlicka, E. (2003) To feel or not to feel: The role of affect in human–computer interaction, *International Journal of Human-Computer Studies*, Vol. 59, pp. 1-32, July 2003

Kort, B.; Reilly, R. & Picard, R.W. (2001). External Representation of Learning Process and Domain Knowledge: Affective State as a Determinate of its Structure and Function, MIT Media Laboratory

Lozanov, G. (1978). Suggestology and outlines of suggestopedy. Gordon and Breach

Markus, H. R. & Kitayama, S. (1991). Culture and the self: implications for cognition, emotion, and motivation. Psychological review, Vol. 2, pp. 224–253

Nielsen, J. (1999). Designing Web Usability: The Practice of Simplicity. New Riders, Indianapolis, Indiana

Oatley, K. & Johanson-Laird, P. (1987). Towards a cognitive theory of emotion. *Cognition and emotion*, Vol. 1, pp. 20–50

Ortony, A., Clore, G., & Collins, A. (1988). The cognitive structure of emotions. Cambridge University Press

Picard, R. (1997). Affective Computing. MIT Press

Picard, R. & Healey, J. (1997). Affective wearables, *Personal and Ubiquitous Computing,* Vol. 1, pp. 231-240

Stiehl, W. D. & Breazeal, C. (2005). Affective touch for robotic companions. *First International Conference Affective Computing and Intelligent Interactions*, Beijing, China

Tzvetanova, Tang and Justice (2006) Modelling Emotional Interfaces Using OutSite and InSite Factors, *Design Computing and Cognition*, Eindhoven, Netherlands, July 10-12

Vicente, A. & Pain, H. (2002). Informing the detection of the students' motivational state: An empirical study. *Intelligent Tutoring Systems, 6th International Conference*, pp. 933–943

17

Understanding Group Work in Virtual Environments: Performance, Creativity, and Presence

Ilona Heldal[1] and Lars Bråthe[2]
[1]*Chalmers University of Technology, SE–41 296 Göteborg, Sweden*
[2] *Volvo Powertrain Corp., SE–40 508 Göteborg, Sweden*

1. Introduction

Virtual environments (VEs) have the following dimensions: content, geometry and dynamics. Experiences in VEs refer largely to *the sensory experience* produced by a computer technology, which often is a 'sense of physical reality ... a construction from the symbolic, geometric, and dynamic [computer generated] information directly presented to our senses' (Ellis 1995, p. 16). In a VE the following aspects are also important: user-involvement, direct interactivity, the possibility to elaborate a sense of being in the three-dimensional computer-generated space, and to receive direct responses from the environment so that the participants experience a control on their actions.

By visualizing three-dimensional spaces and objects, computers can support collaboration. People at the same place or at distributed locations can share similar images and use them for work or leisure. The computer systems that allow these visualization possibilities are termed collaborative virtual environments (CVEs). By providing services such as distance conferencing, shared industrial applications, distance learning, maintaining online groups, and games, CVEs offer several advantages: to overcome travel problems, to avoid ambiguities during the different phases of the collaboration by visualizing the same processes, and being dynamically changeable, which can be time- and cost-effective in comparison with using real models. By visualizing a model around the users at actual scale, it is possible to experience buildings, ships, airplanes, or roads before they are built in order to explore them and select the most suitable alternatives. Other benefits are e.g. to visualize safety-critical situations, to aid rehabilitation and to train when learning, and in general for scenarios that may be hard to explore in reality. Firemen can train by using VEs to rescue, patients can do their rehabilitation exercises or overcome their fears, pilots can train to fly airplanes, and so on. These systems also bring together people with the same interests, who are distributed over space, to interact remotely.

The overall objective of this chapter is to identify issues that contribute to creative, effective and enjoyable group collaboration in CVEs. For this purpose we review theories on supporting performance, creativity, and presence. We examine studies on the contribution of performance, creativity and presence in the use of computer mediated collaboration (see Section 4), and we also use some previous research on creativity support in CVEs (Roberts et al., 2007; Heldal et al., 2007). Many of the already identified supporting factors depend on the quality of how technologies allow seamless interaction and how they support social aspects. This study extends the previous work and exemplifies that a more usable and intuitive CVE does not necessarily support group work better, and shows that the notion of presence is not necessarily unambiguous for determining high quality work in CVEs.

The goal is to find approaches supporting *collaborative* experiences. By reviewing research on differences between individual work and group work and how it is influenced by presence, creativity and performance, the findings will contribute to better understanding of networked collaboration.

2. Motivation and structure

To produce better systems in general, the benefits of defining suitable evaluation methods and guidelines have already been shown. Research has defined methods and identified many different concepts and factors that contribute to developing advanced VEs. Such factors are presence, creativity, performance, enjoyment, interaction, immersiveness, input and output devices etc. However, the factors that contribute to efficient and enjoyable work for single users are not necessarily the same or equivalent in impact on group collaboration.

CVE technologies are complex, diverse, and in many cases without established standards and with 'homemade' adjustments. Their use and impact are increasing, since they offer a number of benefits. Allowing users to interact with each other - or each other's representations - and the same or similar computer-generated graphical images, to see what the others are doing, and to communicate with each other also through visual and auditory channels are clear benefits. A user can write, describe by voice, or show to her remote partners what she means, and whether or how she follows the group activities. Thus, the interaction can be multifaceted. The amount of technical and social factors influencing the collaborative results just blossoms out. To answer the questions 'Under which conditions does collaboration have added value over individual work when using VE technologies?', 'Does a technology supporting creative individuals supports creativity for groups?', and 'What is the relation between the most important factors influencing work in CVEs that have the greatest impact on the outcome?' is the broad motivation behind this study.

A factor that influences an individual in one way does not necessarily influence another in the same way, even if the members of the group use similar technologies. For example, a person can experience high presence, while another finds it low in the same virtual room. If these two people work together, both the ability to experience higher presence for the first person and the collaborative outcome can be lowered, e.g. by unnecessary discussions, technical interruptions, or social misunderstanding (Heldal et al., 2006). For a superior outcome it is not necessarily enough to allow advanced technologies and provide successful networking. How the individuals handle these, how the group is organized, what the main technical characteristics and the social differences are, also have to be taken into account.

Object-focused collaboration is common in creative tasks and is well researched in CVEs, and typically involves problem-solving (Wolff et al., 2006). We use object-focused interaction as the basis for discussion of group work in CVEs.

The paper is structured as follows. Section 3 briefly presents single-user work versus collaboration. In Section 4, performance, creativity, presence and other factors and concepts are examined that are considered to have a great impact on evaluations and outcomes. Section 5 briefly examines relations between these factors, with focus on presence and creativity. Section 6 includes a pragmatic discussion about treating performance as a main goal for examining collaborative work. This is followed by Section 7 with the findings and discussion, and suggestions for future directions. The last section, Section 8, presents the conclusions.

To acquire an overall view of performance for collaboration when people use CVEs, one must examine the following, according to Heldal (2004):

1) how people can work, with special focus on problem-solving,
2) how technologies can support this,
3) what they experience.

Thus, performance in CVEs is described in terms of 1), 2) and 3). We use these types of activities in order to examine creativity and presence contributing to group experiences and outcome for object-focused work.

Since many studies, especially those investigating collaborative creativity, are for networked computer technologies in general, even though the focus is on collaborative work in CVEs, we do not limit this study to examining exclusively VEs, but also consider research from computer-mediated communication (CMC) or computer-supported collaborative work (CSCW). Some relations, e.g. between creativity and group creativity or social creativity, are exploited more for general communication technologies.

3. Single-user work versus collaboration

3.1 Understanding computer-mediated collaborative outcomes

Collaboration is not always easy, yet it is often a necessity in order to reach one's goals in society, organizations, or relations between individuals. In trying to collaborate efficiently, one can experience difficulties caused by, for example, distance, differences regarding motivation, language, culture, lack of agreement upon a set of definitions, or different mental models. To avoid these difficulties, more support for collaboration and better suited equipment is needed.

To find out how a group can be more than the sum of individuals has preoccupied a number of researchers for several decades. By considering various technologies that support work, many old questions become actual again. In general, it is difficult to explore the benefits of group work in terms of individual contribution, task and context, and to obtain measurable and consistent results through several projects. Research, though, has acknowledged that individuals contribute with at most 70% of their optimal individual performance for a well-working collaboration. The results often depend on task, time, group, chosen evaluation method or applied theories (Brown 2000). Brown's research focused on face-to-face collaboration. For the CMC, the CSCW and the CVE studies too, most evaluations treat face-to-face collaboration in real environments as a reference for obtaining superior communication and collaboration results. Even if computer-mediated work can have unique advantages prior to work in physical environments (Walther 1996), it is worth considering the potential for working with physical objects rather than technology-mediated work, where applicable, since naturalness still has unique value (Wolff et al., 2006).

Among the earliest, probably most promising distributed applications are those that support meetings and conferencing. For these, Scott (1999) summarized several group collaboration models in an input, process and output framework that also includes task characteristics for the input, grouped according to McGrath's decision typology: create a plan, choose, negotiate, and execute (McGrath 1884). Neal et al. also argue for the importance of treating, in CSCW evaluation methods, the second-level social system effects such as coupling of work, joint awareness and coordination, which can be more easily approximated by laboratory studies (Neale et al. 2004). Knowing more about normative behaviors and main tendencies can yield benefits for field-work evaluations. Understanding such behaviors is important since including social interaction in the evaluation of collaborative work is crucial.

Much applied research on using VEs concerns handling prototypes and models. Group work for these applications, too, can be supported by knowing more about social interaction (Heldal et al. 2006). The establishment of common grounds, conventions, awareness, trust, naturalness and human proximity (Hinds et al. 2002), time and distance (Poltrock et al. 2003), and knowing the prerequisites for single users or good collaboration (Gutwin et al. 1998) are important roles for these applications as well.

3.2 Towards collaboration in CVEs

Several studies have identified some factors such as presence, performance, intuitiveness, interaction, and leadership as important for VEs (Tromp 2001, Slater et al. 2000, Schroeder et al. 2006). Certain of these may be more closely associated with one specific application or type of VE than with another. For example, desktop systems can be more effective than immersive environments for problem-solving when visualizing large molecules, while immersive systems can be more effective for visual modeling of object-focused collaboration with a few objects (Heldal 2004).

There are also differences when varying some technical factors of an environment. For example, varying latency, field of view, different rendering usage, interaction styles, or varying perspectives for navigation can result in different performance and presence measures (Tromp 2001, Steed et al. 2003, Polys et al. 2004, Steed et al. 2005, Schroeder et al. 2006). For CVEs there are still many problems remaining, for example, the influence of technical interaction, chosen interaction style, the flow of interaction, devices and user interfaces, communication modalities and considering the influence of social interaction (Wilson, 2003). The social interaction and the technical interaction often take place in parallel, or they are interconnected in a non-deterministic way due to the nature of social interaction. Possibly because of the novelty and complexity of the technology, or because it supports applications from several different areas, there are only a few works on approaching e.g. overall outcome or overall usability for CVEs (Schroeder et al. 2006). To approach collaboration in CVEs that can be focused or unfocused, Tromp (2001) has identified three main stages of the collaboration that are embedded in a 'meta-collaboration' context. She divided the temporal structure of the interactions into the beginning of the interaction, proper collaboration, and ending the collaboration (Tromp et al. 2003).

Understanding the task, problem-solving in relation to available or spent time in the environments, and choosing the right strategies are important for increased performance and presence (Schroeder et al. 2006). This can mean quicker plan creation, less time spent for negotiation, and quicker decision-making (McGrath 1984).

3.3 Towards creative collaboration

Creativity is helped by an uncluttered state of consciousness but while creative tools promote this through intuitive and natural interfaces, this naturalness of interaction does not yet extend to distance collaboration. For group creativity to be considered collaborative it must have some common focus (Roberts et al. 2007). Allowing creativity is considered to augment the quality of work (Fencott 1999, Waterworth et al. 2001).

Numerous studies associate creativity with the multiple dimensions of experienced flow defined by Csíkszentmihályi. These are (Csíkszentmihályi, 1996):

1. Clear goals – this means having clearly defined objectives and, during the whole work, immediate feedback so that one knows instantly how well one is doing.
2. To immediately understand one's perceived ability to act. This also means that the task should be suitable to individual skills.
3. Action and awareness should merge.
4. Supporting concentration on the task. This also means that irrelevant stimuli must disappear from consciousness; one should not worry or be concerned about irrelevant issues.
5. The individual should feel a sense of potential control.
6. To feel, however, a loss of self-consciousness, and a sense of growth and of 'being part of some greater entity'.
7. Altered sense of time. Time should be experienced to pass faster.
8. The experience should become autotelic, worth doing for its own sake.

Experiencing creativity as individuals may differ from experiencing group creativity. It is debated whether individual creativity can contribute to group creativity at all (Fischer et al. 2005). Moreover, by using technologies one adds a further level of possible disturbances: experiencing creativity for groups while using technologies (Shneiderman et al. 2007).

Aiming to obtain creative work in CVEs thus raises a lot of questions. How do the application, technology and social factors such as 'joint thinking, passionate conversations, and shared struggles among different people' (Fischer et al. 2005, p. 4) impact upon this? And how is this connected with supporting presence, collaborative presence and social presence?

Handling innovations in a company may also differ from focusing on the need for supporting creativity from the beginning. The starting points for innovation work usually consider identification of the users' and customers' needs, identification of a new market possibility (the work forward to successful business plans), considering new technological possibilities, or simply the conviction of an individual or small group that it is possible to do something in a completely new or simpler way. This often refers to efficiency in the first instance. Thus, the starting point for creative work might be quite different and takes more time and often, unfortunately, is more diffuse. Hence, the composition of the group may also differ; e.g. the members might have been working close together before, or they might be new to each other and coming from different cultures. Thus, they may need different support to perform tasks in a creative way.

4. Factors influencing work

4.1 Performance

One of the major factors that influence performance is the perceived and actual interaction in these technical environments. Interaction can be defined by the following components: affective and emotional, cognitive or intellectual, non-verbal, content or message, and social or personal network segments (McLeish et al. 1973). It is almost impossible to divide and define exactly the different components of the interaction. They are embedded in the content and in the network of relationships. However, if the aim is to improve collaboration in a technical environment, we need to separate these, since both the origins, and the effects of social interaction and interaction mediated via technologies are different. Thus, a separation - at least in these two main categories - contributes to better understanding of issues supporting or disturbing work.

There are differences in overall performance, depending on the time the users have spent in the environment and on aspects of their expertise (Nielsen 1993; Nilsson et al. 2002). The design of a new system does not incorporate either how the variation in the surrounding physical environments will influence the use, or how the social interaction will do so via the technology. Research has demonstrated that time does have effects on the use of media for groups. Ad hoc groups must sometimes handle decisions in organizations through a medium, but this can have negative consequences on their agreements. The long-term use of a certain medium supporting group collaboration has the result that media effects may disappear (Walther 2002).

Sonnenwald showed statistically significant differences with respect to performance and adoption, in the sense that the users developed work-around to cope with the perceived disadvantages of collaborating remotely with scientific systems (Sonnenwald, et al. 2002). It is well known that people, if they can do so, use systems in different ways (Caroll 1995). Disruptive technologies, and the way that they allow *seamful* interaction may also support experiences (Höök et al. 2008). Webster et al. (2001) show that people interact differently in different social contexts. We can also mention here that differences in the attitude towards use exist between members of different national groups (Vöhringer-Kuhnt 2002).
Lampton et al. (2002) pointed to the value of considering proper performance measurements in evaluating VEs. This should support meaningful comparisons and contribute to cost-

effectiveness and safety, among many other reasons. They based their view on a list of problems regarding measurements in evaluations from the American National Standards Institute (1993). Some of the problems were a lack of general theories to guide human performance measurement, difficulties in handling the inverse relationship between operational control and realism, the multiple dimension of behavior, how to measure cognitive tasks etc. Based on ten categories defined by the same institute (time, accuracy, amount achieved, frequency of occurrence, behavior categorization, consumption, workload, probability, space/distance, errors), they discussed performance measurements for VEs (Lampton et al. 2002).

Bystrom and Barfield (1999) have previously analyzed collaborative task performance in a VE. They found that task performance is affected by the presence of others and by the level of control, even though the sense of presence was not correlated with the collaborative experience. They suggest that experiences in VEs should be grouped according to three factors: presence, the quality of VEs, and task difficulty. Another study, by Slater et al., also argued that efficient performance could be a consequence of the VE experience. Subjects in a more realistic environment performed better (Slater et al. 2001; Wolff et al. 2006). Time and efficient workflow also influence effectiveness (Heldal 2004).

Social studies treat technology-mediated collaboration in such a way that the technical factor is often implicitly embedded in the process of social interaction. Yet the technology often matters through its presence, or when a problem occurs during its use. By developing technology that supports mediated collaboration, the nuances of social interaction are not considered. But at a certain stage - and VEs have passed this stage - the technology is mature enough to be evaluated for groups and improved to provide what the users need for collaboration.

Putting the arguments together, these all means that one can not possibly examine and understand interaction (and performance) in VEs without separating and examining social interaction and interaction via technologies. However, how one factor influences the other and the overall experiences during the time of use should also be considered.

4.2 Creativity

As we described previously, creativity has been linked to a state of mind known as flow, considered a precondition for creative experience in numerous works. Flow is defined by Csikszentmihályi (1996) via eight distinct dimensions. Some of these dimensions, however are clear social interactions that can be hard to implement in technologies. Table 1 examines how the certain dimensions can be treated for technology mediated interaction. On the basis of important issues influencing individual, and technology-supported group creativity, we will examine how these issues are considered in different research studies.

As pointed out earlier, to examine creativity (and later presence) for performance in general, we focus on creativity (and later presence) support for problem-solving, experiences, and technical support. Therefore, we shall briefly overview relevant research on: creative problem-solving, creative experiences, and creativity-supporting tools. Many of the studies examining creativity for these three areas originate in considering the dimensions of flow, described above. Table 2 summarizes these and present studies offering possibilities for support it.

Vass et al. defined a framework to support creativity especially for problem-solving based on the dimensions defined for flow. The authors emphasized the importance of considering an appropriate balance between challenges and skills, and of the immediate feedback and the clarity of goals and problem-solving to the sixth dimension, which also means 'No worry of failure'. They also emphasized the value of differentiating time-dependent relations for their workflow model (Vass et al. 2002).

Dimensions	*Challenges for technologies*	*Challenges for groups using technologies*	
		Main success factors- important for social interaction (SI):	**Main success factors – important for interaction via technical devices (IT):**
clear objectives	Well-defined TA	Often assumed to be already known	Usability T, TA, IT.
immediate feedback	Usable, intuitive T and clear TA	Missing feedback (SI) often causes confusion	Depends on how 'transparent' a T is, IT
skills suited to challenges	I, T, TA	Easiest for homogeneous G	Homogeneous use, symmetrical T, usable settings, IT
action and awareness merge	I, T, TA	Size G, transparent T, and allowing I and SG communication	Completely intuitive T. I and SG communication should also be supported
allowing high concentra-tion	I, the usability and intuitiveness of T	Depends on the size of G, SI. Secondly on how T becomes transparent and how it supports I and SG	The T should be completely intuitive to support this
sense of control	I, TA and the usability of T	Concerns what to do next, comfort with 'the social group', I, SG, G, SI, IT, T	Easy to use T, 'enough' challenging TA, IT
loss of self-conscious-ness	Intuitive T, I	Depends on I, the size of the group G and how I and SG are supported. TA, T	Usable and intuitive T, IT
altered sense of time	Mainly I, TA	I, SG, G, SI - if T and IT work	Completely intuitive T and IT
autotelic experience	Mainly I, but also T and TA	I, SI - but also G, SG	Completely intuitive T and IT

Table 1. From individual creativity to technology-supported group creativity. The second column shows main challenges for technology supporting the corresponding dimension for single users. The third and fourth columns are for collaboration in terms of social interaction (SI) and interaction via technical devices (IT). The success factors in terms of individual abilities (I), the capability of technologies (T), tasks (TA), groups (G) and subgroups (SG).

However, the model defined by Vass et al. (2002) cannot necessarily be extended for group work, since it does not consider enhanced experiences for problem-solving and different dimensions for social aspects. This work is important since it explains more granulated influential dimensions of problem-solving and relates to a generic framework aimed to support human needs by using technologies defined by Shneiderman (2002). By considering the dimensions identified for flow, this work suggests certain tasks that have to be considered for designing tools that support creativity: (1) Searching and browsing, (2) Visualizing relationships, (3) Intellectual and emotional support, (4) Allowing free associations, (5) Exploring solutions, (6) Composing artefacts and performances, (7) Reviewing and replaying sessions, (8) Disseminating results (Shneiderman 2002). This framework gives a greater understanding of the connection between specified functionalities needed for creativity (Shneiderman 2007). In general, to understand how certain social aspects can be mirrored and implemented in technologies is important in order to develop better creativity-supporting tools.

What user(s) do	**Mainly Internal vs. external Activities**	**Suggestions for supporting individual creativity**	**Suggestions for supporting group collaboration**
Solve problems	Internal	By considering time-dependent relations, workflow (e.g. Vass et al. 2002) and focus of attention (Heldal, 2004).	Support for integrating individual work in group work (e.g. Fischer et al. 2005). Managing to handle easier interpretations and transparency of others' activities (Heldal et al. 2006), and allowing personal space.
Experience	Internal – high-tech might attract	Implement environments prepared to handle experiences, (e.g. Fencott 1999), and allow seamless interaction (e.g. Wolff et al. 2005).	Common targets, clear objectives, feedbacks, rewards. Separate activities where group awareness stimulates group members.
Handle technologies	External – hard to understand sometimes	Define tasks that should be considered for designing creativity-supporting tools, (e.g. Shneiderman 2002).	Symmetry helps. Otherwise make the group aware of each other's possibilities (Tromp et al. 2003).

Table 2. Examples of studies enhancing how to support creativity for a single user, or for a group.

Creativity-supporting tools in distributed scientific communities need to support flexibility in granularity of planning (Farooq et al. 2005). Roberts later demonstrated characteristics of immersive collaborative environments that can easily provide a seamless workflow through transitions between content and detail in planning (Roberts et al. 2007). Experiencing flow can be impacted by the way in which people handle different events, and by how they build a conceptual map in VEs. According to Fencott, to support creativity, knowledge about social and technical contexts should be considered already in designing VEs, to support VE users in handling *sureties, surprises,* and *shocks* (Fencott 1999).

Another way to understand creativity-supporting tools is the one that examines the origins and context of creative activities. A great pioneer in this work is Fisher with the work done by his group(s). Fischer differentiates between two levels of creativity, viz. historical creativity associated with fundamentally novel ideas and discoveries, and psychological creativity associated with ideas and discovery from everyday work practice. Accordingly, historical creativity can be more easily associated with individual work, while psychological creativity incorporates prerequisites from groups which also can offer prerequisites that support social creativity. Beside functionality, it has been necessary to consider factors, such as cultural diversity, the context of the experiment, individual versus group support, allowing reflection on minority conflicts, and supporting flexibility in granularity of planning. Fischer states that individual creativity is usually integrated in social creativity. The social structure and mindset contribute better-formulated problem areas and stable environments. The collaboration is examined through several applications, e.g. Creation (collaborative drawing art) and Linux; it often has non-simultaneous characteristics, where the contributors take turns at work. During his or her turn, one can make essential contributions, which might be called individual (Fischer et al. 2005).

4.3 Presence

Short, William and Christie introduced measurements of the quality of distributed work in 1976, such as *social presence* as the users' subjective sense of being present in technology in a social setting with another person (Short et al. 1976). Later, presence was identified as a main factor that contributes to an improved experience for VEs. It refers to experiencing being in a place other than where one is physically present, which is possible by using computer graphics. If this sense refers to being there together with one's partner, then we often speak of *copresence* (Slater et al. 2000).

There are many studies that try to define relations between presence and other factors that are representative for VEs. The level of presence has often been related to task performance (Witmer et al. 1998, Slater et al. 1994). At first Slater et al. defined external and internal determinants of the sense of presence. The external determinants include display quality, consistency of presentation across displays, ability to interact, the anthropomorphism of the user representation, and the clarity of causal relationships between user actions and reactions. The internal ones are the representation system and perceptual position. These were defined with the help of neurolinguistic programming (NLP) and three key representations: the visual, the auditory, and the kinesthetic. They examined the effects of various display modalities, interaction techniques, and system algorithms on the reported level of presence. Presence is measured in several ways, by objective and subjective measurements, using questionnaires or external observations (Slater 2003, Heldal 2004). Usually there is a measurement type that fits and is used in more specific areas to be studied. Later, Maya Garau summarized the determinants that are recognized by different

researchers. These are: (1) the extent of fidelity and sensory information, (2) the match between sensors and displays, (3) content, and (4) user characteristics (Garau, 2003).
During collaboration an important aspect is that the partners should be aware of each other and each other's presence. Therefore, an important question here is how awareness relates to presence and to the collaborative experience. Intuitively, it seems that there should be a correlation between presence and copresence, and such that more immersive VEs should provide an enhanced sense of copresence. However, in CVEs this is not necessarily the case. Higher presence does not necessarily result in higher copresence. The collaborative experience of 'being there together' has to do with the real-time information on the others – who the others are, how they are represented and what they are doing. Except for the co-located environments, this information can be transmitted by the different technologies, i.e. it can be externalized (Polanyi 1966). The influence on experiences, though, can differ from one technology to another.

What user(s) do	**Mainly Internal vs. external Activities**	**Suggestions for supporting individual presence**	**Suggestions for supporting group collaboration**
Solve problems	Internal – although an external observer can see it.	Fidelity and sensory information, match between sensors and displays (Garau 2003). Clear interaction, focus of attention (Heldal 2004).	Support for integrating individual work in group work, e.g. creativity (Fischer et al. 2005). Manage to handle easier interpretations, have awareness transparency of the others' activities (Heldal et al. 2006), seamless communication, show intentions and emotions (Slater et al. 2000). Support decision-making etc.
Handle technologies	External – Disturbances Internal – Intuitive Technologies	Screen size, immersiveness, less breaks in presence (Brogni et al. 2003) Seamless interaction (Shneiderman 2002; Heldal 2004).	Consider the dimensions defined by Garau (2003). Symmetry helps (Heldal 2004); otherwise make the group aware of each other's possibilities. Clear object laws (Roberts et al. 2007).
Experience	Both internal and external – Immersive technology, design may benefit	Tracking, real time (Waterworth et al. 2001). Implement challenges (Heldal 2004), seamless interaction (Wolff et al. 2006); for certain applications photorealism helps (Heldal 2004).	To support group awareness, quick feedback, common objectives, allowing rewards, problem-free communication, using rich technologies that transmit human cues, important movements, naturalness (Heldal et al. 2006). Consider cultural differences, leadership, emotion, etc.

Table 3. Possibilities to support presence for a single user or for a group

Another potential explanation of eventual trade-off between potential presence and copresence is that it may be difficult to sustain high sense of presence and also high sense of copresence over time. In either case, it seems that the situations of trade-offs between presence and copresence can be explained by focus of attention: in certain situations it is not possible to focus on both the space and the other at the same time. It can be hard to explain true relationships since presence and copresence are often evaluated *after* the task performance. People sometimes look after each other, point to the other person, or ask questions in the environment, without necessarily having such intentions to strengthen copresence. If the presence is evaluated by questionnaires afterwards, they need to remember these intentions. Sometimes they intuitively use the technology, or use it wrongly, e.g. point with non-tracked hands in immersive environments, in such a way that the other person does not necessarily observe these activities. If, for example, one points unintentionally with the wrong hand, this does not disturb one's presence. The copresence may be disturbed since the activity is not transmitted, but none of the subjects can possibly report it afterwards. Table 3 lists the possibilities to support presence in relation to what people or group do in VEs.

While collaborative and social presence does make a great contribution to user experiences, the way in which this influences overall performance, usability, and particularly effectiveness is not necessarily known (Schroeder et al. 2006). As shown in Table 3, the relation between presence and overall outcome is hard to know. Presence for certain tasks and for certain settings is valuable, but to implement it in technologies is difficult; this would need several individually adjustable features for each person and task for each time.

4.4 Other factors influencing the workflow in CVEs

Time: People's behavior, including the way in which they interact socially and with objects, changes over time when immersed in a virtual environment (Tromp et al. 2003). At the beginning and end people focus on social interaction, while interaction via technical interfaces and the virtual representations plays a more important role for task-focused collaboration. Considering flow in the wider context, we can postulate that time is likely to impact on many of the previously defined dimensions. Time is a dimension of interaction with the environment - for example, immediate feedback and control. It is also a dimension of the individuals themselves: for example, it takes time for action and awareness to merge, and to lose the sense of time (Heldal et al. 2007). As we pointed out earlier, research has demonstrated that time does have effects on the use of media for groups. Ad hoc groups must sometimes handle decisions in organizations through a medium, but this can have negative consequences on their agreements. The long-term use of certain media supporting group collaboration has the result that media effects may disappear (Hinds 2002, Heldal 2004).

Embodiment: To consider social issues when designing new technologies and new applications is relatively new, especially in the context of developing networked VE technologies, but has a great impact on the general outcomes. This work did not treat, for instance, embodiment - even if embodiment and using avatars has a great impact on social issues influencing collaboration flow, for example by reflecting the orientation of the user within the environment and in some cases gestures that can be directed towards the focus of interest (Heldal et al. 2006).

Emotions: Another example that should be studied, especially in connection with creativity and presence and the collaborative outcome, is emotion. Experiencing emotions is an important social resource in managing creative collaborations (Slater 1999).
Furthermore, there are several facilitators that may contribute to enjoyable and effective communication in VEs. Some examples are: transparent **intention**, visualizing and knowing about **attention, motivation, awareness** (Roberts et al. 2007), **praise, recognition** and **rewards** (Roberts 2009). **Common ground, team spirit** and a **sense of belonging** are needed in order to build **trust** and **consensus** (Culnan 1987) - and these qualities are hard to support through communication media. Dourish (2001) explored the meaning behind possible interactions in context, by exploring common trends from tangible and social computing. He argues for considering technologies as 'embedded' in their context of use, in order to support meaningful interaction.

5. Relation between the factors influencing work

There is a huge difference when people solve problems alone instead of together. If the individual can contribute less than 70% of his capability for the group outcome (as we presented before, stated by Brown 2000), it is important to know whether this contribution is best for the group in terms of creativity and performance. Problem-solving requires mental work which is to a great extent individual (Brown 2000). The fact that individual problem-solving also requires high presence is obvious. Following Fischer's argumentation for supporting creativity for individuals and for groups, we note the need of private space for the individual to make it possible to give her best in collaboration (Fischer et al. 2005).

Collaborative problem-solving, as we showed in the previous sections, requires intuitive technology. Via this, the group can interact more easily and support peripheral collaboration that also requires social presence. Studies show that symmetrical settings help (Heldal 2004) and technology can be neglected and used more intuitively (Roberts et al. 2007); however, the group still needs to cope with differences between the group members (Schroeder et al. 2006). Interruptions caused by nonintuitive devices, bad design, or needless social interaction can disturb a member, as well as a group (Hinds et al 2002). On the other hand, as Höök (2008) presented, sometimes disruptive technologies are required for well being. For these cases, however, the interests of individuals (their social need to be aware of things and happenings) steers the requirements. People need fresh air, food, motion and awareness of their social relationships in order to be well-functioning. See Table 4 for examining requirements for individuals and group in terms of presence and creativity for superior results.

Social behavior in a group can support peripheral communication, strengthening group awareness of the members and vice versa. High social presence is required for maintaining peripheral awareness in networked group activities, allowing coordination, supporting decision-making processes, negotiations and choosing strategies. This can be better supported by using different communication modalities, transmitting the right social cues.

To have high social presence is important, for example, for applications exploring museums, cities and collaborative games (Stones 2002). Probably high social presence is required to attain superb experiences. High social presence in turn can allow increased social creativity.

<table>
<tr><td rowspan="2">What user(s) Do</td><td colspan="2">Individual</td><td colspan="2">Collaborative or social group</td></tr>
<tr><td>Presence</td><td>Creativity</td><td>Presence</td><td>Creativity</td></tr>
<tr><td>Solve problems</td><td colspan="2">Both presence and creativity need to be supported.
High presence is needed for individual creativity.
High presence often contributes to high performance (Slater's earlier work).</td><td colspan="2">Differs for proper collaboration versus peripheral collaboration. Also depends on application type, e.g. object-focused task-solving versus learning (Heldal 2004). Maintaining and sustaining group activities needs social skills, high copresence, and social presence. Group creativity requires awareness of the members' activity, i.e. social creativity is favored by high social presence (Fischer et al. 2005).</td></tr>
<tr><td>Handle technologies</td><td colspan="2">To reach high presence, intuitive technologies and natural interactions are needed (Wolff et al 2006). This is a precondition for supporting individual creativity.</td><td colspan="2">One can help the others in networked situations to handle technologies and eventual problems (Heldal 2004). Helping requires different communication modalities. Symmetry or information on asymmetry helps (Schroeder et al. 2006). Naturalistic technologies may support peripheral collaboration, copresence and communicative activities that are required for group creativity (Roberts et al. 2007).</td></tr>
<tr><td>Experience</td><td colspan="2">High individual presence is required for experiencing VEs.
Creativity is less important.</td><td colspan="2">Group maintenance, collaborative activities and awareness are most important for a good outcome. Naturalness, high social presence can help. Time may be influential (Tromp 2001).</td></tr>
</table>

Table 4. How problem-solving, handling technical devices and experiences, is influenced by presence and creativity for a single user or for collaborative settings

Continuous workflow can also contribute to increased presence and creativity in CVEs. This can be maintained by avoiding or decreasing disturbances from the surroundings, which cause breaks in presence and interrupt concentration. Flow can be impacted by the way in which people handle unexpected events. Presence requires the building of a conceptual map that is grounded in the experience of sureties and even of plausible surprises, but is weakened by shocks (Frencott 1999).

Creativity must be combined with knowledge of social and technical context in the design of content, for VEs to provide challenges in handling sureties, interest in handling surprises and support in handling shocks. We postulate, however, that flow requires the transition between handling these disruptions to be seamless. Interacting naturally and intuitively, for example, can also be disruptive or seamful interaction (Höök et al. 2008) – for the aim of certain applications and for specific and expected handlings. In general, hiding the technology so that people can interact naturally with the simulation significantly increases not only performance, but also engagement, motivation, enjoyment, and creativity (Wolff et al., 2006). Since temporal issues are crucial in work and many people work for long periods on computers, it is essential to include the effect of time in using CVEs. For many of the studies performed in the fields studying the usage of VEs, the users do not spend more than 15-30 minutes in the environments; this also influences earlier results. As we showed, time plays a very important role for all factors. The users adapt to using technologies and settings, and avoid hindrances, if they spend longer time in the environments. They also develop work-around to cope with the perceived disadvantages (Heldal et al. 2006).

6. A pragmatic approach

In contrast to using the hard-to-interpret concept of *presence*, it is also possible to give some general advice with a basis in the group members and their human need to be recognized for their achievements. Based on the background from sections 3.2 and 3.3 that collaboration can be divided in three main stages, we consider the following.

The **initial stage** of collaboration can mean: getting to know each other, defining a task to solve or discuss, determining the rules of the group, and building (or acknowledging) trust. All of these activities often require a formal or an informal leader or leader group. In our experience, the emergent leader group often consists of a few people who already know each other quite well and trust each other. The values with this leader in the groups are often well developed. However, there are cases, e.g. for Internet-based communities, where there are no formal leaders (Weisband 2007). Listening, and trying to understand and to explain, are catalytic actions by the leader(s). It would be advantageous (Roberts, 2009) to have high resolution CVEs available at this stage when building trust, as much of this is related also to body language. Probably these VEs would require stronger governance during the first stage. If successful, the group would form a kind of society, a separate partition of the participant's ordinary life, in which the innovative action would take place. This society with rather determined/fixed rules should in some respects be comparable to other virtual *worlds*. In this partition, the participants would have a feeling of belonging, meaning and security.

The minimum requirements for getting into the **second stage** of work and expecting results are: *clear targets* (what is to be achieved?), *clear rules for collaboration* (what is the reward?) and *knowledge of who takes part in the group and their interests.*

With the information available, the participant should experience trust and be able to answer the question: 'What's in it for me?'. The work in the second stage would typically follow the funnel model: create many ideas and nurture them, and then gradually sort forward the best ideas. In this stage it would be supportive to have e.g. homework between meetings in CVEs. The group member would still require stimulation, response and energy from the rest of the group at regular meetings. Here the role of the leader still would be listening, trying to understand, and explaining. Some innovative groups use designers to visualise the ideas that are generated, and this seemingly stimulating interaction between

the *innovators* and the people who visualize appears to be quite fruitful. For that case an efficient sketching tool would be required, a tool that everybody can use, and it is as intuitive as using paper and pen. During this stage it would be desirable to be able to transfer *energy* between participants and to have a system that allows jokes and other rather impulsive actions to keep spirits up.
The **third stage,** finally, with evaluation and praise and rewards, would require displays that make it possible also to read the body language. The possibility to come back and use the group for other work later would very much depend on a fair and well-organized conclusion of the present work.

7. Discussion and future directions

As was shown in the first sections, considerable work has been done regarding evaluation for VEs, but there is much less research on evaluation for CVEs. The work was more concerned with how technology can be connected at all, how it allows sharing of resources without bottlenecks, and how a previous type of interaction can be transmitted (Heldal et al. 2006). By addressing these issues, the technological precondition for collaboration is mostly fulfilled. But even if this is a necessary precondition, there are several other aspects regarding the group and the context of application that have a major impact on the entire process of collaboration.

According to many studies the role of social interaction and social space becomes more important for collaboration (Schroeder 2007, Tromp et al. 2003). The drawback of asymmetrical setups can be overcome by letting people trade places and learn about each other's different capabilities. To evaluate CVEs, some of the problems are inherited from the lack of general theories to guide human performance measurement, difficulties in handling the inverse relationship between operational control and realism, the multiple dimension of behavior, how to measure cognitive tasks and how creativity is supported, etc.
We showed that there are at least three stages in sustainable constructive/creative work. The first stage is getting the group together, defining rules and roles, and establishing common ground, letting members be aware of each other, and formulating tasks and problems. During this peripheral communication, the socio-cultural context plays an important role; questions in relation to organizing work and group activities have to be settled.

The second stage is performing the creative or constructive work - the actual collaboration. In this stage, there are two possibilities. If the problem or tasks are intended to carry out rather moderate changes/innovations, so-called psychological creativity (Fischer et al. 2005), one part of the aim is to get the entire group to arrive at and accept the relatively foreseeable solutions. In this case it is still important to have simultaneous participation of the entire group. Here, supporting individual presence and thus creativity, and seamlessly integrating it into the group work, are very important. Disturbances from the technical devices and from the group can lower both individual and group results. For well-structured problems with clear goals, the personal motivations to contribute in the group are important. For problems and tasks that aim to support learning, exploration, or general social interaction, maintaining both collaborative and individual presence is important. Even though 'isolating' a member can be disturbing for the group, it may still contribute to overall efficiency.

If the purpose is to find a really innovative and so far unknown idea, which Fischer called historical invention (Fischer et al. 2005), the surroundings that support creativity with tools and tasks are important. The environment needs to allow evaluation of alternative choices, using different strategies, easy backtracking and searching. Even tough creativity has the highest importance; the social presence helps to support this. Once the context is set, the group is needed only to keep up the pace and to evaluate the proposed solutions. With this kind of formulation, it is possible and even desired to allow space and time for the group individuals to reflect and come up with ideas. The third stage is concluding the work, or certain work steps, making the solution and its evaluation known and giving rewards (of whatever type they may be). In this stage the group must be collective. Many of the preconditions for starting the work have to be considered for this stage too.

Another aspect that has to be reevaluated for supporting high copresence and creativity is consideration of interruptions. There are many interruptions that disturb individuals endeavoring to contribute their own creativity for working with physical objects in face-to-face conditions in real environments. These interruptions have many old characteristics inherited from face-to-face work, but they can also differ. Problems with devices, user interfaces, networking, who is talking to whom and why, turn-taking, or when the user interface does not transmit personal cues, or wrongly or non-naturalistically transmits certain actions such as pointing, looking, etc., can disturb the personal space needed for individual creativity. Furthermore, we showed that external observations play a great role in evaluating collaborative activities and group work. The observations can distinguish certain critical sequences and activities that the users went through quickly during their work and did not pay attention to.

For the study of CVEs, multiple users play an important role. To see CVEs as extensions of users that support seamless collaboration and creativity as in face-to-face conditions may be too complex and resource-demanding. For this, laboratory studies still are important. As we have seen, making VR systems usable for the average user requires generalization but also tailor-made solutions for specific purposes and technologies. However, one cannot expect that end-users will be able to describe their needs in technical terms and with an overall understanding of the complexity of VEs. Throughout the previous sections we have shown that future work has to consider developing seamlessly distributed work that allows: creative problem-solving, creativity-supporting tools, and allowing creative experiences. This often requires high presence and knowing more about the influence of presence. However, implementing 'presence' may not be necessary, especially for seamful technologies (Höök et al. 2008). The recent literature still lacks a consistent theoretical approach to guide experiential research and technological development towards collaborative applications that support group creativity and allow high experiences. In our opinion, for the first step we have to identify the main dependencies between technology, application types, users, and time (Heldal 2004).

8. Conclusions

By reviewing research on differences between individual work and group work, and how they are influenced by presence and creativity, this chapter has sought a better understanding of networked collaboration and how to support creative, collaborative activities in CVEs. As we have shown, in many cases presence may be either a precondition or a desired prerequisite for creativity; however, it is almost impossible to determine exactly the preconditions for individual presence for certain technologies, applications and groups. A suggestion here is that user experiences should be approached instead of presence.

Allowing creativity is considered to contribute to higher-quality work in general. However, to support group creativity, the peripheral collaboration should be seamless. Results on copresence show that maintaining and seamlessly integrating individual creativity, and allowing subgroup activities that contribute to group results, would be beneficial here. It is found, according to Fischer (2005), that one of the most important prerequisites for successful outcomes is providing enough time and space for individual creativity contributions. This may also be a requirement for supporting small groups within the larger groups. However, future research is needed in order to determine how to resolve certain social issues in technologies for better supporting individuals, subgroups and groups.

Overall, work was examined in terms of three main activities: how people approach problem-solving, how they handle technical devices, and how they experience virtual representations. The analytical distinction has helped us to review the creativity literature for these three areas and to connect it with available presence results, which are essential for evaluating VEs. In relation to methodology we have shown the importance of observations and of examining normative behaviors via laboratory studies.

9. Acknowledgements

The authors are grateful to David Roberts, Robin Wolff, and Jon van Leuven for their help.

10. References

American National Standard Institute. (1993) *Guide to Human Performance Measurements.* American Institute of Aeronautics, Washington DC.

Brogni, A., Slater, M., Steed, A. (2003) More Breaks Less Presence. *Proc. Presence 2003, The 6th Annual International Workshop on Presence,* Denmark.

Brown, R. (2000) *Group processes: dynamics within and between groups.* Oxford: Blackwell Publishers.

Bystrom, K.E., Barfield, W. (1999) Collaborative Task Performance for Learning Using a Virtual Environment. *Presence,* MIT Press, 8(4), pp. 435-48.

Carroll, J.M. (1995) The Scenario Perspective on System Development. In Carroll, J. M. (ed.), *Scenario-Based Design: Envisioning Work and Technology in Systems.*

Culnan, M.J. (1987) Mapping the Intellectual Structure of MIS 1980-1985: A Co-citation Analysis. *MIS Quarterly,* 11(3), pp. 341-53.

Csikszentmihályi, M. (1996) *Creativity: Flow and the Psychology of Discovery and Invention.* New York: Harper Perennial.

Dourish, P. (2001) *Where the Action Is: The Foundations of Embodied Interaction.* MIT Press, Cambridge, Massachusetts.

Ellis, S.R. (1995) Origins and Elements of virtual Environments. In Barfield, W. (ed.), *Virtual Environments and Advanced Interface Design,* Oxford University Press, pp.14-57.

Farooq, U., Carroll, J.M., Ganoe, C.H. (2005) Supporting Creativity in Distributed Scientific Communities. *Proceedings of the International GROUP Conference,* pp. 217-26.

Fencott, C. (1999) Content and Creativity in Virtual Environment Design. *Proc. of VSMM'99.*

Fischer, G., Giaccardi, E., et al. (2005) Beyond Binary Choices: Integrating Individual and Social Creativity. *Human-Computer Studies (IJHCS).* 63(4-5), pp. 482-512.

Gutwin, C., Greenberg, S. (1998) Design for Individuals, Design for Groups: Tradeoffs between Power and Workspace Awareness. *Proc. CSCW'98,* ACM Press, Seattle, pp. 207-16.

Heldal, I. (2004) *The Usability of Collaborative Virtual Environments: Towards an Evaluation Framework.* Ph.D. Thesis, Dept. of Technology and Society, Chalmers, Sweden.

Heldal, I., Bråthe, L., et al. (2006) Analyzing Fragments of Collaboration in Distributed Immersive Virtual Environments. In Schroeder, R. Axelsson, A. (eds.), *Avatars at work and play.* Springer Verlag, pp. 97-130.

Heldal I., Roberts D., Bråthe L., Wolff R. (2007) Presence, Creativity and Collaborative Work in Virtual Environments. In *Lecture Notes in Computer Science, Human-Computer Interaction,* Springer Berlin/Heidelberg, pp. 802-811.

Höök, K., Ståhl, A., et al. (2008). Interactional empowerment. *Proceedings of the ACM SIGCHI Conference on Human Factors in Computing Systems.* ACM Press.

Lampton, D. R., Bliss, J. P., Morris, C. S. (2002) Human Performance Measurement in Virtual Environments. In K.M. Stanney (ed.), *Handbook of Virtual Environments. Design, Implementation, and Applications.* Lawrence Erlbaum Assoc., Mahwah, pp. 710-20.

McLeish, J. M. W., Park, J. (1973) *The Psychology of Learning Group.* Hutchinson, London.

McGrath, J.E. (1984) *Groups: Interaction and Performance.* Englewood Cliffs, NJ: Prentice Hall.

Nielsen, J. (1993) *Usability engineering.* AP Professional, Boston.

Neale, D.C., Carroll, J.M., Rosson, M.B. (2004) Evaluating Computer Supported Cooperative Work Models and Frameworks. *Proceedings of CSCW'04,* pp. 112-21.

Nilsson, A., Heldal, I., et al. (2002) The Long-Term Uses of Shared Virtual Environments: An Exploratory Study. In Schroeder, R. (ed.), *The Social Life of Avatars.* Springer, London, pp. 112-26.

Polanyi, M. (1966) *The Tacit Dimension.* Garden City, NY: Doubleday

Polys, N.F., Bowman, D.A. (2004) Design and Display of Enhancing Information in Desktop Information Rich Virtual Environments. *Virtual Reality,* 8, pp. 41-54.

Poltrock, S., Grudin, J. (2003) Collaboration Technology in Teams, Organizations, and Communities. *Proceedings CHI'03,* Tutorial.

Roberts, D., Heldal, I., et al. (2007) Factors influencing Flow of Object Focused Collaboration in Collaborative Virtual Environments. *Virtual Reality,* 10(2): 119-33.

Roberts, D. (2009) *Reproducing face-to-face interaction.* Presentation in Gothenburg, Chalmers, Sweden, 27 April 2009.

Schroeder, R., Heldal, I., Tromp, J. (2006) The Usability of Collaborative Virtual Environments and Methods for the Analysis of Interaction. *Presence 15*(6), pp. 655-67.

Schroeder, R. (2007) *Rethinking Science, Technology and Social Change.* Stanford Univ. Press.

Scott, C.R. (1999) Communication Technology and Group Communication. In Frey, L.R. (ed.), *The Handbook of Group Communication Theory and Research.* Sage, pp. 431-72.

Shneiderman, B. (2002) Establishing Framework of Activities for Creative Work. Creativity Support Tools, *Communication of the ACM, 45*(10), pp. 116-120.

Shneiderman B., Fischer G., et al. (2007) *Proceedings of the 6th Conference on Creativity & Cognition*, Washington, DC, USA, June 13-15, 2007.

Short, J., Williams, E., Christie, B. (1976) *The Social Psychology of Telecommunications*. London: John Wiley.

Slater, M., Usoh, M. Steed, A. (1994) Depth of Presence in Virtual Environments. *Presence* 3(2), pp. 130-44.

Slater, M., Linakis, V. et al. (1996) Immersion, Presence, and Performance in Virtual Environments. *Proc. ACM Virtual Reality Software and Technology*, pp. 163-72.

Slater, M. (1996) *Co-presence as an Amplifier of Emotion*: Available http://wwwais.itd.clrc.ac.uk/VVECC/proceed/collab/materials/slater/.

Slater, M., Sadagic, A., et al. (2000) Small-group behavior in a virtual and real environment: A comparative study. *Presence*. *9*(1), pp. 37-51.

Slater, M. (2004) How colourful was your day? Why Questionnaires Cannot Assess Presence in Virtual Environments. *Presence* 13(4), pp. 484-493.

Sonnenwald, D. H., Solomon, P., et al. (2002) Collaboration in the large: Using Video Conferencing to Facilitate Large Group Interaction. In Khalil (ed.), *Knowledge and Information Technology in 21st Century Organizations*, Idea Publishing Co., pp. 136-55.

Steed, A., Parker, C. (2005) Evaluating Effectiveness of Interaction Techniques across Immersive Virtual Environment Systems. *Presence* 14(5), pp. 511-27.

Stone J. S. (2002) Applications of Virtual Environments: An Overview. In K.M. Stanney (ed.), *Handbook of Virtual Environments. Design Implementation, and Appl.*, pp. 827-56.

Tromp, J. (2001) *Systematic Usability Design and Evaluation for Collaborative Virtual Environments*. PhD Thesis, University of Nottingham, Nottingham, UK.

Tromp, J., Steed, A., Wilson, J. (2003) Systematic Usability Evaluation and Design Issues for Collaborative Virtual Environments. *Presence*, 10(3), pp. 241-67.

Walther, J.B. (1996) Computer-mediated communication: Impersonal, interpersonal, and hyperpersonal interaction. *Communication Research*, 23, pp. 3-43.

Walther, J.B., Parks, M. (2002) Cues filtered out, cues filtered in. *Handbook of Interpersonal Communication*. Thousand Oaks, CA: Sage Publications.

Vass, M., Carroll, J.M., Shaffer, C.A. (2002) Supporting Creativity in Problem Solving Environments, *Proceedings of the Fourth Creativity & Cognition Conference*, pp. 31-37.

Waterworth, J.A., Waterworth, E.L. (2001) Affective Creative Spaces: the Interactive Tent and the Illusion of Being. *Proc. of the 1st Int. Conf. on Affective Human Factors Design*.

Webster, C.M., Freeman, L.C. Aufdemberg, C.G. (2001) The Impact of Social Context on Interaction Patterns. *Journal of Social Structure*, 2(1).

Weisband, S.P. (2007) *Leadership at a distance. Research in Technologically-Supported Work*. Psychology Press.

Wilson, J.R. (2003) If VR Has Changed, then Have its Human Factors? In Waard, D. et al. (eds.), *Human Factors in the Age of Virtual Reality*, Shaker Publishing, pp. 9-30.

Witmer, B. G. Singer, M. J. (1998) Measuring Presence in Virtual Environments: A Presence Questionnaire. *Presence*, 7(3), pp. 225-40.

Wolff, R., Roberts, D.J., et al. (2006) A Review of Tele-collaboration Technologies with Respect to Closely Coupled Collaboration. *International Journal of Computer Applications in Technology (IJCAT)*, pp. 11-26.

Vöhringer-Kuhnt, T. (2002) *The Influence of Culture on Usability*. Freie Universität, Berlin.

18

An Entertainment-System Framework for Improving Motivation for Repetitive, Dull and Monotonous Activities

Itaru Kuramoto
Kyoto Institute of Technology
Japan

1. Introduction

Much significant research has been done to improve the efficiency of activities, based in large part on continuing improvements in computer power and refinements to computer interfaces. However, such improvements will inevitably reach a limit and even today, in our ordinary daily activities, we are hardly aware of things such as higher CPU frequency. Consequently, we do not expect to see further improvements in efficiency, simply due to improved computer power or refined compute interfaces. if we have little motivation to perform the activities. Although some kinds of activities are automated and others are creative enough to maintain motivation, many dull activities are not yet or cannot be automated.

If we can improve our motivation for some activities, the efficiency and/or productivity with which we perform them can improve. According to the Hawthorne effect, human activity is influenced by psychological effects (Sonnenfeld, 1983). Therefore, a desirable stimulus can improve motivation. To put this effect into practice, I have attempted to introduce entertainment into daily activities for which we normally have a low motivation. Entertainment provides us with fun and escape from dullness; therefore, it is effective for improving motivation.

Entertainment is commonly applied to education, and many studies in computer-supported learning support its value. This area is known as "Edutainment" (Par et al., 2008). However, its application to daily activities is recently being studied in computer science. Applying games to computer administration tasks, as suggested by Chao, points out that the game interface has large power of expression and can be made intuitive for children and non-technical users (Chao, 2001). However, the author did not discuss the effect of entertainment on improving user motivation.

In this chapter, I present a framework of entertainment systems, called EELF (Entertainment-for-Everyday-Life Framework), and propose a method for introducing entertainment directly into repetitive, dull and monotonous activities. I discuss the following:

- The nature of target activities that are repetitive, dull and monotonous
- The structure of EELF
- How EELF stimulates motivation for such activities

I introduce the following four EELF-based systems; Weekend Battle, ExS, MIPS, and VASC.

2. Entertainment for Daily Activities

Many repetitive activities are dull and monotonous but must be done, such as inputting an enormous number of answers to inquiries, jogging every day for health, and performing Hanon piano exercises.

Such activities are generally:

A. Monotonous
B. Not creative
C. Not fun

To stimulate motivation for such activities, I address these three characteristics by introducing entertainment into the activities. The entertainment should satisfy the following three conditions:

1. It should reflect and represent our efforts (corresponding to A).
2. It should provide something new and attractive (corresponding to B).
3. It should be fun (corresponding to C).

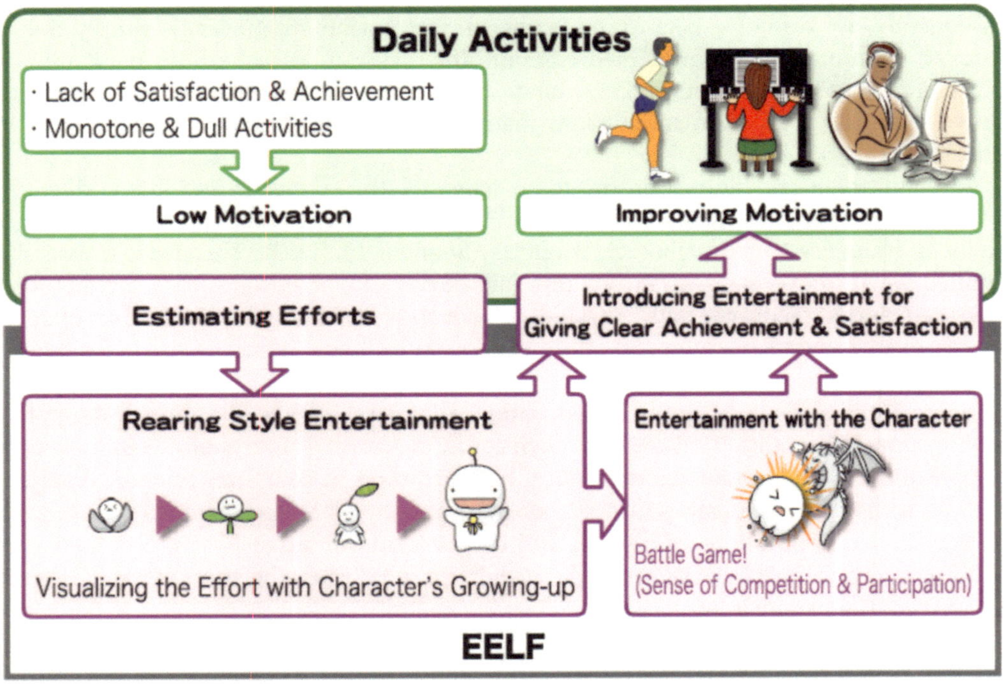

Fig. 1. Overview of EELF

Fig. 2. Sample character representation

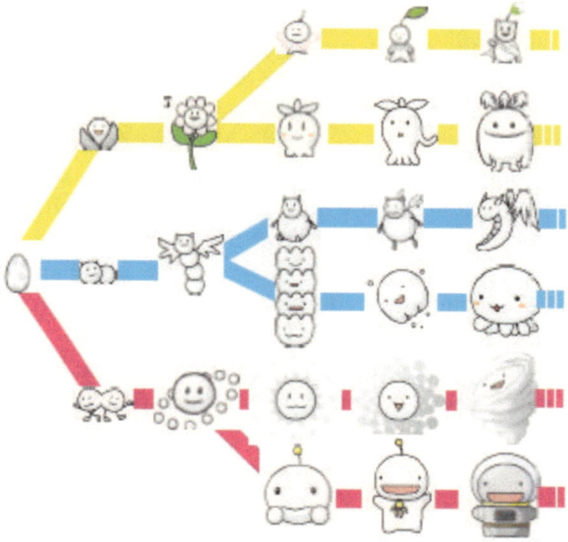

Fig. 3. Sample change patterns for a character

3. EELF

EELF (Entertainment-for-Everyday-Life Framework) is an entertainment-system framework for improving and maintaining motivation for daily activities. It has three components: character (avatar) creation, effort estimation, and competitive game. Figure 1 shows an overview of EELF.

3.1 Character Creation

An EELF-based entertainment system, in response to condition 1, has a character-creation component. Each system user creates his/her own character, or avatar, which grows up

from infancy to adulthood in response to user efforts. The method of estimating effort is described in section 3.2.
Figure 2 shows an example of a character. The character is represented by both graphical images and numerical parameters. Graphical images are needed for attractive and intuitive representation, and numerical parameters are needed for explicit and clear indication of achievement. Many additional parameters add to the variety of the character: however, which parameters apply is mainly determined by the types of user activities.
When a user performs an activity at a certain level, the character changes shape step by step along one of several possible of character growth, but the patterns are unpredictable so as to maintain interest and therefore address condition 2. Figure 3 shows an example of a variety of possible growth pattern.

3.2 Effort Estimation

In EELF, entertainment should not be used to assess activities or reflect the final results of an activity. For example, say a user puts a lot of effort for a certain difficult task, but fails. The user's motivation tends to decrease, and an EELF-based entertainment system should address this situation and not merely reflect the user's final results. Thus, the system must pay attention to not just results but also to effort. We use the word "subjective workload" throughout this chapter to describe the degree of effort.
In general, an activity for which subjective workload must be estimated can be decomposed into a number of components. For example, daily work with an office PC can be decomposed into keystrokes, mouse movements, and so on. Subjective workload is based on the number of components and/or the time spent in performing the components. For example, an office worker might write a certain document without mistakes, and another worker, writing the same document, may make many mistakes, perform many more operations, and spend time repairing the mistakes. The latter worker feels that he/she worked harder than the former worker. Thus, although the products are same, the subjective workload of the latter worker is higher than that of the former worker.
We assume that the subjective workload of a certain activity can be estimated by the formula

$$W = \Sigma a_i x_i \qquad (1)$$

In this formula, W is the subjective workload and x_i is the number of components of the activity. The weight a_i is determined by each activity. How to determine the weight a_i of each implementation of EELF-based entertainment system is described in Sections 4.2, 5.2, and 6.2.

3.3 Competition

Play, an important component of entertainment, has four characteristics (Caillois, 2001):

1. Aĝon: competition
2. Alea: chance, happening
3. Mimicry: simulation, role playing
4. Ilinx: shock, drastic change (such as vertigo)

Character creation has the characteristic of mimicry. It also has the characteristic of alea because users cannot predict the shape of their characters.

Competition can be a particularly important characteristic of entertainment, and address condition 3 of the previous discussion. An EELF-based entertainment system might involve, for example, a battle game with the user's own character. When a character grows up without being taken down, its owner wins the game, and the harder the user performs, the more likely his/her characters wins. The game also makes the user's achievements clear, so introducing a competition game addresses condition 1. Figure 4 shows an example of a competition-game component.

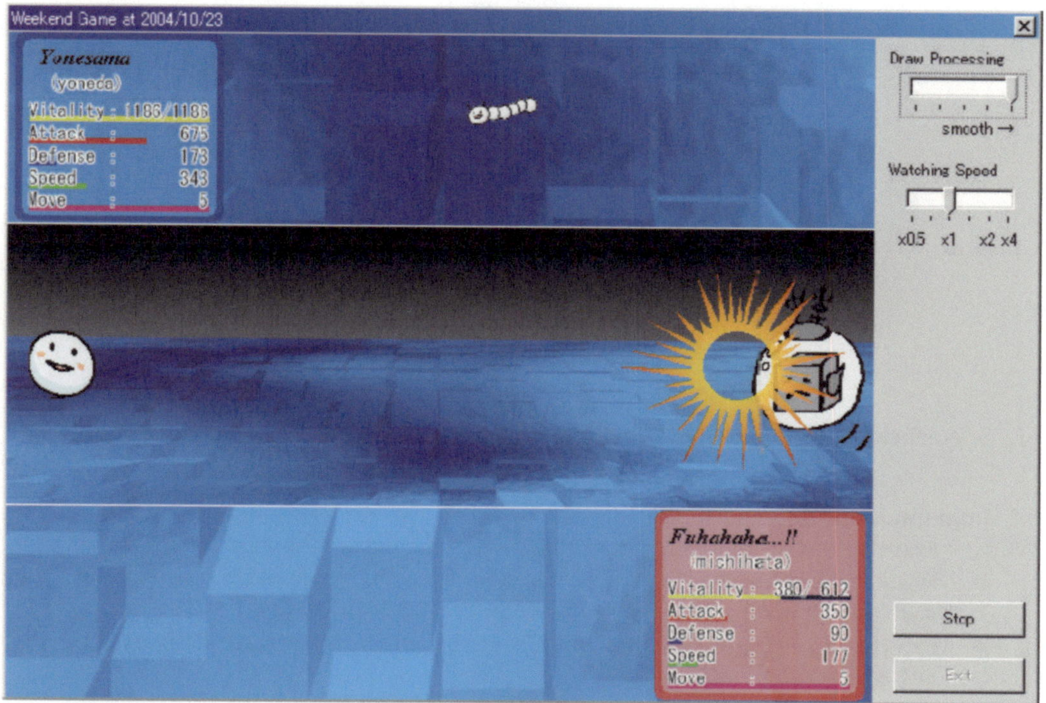

Fig. 4. Weekend Battle: competition-game component

3.4 Distraction Avoidance

There are many other styles of entertainment, such as movies, pictures, animations, and music. However, there are serious problems with introducing some kinds of entertainment into activities because they can distract users from the activity at hand by their heavy visual and/or audible effects. Therefore, EELF-based entertainment systems seek to improve efficiency and productivity, so that they do not interfere with the user activities.

To avoid distraction, extraneous user operations must be prohibited, and heavy visual and audible effects must not be used. However, it is preferable that a user's character should be displayed at all times because it represents his/her achievement of the subjective workload, as mentioned in Section 3.1. To avoid distraction, the character should be displayed so as not to obstruct his/her activities, such as near a certain corner of the display as with some Microsoft Office help agents.

Avoiding distractions a competition-game component is difficult. One solution is that the game is executed automatically, and users can only formulate the strategy of the game. The competition game of Weekend Battle, described in section 4, uses the solution. Figure 5 shows the strategy-setting window. A user can set up his/her desired strategy during free time such as lunch time or coffee break.

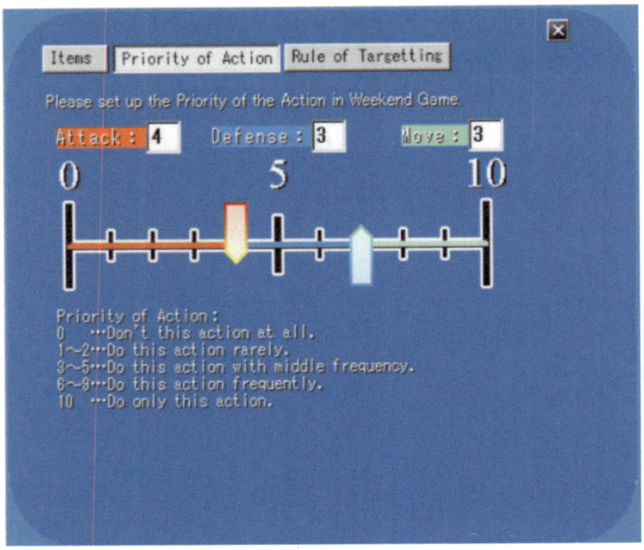

Fig. 5. Weekend Battle: strategy-setting window

3.5. Implementation

We now examine four implementations of EELF-based entertainment systems:

- Weekend Battle: an entertainment system for daily work in an office environment such as preparing documents, presentations, and spreadsheets
- ExS (Exercise Game System): a mobile entertainment system for daily exercise such as jogging and walking
- MIPS (Musical Instruments Practice Supporter): an entertainment system for daily practice of musical instruments
- VASC (Virtual Aquarium for Subjective Competition): an entertainment system for daily work in an office environment, with the same target as for Weekend Battle.

The character-creation and competition-game components of Weekend Battle, ExS, and MIPS are similar, but the effort-estimation component is different. The effort-estimation component of VASC is the same as that of Weekend Battle, but the other two components are different.

The next four sections describe the implementation of the three components and results of experimental evaluations of these systems.

4. Weekend Battle

4.1 Overview

Weekend Battle is an entertainment system for improving user motivation in a computer-aided office work environment. It covers three categories of works:

1. Document preparation by word processor

2. Code preparation by IDEs (integrated development environments)
3. Slide preparation by slide-show applications

It is assumed that users work on individual PC. However, the system can be applied to works that does not involve a PC as long as the workload can be estimated and users have their own displays to show their avatars, perhaps on PDAs.

4.2 Effort Estimation

4.2.1 Components of Effort

The components of PC office work fall into two categories: the amount of computer operations and the work time.

Computer operations are categorized as follows:

1. Number of keystrokes
   (a) Number of alphanumeric keys
   (b) Number of keyboard shortcut (Ctrl-X, Ctrl-C, Ctrl-V, and Ctrl-Z)
   (c) Number of keyboard correction keys (DEL and Backspace)
2. Number of mouse clicks (single or double clicks; left, center, or right buttons)
3. Distance of mouse movements
4. Amount and distance of dragging-and-dropping (left, center, or right drags and drops).

The distance of mouse movement is not the exact length of the trace of a mouse cursor but rather the distance between the points of current and previous clicking. The distance of dragging and dropping is measured similarly, as the distance between the point to start dragging and the point of dropping. Thus, we avoid adding meaningless mouse movements to the subjective workload estimation.

Work time is categorized into writing time, reading time, and thinking time. When a user strikes keys to produce text, the duration is writing time. When he/she reads something on the display, perhaps using the mouse to drag a scroll bar, the duration is reading time. When the user is doing nothing on the PC, the duration is thinking time.

However, it is hard to distinguish between thinking time and reading time because neither involves activity, so both are counted as reading time. Similarly, the time spent using mouse for drawing pictures is counted as reading time, not writing time. Time spent doing nothing is counted as time not working.

We define thresholds T_k and T_r. It is assumed that a user performs a certain operation at time t_1 following the previous operation at time t_0. To what category the time $t_1 - t_0$ belongs to is determined as follows:

1. **if** ($t_1 - t_0 <= T_k$ and the operation is a keystroke) **then** writing time;
2.   **else if** ($t_1 - t_0 <= T_r$) **then** reading time;
3.   **else** he/she is not working.

4.2.2 Subjective Workload Estimation Formula

To determine a_i of Formula 1, a user's 10-min subjective workload for three types of work is gathered. Ten users perform three tasks of each type. An easy task could be finished in a few minutes, a normal task in 5 or 6 min, and a hard task not even in 10 min.

Users perform each of the 9 tasks (3 types × 3 difficulties) for 10 min. After each task, they evaluated the subjective workload of the task on a scale of 0 to 100, 100 implies that they worked hard through the 10 min as judged by themselves. If they finished the task before 10 min, they could do anything they liked, but could not include that activity in their judgement. I also collected all of their operations during the task.

The weight a_i is estimated by the multiple linear regression analysis method. We calibrated the significance level so as to leave at least three parameters in Formula 1. Then we created three formulas for each type of work as follows (the unit of time is the second):

- Word processing:

W_w = (writing time) × 0.178 + (reading time with keyboard) × 0.164 + (reading time with mouse) × 0.211 + (left click) × (-1.26) (2)

- Creating a presentation

W_p = (reading time with mouse) × 0.146 + (Ctrl-C) × 2.22 + (right click) × 0.959 (3)

- GUI program coding

W_c = (reading time with mouse) × 0.0633 + (left drag and drop) × 0.623 + (keystrokes) × 0.102 (4)

4.3 Character Creation

The character-creation component shows the user's character and ability scores on the right-bottom corner the PC display (see Figure 2).

A character has five ability scores for the competition game. Four of them — hit points (HPs), attack points, defence points, and agility points — increase with increasing subjective workload. Each ability score is calculated by its own estimation formula. For example, attack points increase faster than defence points when the users' work application is word-processing software. Speed is generally not a factor, and is not shown by default.

The character-creation component shows a progress bar indicating how much subjective workload is needed to change shape. Subsequent shape changes require increasing amounts of user effort.

The character has a mood (Figure 6). It is happy when the user works hard during a short period and sad when the user does not work. The mood is related to the probability of getting an item. For instance, when a character remains happy for three successive periods, the character can get an item.

The character-creation component provides different functions by time of day, that is, during work and break times. Table 1 shows these functions.

To follow-up the discussion in Section 3.4, the character-creation component does not require any user operation during work time. Excluding the presentation of a character, which is always shown on weekdays, users can view only a summary of the last weekend's game.

At break time, users can manage their characters' settings (Figure 7). They can equip their characters with items for the next competition game, and choose a ratio of actions for the game, including attack, defence and move (Figure 5). In addition, they can set up strategies for selecting the target to fight. Examples include "the character that bites me at the previous turn" and "the character that has the lowest HP." They can select three different strategies, or the same strategy twice or three times.

(a) Happy (b) Normal (c) Sad

Fig. 6. Weekend Battle: possible character moods

Work time	Break time	Function
*	*	Showing an avatar
*	*	Showing a summary of the last battle
	*	Showing the details of the last battle
	*	Showing the details of items that an avatar possesses
	*	Setting strategies for the next weekend battle

(*: provided)

Table 1. Weekend Battle: functions of the character-creation component

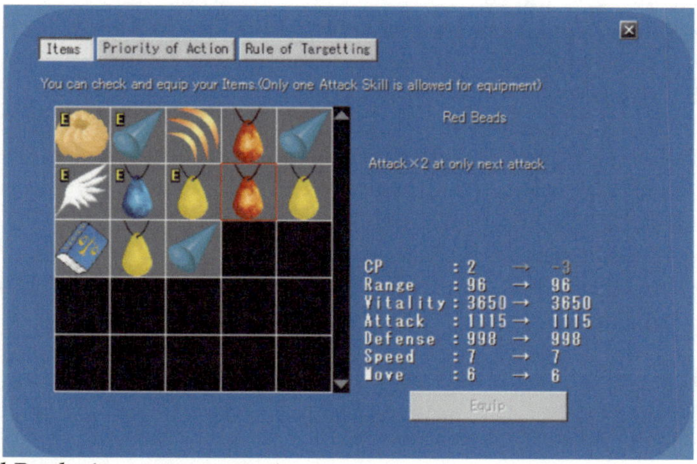

Fig. 7. Weekend Battle: item representation

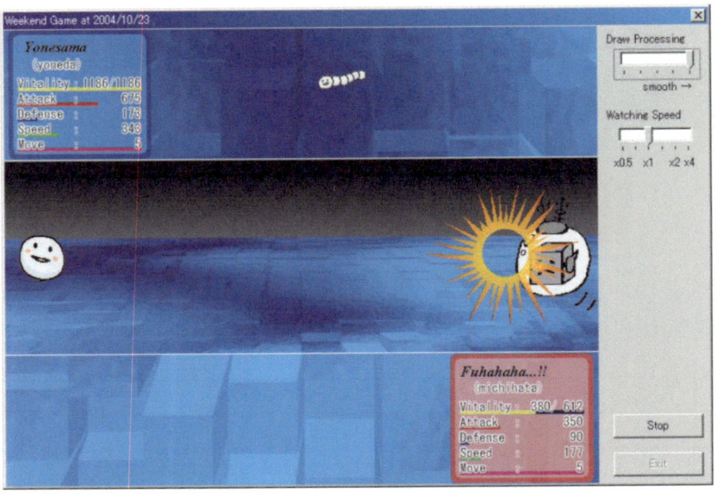

Fig. 8. Weekend Battle: battle representation, with full animation

4.4 Competition Game

A competition game system gathers all users characters and has them fight against each other over the weekend, in other words in a "battle royal." The game is performed automatically according to the strategy that each user has set for his/her character during the previous weekdays. Characters perform their actions in a battlefield. Actions are ordered by ability points, and consist of a movement and one of following for one turn: attack another character, defend self, or use an owned item.

One game has 20 turns. Characters are ranked according to when they go down. If they go down sooner, their ranking is lower. If all characters except one go down, the last one still up is the winner and the game is over. If two or more characters are still up at the end of the last turn, they are ranked according to the ratio of remaining HPs.

Results are logged and it sent to the character-creation component for user viewing during the succeeding weekdays. The component shows the details of the last battle with full animation (Figure 8).

4.5 Evaluation

4.5.1 Methods

I conducted a five-week trial with two user groups (groups A and B), each with eight users, to compare user motivation with and without the entertainment system, with and without the weekend battle, and with different lengths of system use. The evaluation weeks were as follows:

- **Week 1:** Control experiment of group A (without the system).
- **Week 2:** The system is introduced to group A, and control experiment of group B.
- **Week 3:** The system is introduced to group B. A continues to use the system.
- **Week 4:** Both groups continue to use the system.
- **Week 5:** Both groups stop using the system as control experiments.

I compared A at week 1 (abbreviated to A-1, and so forth) and B-2 to A-2 and B-3 to evaluate the effect of the weekday system only because users had not yet played the weekend battle game. I compared A-2 and B-3 to A-3 and B-4 to evaluate the effect of the weekend battle game. A-3 and B-4 differ from A-5 and B-5 in the existence of the entertainment system. This situation is slightly different from the first control experiment as to whether users have experience with the system. In addition, group A is compared to group B for differences in beginning to use the system.

At the end of each week, after watching the weekend battle game of the week, users filled out a questionnaire (Table 2) to determine their level of motivation. Answers ranged from -3 (strongly disagree) to +3 (strongly agree). Q3 is asked on weeks when the system is used and Q4 is asked on only the last week.

No.	Question
Q1	You feel motivated to work
Q2	Your work is fun.
Q3	Weekend Battle is fun.
Q4	You want to use Weekend Battle in future.

Table 2. Weekend Battle motivation questionnaire

4.5.2 Results

Table 3 shows the questionnaire results. The standard deviation is in parentheses. Q1 and Q2 results for weeks with Weekend Battle (Week 2/3 and Week 3/4) are significantly higher than for weeks without Weekend Battle (Week 1/2 and Week 5/5). Thus, Weekend Battle clearly improves user motivation, and makes users feel that their work is more fun than without Weekend Battle.

All the answers to Q3 are positive, so Weekend Battle is clearly perceived as begin fun. The average answer to Q4 is also positive, so Weekend Battle is acceptable in the work environment. Moreover, all users have used it continuously since the end of the experiment.

No.	Group	Week 1/2	Week2/3	Week3/4	Week5/5
Q1	A	-0.60(0.84)	1.50(0.71)	1.20(0 63)	-0.90(1.10)
	B	-0.89(0.93)	0.67(1.12)	0.89(0.93)	-0.89(0.78)
	all	-0.74(0.87)	1.11(0.99)	1.05(0.78)	-0.89(0.94)
Q2	A	-0.10(0.74)	0.40(1.58)	0.50(1.27)	-0.90(1.20)
	B	-0.78(1.09)	0.11(1.05)	0.56(1.24)	-0.89(0.78)
	all	-0.42(0.96)	0.26(1.33)	0.53(1.22)	-0.89(0.99)
Q3	A		1.80(0.92)	2.00(0.67)	
	B		2.11(0.60)	1.78(0.44)	
	all		1.95(0.78)	1.89(0.44)	
Q4	A				1.80(0.92)
	B				1.67(0.50)
	all				1.74(0.73)

(Week x/y: Group A's Week x and group B's Week y)

Table 3. Weekend Battle evaluation results

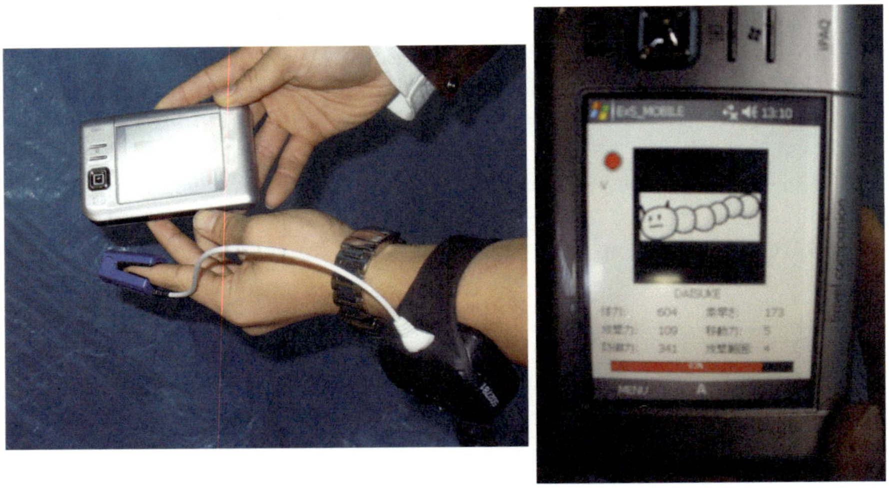

Fig. 9. ExS: equipment and character representation

5. ExS

5.1 Overview

Exercise Game System (ExS) is an entertainment system that supports users' daily exercise for health. Daily exercise can benefit from such a system because achievement is ambiguous and jogging or walking the same route everyday can be boring.

In addition, users may be tempted to to give up daily exercise because of lack of time. ExS cannot rely on special devices that restrict the place to exercise. For example, the dance game Dance Dance Revolution is used now in some schools in West Virginia for reducing student obesity (Toppo, 2006). However, it can be used only in places such as schools, where the required special hardware is available. Mueller et al. proposed a football-based entertainment system that aims to enhance social bonding; however, it also is limited to places where it can be used (Mueller et al., 2003).

The implementation of ExS is shown in Figure 9. It consists of a PDA with GPS (HP iPaq rx5900) that measures jogging or walking speed, and a wireless Bluetooth-communicating heartbeat sensor (NONIN 4100). They are light enough to wear and carry in everyday life. ExS measures user heartbeat rate and velocity of movement at all times, and displays the user's own character on a PDA. Thus, ExS can estimate user effort for exercise anytime, and create the user's character to reflecting exercise effort.

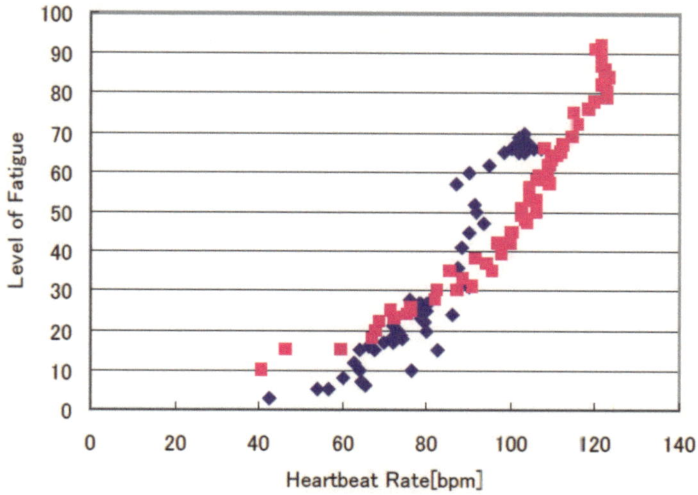

Fig. 10. ExS: relationship between heartbeat rate and fatigue level

5.2 Effort Estimation

When a user exercises, his/her heartbeat rate increased compared to when he/she, for example, sits for office work, stands in a train, or sleeps. Masuko et al. use heartbeat rate similarly for physical entertainment, and change the difficulty of a game according to changes of in a user's heartbeat rate (Masuko et al., 2006). ExS determines that a user is exercising when his/her heartbeat is 20 beats per minute (bpm) faster than usual, as measured before using ExS.

When determining that a user is exercising, ExS must also estimate the user effort during exercise. Figure 10 shows the relationship between user effort and heartbeat rate during jogging. The X-axis is the increase in heartbeat rate from the ordinary condition. Two users jog for 30 min, and reported their level of fatigue every minute. I assume that the level of fatigue directly reflects effort. From the shape of the graph, I estimate effort by the formula

$$E = ah^2, \tag{5}$$

where E is the estimated effort during one minute, a is a constant factor that depends on the user, and h is heartbeat rate.

Even for the same heartbeat rate, different types of exercise might incur different feelings of effort. Thus, the constant factor a varies with the type of exercise. ExS measures the velocity of user movement and classifies the exercise into one of three categories:

- <5km/h: exercise in place
- 5-7km/h: walking
- >7km/h: jogging

ExS has three effort estimation equations, respectively.

5.3 Evaluation

I conducted a trial to evaluate the improvement in user motivation by ExS. The competition system is almost the same as that of Weekend Battle; therefore, evaluation focuses on character creation during exercise. Five users are performed one of three kinds of exercise

each day: 20-min walking, 10-min jogging, and 5-min rope jumping. After three days, they filled out a questionnaire.
Table 4 shows the questionnaire results. Values shown are the averages of all users, where 5 is strongly agree, 3 is moderate, and 1 is strongly disagree. Results indicate that the character-creation component of ExS stimulates daily exercise.

Average score	Question
3.8	ExS stimulates the motivation of daily exercise
4.2	Creating my own character on ExS is fun

Table 4. ExS evaluation results

6. MIPS

6.1 Overview
Musical Instrument Practice Supporter (MIPS) is designed for music students. Music is commonly thought to be fun itself; therefore an EELF-based system may not be required. However, many music students quit their studies, usually because they cannot keep to a regular daily practice schedule. Repeated practice can be dull and monotonous, and often involves repeating a simple and not-very-interesting phrase many times (for example, Hanon piano exercises). It is, therefore, appropriate for an EELF-based support system.
Although MIPS targets students of the electronic piano, it can be used with other musical devices as long as device operations can be measured.

6.2 Effort Estimation
Many factors are considered to affect the effort of piano practice. I conducted a trial to determine the factors and their intensities. I recruited five users who have a little experience playing the electronic piano to practice 10 scores of classic composition. Each practice period was 30 min. I determined the following components of piano practice:

- Number of touches, counting one chord as one touch
- Ratio of the number of accidental notes (played by black keys) to the number of all notes
- Amount of chords, which is the ratio of the number of notes (counting all notes forming the chord) to the number of touches
- Standard deviation of the pitch calculated by MIDI note number
- Difficulty of the score (easy, moderate, or difficult).

After each period, users indicated the level of effort they felt relative to the first period, which is rated as 100. Effort is estimated by the following linear summation

$$E = \Sigma_k a_k p_k, \tag{6}$$

where E is the estimated effort, k is the factor for piano practice mentioned above, p_k is the value of the factor k, and a_k is the constant weight. We determine a_k by the multiple linear regression analysis ($\alpha < .05$). The resulting effort estimation formula is as follows:

$$E = .377 \times p_{\text{stddev}} + 23.2 \times p_{\text{chord}} + 93.6 \times p_{\text{accidental}}. \tag{7}$$

6.3 Character Creation

In contrast to Weekend Battle and ExS, MIPS aims to support learning musical instruments. In learning instruments, the following are essential:

1. The user should practice every day
2. The user should practice for as many hours as possible

To address these points, the method by which characters grow up is modified in MIPS. A parameter of succession of practice is added. To address point 1, in daily character creation, a character sometimes gets an item that temporally improves its power during competition. If a user practices daily for a week, his/her character can get new, unusually strong items. If the user practices daily for two weeks, his/her character can get even more and stronger items. If the user takes a day off, his/her character loses the ability to get these enhanced items. Similarly, to address point 2, if a user practices for an hour, his/her character can get new, unusually strong items. If the user practices for an additional hour, his/her character can get even more and stronger items. At the end of the day, his/her character loses the ability to get these enhanced items.

By these two modifications, a user who practices every day for long hours can create a stronger character than others who practice less.

6.4 Evaluation

A four-week trial was held to evaluate MIPS. Four beginner piano students with some experience on the instrument were asked to practice a certain piece of classical music for four weeks. Two of them used MIPS and two did not. Each weekend, they answered the question "Does MIPS motivate you to practice (+2: strongly agree; -2: strongly disagree)?" Practice logs for all for users were gathered.

Table 5 shows the average motivation scores. MIPS improves user motivation slightly, and thus, can be effective in maintaining and improving motivation. Table 6 shows the average daily practice time. There is no significant difference between users who uses MIPS and those that did not. The influence of MIPS on amount of practice is unclear, however, for the following reason: users were asked simply to practice a classical piece; They were not asked to perform pepetitive exercises such as the Hanon exercises. MIPS can be effective for such repeated, dull practice.

# Week	With MIPS	Without MIPS
1	1.0	-1.0
2	0.5	0.0
3	1.0	0.5
4	1.0	1.0

Table 5. MIPS evaluation results

With MIPS (std. dev.)	Without MIPS (std. dev.)
19.64 (10.25)	32.04 (42.91)

Table 6. MIPS average daily practice times (in minutes)

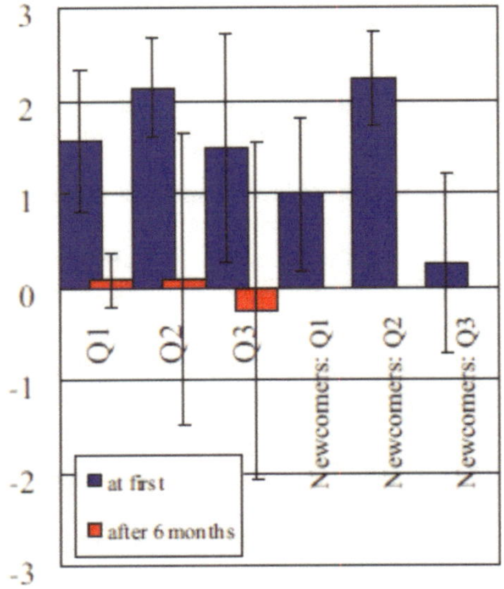

No.	Question
Q1	Weekend Battle improves my motivation for work.
Q2	Creating my character is fun.
Q3	Battle game at weekend is fun.

(-3: strongly disagree; +3: strongly agree)

Fig. 11. Weekend Battle: results of follow-up questionnaire

7. VASC

7.1 Problem with Weekend Battle over Long-Term Use

Weekend Battle is effective for improving user motivation, as discussed in Section 4.5.2. However, there is one problem; its competition-game component depends on objective measurement of the character's ability. Once a certain character's ability score is much higher than another's, the latter cannot generally beat the former, because it is difficult to narrow the gap in scores.

Figure 11 shows the result of a follow-up questionnaire about the effectiveness of Weekend Battle over six-months of use. Its effectiveness after two weeks of use is high, but after six-months it decreases. Thus, the problem becomes paramount by at least six-months of use.

To solve the problem, I created Virtual Aquarium with Subjective Competition (VASC). The character for each user is a fish, and users compare the appearance of their fish by subjective measurement.

7.2 Adding a Subjective Elements to the Competition

The results described previously for the Weekend Battle are for objective measures of competition. Objective competition has two characteristics that can cause problems:

1. There is only one winner
2. The winner depends only on explicit measures as numerical parameters

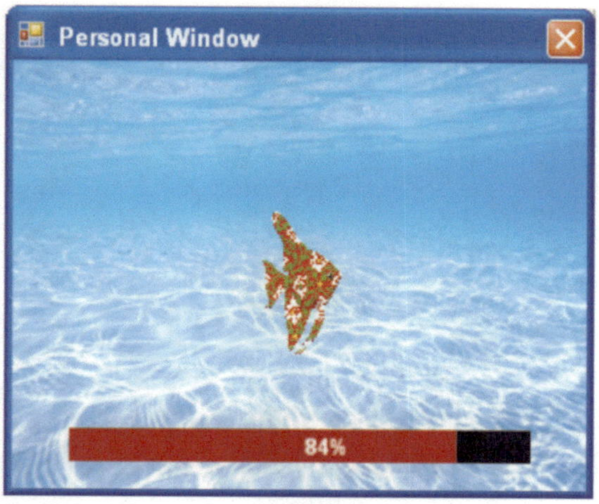

Fig. 12. VASC: character representation (personal window)

In case of Weekend Battle, the only winner is the winner of the competition game. The result of the competition game depends greatly on the characters' ability scores, which increase with increasing subjective workload. Once one character's score is much higher than the other characters' scores, it is difficult for others to win. Closing the gap in scores is difficult because the owners of both the winning character and the other characters continue to work hard and develop their characters.

To solve this problem, I introduced subjective measures for competition, such as prettiness and coolness, to the competition game. As users perform their work, the appearance of their character changes favorably according to their own subjective preferences. Subjective preferences differ among users, and a high score for a particular parameter is not necessarily altogether good.

For example, one user might value height, but another might value a balance between height and width. In this case, the latter user would win the competition even if the former user works much harder.

7.3 Changing the Nature of Character Creation

In VASC, users have their own fish in an aquarium, which can change its appearance as per the user choice. To do so, they use bait, which they earn by working. Figure 12 shows the VASC personal window, which shows the fish owned by a user.

To get the bait, the user must perform a certain amount of effort. This subjective workload is estimated by the same technique as for Weekend Battle. The progress bar at the bottom of the window (Figure 12) indicates the amount of subjective workload required to get the new bait.

Before getting the bait, the user decides on the kind of bait that he/she wants to get. However, he/she does not always get the desired kind. When the progress bar is full, he/she gets a capsule that contains the bait. The probability that the capsule holds the desired bait reflects how hard the user has worked. If he/she works hard enough to fill the progress bar quickly, the probability is high. Thus, the harder the user works, the more likely he/she is to get his/her favorite bait. The user can feed the bait to his/her fish at any time.

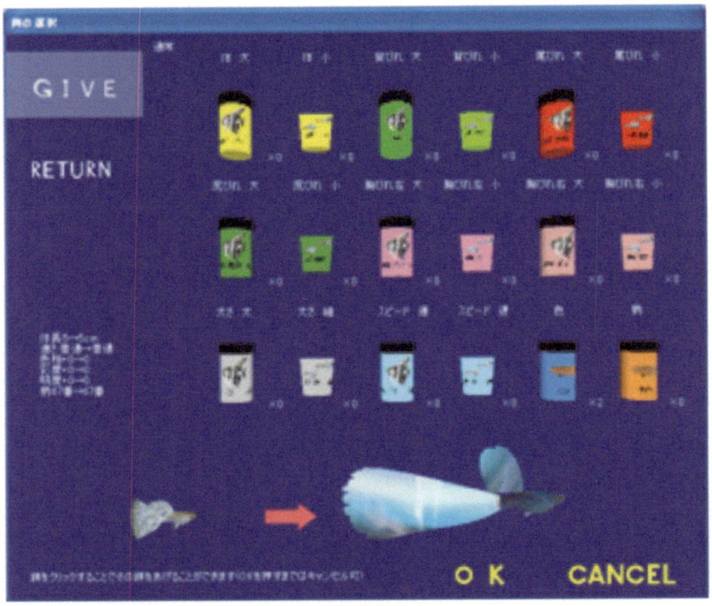

Fig. 13. VASC: feeding window

For subjective competition, fish parameters are as follows:

- Skin pattern (texture)
- Color (hue, brightness, and saturation)
- Length/width of body
- Length of breast fins
- Length of tail fin
- Swimming speed

A user can choose the types of bait to increase or decrease each parameter, but cannot specify the precise result. For example, although 400 different kinds of bait change skin pattern, he/she can only choose "skin pattern" and the patterns that he/she gets are determined randomly. Figure 13 shows the interface for feeding.

7.4 Changing the Nature of the Competition

The amount of bait and the number of capsules are clear objective measures; therefore, I limited objectivity as follows:

1. The probability of getting the desired bait is mentioned in Section 7.3. A user does not always get the bait that he/she wants, and normally does not feed undesired bait. Thus, users who get the same number of capsules feed different amounts of bait to their fish. Therefore, users cannot guess how many capsules other users have only from changes in the appearance of their fish.
2. Users can feed their fish whenever they wish, so the time of use is different for each other. Suppose there are two users who want to make their fish grow larger. At a particular instant, one's fish is larger than another's. However, the user with the larger fish need not necessarily win because the other user might gather and keep his/her favorite bait for later use, while the former might use entire bait right away.

All fish are shown in a shared display of a virtual fishbowl placed in a common space so that all users can compare their fish during break time.

7.5 Long-Term Evaluation

I conducted an empirical trial for about eight months to ensure that VASC stimulates and maintains user motivation during long-term use.

No.	Question
Q1	VASC is fun
Q2	VASC stimulates my motivation for work
Q3	I compare my fish to other ones (Yes/No)
Q4	I want to use VASC in future

Table 7. VASC questionnaire (Q1-Q4)

No.	Reason
F1	Comparing fish is fun
F2	Creating my fish as I like is fun
F3	Gathering capsules is fun.
F4	Gathering many kinds of bait is fun

(a) reasons for fun

No.	Reason
M1	I want to grow my fish as I like
M2	I want to feel my achievement through my fish
M3	I want to get a capsule
M4	I want to get high probability to get my favorite bait

(b) reasons for stimulating motivation

Table 8. VASC questionnaire reasons (Q1 and Q2)

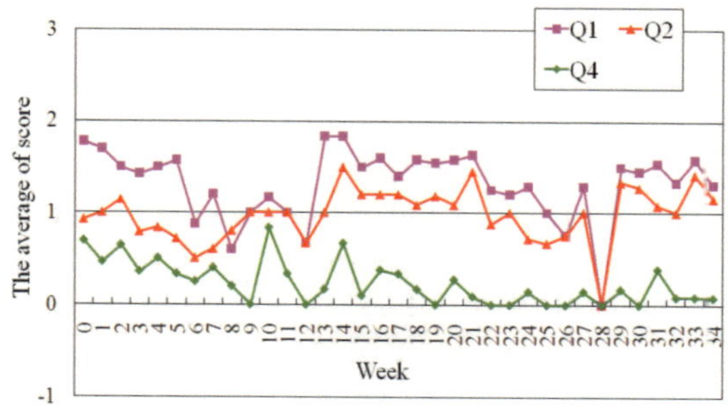

Fig. 14. VASC questionnaire results (Q1, Q2, and Q4)

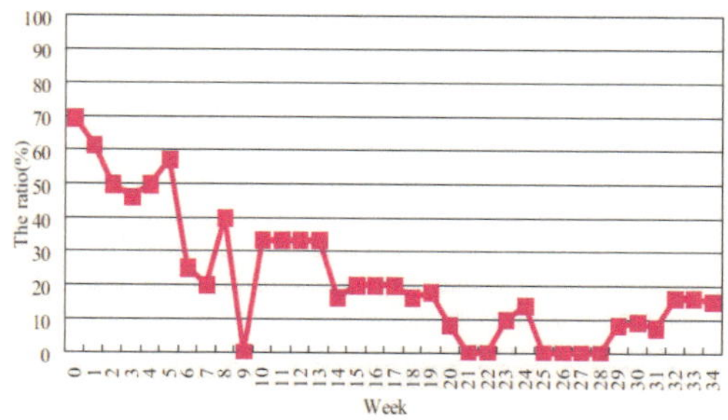

Fig. 15. VASC questionnaire results (Q3)

7.5.1 Methods

I recruited 16 participants (11 males and 5 females) from our laboratory, aged 22-26. All were undergraduate or graduate school students majoring in information science. The period of evaluation was 35 weeks (11 Jun 2007-17 Feb 2008). VASC was installed on their laboratory PCs, and they used them in their daily work. The shared display was placed in a public space in the main room of the laboratory where they take breaks and have lunch.
The users filled out the questionnaire in Table 7 at the end of each week except the first. Evaluation weeks are numbered 0th-34th. For Q1, Q2, and Q4, answers range from -3 (strongly disagree) to +3 (strongly agree). For Q1 and Q2, reasons are selected from Table 8 and multiple reasons are allowed.

7.5.2 Results

Figure 14 shows the results for Q1, Q2, and Q4 by week. Figure 15 shows the ratio of users who answered "Yes" to Q3. Figure 16 shows the reason for fun, and Figure 17 shows the reason for stimulating motivation.
The results for Q1 and Q2 indicate that VASC continued to be fun and stimulated motivation throughout the experimental period. However, users became gradually less apt to compare fish (Figure 15; F1 in Figure 16). It appears that the effect of competition on stimulation and/or fun exists only during early use of VASC.
F2 and F3 ratios remain high. The number of bait capsules and the changes in the appearance of the fish reflect user work achievement. Therefore, showing achievement is one of the most important factors in keeping work fun during long-term use of VASC. In contrast, the F4 ratio increases early (0th-3rd), until about 50% of users say that gathering many kinds of bait is fun, and then decreases gradually until, at the end, it falls to 0% (24th week). Koster points out that such a trend indicates that finding something new is fun, but the fun disappears when users find nothing new (Koster, 2004).
M2 (I want to feel my achievement through my fish) is the most frequently cited reasons (Figure 17). Thus, for the purpose of stimulating motivation, achievement feedback is the most important factor. M3 (I want to get a capsule) is also frequently cited for the same reason. However, Weekend Battle has similar feedback. The difference between Weekend Battle and VASC can be explained by how frequently M1 (I want to grow my fish as I like) is cited. In VASC, the user can control how his/her fish grows, while in Weekend Battle the character can change only in strength. In other words, VASC users can win in many different ways, but Weekend Battle users can win in only one way. As mentioned above, most users lose motivation for creating when the characters of others are much stronger, and VASC can avoid this problem. The F2 ratio supports this view. Users did not lose the fun of creating their fish, so their motivation remained high.

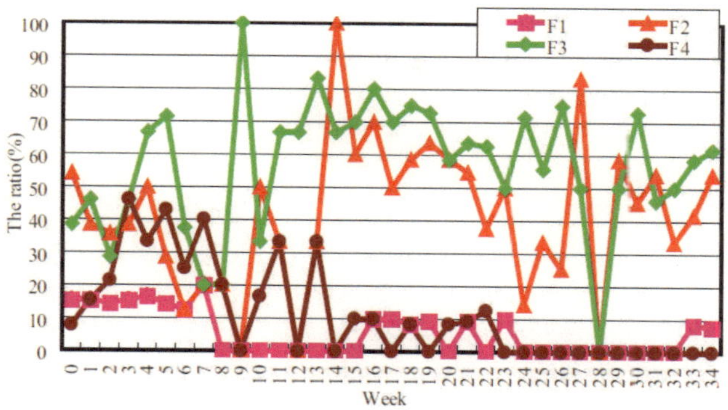

Fig. 16. VASC questionnaire results (F1-F4)

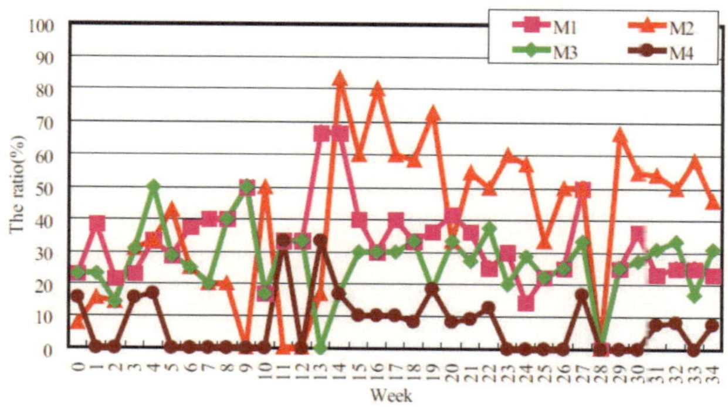

Fig. 17. VASC questionnaire results (M1-M4)

8. Conclusion

EELF is an entertainment-system framework that aims to improve motivation for repetitive, dull and monotonous activities. It consists of three components: effort estimation, character creation, and competition game. For the effort-estimation component, subjective workload of repetitive, dull and monotonous activities is estimated. The user of an EELF-based system has his/her own character, which grows in response to the estimated subjective workload, in the character-creation component. For the competition-game component, the characters of all users are gathered and compared with one another, and a winner is chosen. The fun of character creation and competition can stimulate user motivation for the target activities.

In this chapter, four EELF-based entertainment systems are introduced. Weekend Battle and VASC are systems for improving motivation for daily work with PCs in an office environment. ExS is a system for daily physical exercises. MIPS is a system for repeated practice on a musical instrument. All such activities are so monotonous that motivation to perform them tends to be low. Evaluation results suggest that they can improve and maintain user motivation for these activities. In addition, VASC can do so over long-term use.

In future, I will attempt to understand the mechanism of boredom, which we often see in situations where nothing is new. Boredom decreases motivation and fun; therefore I believe that it is crucial to know about and solve the problem of boredom. I am interested in the fact that most creators of massively multiplayer online role-playing games revise their systems periodically, although not drastically. I think that a suitable revision frequency for eliminating boredom can be extracted.

9. References

Caillois, R. (2001). *Man, Play and Games,* Univercity of Illinois Press, Champaign, IL.

Chao, D. (2001). Doom as an interface for process management. *Proceedings of the SIGCHI conference on Human factors in computing systems(CHI'01),* ACM, pages 152–157.

Koster, R. (2004). *A Theory of Fun for Game Design*. Paraglyph Press.

Masuko, S., and Hoshino J. (2006). A fitness game reflecting heart rate. *Proceeding of the Advances in Computer Entertainment (ACE2006),* ACM, in DVD-ROM.

Mueller, F., Agamanolis, S., and Picard, R. (2003). Exertion interfaces: sports over a distance for social bonding and fun. *Proceedings of the conference on Human factors in computing systems(CHI'03),* ACM, pages 561–568.

Pan, Z. et al.(eds.) (2008). *Technologies for E-Learning and Digital Entertainment (Edutainment2008),* LNCS5093, Springer, Germany.

Sonnenfeld. J. (1983). Academic learning, worker learning, and the hawthorne studies. *Social Forces,* Vol. 61, No.3, pages 904–909.

Toppo, G. (2006). Students going to gym to video dance. *USATODAY.com,* http://www.usatoday.com/tech/gaming/2006-01-24-ddr-gym-class_x.htm, (last visited on 13/04/2009).

DiFac: Digital Factory for Human Oriented Production System

Claudia Redaelli[1], Glyn Lawson[2], Marco Sacco[1] and Mirabelle D'Cruz[2]
[1]*ITIA CNR Institute of Industrial Technologies and Automation, National Research Council*
Italy
[2]*Human Factors Research Group, Faculty of Engineering, University of Nottingham*
England

1. Introduction

The production paradigm of the European Industry sector has changed in the last few years. If large companies have already adopted *virtual reality* tools in their production chains, the Small and Medium Enterprises (SMEs) are still looking for more customised solutions: more suitable for their dimension and less expensive (Consoni et al. 2006, Sacco et al. 2004 and Mancini et al. 2004). As also mentioned in the ManuFuture SRA (Strategic Research Agenda, 2006), the traditional factories have seen dramatic improvements in efficiency and changes in working methods brought about by the introduction of automation and control systems based on digital technology.

Currently, around 230 000 European Manufacturing enterprises with 20 or more employees provide 34 million people with work. (Manufuture SRA, 2006). New technologies appear the most appropriate approach for reinforcing European SME manufacturing ground. As described in the FuTMoN report (uture of Manufacturing In Europe 2015-2020 - the challenge for sustainable development): "Not only does RTD *{Research and Technology Development}* drive new developments in manufacturing, but more importantly, manufacturing is the contextual driver for more RTD"(EC, 2006)

With most influencing factors in a constant, and even turbulent state of flux, the next step is to progress towards what can be described as the 'virtual factory' of the future. This will require a European platform for digital manufacturing engineering, having the capability to create, maintain and use a dynamic system of networks, in which all the actors contribute and add value to the manufacturing chain, without the constraints of physical co-location or rigid partnerships. New products are required to fill markets gaps and customers' expectations, and the new production systems are designed accordingly as a collaborative action with the suppliers. The requirements are detected with an immediate communication between producers and clients supported by new technologies. A company has normally delocalised production sites in different countries and communication is essential for maintaining the corporate line coherence and the production plan. New technologies, such

as Virtual Reality (VR) and Augmented Reality (AR), permit an immediate communication among different entities with a higher participation grade.
The research in DiFac aims to develop various environments to support SMEs working on a product in the design phase, or creating a new production line without physically moving the machinery, or again training workers in a safe and secure situation.
In recognition of their importance to the success of Virtual Environments (VEs), the framework is based on three main pillars: presence, ergonomic and collaboration. They are composed of both tools and methodologies. This is the base on which the tools for supporting the manufacturing activities are developed.
In order to demonstrate the potential of the structure, three validation scenarios have been implemented as pilot cases. Two of these are directly derived from project industrial partners, PRIMA INDUSTRIE and Pantelis Pashalidis & Sons (PPS), and are focused on product development and training. A third scenario is developed following the requirements of a highly committed Romanian industry named "Compa". It works in the automotive sector and applies DiFac results for Factory Constructor. Moreover a European industrial group has participated in the project with a validation role. Their involvement was critical in developing a successful DiFac solution. The DiFac toolset supports collaboration among different sites and users during design, prototyping and manufacturing through an interactive environment to support SMEs delivering better quality products and services. The use of such a technology will definitely lead directly to reinforcing competitiveness in the European industry and solving societal problems since it will provide many benefits, as follows. *Increased Efficiency*: team members will be able to collaborate anytime, anywhere making faster decisions and gaining approvals instantly. *Reduction in Complexity*: employees will be able to seamlessly work together, and extend communication and collaboration beyond their organizational boundaries. *Reduction in Physical Mock-ups*: the DiFac environment will allow testing on digital (virtual) configurations, employing advanced paradigms of immersive interaction and collaborative work without relying on physical mock-ups or experiments and tests. *Enhanced Organizational Intelligence*: the information will be collected and organized in a single place. New members will be able to view all the history and information very fast and to start working with the other members in less time, thus improving productivity. *Better working conditions:* as a result of the above employees will have the opportunity to work with advanced supporting tools that will make their lives easier and safer.
The DiFac European consortium and project is just part of a wider project with Korea and Switzerland for creating a new effective Digital Factory Environment, through the associated Intelligent Manufacturing System (IMS) project.
This chapter presents the innovation behind the three pillars on which the environments are based, and the different technical solutions that constitute the DiFac integrated scenario.

2. A Digital Factory sustained by three pillars

A **Digital Factory** is a comprehensive approach of networking of digital models, methods, and tools - including modelling, simulation and 3D/Virtual Reality visualization- integrated by a continuous data management (DiFac brochure, 2007). The DiFac framework identified three activity areas to address- training, product development and factory design/evaluation.. The objectives of these activities were defined by the industrial partners

of the project including the tasks of the workers, the designers, and the production department. In collaboration with the industrial and development team of the consortium, the characteristics of the three theoretical pillars of the framework were defined in terms of Ergonomics, Presence and Collaboration.
Therefore the basic framework of DiFac (and the main innovation) was to provide understanding of these three main pillar components, with supporting tools and methods, to help the development of specific components from the three main activities in the product/process life cycle.

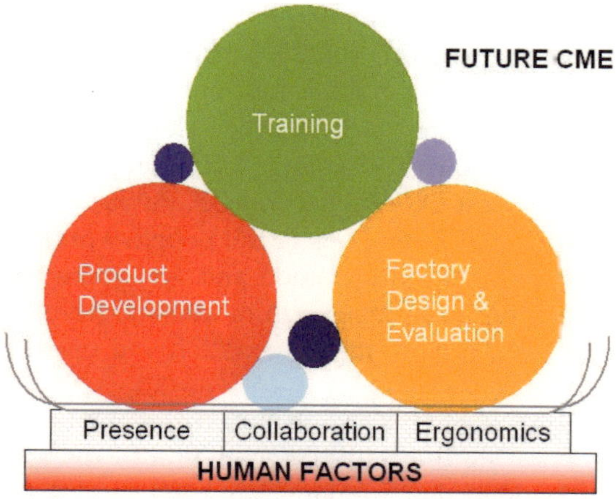

Fig. 1. DiFac framework

DiFac main results are the following:
Product Designer is a collaborative design environment that supports communication and design activities between distributed engineers and designers during the product development phase.
Training simulator includes two different components. First is an Augmented Reality (AR) environment that offers remote technical support for non-standard maintenance operations from headquarters to branches located in different parts of the world. The second is an immersive simulator for workers' training in emergency situations, such as a factory fire.
Factory constructor. With the objective of checking the feasibility of the best Product Designer chosen in the product development scenario, it is composed of different components: a planning table for a first rough design of the production lay out, a VR viewer called "GIOVE" for visualization of the layout even in an immersive way and a web based simulation to identify production bottlenecks and optimize the shopfloor. The pillars approach was considered in every phase of the development. The methodologies developed guided the user in enhancing the existing tools or developing new ones in appropriate ways: always focusing on the human factors. Moreover the resulting environments have been validated according to the methodologies in order to identify the existing gap and propose further improvement for the future.

The following paragraphs contain a definition of the investigated field and the application of the methodologies to the DiFac environments.

3. Ergonomics

Taking proper account of people's needs and capabilities in design, implementation and operation - being human-centered and addressing the human factors - is the province of Ergonomics. As a discipline it is concerned with the theory and practice of learning about human characteristics and capabilities, then using that understanding to improve people's interaction with the hardware, software and people with which they interact, and with the environments in which they do so (Wilson 2005). Poor ergonomics (for example failure to account for the users' end needs; making systems excessively complicated; providing interfaces which do not support the user) has been cited as the reason for failure in many Information and Communications Technology (ICT) projects (Wellington 2006; Beynon-Davies 1999; UK National Audit Office 1999 and UK Public Accounts Committee 2000). In all cases, the abilities, needs and limitations of the people working within these systems or with the equipment have not been understood and accounted for. Conversely, successful products or work systems typically demonstrate that the needs of their users have been addressed during conception, design, implementation and operation (Eason 1997; Wastell and Cooper 1996;).

Within DiFac, the focus throughout the development of the technologies has been on the human factors: that is, ensuring the solutions were usable and satisfying to use. However, consideration was also made of the ergonomics of the factories, products and training, for which DiFac aims to improve the productivity and safety of people at work. For this, the DiFac technologies provide the opportunity for a proactive approach to ergonomics - identifying and resolving ergonomics issues at an early stage in the design process, when changes are less costly to implement, rather than responding to complaints of ill-health in the workplace. This has been achieved by enabling workers to evaluate digital representations of workplaces, thus benefiting from their tacit knowledge of working practices and from the opportunities afforded by visualisation technologies (Chaffin 2001; Laughery 2005 and Lawson et al. 2006).

Concerning the development of the technologies, one of the main research aims was to investigate the suitability of existing ergonomics methods for application to the digital factory. The DiFac project presented many issues typical of any development programme, including: restricted access to the anticipated end-users; limited resources for user-testing and inconsistent availability of prototypes for evaluation work. However, the DiFac project presented some unique challenges affecting the ergonomics evaluation process, including: an emphasis on distributed collaborative working, with the development partners and end-users in several countries with different time-zones, first-languages, cultures and operational stereotypes; a necessity to conduct evaluations remotely due to the geographical dispersion; and an extension beyond typical software and web interfaces to include, for example, virtual and augmented environments.

3.1 Method

The general approach to development was a user-centred participatory design and evaluation process. Involving end-users can improve the solution through the benefit of

their unique insight into working activities. Moreover, they are the people who will ultimately evaluate the success of the technology. This approach has been proven to lead to quality improvements, and a reduction in throughput time and costs. It not only ensures that the technology will match the end-users' needs, but also increases their acceptance of the final solution through an increased sense of ownership. The essential elements of this approach include direct involvement of the end-users, a focus on developing the system to match their capabilities, and an iterative development approach (Vink et al., 2005). End users were involved at every possible stage; when time or availability prevented their involvement, their needs and capabilities were considered inviolable.
Hereafter follows a description of the specific methods used to evaluate the various iterations of DiFac technologies. They were selected based on the priority for end-user involvement, in addition to the specific challenges of DiFac mentioned above.

User requirements questionnaire – a user requirements questionnaire was generated containing questions designed to elicit any mismatches between the technology and user requirements. It was based on qualitative feedback, and included questions such as "What did you like about the system?", "How do you think the system could be improved?"

Systems Usability Scale – SUS (Brooke, 1996) – this was used as it is a quick and easy method to assess usability. It comprises 11 statements related to usability, for example "I think that I would like to use this system frequently" against which the user rates the extent to which they agree or disagree on a 5-point scale.

UNott Heuristics checklist – heuristics are rules of thumb which are followed to help people make judgements quickly and efficiently (Stanton et al. 2005). It was recognised that the users would not always be available for evaluation tasks due to the demands of their jobs. Therefore, a checklist was developed based on the VIEW-IT (Tromp and Nichols 2003) assessment tool, which was originally developed for evaluating usability, input/output devices, and health and safety issues associated with VEs. The DiFac checklist was developed to be completed by Ergonomics experts, and extended the original tool to be suitable for desktop and AR solutions.

The application of the various methods was dependent upon the state of the prototype, as well as the geographical location of the Ergonomist and end-users. An overview is provided in Table 1. In the early stages, development partners generated videos of proposed solutions, based on pre-existing prototypes. Industrial end-users were asked to watch this, and then complete the user requirements questionnaire. This process was conducted remotely, with the users downloading the video and completing the evaluation from their sites, then emailing their completed questions back to the Ergonomist for analysis. Thereafter, prototype systems became available in which users were able to explore and attempt certain relevant tasks before completing SUS as well as the user requirements questionnaire. Again, this process could be conducted remotely. If interim developments were released they would be subject to an expert review using the UNott heuristics checklist. As more detailed working prototypes became available, co-located evaluation sessions were held in which the DiFac end-users and external companies and associations gathered in one location to evaluate the technologies. The participants would receive a demonstration, and then be invited to attempt tasks. They were then asked to complete SUS and the user requirements questionnaire.

Technology stage of development	User-requirements questionnaire	SUS	Heuristics checklist
Early video clips showing proposed solutions	Y (distributed evaluation)		Y
First prototypes	Y (distributed evaluation)	Y (distributed evaluation)	Y
Interim releases			Y
Higher fidelity prototypes	Y (co-located evaluation)	Y (co-located evaluation)	Y

Table 1. Application of the ergonomics methods to the technologies.
Note: Distributed refers to geographical separation of the participants from the evaluator; with co-located the evaluation was conducted with both in the same room

3.2 Results

The overall approach can be considered a success, given the positive response of the end-users and EU reviewers towards the final stages of the DiFac project. The following specific points were noted from the application of the chosen ergonomics methods:

- Asking end-users to evaluate video clips of proposed solutions enabled them to provide feedback at a very early stage of the development process. This helped clarify the user-requirements, and also identify any mismatches in the proposed solutions before any development work had occurred; hence changes were easier to manage than had they arisen later in the development process.
- Conducting distributed evaluations was particularly useful for reducing travel costs. It also minimised the time SME employees were removed from their work places. Most of the distributed evaluations lasted considerably less than one hour.
- The user requirements questionnaire and SUS were useful for identifying significant usability issues and mismatches between system performance and user requirements. However, it was necessary to supplement this process with the UNott heuristic checklist, which enabled a more detailed evaluation of the interface. Through the heuristics checklist the Ergonomist made recommendations for aspects such as navigation, icon design, labelling, window behaviour and movement in the VE; the other methods would only indicate a general problem area and would not generate recommendations of sufficient clarity for a developer to easily respond.
- The UNott heuristic checklist was also useful for tracking changes with development iterations – it was not feasible to ask the user-partners for their feedback at every stage of evaluation, due to the demands of their jobs.
- Despite the aforementioned benefits of the distributed evaluations, the co-located evaluation was invaluable for the Ergonomist to witness first hand subtleties such as body language, facial expressions, and utterances by the industrial end-users when trying out the technologies. It provided the opportunity for all the participants to ask

questions so that direct feedback could be provided and also more detail could be pursued. It was also useful for the developers to witness this rich feedback, rather than summarised feedback from the other methods.

3.3 Conclusions

The methods chosen were appropriate for the ergonomics development of technologies in the digital factory. The combination of methods was necessary to ensure that all elements were captured, from general user requirements to detailed user-interface design. Distributed evaluations enabled end-user input at an early stage in the development, and reduced travel costs, but the process also benefited from co-located evaluations when prototypes became available.

4. Presence

The "natural responses of human and environment to each other" (Sheridan 1996) can be considered a definition of the Presence concept, and the most suitable summary of the sense of Presence is the sensation of "being there" (Ijsselsteijn & Riva, 2003) without physically being in a precise physical place. In a Virtual Environment the sensation of being inside the environment depends on different factors. Within DiFac, the factors were analysed according to the activities to be developed: training, product development and factory design.

Inside the perceptual features important are the graphic vividness, the interactivity and control of the entire environment and its elements. Since the sense of Presence has a strong personal aspect, there are many individual factors: the imagination and suspension of disbelief; identification; personal motivations and goals; and emotional state during the precise moment in which the customer uses the environment. The content of the environment and the story are very important for involvement with the environment, and linked to this, are the social and cultural aspects (Riva, 2008). On this basis, we defined the requirements for different project environments. However, the innovation of DiFac is the measurement methodology. Presence can be measured using many modalities that can be divided into two main areas: subjective and objective. The first evaluates the personal experience in utilizing the environment with a questionnaire, the second calculates an objective amount of data while the user experiments with the environment (e.g. heart beating, blood pressure…)

The innovation of the project is the use of a psychological theory called "Flow" by Csikszentmihalyi (1996). Flow is a subjective state that people report when they are completely involved in a task to the point of forgetting time, fatigue, and everything else but the activity itself. "You're right in the work, you lose your sense of time, you're completely enraptured, you're completely caught up in what you are doing [...] when you are working on something and you are working well, you have the feeling that there's no other way of saying what you're saying" (Csikszentmihalyi, 1996). The intense experiential involvement of Flow is responsible for three subjective characteristics commonly reported: the merging of action and awareness, a sense of control and an altered sense of time.

The state of Flow can be experienced in different fields and doing various activities, but it has always these characteristics:

- flow tends to occur when the activity one engages in contains a clear set of goals

- flow results from a balance between perceived challenges and perceived skills
- when perceived challenges and skills are well matched attention is completely absorbed
- flow is dependent on the presence of clear and immediate feedback

Having these features in a VE should ensure the success of the work to be done in the synthetic environment (Riva, 2008).

DiFac linked Presence and Optimal Experience detected in "classical" Presence factors to determine the sense of being in the environment, and the Flow state to establish the quality of the experience and consequently understand if the use of the virtual environment was near to the Optimal Experience. During the project time framework a new questionnaire was written by merging questions from the Witmer & Singer Presence Questionnaire and the Flow Questionnaire applying to the Virtual Reality a methodology already consolidated for identifying experience in real world. Furthermore the questionnaire checks the balance between skills and challenges, two main components for reaching the optimal state and the disorientation level.

4.1 Method

The questionnaire was scientifically validated as a PhD study in three steps. This first step, was to evaluate a questionnaire initially composed of 135 questions, with a sample of 400 participants (200 male - 200 female) between 18 and 35 years old. Each participant was tested immediately after a set of experiences with various levels of Presence and Flow:

- reading a narrative description of a tennis match
- watching a television programme of a tennis match
- playing a tennis game using a static system console
- playing a tennis game using a dynamic system console: Nintendo Wii TM.

At the end of each trial the participant filled in the questionnaire. The collected data was analysed with SPSS software. It revealed the structural relation among the constructs, and reduced the number of questions to 40. The 40 item questionnaire, now called *Flow for Presence Questionnaire,* was evaluated with a further 100 participants (50 male - 50 female). Each participant experienced a session in an immersive VE of an imaginary city. During the trial, participants completed the questionnaire.

During the third and final study, a sample of 90 participants (45 male - 45 female) was divided into three groups: 30 for each. The VE representing an imaginary city was presented to each group in three different versions: low/media quality and interaction; middle quality and interaction; and high/media quality and interaction. Each participant navigated around the environment for around 15 minutes. The objective of the third study was to verify at different levels of the manipulate variable (media-interaction) the different scores of Presence and Flow using the Flow for Presence questionnaire. Further test wass the use of a portable mini ECG for measuring some objective data. This last study phase is still on going.

4.2 Example Application: the Factory Constructor Case

The Factory Constructor (FC) is a VE that allows the re-planning of an existing shop floor or the design of a new one. The results were collected in Italy with ten users and in Korea with a further 20. The users answered the questionnaire after 15 minutes trial.

Since the Likert scale used was from 1 to 5, where 1 is the lowest grade and 5 is the highest, **3** is the border between the negative and positive score.

The General Index Evaluation Experience is 4,59. This value is linked both to Flow and Presence evaluation. The subject shows here the wish to repeat the experience. It refers to the desire to repeat the experience. The repetitive rate is higher than 3, the environment is good. People enjoyed themselves using the environment: doing their duty easier in a relaxed state.

The Flow General Index is 0,72. This index should be between -1 (poor) and 1 (good). The subjectss experienced a sufficient level of Flow state and this helped the learning/commitment phase (Riva, 2008). The balance between Skill and Challenge is fundamental for the Optimal Experience. The values must be more than 3 to have a good rate. As the **Skills value is 2,83** and **Challenges is 3.55**, the users were a little anxious during the test, as shown in Figure 2 below.

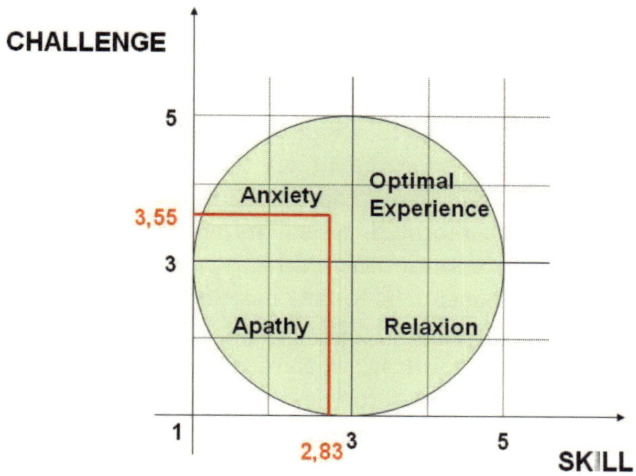

Fig. 2. Users' state based on skill and challenges values during FC test

For keeping a high level of interest, skills and challenges should be balanced. Skills of the FC appear a little low because the subjects were people with no professional need to use the VE and therefore they were expected to have a higher level of difficulty as they did not have the basic skills required for the activities. The technician in a real situation faced with a real production line, real machinery, real people and the economic implications of their decisions, can have a high stress factor and carrying out these activities in a VE could reduce this.

The Presence General Index is 3,69. The sense of being in the VE was quite good, with the value being higher than 3. The subjects felt a good emotional state using the VE, well balanced between personal internal state as influenced by the external environment.

The Disorientation level changes depending on the type of VE. Whenever the environment is immersive, the disorientation level can depend on the hardware (helmet, gloves, glasses…) and personal vestibule system sensitivity. The **disorientation value for the FC is 1,32**. The low score is mostly because the test was made on PC (both desk- and lap-top PC) and not using any immersive hardware. Finally the Coping is strictly linked to the ability to manage unforeseen situations. This value indicates the subject's ability to find the solution in front of unexpected situations or problems. This can be useful for evaluating the interface and the level of the friendly use of it. **The Coping rate was 3,39,** indicating that the instruction section was easy and generally intuitive.

4.3 Conclusions and further development

The *Flow for Presence Questionnaire* can be used step-by-step in a VE development process improving the environment in a loop process, by implementing the critical elements and increasing iteratively the sense of Presence and Flow. Through the iPortal the user can have the questionnaire translated in different languages, and the Excel file containing the questionnaire generates values and a document for understanding them. One of the most interesting aspects of the questionnaire is that even a manager can obtain useful information from the numbers and evaluate the VE and workers' well-being.

5. Collaboration

Collaboration has been defined as "the process of shared creation: two or more individuals with complementary skills interacting to create a shared understanding that none had previously possessed or could have come to on their own" (Schrage, 1990). Through collaborative working practices, a shared meaning can be created about a process, product or event. Collaboration can be co-located, when individuals work together in the same physical space and are able to communicate directly, or remote where individuals are geographically distributed and hence face-to-face meetings may not be possible. A further distinction is one of time: synchronous collaboration is when information is exchanged immediately (e.g. face to face meeting, instant messaging); asynchronous involves collaborative working but at different times (e.g. email, voicemail). Computer mediated communication tools can be used to support coordination and collaboration between geographically dispersed members of a team to coordinate their individual efforts and inputs (Saikayasit, 2008).

An aim of DiFac was to support the future manufacturing plant in a distributed, collaborative working environment, in recognition of the importance of this type of work in today's business climate (DiFac consortium, 2006). To achieve this, seamless collaboration is required amongst workers, machines, suppliers and customers, regardless of their physical location. The tools were required to support distributed design and manufacture, information sharing, decision making and project management, all tasks which require effective collaboration. The project provided an ideal opportunity to test a new questionnaire developed at the University of Nottingham for evaluating the collaboration aspects of new technologies.

5.1 Method

The collaboration questionnaire applied to DiFac was developed at the University of Nottingham in recognition of the lack of existing, validated methods for evaluating collaborative features on emergent technologies (Saikayasit, 2008). It was developed for evaluating the collaborative features provided by tools, and for evaluating the extent of the collaboration these features support. The questionnaire was created such that it could be applied to any collaborative system, yet provide a score on the same scale. It was initially developed through literature and focus groupswith Human Factors experts who were asked to list 10 of the following:

- key functions which collaborative technologies should support
- factors which may result in effective collaboration
- factors which may result in ineffective collaboration

They were then asked to rank the factors from most important to least important. The results of this study were used to formulate an 11-item questionnaire, which can be used to evaluate collaboration. An extract from the questionnaire is shown in Figure 3.

	Strongly disagree	Disagree	Neutral	Agree	Strongly agree
1. The system allowed me to locate other users easily					
2. The system allowed me to identify other users easily					

Fig. 3. Extract from the collaboration questionnaire (Saikayasit, 2008)

The questionnaire was administered in a user-trial of the DiFac technologies. Initially, key features of each technology were demonstrated by a DiFac representative. Thereafter, the participants were given time to explore the systems before being asked to attempt a list of tasks which were typical of the anticipated end-use of the given technology. These included collaborative tasks, where appropriate. Thereafter, the users were asked to complete the collaboration questionnaire for each of the tools.

5.2 Results

The results focus on the utility of the collaboration questionnaire for evaluating new technologies, rather than an evaluation of the collaborative features and support for these offered by the tools.

Firstly, the administration of the questionnaire was simple. It was printed onto 1 A4 sheet, and took less than 5 minutes to complete per technology. The 5-point scale was easy to understand, and complete.

Analysis of the ratings was also straightforward. Median ratings were used for each question. A graph of these can be used to rapidly identify problem areas. For example, Figure 4 shows the results from an early evaluation of the iPortal. It is clear that, in particular, questions 6 and 7 (relating to awareness of others' actions and indicating a location on a shared file) require improvement.

Unfortunately, one potential issue arises as a result of the simplicity of the questionnaire. The evaluation criteria (and questions) are the same for all technologies. However, the type of collaboration required for an expert and novice emergency training simulator is different to that for a product design tool. In the DiFac application, this led to some confusion as some of the tools received a poor score for one or more aspects of collaboration, but in reality the Human Factors specialists recognised that these were not necessary for the type of collaboration required by the tool. Therefore, the effects of this problem can be mitigated through expert analysis of the results.

A problem experienced as part of the evaluation, but not strictly related to the questionnaire, was that quite often the collaboration features did not work on the prototype technologies when tested away from the development partners' sites. This was partly due to different operating systems, and as a result it was difficult to explore fully the collaborative nature of the system..

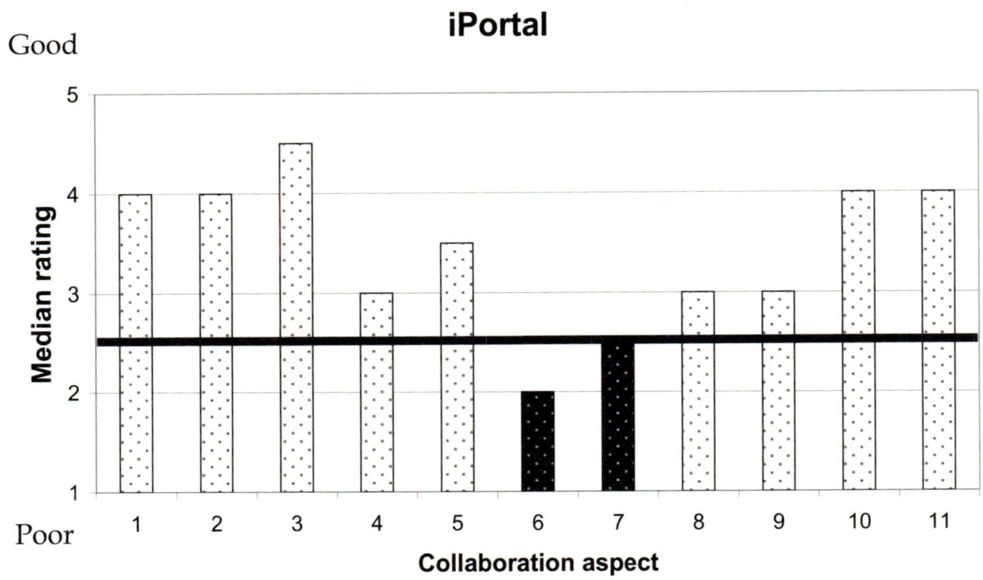

Fig. 4. Example results from an interim application of the collaboration questionnaire

5.3 Conclusions

The collaboration questionnaire (Saikayasit, 2008) was a useful tool in the development of the DiFac technologies. It was quick to administer, easy for participants to understand, yet enabled simple identification of the aspects of collaboration receiving a poor score. It was found to be improved through expert input, in particular if an aspect of collaboration which was poorly rated was not necessary for the application. Future research could enhance this aspect of the tool, for example by clarifying the types of collaborative tasks for which the questionnaire is most suitable.

6. DiFac Integrated Scenario

The following section presents a concrete scenario to illustrate the use of the DiFac toolset. It concerns the design and production of a new customised laser cutting machine.

The following hypothetic companies are the participants of the Integrated Scenario, although they mirror the real enterprise partners of the DiFac consortium:

- SECONDA company which is a laser machine producer (in the consortium PRIMA INDUSTRIE is an Italian producer of 2D and 3D laser cutting machines)
- PACOM company, a customer interested in purchasing a cutting laser cell (COMPA is a Romanian automotive industry)
- A new IT company providing the DiFac Solution. This is composed of the R&D DiFac partners, who worked on the different solutions, headed by ROPARDO, who developed DiFac iPortal.

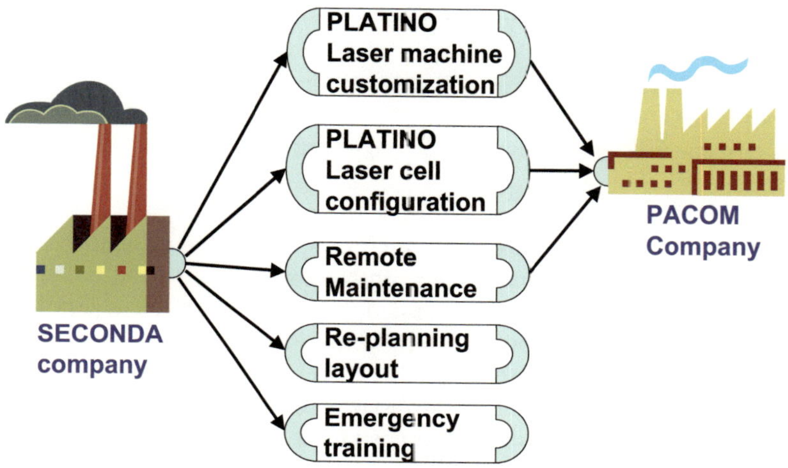

Fig. 5. Integrated scenario sub projects

Here follows the story of the scenario. PACOM orders a new laser cell from SECONDA. The order is composed of a PLATINO laser cutting machine which has to be customized in order to meet special customer's needs.

The SECONDA general manger, taking advantage of collaborative, presence and ergonomics features provided by the DiFac solution, creates a new internal project whose main goal is to design and assemble the new laser cell named "*New PLATINO laser cutting cell.*" For producing the new Platino machine, there are three main goals to be reached: design a customized Platino cutting laser machine, design the laser cutting cell and consequence of the new product, and re-plan some parts of the actual shop floor.

When the design phase starts, two designers in different locations work on the design of the laser machinery in a collaborative way in real time. They develop two different possibilities, which are presented to the General Manager. To help decide which design to progress, the designer starts an evaluation session using the DiFac decision support system. This includes evaluation criteria including for example, weight, benefits and costs. The team members (General Manager, Assembly Engineer, Designer and Factory Planner) rate the design against these criteria, to help support the decision-making process. When the selected design is sent to the production sector, there are implications for the production process due to the modified components. To better assess these implications, the process is analysed with Factory Constructor. The new shop floor can be visualized in an intuitive and user-friendly way thanks to the Presence evaluation done during its development. The workers

can verify the effective ergonomics of their own workstation and give back some suggestions to the Factory Planner. The proposed new layout passes through a web-based simulation tool that detects a bottle-neck in the production line. This is used to identify a solution, implemented by the Factory Planner.
Since the shop floor has been re-planned, it is very important that workers are retrained to manage emergency situations. This is achieved through a simulation environment, in which workers can learn emergency response procedures.
The virtual prototype design tool allows the project manager to present the new machine to the customer who can make some changes in collaboration with the project designer. When the machine has been settled at PACOM, the DiFac system provides the maintenance procedures. The customized maintenance procedures, modified for the personalized Platino machine, can be uploaded on the iPortal to provide an efficient remote maintenance service. A technician is available for specific remote maintenance services using the Augmented Reality techniques.
The integrated scenario has been written as a test bed for DiFac solutions. It demonstrates the following aspects:

- The DiFac solution supports group work in an immersive and interactive way, for concurrent product design, factory design and optimisation as well as worker training in dangerous moments or for machine maintenance.
- The various partners' results are integrated into a comprehensive solution: changes in the data handled by a component are reflected in other components and data can be exchanged between the software tools where it is needed.
- The outcomes of the 3 pillars (i.e. Presence, Collaboration and Ergonomics) have increased the tools' functionalities, composing the DiFac solution, from the key pillars of collaboration, presence and ergonomics
- DiFac solution is modular and scalable

7. Conclusion

The DiFac project has concentrated its attention on the realisation of the "digital factory" tools taking into consideration human aspects. This paper has presented the three main pillars above which the framework is built: ergonomics, presence and collaboration are considered to be the foundation for human oriented production systems. In building up the environments for training, product development or production design the three pillars were analysed and specific methodologies and guidelines developed.
The first application of the presented methodologies gave a positive score in the evaluation of the environments. The validation process was also conducted in order to collect external industrial's evaluations.
The complete solution will be soon available trough the DiFac iPortal, where the users can use the project pillars as integrated part of the Software solutions for better customization of their results.

8. References

Beynon-Davies, P. (1999). Human error and information systems failure: The case of the London ambulance service computer-aided dispatch system project. *Interacting with Computers,* 11(6), pp. 699-720.

Brooke, J. 1996. SUS: A Quick and Dirty Usability Scale. In: *Usability Evaluation in Industry,* Jordan, P.W., Thomas, B., Weerdmeester, B.A, McClelland, I.L. (Eds), pp189-194, Taylor and Francis, ISBN: 978-0748404605, London

Chaffin, D.B. (2001). *Digital human modelling for vehicle and workplace design.* Society for Automotive Engineers, ISBN: 978-0-7680-0687-2, Warrendale, PA

Chryssolouris G., Pappas M., Karabatsou V., Mavrikios D. and Alexopoulos K., "A Shared VE for Collaborative Product Development in Manufacturing Enterprises", *Collaborative Product Design and Manufacturing Methodologies and Applications* (ISBN: 978-1-84628-801-2), Li W.D., Ong S.K., Nee A.Y.C. and McMahon C. (Eds.), Springer Series in Advanced Manufacturing, Springer-Verlag, London (April 2007).

Consoni Florenzano Souza, M., Sacco, M., Vieira Porto, A.J. (2006), Virtual manufacturing as a way for the Factory of the Future. *Special issue on E-Manufacturing and web-based technology for intelligent manufacturing and networked enterprise interoperability, Journal of Intelligent Manufacturing,* 17/6, Springer Verlag, ISSN 0956-5515.

Csikszentmihalyi, M., (1996). *Creativity: Flow and the psychology of discovery and invention.* New York: Harper Collins

Csikszentmihalyi, M., Beyond (1977). *Boredom and Anxiety, second printing.* San Francisco Jossey-Bass

Csikszentmihalyi, M., and LeFevre, J. (1989). Optimal Experience in Work and Leisure, *Journal of Personality and Social Psychology,* 56 (5), 815-822.

DiFac consortium (2007). *DiFac project brochure,*

DiFac consortium (2006). Annex I - "Description of Work". IST5-035079.

Eason, K.D. (1997). Understanding the organizational ramifications of implementing information technology systems. *In: Handbook of Human-Computer Interaction,* M. Helander, T. Landauer, P. Prabhu (Eds), pp.1475-1495 (2nd ed), Elsevier, ISBN 0-444-81876-6, Amsterdam

EC (2006). *Manufuture: Strategic Research Agenda, report of the high-level group,*

EC (2006). *Future of Manufacturing In Europe 2015-2020 – the challenge for sustainable development*

Hoffman, D.L., Kalsbeek, W.D., and Novak T.P. (1996). Internet and Web Use in the United States: Baselines for Commercial Development, Special Section on *Internet in the Home,* Communications of the ACM, 39 (December), 36-46.

Ijsselsteijn, W., Riva, G. (2003). Being There: The experience of presence in mediated environments, *Being There: Concepts, effects and measurement of user presence in synthetic environments,* G. Riva, F. Davide, W.A IJsselsteijn (Eds.) Ios Press, Amsterdam, The Netherlands

Laughery, R., (2005). Simulation and modelling for analysing human performance. In: *Evaluation of Human Work,* Wilson, J. R. and Corlett, N. (Eds.), Taylor and Francis, pp. 219-238, ISBN 978-0-415-26757-1, London.

Lawson, G., D'cruz, M., Wilson, J.R., Smith, S., Bourguignon, D., Pentenrieder, K. & Pavlopoulos, C. (2006). *D3 Ergonomic requirements for human safety and productivity.* DiFac IST5-035079. Nottingham: The University of Nottingham.

Mancini, F., Viganò, G., Liao, Z., Sacco, M., Boër, C.R. (2004). The Virtual Factory: A Semi-immersive Interactive 3D Environment. *SCSC 2004, Summer Computer Simulation Conference*, San Jose, CA, USA.

Pappas M., Karabatsou V., Mavrikios D. and Chryssolouris G. (2006) "Development of a web-based collaboration platform for manufacturing product and process design evaluation using virtual reality techniques", *International Journal of Computer Integrated Manufacturing*, (Vol. 19, No. 8, Dec. 2006), pp. 805-814.

Riva, G., (2008) Psicologia dei nuovi media, il Mulino ed.,

Saikayasit, R. (2008) *Supporting distributed collaboration.* Internal report, University of Nottingham, Nottingham.

Schrage, M (1990). *Shared Minds: The New Technologies of Collaboration,* Random House, ISBN: 978-0394565873, New York

Sheridan, T., B, (1996). Further Musings on the Psychophysics of Presence. *Presence: Teleoperators and Virtual Environments* 5(2): 241-246

Stanton, N., Salmon, P., Walker, G., Baber, C., Jenkins, D. (2005). *Human Factors Methods: A Practical Guide for Engineering and Design.* Ashagate Publishing Ltd., ISBN: 978-0754646617, Hampshire, England

Tromp, J.G. and Nichols, S., (2003). VIEW-IT: A VR/CAD Inspection Tool for use in Industry. *Proceedings of 10th International Conference on Human-Computer Interaction,* Crete, Greece, June 2003, Lawrence Erlbaum, London.

UK National Audit Office, (1999). *The Passport Delays of Summer 1999.* Report by the Comptroller and Auditor General, 27th October. London: The Stationery Office.

UK Public Accounts Committee, (2000). Improving the Delivery of Government IT Projects. House of Commons, London.

Vink, P., Nichols S., and Davies R.C. (2005). Participatory Ergonomics and Comfort. In: *Comfort and Design*, P.Vink (Ed), pp. 41-54, CRC Press, ISBN: 0-8493-2830-6, Florida

Wastell, D.G. and Cooper, C.L., (1996). Stress and technological innovation: A comparative study of design practices and implementation strategies. *European Journal of Work and Organizational Psychology*, 5, pp. 377-397.

Wellington, SB. (2006) Poor requirements-defintion equals ICT failure. *Computerworld,* 9 November, 2006

Wilson, J. R. (2005). Methods in the understanding of human factors, In: *Evaluation of Human Work,* Wilson, J. R. and Corlett, N. (Eds.), Taylor and Francis, pp. 1-31, ISBN 978-0-415-26757-1, London.

Witmer, B. G., & Singer, M. J., (1998). Measuring presence in virtual environments: A presence questionnaire. *Presence: Teleoperators and Virtual Environments, 7,* 225-240

Web Users' Implicit Feedback Inference Based on Amount of Simple Interaction Logs at Browser Side

Jinhyuk Choi and Geehyuk Lee
Korea Advanced Institute of Science and Technology
Republic of Korea

1. Introduction

In order to provide personalized service to web users, the first thing to do is to find the web pages that contain interesting and useful contents among all visited web pages. So far, many researchers have attempted to do the task using various usage logs – viewing time, scrolling, bookmarking, saving, printing and so on - that can be collected without notice to users while they visit web pages. Consequently, it has been important things for many researchers to find useful logs that indicate users' interest level efficiently. However, it is still challengeable to find useful logs that can be considered as good implicit interest indicators. In other words, we need an efficient and effective method to elicit users' interest implicitly under current web environments. In addition, although a lot of researchers have focused on implicit elicitation of users' interest level for contents of web pages, many other influential factors that may make users interact with web pages have been also investigated [Kelly, 2004; Fogg et al., 2003; Wathen & Burkell, 2002; Chi et al., 2001; Kim & Allen, 2002; Kellar et al., 2007; Rieh, 2002]. For examples, users may show more interactions on web pages that contain difficult or even on web pages that have more complex layout structures irrespective of interest level. Therefore, various other influential factors also should be investigated carefully. As we can see in figure 1, it is necessary to analyze the factors and usage logs to understand web usage patterns. We are going to find various influential factors that can be identified by computer system while users browse the web.
To find the factors correctly, it is also important to develop a tool to assess users' feedbacks about a web page. Such tools may run on the browser-side or on the server-side, but we are more interested in browser-side tools because they do not restrict information sources to a specific website and also because they can derive timely information from dynamic web sites whose contents may change frequently. One of the important requirements of a good browser-side

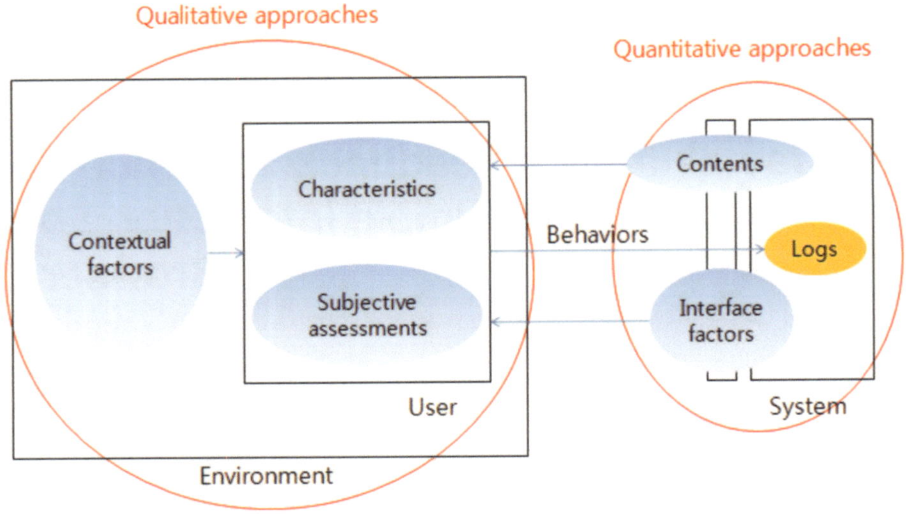

Fig. 1. The concept of influential factor analysis based on interaction logs

tool is that it should preserve the web browsing environment as much as possible, which in turn means that it should not depend too much on the implementation details of diverse web browsers. We supposed that one of such tools for monitoring users' interests may be built simply based on the amount of processed Windows GUI messages while users are reading a web page.

In these perspectives, we designed several experiments to see whether influences of the factors can be inferred based on the Windows GUI messages efficiently at browser side. We also built a software module, called the Browser Monitoring Module (BMM), which runs behind the Internet Explorer and counts Windows GUI messages. Our experimental results showed that the amount of message traffic, though it may sound simplistic, is indeed an effective indicator of users' interests about a web page and some influential factors. Therefore, we concluded that we can use the BMM for our future designs of various user-adaptive services, for example, personalized web browsers, personalized search engines, recommendation systems web usage mining, and so on.

2. Related work

Many studies have implicitly measured web users' interest. Server-side analyses have shown good performance and have been successfully applied to consumer analyses of commercial web sites. The users' interest at the server-side can be analyzed more easily because relevant information can be found in log files maintained by the server. For example, from the log file, the users' login/logout time, the web pages that users have visited, users' IP addresses, and so on can be obtained. However, the server-side analysis has critical limitations - only users on a specific site can be analyzed and the contents of a server are not sufficient to construct a general user model. On the other hand, through a browser-side analysis, the users' interest can be analyzed from various sites and a user model can be constructed using a wealth of information. Therefore, many researchers have focused on browser-side analyses. However, this form of analysis also brings forth certain challenges, largely because there are no standardized methods to determine what users' activities are relevant to users' interests. Finding relevant activities is important in that an explicit user feedback method (e.g.: think aloud protocol, post interview) cannot be applied in natural web browsing environments.

In order to predict users' interest implicitly at the browser side, a modified web browser was built [Claypool et al., 2001]. This browser monitors the number of mouse clicks, mouse movement, the scrolling amount, and the elapse time on a page. From this method, it was found that a user's interest for contents of a web page is correlated not with a unit activity but a combination of several activities. However, with regard to measuring the amount of scrolling, the authors counted only the number of mouse clicks on the scrollbars and measured the duration of scrollbar usage. However, users may also use up/down keys or a mouse wheel to scroll the windows. In [Goecks & Shavlik, 2000], the authors measured the number of command-state changes to detect scroll activity and assessed status-bar-text changes for mouse activity. Changes may occur according to the activities but they may also arise by performing a different activity. In [Hijikata, 2004], the authors collected the results of several activities for analyzing user behaviors but the methods of detecting the activities were not described in detail. In [Reeder et al., 2000], the authors built Weblogger, a tool to detect several activities on Internet Explorer. However, the detection of all events from a browser is not an easy task. In [Kelly & Belkin, 2004], the method of using the length of time a user views a document in his/her web browser as implicit feedback was investigated and their conclusion was that there is no significant relationship between display time and document preference. However, they only addressed display time. In [Seo & Zhang, 2000], the authors used bookmarking as a relevant activity, but this approach is inadequate for dynamic websites whose contents may change frequently.

In numerous studies, the activities during task-oriented web browsing, such as using search engines, information seeking, and problem solving, exert been analyzed. For example, in [Badi et al., 2006], the authors analyzed various user activities and document properties, but their focus was limited to organize some links for class material as high school teacher. Users browse the web not only for searching important information but also for entertainment or distraction. In other words, one of the purposes of web browsing is merely to seek enjoyment.

Moreover, other factors that may have influences on users' activities have been studied. The factors may belong to one of three categories - contents attributes, user characteristics, and context. As one of the factors in contents attributes, in [Kelly, 2004], the familiarity of topics has been discussed and in [Fogg et al., 2003; Wathen & Burkell, 2002], information credibility has been considered and important factors of credibility were suggested. Information scent [Chi et al., 2001] has been understood as an influential factor on user activities and cognitive authority and information quality were also suggested [Rieh, 2002]. Structural complexity and reading pattern are still on debate. For user characteristics, cognitive style and problem solving style were studied [Kim & Allen, 2002]. Context factor that has been mostly discussed was user's task at hand [Kellar et al., 2007]. And finally, in [Kelly & Belkin, 2004], the relationships between display time and various factors - task, topic, usefulness, endurance, frequency, stage, persistence, familiarity, and retention were investigated. However, in spite of the fact that there are many factors that may have influences on users' activities, the previous researches have mostly focused on interest.

3. Our approach

We analyzed several methods that have been proposed thus far in order to identify some requirements. First, web user analyses should be conducted at the browser side and in a real time manner. In addition, it is necessary to find simple but effective methods for detecting user activities that can be used as a measure of interest and influences of other factors with minimal unnatural change to the web-browsing environment. The last aspect is that evaluation of the proposed method should be conducted with natural tasks such that users read web pages without any specific goals in mind. To meet these requirements, BMM detects Windows GUI messages while users are reading web pages and thus it is possible to measure user activities in real time without any interruption to the users. We also evaluated the proposed method under a natural web browsing environment in which users could read web pages of various topics in a desired manner.

3.1 Simple log data at a browser side

In order to analyze users' implicit interest at the browser side, we have to monitor several usage logs, for example, the viewing time, scroll movement, sequences of visited URLs, keyboard typing, and so on. In our research, we have chosen several usage logs to record while users view different Web pages. The viewing time that has mainly been investigated in the related researches so far is the time during which users remain on a particular web page. The mouse wheel counts the number of WM-MOUSEWHEEL messages. For mouse and scrollbar movement, we measured the distance between two consecutive positions of the mouse cursor and scroll bar at regular intervals and summed the distances. We also counted the number of processed WM-PAINT messages, as WM-PAINT messages are processed when users change the size of their browser window, scroll within the window, move their mouse cursor, and so on. The number of mouse clicks and keyboard typing were also considered. We believe that these activities are good indicators of user interest regarding the contents of Web pages. We have chosen these logs because they can be measured without much effort. However, for scroll movement, we were unable to obtain the position of the scrollbar on some of the Web pages, and the WM-PAINT messages can be affected by the dynamic content of certain Web pages. This means that we have to be careful when using these data as logs for measuring user activities. We did not record some of the behaviors that have been considered by other researches - bookmarking, saving, printing, and coping and pasting - because users do not always show those behaviors on every valuable Web page, and hence their records do not suit our purpose. We collected some physical data of Web pages - the scroll height and file size - of each visited Web page.

3.2 Various subjective feedbacks

There are several factors that make users interact with web pages. For example, a user may stay for relatively long time at a specific web page because there are interesting contents or the user feels that the contents are more difficult than others. Sometimes the user may roll the mouse wheel more frequently on one Web page than on others because it may not easy for him/her to find necessary information from the pages. Therefore, we selected some factors that may exert an influence on user interactions with web pages - interest, credibility, complexity, and difficulty. Because these factors are inherently subjective and cannot be measured with only usage logs, we collected various types of feedback regarding the current context directly from users.

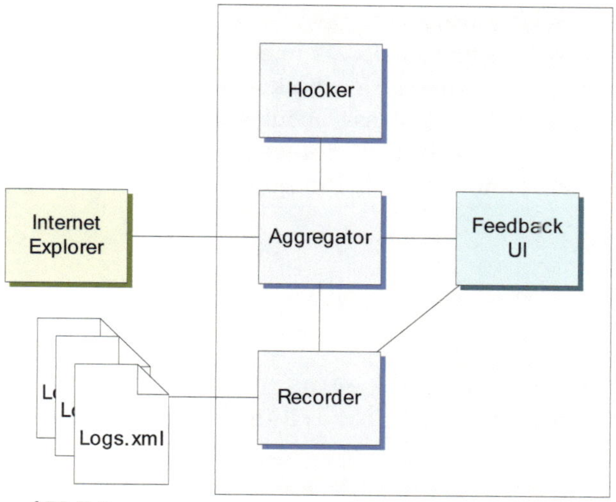

Fig. 2. The structure of BMM

3.3 Data logging software – Browser monitoring module (BMM)

In some of the previous researches, custom-built browsers have been used [Kellar et al., 2007], as have some specialized logging software that works "in stealth mode" [Kelly & Belkin, 2004]. Although there are several merits in using custom-built browsers, because various data can be collected easily, we developed a browser-monitoring module (BMM) that runs behind Internet Explorer without any modification to the browser, as we wanted to preserve the natural state of the Web browsing environment as much as possible.

BMM is a type of monitoring software that was developed to detect Windows GUI messages while users read Web pages, and thus it is possible to measure user activities in real-time without any interruption to the users. BMM uses a global hooker library, written in C++, which runs in the background and hooks all Windows operating system events. In addition, using Windows Shell API, BMM can collect all instances of currently running Internet Explorers through the COM object. In addition, necessary properties of Web pages can be obtained from the COM object. BMM is written in C#, running under a Windows platform with .NET Framework 2.0.

BMM consists of four components - hooker, data recorder, data aggregator, and feedback window. The data to hook are the number of keys pressed, events of program focus changes, number of WM_PAINT events, mouse click and mouse wheel messages, and so on. Basically, the hooker catches every message passed within the operating system, so we should filter out irrelevant messages to record only necessary data for our studies. For instance, because a WM_PAINT message is invoked whenever the O/S needs to re-draw some parts of a window, we have to be able to ignore the messages from unfocused windows and count the number of messages that are invoked for only the currently focused browser window. The aggregator can acquire several properties of web pages by using a Document Object Model (DOM). Acquired properties are the viewing size of a document (in pixels), file size (in bytes), current location of the scrollbar, and character set of the page. The location of scroll bar is periodically updated so that the total displacement of the scrollbar can be estimated. However, a critical issue arises at several 'fancy' Web pages that have different structures from standard Web documents, eventually yielding no data while accessing the DOM property. The data aggregator also aggregates all data from these multiple components, and the data recorder stores the aggregated data in a human-readable XML format for future analysis. After Web searching, using the feedback window, users can review the visited Web pages and choose radio buttons that ask about several types of assessments about the contents of each Web page. If the users do not want to answer questions regarding some of the Web pages, they can even remove the records easily. In figure 2, the structure of the BMM is shown.

4. Experiment 1

4.1 Procedures

In the first experiment, we analyzed viewing time and 3 GUI messages - WM_PAINT, WM_MOUSEWHEEL, and WM_MOUSEMOVE - and formulated the following hypotheses.

1. The number of processed GUI messages is relatively higher on web pages that contain interesting contents.
2. The amount of information in a web page affects the number of processed GUI messages.

Under the above assumptions, we conducted experiments to verify the positive relationship between the amount of processed GUI messages and users' interest for the content. First, we collected 120 text-based web pages offering information on various topics – Politics, Economics, Education, Engineering, Entertainment, Science, Health, and Sports – with varying content size. 25 subjects read each page in their own desired manner. To obtain appropriate data, the subjects were not told that some activities would be measured while they read the web pages. During the experiments, user activities while reading a web page and some measurable data were recorded in a log file for future analysis. In addition, whenever a subject finished reading a web page, a small window appeared wherein the


```
<BMMDataTable>
  <Site>http://www.google.com/</Site>
  <StartTime>08-04-03 01:21:59</StartTime>
  <EndTime>08-04-03 01:22:11</EndTime>
  <Time>12.0625</Time>
  <MouseMove>1156.72067255927</MouseMove>
  <MouseClick>2</MouseClick>
  <MouseWheel>2</MouseWheel>
  <KeyPress>0</KeyPress>
  <Scrollbar>35</Scrollbar>
  <WMPaint>305</WMPaint>
  <DocumentSize>1712240</DocumentSize>
  <FileSize>245</FileSize>
  <Interest>4</Interest>
  <Credibility>4</Credibility>
  <Complexity>3</ Complexity >
  <Difficulty>2</ Difficulty>
</BMMDataTable>
```


Fig. 3. An example log record produced by the Browser Monitoring Module

Message	p-value
WM_MOSEMOVE message	0.0006
WM_MOUSEWHEEL message	0.000036
WM-PAINT message	0.000013
Viewing time	0.00000032

Table 1. Results of statistical significance analysis. The p-value shows us that there is a strong relationship between the number of each message and interest level.

subject recorded his/her interest and preference level for the contents of the page. There are 5 levels of interest, and subjects recorded their interest for the contents of a web page accordingly. Due to some malfunctions of the BMM in the users' browsing environment and failures to properly obtain user feedback, 5 users' log files were excluded. Therefore, we analyzed 20 users' log files.

In figure 3, an example of a log record is shown. BMM records several data - the visited URL, the number of typed keys, the number of GUI messages, file size of the web page, viewing time, and feedback levels as obtained from the user's feedback. Each element represents log data of a web page that user visited. Among these data, the number of GUI messages, the file size of the web page, viewing time, and user feedback were analyzed in this experiment.

4.2 Evaluation

The main objective of the experiment was to determine whether there is a positive relationship between the number of processed GUI messages, which is normalized by the information size, and the users' interest level. We measured the amount of users' interaction on a web page as follows.

$$U_i = \frac{w_i}{f_i}, \quad V_i = \frac{t_i}{f_i} \quad (i\text{: index of web page}) \tag{1}$$

In Eq. (1), w_i is the normalized value of the number of processed GUI messages on the i-th web page, t_i is the normalized value of the elapsed time on the i-th web page, and f_i is the file size of the i-th web page (amount of information). Because the absolute number of each user's processed messages varies according to the user's habit, we normalized each user's w_i and t_i using min-max normalization and took the average of all users' U_i and V_i according to each interest level. From figure 4 and table 1, it is observed that the users caused the browser to process more GUI messages for interesting web pages. For example, the value of U_i at interest level 5 is much higher than that of level 1 in all cases. We verified that the results are statistically significant on the basis of a one-way ANOVA test (p-value < 0.01). The pattern is most distinct in the case of WM_PAINT message - the value of U_i increases according to the interest level. We also observed that there is a strong positive relationship between the viewing time and interest level, but there remains debate as to whether viewing time can be used as a measure of interest. [Kelly & Belkin, 2004]

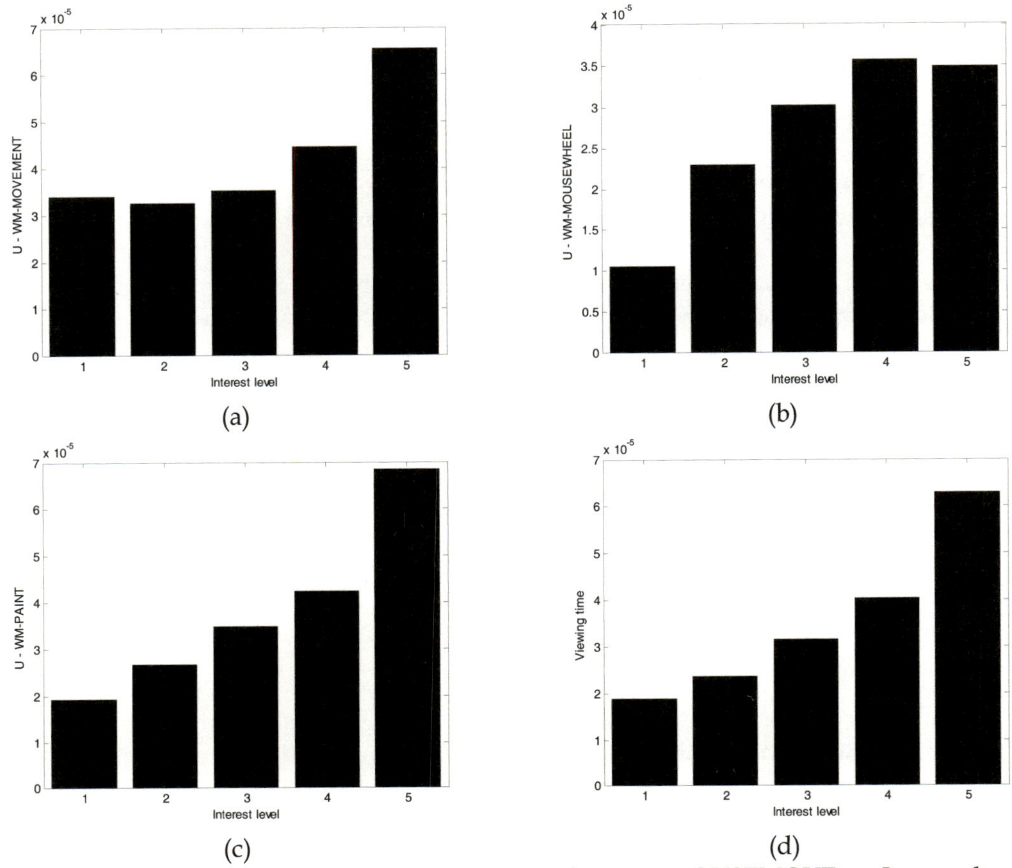

Fig. 4. Analysis of experimental result: (a) U-value for WM_MOUSEMOVE vs. Interest level, (b) U-value for WM_MOUSEWHEEL vs. Interest level, (c) U-value for WM_PAINT vs. Interest level, (d) Viewing time average vs. Interest level

4.3 Conclusion of experiment 1

In this experiment, we used the number of processed GUI messages to predict users' interest, as the messages are processed whenever users perform certain activities while reading web pages. It was found that the proposed method is simple and easy to develop while still being adequately effective. The results of our experiments showed that if a user engages in more activities that make the system process more GUI messages while reading a web page, even in the event that the page offers relatively little information, it can be inferred that the page contains interesting or preferable content. This provides an important guideline to follow, because finding preferable web pages is the first step of user modeling procedures and personalization services.

In this work, we considered only text-based web pages for ease of defining the amount of information on a web page. However, web pages contain an abundance of multimedia objects such as pictures and videos. Subsequent experiments should consider the use of a well-defined measure for the amount of information in such web pages. Also, because users' interaction is believed to be influenced by the layout of a web page, this aspect will also be taken into consideration in later works.

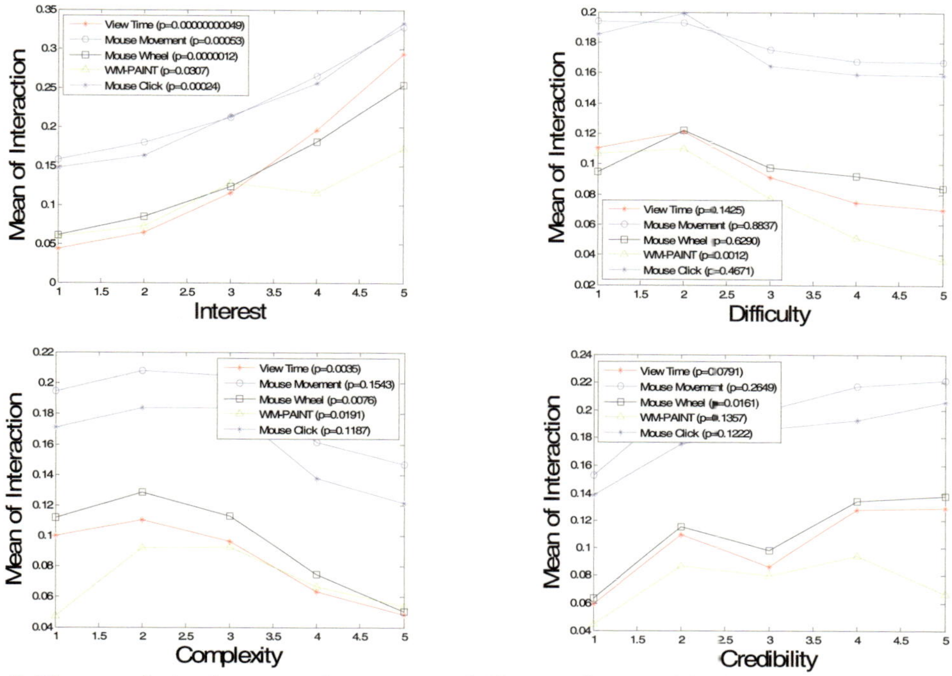

Fig. 5. The correlation between the amount of all usage logs and feedback levels

5. Additional experiment

5.1 Experiment 2

In the second experiment, we collected 160 web pages offering information on various topics - Politics, Economics, Education, Engineering, Entertainment, Science, Health, and Sports - with various content sizes in which text, images, tables and videos are all presented naturally with various layouts. 20 graduate students read each page in their own desired manner. We just gave the list of numbers to click without showing any information about the contents of web pages in advance because we want to exclude any effect of information

	Viewing time	Mouse move	Mouse click	Mouse wheel	WM-PAINT
Interest	0.771	0.545	0.686	0.559	0.507
Difficulty	-0.476	-0.340	-0.532	-0.418	-0.057
Complexity	-0.309	-0.178	-0.148	-0.196	-0.599
Credibility	0.507	0.203	0.411	0.289	0.241

Table 2. The correlation coefficients between the amount of usage logs and feedback levels - the results of the second experiment

scent [Chi et al., 2001]. To obtain appropriate data, the subjects were not told that some of activities would be recorded while they are viewing the web pages. The subjects' activities and some necessary data were recorded in a log file for future analysis. After browsing all the web pages, the subjects were instructed to review the visited web pages and answer some questions about their feedback level - interest, difficulty, complexity and credibility - in 5 point scales through the feedback window.

5.2 Experiment 3

This experiment was an extension of the previous experiments and conducted under more natural environment that subjects can do their web searching task on their own phases. The usage logs and feedbacks to record were same with the first experiment. We gave the subjects two tasks to perform. The first task is a kind of information gathering that requires accuracy, trust, efficiency, and responsibility about the search results. The subjects had to find some laboratories in universities or companies that research similar topics with the subjects' own research topics and read carefully each page to judge the relevance of the information. We encouraged the subjects to perform this task as normally as possible. The second task is a kind of information gathering and browsing that can perform without any burden or responsibility about the search results. For examples, the subjects can search some

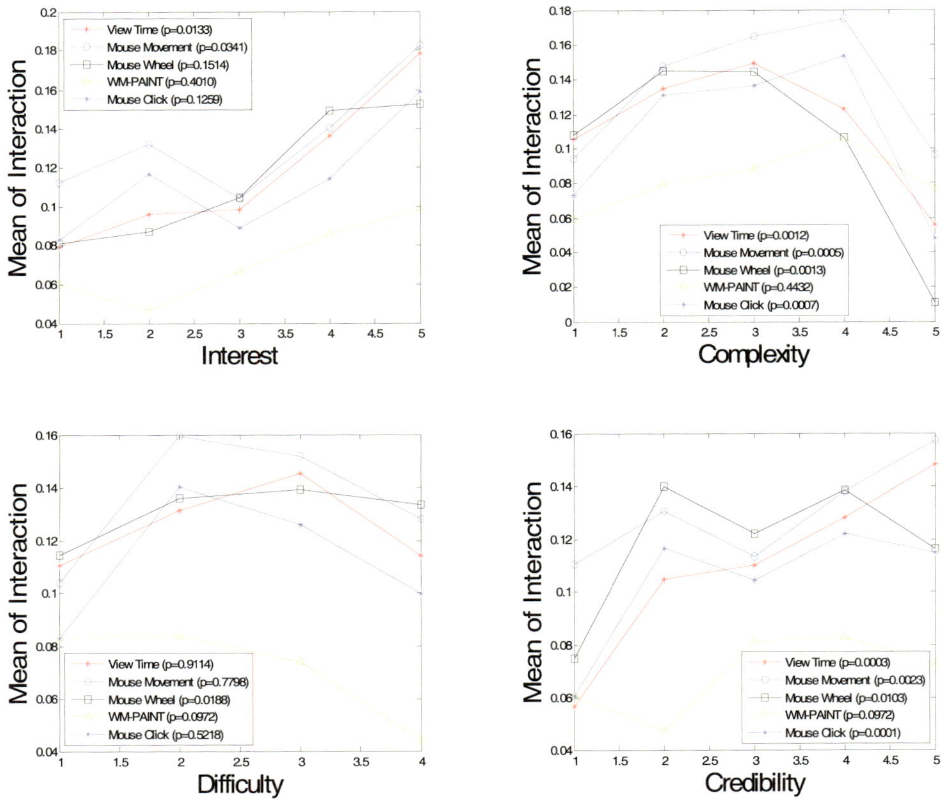

Fig. 6. The correlation between the amount of all usage logs and credibility levels

information about their hobbies, favorite products to buy, famous tourist spots, favorite sports or movie star and so on. We also encouraged the subjects to perform these tasks as normally as possible.

Differently with the first and second experiments that controlled the subjects' activities in that the subjects could only visit the collected Web pages without any pre-information clues, in this experiment, the subjects could visit any Web page that they wanted and use any search engine or portal site they wanted to use. Therefore, we observed a lot of re-visitation patterns. Thus, during the feedback phase, we let the subjects delete the logs of Web pages that they just used to find other Web pages to visit. In this way, we excluded the navigational Web pages [Fu et al., 2001].

5.3 Result of experiment 2

Actually, we thought that there are supposed to be some differences between the result patterns of the first experiment and that of the second experiment because the types of web pages are quite different. However, there were no big differences between the results. The figure 5 and table 2 shows us that there were also positive correlations between the amount of all usage logs and interest levels similarly with the results of the first experiment. In addition, we also found significant differences of the amount of usage logs among the interest levels. This means that the type of web pages is not important factor. Differently from the result of interest levels, difficulty and complexity levels showed negative correlation with the amount of usage logs. The credibility levels showed no big correlation with the amount of usage logs. From the results, we concluded that interest level has the most significant influence on the amount of usage logs and users are inclined to leave quickly web pages that have difficult contents or complex structures without much interaction.

5.4 Result of experiment 3

In figure 6 and table 3, we can see that the viewing time and the amount of mouse movement have positive correlations with the interest levels and the differences among the interest levels also statistically significant. The amount of mouse wheel, mouse clicks and processed WM_PAINT messages also showed positive correlations with interest level but the differences were not statistically significant. The amount of usage logs increased according to complexity levels but dropped steeply at level 5. The difficulty levels showed no big correlation with the amount of usage logs. The most interesting pattern that we found in the results of the third experiment was that the amount of usage logs showed positive correlation with the credibility levels and the difference of the amount of usage logs among the credibility levels were statistically significant. This result was not found in the results of the second experiment in which users browsed pre-collected web pages without proximal cues. Therefore, we concluded that the usage logs are under influences of credibility levels as well as interest levels in ordinary web browsing environments.

6. Interest level inference

Because we found that there are positive relationships between interest levels and the amount of usage logs from the results of our experiments, we used the usage logs for the training of decision trees and Bayesian networks to infer the interest levels. For construction

	Viewing time	Mouse move	Mouse click	Mouse wheel	WM-PAINT
Interest	0.396	0.301	0.119	0.245	0.229
Difficulty	0.307	0.073	-0.124	0.182	-0.330
Complexity	-0.315	-0.129	-0.533	-0.162	0.040
Credibility	0.609	0.414	0.288	0.412	0.389

Table 3. The correlation coefficients between the amount of usage logs and feedback levels - the results of the third experiment

and testing of the machine learning models, the logs were normalized to each subject's scale in order to ignore the variances that can be included due to differences in viewing style and we applied a 10-fold cross validation. Actually, it was not easy to infer 5 interest levels exactly - the classification accuracy was below 50%. Therefore, we merged levels 1 and 2 into a low-interest group and merged levels 4 and 5 into a high-interest group to see the accuracy of binary classification. The overall classification accuracy was 82% using Bayesian networks that are constructed by Simulated annealing algorithm and 84% using Decision trees.

7. Conclusion

Thus far, numerous researchers have attempted to obtain users' preferences or interests implicitly for the contents of web pages by observing their interactions on a browser. This information could then later be used for information filtering, recommendation applications, and adaptive user interfaces. However, due to the limitations of interaction channels between users and computers - i.e., only a mouse and keyboard - predicting users' interests is not an easy task.

In this chapter, we mainly used the number of processed GUI messages to predict users' interest, as the messages are processed whenever users perform certain activities while reading web pages. It was found that the proposed method is simple and easy to develop while still being adequately effective. The results of our experiments showed that if a user engages in more activities that make the system process more GUI messages while reading a web page, even in the event that the page offers relatively little information, it can be inferred that the page contains interesting or preferable content. This provides an important guideline to follow, because finding preferable web pages is the first step of user modeling procedures and personalization services.

In our first experiment in which we considered only text-based web pages, we found that if a user engages in more activities that make the system process more GUI messages while reading a web page, it can be inferred that the page contains interesting contents. In later experiments, based on new results of our extended experiments using natural web pages that contain images, frames, videos, and so on, we further confirmed that users have tendency to interact more on the interested web pages. This result looks natural and simple but it is very important fact that we can infer users' interest for web contents based on the amount of simple interaction logs that can be measured easily. The amount of log data can be measured without any modification to current browsing environments so that our method can be applied very easily.

Many previous researches [Fogg et al., 2003; Wathen & Burkell, 2002] already have focused on credibility on the web and it is currently considered as important factor to improve web environment by usability researchers, media researchers, web designers, psychologists, HCI practitioners, and so on. However, influence of the information credibility on users' interactions on web pages has not been clearly investigated. From our experimental results, we showed that users interact more on web pages that contain credible contents and the pattern may be clear in natural browsing environments. We think the results may come from the fact that users select their links using various information scents, therefore, the interest or usefulness of the contents may be partially determined in advance so that users may interact more on web pages that contain credible contents. Because current web environments give users multiple methods to find interesting contents - search engines, portal sites, commercial sites, and so on - credibility as well as interest plays an important role to make users interact with web pages. From this result, it is apparent to us that we are supposed to consider what makes the contents of web pages more credible as well as interesting in order to attract users' attention to our web sites.

Many web personalization systems make use of a user's activity logs at the web browser in order to build a user model. A user model here is simply a structured summary of web pages where a user exhibited high activity. A web personalization system then uses a user model to determine whether a new page is recommendable or not by computing content similarity between the new page and a user model. It is important to realize at this point that the high-activity web pages do not only reflect a user's topics of interest but also a user's way of assessing the credibility of a web page. If a personalization system intends to recommend a page that is both interesting and credible to a user, it should not only depend on content similarity but also utilize a user's way of assessing credibility of a web page, which can be inferred from the same web pages that provide keywords for a user model. A better user model should not only contain topic keywords but also contain page attributes that a user thinks important for a web page to be credible. In some previous researches [Fogg et al., 2003; Wathen & Burkell, 2002], several important factors for web credibility have been discovered, and we recognize easily that many of the factors cannot be explained by content similarity only. A new method to integrate the credibility factors into a recommendation model is highly desired. Currently, from this point of view, we are also carrying out some extended experiments based on long-term monitoring of over 10 subjects to verify whether we can find some relationships among activity logs, credibility levels, and some credibility factors for the purpose of developing an initial user model in which the credibility factors are also integrated.

8. References

Badi, R.; Bae, S., Moore, J. M., Meintanis, K. Marshall, C. C. (2006). Recognizing User Interest and Document Value from Reading and Organizing Activities in Document Triage, Proceedings of International Conference on Intelligent User Interfaces, pp. 218-225, Sydney, Australia, January 2006. ACM.

Chi, E. H.; Pirolli, P., Chen, K., Pitkow, J. (2001). Using information scent to model user information needs and actions and the Web, Proceedings of the SIGCHI conference on Human factors in computing systems, pp. 490-497, Seattle, Washington, United States, March 2001. ACM.

Claypool, M.; Le, P., Waseda, M., Brown, D. (2001). Implicit interest indicators, Proceedings of International Conference on Intelligent User Interfaces, pp. 33-40, Santa Fe, New Mexico, United States, January 14 ? 17. ACM.

Fogg, B. J.; Soohoo, C., Danielson, D. R.,Marable, L., Stanford, J. & Tauber, E. R. (2003). How do users evaluate the credibility of Web sites?: a study with over 2,500 participants, Proceedings of the 2003 conference on Designing for user experiences, San Francisco, California, pp. 1-15

Fu, Y.; Creado, M. & Ju C. (2001). Reorganizing web sites based on user access patterns, Proceedings of the tenth international conference on Information and knowledge management, pp. 583-585, Atlanta, Georgia, USA, October 2001. ACM.

Goecks, J. & Shavlik, J. (2000). Learning users' interests by unobtrusively observing their normal behaviour, Proceedings of International Conference on Intelligent User Interfaces, pp. 129-132, New Orleans, Louisiana, United States, January 09 ? 12, ACM.

Hijikata, Y. (2004). Implicit user profiling for on demand relevance feedback, Proceedings of International Conference on Intelligent User Interfaces, pp. 198-205, Funchal, Madeira, Portugal, January 13 ? 16, ACM.

Kellar, M.; Watters, C. & Shepherd, M. (2007). A field study characterizing Web-based information-seeking tasks, Journal of the American Society for Information Science and Technology, 58(7), pp. 999-1018, May 2007. John Wiley & Sons."

Kelly D. & Belkin N. J. (2004). Display time as implicit feedback: understanding task effects, Proceedings of the 27th annual international ACM SIGIR conference on Research and development in information retrieval, pp. 377-384, Sheffield, United Kingdom, July 2004. ACM.

Kelly, D. (2004). Understanding implicit feedback and document preference: A naturalistic user study, Ph.D. Dissertation, Rutgers University

Kim, K. & Allen, B. (2002). Cognitive and task influences on Web searching behaviour, Journal of the American Society for Information Science and Technology, 53(2), pp. 109-119, January 2002. John Wiley & Sons.

Reeder, R. W.; Pirolli, P. & Card, S. K. (2000). WebLogger: A data collections tools for Web-use studies, UIR Technical report UIR-R-2000-06 (2000), Xerox PARC.

Rieh, S. Y. (2002). Judgment of information quality and cognitive authority in the web, Journal of the American Society for Information Science and Technology, 53(2), pp. 145-161, January 2002. John Wiley & Sons.

Seo, Y. & Zhang, B. (2000). Learning user's preferences by analyzing Web-browsing behaviours, Proceedings of the fourth international conference on Autonomous agents, pp. 381-387, Barcelona, Spain, June 2000. ACM.

Wathen, C. N. & Burkell, J. (2002). Believe it or not: Factors influencing credibility on the Web, Journal of the American Society for Information Science and Technology, 53(2), pp. 134-144, December 2001. John Wiley & Sons.

21

How can we make IT appliances easy for older adults?: Usability studies of Electronic Program Guide system

Noriyo Hara[1], Toshiya Naka[1] and Etsuko T. Harada[2]
[1]Panasonic Corporation, [2]Hosei University
Japan

1. Introduction

New information appliances, typically personal computers (PCs), cellular phones or car navigators, have so many functions with great varieties that many elder users have difficulties to use them. Manuals are too thick to read up before starting to use. On the other hand, TV set has been a very common consumer appliance that has been used by most elderly without serious difficulty. In recent years, however, new information technologies are applied to conventional home appliances including TV set, resulting in a lot of problems of usability, especially for elder users. It might cause inequality of chance to access many information resources and resulting in digital divide, one of the most serious social problems.

In order to make IT appliances elder-friendly, so-called "universal design" has been a popular approach. Many appliances equipped with large fonts and large buttons claim a universal design (Hasegawa et al. 2005; Zhao et al. 2007) to ensure easy access to use. Even though the adaptation of these physical designs is important and effective, this approach does not cover all of problems of difficulty in using for elder users, because this approach aims only to compensate declines of sensory- and motor-functions with aging. There are also solid changes of cognitive functioning with aging, based on changes of brains and neural activities and resulting complex phenomena related to lots of social and adaptive factors (Craik & Salthouse, 2008; Harada, in press). Effective support in IT design for these cognitive aging should be considered and investigation of this new approach is important.

Another factor of difficulties in using for elder users is lack or shortage of experience in using IT appliances in general. People living in these days have been making up a generic mental model of IT appliances while they use many kinds of them. Mental model is a kind of knowledge, which offer expectations and indicate assumptions of system behaviour when users try to use (Gentner & Stevens, 1983; Norman, 1988). Users may use general mental model when they try to use a new appliance or service, and then develop more specific mental models for each specific appliance based on their own interactions (Akatsu & Harada, 2008). Many elder users have few experiences on IT appliances resulting in difficulties in using new one because they have only poor mental models for them.

Harada proposed the three-layered model of cognitive aging and usability, consisting of "declines in cognitive functions", "shortage of knowledge and mental models of objects" and "attitudes and strategies based on meta-cognition and value system". Three layers are cross- linked to each other, and are affecting interactions between older adults and IT appliances (Harada & Akatsu, 2003).

Reported experimental studies comparing older adults with younger adults in using IT appliances showed effects of aging which were mixture of cognitive aging and shortages of mental models applicable to usages of appliances. For example, Harada et al. analyzed older users' behaviours of automatic teller machine (ATM), L-mode telephone and other IT-based appliances, and reported some typical features of older adults including difficulties in awareness of changes in an information displayed and error repetitions (Harada et al, 2002; Ogata et al., 2005). Kitajima et al. proposed a test battery for attentional function with aging, and reported that different groups of users whose performance declined in a different subtest showed differential problems in mobility within the train station (Kitajima et al., 2005).

On the basis of these preceding studies, this study had two purposes. One was to investigate effects of cognitive aging and shortages of mental models independently on learning the operation of a new appliance. The other is to explore possibilities of making IT design supportive to learn for elder users, providing errorless environment.

2. Experiment I: Are there really aging effects on using IT appliances or just effects of past experiences of the use of similar appliances?

In experiment I, in order to investigate effects of cognitive aging independently from lack of mental models, the usability testing of EPG system was performed with older and younger adults of different experiences on PCs. (Hara et al., 2005)

2.1 Methods

2.1.1 Participants

Fifteen older adults (8 male and 7 female, mean age: 68.8 years, ranging 65-73) and younger adults (8 male and 7 female, mean age: 20.8, 18-25) participated in the experiment voluntarily and were paid for participation. All participants had no experienced in using EPG system before the test. Half of older participants had substantial experience in using PC, while the remaining half did not have any experiences. Among younger adults, half were PC beginners and the other half were rather experienced PC users. It was impossible to find younger adults without experiences of PC usage. Table 1 shows participants' experiences in using scheduled recording of VCR and a cellular phone. Two groups in younger adults were not different from each other with these experiences, in contrast with older adults groups. The without-PC experiences group of older adults had little experiences with other equipments also, indicating the larger individual differences of mental models of IT appliances in older adults compared with younger adults.

Age	Older adults		Younger adults	
PC experience	With	Without	Experienced	Beginner
Number of participants	8	7	7	8
Cellular phones	5	0	7	8
Cellular phones mail	1	0	6	8
Scheduled recording of VCR	5	0	5	6

Table 1. Number of participants who had experience of cellular phones and the scheduled recording.

2.1.2. Evaluated system

In this study, we adopted an Electronic Program Guide System, abbreviated as EPG system as the target system of our usability testing. EPG in Japan provides a TV program listing in a format of 2-dimensional matrix of TV-channels and time of the day, which looks similar to the TV program guide in traditional Japanese newspapers (Figure 1). Each program is located at the intersection of the time and the channel. The EPG data including additional information are provided with digital broadcast and displayed on call on the TV screen. The TV set offers many functions e.g. scheduled recording when the program is clicked. There were three reasons why we used the EPG system in this study. At first, the EPG is a quite new system added to TV sets or recorders, which are commonly used daily appliances familiar to everyone including elders. As the second, the user interface of the EPG system is quite different from that of classic TV sets, and similar to the GUI of PCs. Specifically, operation of system depends on information displayed on the screen. Finally, the EPG system is expected to become a widely used standard function of digital TV/ broadcasting system which should be easy to use for all users.

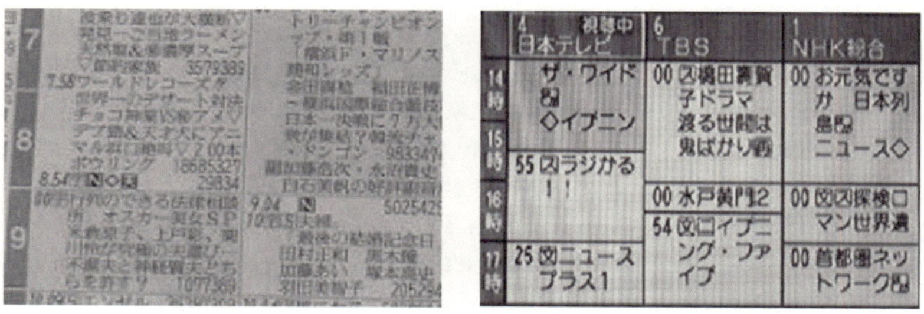

(a) (b)

Fig. 1. A TV program listings in Japanese newspaper (a) and in EPG system (b). They aer provided in a format of 2-dimensional matrix of channel and time

In experiment I, a digital high vision TV set (TH-32D30T, Panasonic Corp.) was used for the usability testing for EPG system. Its standard remote controller used in the test is shown in Figure 2. The controller has many buttons, which can be categorized to 4 groups. To use the EPG functions with this controller, users should perform four types of elementary actions associated to different set of buttons, as follows.

- Direct button action: for example [power] and [channel] buttons are directly associated to the system functions. When they are pushed associated actions are immediately invoked.
- Cursor action (move-and-select): the cursor indicates current focus on the items shown on the screen. Users move the curser with [up][down][left] and [right] buttons and push [execute] button to make choice.
- Colour button action: [blue], [red], [green] and [yellow] buttons are on the EPG remote controller. Each button is directly associated to a system function like direct action buttons, however, the association is not static but dynamically changed depending system state; they are available only when the definition of their functions is displayed on the screen. The colour buttons are defined in the EPG specification and common for all EPG systems.
- Menu selection: because of richness of functions, many complex functions are offered in a multi-layered menu tree structure. Users reach to desired system function in the menu by making step-by-step selections at each layer with cursor action. It is necessary for effective use to understand the menu structure as well as the concept of menu selection.

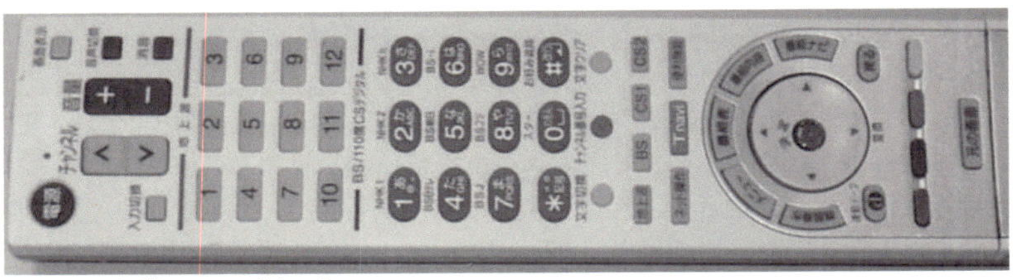

Fig. 2. Remote controller used in the test

The direct action buttons are simple and equipped on conventional TV sets and were familiar even to older groups. Cursor actions and menu selection are derived from IT systems and cellular phones, and they may have been quite new way of use for older adults who had no experiences on PCs or Cellular phones. Colour buttons are characteristic of digital TV and EPG system, and were new to all of the participants.
Usually, there is some distance between the TV screen and users who operate the remote controller. Users have to move their view focus to and fro between the TV screen and the remote controller, and need to remember information on the screen to operate the remote controller on the basis of information displayed. Both of these costs are to be paid by users for context-dependent button actions, i.e., cursor action, colour button action, and menu selection. It may have been additional problem for older users.

2.1.3 Tasks

A series of tasks are prepared for the usability testing;

1. Turn on the TV set and view a instructed terrestrial channel, and then view a BS channel. Younger participants were asked additional task to view a BS which need to be input by a channel number.
2. Display the electronic program listing of the terrestrial broadcasting, scroll down the screen, and see programs at 19:00 on the same day; do the same task with listing for the BS.

3. See additional information by EPG for a program assigned by instruction.
4. Display the electronic program listing, and see a programs at 12:00 on the day after tomorrow (changing the date).
5. Find a movie program on the same day by EPG (search by category); and then find a sports program on the next day (search by category).
6. Find a program with a given performer (search by performer's name).
7. Setup a scheduled recording of a program found at the task 6.
8. Setup a scheduled weekly watching of a program assigned by instruction; then cancel that scheduling.

Task 1 was pure conventional operation of TV set, but the tasks from 2 to 4 were intended to see the performance of program listing operation. Tasks 5 and 6 were to see the performance of EPG search operation, and tasks 7and 8 were for reservation operation for recording or viewing. Every task was given with a written document which did not include any words shown on the controller as labels.

2.1.4 Procedures

The experiment was executed with each participant individually. After coming to the lab, participants were told about the experimental objectives and they filled in a questionnaire about personal background and experiences with IT-based systems. Following instruction and demonstration by the experimenter, participants performed a practice session of thinking-aloud method while solving a Tangram puzzle.

After the experimenter explained the EPG system only with conceptual description, the usability test was performed task by task. No system manuals or prior verbal guidance about operations were given. The task was presented by a written card, and participants were requested to read the task aloud at first, and then start the task. Participants were requested to make a guess how to solve the task and try on it, with prompting to think aloud when keeping silent. When a participant seemed to reach to a deadlock, the experimenter asked the participant about his/her problem at that point, then gave them a minimum help to get out of the trouble. After all tasks completed, the experimenter interviewed the participants. The experiment lasted two hours for elder adults, and about one hour for younger participants. Because of the testing time limitation, task 6 was skipped for some older participants.

Utterance of participants was recorded by an IC sound recorder, and three video cameras recorded the operation on the remote controller, information on the TV screen and participant's behaviour as a whole. All button actions on the controller were monitored and recorded at the infra-red receiver.

2.2 Results and implications

All utterance and behaviour of participants were transcribed for analysis. The achievement of each task was coded as 3 categories: succeeded by oneself, succeeded but with experimenter's help, or failed. Statistical significance was determined by one-sided Fisher's exact test unless otherwise indicated. In this paper, results were reported in three kinds of different button actions described earlier.

2.2.1 Troubles with Cursor actions

When pushing [Program Guide] button to display the electronic program listing on the screen, a cursor with yellow frame in the table is shown indicating the current focused program. This focused program can be moved up and down (along with the time axis) and right and left (along with the channel axis) with four cursor buttons. To select the focused program for the extended functions, [Enter] button should be pushed. Participants experienced these cursor actions of EPG in Task 2 at the first time. Younger participants had no difficulty in cursor operations and selection. However, older participants showed some difficulties in understanding the difference between focused and non-focused programs. They needed to become aware that the cursor could be moved and to learn how to move the cursor. Half of the older-PC users and all seven participants in older non-PC user group could not find out the down scroll cursor operations without experimenter's help. There was no significant difference between PC user and non-PC user groups. As for the side scroll cursor operations, one fourth in the older-PC user group and six of seven in older non-PC user group succeeded after the experimenter's help ($p<0.05$, older PC user group vs. non-PC user groups).

Understanding the possibility of scroll may have come from knowledge or models of IT appliance operations, or may have been interfered by perceptual constraints which were strong in older adults. In any cases, stretch of the knowledge of paper-based 2-dimensional program listing to EPG system was the key to solve the difficulty in using IT-based display for older adult users.

2.2.2 Troubles with Colour button action

Among the buttons on the controller, the colour buttons have highly context-dependent and quite new for all participants. Colour button actions were expected to be used to change date of the electronic program listing in the tasks 4 and 8. Table 2 shows the number of participants who noticed the display of colour button functions on the screen and used it. Some users completed the tasks without using colour buttons (for example, with a long scrolled down until the next day). Most younger participants noticed the colour button functions by themselves, and no hints were necessary at all. On the contrary, among the older participants, only three in PC user group and one in non-PC user group noticed the colour button functions shown on the screen by themselves.

Age	Older adults		Younger adults	
PC experience	With	Without	Experienced	Beginner
Number of participants	8	7	7	8
By oneself (Task4)	3	1	6	6
With experimenter's help	3	5	0	0
No use	2	1	1	2
By oneself (Task8)	6	1	7	8
With experimenter's help	2	6	0	0

Table 2. Awareness of colour button functions

There observed some errors that colour buttons were pushed while they were disabled. Most of these errors with colour buttons were caused by colour design of the screen. We call this type of error as "Colour slip", which was caused by direct but wrong association induced by common colours. Typical examples of utterances while pushing buttons were shown in Table 3. At this time, yellow-coloured area in the electronic program listing indicated the focused program. The participant erroneously associated the yellow colour on the screen with the yellow button, and pushed the yellow button repeatedly. Similar behaviour was seen in several other older participants (Table 4). The PC experiences in older participants seem to have had no effects on these kinds of behaviours.

Participant:	May I push the yellow button? Am I right?
Experimenter:	What do you think is meant by the yellow colour? How do you think why that part is yellow-coloured?
Participant:	I guess I should push the yellow button. Ah, is it wrong? (She pushes the yellow button.) No, it won't work, why? (She pushes the same button again.)

Table 3. Example utterance with colour slip

Age	Older adults		Younger adults	
PC experience	With	Without	Experienced	Beginner
Number of participants	8	7	7	8
None	4	2	5	8
Once	2	3	2	0
Many times	2	2	0	0

Table 4. Number of participants who needlessly pushed 4 color buttons (for all tasks)

Two younger participants also pushed colour buttons by errors. However, their errors did not look like resulting from "colour slip", but from logical searching/testing for a proper operation. The most distinguished differences from older participants was that younger participants never repeated pushing colour buttons; i.e., once they found that the buttons did not related to the expected functions and that the colour of the display had no meaning, they easily abandoned the colour buttons, and tried other buttons without repeating the same errors. Thus was indicated that colour slips seems to have come from poor understanding of the EPG system and/or strong effects of distraction by colours.

2.2.3 Troubles in Structured menu action

From tasks 5 to 8, it is necessary to operate menu-driven functions to achieve the task goal. The multi-layered, tree structured menus is common in PCs but has hardly used in conventional TV sets just to watch TV programs. For the task 5, finding out a movie on the same day, four stages of menu and sub-menu selections were required after invoking menu by pushing [menu] button. The first selection, i.e. the root menu, was to select the action type (search for a program, schedule a recording, etc.), and the second step was the selection of search method (search by category, search-by keyword, etc.). After the "search by category" was selected, program categories (movies, sports, etc.) were displayed and to be selected, then finally, sub-categories for "movie" (domestic movies, foreign movies, etc.) was to be selected.

Table 5 shows the number of participants who could pass each step without experimenter's help. Some in younger PC beginners group had difficulty with opening the "menu". (not shown). As for menu selection, all younger participants could perform correct operations, regardless of rich experiences of PC use.

Age	Older adults		Younger adults	
PC experience	With	Without	Experienced	Beginner
Number of participants	8	7	7	8
1. Action "Searching for"	2	0	7	8
2. Method "By category"	6	0	7	8
3. Category "Movie"	6	4	7	8
4. Sub-category "Japanese Movie"	8	4	7	8

Table 5. Number of participants who passed the each step of task 5

On the other hand, all of older participants showed difficulties at the first stage, regardless of PC experiences. Interestingly enough, these difficulties seems to have been gradually reduced along with going down to the stages for both groups, but the rate of reduction was different with PC experiences. Although most of the older PC user group had little difficulty at the second step, non-PC user group still showed severe difficulties, whose performance were improved at the third and fourth stages. Statistical analysis confirmed that the PC experience did not affect the performance at the first step, but there was a significant difference at the second step ($p<0.01$). On the third stage, the differences did not reach significant, however, on the last fourth stage there was a tendency for the difference ($0.05 < p <0.1$). Older PC user group showed increase in the number who completed by themselves at the step from the first to the second stage ($p< 0.1$), while the group without PC experience showed increase at the step from second to the third stage ($p<0.05$).
The cause of this observation seems multiple factors. One reason of the increased success rate by older participants might be learning of move-and-select operation in the menu structure. The differences between two groups of older participants should have been related to this learning, because of their prior experiences of using menu interfaces of PC. There seemed to be other reasons related to the characteristics of menu structure. In structured menu operations, the menu items at earlier stages are more distant from the final goal, and with going down the menu structure, the distance become smaller. It was also suggested that the lack of the mental model or system knowledge disturbed the ability to keep their own goal in mind while operating the menu selection and/or understanding external stimuli such as displayed items (De Yong, 2001).
In addition, the feature of item selected at each stage was also different in the structured menu. In the target EPG system, the first stage was the selection of actions which were described by verbs, and second stage was for the selection of methods which were described by adverbs. At the third and fourth stages, menu items were objectives of the action and expressed as nouns, i.e., concrete objects. The action of selection may have easily been connected to nouns, especially concrete objects, with similarity to the selective actions in everyday life. From this view point, selecting an abstract verb may be unfamiliar actions, and needs to be learned.

These characteristics of structured menu systems are coming from the root of PC interfaces or cultures, and the way to avoid of this is not clear. However, the results showed some aspects of possible difficulties for older adults when using PC and IT-based appliances.

2.3 Discussions

The results above showed absolute differences between younger and older adults in using the EPG system at the first time. As long as the final achievement, younger adults had very little problems using EPG system in the usability testing, without regard to experiences of PC usage. On the other hands, older adults, regardless of PC experiences, showed a lot of problems interacting with new systems. There were also effects of experiences observed in older participants groups, even though the significance of effect seems much smaller than aging. With PC experiences participants could take advantages of help by experience, and showed a little bit better performances than older adults with no PC experiences.

Some younger adults could not use the new system and new functions without embarrassments. They made errors at the first time and hesitated to use. However, they were able to overcome and find out the ways to use by themselves while trying to use them. It is implied that for usage of an IT system especially a new one, the key factor affected by aging is learning, with which users acquire some specific mental models of the target system (Harada et al., in press). The knowledge or mental models users already have, has rather small facilitative effects and cannot cover the whole range of aging effects.

Causes for these poverty of learning must be complicated and many factors of cognitive changes are related. Among them, one of the most important issues should be error. Older adults experience more errors, and while recovering from the error, they often make another erroneous operation, which makes older adults difficult to understand the situations. In addition, older adults have tendencies to repeat the same errors in consecutive trials, which is reportedly one of characteristic behaviours for older adults (Harada & Suto, 2008). With these repetitive errors, it is quite difficult to understand the reason of errors and to learn how to use the appliance.

Based on this hypothesis, we planned the following experiment to make IT appliances more easy to use for older adults by making a supportive learning environments by keeping the users away from errors.

3. Experiment II: Can we make IT appliances easy to use by supporting learning?

As mentioned above, it was observed that younger adults could learn how to use the EPG system while they tried to use it, but older adults could not. As a hypothesis, one of the most serious obstacle factors for older adults' learning is experience of errors, especially repetitive errors.

In general, experience of errors provides rich information and it is said that people can learn more from errors than from success. However, for amnesic (memory-impaired) patients, it is difficult to learn from experiences with errors and some successful alternative ways for them to learn, called "errorless learning" were reported (Baddeley & Wilson, 1994; Evans, 2000). The same tendency was observed with healthy older adults (Anderson & Craik, 2006). In addition, older adults do not attend to negative information in general, compared with younger adults (Carstensen et al., 1999).

In the Experiment II, for the purpose of finding the ways to make IT system easy to learn especially for older adults, we examined the effects of environments in which users were supported to be kept away from serious errors with guidance, suggestions, or more conceptual information (Hara et al., 2007). Because of difficulties in making these environments by a system, the experimental settings were supplied by human experimenters with defined rules when/what/how to intervene to users. To ensure that the effects came from the environmental intervention but not the amount of information provided, two groups were set up. To the experimental group named "early-supported" group, helpful information or suggestions were given at the time it was necessary and errors or troubles were anticipated. The same information was given to the other group named "late-supported" group after making errors or end of the daily tasks.
Another purpose of the Experiment II was to see the effects of repeated basic operations. While it is difficult to learn mental modes or some conceptual local rules by older adults, it is known that there are tacit perceptual-motor learning, e.g., inputting a same long line of characters (Harada & Akatsu, 2003), or that it is possible to learn basic operations with supportive cares leading to successive usages (Harada et al., in press). To see the effects of repeated practice on the operations trained, and also observe its effects on operations of other functions, consecutive three-day test was performed on each participant individually. The tasks were organized to ensure repeated trial of basic operations. The repeated basic operations were performed by both early- and late-supported groups.

3.1 Strategies for supported learning

3.1.1 Strategy 1: making environments to avoid experiencing errors

To keep users away from experiencing serious errors, help / guidance / suggestions / explanations were provided by the experimenter during the test at different timing depending on the group. The following two types of information were given:
General concepts: useful general information about the system was given just before starting the related tasks to the early-supported group. To the late-supported group, the same information was given at the end of the day after all tasks had done. The information was provided by the experimenter

- The screen shown by EPG system consists of various different areas including TV program listing, commercial (PR) information and operational instruction areas. The screen image was shown with this message.
- The system has two separate storage areas, which are HDD and DVD.

Context-dependent guidance information: following helpful messages were given as needed. The early-support group was given with these messages immediately when they were applicable. The late-supported group was given after they showed difficulties.

- Invalid operation: e.g. the button you are pushing is invalid at this moment.
- Explanations of current status: e.g. the TV program listing is shown now.
- Suggestions: e.g. please pay attention to the on-screen message.
- Solution: e.g. please push the red button for your purpose.
- Goal reminder: e.g. please confirm the target of your task. This message was given when participants forget the final goal of the task they were tackling during the test.

3.1.2 Strategy 2: Repeated Practice of Basic Operation

In order to ensure that participants were able to learn the skills of basic operations, repetitive practices of basic operation were incorporated in the series of tasks. The basic operations repeated were as follows. They were the fundamental functions of the EPG system. Each basic operation was repeated several times in the series of tasks.

- Examine TV program listing
- Setup scheduled recording
- Review recorded programs

Figure 3 shows the operation schema of EPG system. The relation between basic operations and more complicated operations were described.

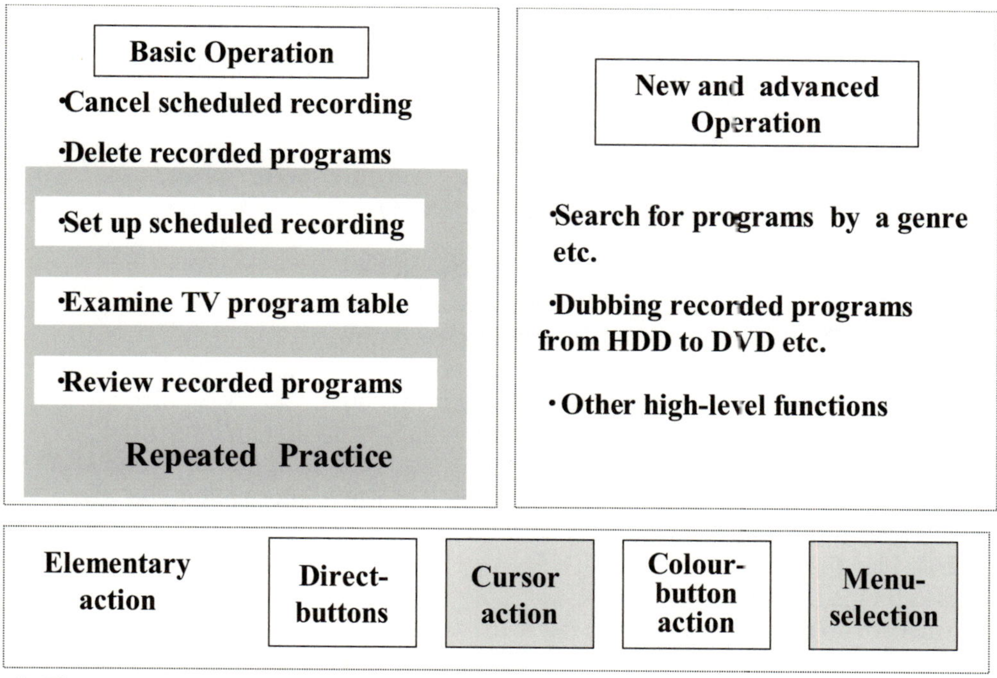

Fig.3. The operation schema in the EPG system

3.2 Methods

3.2.1 Participants and condition

Participants were five older (4 male and 1 female, mean age: 69.8 year, ranging 68-73) and 5 middle-aged adults (1 male and 4 female, mean age: 59.6, 51-65), who did not have substantial experiences of PC operation nor cellular phone mail, but had some experiences of using VCR. The familiarity with VCR was tested with easy operation tasks. The participants were stratified by age and VCR familiarity and were randomly assigned to the early-supported group (3 male and 3 female totality 6) and to the late-supported group (2 male and 2 female totality 4).

3.2.2 Tasks

The tasks of the Day1 were as follows:

1-1: Turn on the TV set.

1-2: Display the Electronic program listing and identify a TV program on the day.

-- General concept information about EPG screen layout was given only to the early-supported group. The same information was given to the late-supported group at the end of the day.

1-3, 1-4: Display the Electronic program listing and identify TV programs on different days.

1-5: Setup scheduled recording for three programs assigned by instruction.

1-6: Play recorded programs.

1-7, 1-8: Setup scheduled recording for a participant's favourite programs.

1-9: See the lists of already scheduled-recording-programs

1-10: Cancel a/some specified scheduled-recording-program(s)

Tasks 1-2 to 1-4 were placed for repeated basic cursor operations. The users were expected to become familiar with the information shown on the screen such as context-dependent functions of colour buttons. Task 1-5, 1-7 and 1-8 were placed for repeated scheduled-recording with cursor, enter and colour buttons.

The tasks on the Day2 were as follows:

2-1: Turn on the TV set and setup scheduled-recording

2-2 to 2-4: Do operations related to playing recorded contents.

2-5 to 2-9: Do operations related to scheduled-recording.

2-10, 2-11: Do operations related to playing recorded contents.

2-12: Search for movie programs assigned by instruction..

2-13: Search for programs of favourite genre

-- General concept information about storage areas consisting of HDD and DVD were given only to the early-supported group. The same information was given to the late-supported group at the end of the day.

2-14: Play the program on the DVD.

The tasks on the Day3 were as follows:

3-1: Turn on the TV set and setup the scheduled-recording.

3-2, 3-3: Do operations related to playing recorded contents.

3-4, 3-5: Do operations related to scheduled-recording.

3-6: Play the programs on the DVD.

3-7: Dubbing of three recorded programs from HDD to DVD.

3-8: Do operations related to scheduled-recording.

3-9: Do operations related to scheduled-recording and cancel duplicated reservation.

3-10: Start recording current program on air

3.2.3 Evaluated system

In Experiment II, a DVD/HDD recorder (EH-60) with TV monitor (TH-32D30T) was used as the similar EPG system as Experiment I. Button locations of the remote controller, TV program listing layout on the screen, and menu tree structure were almost the same as those of Experiment I.

Some buttons on the remote controller were hidden to minimize confusing factors. For example, a button's label "Chapter" was hidden since many participants in Experiment I were uncertain about the meaning and the function of the button and showed fears to use it. This button was available only for the edition of a video.

3.2.4 Procedures

The experiment was performed on consecutive three days with each participant individually. Each day had one session lasting less than two hours. A few days before the experimental session, each participant was tested for VCR operation and was interviewed about personal backgrounds and experiences of IT-based system operations.

3.3 Results

The first obstacle for the users was the cursor action in Task 1-2, where the users were requested to display the program listing and identify the TV programs. All users of both experimental groups needed suggestions by the experimenter to complete the task, implying that two groups were equally not familiar with EPG operation at the start of the test. The result was also similar to the Experiment I as compared to the older adults without PC experiences group, suggesting that participants' performance levels of two experiments were equivalent.

3.3.1 Effects of General concept Information

The second obstacle for the users was the colour button action in Task 1-3, where the colour buttons were assigned to functions to change the date of the TV program table. Only the early-supported group was given with information about general concept of EPG screen layout just before tackling the task. Although the general information was not directly focused on colour buttons, it could be a good suggestion and help for users to become aware of the colour button actions. Table 6 shows the number of participants who completed the task by themselves, i.e. who found the colour button function shown on the screen. Performances were not different in the two experimental groups, suggesting that the general information about screen layout turned out to be ineffective.

Group	Late-supported	Early-supported	Total	Experiment I
Number of participants	4	6	10	7
By oneself (Task1-3)	2	3	5	1
By oneself (Task1-4)	4	4	8	1

Table 6. Awareness of colour button functions

Another general concept information regarding HDD and DVD was given to the early-supported group before Task 2-14, where the users were requested to watch the programs recorded in the DVD. However, the number of users succeeded by oneself in Task 2-14 was two of six in the early-supported and two of four in the late-supported groups, with no significant differences. Again, giving general concept information before the task was not helpful to users.

This result suggested that general information without clear focus on the target operation was not helpful, at least for older adults, even if they were provided before tackling the related task. It seemed difficult for participants to understand the relationship between general information and an actual operation.

3.3.2 Effects of Repeated Basic Operations with Context-dependent Help

In this experiment, target basic operations were incorporated in different tasks, offering repeated practices of them in various contexts. One of repeated basic operations was scheduled recording, which was incorporated in Tasks 1-5, 1-8, 2-1 and 3-1. The performance of these tasks is shown in Table 7. At the first trial (Task 1-5), the performance was almost the same between two experimental groups. However, the next task performance (1-8) was better in the early-support group than task 1-5 (p=0.015). No significant improvement was observed in the late-supported group, suggesting that the context-dependent help information given to the early-supported group facilitated learning of the basic operations. The early-supported group seemed to acquire elementary actions more effectively than the late-supported group. The performance on the day 2 in the early-supported group was a little bit worsened back, however, it improved again on the day 3, suggesting that stable knowledge was acquired.
Other task performances also showed improvements by the repetition. For example, the performance in Task 1-4 seemed better than in Task 1-3 (Table 6), even though it was not statistically significant. Similar improvement was observed with other repeated basic operations. It was notable that such improvement was not observed in the experiment I, where help-guidance by the experimenter was not provided before participants voluntarily giving up or falling into deadlock after making repeated errors. Too late help-guidance was not effective nor helpful. These results suggest that older adults can learn by repeated successful practice with timely help-guidance but not by trial-and-errors.

Group	Late-supported			Early-supported		
	Achieved	Suggestion	Solution	Achieved	Suggestion	Solution
Task 1-5	1	1	2	1	1	4
Task 1-8	2	1	1	6	0	0
Task 2-1	2	0	2	3	3	0
Task 3-1	3	1	0	5	1	0

Table 7. Number of participants who achieved "scheduled recording"

3.3.3 Improvement with New and Complicated Tasks

The other obstacle in this experiment was the menu selection action. Task 2-12, TV program search, was quite new to participants as described in the Experiment I. The performance at each stage in four steps of the search menu selection was shown in Table. 8. At the first stage, selecting the action, it is possible to skip of this selection by taking alternative path Five of ten participants in this experiment found and used this alternative path, which never happened in the Experiment I.

Group		Late-supported	Early-supported	Total	Experiment I
Number of participants		4	6	10	7
1. Action	"Searching for"	2	1	3	0
	Alternative path	(2)	(3)	(5)	-
2. Method	"By category"	3	5	8	0
3. Category	"Movie"	4	6	10	4
4. Sub-category		4	6	10	4
Change of date		3	6	9	-
Scheduled recording		2	4	6	-
No try		2	1	3	-

Table 8. Number of participants who passed each step of menu selection.

Surprisingly enough, the performance of both early- and late-support groups especially at the first and the second steps was better than that in the experiment I ($p<0.01$). The menu selection action itself was new to participants in the present experiment, too. The difference between two experiments was that this task was assigned to the day 2 in this experiment and that participants were able to experience many times more basic operations. So it is suggested that acquisition of basic operations by repetition can facilitate learning of more complicated operations. Actually the screen design of the program listing attained as search result in task 2-12 was quite different from usual TV program listing repeatedly presented to participants. With this "new" screen, participants were asked to change date or to setup scheduled recording. They needed to get the meaning of cursor actions or colour buttons on the new screen. Although it is difficult for older users to get the new meanings of actions by watching the screen in general, most participants had no problems in Task 2-12 in this experiment. They found the proper operation just with the interaction with the system, which was never observed in the Experiment I.

3.4 Discussions

As shown above, it was shown that older adults learn elementary actions with repeated successful basic operations. Timely context-dependent help-guidance information facilitated learning. In addition, the learning of the basic operations facilitates the learning of other new and more complicated operations effectively. In contrast, general and unfocused concept information did not help older participants to use closely related target operations at all.

Another interesting factor observed was the value of personalized purposes. On the task 1-1 to 1-4, TV programs to be handled were pre-assigned by instruction. However after task 1-7, participants were asked to do the similar actions with TV programs which they prefer to see. When they had such chance to select their own favourite programs, the performance was better. It may be attributed to their higher motivation. Unfortunately this result was contaminated with task order and may be affected by repetition or learning. So the effect was not confirmed by comparison. Such motivational aspects by personalized purpose seems to affect learning, too. Some participants told at Task 1-7, "I like to see this program, so I want to make scheduled-recording of it", and started searching the EPG voluntarily.

Effects of these kind of user's attitudes and/or powers of personalized purposes should be investigated with more systematic methods.

4. General Discussion

As the results of experimental usability testing of the EPG system, Experiment I showed younger adult users can learn how to operate IT appliances while they are trying to use it without reading manuals and any conceptual learning before. It may be achieved with so called "trial-and-error" fashion, or by hypothesis-testing methods. These results gave us a question why older users have difficulty in learning to use IT appliances during trial. What is the differences in the learning between younger and older adults?

In order to learn to use IT appliances by "trial-and-error" fashion or hypothesize-and-test manner, there should be multiple steps to be succeeded, which is similar to the seven stages model of user-computer interaction (Norman 1988): 1) Set a goal, 2) Select an yet untried action, 3) Try the action, 4) Receive the feedback, 5) Compare results to the goal, 6) If failure, step back to 2). To set a goal and to compare results to the goal, the user should keep the goal in his/her working memory, i.e., necessity of a goal maintenance (De Yong, 2001). To select one of yet untried actions, she/he should remember what was already tried, i.e. necessity of output monitoring (Marsh et al., 2007). To receive feedback, the user should be aware of what is shown and how it is changed (sensitivity of display changes; Harada & Akatsu, 2003). Older adults have various obstructive factors for these processes, because of declined memory and/or cognitive control functions (Craik & Salthouse, 2008), which induce the poor learning processes. In addition, many of IT appliances' functions are invoked by a series of interactive actions in nested structures, then the feedback from the system for each action is sometimes far from the final goal. With these structures, users should memorize the cascades of goals, and it makes the stage 5) difficult. Actually, it is not easy to distinguish successful actions from failures clearly in the level of elementary actions (like cursor actions or menu selections) for older adults, especially when they do not have enough knowledge or mental models of the target system.

In addition to these cognitive functional factors, older adults often have attitudes or mental sets to IT systems, and have prejudice-like beliefs that they cannot use or learn IT system (Harada & Akatsu, 2003). These attitudes should be related to the phenomena called "stereotype threat", e.g., older adults showed worse memory performance when they were told or believed that the task was measuring memory than when they think the task was not related to memory (Hasher et al., 1999). Actually, older adults showed different attitudes to IT appliances which look like "very computer-like" from those which seem not-a-computer. These attitudes, computer threat, might get stronger, if they by themselves have experiences of failures to use or learn a new IT systems. With a lot of experiences, they may even get a "learned helplessness" (Seligman & Maier, 1967; Norman, 1988). Such negative attitudes of older adults must make it difficult to learn to use IT appliances. These negative attitudes are often observed in relation to experienced errors. When older adults make many errors, they are easy to lose motivation to learn the target system. This makes them passive to interactions with systems, which makes more errors. This loop can be called "harmful error spiral", which seems a fundamental factor for difficulty in learning operation. Our basic idea was to stop this harmful error spiral and to offer a reverse rotation; leading to success spiral that users experience success, they learn operation by the success, and are motivated, resulting in less errors. The models of harmful error spiral and success spiral are shown in Figure 4.

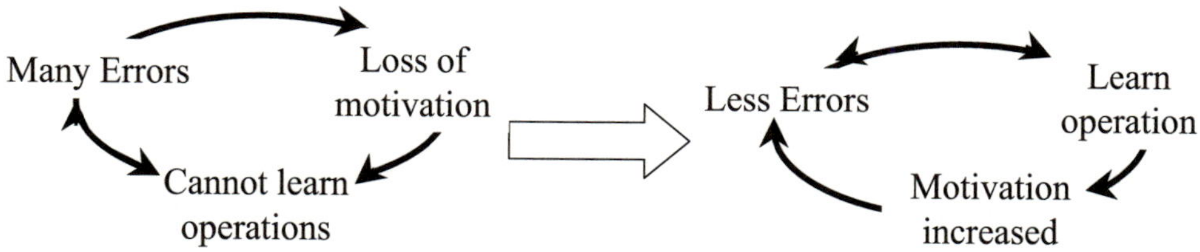

Fig. 4. Models of harmful error spiral and success spiral

To get rid of this learning poverty, we tried to provide older adult users with errorless learning environments, in which they would learn from successful experiences. The basis of the errorless learning is: 1) insufficient understanding of the basic operation induces many errors, and 2) consecutive or repetitive errors prevent users from learning the basic and more advanced operations. That is, reduction of errors is expected to facilitate learning.

The results were interesting. Not only basic operations actually repeated but also untrained complex operation was learned better. In addition, the older users started the voluntarily learning. However, general information provided had no effects on learning and improving better performances.

Errorless learning with repetitive basic operations seems to have the following advantages. Older users become aware of basic button layout by repetitive practice. They can operate the remote controller focusing on the video screen but not watching the panel on the controller. Then they will not miss the changes on the screen. They learn basic system behaviour and form mental models. Then they expect what happens with basic operations. Appropriate help-guidance makes users oriented in the context of actions and helps them understand what was wrong. Success experience induces the change of mindset to be positive and motivate them to try more. As a result, the difficulty in the older users is reduced, leading to mode change to the success spiral from harmful error spiral.

The number of practices or repetitions of each basic operation was not so huge in this experiment. A few times of repetitions with fairy long interval between repetitions seems effective enough. However the order and task structures was important for effectiveness: the key of this repetition effect must be the successful experience offered first.

Our results were just observed in a laboratory environment at present. In actual home use, users often have to operate new IT appliances alone. They are sometimes disturbed. They can give up whenever they want without jumping over the first hurdle. How can we implement the repetitive practice and errorless learning environment in the design of utility appliances to break harmful error spiral? Among the help-guidance messages given in this study, "invalid operation" and "current status" messages can be implemented in the system with relative ease. The "suggestion" and "solution" messages should match what the user wants to do, and are difficult to be implemented in the system. Complete feedback of "invalid operation" and "current status" should be helpful because users can learn context of operation. If feedback is inappropriate, users are confused and will not understand system behaviour and learn operation. It seems helpful to incorporate good messages for common situations of errors which are often observed.

Another problem to be solved is how to judge achievement of the learning of the basic operation. In our observation, when an older user proceeded to next operation before establishing good comprehension, he/she got confused by new operation. Specifically, a participant learned the operation of scheduled recording. Thereafter she learned the operation of program review, and then, she forgot what she learned first with scheduled recording.

Our results suggested the importance of breaking harmful error spiral in self-learning environment with repetitive practice in home use. It is still to be investigated how to make environments to support and facilitate the repetitive practice of basic operations and errorless learning in actual daily life. It is also to be discussed whether our method is effective in other new IT appliances. We are convinced that our approach is applicable to not only older users but all who feel difficulty in using new IT appliances.

5. Conclusion

Older adults have difficulties in using unfamiliar IT appliances. In order to investigate effects of cognitive aging and lack of mental models, the usability testing of EPG system was performed with older and younger adults of different experiences on PCs. Experimental results showed PC experiences did not save difficulty of new operations but facilitated learning of operations. Younger adults learn to use IT applications by trial-and-errors or hypothesis-testing method. Older adults especially those without PC experiences, could not learn GUI operation by this trial-and-errors fashion during using. Repetitive errors characteristic to older adults seemed to make it difficult to learn operations, resulting in loss of motivation to use new appliances

To find a different way for older adults to learn operations effectively, we proposed two methods. Our strategy was to keep users away from serious errors with help-guidance and repeated practice of basic operation. Unfocused general conceptual information was not helpful for learning new operations. Repeated practice of basic operations with timely help-guidance messages facilitated the acquisition of basic operation and system behaviour, resulted in making them easy to learn new and complicated operations. It was suggested that older adults could learn better from successful operations than from trial-and-errors, which may induce harmful error spiral. It is notable that they start to learn operations in trail-and-errors fashion after they got mental models of basic operation. This learning method from success trial seems effective for not only older adults but also all users. It is necessary to investigate how to avoid error spiral in self-learning environment in daily actual life.

6. References

Akatsu, H. & Harada, E. T. (2008) Emergent usage of Artifacts : A Comparative Analysis of Interactions with a Single Function Artifact, between Younger and Older Adults, The Japanese Journal of Ergonomics, 44(5), pp.268-278.

Anderson, N. D. & Craik, F. I. M. (2006). The mnemonic mechanisms of errorless learning. Neuropsychologia, Vol. 44 (14) pp.2806-2813

Baddeley, A. & Wilson, B. A. (1994). When implicit learning fails: Amnesia and the problem of error elimination. Neuropsychologia, Vol. 32(1), pp.53-68

Carstensen, L. L.; Isaacowitz, D. M. & Charles, S. T. (1999). Taking Time Seriously: A Theory of Socioemotional Selectivity. American Psychologist, 54(3), 165-181.

Craik, F. I. M. & Salthouse, T. A. (Eds) (2008). The handbook of aging and cognition (3rd ed.). New York, NY: Psychology Press.

De Yong, R. (2001). "Adult age difference in goal activation and goal maintenance", European Journal of Cognitive Psychology. 2001, 13, pp.71-89

Gentner,D. & Stevens, A. L. (1983). Mental Models. Hillsdale, NJ: Lawrence

Evans, J. J.; Wilson, B.A., Schuri, U., Andrade, J., Baddeley, A., Bruna, O., Camavan, T., Della Sala, S., Green, R., Laaksonen, R, Lorenzi, L. & Taussik, I. (2000). A comparison of "Errorless" and "Trial-and-error" Learning Method for Teaching Individuals with Acquired Memory Deficits. Neuropsychological Rehabilitation, 2000, 10 (1), pp.67-101

Hasegawa, S.; Omori, M., Matsunuma, S. & Miyao M. (2005). Visibility of graphic text on mobile phones among elderly people. 5th International Conference on Gerontechnology

Hara, N.; Murase, C., Isono, M., Nambu, M. & Harada, E. T. (2005). How can we make IT Devices Easy for Elderly People? : usability testing of electronic program guide system. 5th International Conference on Gerontechnology

Hara, N.; Naka, T., & Harada, E. T. (2007). How can we make IT Devices Easy for older adults? - Effects of repetitive basic operation training and help-guidance on learning of Electronic Program Guide system. HCI International 2007

Harada, E. T.; Akatsu, H., Sawashima,H., Nambu, M. & Ishimoto, A. (2002). Cognitive Characteristics of Elder Users: Data Corpus from Massive Usability Tests of Four IT devices. 1st meeting of Gerontechnology (SIG) in Japan Ergonomic Society (In Japanese)

Harada, E. T. & Akatsu, H. (2003). Usability for old users. In: Cognitive Studies of Human-Artifacts Interaction: What is "usability"?, E.T. Harada, (Ed.), pp. 119-138. Kyoritsu-syuppann, ISBN4-320-09440-9, JAPAN (In Japanese)

Harada, E. T. & Suto, S (2008). Error Repitations and cognitive control: Why does it happen outside the psychology lab? Cognitive Aging Conference, 2008

Harada, E. T., Mori, K., & Taniue, N. (In press). Cognitive aging and usability of IT-based equipments: Learning is the key. Japanese Psychological Research

Harada, E. T. (In press). What do cognitive aging studies tell us? Some implications from aging investigations on human memory and cognitive engineering studies. Japanese Psychological Review (In Japanese)

Hasher,L.; Zacks, R. T. & May, C. P. (1999). Inhibitory control, circadian arousal, and age. In D. Gopher and A. Koriat (Eds.), Attention and performance XVII: Cognitive regulation of performance: Interaction of theory and application. Attention and performance. Cambridge, MA: The MIT Press, pp. 653-675.

Kitajima, M.; Kumada, T., Akamatsu, M., Ogi, H. & Yamazaki, H. (2005). Effects of cognitive ability deficits on elderly passengers' mobility at railway stations: Focusing on attention, working memory, planning. 5th International Conference on Gerontechnology

Marsh, R. L.; Hicks, J. L., Cook, G. I. & Mayhorn, C. B. (2007). Comparing Older and Younger Adults in an Event-Based Prospective Memory Paradigm Containing an Output Monitoring Component. Aging, Neuropsychology, and Cognition, 14, pp.168–188

Norman, D. A. (1988). The psychology of Everyday Things (1988) New York: Basic Books
Ogata, K.; Harada, E. T., Nambu, M., Mori, K. & Niizeki, R. (2005). A cognitive engineering study of informational care systems at home: From the usability test focusing on workload. 5th International Conference on Gerontechnology
Seligman, M. E. P. & Maier, S. F. (1967). Failure to escape traumatic shock. Journal of Experimental Psychology, 74, pp.1-9.
Xia, Z.; Jin, J., Plocher, T & Kiff L. (2007). Touch Screen User Interfaces for Older Adults: Button Size and Spacing. HCI International 2007

22

Elderly people as Web seekers: Needs, strategies and difficulties

Jérôme DINET and Robin VIVIAN
University Paul Verlaine - Metz
France

1. Introduction

The aim of this chapter is to determine the information needs of elderly, specifically the online information needs, the strategies used by these specific end-users to search for online information and their difficulties. Because in our new millennium individuals aged 60 years and older constitute one of the fastest growing age groups (Billip, 2001; Lawhorn, Ennis and Lawhorn, 1996) and because the populations of the developed countries are becoming older while computer use is increasingly affecting wide aspects of life, it is more and more important to understand specific information needs and strategies used by elderly end-users in their search for information through a computer.

The information needs of elderly must be established, as must the most acceptable method of provision of this information. What this group of people wants and what is acceptable to them should determine the criteria for information provision. All too often so-called experts make assumptions about what people need. But, as Barrett (2000) said, "the true experts on the information needed by these specific end-users to enable them to live as they want to and to participate in society, are the people themselves. [...] It is necessary to explore how elderly people live and what their day-to-day difficulties are, the support and information that they and have and are aware of, what further support and information they need, and how they would prefer to get the information".

2. Online information needs of seniors and their difficulties

2.1 Previous studies

One of the first studies investigating the information needs for elderly people is the study conducted by Epstein (1980). This study included personal interviews with 900 people aged 65 and over in 6 areas in England. Interviewees were not asked directly what information they needed or wanted, but asked what their most worrying problem had been in the past year. The most common types of problems were health and financial, together accounting for 62 per cent of all problems.

In a vast study (of 5060 questionnaires sent out, 1936 completed questionnaires were returned), Barrett (2000) investigated the real information needs of seniors in UK. Several interesting results have been obtained. First, the elderly participants demonstrated a general lack of awareness of the vast amount of information on practical help, services, health, benefits and equipment available to them and how to access it. Second, this group of respondents has information needs in three specific information areas: financial and practical help; how to adapt their homes and the products available to make life easier at home; whom to contact for advice on all these matters. A large majority of respondents wanted to be told where they could get this information locally. In other words, this study identified finance and benefits, community care (support, services and practical help at home), and housing as major areas of information need for elderly people.

In the same way, in her study of the information needs of people aged 50 and over in Scotland, Troup (1985) conducted a questionnaire survey including a question to discover the broad areas on which respondents wanted more information. For those that said they needed more information (77 per cent of respondents), the most frequent areas were money/housing (24% of responses), leisure opportunities (21 %) and health matters (21 %). Troup (1985) also carried out a series of group meetings involving some 40 people over the age of 50 in Scotland. She found general agreement among the participants that there was a great need for information for elderly people on a wide variety of topics. All aspects of finance, housing and benefits were considered to be the areas of most importance and where there was greatest need. Information on leisure opportunities was also considered important, but information on health was not.

In the study conducted by Tinker, McCreadie & Salvage (1993), 50 elderly interviewees (age 60 and over) were presented with various situations where information needs could arise and where there may be uncertainty about what to do. In each of 5 towns, half of the people interviewed were judged to be "in touch" with information services (attended an Age Concern Centre) and half were "not in touch" (no involvement with clubs, day centers, voluntary work or additional church activities). What information was required, where it has been obtained, and whether it was adequate was determined for each situation experienced by an interviewee, otherwise a situation was treated as a "what if" scenario. It was found that, in the 6 months preceding the interview, the elderly people were most likely to have experienced or thought about becoming less capable (48% of interviewees). This was followed by the practical domestic problems of getting repairs done in the home (34%), buying something for the home (32%), and finding help with the garden (24%). Ninety three per cent said that their needs had been met when they had sought information about a specific concern.

Older people lack precision using direct and indirect input devices, such as the electronic mouse. Difficulties using the mouse, which can be regarded as the most common type of indirect input device for computer systems are primarily accounted for by age-related changes in spatial abilities and manual dexterity (Fisk, Rogers, Charness, Czaja & Sharit, 2004; Sayago & Blat, 2007). Overall, there is widespread agreement in the literature that most widgets ought to be enlarged and the number of clicks / steps minimized as much as possible. These usability recommendations are suggested by guidelines for designing user interfaces for older adults (Hodes & Lindberg, 20002; Jastrzembski, Charness, Holley & feddon, 2005; Morrell, Dailey & Rousseau, 2003).

Older adults had more difficulty than younger adults when searching for information on the Web. However results obtained in recent studies revealed that the age-related effect resulted from ineffective search strategies and amount of Web experience rather than age per se (Stronge, Rogers & Fisk, 2006). In other words, the seniors' difficulties are related to the selection of inefficient search strategies, which may have been attributable to a lack of knowledge about available Web search strategies.

Because older people tend to need a reduced number of functionalities and require few elements per Web page (Arnott *et al.* 2004; Chadwick-Dias, McNulty & Tullis, 2003), in their paper, Sayago & Blat (2007) have focused on this requirement of simplicity for elderly end-users. More precisely, Sayago & Blat (2007) have focused on three strategies to find online information, which are likely to be the most predominant ones: basic search (Google); advanced search (Google Advanced Search); and directories (Yahoo! Directory). To be as much relevant as possible to real-life scenarios, seniors ranging in age from 65 to 74 were asked to conduct two information search tasks they could be interested in and were more complex than those with which they were familiar with: to find the exact dates when the film "X-Men" and to find the synopses of Iliad and Odyssey and their historical contexts. Two main results have been obtained: difficulties using the mouse have a stronger effect on the total search time than difficulties in typing queries and that older people found online information 3 times faster by using basic search (Google) than by means of advanced search (Google Advanced Search) or directory (Yahoo! Directory). According to Sayago & Blat (2007), the directory was the slowest because of difficulties using the mouse and information overload. Despite providing fewer but the most precise results, advanced search was slower than basic search mostly due to the complexity of its interface.

Nevertheless, very little research has gone into evaluating the usability of seeking online information strategies with older people and there are many unanswered questions. Finding online information is a process, which involves a series of cognitive activities, and investigating the effect of age-related changes in cognition on the time spent by elderly adults in each step is an interesting future research area.

Finally, an increasing number of elderly people use computers and the Web to search for information, especially health/medical-related information (Fow & Fallow, 2003; Karavidas *et al.*, 2004; Meischke, Eisenberg, Rowe, & Cagle, 2004). Our modern industrial societies make it increasingly necessary for seniors to deal with expert information in many areas of everyday life, as a patient, client or customer. Elderly often retrieve health/medical information from the Web, which used to be available to experts exclusively (Bromme, Jucks, & Runde, 2005; Williamson, 1995, 1998). Today, seniors can have immediate access to a vast amount of health-related Websites, which are only a mouse-click away. The information they retrieve may help them to understand the assets and drawbacks of different therapeutical alternatives and eventually make a knowledge-based decision about their compliance with a suggested therapy (Morahan-Martin, 2004).

2.2 Health/medical information seeking from the Web

Individuals receive health information from a variety of information channels, including friends, family, health care providers, and the media (Johnson & Meischke, 1991; Meischke, Eisenberg, Rowe, & Cagle, 2004; Meischke *et al.*, 2004). These channels have inherent differences in their capabilities for handling health information. For instance, the traditional media (e.g., television, radio, and newspapers) may be an excellent source for increasing the public's awareness of behaviors that help prevent heart disease, because it tends to provide information of a fairly general nature to a large audience with considerable speed and efficiency. However, interpersonal channels (e.g., doctors, nurses, friends, and family) may be more effective in persuading people to adopt health behaviors, because they are characterized by immediate feedback and situation specificity. In general, research shows that people receive most of their health information from media channels even though these channels are rated as less credible than interpersonal channels (Johnson & Meischke, 1991; Meischke *et al.*, 2004). The same seems to be true for information seeking on heart-related matters (Fox & Fallow, 2003). They are called "health seekers". A majority of health seekers go online at least once per month for health information. A great majority of health seekers say the resources they find on the Web have a direct effect on the decisions they make about their health care and on their interactions with doctors. Three quarters (73%) of health seekers say the Web has improved the health information and services they receive (Fox & Fallow, 2003). The most frequently mentioned health topic searched for online pertains to "specific disease or medical problem". Although there is a great deal of optimism about the Internet as a health information source, there are some concerns that dampen this enthusiasm. For instance, there is a great deal of debate on both the quality and quantity of health information on the World Wide Web (Katz & Aspden, 2001). Several studies show that health information on the Internet is not always accurate or complete (Tatsioni *et al.*, 2003; Eysenbach, Powell, Kuss, & Sa, 2002; Lee et al., 2003). In addition, even if it is accurate, people cannot always find the information they want online (Meischke, Eisenberg, Rowe, & Cagle, 2004; Meischke *et al.*, 2004). This means that people who are less familiar with computers, such as the elderly, may have a particularly hard time finding useful and accurate information on heart and treatment.

So, since many years, a lot of studies explore computer use and health-related information needs among the elderly adults. Three main types of research have been identified by Frase (2004): (a) studies involving interviews and/or focus groups of seniors (e.g., Karavidas, Lim, & Katsikas, 2005), (b) surveys given to organizations that offer information and/or services to senior users (e.g., Mühlhauser & Oser, 2008), and (c) experimental studies in which seniors are observed using computers to find information (e.g., Becker, 2004; Czaja and Lee, 2001; DeOllos and Morris, 2000; Ellis and Allaire, 1999; Selwyn, Gorard, Furlong and Madden, 2003). Even if these three types of studies provide very interesting information in the effective online information needs for elderly people, there are two several methodological limitations (Frase, 2004; Tolbert, 1993):

(1) the first one is the variation in age range. This variation in age range is mirrored by the ages used in the scientific literature: some studies chose 50 years as the beginning age (Czaja, Sharit, Nair ad Rubert, 1998; Hawthorn, 2000), others chose 60 years, and still others chose 65 years. Dee & Bowen (1986) note that social gerontologists separate "the old" into three groups: the "young old", aged between 60 and 75; the "old old", aged between 75 and 85; the "very old", those aged over 85" (pp. 16-17). Other studies (Chatman, 1991; Wilkinson & Allen, 1991) discussed a variation of that breakdown: the young old or young elderly, aged 50-64; the middle old or active elderly, aged 65-74; and the old old or older elderly, aged 75 and older. Moreover, the age rank is often very large: for instance, in the study conducted by Karavidas *et al.* (2005) to determine the effects of computers on the retired older adult users, the participants were ranged in age from 53 to 88;

(3) the second one concerns the origins (socioprofesional, ethnics, etc.) of the samples recruited which prevent us to generalize results For instance, in the study conducted by Karavidas *et al.* (2005), participants consisted of retired older adult computer users living in private residences throughout South Florida most of whom belonged to various computer clubs. On the other hand, origins are not controlled and are "mixed" in other studies. But, previous researches suggest that individual and demographic variables are important predictors of information-seeking behaviors for elderly adult population, such as health beliefs (Johnson, Meischke, Grau, Johnson, 1992), personal experience (Meischke & Johnson,

1995), age (Turk-Charles, Meyerowitz, & Gatz, 1997), ethnic background (Hsia, 1987), sex (Karavidas, Lim and Katsikas, 2005) and education (Benjamin-Garner *et al.*, 2002).
So, the first study presented here investigates the Web interests and needs, and impacts of computer knowledge on seeking for health/medical information from the Web among 47 French seniors aged between 68 and 73, by using interviews with a semi-directed questionnaire.

3. Study 1. Why, where and how do elderly people search for online information?

Seniors' perceptions of the Web and of the information searching activity in general were assessed by a paper-and-pencil questionnaire (a Likert response scale) elaborated on the basis of a series of interviews and used in a previous research conducted with younger Web searchers (Dinet, Marquet & Nissen, 2003). Questions concerned: perceptions about the nature of health-related information found in the Web; 'strategies' of access to the interesting Websites and the reliability of different information resources (libraries, television, Web, etc.) about health/medical information. One individual factor was manipulated: Computer knowledge (low vs. high). Computer knowledge were evaluated by using the computer questionnaire elaborated by Lim, Bonge, Pellegrini, & Montagna (2001) and used in other studies (e.g., Karavidas, Lim & Katsikas, 2005).

3.1 Participants

47 seniors volunteers (19 males and 28 females), aged between 68 and 73 were recruited to participate in this study. If all the participants were Web users, two groups were constituted according to their computer knowledge: 24 seniors were considered with low level of computer knowledge and the Web (Low-CKnow) while 23 seniors were considered skilled with the computer and the Web (High-CKnow).

3.2 Material and procedure

Assessment of computer knowledge. To assess computer knowledge, participants completed the computer questionnaire elaborated by Lim, Bonge, Pellegrini, & Montagna (2001) and used in other studies (e.g., Karavidas, Lim & Katsikas, 2005). The computer questionnaire subscales tapped into: (1) software knowledge, (2) hardware knowledge, (3) general computer knowledge, and (4) Internet knowledge. Previous reliability analyses estimâtes (Lim, Karavidas & Katsamanis, 2001; Karavidas, Lim & Katsikas, 2005) of the coefficient α ranged from .86 to .93.
Assessment of needs and information search strategies. A paper-and-pencil questionnaire was elaborated on the basis of a series of interviews with open questions, conducted with six seniors who were not asked to fill it. This qualitative method provides a rich data set for studying seniors' perceptions of the Web and was appropriate to the exploratory nature of this study. During this interview, the six seniors were asked to explain what kind of information they found on the Web, to discuss the types of electronic resources they had access to, and their perceptions and opinions about the information they can find using different information resources. The researcher asked the following questions: (1) "Why do

you search for information on the Web?" (2) "How do you find an interesting Web site?" and (3) "In general, where do you find interesting information?"
On the basis of the responses obtained from these six interviews, several questions for a paper-and-pencil questionnaire items have been created (that can be rated on a 0-to-6 Disagree-Agree answer scale). The questionnaire used in this study was a Likert scale which is a way of generating a quantitative value (numerical) for a qualitative questionnaire (i.e., strongly disagree, disagree, undecided). For an ascending five (or six, or seven or eight, etc.) point scale, incremental values are assigned to each category and a mean figure for all the answers can be calculated. Each participant was asked to rate each item from the 0 ("strongly disagree") to 6 ("strongly agree") response scale. A forced-choice answer scale with an even number of responses and no middle neutral or undecided choice was used. In other words, the participants were obliged to decide whether they lean more towards the agree or disagree end of the scale for each item.
Moreover, the first section of the questionnaire consisted of questions related to demographic factors such as age, gender, and had questions concerning Web use, such as how long they had been using the Web and the average time they spent on it.

3.3 Main results

The measures from the computer questionnaire (Lim, Karavidas & Katsamanis, 2001) used in our study were general computer knowledge, software knowledge, hardware knowledge, and Internet knowledge. The estimated reliability α coefficients were .79, .84, .95, and .92, respectively. The computer knowledge subscales were correlated as expected (Table 1). So, on the basis of the global score obtained with the computer knowledge questionnaire, two groups were constituted: "Low computer knowledge group" or Low-CKnow (*N* = 24) and "High computer knowledge" or High-CKnow (*N* = 23).

Scale	General Know.	Hardware Know.	Software Know.	Internet Know.
General Know.	-	.85**	.72*	.64*
Hardware Know.		-	.73*	.81**
Software Know.			-	.84**
Internet Know.				-

Table 1. Intercorrelation among the computer subscales (N = 47; *Note*:* p < .05. ; ** p < .01).

We asked the respondents about their Internet behavior. In our study, 65% of the respondents indicated using the Internet to search for health/medical information. Other commonly cited reasons included reading news (51%), searching for product or auction information (37%), researching hobbyrelated topics (33%), searching for travel information (12%), and tracking investments (10%). Some differences have been found with results obtained by Karavidas, Lim & Katsikas (2005) because populations recruited in their study and recruited in our study are different from an ethnic and sociodemographic point of view. Moreover, results indicated that there were proportionately more users with High computer knowledge (High-CKnow) who reported using the Internet to search for health- or medical-related information (High-CKnow, 68.6%; Low-CKnow, 42.4%), $\chi 2$ (1, *N*) = 56, p = .002. When asked to indicate how the computer has enhanced their lives, the largest reason provided was their ability to maintain social

contact (48%) followed by ease of access to information (31%). Be as it may, to search for health/medical information is the major reason to use the Web for all our 47 participants.
Eight reasons were proposed to the seniors to describe why they search for health/medical information on the Web. Table 2 shows that the "patterns" of the opinions are similar whatever the group (Low-CKnow *vs.* High-CKnow).

	Computer Knowledge				
	Low		High		*p*
	M	SD	*M*	SD	
On the Web ...					
I can find information in a quicker way	4.3	0.7	4	0.6	.32
I can find more information	4	0.5	3.8	0.6	.24
I can find more recent information	3.9	0.7	3.8	0.5	.18
I can find more interesting information	4.6	0.8	4.2	0.6	.17
I can find more beautiful information	2.6	0.6	2.2	0.4	.09
I can find information with clearer examples	2.6	0.9	2.3	0.8	.11
I can find all the information I need	2.6	0.7	2.5	0.5	.23

Table 2. "Why do you search for health/medical information on the Web?" Average scores of the answers

From the seniors' perspectives, the reasons are (in decreasing order): (1) the interest of the information found on the Web; (2) the quick of access; (3) the quantity; (4) the recency; (5) the superiority of the Web to give information; (6) the possibility to learn how to search for information through the Web; (7) the aesthetic of information; and (8) the accuracy and the number of examples. Several multivariate analyses (MANOVAs) were computed. There appear to be one general trend: low experienced seniors' (Low-CKnow) scores are always superior to high experienced seniors' (High-CKnow) scores. So, seniors with a high degree of computer and Web experience could become less confident and more critical than seniors with little Web experience.
Seven strategies to get access to interesting Web sites related to health were proposed. Table 3 shows that seniors' strategies for accessing interesting Web sites are partially dependent from their computer experience (Low-CKnow *vs.* High-CKnow).

	Computer Knowledge				
	Low		High		*p*
	M	SD	*M*	SD	
Through search engines	4.5	0.3	2.8	0.4	.003**
At random	2	0.6	1.5	0.8	.23
Through TV	3.5	0.9	3	1.2	.31
Through friends	5	1.1	4.4	1.3	.18
Through magazines	4.8	0.8	4.4	0.7	.42
With radio	2.4	0.6	2	0.8	.27
Through other Web sites	3.7	0.3	1.3	0.2	.001**

Table 3. "How do you find an interesting Web site about health/medical information?" Average scores of the answers

Whatever their computer knowledge, the strategies used by our participants can be dispatched into three categories (in decreasing order of preference): (1) friends, search engines, and magazines; (2) other Web sites and television and (3) radio and random. Results show that the scores of the seniors with high experience (High-CKnow) are always inferior to those with low experience (Low-CKnow), even if differences are only significant for two strategies: through search engines (p = .003) and through other Websites (p = .001). This means that the reliability of seniors in different 'strategies' to get access interesting Web sites related to health/medical information tend to decrease with experience, whatever the strategy used.

So, in accordance with some previous studies on the needs for information for elderly users (Williamson, 1995, 1998), the topics of interest for our participants were (in decreasing order): (1) health, (2) news, and (3) leisure activities (e.g., holidays, hobbies and travels). Other topics included consumer, housing and accommodation, safety, environment, pharmaceuticals, family and personal, education, and services.

4. Study 2. Impact of metamemory skills

An important aspect of the elderly adult population is the proportion having some type of disability: chronic disabilities include arthritis, hearing impairments, cataracts, hypertension, heart diseases, and diabetes, among others. Unlike younger adult users, there are physiological factors due to the normal aging process affecting older adults' use of the Internet. The normal aging process, including vision, cognition, metacognition and physical impairments, has an impact on Web usability (Karavidas, Lim & Katsikas, 2005; Selwyn, 2003). In other words, as adults are aging, their vision, cognition, metacognition, and physical skills are declining with an important impact on their ability in performing many tasks such as the information search on the Web. Unfortunately, little attention has been paid to the understanding of the impacts of these cognitive and metacognitive impairments on the information search activity performed through a digital environment.

Metamemory is defined as knowledge of one's memory abilities and functioning (Flavell, 1979). Two levels of metamemory can be identified (Nelson & Narens, 1990): monitoring concerns knowledge of the information being processed while control concerns knowledge of the strategies that enable to improve information processing. However, these two levels are strongly dependent on one another and it is difficult to distinguish the both experimentally (Lazonder & Rouet, 2008).

Poor metamemory appears to be a characteristic of elderly adults (Lovelace and Marsh, 1985; Turvey *et al.*, 2000) due to a selective decline in frontal lobe functioning related in executive functioning (for a synthesis, see Souchay & Isingrini, 2004). Even if some studies have demonstrated little relationship between memory complaint and impairment (West, 1996), others studies have suggested that an older person's metamemory is mostly accurate (Souchay & isingrini, 2004; Turvey *et al.*, 2000). For instance, in the study performed by Turvey *et al.* (2000), researchers examined memory complaint in a large national sample of 5 444 people aged ≥70, by using a longitudinal cohort study with two waves of data collection spaced 2 years apart. Participants were asked if they believed their memory was excellent, very good, good, fair, or poor. They were then administered a cognitive assessment. Results have shown that if people's assessment of their memory matched their actual performance on cognitive measures in general, large portions of the sample inaccurately assessed their

memory skills. In other words, poor metamemory appears effectively to be a characteristic of elderly persons.
Nevertheless, little attention has been paid to the investigation of the searching strategies used by elderly people when looking for information, even if some studies have shown that an older adult's performance on working memory tasks decline with age, s/he has a reduced ability to discern details in the presence of distracting information, and s/he has difficulties to search for information accurately and quickly (Becker, 2004; Lazonder & Rouet, 2008).
According to the recent theoretical models elaborated to describe the cognitive and metacognitive processes involved in the information search tasks (David, Song, Hayes and Fredin, 2007; Rouet & Tricot, 1998; Dinet & Rouet, 2008), the role of metacognitive skills such as metamemory in searching complex environments is crucial. In case of Web searching, these metacognitive skills pertain to a person's ability to plan a search (including the selection of appropriate search strategies), monitor the progress of the search process, and evaluate search outcomes in terms of relevance, reliability and authority (e.g., Branch, 2001 ; Lazonder & Rouet, 2008). In accordance with these recent models (Dinet & Rouet, 2008; Lazonder & Rouet, 2008; Rouet & Triot, 2008), the information search activity involves several cyclic processes and consists of three stages: preparation, exploration, and consolidation. The preparation stage begins when the end-user prepares to make choices from a menu of links in a hyperlinked system. In the exploration stage, the user navigates and explores the results of the choices and processes the information. After exploring and processing information, the end-user consolidates by evaluating the results against the goals set during the preparation stage. The outcomes of the evaluation stage play an immediate role on recalibration of goals that are carried into the preparation phase of the next cycle. The model is ideally suited for information seeking situations in which goals are emergent, which means that at the beginning of the information seeking task, the user has vague goals, which are refined during the searching process. So, using a vague goal as a starting point, user seeks different types of online information, perhaps beginning with the results from a search engine. With emergent goals, the definition of success in finding the right information evolves during the searching process and the criteria for success vary by different levels of fit between information sought and information found. The user may evaluate the information as 'this is not exactly what I was looking for, but it seems interesting', or 'I will keep this in mind and continue looking for something that fits more precisely into what I am looking for'. Because the user must remember her/his search topic during her/his information searching process and because she/he must decide to begin or to stop one of the three stages (i.e., preparation, exploration, and consolidation), metamemory is essential.
So, because poor metamemory appears to be a characteristic of elderly persons and because metamemory is essential during the information searching process, the main goal of this experiment was to investigate the impacts of metamemory skills on the information search activities performed by elderly end-users.

4.1 Participants

In this experiment, 50 French end-users volunteers (32 males and 18 females), aged from 66 to 71 years were recruited to participate. Each of them was individually asked to search for

information about three specific topics in the World Wide Wed by using a specific search engine (Google.fr).
The 50 participants recruited for this experiment had a range of experience with computers and the World Wide Web. Participants had been using a computer for an average of 63.7 months (SD = 22.67) and they all spent an average of 12.32 (SD = 5.71) hours per week using a computer. While all the participants had used the World Wide Web at least once, there was quite a wide range of experience. On average, seniors recruited had been using the Web for 26.34 months (SD = 8.21) and spent 5.15 h (SD = 3.17) per week using the Web.

4.2 Material

Assessment of computer and Web knowledge. To assess computer and Web knowledge, participants completed a computer questionnaire elaborated by using all the items created by Lim, Bonge, Pellegrini, & Montagna (2001; Karavidas, Lim & Katsikas, 2005) and by adding some items extracted from the questionnaire used by students in University of Washington to assess their computer and Web knowledge. So, our final computer questionnaire subscales tapped into:
(1) software knowledge, with 15 questions (e.g., "Do you know how to change text fonts, size, color and style?");
(2) hardware knowledge, with 14 questions (e.g., "If you have a program on a diskette or a CD, do you know how to tell the computer to RUN it?");
(3) general computer knowledge, with 15 questions (e.g., "Do you understand and use the functions of the left and right mouse buttons?");
and (4) Web knowledge, with 15 questions (e.g., "Do you know the difference between a search engine, subject directory and a meta-search tool, and know when it is most advantageous to use one over the other?").
For each of these 59 questions, each participant was asked to check one of the three following response : "no or unlikely" (= 0), "not sure, but likely" (= 1), or "yes" (= 2). So, a global score (from 0 to 118) was computed for each respondent.
Assessment of metamemory. A Likert scale elaborated by Fort (2005) was used to assess the metamemory of the participants. Each participant was asked to fill this questionnaire before to perform the three information search tasks. This questionnaire is a Likert scale with 41 items about the three dimensions involved in the metamemory identified by Fort (2005): 11 items about the stereotypes about memory aging (e.g., "I remember very well where I went"); 15 items about the subject's beliefs about one's abilities (e.g., "Now, I remember less well than before"); and 14 items about his/her knowledge about strategies and strategy uses (e.g., "You write your appointments on a calendar to help you remember?"). For each of these 41 items, each participant was asked to check "no" (= 0) or "yes" (= 1). On the basis of the mean result computed for all the participants, two groups were constituted: participants with low metamemory skills (Meta-; n=32) and participants with high metamemory skills (Meta+; n=18)

4.3 Procedure

Individually, participants were asked to perform three different information search tasks through the use of Google.fr. On the basis of results obtained in previous studies (Dinet, submitted; Karavidas, Lim & Katsikas, 2005), these search topics were chosen to provide real life examples that showed relevant to our participants and they focused on:

- health: "Can you find Web sites to get information on the causes, symptoms, treatment and prevention of senior's health",
- finance: "Can you find Web sites about the financial planning guidelines to seniors",
- and travels: "Can you find Web sites related to an adventure travel tour operator that runs small group for people over 60".

Each participant received the same instructions and followed the same experimental procedures as all the others. All the sessions took place in a quiet room equipped with one computer. One week before they attended their session, the participants had completed the computer and Web knowledge questionnaire. Moreover, a background questionnaire gave for each participant the gender, age, personal experience in the use of a computer, and the number of hours spent in a week searching on the World Wide Web.

At the beginning of a session, the experimenter presented the procedures to the participant. S/he was then given the paper with the three questions (health, finance, and travels), and s/he was asked to search for information on the World Wide Web to find answers to these three questions.

The participants were allowed a maximum of 50 minutes to complete each information search: the experiment began as soon as the participant turned the sheet over -with the three questions on it- to read them and finished 50 minutes later. The participant could ask questions to the experimenter before the search for information actually started. If s/he had no questions and said s/he was ready, the experiment could start. Finally, an informal interview took place after the participant had finished their information search task at the computer.

The search engine used by the participant in this study was Google fr with Internet Explorer 6.0, as these electronic tools were commonly used in France. The same experimenter was with the participants all the time while they were searching for information on the World Wide Web. He did not intervene in the participant's activity during the search for information process, except when it was absolutely necessary to help them (for instance should an electronic bug or a technical problem happen).

4.4 Main results

Based on the results obtained with the Lickert scale used to assess the metamemory skills (Fort, 2005), two groups were distinguished: participants with low metamemory skills (Meta-) and participants with high metamemory skills (Meta+). As Table 4 shows, computer and Web knowledge were equivalent for the two groups.

		Group				
		Meta-n=32		*Meta+n*=18		
		M	SD	*M*	SD	*p*
Age (years)		69.3	3.4	72.1	2.6	.23
Metamemory skills	Stereotypes about memory aging (from 0 to 11)	4.3	1.8	8.8	1.7	.001**
	Subject's beliefs (from 0 to 15)	3.9	2.1	11.3	0.9	.001**
	Knowledge about strategies (from 0 to 14)	4.2	1.5	10.2	1.2	.002**

	Σ	12.4		30.3		.002**
Computer and Web knowledge	General Knowledge (from 0 to 30)	23	7	20	6	.18
	Hardware Knowledge (from 0 to 28)	21	5	19	9	.21
	Software Knowledge (from 0 to 30)	17	4	19	6	.19
	Internet Knowledge (from 0 to 30)	19	7	21	5	.18
	Σ	80		79		.23

Table 4. Distribution of participants in the two groups, Meta- and Meta+ (N = 50). *Note1*: "*M*" means Mean and "SD" means Standard Deviation; *Note2*: * p < .05 ; ** p < .01

The measures from the computer and Web questionnaire used in our study were general computer knowledge, software knowledge, hardware knowledge, and Web knowledge. The estimated reliability α coefficients were .79, .84, .95, and .92, respectively. As analyses revealed, the computer and Web knowledge subscales were significantly correlated as expected for the two groups (Meta- and Meta+).

As Table 5 shows, the average time spent to perform the information search tasks for participants with high metamemory skills (Meta+) is always inferior than the average time spent to perform the same activity for participants with low metamemory skills (Meta-). This difference is significant whatever the search topic (Health: $F(1\text{-}48) = 10.84$, $p < .0001$; Finance: $F(1\text{-}48) = 8.43$, $p < .0001$; Travels: $F(1\text{-}48) = 5.31$, $p = .002$). In other words, there is a significant impact of metamemory skills on the time spent to perform the information search activities performed by elderly end-users.

		Group				
		Meta-N=32		*Meta*+N=18		
Search topics	Indicators	*M*	SD	*M*	SD	*p*
Health	Answer time (in min.)	16.3	3.5	8.4	4.1	<.0001**
	Number of Web sites explored	9.5	3.2	8.9	2.3	.12
	Number of relevant Web sites	5.4	2.8	4.3	2.9	.10
Finance	Answer time (in min.)	24.7	5.1	11.8	6.9	<.0001**
	Number of Web sites explored	10.4	2.8	11.1	2.2	.11
	Number of relevant Web sites	3.5	1.9	4.2	2.3	.09
Travels	Answer time (in min.)	17.1	3.8	10.3	2.4	.002**
	Number of Web sites explored	9.3	3.1	7.6	4.2	.09
	Number of relevant Web sites	3.4	2.1	4.4	3.1	.13

Table 5. Impacts of metamemory skills on performance in an information search task. *Note*: * p < .05 ; ** p < .01.

For the number of Web sites explored and for the number of relevant Web sites found, results show no significant difference between our two groups (Meta- *vs.* Meta+), whatever the search topic (health, finances, and travels).
In other words, results obtained in this second experiment have mainly shown that there is a significant impact of metamemory skills on the time spent to perform information search activities performed by our participants. More precisely, the time spent to perform the information search tasks for participants with high metamemory skills is significantly inferior than the average time spent to perform the same activity for participants with low metamemory skills, whatever the search topic considered (health, finance, or travels). These results are consistent with the general view that age-related decline in cognitive functioning is partly due to executive dysfunction (Moscovitch & Winocur, 1992; Souchay & Isingrini, 2004; West, 1996).

5. Discussion and perspectives

Because some psychological and neuropsychological research suggests that it is hard for elderly people to develop new skills and because the ability to use information and communication technology is now assumed to be a prerequisite to living in our societies (Asla, Williamson & Mills, 2006; Curzon, Wilson & Withney, 2005; Selwyn, 2003), then understanding more about all aspects of information and communication in relation to elderly people is becoming increasingly crucial considering the changing demographic profile of communities and the implications for society. Second, our results confirm that the role of metacognitive skills such as metamemory in searching complex environments is crucial, according to the recent theoretical models (David, Song, Hayes & Fredin, 2007; Rouet & Tricot, 1998; Dinet & Rouet, 2008).
According to many authors (e.g., Alpass and Neville, 2003; Coulson, 2000; Groves and Slack, 1994; Karavidas, Lim and Katsikas, 2005), computers and the World Wide Web present two main opportunities for elderly adults: on the one hand, minimizing social and psychological problems through computer usage because computers and the Web can present unique opportunities for them to socialize and establish social networks that can help alleviate loneliness and alienation; on the other hand, improving quality of life with computers by increasing levels of independence. In addition, this increased perception of independence included engaging in more social activities and manifesting more positive attitudes. Another benefit of the newfound independence is higher confidence in one's ability that ultimately leads to higher levels of life satisfaction. Computers add a "functional dimension" in the lives of seniors that may contribute to a better self-concept.
Finally, this will require a considerable amount of research in forthcoming years if end-users have specific impairments because the normal ageing process, including vision, cognition, metacognition and physical impairments, has an impact on Internet usability.
Because an increasing number of elderly people will need to use computers and computer related systems in the future to avoid social exclusion and so as to be able to live more independently, there are considerable social and economic reasons why interface designers should rise to the challenge of designing interfaces which are usable by elderly people (Hawthorn, 2000; Zajicek, 2004). The number of seniors is growing more quickly than that of all the other segments of the population. This will impact on the cost of social care unless technological solutions can be found to enable people to stay longer in their homes (Czaja &

Lee, 2001; Lawhorn, Ennis & Lawhorn, 1996). Designers of interactive electronic products must take into account the special needs of such a significant population who often find current products difficult and complicated to use (Becker, 2004; Billip, 2001; DeOllos & Morris, 2000). Failure to do so will result in this large and growing group of citizens becoming marginalized through lack of access to information and services and also excluded from the use of interactive electronic products such as stair lifts and alarm systems that could help them to live longer in an independent way. As Zajicek (2004) said, even if there is also legislative pressure for the development of systems that are accessible to older and disabled people, unfortunately, the industry sector has not yet recognized the significant benefits of more accessible design and most providers continue to produce products that are primarily aimed at younger people.

6. References

Alpass, F.M., & Neville, S. (2003). Loneliness, health, and depression in older males. *Aging and Mental Health*, Vol. 73, 212–217

Arnott, J.L., Khairulla, Z., Dickinson, A., A.Syme, N.Alm, R.Eisma and P.Gregor (2004). E-mail Interfaces for Older People. In *IEEE International Conference on Systems, Man and Cybernetics*, 2004, pp: 111-118

Asla, T., Williamson, K., & Mills, J. (2006). The role of information in successful aging: The case for a research focus on the oldest old. *Library & Information Science Research*, Vol. 28, 49 - 63

Barrett, J. (2000). The information needs of elderly, disabled elderly people, and their carers. *Research report published by the Disability Information Trust*, retrieved online: http://freespace.virgin.net/julie.barrett/ April 14, 2009

Becker, S. (2004). A study of Web usability for older adults seeking online health resources. *ACM Transactions on Computer-Human Interaction*, Vol. 11, No. 4, 387–406

Billip, S.H. (2001). The psychosocial impact of interactive computer use within a vulnerable elderly population: a report on a randomized prospective trial in a home health care setting. *Public Health Nursing*, Vol. 18, 138–145

Branch, J. L. (2001). Junior high students and thinks alouds: Generating information-seeking process data using concurrent verbal protocols. *Library & Information Science Research*, Vol. 23, 107–122

Chadwick-Dias, A., McNulty, M. and Tullis, T. (2003). Web Usability and Age: How Design Changes Can Improve Performance. In *Proceedings of the 2003 Conference on Universal Usability CUU'03*, (Vancouver, British Columbia, Canada), pp: 30-38

Coulson, I. (2000). Introduction: Technological challenges for gerontologists in the 21st century. *Educational Gerontology*, Vol. 26, No. 4, 307–316

Czaja, S. J., Lee, C. C. (2001). The Internet and Older Adults: Design Challenges and Opportunities. In N. Charness, D.C. Park, D.C. and B.A. Sabel (Eds.), *Aging and communication: Opportunities and Challenges of Technology*. Springer Publishing Co, New York

Czaja S.C.J., Sharit J., Nair S. and Rubert M. (1998). Understanding sources of user variability in computer-based data entry performance. *Behaviour & Information Technology*, Vol. 17, No. 5, 282–293

Curzon, P., Wilson, J., and Whitney, G. (2005). Successful strategies of older people for finding information. *Interacting with Computers*, Vol. 17, 660 - 671

David, P., Song, M., Hayes, A., and Fredin, E.S. (2007). A cyclic model of information seeking in hyperlinked environments: The role of goals, self-efficacy, and intrinsic motivation. International Journal of Human-Computer Studies, 65(2), 170–182

DeOllos, I. Y. and Morris, D.C. (2000). The Internet as an information resource for older adults. *Journal of Educational Technology Systems*, Vol. 28, 107–122

Dinet, J. (submitted). Elderly people as Web seekers: Why, where and how do they search for health/medical information. *Canadian Journal on Aging*

Dinet, J. & Tricot, A. (2008). Recherche d'information dans les documents électroniques. In A. Chevalier & A. Tricot (Eds.), *Ergonomie cognitive des documents électroniques* (pp.35-69). Paris, Presses Universitaires de France

Ellis, R. D., & Allaire, J. C. (1999). Modeling computer interest in older adults: The role of age, education, computer knowledge, and computer anxiety. *Human Factors*, Vol. 41, No. 3, 345–356

Epstein, J. (1980). Information needs of the Elderly, Final Report, June 1980. *A Study Commissioned by the Department of Health and Social Security*. Research Institute for Consumer Affairs, London

Fisk, A.D., Rogers, W.A., Charness, N., Czaja, S.J. and Sharit, J. (2004). *Designing for older adults. Principles and Creative Human Factors Approaches*. CRC Press

Flavell, J. H. (1979). Metacognition and cognitive monitoring: a new area of cognitive-developmental inquiry. *American Psychologist*, Vol. 34, 906–911

Fort, I. (2005). La métamémoire: Analyse de sa mesure par questionnaire. *Psychologie Française*, Vol. 50, No. 2, 195–210

Groves, D.L., & Slack, T. (1994). Computers and their application to senior citizens therapy within a nursing home. *Journal of Instructional Psychology*, Vol. 21, No. 3, 221–227

Hawthorn, D. (2000). Possible implications of ageing for interface designers. *Interacting with Computers*, Vol. 12, 507–528

Hodes, R.J. and Lindberg, D.A.B. (2002). *Making Your Web Site Senior Friendly*, National Institute on Aging and the National Library of Medicine

Jastrzembski, T., Charness, N., Holley, P. and Feddon, J. Input devices for web browsing: age and hand effects. Universal Access in Information Society, 2005, 4. pp: 39-45

Karavidas, M., Lim, N.K., and Katsikas, S.L. (2005). The effects of computers on older adult users. *Computers in Human Behavior*, Vol. 21, No. 5, 697-711

Lazonder, A.W., & Rouet, J.-F. (2008). Information problem solving instruction: Some cognitive and metacognitive issues. *Computers in Human Behavior*, Vol. 24, No. 3, 753-765

Lawhorn T., Ennis D., Lawhorn D. C. (1996). Senior adults and computers in the 1990s. *Educational Gerontology*, Vol. 22, 193–201

Lim, N. K., Bonge, D. R., Pellegrini, A., & Montagna, S. (2001). *Computer anxiety, computer knowledge, and computer liking: Updated computer scales for the new century*. Unpublished manuscript, Carlos Albizu University at Miami

Lovelace, E. A., Marsh, G. R. (1985). Prediction and evaluation of memory performance by young and old adults. *Journal of Gerontology*, Vol. 40, 192–197

Meischke, H., Eisenberg, M., Rowe, S.R. and Cagle, A. (200)5. Do older adults use the Internet for information on heart attacks? Results from a survey of seniors in King County, Washington. *Heart & Lung: The Journal of Acute and Critical Care*, Vol. 34, No. 1, 3-12

Morrell, R.W., Dailey, S.R. and Rousseau, G.K. (2003). Applying Research: The NIHSeniorHealth.gov Project. In N. Charness and K.W. Schaie (Eds.), *Impact of Technology on Successful Aging*. New-York, Springer Series Societal Impact on Aging

Moscovitch, M. and Winocur, G. (1992). The neuropsychology of memory and aging. In F.I.M Craik and T.A. Salthouse (Eds.), *The handbook of aging and cognition* (pp 315–372), Hillsdale, Lawrence Erlbaum Associates

Nelson, T.O., & Narens, L. (1990). Metamemory: a theoretical framework and new findings. In G. Bower (Ed.), *The psychology of learning and motivation* (pp 125–140), New York, Academic Press

Rouet, J-F., & Tricot, A. (1998). *Les hypermédias: Approches cognitives et ergonomiques*. Paris: Hermès

Sayago, S. & Blat, J. (2007). A preliminary usability evaluation of strategies for seeking online information with elderly people. *Proceedings of the 2007 international cross-disciplinary conference on Web accessibility* (W4A) (pp 54 - 57), Banff, Canada

Selwyn, N. (2003). Apart from technology: understanding people's non-use of information and communication technologies in everyday life. *Technology in Society*, Vol. 25, 99 - 116

Selwyn, N., Gorard, S., Furlong, J., & Madden, L. (2003). Older adults' use of information and communications technology in everyday life. *Ageing & Society*, Vol. 23, 561–582

Souchay, C., & Isingrini, M. (2004). Age related differences in metacognitive control: Role of executive functioning. *Brain and Cognition*, Vol. 56, No. 1, 89-99

Stronge, A. J., Rogers, W.A., & Fisk, A.D. (2006). Web-based information search and retrieval: Effects of strategy use and age on search success. *Human factors*, Vol. 48, No. 3, 434-446

Tinker, A., McCreadie, C., & Salvage, A. (1993). *The information needs of elderly people – an exploratory study*. Age Concern Institute of Gerontology, London

Troup, G. (1985). Information and older people in Scotland (needs and strategies). *Report of a one year research project funded by Age Concern Scotland Development Advisory Resource Group and the Scottish Education Council*, January 1985

Turvey, C.L., Schultz, S., Arndt, S., Wallace, R.B., & Herzog, R. (2000). Memory complaint in a community sample aged 70 and older. *Journal of the American Geriatrics Society*, Vol. 48, No. 11, 1435–1441

West, R. (1996). An application of prefrontal cortex function theory to cognitive aging. *Psychological Bulletin*, Vol. 120, 272–292

Williamson, K. (1995). Older adults: information, communication and telecommunications. *Unpublished doctoral dissertation*. RMIT, Monash, Australia

Williamson, K. (1998). Discovered by chance: The role of incidental learning acquisition in an ecological model of information use. *Library & Information Science Research*, Vol. 20, 23–40

Zajicek, M. (2004). Successful and available: interface design exemplars for older users. *Interacting with Computers*, Vol. 16, No. 3, 411–430

Seamless-based infomobility applications to support the needs of all travellers

Evangelos Bekiaris, Maria Panou and Konstantinos Kalogirou
Centre for Research and Technology Hellas – Hellenic Institute of Transport
Greece

1. Introduction

Mobility often depends on the possibility of getting access to information both in terms of planning before travel and orientation during travel. The population in Europe with problems using information and communication technology is estimated to be 22.25% (Gill, 2004). Over 30% of the population can't use emerging mainstream web services and benefit from the eSociety and ICT applications, as unfortunately, little consideration has been given to the accessibility of these services by people suffering from motor, communication (illiteracy, dyslexia), hearing or visual limitations, which have an imminent negative effect to their mobility. The main reasons are the inappropriate interfaces and the lack of adequate integrated services and content that covers holistically an application area, leading to the need to visit various web-places from different service providers to collect the relevant info; which is neither practical nor economical.

2. The ASK-IT project – an overview

ASK-IT IP (co-financed by the eInclusion initiative of the IST Program of EC), developed a novel application consisting of prototypes and systems which automatically interfaces services from different service providers, in a transparent to the users way. Thus, ASK-IT manages to take everybody everywhere with a good level of comfort, providing pre-trip and on-trip information and support by telematic services; seamlessly throughout the trip, in a personalised way, according to individual user needs and preferences. In specific, ASK-IT developed a set of new, fully accessible tools, to support key functionalities for all, including travelers with functional limitations, among which are accurate indoors and outdoors localization, accessible route planning and guidance for car drivers, PT users and pedestrians.

ASK-IT is thus a universal system for all, which however takes specific care to satisfy the needs of ALL citizens, including mobility impaired (MI) users, such as:

- blind and partially sighted people;
- deaf and people with hearing problems;
- people unable to walk, i.e. wheelchair users;

- people who have difficulty in walking and bending limbs;
- people with medical problems affecting balance and stamina;
- people with cognitive impairment;
- people who are illiterate.

2.1 The Ontological framework used

In order to realise its vision, ASK-IT developed, among others, an open ontological framework, covering the contents that correspond to the above fields. For each type of content and each element within it, all accessibility attributes have been incorporated into the ontology. For example, the height and width of doors at a hotel, the existence or not and the width and height of steps at entrances or stairs, the existence or not and the inclination of ramps, etc. These ontologies are public and any new service provider can use them to develop ASK-IT compatible services. Thus, services are based upon a common ontological scheme, which can interface existing services through an online service alignment tool and a multi-agent system for service delivery, including personalized agents at the user's device and Web-based agents for service discovery.

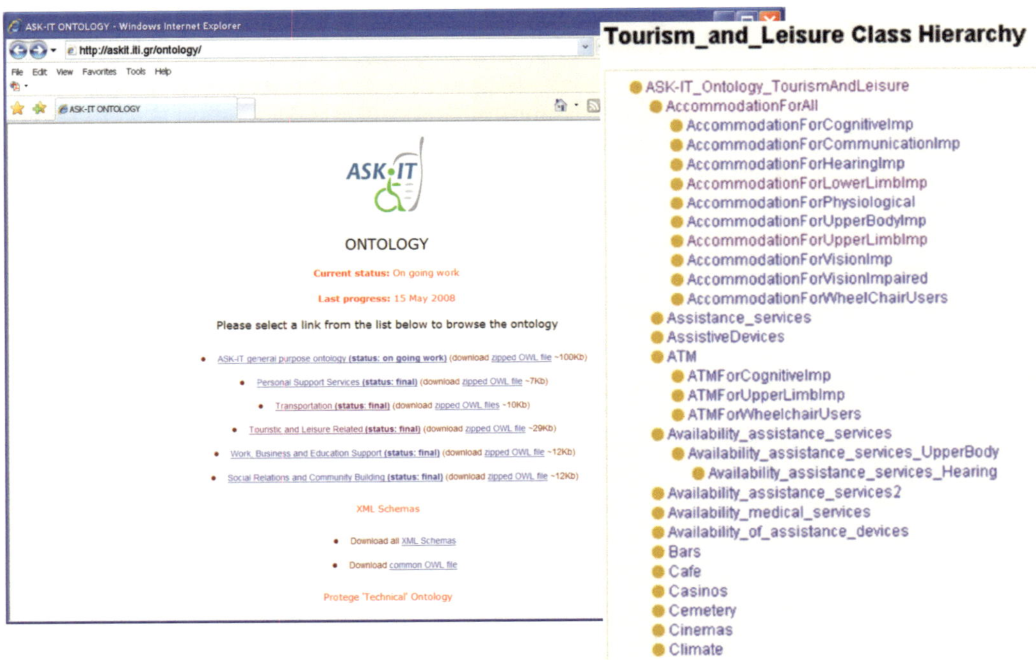

Fig. 1. Extract of the ASK-IT ontology.

Ambient Intelligence has been achieved by introducing personalisation to the content management (intuitive semantics), search functionality (intelligent agents for service provision), as well as the usability (self configured UI). The relevant GUI is self-configurable to the user type, as well as the device used, thus allowing users to get ASK-IT services through PC, tablet PC, mobile PC, PDA, mobile phone, automotive screen or even specialised domotic devices. The UI is adaptable to each device properties and capabilities. It tailors the service to the user's preferences, needs and habits as well as to the context of use. It then introduces this intelligence to the body, personal, local and wide area networks, and the integrated, secure service platform. Thus, the intelligence is diffused on all aspects of service provision; else the unintelligent parts (i.e. content, functionality or interface) would cancel and limit the benefits of the intelligent ones. On the other hand, intelligent sensors were not developed, but interfaced from other research initiatives (such as SENSATION IP), to limit the work to the required for the service provision and result to a low-cost, modular, s/w-based system.

3. Applications and services in the Greek pilot site

Substantial developments were realised in the Greek pilot, resulting in a total of 10 connected services to the ASK-IT platform. A number of services already existed, including traffic and travel information services, demand responsive transport services, personal assistance in the airport, etc. Besides the existing services and infrastructure, many more services were created, in order to cover the ASK-IT application areas. For existing web services and applications, the existing content was updated and connected to the ASK-IT ontologies. The list of the available services follows below:

1. Accessible POIs (Athens & Thessaloniki), with transportation means info
2. Accessible multimodal routing
3. Personal support services
4. Social services
5. E-learning & e-working services
6. Domotics
7. In-vehicle services

A short description follows below for each of the above service types.

3.1 Accessible POIs and routes between POIs/stations

Accessibility data gathering was realised with the on-site visit of a specialized team, that stored the data electronically, according to specific evaluation forms (loaded on a PDA). Thus, accessibility information was stored on a PDA. Then, locally stored data was transferred to the ASK-IT SQL database and populated the corresponding Web services. Detailed info has been gathered for the accessibility of the POIs (hotels, restaurants/cafes, entertainment centers/venues, theatres/ cinemas, cultural facilities, sport venues, parks, bank ATM, shopping centers), the accessibility of the transportation means and stations, nearby the POIs as well as main public transport terminals (main bus, train and metro stations, airport). In total, 234 POIs were evaluated in Athens (including the Athens International Airport). The accessibility of 111 POIs from Thessaloniki city centre was included in the system by connecting already available content from a local project of the University of Macedonia to the ASK-IT platform.

Also, the most accessible pedestrian route, from the nearest stop/station to the selected POIs or from a POI (e.g. hotel) to another nearby (e.g. restaurant) is proposed, per ASK-IT user group. Over 50 pedestrian routes were evaluated in Athens and more than 20 in Thessaloniki.

A 3-level accessibility scheme is used, with a colour coding, distinguishing between the accessibility level of each POI/route. The results are shown according to the following table:

ASK-IT accessibility level	ASK-IT colour coding
0. Not checked	Black or grey
1. Not accessible	Red
2. Semi-accessible	Orange or yellow
3. Fully accessible	Green

Table 1. ASK-IT accessibility levels and corresponding colour coding used.

3.2 Accessible multimodal routing

A new mode of route guidance was developed, namely accessible route guidance. The system knows the user's particular problems (i.e. use of walking stick, wheelchair, or blind, or ...) and the accessibility attributes of the routes and matches them (by semantic search), resulting to the proposition to each user of a route that is accessible for him/her (i.e. without stairs or with ramp/lifts, etc.).

Fig. 2. Routing application on the mobile phone.

In addition to it, multimodal route planning is supported (including rerouting during trip in case of need, i.e. service disruption or change of plans by traveller), again taking into account the user abilities, as well as preferences (i.e. maximum number if transportation mean choices he/she usually accepts) for selecting the multimodal trip as well as for selecting the suggested POIs to visit (i.e. type of restaurants he/she prefers, type of hotel he/she usually books). The personalisation of information is according to the parameters defined in Panou, 2008 (PhD Dissertation).

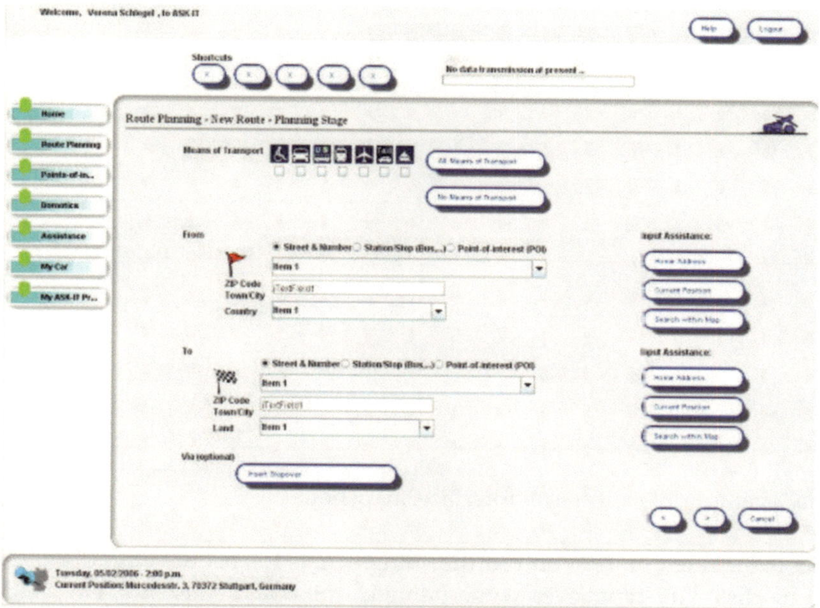

Fig. 3. Personalised multimodal route planning within ASK-IT.

3.3 Personal support

This service allows the users to rent special equipment before their arrival at the airport or a hotel. Such equipment are wheelchairs and Braille maps. For the purpose of the tests, Braille maps were prepared for the centre of Thessaloniki.

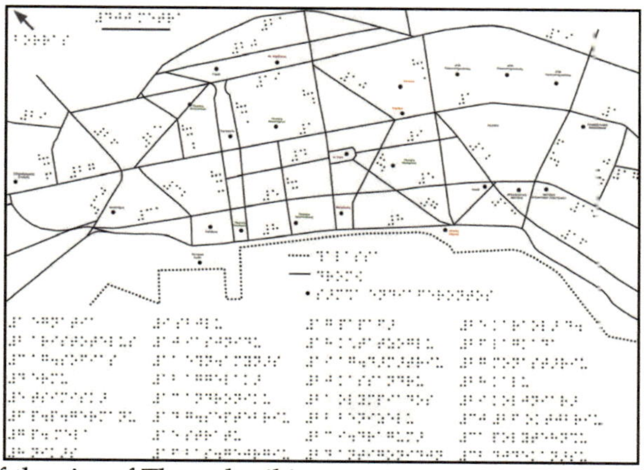

Fig. 4. Braille map of the city of Thessaloniki.

3.4 Social Events

CERTH/HIT developed the ASK-IT Social Events application. It is a web-based dynamic application that allows storing events in ASK-IT database (e.g. events not provided by Web service providers). The editing, deleting or adding of a new entry is allowed only to registered users.

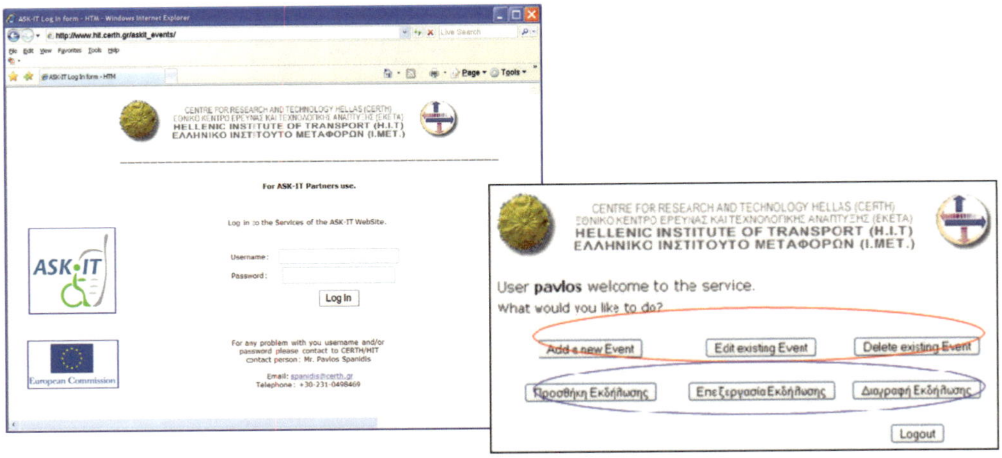

Fig. 5. Social events application user interface snapshots.

Information is included on past and forthcoming events for people with disabilities. Search is possible by disability type, event type (athletic, musical, conference, etc.) and date. The application can run on the mobile phones and PDAs. Below, the way that the application appears on the mobile phone is shown:

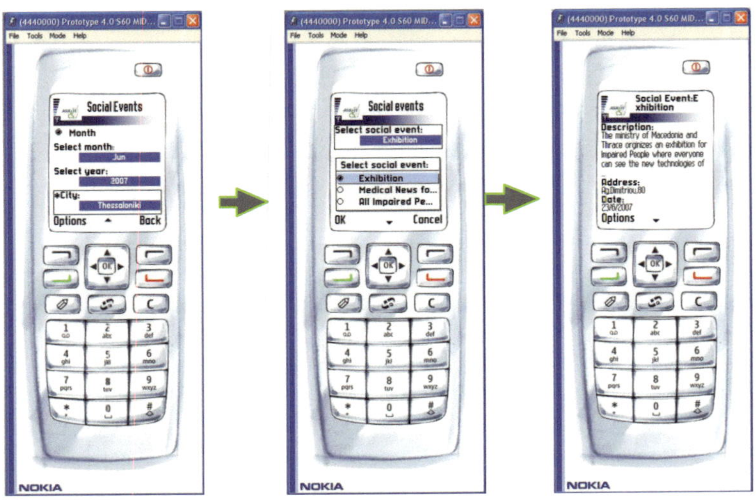

Fig. 6. Social events application on the mobile phone.

3.5 E-learning & e-working services

With the e-learning applications, the MI user is able to follow specific e-learning programs (e.g. Open University, national institutes, foreign languages lessons through internet, etc.). Also, a number of tasks can be performed with the e-working service, i.e. (Zabulica V., 2008):

- Receive / send e-mails, multimedia files.
- Download application from a website (i.e. company web site).

- Connection to a teleconferencing session.
- Participation in a collaborative work session.

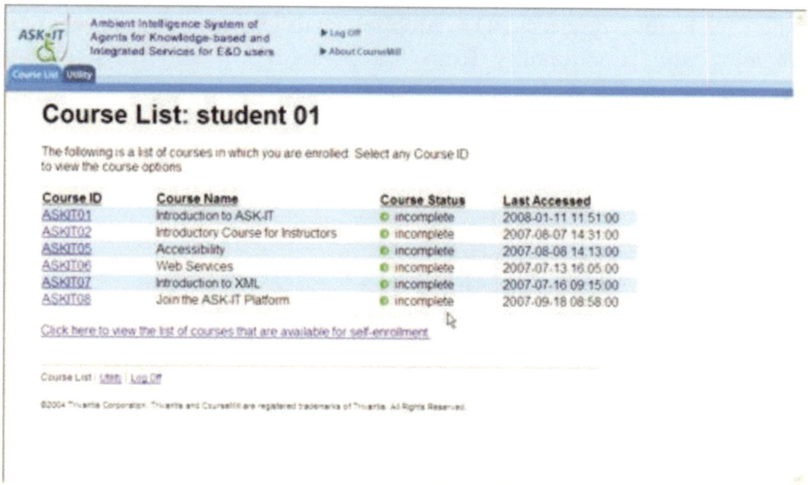

Fig. 7. Screenshot from the eLearning service of ASK-IT.

3.6 Domotics application

The Greek domotic pilot site has been designed and implemented from scratch for the purpose of ASK-IT and employs a wide variety of communication technologies and standards. From a top level point of view it makes use of both wired and wireless network communication mediums and the core of the system is based on OSGi middleware technology to form a Service Oriented Architecture. The domotic modules are integrated to the ASK-IT project by providing a User Interface under the common ASK-IT client software, and thus providing a centralised place for accessing all ASK-IT services (route planning, e-learning, etc.).

The general concept was to provide a safer, more secure and comfort environment for elderly and mobile impaired users (MI users) and to improve their overall wellbeing (Genoux et al., 2007). Taking this into consideration, the Greek demonstration site has been designed having a typical environment of a mobile impaired user in mind.

Fig. 8. Greek pilot site domotics room (at CERTH/HIT)

The UI developed for controlling the domotics in the Thessaloniki pilot site is integrated into the main ASK-IT services client UI and is designed with the same "look and feel". There are two versions available, one for large screen displays (desktop PC, laptop, media centre) and one smaller for mobile devices (PDA, mobile). Both UIs have been designed separating the business logic and functionality from the presentation and thus a more modular approach has been utilized. This is very important since it makes possible for other domotic sites to integrate with less development the ASK-IT services and domotics UI with their current infrastructure. The following screenshots present the two different UIs for both the mobile devices and large screen displays.

Fig. 9. UI of the domotics application at the mobile devices (PDA, mobile phone).

The laptop, desktop and media centre computers share the same application and size constraints. The following screenshots are from the UI of these devices.

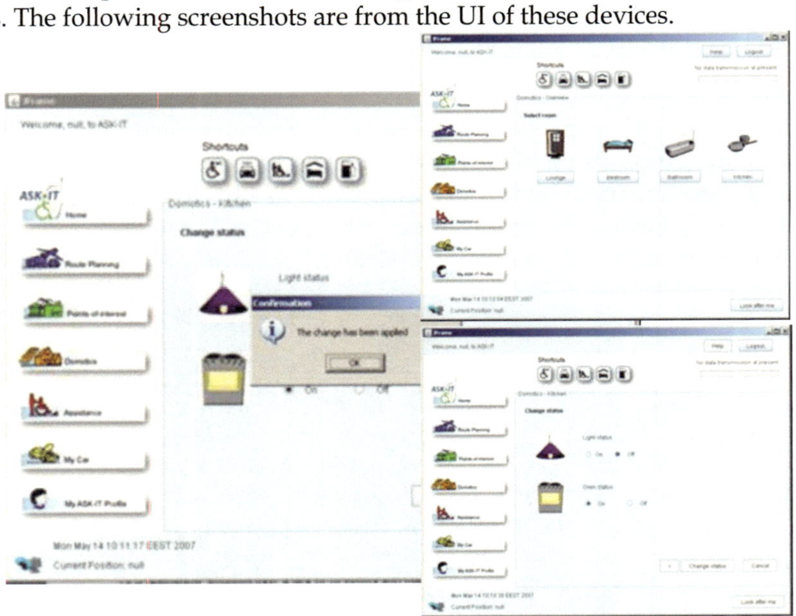

Fig. 10. Screenshots of the large screen displays UIs (laptop, desktop and media centre computers).

The pilot-site in Thessaloniki uses a touch-panel based User Interface device. In general, this device has been customized to the special needs of elderly & disabled users. Furthermore, it is appropriate for dyslexic persons, because the UI concept is based on images instead of text.

3.7 In-vehicle application

To secure safe operation of ASK-IT services while driving, a specific context-aware system for in-vehicle ASK-IT services provision has been built. The UI of the services is thus adapted when the vehicle is travelling with a speed over 15km/h (i.e. visual elements are minimised, technical interactions are frozen, ...) and also ASK-IT info is delayed or cancelled when other info/warning comes from Advanced Driver Assistance Systems (ADAS). The in-vehicle system has been also adapted for specific user types categories, i.e. people with hearing impairment, colour blindness, illiterate /dyslectic, upper limbs impairment and neck problems (Visintainer et al., 2007). The ADAS that have been selected, implemented and integrated to the CERTH/HIT test vehicle to demonstrate the proposed algorithms and UI adaptation are:

- Adaptive Cruise Control (ACC) and Collision Avoidance System (CAS).
- Lane Departure Warning (LDW).

The driver keeps receiving the ASK-IT info from his/her ASK-IT nomad device. No transfer to an in-vehicle system takes place. The ASK-IT nomad device is connected to the car through a Bluetooth gateway. Thus, the ASK-IT services HMI adaptation for the MI users is according to the one developed for ASK-IT. Only the related ADAS HMI is thus adapted, when needed. ADAS algorithms have been adapted in terms of timing, modality and intensity of warning.

As a general rule, ADAS warnings have priority over all ASK-IT UCs. Thus, when an ADAS message is given, the ASK-IT messages will be interrupted or delayed by 20 seconds. Exceptions are the ASK-IT use cases related to emergency issues, which have top priority and follow their functionality in parallel to ADAS operation. For example, if a lane departure warning comes when the driver has pushed the emergency button requesting help, then: the LDW warning is given to the driver, while at the same time the car is being braked and the alarms are being activated. When the Center sends the feedback that help is coming, the driver is being informed. Another exception is the relevant use cases where the user has to turn to the next junction, the ADAS warning will come first but then the indication to turn may come after it with less distance than 20sec, so as not to lose the junction. This distance may never be less than 3sec.

The in-car module consists of two components; the server and client modules. The server module resides at PDA device and the client module resides at car's PC.

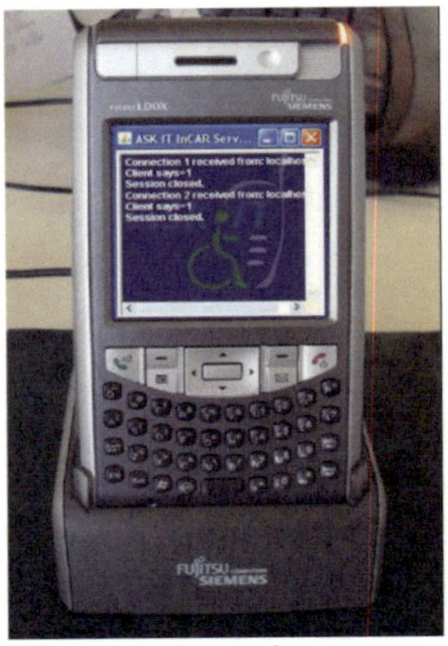

Fig. 11. Server's application

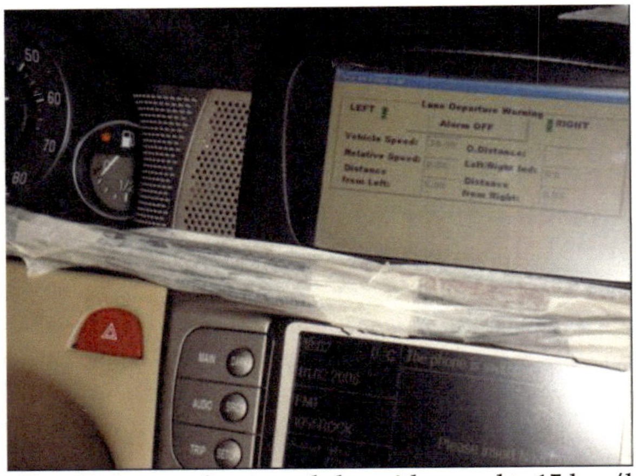

Fig. 12. In-car client module, with speed > 15 km/h

4. System evaluation in the Greek pilot

ASK-IT services have been installed in 8 sites Europewide, where significant accessibility content and infrastructure existed beforehand (to minimise efforts) but with many different IST technologies and sociological characteristics (to demonstrate interoperability). The ASK-IT sites were: Athens-Thessaloniki (GR), Bucharest (RO), Genova (IT), Helsinki (FI), Madrid (ES), Newcastle (UK), Nuremberg (DE) and The Hague (NL) as satellite site. Roughly 50 users tested ASK-IT services per site. Several hundreds of POIs and PT hubs and routes, as well as pedestrian routes have been connected to ASK-IT in each site, including a total of roughly 50 different service and content providers integrated into ASK-IT platform. Furthermore, cross-site Pilots between these sites guaranteed the seamless service delivery across Europe.

The Greek pilot site is a combined site, taking place in the two largest cities of Greece, Athens and Thessaloniki. All the above described services were evaluated with users with motor disabilities, as well as hearing problems and dyslexia. Participants were recruited by three supportive, non-profit, non-Governmental organizations. Moreover, mobility-impaired individuals were referred by employment counseling services.

The ASK-IT services enjoyed high levels of user acceptance from participants of the Athens-Thessaloniki pilot site. The easiness of use is highly related to the HMI issues. 72% of participants found ASK-IT easy or very easy to use at the start, and 74% found it easy or very easy to learn.

The following graph provides a visual image of the users' feedback, where the percentage of users that provided positive replies can be distinguished. The results are very encouraging.

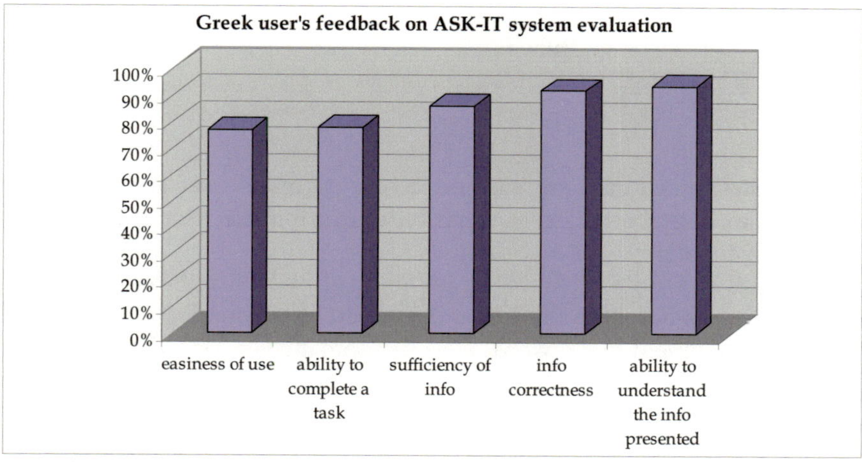

Fig. 13. Percentage of users with positive replies.

The personalisation service was accurate in terms of people's preferences for 89% of participants. Overall, 92% of people found ASK-IT met their needs. Security and privacy is seen as important or very important and all were satisfied or very satisfied with the perceived security of ASK-IT.

In terms of the graphical user interface, 84% of people found it easy or very easy to use it, of which 96% of participants found clear or very clear. 70% of participants found the text to be clear or very clear and 98% found the colour contrast to be clear or very clear. 71% of people suggested that the buttons and keypad are easy or very easy to use, although 65% would like additional buttons.

The responses regarding the ASK-IT services most cited as improving accessibility are shown below:

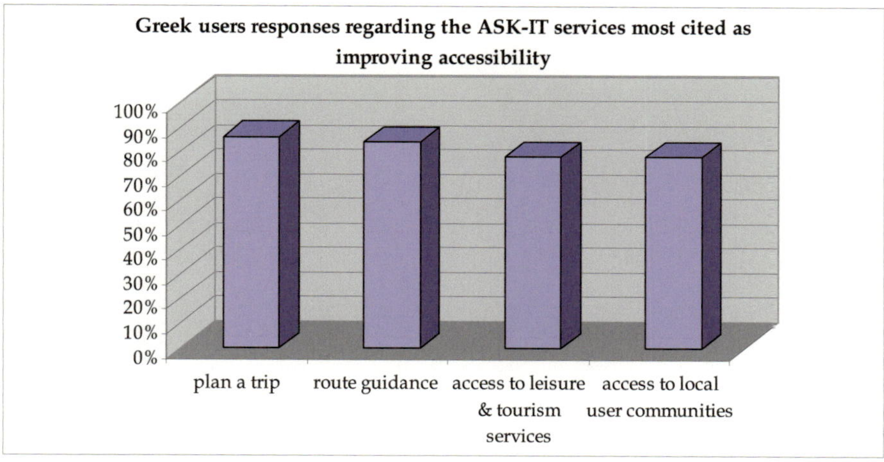

Fig. 14. Percentage of users suggesting the most important services for improving accessibility.

All participants would consider using ASK-IT in the future. The main factor that would influence their decision is the cost of equipment.

5. Conclusion

The findings from Athens-Thessaloniki are very positive in terms of user acceptance and usability. There appear to have been very few problems during the user trials. All the services are valued relatively highly.

ASK-IT research continues in OASIS IP (www.oasis-project.eu) which uptakes the ASK-IT ontology and further enhances it, within the scope of an open Hyperontological framework and further develops the alignment tool towards a semi-automatic version. Also, limitations of mobile devices reported by the users that obstruct them to use ASK-IT services intuitively, are dealt into AEGIS IP, that strives to make the next generation of mobile devices, desktop and rich internet applications fully accessible (www.aegis-project.eu).

6. References

Genoux F., Bekiaris E., Linaras C., Telkamp G, Heck H., Hanekamp N., Gaeta E., ASK-IT Deliverable 2.5.1 "*ASK-IT Interface to Domotic Applications*", December 2007.

Gill J. M., '*Smart Cards: Accessibility and Social Inclusion*'. National Smart Card Project, March 2004, 37 pp.

Panou M., PhD Dissertation '*Advanced personalized travelers' warning and information system*', Aristotle University of Thessaloniki, 2008.

Visintainer F., Bekiaris E., Panou M., Kalogirou K., Mourouzis A., Pagle K., ASK-IT Deliverable 2.6.1 "*ASK-IT gateway to ADAS/IVICS*", December 2007.

Zabulica V., ASK-IT Deliverable 2.8.2 "E-learning & e-working modules", March 2008.

24

The Continuity of Disability, Diversity and Personalisation: an Emerging Challenge for HCI

Sebastiano Bagnara[1] and Simone Pozzi[2]
[1] *Faculty of Architecture, University of Sassari, Alghero, Italy*
[2] *Dept. of Communication Sciences, University of Siena, Italy & Deep Blue, Rome, Italy*

1. Introduction

In the famous short novel "The Country of the Blind", H.G. Wells describes an isolated community, whose members have become blind long ago. The blind men have entirely redesigned their village to suit their blindness: sensory paths radiate from the village centre to the fields, houses are windowless to better protect from heat and from cold, the villagers have even changed their circadian rhythms, as they work at night when there is no sun heat. One day a traveler, named Nunez, arrived in this village. After discovering the blindness of the inhabitants, Nunez started thinking that "in the country of the blind the one-eyed man is king". He thought he would eventually rule the village because of his superiority, because he could see. However, Nunez soon discovered that the sense of sight was not highly valued by the blind villagers. They no longer had a concept for sight and their village had been shaped in such a manner that Nunez could not demonstrate any practical advantage over them. Indeed, he found himself to be the disadvantage one. He was not able to see where to walk inside the dark windowless houses and kept stumbling. He could not become a member of the community because he was still able to see.

The story of Wells illustrates some subtle aspects of the relationship between disability and human activity:

- Disability is related to a specific setting and to a specific activity (e.g. windowless houses and night work). There are "objective" physical, cognitive and social abilities/impairments, but disability is better thought of as the outcome of these in relation to an external setting and activity. Limitations are engendered by the relation between (i) our physical, cognitive and social characteristics, (ii) the activity to be carried out and (iii) the setting.
- A well-thought design of the setting (i.e. of assistive tools) can overcome what we would expect to be our limitations. Humans are able to exploit external tools to overcome their impairments and achieve a proficient performance.
- Being a relational concept, disability is more a statistical measure of the "standard relation" between human characteristics and the activity, than an "objective" parameter. Instead of being the king, Nunez is the disabled one in the country where everyone is blind.

Our paper moves from these points to reflect on the relationship between HCI and disability. We propose to consider disability not as an isolated niche of HCI study. It is rather part of a more general challenge, that HCI is facing as a discipline in its applications and studies (a similar claim can be found in Lewis, 2006). Our claim is that HCI is not yet fully equipped to cope with the increased complexity and variety of our technological life, of which disability is only a specific part.

2. Dovetailing and internalisation

The field of HCI studies on disability has definitively certain peculiarities. HCI researchers do need to study the nature and causes of specific physical or cognitive conditions, in order to design user-friendly technologies. But it also shares the basic goal of the general HCI endeavor "Human-computer interaction is a discipline concerned with the design, evaluation and implementation of interactive computing systems for human use and with the study of major phenomena surrounding them" (Association for Computing Machinery, 2008).

At the core of HCI studies is indeed the special relationship that we as humans are able to establish with technological devices. As well put by Andy Clark (Clark, 2003), humans are increasingly becoming "natural-born cyborgs". Key concept in his reasoning is the one of 'dovetail'. By interacting with tools and external elements, we put our cognitive skills in connection with these external elements, to form a new unity, new cognitive skills, new abilities, where it is hard (and not very meaningful) to distinguish between the contribution of our mind and that of external tools. "Ours are essentially the brains of natural-born cyborgs, ever-eager to dovetail their activity to the increasingly complex technological envelopes in which they develop, mature, and operate" (pg. 26).

On the same line of thought, we should also mention the Distributed Cognition approach (Hutchins, 1995; Norman, 1988). While mainstream cognitive science sees human cognition as happening inside the heads of individual actors, Distributed Cognition describes cognition as happening in the fabric of 'human-external world' interactions. In particular, Distributed Cognition has studied how people modify the external environment to save attention, memory and computational efforts. They recruit external elements to reduce their own cognitive effort (Kirsh, 1995), they produce pre-computed solutions (e.g. tools and procedures) to frequently encountered problems and preserve these solutions through cultural transmission (Hutchins, 1995).

Behind such approaches lies a theoretical tenet that has gained momentum since the eighties, as a reaction to the cognitive revolution of the fifties. It claims that cognition is not only in our head, but results from the connection between our head and the external world, in particular between our cognition and our tools.

We all have experienced the sensation of a tool becoming transparent to our perception. It becomes so part of our daily life, that we no longer perceive it as an external device. This happens for very simple tools (e.g. a hammer, sport equipments, a pen, etc.), as well as for more complex devices (e.g. computers, mobile devices, clutch and pedals in our car, etc.). Noticeably, blindness was again taken as an example to elaborate on this concept by Bateson in a very famous excerpt: "Suppose I am a blind man, and I use a stick. I go tap, tap, tap. Where do *I* start? Is my mental system bounded at the handle of the stick? Is it bounded by my skin? Does it start halfway up the stick? Does it start at the tip of the stick? But these are nonsense questions. The stick is a pathway along which transforms of difference are being transmitted. The way to delineate the system is to draw the limiting line in such a way that you do not cut any of these pathways in ways which leave things inexplicable. If what you are trying to explain is a given piece of behaviour, such as the locomotion of the blind man, then, for this purpose, you will need the street, the stick, the man; the street, the stick, and so on, round and round. But when the blind man sits down to eat his lunch, his stick and its messages will no longer be relevant—if it is his eating that you want to understand" (Bateson, 1972, p. 434). However, we also know that too often a tool gets in our way while we try to perform a certain task, e.g. troubleshooting our word processor, pc and printer is a good example of tools getting between us and our goal.

These two polarities of human-tool interaction can be summarised in two categories first introduced by Heidegger: 'ready-to-hand' and 'present-at-hand' (Heidegger, 1927/1962, cited in Chalmers, 2004). *Ready-to-hand* tools are transparent when we use them, "literally visible, effectively invisible" (Weiser, 1994a, p. 1). They are dovetailed with our cognition. *Present-at-hand* tools concern us not because we are using them, but because we are consciously observing and analysing them. A tool like a hammer may become *present-at-hand* when it breaks and loses its usefulness, or at the first encounter, when we do not know how to interact with it.

These two poles may be conceived as separate, but reality is that we continuously move between the two poles in our daily activity. Tools become *ready-to-hand* usually after some usage, they may revert to *present-at-hand* in case of breakdowns in the activity and, to a certain extent, the more we shift between the two modes, the more we are able to effectively master a tool and make it fully transparent in our activity. In order to understand these two modes of human-tool interaction we need to conceive the interaction as a process, with learning and development taking place through practice.

When a tool becomes *ready-to-hand*, it does not only disappear from our awareness. It also re-structures the way we think and the way we see the world. It becomes part of our cognition, in the sense that we begin perceiving the world and thinking of possibilities of action through the tool's affordances. This process has been described by Vygotsky in his cultural-historical approach (Vygotsky, 1978, 1986), by analysing the internalisation process. Oversimplifying for clarity's sake, Vygotsky's "General Law of Cultural Development" states that subjects internalise external tools (material and non material ones, like language and signs) and form analogue cognitive functions inside their brains. For instance, the process of thinking is formed by the progressive internalisation of speaking.

The key common point in the above discussion is that of brain plasticity. As a product of their functioning, our brains internalise tools. Our tools become part of our brain. It is not something we have to try hard for, it is like second nature. And it applies to any tool.

This is a challenge for HCI: how to design tools that effectively dovetail with our cognition? Certainly by supporting both ways of functioning, i.e. *ready-to-hand* and *present-at-hand*. I may prefer not being aware of the tool when using it, but I definitively have to understand its way of working at the first use, or if I want to avoid/solve breakdowns. Even though some design approaches (Dourish, 2001; Weiser, 1991) have advocated a decisive move in the direction of invisible tools ("a good tool is an invisible tool", Weiser, 1994b), we maintain that both modes are necessary for good HCI. As well put by Norman, a tool is user-friendly as long as the designer makes clear its way of functioning to the user, thus bridging the gap between the user's mental model and the actual system model (Norman, 1988). In order to do that, the user needs to shift continuously between experiential cognition (*ready-to-hand*) and reflexive one (*present-at-hand*).

3. Changes in the nature of work

HCI is an applied science, whose objectives reflect the changing priorities of human societies. In its history, Ergonomics (the direct father of HCI) has always tackled those issues that mostly mattered to its contemporary societies: physical ergonomics and work related diseases in the Tayloristic era, selection and training during the Second World War, human error in nuclear power plants and aviation in the Eighties, to name but a few. HCI has flourished during the 'information revolution', when the Tayloristic era came to its end, and computers became central to our everyday life. Indeed, most of today work is very far from that of twenty-five years ago. At that time, industrial work prevailed: it was very simple, usually performed in dedicated place, permanent, repetitive, and boring. It did not require mental effort, and was predominantly manual. Clerical work was similar, even though implied routinary mental, rather than manual, work.

If we are to understand the role HCI can play in designing assistive technologies, we need to reflect on the changing characteristics of modern societies. Ergonomics itself has moved from a science of correction (correct and eliminate work related problems), to a science of compatibility (design systems so that they are compatible with humans' limitations), to being primarily concerned with the notion of 'fit' (design man-machine systems so that the various elements best fit with each other).

The actual prevailing form of work shows some striking features (Malone, 2004; National Research Council, 1999). From the demographical point of view work is heterogeneous. The diversity in human resources is growing in terms of gender, race, education, culture and status. Communication has become a key topic to keep such heterogeneity organised.

Work is becoming more dynamic and boundaries among various jobs have become weak and permeable (Davis & Meyer, 1998). Jobs are often complementary and affect each other. Many workers are engaged in more parallel tasks, sometimes exploiting different competencies. However, new work forms tend to rely on the same technological infrastructure. Compared to the Tayloristic era, today's workplaces are more similar, all implying the use of a personal computer. Another key difference is that no one could have taken home her/his working tools from the Tayloristic factory, while working tools are now part of our houses and of our personal life. Nowadays, it is possible to work at home: technology is everywhere, and employers expect people to have the skills required to manage this technology. Those who lack these skills are at risk of being cut off from work. This digital divide is not limited to work but is also present in everyday life and affects people's social relations.

Work is differentiated. The supply side is no longer setting the pace of the market. The demand side is doing it. Contrary to the supply side, demand is driven by desires, thus differentiated by nature and changing rapidly. Work has to cope with such variability. Work aim is to deliver novelty and innovation, thus constantly requiring novel activities in uncertain conditions (Bauman, 2000).

Work is socially intense. There is horizontal and vertical flexibility. One person may work in parallel on more than one project, taking a different role in each of these. S/he may be the boss, or the project manager in some projects, to then take a more marginal role in others.

S/he may sometimes offer her/his expertise, some others seeking expertise. Interruptions and distractions are the fabric of such a multi-tasking work, driving away from reflection to action.
Work is mentally demanding and implies responsibility. It is made of often quite new activities to be performed in unfamiliar settings. In these days, markets are characterised by uncertainty, consequently work goals are never clear or defined, and the value of work depends by its originality.

4. Disability as limitation of activity

Work transformation clearly affects also the inclusion of disabled people at work. And it has not gone unnoticed by the World Health Organisation (WHO), that in twenty years has changed the basic definition of disability.
In 1980, WHO introduced a clear distinction among impairment, disability, and handicap, and for each term listed various categories, with the relating characteristics, in order to make a classification. It could be interesting to review some of these categories. 'Impairments' are related to the capacity of a person: intellectual, psychological, linguistic, auditory, visual, skeletal, and so on. 'Disability' is connected with the activities performed by a person: behaviour, communication, taking care of oneself, dexterity, and so on. Finally, 'handicap' reveals itself as a deficiency in physical autonomy, work, social inclusion, and economic autonomy of a person. For example, according to these definitions, a blind person is a person who suffers from a *visual* impairment, which causes a *communicative* and *locomotive* disability; it means also handicap, for example, in the *mobility* and in the *occupation*. Therefore, one type of impairment can cause various disabilities and involve different handicaps. In a similar manner, one type of handicap can be linked to different disabilities, which can derive from various impairments.
While the impairment is permanent for a person, disability depends on the activities that he/she has to do and the handicap expresses the disadvantage that he/she has with regard to others (so called "normal people"). The significant aspect of the first document of the WHO was that it associated the state of a person not only to functions and structures of the human body, but also to individual activities. The key concept is 'normality'. The degree of handicap is defined with reference to the standard (the one given to "normal people"): It is the gap that must be overcome to become normal.
It is apparent that 1980 definitions of WHO were basically coherent with the work of that time. There are a lot of different jobs. Each one is executed in a standard way. Handicap underlines the gap from the "normal" mode of working caused by the disability. The inclusion of a disable person will be easier as the gap is smaller. There are even jobs where the work is not affected by an impairment at all. For the blind people, the occupation of telephonist is one of these. The new Information Technology sector seemed to be one area where many impairments are insignificant.
In June 2001, the WHO published "Classification of Functioning, Disability and Health". The title is indicative of substantial changes. The aim was no more to describe the handicap, but the state of wellbeing of a person, by focusing on her/his own physical state, but also on the different ways that a person interacts with the outside world, and the impact of external events on a person. There is no reference to any disorder, structural or functional, without linking it to the state of 'wellbeing'.

Therefore the WHO classification includes not only the physiological and cognitive functions (mental, sensorial, vocal, immunological and cardiological functions, etc.) and the physical structure of a person (the nervous, visual and auditory systems, the vocal apparatus, the cardiovascular and respiratory systems, etc.), but also the activities that guarantee inclusion and social participation (learning, communication, interaction and interpersonal relations, community life, etc.), and environmental, i.e. natural (the environment), artificial (technology), and social (support, attitude, services, etc.) factors. The classification system covers every aspect of human health, arranging them in two different domains. The first is the *health domain,* which includes the action of seeing, hearing, walking, learning and remembering, etc. This is directly related to physical structure and functions. The second, the *health-related domain* which includes mobility, education, participation in social life and similar, refers to activities and environmental and social factors.

It is important to underline that the WHO definition does not only concern persons with disability but everybody: it has a universal use and value. There are hundreds of different categories. Any person can be associated with one or more *categories* that characterise his/her 'functioning'. The classification is 'positive'. It starts from the 'normal' level of functioning, considers if a person differs from this norm, and how far they are from it. The term 'handicap' is abandoned and the term 'disability' is extended to cover the *limitation of activity* and *restriction on participation.* For the function and structure of the body, the qualifier can assume values from zero (no impairment) to four (severe impairment, equal to 96-100%). Similar qualifiers exist for the activities that do not refer to impairment, but to *limitations,* and for *participation* it is said that there are *restrictions.* In short, concerning environmental factors there are *barriers.*

In our view, the new WHO definitions and classifications are strongly related with the changes in work (not to say in the attitudes of disabled people toward them) that had taken place during the years. Moreover, all this has been strongly influenced by the information technology. In summary, handicap is now seen as a form of diversity in a society where all are diverse and need some kind of assistance.

5. HCI as science of diversity

It is work itself that demands for an increased diversity, because it has become more complex, more technology enmeshed, because it mixes the traditionally separated moments and spaces of work life and personal life.

Disabilities have to be seen as some of the forms of diversity we should take care of, since, as for technologies, difficulties and benefits concern everyone. It depends on the tool, and the context. Difficulties can arise or change at any time; it is not possible to overcome them once and for all. This perspective implies the concept of disability must be replaced by the idea of diversity. From the point of view of diversity, people have not to be qualified as disabled, but rather as more or less diverse from others with respect to their working situation and the degree of their IT competence (Hull, 2004). Everyone is, in a way, disabled with respect to digital technology. To overcome their personal digital divide (subjective and contextual), everyone needs to personalise technology (Obrenovic et al., 2007). The needs of disabled people are cases in the general necessity to personalise IT. But every person, either normal or disabled, continually needs more personalised and specific solutions. Disabled people may live in greater symbiosis with technology, so they are probably the most evident case of human-machine symbiosis.

The challenge for HCI (in other words, the demand that society is posing on HCI) is to turn itself into a science of diversity and to achieve a smooth interplay between user studies and design. This transition has not been completed yet, even though it is acquiring increasing importance in the HCI community (Harper et al., 2008). In this section, we will briefly sketch the main open issues that, in our opinion, HCI has to address to turn itself into a science of diversity. We will present three aspects:

- From work to self-realisation
- A new pace of learning
- Digital ecosystems

5.1 From work to self-realisation

Ergonomic studies were initially born to address work-related problems. Work was conceived of as physical and mental strain, which is for instance reflected in the French word for work 'travail', literally 'toil', 'pain'. Ergonomics set out to reduce or eliminate this pain. In the Nineteen century, machines entered workplaces, thus becoming the first source of strain. It was by interacting with machines that humans started working in unhealthy conditions (e.g. high temperature, dirtiness, noise, etc.), also at risk of being killed or seriously harmed by the machine itself. This is why ergonomics traditionally considers human-machine interaction as the locus where work-related problems are engendered.

The approach has been changing in the last few years. HCI needs to address not only work-related problems, but it should also cover leisure and entertainment (Bodker & Sundblad, 2008). HCI researches now need to go beyond 'human needs' and also focus on 'desires'. People nowadays engage in interactions with the machines not only to work, but most of all for the experience of it, to fulfil personal goals and desires. HCI cannot restrain itself to merely correcting interaction problems, it has to contribute to the creation of fulfilling experiences. The Apple iPod does not solve any music-related problem. It instead leverages on the experience of listening to our favourite music.

The same reasoning should apply to HCI and disabilities. HCI should not be primarily focused on solving impairments, it should also include in its objectives the creation of rewarding experiences of use (Yesilada et al., 2007). In a recent interview, Donald Norman aptly pointed out that assistive devices should be also aesthetically pleasing ("CNN Designers challenged to include disabled", available on the Web on Norman's site www.jnd.org/). If we consider social networks the reasoning is straightforward. A social network is valuable not because of its usability, but because it serves as an attracting pole for a community of people (Hart, 2008). This source of value does not change if an user interacts with it with the aid of assistive technologies.

Gaming is another case of such a general change of approach. HCI researches on gaming cannot primarily concentrate on functional aspects of the interaction (Desurvire et al., 2004). Game interfaces are windows on complex set of activities. Users enter game world through the interface. The interface is the access door to an ongoing narration, which is nowadays often a collective one.

HCI has not completed yet this transition, from an applied science of correction to the science of analysing and designing rewarding human-machine interaction. Many researches are going in this direction (Garrett, 2002; Lundgren, 2008; McCarthy & Wright, 2004).

However, design is still considered by many as a form of art, while HCI methods and techniques mostly provide support for the evaluation of technologies, or for activity analysis (Norman, 2006).

5.2 A new pace of learning

A second challenge for HCI comes from the current pace of change. We are not only referring to technological innovation. We are mostly concerned with the rate of change of human desires. If HCI had to correct interaction problems, we may expect these problems to be fairly stable. That is why we have design heuristics and principles. Desires are instead by their very nature dynamically changing, as they are referred to the whole of a person, including social relationships, values and culture. Desires concerns one's own lifestyle, thus making their nature a really dynamic one. One person may even have contradictory desires, subject to drastic changes over time. Desires' development proceeds by leaps, hard to predict, not at all in linear trends.

A side effect of such a dynamic is that new desires fade away as quickly as they have emerged. This has a cost for both HCI research and for users themselves. HCI has to be ready to address new desires, to move away from them as they become less relevant, to pick up new challenges. Which often implies adopting different sets of methods and techniques. On the other hand, users invest their time in learning how to interact with a tool, to then relearn its new releases, to eventually start again from scratch in case another tool becomes available. This require HCI to support new learning styles and paces. Users no longer progress from a *present-at-hand* modality to *ready-to-hand* modality in a linear way (to then eventually devote their time to fully master the tool). Learning is not only a vertical process of progressively mastering a fixed body of knowledge. It is also a horizontal movement of transcending domain boundaries. As well put by Engeström (Engeström, 1987), the crucial learning activity for experts is learning what is not yet there. Users need to learn how to move from one tool to a new one in a quick and efficient manner.

There are two key points in the above line of reasoning. On the one hand, learning has changed its nature by becoming more transversal and dynamic, which requires users and researchers to be highly flexible. On the other hand, the actual bottleneck in such learning dynamics is represented by our attentional resources, scarce by nature. Our society is increasingly characterised by a fierce competition for attention. Different inputs are competing for the attention of users, customers, audience, etc. (Bagnara, 2008; Davenport & Beck, 2001). The consequence is that the turn-over among different inputs is very fast, while it gets risky to actually invest lot of resources (attention and memory) in any of them. We may pick a totally wrong "investment", but even if we select the right one, we may end up having a too short time to actually profit from it. There is no point in becoming a proficient Facebook user, if another social network is likely to take its place in two-three years (or even less). Users and researchers then need to devise new strategies to manage their attentional resources.

The line of reasoning for disability should be similar. Users need to learn how to adapt to assistive devices' rate of change. HCI has to adapt its methods and techniques to such a pace, possibly supporting users in the continuous learning activity required by innovation. Disable people see the continuous change in the technologies, in the way they have to interact with them, in the skills needed to operate with them, and in the knowledge required to understand them as requiring an endless effort to cope with (Bagnara & Failla, 2007). But most of all, we would need more disciplined ways of supporting users in managing their attentional resources. The use of aggregators of social preferences (e.g. like Trip Advisor, Delicious, Stumble Upon, or the Amazon's recommending system) is just a first instance.

5.3 Digital ecosystems

The third issue impacts directly on the already mentioned movement that an user does from a *present-at-hand* modality to *ready-to-hand* modality. Ubiquitous computing (and Ambient Intelligence) means a more pervasive presence of computer, but it may also bring by a qualitative change in the interaction type. Computers will start interacting with each other, often independently from any user's input. Will this digital ecosystem ever be *present-at-hand*?

As mentioned above, some HCI researchers maintain that "a good tool is an invisible tool". This may be true in many respects, but what about the perceived degree of control over technologies? What about troubleshooting activities? How can we form our model of the system functioning, if the system works almost independently from our inputs? Both degree of control and troubleshooting rely to a large extent on the *present-at-hand* modality, on conscious analysis and reflection. If computers are invisibly weaved into our world and if they start to invisibly interact with each other, the user is likely to have little (if any) visibility on their behaviour. We may also expect this complexity to cause emerging properties, even hard to detect and to intervene on in case needed.

The challenge for HCI is to analyse and design human-computer interactions, computer-computer interactions, but most of all the degree of control that users should have on these digital ecosystems. We would need to design new interfaces to enable control of digital ecosystems, to represent their state in a comprehensible manner and support intervention. For instance, Smart Homes (and other applications of Ambient Intelligence) are often based on "smart monitoring" of people living therein, but they afford humans limited control on the system. Sensors are deployed in home environment to monitor movements, to track behaviours and interactions with household objects (Kimel & Lundell, 2007), to detect potential critical incidents (de Ruyter & Pelgrim, 2007). A sense of tele-presence is created, but the real users of these systems are seldom those being monitored. They serve to care-givers, or family members, or therapists and doctors. Self-monitoring is seldom implemented, direct control over Ambient Intelligence almost never.

There is a second issue at stake here: users may end up 'dovetailing too much' to the digital ecosystem, thus losing their capacity to switch to a *present-at-hand* modality. We have the case today of too *ready-to-hand* tools in the form of 'technological addictions' (Young, 1998). For instance, email monitoring has become a task in itself for many office workers, instead of being a communication tool (Renaud et al., 2008). In this case, it seems we have lost the capability of reflecting on the tool. The tool is "too transparent". Instead of getting in our way while we try to communicate with fellow colleagues and friends (thus stimulating reflection), it directs our behaviour on the basis of its rhythms (i.e. it checks email every five minutes), creating a Narcissus effect.

Disability and assistive technologies are again a "not that special" case of the above dynamics. Assistive technologies often form a deeper symbiosis with their users, so HCI needs to pay a special attention to loss of control, invisibility, Narcissus effects. Our claim here is not that we should avoid designing for the *ready-to-hand* modality, rather that HCI should devise methods and techniques to explore the tensions between the two modalities and find means to identify the appropriate trade-off.

6. HCI porous borders: personalisation as the overlap of diversity and disability

One of the avenues that HCI has been more actively pursuing to address the goal of designing for diversity is that of personalisation. Personalisation addresses diversity of users by means of malleable tools, that can shaped as preferred by each user, for instance by changing the interface layout, activating special features, providing automation for frequently performed actions. Some computer applications do not even require the user intervention to adapt, as they self-modify themselves by tracking the user's frequent behaviours. For instance, Microsoft Office cascade menus automatically "shorten" themselves, displaying only those options that have been frequently chosen by the user.

It should then not come as a surprise that the main claim of this contribution is to a large extent already true in the area of personalisation. When we discuss the need to personalise technology, there is no 'HCI for disabled people' *versus* 'HCI for normal people'. The need is the same, maybe just more pressing for assistive technologies, probably with some additional constraints. HCI research on the personalisation of assistive technology can be rightly conceived as research on diversity, and for this very reason it often has a fallout on domains different than assistive technologies.

However, as far as disability is concerned, the need for personalisation has to be addressed at a qualitatively different level. This is not because disabled people possess qualitatively different needs and preferences than the "normal user" (this is exactly the assumption we are arguing against in this contribution). The point is that disability adds a further level of complexity to human-computer interaction, by introducing an additional source of changes in the user's preferred interaction modalities. A source that is complex and very dynamic for two main reasons. Firstly, users do not only show a variety of disability. Many experience a combination of disabilities, especially when combined with aging. Secondly, users' needs fluctuate in time, both in the long term because of aging, but also in the short term, due to fatigue or other immediate needs. As well put by Hanson and Richards (Hanson & Richards, 2005) "users have complex, interacting, and changing abilities". HCI has then to address 'dynamic diversity' (Gregor et al., 2002; Hanson & Richards, 2005), which means fluctuations in time and combination of different disabilities.

To summarise the line of argument in few words: each user has some preferred ways of interacting with her/his computer, which may change driven by needs, desires or everyday contingencies. Personalisation addresses such differences and changes. Disability can be conceived as another source of change in the user's favoured interaction modalities, one which brings about very dynamic and significant changes. And so it is ageing.

To demonstrate such a contiguity between HCI research on disability and HCI research in general, the rest of this section will discuss cases of personalised applications/technologies that successfully flourish (or have flourished) in the assistive technology domain and beyond it.

6.1 When an accessible system is a better systems

The first case shows how ergonomic improvements introduced to accommodate disabled workers may engender a beneficial fallout also for non-disabled workers. Seated working positions are nowadays common in assembly line production. However, their first appearance was due to the duty for employers to modify or adjust work to accommodate disabled workers. In a famous case from the Seventies (an assembly line of an Alfa Romeo factory), such a modification initially brought to two separate assembly line working positions, the seated one for disabled people and the standing one for the "normal worker". One system for disabled, one for non disabled. But it did not take long for non disabled people to realise that the seated position could actually bring some benefits to them as well, in terms of comfort and work-related physical strain. So, unless in those cases where other ergonomic considerations suggested not to do so, the whole assembly line was restructured according to the seated position. Ergonomics research on disability had been a driver to improve well being for all the workers.

Another case is mentioned in (Hanson & Richards, 2005). The authors present a system to improve web accessibility for people with limited dexterity and vision. Over-summarising for clarity's sake, the system magnifies web pages to ease navigation and reading. In order to do so, it has to be able to distinguish the various parts of a page, to selectively magnifies those that convey information of actual interest to the user. For instance, it needs to distinguish between the navigation bar and the page main content, in order to render the page with less visual clutter and fewer navigation options. The system can use the 'skip navigation tag' for this purpose, a HTML tag initially conceived as a way for screen readers (for blind people) to skip directly to the main content on a page. "the skip navigation tag also allows our software to do a better job of rendering pages for low vision users [...] These are examples in which conformance to standards and guidelines results in a more usable page for those not using the initially targeted assistive device. Thus, rather than eliminating the need for accessibility markup, our software capitalizes on its presence to give any person a more useable Web page" (idem, pg. 245).

6.2 Beyond mouse and keyboard: research on multimodality

A second group of examples relates to HCI research on multimodal interaction. This field covers research on input methods different than those based on keyboard and mouse, the application of which spans from mass market product to assistive devices (for a review see Hinckley, 2009; Samman & Stanney, 2006). To name but the principal research areas, interfaces based on speech recognition, pointing, gaze direction or gesture recognition can be exploited to ease human-computer interaction for people with reduced dexterity or motor impairments, but can also be implemented to support hands-free tasks, for instance to reduce risk of infections in pre-operatory debriefs for surgeons, during operations to cut operation time, to have a military aircraft pilot fly the aircraft while gaze-pointing at a target. Another particular case is that of Brain-Computer Interfaces, where the user may self-regulate brain activity (detected by the EEG - electroencelogram - electrical activity of the brain) in order to move a cursor on the computer screen. Again, this interaction modality is an alternative to conventional input devices, which may be particularly useful for people with disabilities. But it can be also used in other situations, not related to assistive technologies.

Unlike the previous assembly line case, these are not cases of assistive technologies fallout to other application domains. Rather we observe concurrent research efforts on the development of a specific set of technologies, whose characteristics may suit the diversity of different users/activities (i.e. particular conditions of operations, or disabled people).
Under the same category, we may also mention 'sonification', i.e. the use of nonspeech audio to convey information. "Sonification is typically used in situations where the user's eyes are busy elsewhere, such as in a laboratory or production line; where extracting temporal information is important; or where the data presentation requirements exceed the bandwidth of visual means" (Walker & Kramer, 2006). Successful applications can be found in the healthcare domain (for instance the hearth rate sound during surgery), or to convey additional information in Geographic Information Systems (e.g. abrupt changes in height or depth). The same technique is also exploited in assistive devices, typically for visually impaired users, for instance to support the exploration and construction of graphs and diagrams (Metatla et al., 2008), or the interaction with computer devices (Yalla & Walker, 2008).
The last example we would like to briefly mention for multimodal interaction is that of gesture-based interaction. On the one hand, gesture research is a natural province of research on technology accessibility. For instance, compared to point and touch interfaces, gesture-based interfaces are easier to use by people with diminished visual acuity (Kane et al., 2008; Moffatt et al., 2008). Research on Sign Languages (and by extension assistive technologies based on Sign Languages) is also concerned with gestures (Huenerfauth, 2008). On the other hand, the iPhone interaction modality (based on gestures, rather than on touch) has brought gesture-based interfaces to the mass public.

7. The niche and beyond: new (economic) drivers for assistive technologies?

We have discussed in the preceding sections how HCI is now facing the challenge of an ever increasing diversity. HCI application fields are not stable at all, they cover a large variety. This means an enlarged scope for HCI research. It also means including human values in HCI leading principles. Technologies are not neutral, they have an impact on social and cultural values. Such an impact is probably the only sensible criterion to steer design. This is similar to the shift from a technology-driven approach to an user-centred one, provided that we complement the old-fashioned criteria (e.g. efficacy, efficiency, usefulness) with social ones. HCI should be able to analyse the multi-faceted issues brought by technological innovation, be those of a cultural, social, political, or even ethical nature. From technology-driven, to user-centred, to human-centred.
To address this change, Harper et al. (Harper et al., 2008) suggested that HCI should focus on two immediate challenges. Firstly, user-centred design should explicitly include the analysis of social issues in the development process, in order to design human-centred innovation. Secondly, HCI should develop methods and techniques to foster dialogue with the humanities. Design trade-off are likely to increasingly concern socio-cultural aspects, with their large variation across different contexts and communities (Medhi, 2007). The concept of privacy means something different in our workplace or in our family, in a small town or in big cities.
HCI no longer studies the interaction between technology and an undifferentiated user (that has to be defined as broadly as possible to fit anybody), rather we need tools to address every user's needs and diversity. Even very peculiar ones.

A potential pitfall here is that of designing overly specific solutions. While it is true that every user is different, it is not feasible to have a different design solution for each one. HCI should work on disciplined ways of overcoming the gap between users and design. Disciplined ways of considering the user characteristics, using them as design leverages, and at the same time being able to identify unnecessary peculiarities. Possibly designing user-friendly tool personalisation, so that each user can customise to a certain extent the tool.
Design to overcome handicaps has been until now (for the large majority) a clear case of over-peculiar innovations, that is innovations that could not benefit any other user than the ones initially targeted. Our proposal is to consider it no longer as a niche, but rather as the most challenging endeavour of a widespread, general approach: dovetailing with diversity to design human-centred innovations (Marcus, 2003). Disability can be regarded as one among many sources of change in the user's favoured interaction modalities.
'Limitation of activity' and 'restriction on participation' are two key concepts not only for disabilities, but also for HCI in general. They are not only related to physical, cognitive or social impairments, but also strongly due to the changing nature of society, work and IT use. If HCI succeeds in this transition, the disability niche may eventually turn into a research intensive one, not solely devoted to assisting a minor part of the population, not to design and manufacture devices that are of some use only for disabled people, rather to function as an incubator for potentially profit-earning innovations. HCI has always been characterised by the successful fallout of technologies from one application to other ones, typically carrying out research in research intensive domains like the military, the industry, or transportation systems, to then transfer those innovations to mass-markets. This dynamic has increased HCI capability of attracting budget for its researches. The assistive technologies niche may become one of these research intensive niches, where research, pressured by complex problems, makes unexpected developments, devises solutions and then transfers them to other domains. Researchers in this niche should be well equipped to address the ever increasing diversity of contemporary society, and to devise effective ways of dovetailing with it.

8. References

Association for Computing Machinery (2008). Definition of HCI, Retrieved August, 2008, from http://sigchi.org/cdg/cdg2.html

Bagnara, S. (2008). L'economia dell'attenzione. In: *Attenzione e cognizione*, R. Nicoletti, E. Ladavas & P. Tabossi (Eds.), Il Mulino, Bologna, Italia

Bagnara, S. & Failla, A. (2007). From Handicap to Diversity. In: *Lecture Notes in Computer Science*, Vol. 4554, pp. 613

Bateson, G. (1972). *Steps to an Ecology of Mind*, Ballantine, New York, NY

Bauman, Z. (2000). *Liquid modernity*, Polity Press, Cambridge, UK

Bodker, S. & Sundblad, Y. (2008). Usability and interaction design-new challenges for the Scandinavian tradition. *Behaviour and Information Technology*, 27, 4, 293-300

Chalmers, M. (2004). A Historical View of Context. *Computer Supported Cooperative Work*, 13, 3, 223-247

Clark, A. (2003). *Natural-Born Cyborgs: Minds, Technologies, and the Future of Human Intelligence*, Oxford University Press, Oxford, UK

Davenport, T. H. & Beck, J. C. (2001). *The Attention Economy: Understanding the New Currency of Business*, Harvard Business School Press, Cambridge, MA
Davis, S. & Meyer, C. (1998). *Blur: The Speed of Change in the Connected Economy*, Warner Books, New York, NY
de Ruyter, B. & Pelgrim, E. (2007). Ambient assisted-living research in carelab. *interactions* 14, 4, 30-33
Desurvire, H.; Caplan, M. & Toth, J. A. (2004). Using heuristics to evaluate the playability of games, *Proceedings of Conference on Human Factors in Computing Systems*, pp. 1509-1512, New York, NY
Dourish, P. (2001). *Where the Action Is: The Foundations of Embodied Interaction*, Mit Press, Cambridge, MA
Engeström, Y. (1987). *Learning by expanding: an activity theoretical approach to developmental research*, Orienta, Helsinki, Finland
Garrett, J. J. (2002). *The Elements of User Experience: User-Centered Design for the Web*, New Riders Publishing, Thousand Oaks, CA
Gregor, P.; Newell, A. F. & Zajicek, M. (2002). Designing for dynamic diversity: interfaces for older people, *Proceedings of ASSETS - 4th international ACM SIGACCESS conference on Computers and Accessibility*, pp. 151-156, Edinburgh, Scotland
Hanson, V. L. & Richards, J. T. (2005). Achieving a more usable World Wide Web. *Behaviour & Information Technology*, 24, 3, 231-246
Harper, R.; Rodden, T.; Rogers, Y. & Sellen, A. (Eds.). (2008). *Being Human: Human-Computer Interaction in the year 2020*. Cambridge, UK: Microsoft Research Ltd.
Hart, J. (2008). Exploring the Facebook experience. *Interfaces*, 77,
Hinckley, K. (2009). Input Technologies And Techniques. In: *Human-Computer Interactions. Fundamentals*, A. Sears & J. A. Jacko (Eds.), pp. 137-152, Taylor & Francis, Boca Raton, FL
Huenerfauth, M. (2008). Evaluation of a psycholinguistically motivated timing model for animations of american sign language, *Proceedings of ASSETS - 10th international ACM SIGACCESS conference on Computers and Accessibility*, pp. 129-136, Halifax, Nova Scotia, Canada
Hull, L. (2004). Accessibility: it's not just for disabilities any more. *interactions*, 11, 2, 36-41
Hutchins, E. (1995). *Cognition in the wild*, MIT Press, Cambridge, MA
Kane, S. K.; Bigham, J. P. & Wobbrock, J. O. (2008). Slide rule: making mobile touch screens accessible to blind people using multi-touch interaction techniques, *Proceedings of ASSETS - 10th international ACM SIGACCESS conference on Computers and Accessibility*, pp. 73-80, Halifax, Nova Scotia, Canada
Kimel, J. & Lundell, J. (2007). Exploring the nuances of Murphy's Law---long-term deployments of pervasive technology into the homes of older adults. *interactions*, 14, 4, 38-41
Kirsh, D. (1995). The intelligent use of space. *Artificial Intelligence*, 73, 1-2, 31-68
Lewis, C. (2006). HCI and cognitive disabilities. *interactions*, 13, 3, 14-15
Lundgren, S. (2008). Designing games: why and how. *interactions*, 15, 6, 6-12
Malone, T. W. (2004). *The Future of Work: How the New Order of Business Will Shape Your Organization, Your Management Style, and Your Life*, Harvard Business School Press, Cambridge, MA

Marcus, A. (2003). Fast forward: Universal, ubiquitous, user-interface design for the disabled and elderly. *interactions,* 10, 2, 23-27

McCarthy, J. & Wright, P. (2004). Technology as experience. *interactions,* 11, 5, 42-43

Medhi, I. (2007). User-Centered Design for Development. *interactions,* 14, 4, 12-14

Metatla, O.; Bryan-Kinns, N. & Stockman, T. (2008). Constructing relational diagrams in audio: the multiple perspective hierarchical approach, *Proceedings of ASSETS - 10th international ACM SIGACCESS conference on Computers and Accessibility,* pp. 97-104, Halifax, Nova Scotia, Canada

Moffatt, K.; Yuen, S. & McGrenere, J. (2008). Hover or tap?: supporting pen-based menu navigation for older adults, *Proceedings of ASSETS - 10th international ACM SIGACCESS conference on Computers and Accessibility,* pp. 51-58, Halifax, Nova Scotia, Canada

National Research Council. (1999). *The changing nature of work: Implications for occupational analysis.* Washington, DC: National Academy of Sciences.

Norman, D. A. (1988). *The psychology of everyday things,* Basic Books, New York, NY

Norman, D. A. (2006). Interaction design is still an art form: ergonomics is real engineering. *interactions,* 13, 1, 45-60

Obrenovic, Z.; Abascal, J. & Starcevic, D. (2007). Universal accessibility as a multimodal design issue. *Communications of the ACM,* 50, 5, 6

Renaud, K.; Ramsay, J. & Hair, M. (2008). Think before you link: controlling ubiquitous availability. *interactions,* 15, 6, 65-68

Samman, S. N. & Stanney, K. M. (2006). Multimodal Interaction. In: *International Encyclopedia of Ergonomics and Human Factors,* W. Karwowski (Ed.), Taylor & Francis, Boca Raton, FL

Vygotsky, L. S. (1978). *Mind in society : the development of higher psychological processes,* Harvard University Press, Cambridge, MA

Vygotsky, L. S. (1986). *Thought and language,* MIT Press, Cambridge, MA

Walker, B. N. & Kramer, G. (2006). Sonification. In: *International Encyclopedia of Ergonomics and Human Factors,* W. Karwowski (Ed.), Taylor & Francis, Boca Raton, FL

Weiser, M. (1991). The Computer for the 21st Century. *Scientific American,* 265, 3, 94-104

Weiser, M. (1994a). Creating the invisible interface, *Proceedings of ACM Conference on User Interface Software and Technology (UIST94),* New York, NY

Weiser, M. (1994b). The world is not a desktop. *interactions,* 1, 1, 7-8

Yalla, P. & Walker, B. N. (2008). Advanced auditory menus: design and evaluation of auditory scroll bars, *Proceedings of* ASSETS - 10th international ACM SIGACCESS conference on Computers and Accessibility.

Yesilada, Y.; Stevens, R.; Harper, S. & Goble, C. (2007). Evaluating DANTE: Semantic transcoding for visually disabled users. *ACM Transactions on Computer-Human Interaction,* 14, 3, 30

Young, K. S. (1998). Internet Addiction: The Emergence of a New Clinical Disorder. *Cyberpsychology and Behavior,* 1, 237-244

Micro Scenario Database - An Approach to Make the Collaboration between the Human Science and the Engineering More Substantial

Masaaki Kurosu
The Open University of Japan (Japan)
The Graduate University for Advanced Studies (Japan)

1. Introduction

More and more ICT (Information and Communication Technology) related products, systems and services have appeared in the market. But it is frequently pointed out that many of them are difficult to use, not so much effective or not so much efficient - in other words, lack the usability. Some of them were intended to provide users a new functionality but failed in giving them a satisfaction by the use of them. It is because the designer and engineers of such artifacts (products, systems and services) did not understand the real need of the user and the real information about the context of use. It is frequently observed that the designers propose new artefacts just based on their own experience and on their own intuition. It is quite natural that such artefacts thus designed will not have the validity that matches to the reality.

This situation let the author consider about the desirable way for giving the designer and engineers of such artefacts the adequate information about the user. The idea of the micro scenario database described in this chapter thus came up to the mind of the author who has been involved in the development of the micro scenario method.

This chapter will give the reader an idea on what the micro scenario method is and how the micro scenario database will be effective and efficient for providing designers and other stakeholders about the user characteristics and the context of use information.

2. Who is the Real User?

2.1 Typical User Image

There is an anecdote that the typical user image that designers and engineers have in their mind is "a male of his 30's who has a certain level of ICT knowledge". The reason why products are difficult to use for "female" or "senior people" or "those who have not such level of knowledge" is that they are out of the range of the user's image that designers and engineers are assuming. But the image they have is the image of their own. In other words, designers and engineers are mostly men and the age range is from 20's to 40's with the biggest population in 30's. Besides, because they are designers and engineers, they have the knowledge and skill for using ICT-related artifacts.

If the artifacts are designed based on the user's image as described above, it is quite natural that they are difficult to use for people who have different characteristics from them. This kind of gap will occur when designers and engineers do not seek for or do not use the information about the real users.

2.2 Diversity of Users

There is a variety of characteristics among real users as shown in Table 1. This table differentiates the traits, the situation and the attitude. The traits are characteristics of people as a "point" in the multi-dimensional space of characteristics and the situation is a "surroundings" of that point. The Attitude is a "tendency" to move from that point. In other words, traits are the static characteristics and the attitude is the dynamic characteristics.

The traits include the biological traits such as age, generation, sex & gender, physical traits, cognitive traits and body dimension. They also include the psychological traits such as mental traits, knowledge and skill, cognitive style and learning style, and the social traits such as language, culture, historical background and educational background. The situation include the mental situation such as emotional condition and level of consciousness, the social situation such as economic situation, degree of freedom, lifestyle and social position, and the other situation such as urgency, geographical situation, physical condition and temporary condition. And the attitude includes individual preference, political attitude, religion, regression to tradition, and social attitude.

Considering the existence of such a big differences among people as shown in this table, it is evident that we should consider the diversity of people when designing the artifact. Something that is favored to some person may be disliked by other person, and something that is usable to somebody may not be usable to others.

We have a tendency to consider about other people based on the information of ourselves. But the imagination has a limitation and we need some information obtained from the real world. That is the point where the field work techniques including the observation and the interview are expected to play an important role for the design of artifacts.

But before going to the discussion of such empirical approach, the author would like to focus on the persona and the scenario methods that have become popular recently for making the design of artifact more empirically valid.

2.3 Persona and Scenario

Persona is an arbitrary description of the user and helps engineers and designers to design the artifact more realistically. Scenario is a description of the situation and the use of some artifact and helps engineers in which way their development should be directed. Scenario-based design is a design framework proposed by Carroll to describe the situation so that the program for solving those problems should be directed properly. Both methods have now become popular and are widely used in the planning process.

Traits	Situation	Attitude
Biological Traits - Age, Generation (Senior, Middle-aged, Young, Children, Baby) - Sex, Gender (Male, Female, Gender Identity Disorder) - Physical Traits (Upper Limb Disorder, Lower Limb Disorder, Paralysis, Pregnancy, Hurt, Handedness, etc) **Cognitive Traits** - Visual - Disorder: Poor-sightedness, Inborn Blindness, Acquired Blindness, Color-Blindness, etc. - Hearing Impaired - Cognitive Impaired **Body Dimension** - Height, Weight, Hand Size, Arm Length, Leg Length, Flexibility, Hand Power, Fine Operation, etc **Psychological Traits** - Mental Traits (Psychosis, Neurosis, Personality Disorder, Mental Retardation, etc) - Knowledge and Skill (Novice, Expert) - Cognitive Style (Systematic Cognition, Unsystematic Cognition, etc) - Learning Style (Strategic Learning, Ad-hoc Learning, etc) **Social Traits** - Language (Japanese, English, Chinese (Mandarine, Cantonese, etc), etc) - Culture (Ethnic Culture, Nation Culture, Local Culture, Family Culture, Generation Culture, etc) - Historical Background (Ruling Class, Ruled Class, Oppressed Class, etc) - Educational Background (Junior High, High School, College, Graduate School, etc)	**Mental Situation** - Emotional Condition (Stable, Unstable, Urgent, etc) - Level of Consciousness (Sleep, Indistinct, Aroused, Over-excited) **Social Situation** - Economic Situation (Income Level, Regularity of Income, etc) - Freedom (Free Situation, Staying in the Office or School, In Custody, etc) - Lifestyle (Workaholic, LOHAS, DINKS etc) - Social Position (Salaried Employee, Self-Employed,) **Other Situations** - Urgency (Normal Situation, Urgent Situation) - Geographical Situation (Living in a Big City, in a Small City, or in an Isolated Place, etc) - Physical Condition (Temperature, Humidity, Illumination, Noise Level, etc) - Temporary Condition (Carrying a Heavy Baggage, Wearing a Bulky Clothing, etc)	- Individual Preference (Many Preferences, No Preferences, etc) - Political Attitude (Left-winged, Right-winged, Neutral) - Religion (No Religion, Buddhism, Islam, Christianity, Newly-risen Religion, etc) - Regression to Tradition (Conservative, Innovative, Radical, etc) - Social Attitude (Individualism, Collectivism, Anti-socialism, etc)

Table 1. The Diversity among People

An example persona is shown in Figure 1. As can be seen, the persona contains descriptions on name, gender, age, occupation, personality characteristics, birth place, current address, academic background, family members, hobbies, licenses and other general information with a photograph. Although it is an artificial profile of a person, it will give engineers and designers who read that profile, a realistic image of the user. Besides, the persona contains such descriptions as the history of use for the PC, the internet and the cell phone depending on the focus of development. Furthermore it contains the background information that is related to the focus. It is a general scenario describing how the persona will act in terms of the device or the system that are the focus of development.

Name Shoichi Nomura
Gender Male
Age 63
Occupation Farmer
Personality Serious. Accomplish anything he started. Highly cooperative and has many friends. Willingly take the role of leader for the local festival.
Birth Place Furukawa city, Miyagi Prefecture
Current Address Furukawa city, Miyagi Prefecture
Academic Background Furukawa Agricultural High School
Family Mother (85 yrs.)、Wife (62 yrs.)、Eldest son (38 yrs.)、Wife of eldest son (35 yrs.)、Second son (33 yrs. In Tokyo)、Grandchild (7yrs. Daughter of the eldest son)
Hobby Comic story
License Driver's license for special big cars, Driver's license for regular cars, License for agricultural machinery, License for poisonous substance
History of Use for PC 1 year
History of Use for Internet 1 year
History of Use for Cell phone 2 years、Still using the first cell phone he purchased.
Background He started to help his family farmhouse business after graduating the Agricultural High School. Because he had a high level of knowledge and skill for the machinery and electronics, he started to introduce various machines into the farmhouse business. He obtained licenses for using his farmhouse business by just studying by himself. But he is no good for the information technology. He started to use the PC and the Internet stimulated by the eldest son, but he is not yet well-accustomed to them and has no specific purpose. Just two years ago, he started using the cell phone by the encouragement of his children. He is using only the calling function now and would like to use it more practically. His wife and eldest son also have a cell phone. Financially he is want for nothing. His mother is sickly and is lying in bed almost all the time.

Fig. 1. Sample Persona

Although the persona and the scenario method brought engineers and designers the information about the realistic image of the user and the realistic description on the use of the artifact, they are not real and are just the outcome of the imagination. It is true that the engineers and designers can get much stimulation and suggestion for their creativity by reading such descriptions. But there is no guarantee if the outcome of their creativity will fit to the real users because the information contained in the persona and the scenario is not real but just the outcome of imagination.

Another problem that have to be pointed out is that the number of persona will usually be limited to several at the maximum. But as can be realized by looking at Table 1, several persona descriptions will not cover the whole range of diversity even if the relevant dimension of people for the design of specific artifact are limited to some of the dimensions listed in Table 1.

What is necessary is more realistic information about the user and the context of use, and the persona description and the scenario description should be more real so that the development of artifact can be valid for the actual usage of that artifact. This is the point that the persona and the scenario descriptions should be based on the real data obtained from the field work of which micro scenario method is emphasizing.

3. Micro Scenario Method

The micro scenario method (MSM) is another approach that directly brings the information about the user, the situation and the problem. Unlike the conventional persona and scenario methods, the MSM uses the real information obtained from the field work thus the information contained in the persona and the scenario is real. From another viewpoint, it is an efficient way to summarize the qualitative information and brings engineers a better understanding of the user. In this aspect, it is similar to the Grounded Theory Approach (GTA) originally proposed by Strauss and Corbin in 1998. But the MSM is more goal-oriented where the goal is the development of the artifact. The initial steps of fragmenting the facts found in the field research and summarizing the problem based on the similarity are similar, but the problem list that will soon be used to seek for the solution is different. It is because the MSM is more goal-oriented.

Following is a general procedure in the MSM. Figure 2 describes the whole steps of the MSM

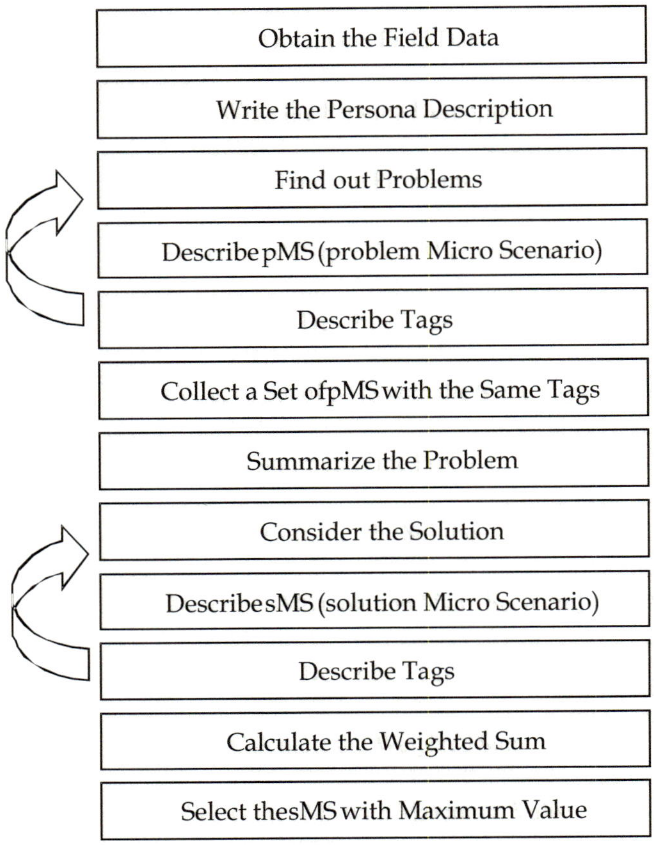

Fig. 2. Steps in the MSM

(1) Obtain the Field Data

First of all, the researcher should visit the informant and conduct the interview by watching the environment. This is fundamentally the same with the contextual inquiry proposed by Bayer and Holtzblatt (1998). The researcher tries to get the fundamental information about the informant including the general information as is described in Figure 1 and then focus on the topics of the research. If the research is on the educational issue, the researcher should first ask about the life history of informant focusing on the education; the school environment, the subject and the material used for each lecture, the teacher's skill and attitude, the favourite subject, the companion, the school fee, the parents' attitude toward the education, the homework, the motivation to learn, etc. In order to get sufficient information, the informant has to provide a list of questions in advance. But it is recommended to adopt the semi-structured interview because the structured interview is too narrow-scoped to get additional information and the non-structured interview has a chance to miss some key information. The researcher is recommended to use the digital recorder in addition to writing the field note. The researcher then asks about the opinion of the informant on the educational policy, the educational environment, important points at the school, the opinion for the e-learning, etc. depending on his/her interest. Usually the research will take about two hours considering the fatigue of the informant. And if more information is needed, visit the informant on the other day.

(2) Write the Persona Description

Based on the information obtained from the contextual inquiry, the researcher describes the persona. The persona description should include the characteristics of the user and the background contextual information about the life of the informant. This information is common to any of the problem micro-scenario and should be referred to afterwards in order to get a better understanding of the pMS. Previously, the persona was called the ground information because this information forms the ground or the base for describing and interpreting the pMS. But it is now called the persona because it was revealed that there is no fundamental difference between the persona and the ground information in its contents and description.

(3) Find out Problems

This step is similar to the open coding of the Grounded Theory Approach in that the fragmental information will be extracted from the field data. But this step in the MSM differs from the open coding of GTA, because only something that was regarded as a problem will be picked up whereas the open coding of GTA picks up any fragments from the original data. The difference lies in the fact that the MSM is a problem-solving activity and the GTA is an open stance theory construction approach. The criterion regarding what to pick up as a problem differs from research to research and depends on the focus of attention or the goal of the research. Some problem will be mentioned as the problem by the informants themselves. But other problem might not be noticed even by the informants. Hence, this step is quite dependent on the sensitivity of the researcher.

(4) Describe pMS (problem Micro Scenario)

Usually the scenario is a FULL description of something including the information about the people who appear in the scenario. But in MSM such information as the characteristics of the informant and the contextual information of the informant will be separately described as the persona, only the description of a problem should be written as a pMS. Important point here is that each pMS describes just a micro problem, in other words, a fragment of the problem. If a problem found in the previous step has 2 or more problem fragments as in the case of problem description as follows: "the informant attended the elementary school where only 2 teachers were in the whole school of 30 pupils and the level of lecture was low because teachers had to take care of different level of pupils from 1st graders to 6th graders". Each fragmental description of problem, i.e. pMS, should be "2 teachers had to take care of 30 pupils ranging from 1st graders to 6th graders" and "the level of teaching was not high because the teacher had to take care of the young pupils".

(5) Describe Tags

Tag is a keyword that represents the key content in the pMS. In above case, "small number of teachers", and "different level of pupils" will be the tags for the pMS "2 teachers had to take care of 30 pupils ranging from 1st graders to 6th graders". Thus the tag is a [list of] word[s] that represent the key content of the pMS. Important point here is that the same tag description should be used all through the pMS and Tag extraction process. It is not good to use "small number of teachers" and "lack of teachers" for different pMSs although they are fundamentally meaning the same thing. The reason is that the tag will be used in the later stage of analysis as a key for the information retrieval. The steps (4) and (5) will be repeated until all the problem fragments in the problem description in (3) will be converted into pMS and tags. Then the steps (3) + (4) (5) will be repeated until the whole information obtained from the field work will be analyzed.

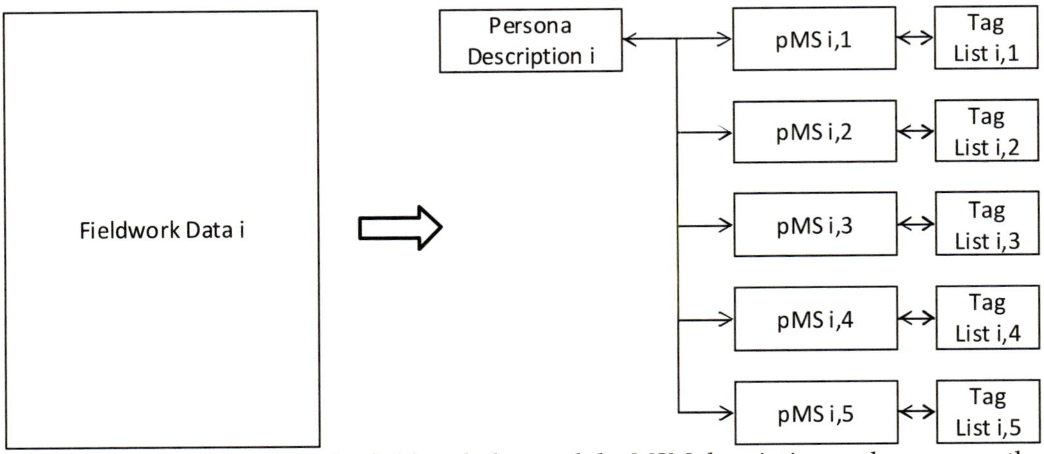

Fig. 3. Relationship between the fieldwork data and the MSM description as the persona, the pMS, and the tags.

(1)-(5) Repeat this activity until the Saturation

Steps from (1) to (5) should be repeated until the researcher will think that the sufficient data was obtained. In the GTA, it is called the "saturation" that means the moment when the repetition of field work for different informants only gives the similar set of problems and no new finding are collected even if the researcher tried to get new information from a different type of informants. The timing when this saturation will come differs from research to research and usually depends on the size of the focus of the research. There is a research where 6 informants are thought to be enough but there is another case where more informants are needed even after taking the data from 18 informants. Every time when the research is repeated, the data described in Figure 3 will be accumulated.

(6) Collect a Set of pMS with the Same Tag

When it was thought that the researcher have collected enough data, then the researcher moves to this step. This step and the step (7) are for summarizing the problem. Figure 4 describes the situation where 3 sets of data were obtained from 3 different informants. By looking through the tag information, list up all pMSs that have the same tag, i.e. that relate to the same kind of problems. It is recommended to use MS Excel or some database software for recording the pMS and the list of tags. It is quite easy to get a set of pMS that have the same tag by using such a computer program. It is not necessary to repeat this process for all tags but should be done only for the tags that seemed to be important for the researcher. In the case of Figure 4, the second (because the order of pMS is arbitrary, the order doesn't have any significance but just a nominal meaning) pMS for the 1st informant and the first pMS for the 3rd informant were found to have the same tag in their tag lists.

(7) Summarize the Problem

The next step is to summarize the problem that is to take out the common and fundamental information from each pMS that has the same tag information. It is sometimes useful to refer back to the persona information when it is difficult to interpret the fragmental pMS. The problem description in Figure 4 is such a de-contextualized description of the problem. This step should be repeated until all the necessary retrieval of tag will have done. There will be a set of problem descriptions after this step. An example of the problem description is "the lack of sufficient number of teachers for the numbers of pupils".

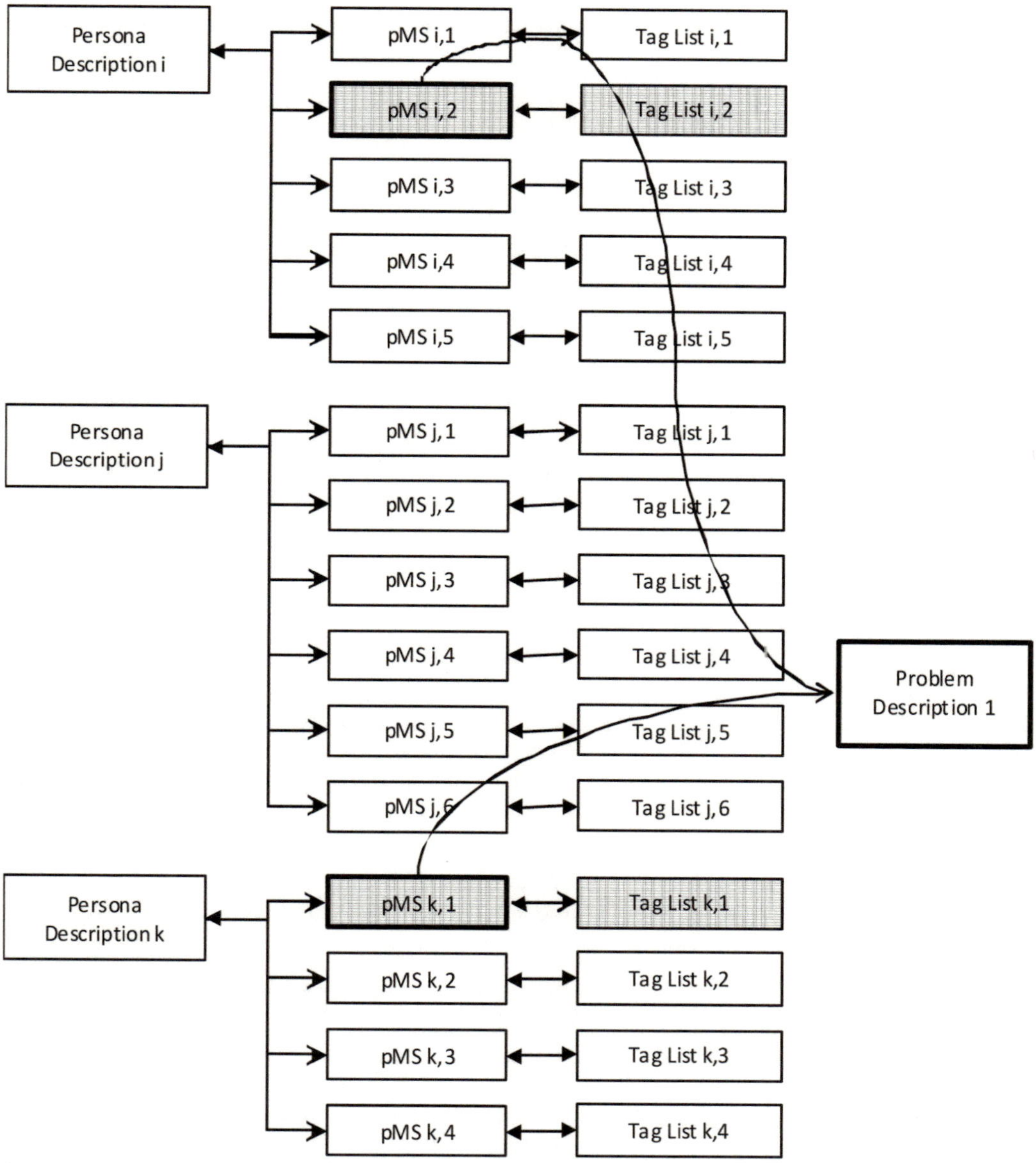

Fig. 4. Summarizing the problem by using the tag information

(8) Consider the Solution

The MSM has two phases, one is focusing on the problem and another is focusing on the solution. The latter phase starts from this step. This step is not supported by any kind of method. But just the imagination of participants who will join in the stakeholders session will be the only source of ideas to solve the problem. Hence, it is recommended that a variety of stakeholders should get together in this idea generation step including other teachers, the school manager, the designer, the social worker, the local government officers, members of the PTA, etc. in the case of this school issue. Sometimes it will take a long time for considering the solution and usually a set of solution ideas will have to be listed. Usually, one session takes just one problem for about 2 hours and the rest of problems should better be discussed on other days.

(9) Describe sMS (solution Micro Scenario)
If the problem description in (7) were "the lack of sufficient number of teachers for the numbers of pupils", tentative ideas to solve the problem will be "to hire more teachers", "to merge this school to another adjacent school which is much bigger with more number of teachers", "to hire some part-time teachers", etc. These fragmental ideas form the sMS. In the example of Figure 5, three sMS were proposed.

(10) Describe Tags
For the sMS, the tag information is useful but in a different sense from the tag for pMS had. In this case for sMS, tags are criteria for evaluating each solution idea. So the same set of tags will be used for all the sMSs proposed. Thus it could be described as a matrix in Figure 5. The first step is to list up all the relevant criteria for evaluating the pMS. Then write a matrix and evaluate each idea in terms of each tag or the criterion. In the example of Figure 5, tags are the total cost, the preparation time, the distance to school and the mental problems of children. And the point for, for example, the first sMS is 3, 4, 4, 3 respectively.

(11) Calculate the Weighted Sum
Next step is to weight each tag for its importance. It is because each tag does not necessarily have the same weight. There are important aspects but at the same time trivial aspects. In the case of Figure 5, weights are 8, 4, 6, 5 respectively. Then calculate the weighted sum for each sMS by adding the multiplication of weight and point for each tag criterion. In the first case of Figure 5, 8 x 3 + 4 x 4 + 6 x 4 + 5 x 3 = 79, and 79 is the weighted sum for the first sMS.

(12) Select the sMS with Maximum Value
The final step is to select the sMS with the highest weighted sum. In the case of Figure 5, the second sMS got the highest score of 97 and after a discussion for confirming the result, it will be adopted to solve the problem.

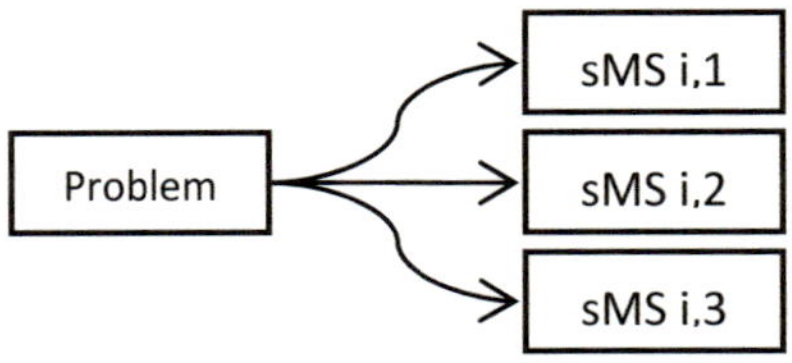

Total cost	Preparation time	Distance to school	Mental problems	WEIGHTED SUM
Weight = 8	Weight = 4	Weight = 6	Weight = 5	
3	4	4	3	79
4	5	5	3	97
5	5	1	2	76

Fig. 5. The process to deal with the sMS with tags and their weights

As have been described, the MSM is a problem solution method based on the qualitative field work data. But the former half of the method for describing problems as a set of pMS and tag can be used in another way. These data can be stored and be referred to afterwards from a bit different viewpoint. The data will serve as a good source of information in a specific format and if the same tag will be used later, the data will give a different insight. This is the base for an idea of micro scenario database that will be described in the next section.

4. Database of Micro Scenario

It is quite natural that the engineers will have the idea to collaborate with human science professionals so that their development can be more human-centered, i.e. more effective, more efficient, more interesting, and more useful. But based on the experience of the author, it is quite difficult for the collaborative project between engineers and human science professionals to be successful. In one extreme case, the project member that include the engineers and the human science professionals go in parallel from its start and finalizes in such a state as each result being still parallel under the title of an integrative approach. It is quite regretful that such an integrative approach fails by spending a big amount of budget and a long period of time.

Such a misfortune can be caused by some reasons. One big reason is the difference of language or the difference of the scheme among different disciplines. Engineers expect human scientists such as psychologists to give them the information regarding the adequacy of their engineering devices or systems. But the psychological findings are based on the psychological scheme and can not easily be translated into the engineering scheme. This is due to the goal of each discipline. The engineer seeks for inventing and developing some devices or system that are new. But the psychologist looks for the new fact about the nature of human being. Because the psychology is one domain of science, the fact finding and the truth seeking are the fundamental stance of psychologists. There are, of course, applied psychologists who put more emphasis on the application of psychological findings. But the number of such psychologists is not large and furthermore the engineers tend to expect to get new finding from fundamental psychologists rather from applied psychologists.

Another big reason is the temporal factor of the collaborative project. Usually, all the project members start their activity at the same time in such a collaborative project. Human science professionals or sometimes social science professionals start their research activity that they believe to bring about very valuable results in terms of the project goal. But, quite naturally, the research will take a certain amount of time during which the engineers are not waiting for the result to be available for them but will carry out their own approach. Hence, it frequently happens that when the result of the human science research are summarized, the development on the side of engineers have already advanced to a certain stage from which the modification of the development will be difficult. As a result, human engineer professionals summarize their own findings as a report whose content will nothing to do with or in a different direction with the technological development by the engineers.

The idea of the micro scenario database was conceived of for minimizing the risk of such misled integrative approach between the engineers and the human science professionals. Figure 6 describes how the collaboration paradigm should change.

The upper figure shows how the current collaboration projects between engineers and human science professionals or social science professionals are going on assuming the abscissa as a time. They start and end the project at the same time, thus the findings of the human science or the social science may not be able to be used by the engineering development.

The lower figure shows the conceptual scheme for the collaborative project using the micro scenario database. The fundamental idea in this figure is as follows.

(1) A big project starts with just human science professionals and social science professionals. In that project a number of field work will be conducted in terms of various aspects of human life including the education, the medical treatment, the local government, the unemployment, the development of depopulated area, etc. Obtained data, for example, about the education will, for some part, include something about the unemployment or the local government issues. By conducting the multi-focused field work, mutually linked information will be obtained. Thus it is far better than the research with just one focus.
(2) The second step is to pick up problems and write down pMSs and tags. Important point is to provide a list of tags to be used in advance. Thus the pMSs containing the same subject will be retrieved by just entering the tag. Of course, it could also be useful to provide a thesaurus for the tag. If it is provided, it is easier to input the tag and retrieve the pMS. pMSs and tags will be stored in a big database from which any information can be retrieved by entering the keyword (tag).
(3) When the engineers want to start a new project that is related to the human user, they simply retrieve relevant pMSs by entering the keyword (tag) to the system. They will be given pMSs that are related to the subject for which they are going to develop some devices or systems. Sometimes, the partial collaboration of the human science professionals will be necessary for adequately interpreting the pMSs.

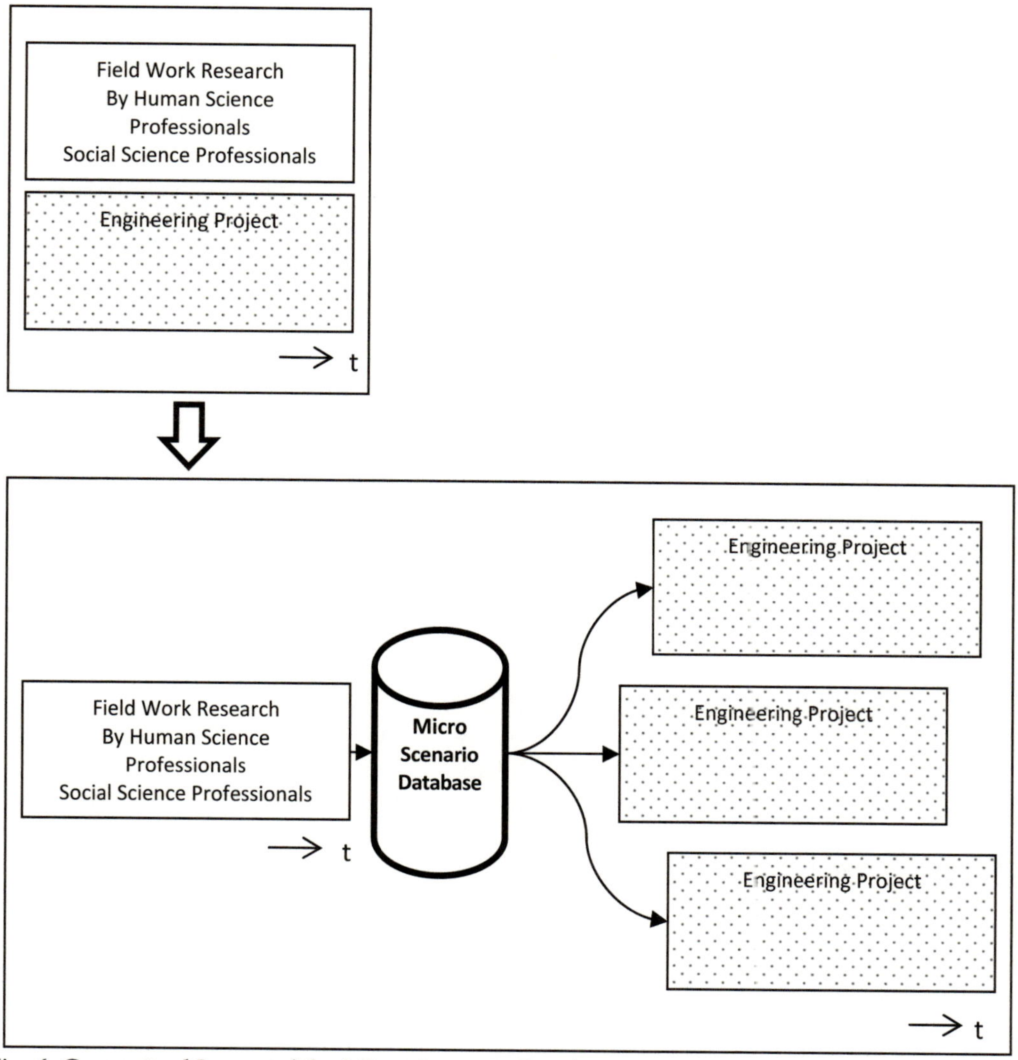

Fig. 6. Conceptual Image of the Micro Scenario Database

The micro scenario database will thus facilitate the collaboration between the human science (social science) professionals and the engineers or the designers. Some of the information in the database will be obsolete after a certain length of time, so the field work research to maintain the database should be conducted once per a few years.

5. Conclusion

In this chapter, the diversity among people was explained at first and it was pointed that the diversity of user of any devices or systems should be covered before the beginning of the development process. After reviewing the current persona and scenario method, the micro scenario method was introduced as to summarize the problem information as the pMS and to lead the solution as the sMS. Then the idea of the micro scenario database was introduced.

The author believes this will surely enhance the effective and efficient collaboration between the human science or the social science professionals and the engineers.

6. References

Beyer, H. and Holtzblatt, K. (1998) Contextual Design - Defining Customer-Centered Systems, Morgan Kaufmann

Carroll, J.M. (ed.) (1995) Scenario-Based Design: Envisioning Work and Technology in System Development, Wiley

Daimoto, H. Araki, S. Mizuno, M. and Kurosu, M. (2007) Application of Micro-Scenario Method (MSM) to the Educational Problem-solving - A Case Study for the Mother Tongue Maintenance for Immigrated Children, HCI International 2007

Kurosu, M. (2003) Analysis of Field Data by Applying Micro-Scenario Method (in Japanese), Human Interface Symposium 2003

Kurosu, M. (2003) Applying Fieldwork Methods for Investigating the Context of Use of Multimedia Education, JALTCALL2003

Kurosu, M., (2004) Micro-scenario method for designing and re-designing the e-Learning system, E-Learn 2004

Kurosu, M. (2004) Micro-scenario method: a new approach to the requirement analysis, WWCS 2004

Kurosu, M. (2004) Micro-scenario method: a new method to the requirement analysis (in Japanese), Human Interface Society SIGUSE

Kurosu, M., (2005) Micro-scenario method - interface design based on the context of use information (in Japanese), Design IT, 2005

Kurosu, M., (2006) Scenario creation by using the micro-scenario analysis system (in Japanese), JPA, 2006

Kurosu, M. (2006) Micro Scenario Method (in Japanese), Report of NIME

Kurosu, M. (2007) Micro-Scenario Database for Substantializing the Collaboration Between Human Science and Engineering, HCI International 2007

Kurosu, M. and Kakefuda, A. (2005) Application of Micro-Scenario Method (MSM) to the Educational Problem-solving - A Case Study for the Mother Tongue Maintenance for Immigrated Children, CATE 2005

Kurosu, M., Kasai, H., Hirasawa, N., and Go, K., (2006) Analysis tool for micro-scenario (in Japanese), Human Interface Society SIGUSE, 2006

Kurosu, M., Nishida, S., Osugi, T., and Mitsui, M., (2003) Analysis of Field Data by Micro-scenario Method" (in Japanese) Proceedings of Human Interface Symposium, 2003

Ohnishi, J. and Go, K., (2002) Requirement Engineering (in Japanese), Kyoritsu-shuppan

Strauss, A.L. and Corbin, J.M. (1998) Basics of Qualitative Research: Techniques and Procedures for Developing Grounded Theory, SAGE

General Interaction Expertise: A Multi-view Approach to Sampling in Usability Testing of Consumer Products[1]

Ali E. Berkman
NANObiz Ltd. - UTRLAB User Testing and Research
Turkey

1. Introduction

With the diffusion of digital technologies, problems that have been witnessed in the domain of personal computers since 1980's (Shackel, B & Richardson, S., 1991) began to be observed in the use of once-humble products (Thimbleby, 1991). Together with this, conventional paradigm of consumer ergonomics was no more sufficient to embrace all the dimensions of user - product relationship.

Relatively complex cognitive processes that were in charge necessitated adoption of methods that traditionally belong to the domain of HCI. In a survey carried out in 1996, including 25 federated societies of IEA, 'usability of consumer products' was ranked as the third most important emerging area in ergonomics, leaving 'human computer interface' behind (Helander, 1997). Since 1990s, it is no more uncommon to come across with cases that consumer product are evaluated using techniques pertaining to HCI (e.g., Connel, Blandford & Green, 2004; Garmer, Liljegren, Oswalder & Dahlman, 2002; Lauretta & Deffner, 1996).

Being a fundamental technique in HCI, usability testing is one of the most frequently applied techniques in both design and evaluation. As the observation of participant behavior forms the backbone of the technique, it is empirical and somewhat objective in character. Given this, usability testing is one of the most frequently resorted techniques when a systematic approach is required for eliminating evaluator biases as much as possible (Potosnak, 1988).

In the case of consumer products, while applying HCI-specific methods, adherence to conventions valid for HCI in a 'verbatim' fashion may cause incompatibilities. Most of the time problems arise because of dissimilar system paradigms of two domains; particularly

---

1 Partially based on the article: General Interaction Expertise: An Approach for Sampling in Usability Testing of Consumer Products (Berkman, 2007).

with respect to how 'user' is defined. Although it is possible to anticipate a wide user population within contemporary HCI theories and practice, 'user' is traditionally conceptualized as a professional, using a tool for sustaining her/his activity within the work domain. Such a tendency may be observed in the fundamental works in the usability literature (e.g. Nielsen, 1993; Dumas & Redish, 1993). Based on professional activity, users can be defined in terms of their occupations and abilities/skills they are expected to possess. Added to this 'screening' effect is the homogenizing effect of personnel selection and training. Therefore, the user profile exhibits a relatively homogenous profile.

Given these, for professional products, it is usually possible to determine the characteristics of target users and 'choose' the ones that represent the actual population as participants, with the help of observable attributes such as job experience, education, age etc. In the case of consumer products, working on homogeneous 'subsets' is not plausible most of the time, given the fact that such products are usually intended for a larger portion of the population. For example, everybody in the world is a potential user of a cellular phone produced for global markets. Therefore, diversity to be accommodated is quite large and many user characteristics, that vary both quantitatively and qualitatively, should be considered.

1.1 Do we really test the interface?

Causes and consequences of the heterogeneity of user population in the case of consumer products may best be illustrated with a speculative example:

Suppose that during the development process of an innovative cellular phone, the manufacturer wants to see whether users will easily adapt to the innovative interface. Furthermore, the manufacturer wants to compare the performance of this innovative design with its competitors and needs to verify that basic functions can be easily used by all users. Although, usability testing would be the right choice to fulfill those needs, results of the test would not be able to yield unambiguous results.

Firstly, the possibility that variance observed in user performance may be explained by individual differences causes methodological problems, and is hard to neglect especially in the case of consumer products. Some participants may not be able to complete even a single task successfully; interpretation of this result would really be trivial. Was it the interface's design that caused too much problem for the participants? Was it the participants' lack of experience with such innovative modes of interaction?

Secondly, when the task is to compare the design with its competitors a methodological problem with 'experiment design' arises. Suppose that interface (A) is decided to be compared with three other products (B, C and D). It is evident that a single test where each participant experiences all the interfaces is not possible, since such a test session would take too much time and it would be difficult to isolate and eliminate the effects of positive – negative transfer among interfaces. Therefore, one would look for experiment designs with more than one group. For example, there may be three groups where each competitor is compared with interface A, so that each participant uses only two interfaces instead of 4. In such a design, participants in each group should be comparable with regards to individual differences that may directly influence the test results.

Thirdly, the manufacturer in the example above would never know whether the sample was representative enough to infer that 'basic functions can be easily used by all users', regardless of the level of success observed in the tests.

The primary aim of any usability test should be to observe the effect of interface design on user performance, and eliminate all other interfering factors. Individual differences should be regarded as the most important factor to be eliminated or controlled since early studies show that huge variability in performance can be explained by individual differences among users, regardless of design or other factors (Egan, 1988). Experiential factors, among other individual differences, are known to have a significant effect on performance (e.g. Nielsen, 1993; Dumas & Redish, 1993).

Despite the famous phrase reminding participants that what is tested is the interface not their abilities, it is usually the participant's familiarity with digital interfaces that is being reflected in results.

1.2 When does heterogeneity really cause problems?

Although, the fact that experiential factors have a considerable effect on results indicates that a methodological flaw is present, this is not a criticism brought to the methodology of usability in general. Most of the time usability tests are conducted to uncover major problems and to have a rough idea about the fit between user and the system. It may be assumed that whether a test would be carried out in 'discount usability situations' (Nielsen, 1993) or for strict, inferential purposes (Potosnak, 1988) may determine how meticulously should external factors be controlled.

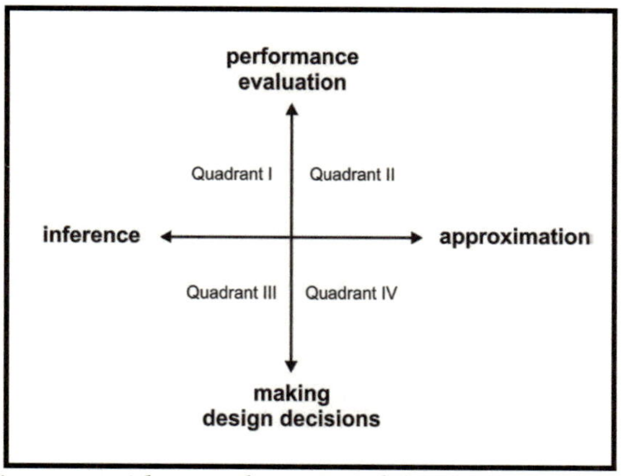

Fig. 1. Types of usability tests with regards to aim of the test and methodological approach

Usability tests are either carried out for summative (Quadrants 1 and 2 in Figure 1) or formative purposes (Quadrants 3 and 4 in Figure 1). In general, aim is to evaluate or measure user performance in the former and to diagnose usability problems and generate results that will give way to design decisions in the latter. Regardless of the nature of research and the motivations behind, representative sampling and heterogeneity of user population are issues to be keen on for obtaining plausible results, unless the only function of observations is to inspire usability experts who rely heavily on their expertise for anticipating usability flaws. However, it should be noted that when a valid inference is to be made with the results of a usability study, control over factors pertaining to sampling that may affect test results becomes even more vital.

Although the main discussions in sampling literature concentrate on the discussions on sufficient sample size to discover the majority of usability problems (see Caulton, 2001 for a review), the probability of experiencing usability problems in a user test seems to be related with experiential factors. Therefore, all types of homogeneity assumptions, regarding age, gender, occupation, experience may prove to be inaccurate. If this is the case, then, even diversity and significance of the problems observed in a discount situation may not be plausible unless the sample is checked for serious biases in terms of expertise levels of the participants involved. With a small sample size even some of the most serious problems may not be encountered by the participants if the sample is heavily skewed in terms of experiential factors.

1.3 Structure of the chapter

In this chapter, two approaches in order to accommodate the effects of individual differences among participants in usability testing of consumer products will be proposed.

In Section 2, after discussing how experiential factors are conventionally handled in usability tests, a working model that suggests a triadic relationship between experience, actual performance, and self-efficacy will be presented. In this regard, how expertise is constructed through a personal history of individual experiences with technological artifacts, and how these acquisitions are reflected upon mechanisms of self perception will be discussed.

In Section 3, an approach based on performance observation will be illustrated by presenting the development process of a prototypical apparatus test, aimed at assessing the expertise.

In Section 4, a complementary approach based on the concept of self-efficacy will be put forward. In this part, a scale developed in order to measure a construct defined as General Interaction Self-efficacy will briefly be presented.

Finally in Section 5, the conclusions drawn and further studies will be discussed.

2. A triadic model of experience, actual performance and self-efficacy

2.1 Conventional approach to experiential factors

Although, representative sampling of participants finds support in usability literature, suggestions about factors to be considered are divergent. Furthermore, it is hard to come across suggestions about how to handle experiential factors.

Nielsen states that "sample should be as representative as possible of the intended users of the system" (1993, p. 175). According to him, in order to achieve this for the systems with large intended populations like consumer products, anyone can be a participant. He suggests that age and gender are among the most critical factors as these may be significant in some cases. He further adds that both novices and experts should be involved in tests. He enumerates experiential factors as computer experience, experience with the particular system, and domain knowledge. Finally, he adds that some "less immediately obvious" factors such as basic abilities are known to play role. Chapanis argues that "human characteristics that are important" (1991, p. 375) are sensory capacities, motor abilities, intellectual capacities, learned cognitive skills, experience, personality, attitudes and motivation. Dumas and Redish (1993) suggest that participants should be chosen directly from target user population when possible. They state that experience and motivation are two important factors to explain differences among people, and propose a similar construct of experience with Nielsen (1993). The experiential factors to be considered are listed as work experience, general computer experience, specific computer experience, experience with the particular product, and experience with similar products (p. 122). The studies reviewed above exhibit a common attitude in the sense that they consider experience as an important factor and how they define it.

In pre-test questionnaires administered before usability tests and some tools developed for measuring computer experience, experience is usually, if not always, defined as quantity, frequency and duration of participation to a task, interaction with a class of applications, a specific application, or computer systems in general (e.g. Bunz, 2004; Kinzie, Delcourt & Powers, 1994; Igbaria, Zinatelli, Cragg & Cavaye, 2001). Such an approach seems to be valuable and has practical appeal for investigating the influences of experiential factors on various measures. Moreover, the fact that such information may readily be extracted by asking frequency-of-use questions before tests has many practical merits. Nevertheless, it is better to treat such information as a nominal variable to distinguish users having some experience and users having none.

The problem of defining experience in above-mentioned terms arises when experience is treated as a ratio variable that confounds performance, or as a substitute for a variable representing the transformations occurred during learning process. For example, let us think of two individuals that have some experience with computers. Assume that individual A has 6 years of computer experience and uses computers 3 times a week; whereas individual B has 12 years of computer experience and uses computers every day. It is not safe to assume that individual B is a higher level of expert than individual B and her/his performance will be better due to this difference since there is no one-to-one relationship between what is experienced and what is retained.

People show great variability even after attending a formal education program to the extent of knowledge and skills they acquired (Ackerman & Humphreys, 1990). This is actually one of the motives behind the study of individual differences. The concept of expertise seems to be a proper starting-point for arriving at a better way of approaching experiential factors. Expertise is defined as "aspects of skill and general (background) knowledge that has been acquired…" (Freudenthal, 2001, p. 23). With such an approach *experience* is treated as a causal variable rather than a reflective one.

2.2 Definition of General Interaction Expertise

In a usability test, most of the time, if not always, participants' experience a novel situation. In other words, either a new interface is being tested or participants are asked for completing novel tasks with a familiar interface. It is observed that participants try to grasp designer's model by navigating within interface and trying to complete the tasks assigned to them. Some participants may predict the model with quite ease before a thorough experience. While others may never form a working model of the system that conforms with the actual model and keep experiencing problems.

Therefore, in essence, in usability tests participants are asked to adapt to a novel interaction situation. It is argued that a test participant's expertise level acquired by experiencing a diversity of interfaces is one of the most determining factors that affect how s/he copes with this novel situation. Term suggested for this construct is General Interaction Expertise (GIE) (Berkman & Erbuğ, 2005), and may be briefly defined as:

> ***General Interaction Expertise (GIE)*** *is acquired by experiencing several interfaces and helps users to cope with novel interaction situations.*

2.3 Triadic model

In this study, the model suggested in Figure 2 will be utilized for comprehending the relationship between what is experienced (experience) and manifestations of what is retained (GIE)— i.e. expressions of permanent cognitive changes, as actual performance and self-efficacy belief.

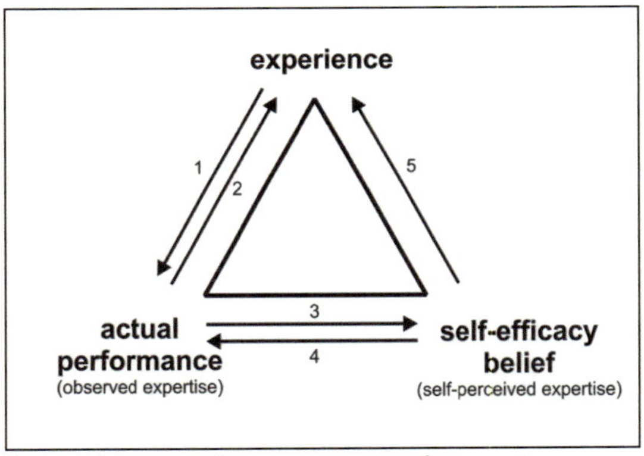

Fig. 2. Triadic model of experience and components of expertise

This triadic model is in line with Bandura's social learning theory (1986). Before going into detailed discussion of the reciprocal relationships among the components of this model, the concept of self-efficacy should be briefly discussed.

Bandura suggests that as individuals experience a domain they simultaneously grow a self system called self-efficacy, which is a reflection of their actual performances. However, being more than a mere reflection this system also influences cognitive processes and actions.

While discussing what is excluded and what is included to the term 'self-efficacy', Bandura asserts that self-efficacy is more than the possession of the required underlying skills for completing a particular task (1986). He maintains that "competent functioning requires both skills and self-beliefs of efficacy to use them effectively" (p.391). Therefore, self-efficacy is proposed as a generative entity that makes it possible to use skills, yielding a desired outcome, within various contexts. In this regard the concept is markedly different from outcome expectancies and can be delineated as an individual's self-belief in attaining a certain level of performance. Bandura views self-efficacy as a functional mechanism rather than just a self reflection on one's own capabilities. Stemming from this argument, it is suggested that it partly determines which actions are undertaken and which social milieus are involved with. Therefore, as self-efficacy about a domain starts to grow, through its effects on choice behavior, it starts to determine what is experienced and what is avoided by the individual, partly influencing the course of personal development.

Another effect of self-efficacy beliefs is about breakdown conditions. It is argued that individuals with high self-efficacy beliefs do not easily give up when faced with obstacles and may even expend greater effort as they may tackle the problem as a challenge. Thus, it is asserted that individuals with strong self-efficacy beliefs tend to invest more effort and persist more in sustaining it.

A third effect of having strong self-efficacy beliefs is on the efficiency in converging cognitive resources on accomplishing the task at hand. Individuals with low self-efficacy tend to concentrate more on their limitations and shortcomings when they cannot proceed. Strong self-believers, on the other hand, concentrate on how to solve the problem and put more effort in dealing with 'external' problems.

Proceeding from this general conception of self-efficacy and related mechanisms that stem from Bandura's cognitive theory, it may be proposed that a user with strong self-efficacy regarding interaction may be expected to have a personal history of interaction where positive experiences are dominant, tendency to use digital interfaces more often, exhibit persistent behavior in breakdown situations, and not to exhibit self-blaming behavior in case of an error.

2.4 Construction of GIE

In order to discuss how GIE is constructed, each link between the elements of the triadic model should be examined.

2.4.1 Experience - Actual performance (1)

The suggested relationship between experience and actual performance (see arrow 1 in Figure 3) is tried to be illustrated by exploiting the elaborated taxonomy suggested by Smith (1997).

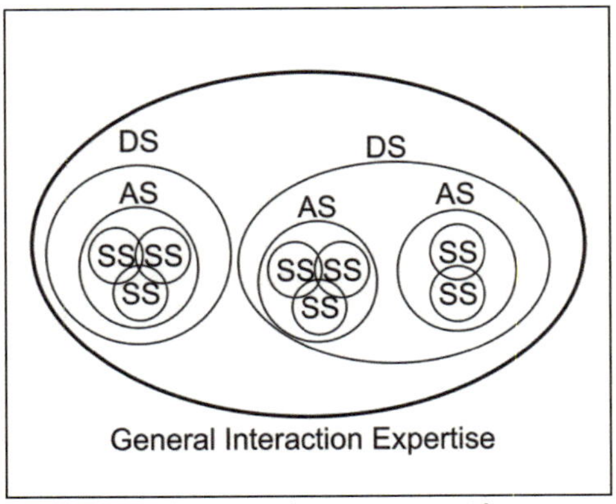

Fig. 3. GIE, domain specific knowledge, application-specific component and system-specific component

It may be suggested that as individuals interact with a specific product they acquire a system-specific component of expertise (SS). After experiencing a number of similar systems for carrying out the same task—i.e. listening to music—an application-specific component (AS) of expertise is formed. Therefore, as people use specific systems with similar functionalities they acquire an AS together with individual SS components. Domain-specific knowledge (DS), on the other hand, consists of all the knowledge and skills required for carrying out a specific task. For example, etiquette of unmediated face-to-face communication may be situated within DS of communication.

Coming across a variety of SS, AS, and DS, several schema-based expertise (see Preece, 1994) are acquired, which help individuals to manage known and novel but familiar systems. Even if users face a totally novel application area, their expertise help them to orientate to the new system, provided that prior expertise acquired bear sufficient commonalities with the novel situation.

Therefore, although it was illustrated as if separate areas of AS and DS do not overlap in Figure 3, they actually do in reality. Moreover, the areas of intersection among separate areas of SS are larger than depicted. This taxonomy is further clarified with a concrete example about using a washing machine in provided in Table 1.

GIE	*Interaction*	Power on/off pictogram, navigating through menu structure, how cancel button functions...
DS	*Washing garments*	Procedure of washing, effects of temperature on textile and dyes, how to spare hot water, how to identify a well-washed cloth…
AS	*Washing with a machine*	Certain controls and displays specific to washing machines, functional model of washing machines, how to save energy, safety precautions …
SS	*Washing with a specific model of washing machine*	Program A, program B, specific pictograms, menu hierarchies, procedures, key combinations …

Table 1. Using a washing machine with a digital interface

2.4.2 Actual performance – experience (2)

The relationship between experience and expertise is suggested to be a reciprocal one (see arrow 2 in Figure 3). It may be argued that as an individual's expertise is observed to be improved over time, a social image will be formed and probability of coming across with novel interaction situations may eventually increase. For example, if an individual is known to be good at handling novel interaction situations, individuals may start to consult her/him frequently. Thus, if an individual's observed expertise becomes prominent it may affect what will be experienced by her/him. On the other hand, if an individual is observed to be a poor performer then other individuals will not ask for help or encourage the individual to get involved in novel interaction situations.

2.4.3 Actual performance – self-efficacy (3)

As mentioned earlier, as individuals experience a diversity of interfaces they form a self-efficacy belief (see arrow 3 in Figure 3). This belief may be strong or weak depending on how the outcome of the experience was perceived by the individual. In other words, an individual's performance in novel interaction situations will be reflected in the form of self-efficacy belief.

2.4.4 Self-efficacy – actual performance (4)

As individuals grow self-efficacy beliefs about interaction, their actual performance with interfaces are influenced through several mechanisms (see arrow 4 in Figure 3). As discussed earlier, people with a strong self-efficacy belief are good at overcoming breakdown situations and converging cognitive resources to problem solving. People with low self-efficacy may tend to get frustrated easier, ask for help or may be prone to quit when confronted with a problem.

2.4.5 Self-efficacy – experience (5)

Individuals with strong self-efficacy beliefs with regards to interaction are expected to extensively use digital interfaces and to frequently get involved in challenging interaction situations. Individuals with a low self-efficacy may choose not to use digital interfaces and try to avoid challenging interaction situations as much as possible.

2.5 Actual performance and self-efficacy as manifestations of GIE

As defined by Cronbach and Meehl (1955), a construct is an attribute postulated to be possessed by individuals and reflected in behavior. It is developed "generally to organize knowledge and direct research in an attempt to describe or explain some aspect of nature" in a scientific inquiry (Peter, 1981, p. 134). It is only possible to make inferences about the attribute by examining its surface manifestations. Therefore, constructs can be observed indirectly.

As depicted in Figure 3, GIE was treated as a construct, which is manifested in actual performance and self-efficacy beliefs. Although it was mentioned that there is a reciprocal relationship between experience and expertise (see 2.4), treating experience as a manifestation of GIE is methodologically inappropriate since 'what is experienced' is not a reflection but one of the causes of GIE in the first place.

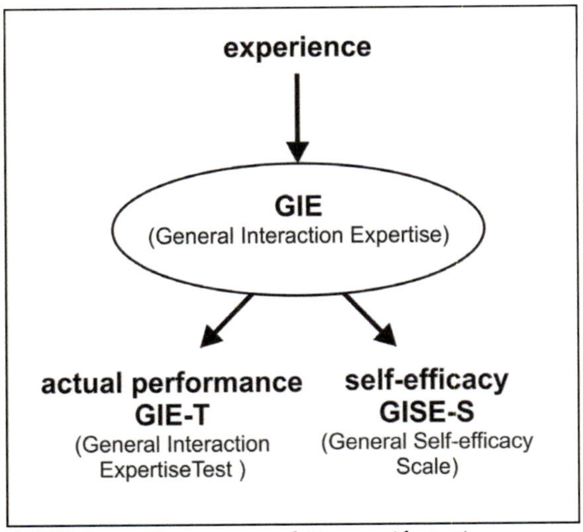

Fig. 3. The construct of GIE, its main cause and its manifestations.

3. Assessment of actual performance

In this section, the method devised for assessing 'actual performance' component of GIE will be explored. The first step in developing a tool for assessment was suggesting a way of recognizing expert behavior. For this purpose, a diversity of cognitive theories was examined and automatic loops of execution - evaluation and problem solving were judged as types of behavior where expertise could be assessed based on performance observation (see Berkman & Erbuğ, 2005). In the following paragraphs the theoretical basis for this measurement strategy was briefly put forward.

3.1 Automated processing

Everyday activities that people carry out are usually composed of automated processes. It is possible to handle such tasks while attending to another one. Such a process of automation is observed in many of the sensory-motor tasks that are practiced frequently. After a sufficient period of experience, even demanding cognitive processes are observed to become automatic (Preece, 1994). From information processing perspective the phenomenon may be explained with the theory of automatic and controlled processing. Automatic processes demand little effort, may be unavailable to consciousness, and maybe identified by their fluency; whereas controlled processes, tap a considerable amount of cognitive resources and are slower than automatic processes (Sternberg, 1999). According to Ackerman (1987), after sufficient practice under consistent task conditions, controlled tasks may become automatic. For consistent tasks, improvements in performance are limited with individual's sensory-motor capacity or motivation to perform better.

Even it has sprouted from a different school of thought, Activity Theory provides a similar explanation to the process of learning. According to Vygotsky (1978) when people get involved in an activity, they make plans that help them to formulate actions, which are meant to satisfy certain sub-goals. Actions, then, are actualized by a set of operations. After individuals gain certain expertise, actions and even whole activities are carried out as routine operations. However, when conditions vary, a simple operation will be handled as an Activity in itself (see Koschmann, Kuuti & Hickman, 1998 and Bodker, 1991 for a complete model).

Both theories have common points that give clues about ways of recognizing expert behavior:

- The extent of expertise gained by practicing a task may be predicted by whether the task is automated, still under conscious control, or both.

- After a certain level of automation is attained in a specific task, gains can be transferred to other tasks with similar conditions.

Therefore, sensory-motor fluency observed in an easy task with a familiar interface may be an observable indication of expertise. Individuals with a high level of GIE would have been gained expertise by practicing similar tasks and may be expected to switch to automatic behavior after a concise orientation period.

3.2 Controlled processing

According to Norman (1990), in order our goals to be fulfilled individuals should be able to perceive and evaluate the current state of the world. The evaluation is then followed by a set of actions for changing the state of the world so that goals are accomplished.

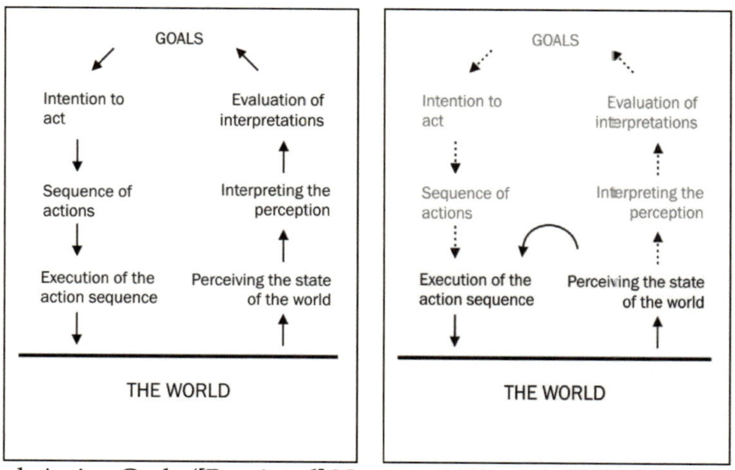

Fig. 4. Left: Task Action Cycle ([Reprinted] Norman, 1990 p.47), Right: The Action cycle bypassed (after Norman).

The steps of the cycle presented in Figure 4 are run until the goals are accomplished and "the world" is in the desired state. However, whether the flow is smooth or constantly interrupted, whether a single iteration is enough or the cycle is run many times may vary. Cycle may be so internalized by the user that both concretizations of goals and interpretation of the world may be minimally crucial. Taken to the extreme, executions may dominate the cycle, minimizing even the need for feedbacks. A secretary making a fair copy of a hand-written letter without getting feedback from monitor or keyboard is an illustrative example for such an extreme case of execution-dominated behavior. This type of interaction may be characterized by automatic processing as it was discussed previously.

On the other extreme, there may be cases where sequence of actions is not readily available to the individual, or "interpreting the perception" is not possible. This usually occurs when people confront with serious problems, or when they came across with a totally novel interface. In such cases, translation of intention to act to a meaningful sequence of actions and to transform perceptions to evaluations may be problematic. With similar concerns, Sutcliff et al. (2000) propose certain elaborations which transform Norman's model so that the level of detail is sufficient to discuss breakdown and learning situations.

In Figure 5, certain shortcuts and sub-cycles are suggested to embrace rather extreme cases mentioned above.

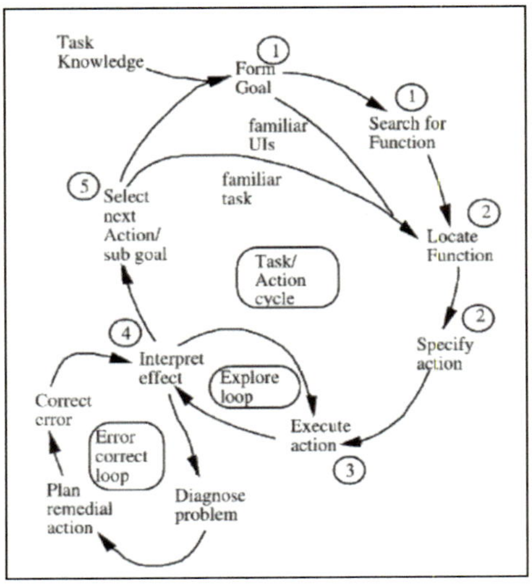

Fig. 5. Task Action Cycle revised by Suttcliff et al. (2000, p. 45)

Mack and Montaniz (1994) state that such extreme cases are represented by different sets of behaviors. They claim that when users are engaged with "well-understood" (p. 301) tasks, they often exhibit goal-directed behavior and utilize routine cognitive skills. However, when task or interface is a novel one, behavior is dominated by problem-solving type of activity.

As far as the elaborated model suggested by Sutcliff et al. (2000) is concerned, this type of behavior is represented by "error correct" and "explore" loops (see Figure 5). While discussing learning through experiences, Proctor and Dutta (1995) typify this problem solving - learning behavior with cases of learning to operate complex devices without instructions. In a typical usability test this is encouraged to see whether interface provides an intuitive mode of interaction. Therefore, it is possible to state that, in almost every usability test, participants are first confronted with a problem-solving activity, hopefully followed by relatively smooth, uninterrupted task-action cycles.

In an experiment conducted by Shrager and Klar (1986, ctd. in Proctor & Dutta, 1995) on learning a complex device without instructions, it is observed that after an initial orientation phase where participants learn how to change device state, they started to systematically investigate the system by generating hypotheses about ways of attaining task goals. These hypotheses were then tested and the ones that survived helped participants to construct and refine the device model. Therefore, in terms of Mack and Montaniz (1994), systematic investigation phase represents problem-solving activity.

All the studies reviewed above indicate that some sort of problem-solving activity takes place especially when users are involved in novel interaction situations.

3.3 Development of General Interaction Expertise Test (GIE-T)

Based on theories discussed above, it is suggested that GIE may be manifested in two fundamental types of behavior, which are automatic loops of execution - evaluation and controlled problem-solving. In order to assess expertise by observing actual performance on tasks that target these two types of behavior, GIE-T that consists of two prototypic apparatus tests were developed.

3.3.1 GIE_XEC

The following set of heuristics guided the development process of GIE_XEC test:

- Task content should be neutral, so that prior knowledge specific to systems, applications and domains should not alter performance.
- Test should not contain tasks that require cognitively complex processes.
- Test should not be comprised of tasks that require novel modes of interaction.
- Test should be comprised of familiar sub-tasks in order to maximize the effects of experience with digital interfaces on performance.

The task consisted of three simple sub-tasks, assumed to fall into automatic loops of execution and evaluation domain defined previously. In order to eliminate the effects of task content on performance, generic tasks were designed. Thus, the effects of SS, AS, or DS were ruled out. Task difficulty and novelty was tried to be adjusted to a level so that indications of automatic processing and fluency in completing sub-tasks would indicate that participant has a level of expertise. Furthermore, it was expected that participants with a relatively higher degree of expertise would exhibit automatic behavior after a very brief period of adaptation to specific conditions of hard and soft elements of interface.

Before the administration of the test, step-by-step instructions were provided; goals and methods of achieving them were clear. A trial session was provided for participants to familiarize themselves with interface and sub-tasks. After the trial, participants were asked to complete 5 identical trials in order to further increase the ratio of automatic behavior observed during performance. Steps to complete one trial were as follows:

Sub-task 1: Navigate and choose modify ('değiştir'),
Sub-task 2: Navigate and choose 'P',
Sub-task 3: Complete the required modifications and choose confirm ('onay')

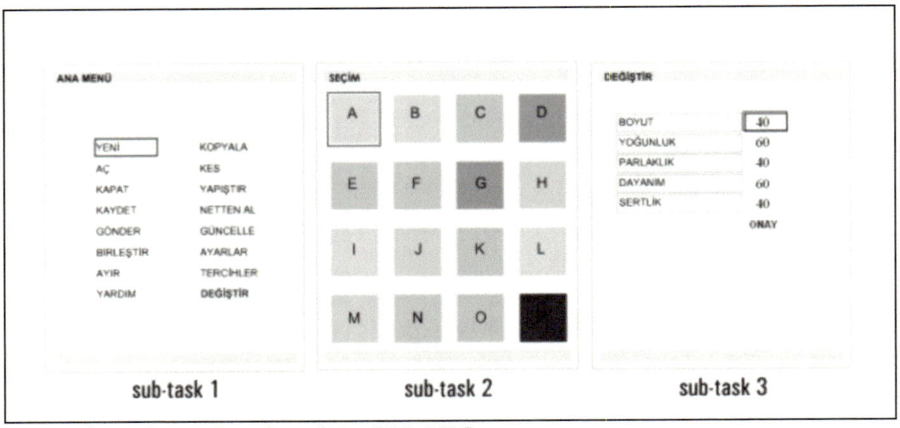

Fig. 6. Screenshots for each sub-task in GIE_XEC

According to the initial findings, performance in GIE_XEC test may simply be represented by means of elapsed times recorded in 5 successive trials (see Berkman, 2007 for further discussion).

3.3.2 GIE_PS

The following set of heuristics was utilized in the design of apparatus test that target problem-solving behavior:

- Goals states and current state of the device should be apparent to the participants. Participant's performance should not be hindered while trying to understand the goal state or compare it with the current state.

- Task should not require domain knowledge or a specific ability.

- Task should be easy to complete without the interface. If the task would be handled in an unmediated manner, all of the participants should be able to complete it (e.g. with paper and pencil, or verbally).

- The task difficulty should be related with how the problem is represented, flexibility in refining the representation, and selection of appropriate methods to control both external and internal processes.

- Task should be complex enough to decrease the probability of success by chance.

- Completion of the task should not require long procedures. This would ensure that the ratio of time spent on problem solving to time spent on keystrokes is huge and determined by efficiency in problem solving activity to a great extent, rather than execution - evaluation loops.

Among many other alternatives a problem situation was chosen to be developed as an apparatus test.

Participants were asked to form a pattern of shapes so that it reproduces the goal pattern. The interface elements were a display and five push buttons. Three buttons were located so that each of them coupled with a single-digit numerical display. A button labeled with an arrow pointing towards the screen was positioned on the right (redraw button). Another button labeled "done" ("tamam") was positioned between the goal pattern and display. By pushing that button, participants would be able to indicate that the task was successfully completed (see Figure 7.).

Parameters that could be manipulated were not described to participants. At the beginning of the test, the aim of the test was briefly described, together with some limited instructions about the task.

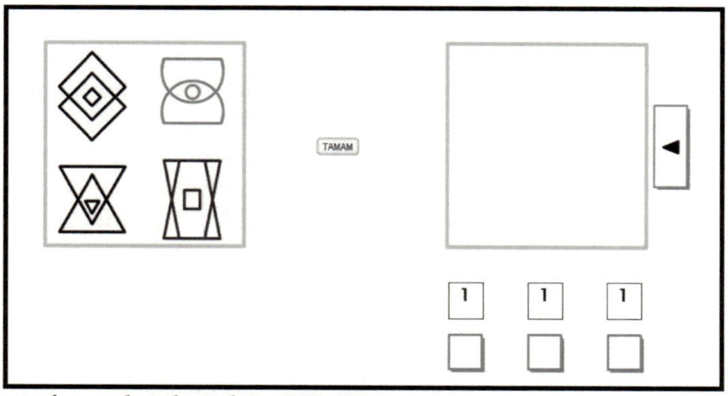

Fig. 7. Screenshots for each sub-task in GIE_PS

A typical sequence of actions taken by an expert user for accomplishing the task would be as follows:

1. Select the slot to be filled with the leftmost button,
2. Modify the type parameter with the middle button,
3. Select the appropriate value for the color parameter with the rightmost button,
4. Press redraw button to see the results,
5. After the goal state is reached, press the button labeled "done".

According to the preliminary studies, GIE_PS test should be regarded as a pass-fail item (see Berkman, 2007). Although, elapsed time was considered as a measure that could yield more precise results, it was observed that some participants were not able to solve the problem and quit the task or were asked to quit.

3.4 Validity of GIE-T

In order to evaluate the validity, both tests were administered in usability tests of consumer products with digital interfaces, such as washing machines and dishwashers. Results show that GIE_XEC and GIE_PS scores correlate with effectiveness scores. Participants scoring high on apparatus tests were observed to be more successful in completing usability scenarios. The correlation coefficients yielded with individual and combined scores of apparatus tests were in the range of 0.46-0.76.

In a usability test where a dishwasher with a menu-driven interface was tested with 15 participants, GIE_XEC scores were observed to be highly correlated with the number of tasks completed (0.68). In an experiment, composed of three sub-tests, where 3 washing machines were compared with a primary interface, both GIE_XEC and GIE_PS scores correlated significantly with test results (0.69 and 0.46 respectively). Furthermore, when scores were combined with a linear model, correlation further increased (0.76).

Although there is still much to do in order to develop and investigate the validity of the GIE-T as it is presented in this study, initial results show that systematical assessment of 'actual performance' or similar constructs may increase researcher's control over experiential factors. The following points summarize the outcomes of studies completed so far and what can be done in the future.

Although a small number of sub-tasks seem to be sufficient in recognizing expert behavior during automatic processes, several pass-fail items are necessary in the assessment of problem-solving behavior. Apparatus tests that would be developed in accordance with the afore-mentioned heuristics would yield similar results in terms of assessing GIE and predicting performance in usability tests. Therefore, researchers can tailor their own apparatus tests when cost of development is not a problem. Although quite an ambitious goal, standardized tests may be developed for setting normative standards. This way, results of individual studies would be comparable. It is recommended that apparatus tests should be updated from time to time in order to make sure that they comply with the contemporary culture of interaction as much as possible. Finally, it should be noted that observing participants before the actual usability tests has merits of its own. Observing how participants behave beforehand may provide the following information that may be helpful in moderating tests:

- Tendency to develop test anxiety,
- Reactions to the idea of being tested in general,
- Tendency to exhibit self-blaming behavior,
- Tendency to get frustrated,
- Ability to tolerate failure,
- Tendency to feel challenged,
- Frequency and style of requesting help.

4. Assessment of self-efficacy – General Self-efficacy Scale (GISE-S)

As far as measurement strategy proposed in this study is concerned, assessment of self-efficacy has a twofold character. First, by definition, it is suggested that one of the manifestations of GIE is self-efficacy belief. Thus, assessment of self-efficacy is proposed as a means for measuring GIE and for complementing the performance measurement approach adopted in GIE-T. Second, like many other tools developed for measuring attitudes (Spector, 1992) a paper-based tool would be appropriate for assessing self-efficacy, which will provide the opportunity to assess GIE with a tool that is easier to administer, even in groups and without any equipment or trained administrators.

4.1 Development of GISE-S

In order to identify the essential steps that will form the development procedure, both basic material on fundamentals of scale development (e.g. Crocker & Algina, 1986; Spector, 1992; DeVellis, 1991; Netemeyer, Bearden & Sharma, 2003) and focused discussions on technical and theoretical issues were reviewed. After the comparative examination of the selected procedures, some attributes that are common in all of them were identified. The steps followed in scale development were listed below:

1. Construct definition
2. Development of item pool
3. Expert review
4. Initial item tryout
5. Major data collection
6. Preliminary reliability and validity studies

The concept of 'self-efficacy' is frequently utilized to measure and even predict performance. According to Pajares, "what people know, the skills they possess, or what they have previously accomplished are not always good predictors of subsequent attainments because the beliefs they hold about their capabilities powerfully influence the ways in which they will behave" (1997, ¶7). In line with this view, researchers developed many scales that targeted 'computer self-efficacy' (e.g. Murphy, Coover & Owen, 1989; Compeau & Higgins, 1995). Suggested as 'more than just a mere reflection of performance', the concept of 'self-efficacy' was considered as a framework for defining the construct that will form the backbone of the scale under development. However, there are some pitfalls to be avoided when defining the specific construct and scale development.

According to Compeau & Higgins (1995), concentrating on individual sub-skills rather than self-efficacy beliefs for accomplishing tasks is a misconception exhibited by some researchers.

While discussing the common errors in assessment, Bong (2006) maintains that self-efficacy should not be confused with other self-referent constructs such as self-esteem and self-concept. Bong maintains that constructs that claim to be a type of self-efficacy should concentrate on one's confidence in accomplishing a task, and not self-worth or self-perceptions regarding a specific domain.

Another error to be avoided is stated as ignoring the context-specific nature of self-efficacy constructs. Consequently, measurements should not be based on self-assessments done in vacuum and respondents should not be forced to weigh their self-confidence on highly abstracted situations. Finally, Bong (2006) warns that beliefs that match what is to be predicted should be looked for. In other words, it is asserted that the predictive power of self-efficacy is maximized when these beliefs are about tasks that are in relation with the criterial variable.

Bandura (2006) states that perceived capability should be targeted by items "phrased in terms of can do rather than will do" (p.308) so that intentions are not mistaken for self-efficacy perceptions. Another crucial elaboration made by him is the danger of focusing on outcome expectancies.

4.1.1 Construct definition

General Interaction Self-Efficacy (GISE) is specified as individuals' self-efficacy perceptions as far as learning new devices. Although core definition seems to be too specifically formulated, it will be primarily utilized in relation with usability tests where participants get involved in a novel interaction situation. Therefore, long-term appropriation of digital products, or long-term transformations witnessed in the nature of interaction should be excluded.

> ***General Interaction Self-Efficacy (GISE)*** *is a judgment of capability to establish interaction with a new device and to adapt to novel interaction situations.*

In accordance with this definition, GISE has two facets. First of all, GISE is related with learning to use new devices. In this regard, it is the capability to learn how to use a new device under unfavorable conditions, as well as ability to sustain adaptation in the absence of factors that enhance the process. Secondly, it is the ability to reorient, recover interaction and survive in a multitude of breakdown situations.

4.1.2 Development of item pool

Scale development may be regarded as a subtractive process where refinement of a large set of items is done in successive steps. In each step, items that are observed to exhibit certain flaws are eliminated. Therefore, quality of a scale is determined by the quality of items in the initial item pool.

There are no well-established theories in the self-efficacy literature that may be helpful in content sampling during item generation. In order to grasp the users' perceptions about factors that influence the adaptation processes positively or negatively an empirical study was conducted. Data collection was done with a self-administered questionnaire, titled Learning Electronic Devices Questionnaire (LEDQ), which consists of open-ended questions. Respondents were asked to report favorable and then unfavorable situations for learning electronic devices.

A total of 550 expressions were gathered from 102 respondents. 287 of the expressions were negative whereas 269 were positive. After the elimination of some problematic expressions 425 of them were retained for item generation. In order to have an understanding of the content domain and the distribution of expressions, data was categorically arranged. In Figure 8, the semantic model extracted was provided.

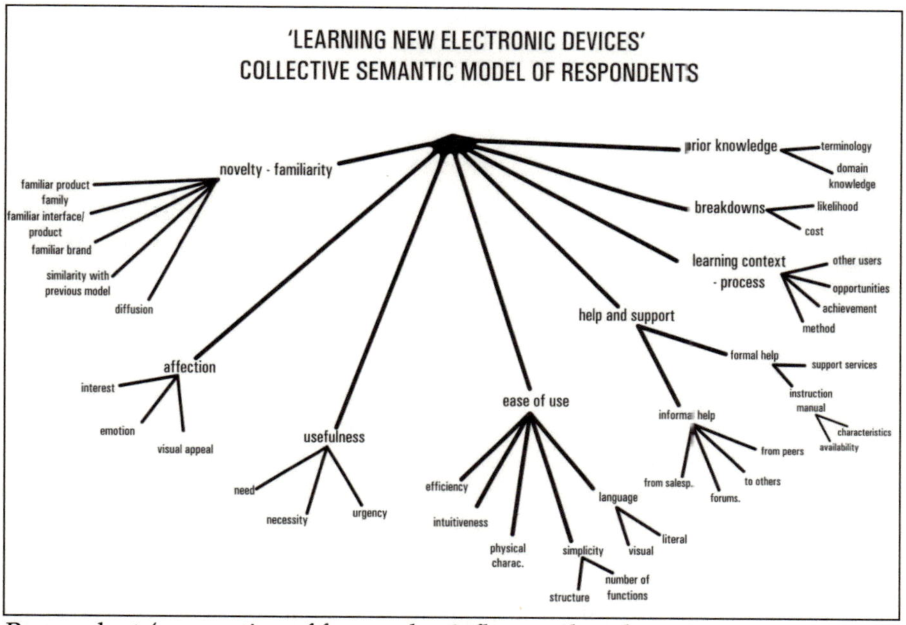

Fig. 8. Respondents' perception of factors that influence the adaptation process.

It should be noted that the model depicted in Figure 8 should not be mistaken for a factual model based on empirical findings. The rationale behind constructing such a model was to gain insight about users' perceptions about adaptation to new interfaces, guiding the item generation and item reduction processes.

Item generation was based on the expressions extracted and a well-established guideline on user interface design (Nielsen, 1994). At the end of the process a total of 242 items were generated. In Table 2 a sample of items were provided[2]. After giving instructions on how to rate the items and a short exercise, respondents were asked to rate their confidence in learning a new device under circumstances depicted in each item.

If I did not use a device with a similar function	(0-10): _____
If it is not a widely used device	(0-10): _____
If I do not really need that device	(0-10): _____
If device is complex to use	(0-10): _____
If I could not grasp how device functions	(0-10): _____

[2] Note that items were generated and tested in Turkish. Translations were provided for illustrating the content of scale and the style of items.

If I frequently need to resort to instruction manual	(0-10): _____
If technical terms were used in device	(0-10): _____
If there is no one to show how to use	(0-10): _____
If there is no one around that I can ask for help	(0-10): _____
If instruction manual is hard to understand	(0-10): _____
If I cannot manage to use it after a couple of trials	(0-10): _____
If error messages are hard to understand	(0-10): _____
If device is hard to control	(0-10): _____

Table 2. Sample of items in GISE-S

4.1.3 Item reduction

Item reduction was done in three successive steps. First, items were rated by five experts and surviving 104 items were tested in a pilot study (N=52) and remaining 92 items were administered to a sample of 442 respondents.

4.1.4 Factor structure

After the final data was gathered, an explorative factor analysis was conducted in order to determine the number of factors and uncover factor structure. In the first iteration, complying with Kaiser Guttman criterion, a 9-factor solution was arrived at. A close inspection of the item groupings indicated that 9-factor solution is quite comprehensible. When items included in these factors were evaluated it was evident that the preliminary semantic structure suggested (see Figure 9) was almost reflected in the factorial structure derived after the factor analysis. However, due to the fact that Factor 9 and 8 were not sufficiently loaded by any items (loadings below 0.50); a 7-factor solution was forced in the second iteration.

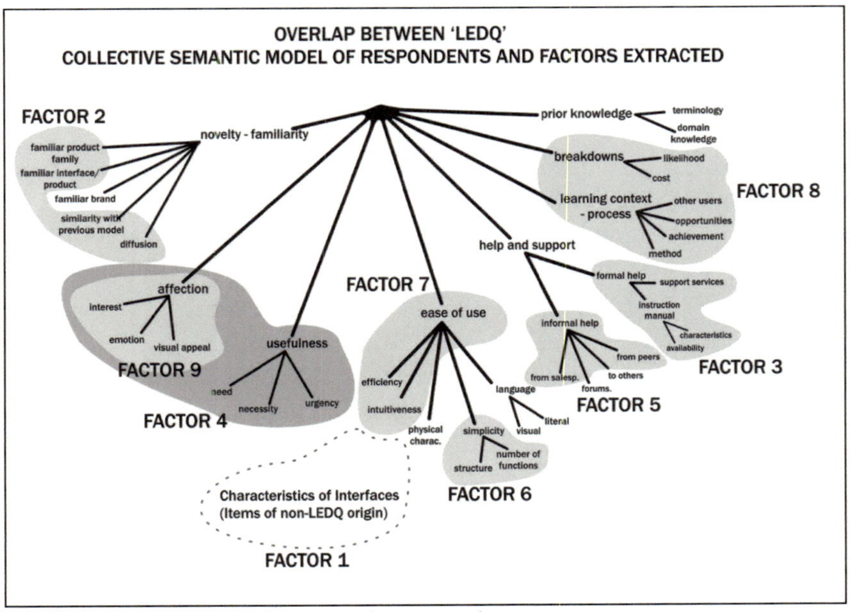

Fig. 9. 9-factor solution after exploratory factor analysis

In the second iteration, item groupings in the 7-factor solution were still theoretically comprehensible. The remaining factors and sample items were listed in Table 3.

Factors	Sample items
1. Interface characteristics	If it is hard to cancel what I have done If error messages do not lead me to a solution If I do not know the abbreviations used in device
2. Familiarity	If it is not a widely used device If it does not bear resemblance with previous models If it is different from devices I used before
3. Formal help	If instruction manual is not informative If it does not have an instruction manual If instruction manual is not clear
4. Informal help	If there is no one to show how to use If there is no one around that I can ask for help If the salesman does not show how to use
5. Motivation to learn (affection and usefulness)	If it has functions that I will not use If it is not interesting for me If it is not a useful device for me
6. Simplicity	If it has too many buttons If it is complicated If it has too many functions
7. Intuitiveness	If I cannot quickly find what I need If I cannot figure it out by just common sense If basic functions are hard to use

Table 3. Factors and sample items

4.1.5 Initial validity studies

During major data collection, some additional data were gathered in order to conduct a preliminary validity analysis. These additional data consisted of age and number of types of electronic devices experienced (NED). Initial findings indicate that there is a positive correlation among NED and a coarse estimate[3] of GISE-S score (EGISE-S). Age correlated negatively both with NED and EGISE-S score. The highest correlation coefficient was observed between NED and EGISE-S score (see Figure 10). Scale should be finalized and additional data should be collected from a different sample in order to have a reliable analysis. However, it should be noted that initial findings are in line with the hypothesized relationship between experience and self-efficacy (see 2.4 and Figure 10).

---

[3] Since scale was not fully developed when the data was collected it was only possible to calculate a coarse estimate of GISE-S score.

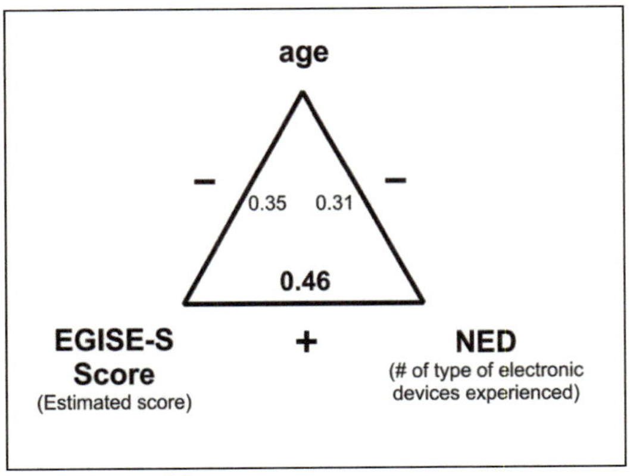

Fig. 10. Relationship between variables

5. Conclusion

Initial results show that there is prospective evidence to show that GIE model proposed here may prove to be useful for measurement purposes. Preliminary analyses indicate that in their fully-fledged forms, GIE-T and GISE-S may be valuable tools for sampling or may be administered when control over experiential factors is necessary. Depending on the nature of research, tools may be administered in combination or individually, or just in reduced forms. GISE-S, being a paper-based tool, has certain advantages over GIE-T such as cost and ease of administration. However, administration of GIE-T provides the opportunity to observe actual performance of participants. A variety of real-life studies where tools are administered in parallel to running usability projects are necessary to weigh cost-effectiveness of both tools.

Measurement of GIE may be helpful for justification of certain assumptions regarding participant profile, as a way of manipulating GIE as an independent variable, or for ascertaining that the effects of GIE on test results were kept to a minimum. Furthermore, if normative standards are determined, the tool may also be used to evaluate usability of interfaces in absolute terms. In other words, it would be possible to identify interfaces that require high levels of GIE and those do not. A final merit of pre-evaluating participants would be to detect the individuals that exhibit intolerable levels of test / performance anxiety before the actual usability test.

Additional studies are necessary for refining GIE-T and GISE-S, increase the prototypic tools in variety and finally justifying that acceptable reliability and validity levels are attained in various research settings.

6. References

Ackerman, P. L. (1987). Individual differences in skill learning: An integrating of psychometric and information processing perspectives. *Psychological Bulletin*, 102,1, 3-27, 0033-2909

Ackerman, P. L. & Humphreys, L. G. (1990). Individual differences theory in Industrial and Organizational Psychology. In: *Handbook of Industrial and Organizational*

Psychology (2nd ed.). M.D. Dunette & L. M. Hough (Ed.), 223-283. Consulting Psychologists Press, 0471886424, California

Bandura, A. (1986). Social foundations of thought and action. Prentice Hall, 013815614X, New Jersey

Bandura, A. (2006). Guide for constructing self-efficacy scales. In: *Self-efficacy beliefs of Adolescents.* F. Pajares and T. Urdan (Ed.), 307-337, Information age, 1593113668, Connecticut

Berkman, A. E. (2007). General Interaction Expertise: An Approach for Sampling in Usability Testing of Consumer Products, In: *Human-Computer Interaction Interaction Design and Usability.* Julie A. Jacko (Ed.), 397-406 , Springer, 9783540731047, Berlin

Berkman, A. E. & Erbuğ, Ç. (2005). Accommodating individual differences in usability studies on consumer products. In: *Proceedings of the 11th conference on human computer interaction,* 3 [CD-ROM]

Bodker, S. (1991). Through the interface. Lawrence Erlbaum, 0805805702, Hillsdale

Bong, M. (2006). Asking the right question: how confident are you that you could successfully perform these tasks? In: *Self-efficacy beliefs of Adolescents.* F. Pajares and T. Urdan (Ed.),287-307, Information age, 1593113668, Connecticut

Bunz, U. (2004). The computer-email-web (CEW) fluency scale—development and validation. *International Journal of Human-Computer Interaction,* 17, 4, 479-506, 1697-9613

Caulton, D. A. (2001). Relaxing the homogeneity assumption in usability testing. *Behaviour & Information Technology,* 20, 1, 1-7, 0144-929X

Chapanis, A. (1991). Evaluating usability. In: *Human factors for informatics usability.* B. Shackel & S. Richardson (Ed.), 360-395, Cambridge University Press, 0521365708, Cambridge

Compeau, D. R. & Higgins, C. A. (1995). Computer self-efficacy: Development of a measure and initial test. *MIS Quarterly,* 19,2, 189-211, 0276-7783

Connell, I., Blanford, A. & Green, T. (2004). CASSM and cognitive walkthrough: usability issues with ticket vending machines. *Behaviour & Information Technology,* 23,5, 307-320, 0144-929X

Crocker, L. & Algina, J. (1986). Introduction to classical and modern test theory. Holt, 0030616344, New York

Cronbach, L.J. & Meehl, P.E. (1955) Construct validity in psychological tests, *Psychological Bulletin,* 52, 281-302, 0033-2909

DeVellis, R. (1991). Scale development: Theory and Application. Sage, 9780761926054, California

Dumas, J. S. & Redish, J. C. (1993). A practical guide to usability testing. Ablex, 1841500208, Norwood- NJ

Egan, D. E. (1988). Individual differences in human-computer interaction. In: *Handbook of human-computer interaction.* M. Helander (Ed.), 543-565, Elsevier, 0444705368, New York

Freudenthal, D. (2001). The role of age, foreknowledge and complexity in learning to operate a complex device. *Behavior & Information Technology,* 20, 1, 23-35, 0144-929X

Garmer, K. Liljegren, E., Osvalder, A. & Dahlman, S. (2002). Application of usability testing to the development of medical equipment. *International Journal of Industrial Ergonomics,* 29, 145-159, 01698141

Helander, M.G., 1997. The human factors profession. In: *Handbook of Human Factors and Ergonomics,* Salvendy, G., (Ed.), 3–16, Wiley, 0471116904, New York

Igbaria, M., Zinatelli, N., Cragg, P., Cavaye, A. L. M. (1997). Personal computing acceptance factors in small firms: a structural equation model. *MIS Quarterly*, (September 1997), 279-305, 0276-7783

Kinzie, M. B., Delcourt, M. A. B., Powers, S. M. (1994). Computer technologies: attitudes and self-efficacy across undergraduate disciplines. *Research in Higher Education*, 35, 6, 745-768, 0361-0365

Koschmann, T., Kuuti, K. & Hickman, L. (1998). The concept of breakdown in Heidegger, Leont'ev, and Dewey and its implications for education. *Mind, Culture, and Activity*, 5, 1, 25-41, 1074-9039

Lauretta, D. & Deffner, G. (1996). Experimental evaluation of dialogue styles for hybrid telephone-based interfaces. *Behaviour & Information Technology*, 15,1, 51-56, 0144-929X

Mack, R. & Montaniz, F. (1994). Observing, predicting, and analyzing usability problems. In: Usability inspection methods, J. Nielsen (Ed.) 295 - 34, John Wiley & Sons, 0471018775 , New York

Murphy, C. A., Coover, D., Owen, S. V. (1989). Development and validation of the computer self-efficacy scale. *Educational and Psychological Measurement*, 49, 893-899, 0013-1644

Netemeyer, R. G., Bearden, W. O., & Sharma, S. (2003). Scaling procedures. Sage, 0761920277, California

Nielsen, J. (1993). Usability engineering. Academic Press, 0-12-518405-0, Boston

Nielsen, J. (1994). Heuristic evaluation. In J. Nielsen, and R. L. Mack (eds.), *Usability Inspection Methods*, 25-62, John Wiley & Sons, , New York:

Norman, D. A. (1990). The design of everyday things. Currency, 0385267746, New York

Pajares, F. (1997). Current directions in self-efficacy research. In: *Advances in motivation and achievement Vol. 10,* [online version] (www.des.emory.edu/mfp/effchapter.html retrieved in 12.11.2006)

Peter, J. P. (1981). Construct validity: A review of basic issues and marketing practices. *Journal of Marketing Research*, 18, 133-145, 0022-2437

Potosnak, K. (1988). Recipe for a usability test. *IEEE Software*, (November 1988), 83-84, 0740-7459

Preece, J. (1994). Human - Computer Interaction. Addison-Wesley, 0201627698, Harlow

Proctor, R. W. & Dutta, A. (1995). Skill acquisition and human performance. Sage, 0803950101, London

Shackel, B. & Richardson, S. (1991). Human factors for informatics usability. Cambridge University Press, 0521365708, Cambridge

Spector, P. (1992). Summated rating scale construction: An introduction. Sage, 9780803943414 ,California

Sternberg, R. J. (1999). Cognitive Psychology. Harcourt Brace College, 0155085352, Orlando Publishers.

Sutcliffe, A., Ryan, M., Doubleday, A. & Springett, M. (2000). Model mismatch analysis: towards a deeper explanation of users' usability problems. *Behaviour & Information Technology*, 19 ,1, 42-55, 0144-929X

Thimbleby, H. (1991). Can anyone work the video. New Scientist, (February 1991), 40-43, 0262-4079

Vygotsky, L. S. (1978). Mind in society: the development of higher psychological processes. Harvard University Press, 0-674-57629-2 , Cambridge

Model-based User Interface Generation from Process-Oriented Models

Thomas Schlegel
Institute for Visualization and Interactive Systems, Universität Stuttgart
Germany

1. Introduction

Usability and software ergonomics play an important role in software product quality and success today. While software engineering has lead to structured approaches and processes for improving quality, usability issues and user interface design are often still regarded as rather optional or late-phase activities. A reason for this gap is that user interface design is either executed ad-hoc and unmanaged by software developers during application development or as a separate activity with only loose coupling to other elements of the software development process.

Already in the late 1980 models and systems for user interface design support have been developed by researchers, followed by first interpreter-based or generative approaches for transforming interaction-oriented descriptive models into user interface prototypes or even full applications. Different types of models or even model sets were created to provide enough semantics for user interface generation.

While generative approaches in software engineering like OMG's Model-Driven Architecture (MDA) were comparably successful in practice also, dedicated modeling and generation approaches for user interfaces were not as successful. The problem of most approaches is that complex and separate models for the user interface only have to be created, which do not integrate well with the software engineering processes and models. Especially where additional effort has to be spent and models only benefit the dialog layer, acceptance by software developers and even potential users has been low.

Especially the development of interactive software has proven to require the involvement of software engineering methods as well as usability aspects. To give emphasis to quality aspects - especially usability - in software development projects, different methodologies have been invented, ranging from checklists to dedicated modeling approaches, complete User Interface Development Environments (UIDE) and User Interface (UI) generators. Approaches trying to focus on usability issues only for the most part have not had much impact on practice and further research because of their incompatibility to existing software engineering models and processes that are used in software development.

A key factor here is the integration of concepts, perspectives, processes and models of usability experts, software engineers and other project-critical stakeholders (Alexander & Robertson, 2004) but still allow for early-phase models and prototyping approaches that have proven their strength in interactive system development. The communication between stakeholders as well as the creation of artifacts is and will be based on the successful use of common models shared when developing software that provides a user interface.

As a consequence, this chapter presents an integrated modeling approach that allows to start with basic specifications such as essential use cases followed by an incremental and iterative refinement and enhancement towards an extensive specification of interaction and system reactions. The fundaments of this Interaction Modeling Language (IML) were developed in conjunction with a user interface generator approach for the creation of graphical user interface prototypes based on a flow-centric interaction specification using IML. This suitability for automatic processing eases the deduction of interactive prototypes from user-oriented models already in early phases of software development projects.

2. Existing Modeling Approaches

An extensive model landscape has been developed in the last decades for analysis and design in software development with regards to user-oriented approaches. This section provides an overview necessary to understand the current model and model integration discussion.

2.1 HCI Models for Task Analysis and Modeling

The goal of finding a modeling technique that serves for task analysis and modeling has produced a variety of different techniques in the human-computer interaction domain, ranging from psychological to rather technical methods.

Some of them are described in the following to give an impression of the wide range and provide hints for developers and research projects that may have special requirements pointing to one of those methods.

ETIT analysis assumes that users have to map intern tasks (IT) to extern tasks (ET). Using a matrix it is possible to estimate the effort for knowledge transfer for similar tasks.

GOMS (goals, operators, methods, selection rules) takes over the notion of goal, sub-goal, operator method and selection rule from the problem solving theory. Goals are subdivided into sub-goals; activities arise from the application of operators, which transform to methods - i.e. high-order operators - by control structures.

CLG (common language grammars) are better suited for command based systems. It differentiates a task layer with extern tasks, a semantic layer with intern tasks, a syntactic layer with concepts and commands and an interaction layer with actions and presentation.

TAGs (task action grammars) do not have this focus on commands, which makes them suitable for other user interfaces, too. They provide a meta language for the description of task description languages. A tag model contains task elements (features), a list of tasks and dedicated elements and substitution rules (grammar) for the production of activities.

CCT (cognitive complexity theory) helps determining the cognitive complexity of a system by judging the knowledge necessary. CCT has been developed from GOMS by projection of the procedural descriptions to conditional and action rules.

Task cases or essential use cases describe the interaction of user and system in natural language with only little structure like dialog or card form. (Constantine, 1995)

These models target behavioral modeling, which is more or less procedural, and often have no relationship to software engineering models. As most of these models are completely incompatible with modern object-oriented software development approaches, they are often used by a small group of specialists only, which makes the models only rarely useful as a model basis for software development projects and integration with software engineering. With the rise of UML (OMG, 2007; OMG, 2007b) use cases in a combined graphical and textual form have been introduced to software engineering practice as black box modeling concepts.

2.2 Models for Task Sequencing

Describing sequences has also lead to many different models trying to capture the interaction dynamics. Many of these are based on concepts similar to Petri nets (Reisig, 1986):

- Data-Flow Diagrams (DFD; DeMarco, 1979)
- State-Charts (Harel, 1987)
- Event Schemata (Martin & Odell, 1992)
- EPC (Scheer, 1994)
- UML sequence diagrams (OMG, 2003)

Others have been described by (Larson, 1992) and (Janssen et al., 1993). They have often been used as the dynamics description part of models for user interface generation and have also had success as partial interaction models.

2.3 Object-Oriented Methods

With object-oriented paradigms becoming popular in the field of programming languages under the notion of object-oriented programming (OOP), modeling concepts also have turned in this direction to keep paradigms of models and code compatible.
In the early nineties, for example OBA (Rubin & Goldberg, 1992), OOA (Coad & Yourdon, 1991) and OOA&D (Martin & Odell, 1992) have been published, all aiming at an object-oriented analysis and providing a basis for the following object-oriented design. (Janssen et al., 1993)
The concepts of OMT (Rumbaugh et al., 1991) and OOSE (Jacobson et al., 1992) were integrated with the approach of Booch to form todays industrial quasi-standard Unified Modeling Language (UML; Scott, 2004) for object-oriented analysis and design, while the OPEN modeling language (OML; Firesmith et al., 1998) has been developed as a sort of competitive language to UML. A comparison of both languages from the perspective of OML can be found in (Henderson-Sellers & Firesmith, 1999), where it is argued that UML can only be considered as hybrid object-oriented and is strongly focused on C++ implementations.
Although, with the Meta Object Facility (MOF; OMG, 2002), OMG strongly pushes UML into the direction of model integration, which will lay the fundament for emerging integrated modeling approaches like the one presented in this chapter.
With the introduction of semantic web technologies, the semantics of models and their (semi-)automated interpretation / inference have become more important leading to more powerful models, which still focus mainly on structural aspects like data structures, types and dependencies.

2.4 Process-oriented Approaches

Besides modeling approaches, many forms of user-oriented software development methodologies have also been discussed.

One popular example is user-centered design, which is an approach for integrating the user into development of software and in newer publications also to hardware and services (Vredenburg et al., 2002), for example using a User Centered Design Process (ISO, 1999). The User Centered Design Process involves users in an iterative process. It strongly involves early evaluation of the user interface, for example using paper prototypes, to gain user feedback as fast as possible and let users actively participate in the development activities. Research on possibilities for integration with software engineering has also been carried out (Metzker & Seffah, 2003).

Usage-centered design on the other hand has emerged from a software engineering perspective and therefore aims at integrating user-oriented models like task descriptions into model-based software development processes ranging from very structured to agile methods like extreme programming (XP; Beck, 1999). Instead of user testing, the focus here lies on improving usage based on models. A short comparison of user centered design and usage-centered design can be found in (Constantine et al., 2003; Constantine & Lockwood, 2002).

2.5 Model-based Development

The problem with these rather complex, often data-centered or object-oriented models in UI generation - e.g. OOA (Hofmann, 1998) - is that users and customers usually only request and accept models that are easy to understand and support their workflows and view of the system. Developers on the other hand may accept such models but will not invest the effort for the creation of models that are not able to save enough effort in later phases or are not at least effort-neutral in practice.

Recognizing this problem and the necessity of an integration of usability and interaction aspects into existing software engineering models, different interaction-oriented description concepts have been developed, improving and extending existing software engineering modeling languages like UML. One example for such an extension is UMLi (Pinheiro da Silva, 2000), an UML extension for interaction design. This extension of common concepts allows easier roll-out than the dedicated models described above. Unfortunately, generative processing is not possible with most of them due to missing formalization.

For broad acceptance in software development practice, models have to integrate seamlessly into one or more of the common models created, like UML use case diagrams and descriptions, class diagrams etc. (OMG, 2003; Henderson-Sellers & Firesmith, 1999). As such description techniques are broadly used, enhancements to these models show easier acceptance by developers.

While these functional and technical aspects were the main criteria in the past, nowadays interaction and non-functional requirements have gained high importance in conjunction with topics like software quality and usability. This requires a stronger involvement of non-developers and the adoption of models for rather "soft" aspects like user interfaces. Additionally, applied software development processes have shifted from straight forward models like waterfall to iterative, incremental and sometimes agile approaches to allow back coupling (Pressman, 1997).

Prototyping has become popular for leading to better integration of customers and users, transforming formerly incomprehensible requirements into visible and understandable artifacts that can serve as a basis for further discussion in order to integrate all stakeholders and achieve a win-win-situation. Building these models, software developers often encounter the dilemma of either spending too much effort in prototype development or not considering user and customer requirements as much as these deserve.

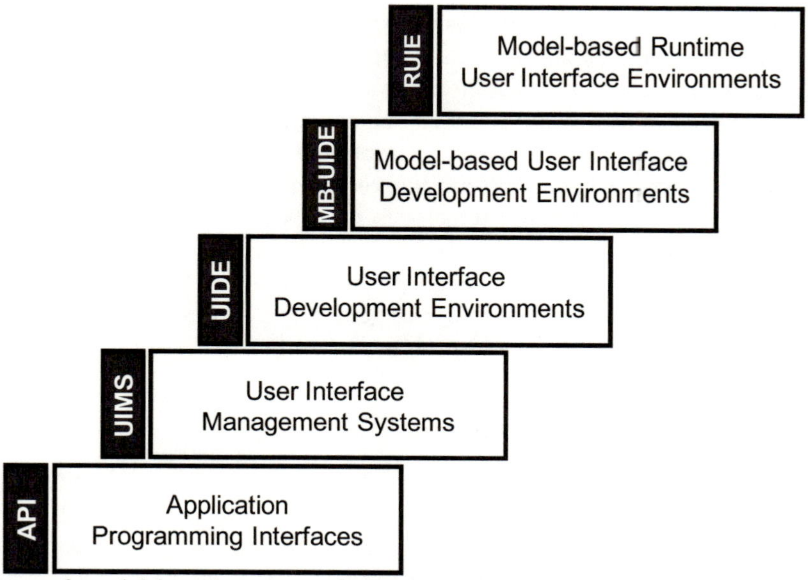

Fig. 1. History of model-based user interface generators.

In the beginning of user interface development, Application Programming Interfaces (API) where chosen for the creation of user interfaces to avoid reinvention and deviation of interaction concepts for each application. More abstraction as well as easier and more flexible definition of interactions became possible by using User Interface Management Systems (UIMS), which interpreted interaction descriptions on runtime.

Better support for design-time modeling was introduced by User Interface Development Environment, some of which are still in use and development.

Targeting direct output of software development artifacts from user- and usage-oriented models through automation, starting in the late 80s, model-based user interface generators have evolved as an answer to usability integration and prototyping. There are many examples for user interface generators that already bring appropriate models with them, e.g. (Janssen et al., 1993).

For such a model-based user interface (UI) development and UI generation, researchers have already suggested approaches using different types of models such as task models, domain models and presentation models like in Teallach (Barclay et al., 1999) or OOA-Models like in JANUS (Balzert et al., 1996). These types of models are intended for utilization in user interface development environments or even user interface generators. Being highly developed, most of these models lack simplicity – in the meaning of easy creation – and often have only rare connection to other models in the software development process besides their ability for user interface generation.

There are three different types of approaches that have been developed for generating a user interface from a declarative model (Pinheiro da Silva et al., 2000): Interpreters like ITS (Wiecha et al., 1990), UIMS generators like TADEUS (Schlungbaum & Elwert, 1995) or FUSE (Lonczewski & Schreiber, 1996) and source code generators like JANUS (Balzert et al., 1996) and Mastermind (Szekely et al., 1995).
Today, applications are moving from the desktop into the network by Application Service Provision (ASP) and Service-Oriented Architectures (SOA; Erl, 2005). This also has a high impact on user interfaces: when services or whole interactive processes are executed for example using BPEL (OASIS, 2007), BPEL4People (IBM et al., 2007) and WS Human Task (IBM et al., 2007b), user interfaces change from process to process and have to serve as input and output interfaces for complex processes and services assembled from atomic ones. For this reason, generative and model-based concepts are a possible solution, but have to be transferred and enhanced to cope with runtime requirements to form Model-Based Runtime User Interface Environments (RUIE), which can be expected to play a major role in future systems.
In the following, we will explain a concept for advancing towards model-based and generative concepts suitable for user interface generation on design-time, which forms the basis for potential future generative approaches on runtime.

3. An Interaction-modeling Approach

For the analysis and requirements phase, pure object-oriented models like OOA are too far away from the mental models of non-developing stakeholders like users and customers and are too static to describe the processes rather than pure entities in requirements gathering. This is the reason why more narrative and informal representations like use cases have gained importance, which may still be embedded into an object-oriented framework - like UML use cases - but are informal enough to let all stakeholders participate in the creation process.
While UML use cases (Jacobson et al., 1992) are defined as a representation of a systems view (Rumbaugh et al., 1999), task cases - also called task descriptions (Rumbaugh et al., 1999) or essential use cases (Biddle et al., 2001) - have been developed to allow for easier expression and focus more on the user and his/her intentions. Starting with this simple but impressive modeling technique, users and customers can join the analysis process, because they are able to contribute in their own words and with natural language concepts.
This trend shows that flow-oriented, natural language based and semi-structured description methods yield high potential for successful requirements analysis and negotiation to software development projects.
Due to different aspects and people working with task cases and use cases, these two - originally very similar - techniques are often used in parallel, even in modern approaches for software engineering and usability integration, like usage-centered design.
It is also possible to refine, expand and integrate essential use cases into system use cases. Merging both concepts together with the ability of stepwise refinement (top down) or - the other way round - construction from almost atomic interactions (bottom up) provides a sustainable concept for interaction modeling. Thus, development projects are no longer forced to develop two or more sparsely connected models in parallel for interaction flow description.

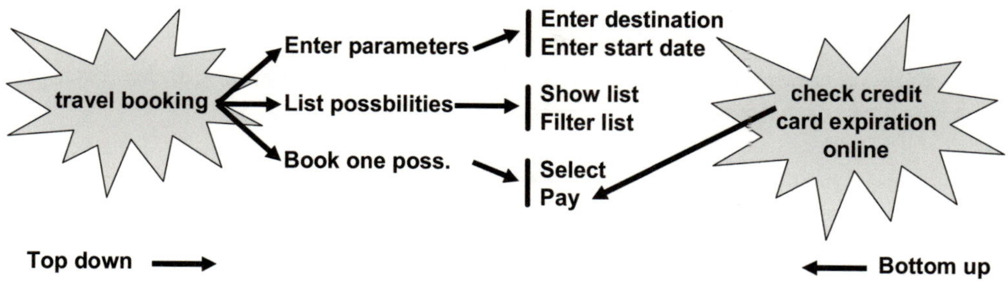

Fig. 2. Starting with the overall task (top down) or an idea for improvement (bottom up) should both be possible with an incremental model.

Beginning with essential use cases that completely abstract from technical and implementation details (Constantine & Lockwood, 2002), it is possible to identify the task descriptions that are fundamental for the interactive software in development. As they are easy to write and widely recognized by both, user interface designers and software requirements engineers, they form at least a first step in many development approaches.

Over the last years, UML use cases have become a very popular method for descriptions in the analysis and specification tasks of software development projects. Easy graphic modeling and free description of workflows for each use case allow for modeling and understanding by non-developers, which has been the basis for their success in practice. The advantages of ease and flexibility for the early stages become a problem when these specifications are to be used in design and development - especially in user interface prototype generation.

Therefore, we propose a model that includes mechanisms for structuring and detailing the initial use cases with regards to user interaction. This will help to preserve all information provided in the basic use case and allow for discussion of the model. But it will also give the developer the ability to use this extended and more structured use case model in the complete development cycle, providing a consistent requirement and interaction model and the ability of out-of-the-box user interface generation.

Already task descriptions (Rumbaugh et al., 1999) provide the ability to transform them to a requirement specification or directly use them as initial descriptions for requirements. However, this ability improves much when detailing and expanding them to a complete and more structured use case set. Here, it is important to abandon the idea of writing use cases from a technical or system perspective. Rather the user perspective should be used, when describing the interactions with the system. This makes a parallel description nearly obsolete and provides a strong model, which can be used as a basis in further development steps.

3.1 IML Model Contents

One example for such an extension of the use case paradigm is an XML-based description we call Interaction Modeling Language (IML; Schlegel et al., 2004).

Following different element and structuring proposals of practitioners, which can be found for example in (Ambler, 2000), it is possible to provide an initial structure for a complete use case specification. As we will use it as a basis for a generator approach, we have subdivided

it into three main parts, which are again hierarchically subdivided: Project definition, data definition and use cases.
Figure 3 shows a condensed example view of an IML-Model containing these three parts: Project definition, data definition and only one IML use case.

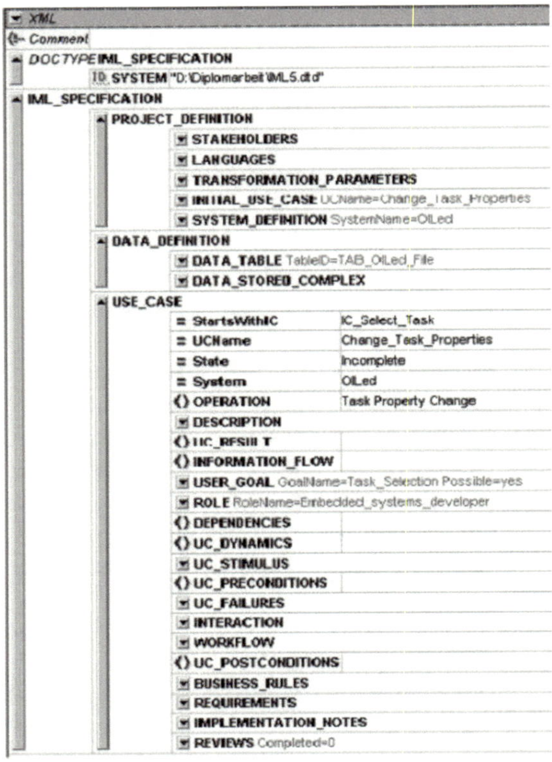

Fig. 3. Sample IML model (XML-based).

3.1.1 IML Project Definition

The first part provides a project definition that embodies necessary information for handling and the later generation, including actors, roles, stakeholders and natural languages used. Actors and roles are employed for identifying the "user type" interacting with the system in the use case interaction definition. Including stakeholder descriptions in the definition is important to ensure model inherent requirements traceability even if stakeholders leave the development project.
The natural language support allows for easy localization providing a verification or transformation engine with the information necessary for checking model completeness for each destination language. Therefore, all translations of descriptions, notifications etc. in the use case part must be stored together with their interaction context in the model. Translation quality will also benefit directly from the contextual and semantic information available in the model context.

3.1.2 IML Data Definition

Developers often complain about a lack of initial data specification in the field of use cases and similar methods. When this is missing and cannot be added once entities become clearer with the project advancing, interactions are only loosely coupled with the application logic and cannot benefit from the semantics available with the data definition

For this reason we have integrated a facultative data section in IML, which allows specifying implementation-neutral entities like data pools but also predefined types that can be easily transformed into programming language types.

The data definition is initially empty and is completed while performing the incremental use case modeling when data sources and sinks are needed. It can also be completed during the use case model refinement and transition to design. The defined data pools serve as a connecting basis for the interaction specification to define entities that are used in different interaction steps or sequences, e.g. "postal address". For the generation of a complete prototype, it is even possible to define database access at this point.

3.1.3 IML Use Case Definition

The third part is what practitioners normally refer to as use case description, containing facultative and obligatory parts that are to be completed during the specification. The elements defined here are a result from necessities in practice and model requirements. These include among others

- unique use case name
- actors / roles interacting
- dependencies
- dynamics
- results
- business rules (e.g. initial credit 1000 Euro)
- additional requirements (e.g. maximum response time)
- review / evaluation marks
- implementation notes

The list should be adapted to the development project type and special process-related requirements, e.g. CMM (Paulk et al., 1993) criteria.

Entries that may be – in some basic form – already included in task descriptions (Rumbaugh et al., 1999) are:

- pre- and post-conditions plus triggers
- purpose / user goals
- frequency of use
- critical scenarios

An additional work context description (Rumbaugh et al., 1999) to identify the context of use (for example "novice at cash desk") is at least partially covered by the actor and role definitions. Preconditions and triggers have to be differentiated: a precondition is a state that has to be active or achieved before being able to start the use case, while a trigger starts the use case actively.

With many facultative parts and wildcard items, IML allows for an incremental development. As the focus for this chapter lies in the interaction description, requirements and consistency elements mentioned above are not discussed in further detail.
IML use cases are structured hierarchically, while standard use cases describe sequences line by line. These workflows described textually in a basic use case are – as a first step – included and structured in the interaction part of the above IML use case interaction specification, which is mandatory in an IML model.
To achieve this, simple sentences have to be transformed to an XML structure preserving and expanding the information already contained in the standard use case description. If this should be necessary in further project phases, the structured descriptions can easily be re-transformed into natural language statements.
A top level structure, which is already used by use case writers in non-IML use cases is the identification of a use case's usual workflow, which helps to divide the interaction description of a use case into a regular flow and a set of alternative flows (Schlegel et al., 2004) – also called "variants"(Rumbaugh et al., 1999).

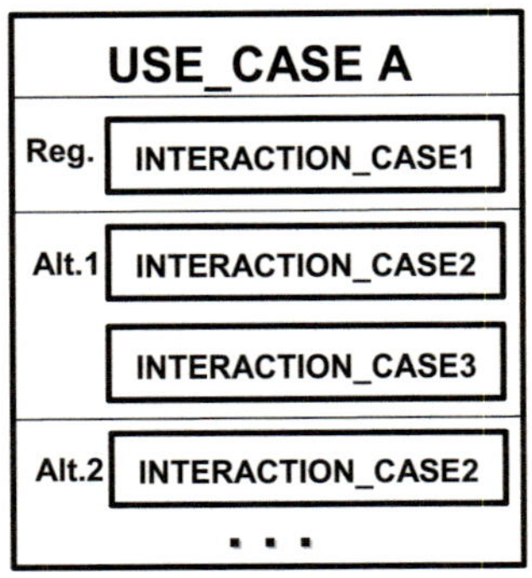

Fig. 4. Use case structured with regular and alternative flows.

While the structure of both is similar, the regular flow represents the entry point for the user interface generator or developer to start with. Actions in the alternative flows are referenced from the regular flow or in some cases triggered directly.

3.2 InteractionCases

So far, the IML concept mainly complies with the standard concept of use cases already used in practice. However, it structures them more consequently and allows or forces the presence of additional information.
Textual descriptions in UML use cases usually include a variety of different steps that are necessary to accomplish a use case. But often these steps do not share a common topic from the perspective of an interaction designer, because they always traverse a complete process or provide solutions to a problem from the application domain point of view. Also, coherence of interaction and semantic grouping of interactions belonging together is not part of a common use case definition.

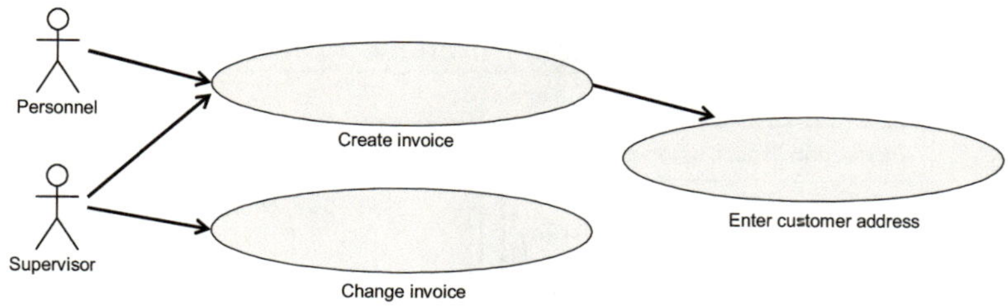

Fig. 5. Example for a use case diagram.

The key approach for structuring and refining basic use cases is therefore to subdivide them into more "atomic" components using the concept of InteractionCases, which we have developed extending the use case paradigm.

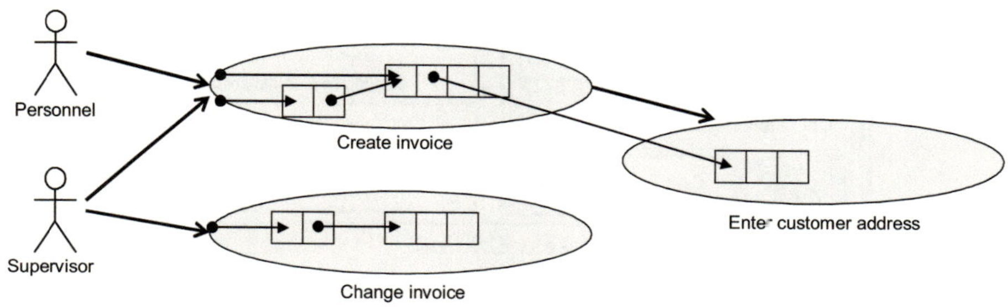

Fig. 6. The same Use case diagram with InteractionCases and the InteractionCase flow marked for each actor.

We define an InteractionCase as an interaction sequence that is strongly independent from other sequences and consists of one or more system or user actions that are part of the same use case. One one hand, these actions form a procedure that should not be split up further in order to concentrate all information necessary for an interaction, meaning to make the InteractionCase as big as necessary. On the other hand, an InteractionCase shall not contain steps that belong to a different context, making it as small as possible. This concept transfers the principle of strong internal cohesion and loose coupling with other components from Information Hiding (Parnas, 1972) to interaction specification.

For example, in an order process, the entry of the address for dispatch could be an InteractionCase, because it has only loose coupling to the price calculation step but high cohesion in its content. For this reason, an InteractionCase contains all steps that belong together as one interaction flow.

As shown in the figures, the steps necessary to enter a complete address together form one InteractionCase, whereas "Calculate Price" is a different task - and probably also a different screen in the final user interface. Therefore, the workflow for price calculation is being separated from the address entry interaction flow by encapsulating it into a second InteractionCase.

Other InteractionCases like error handling and more unlikely selections are located in the alternative interaction flow sections attached to the common use case "Purchase Articles". The different atomic interactions like entry of first and last name additionally can be grouped semantically within their InteractionCase.

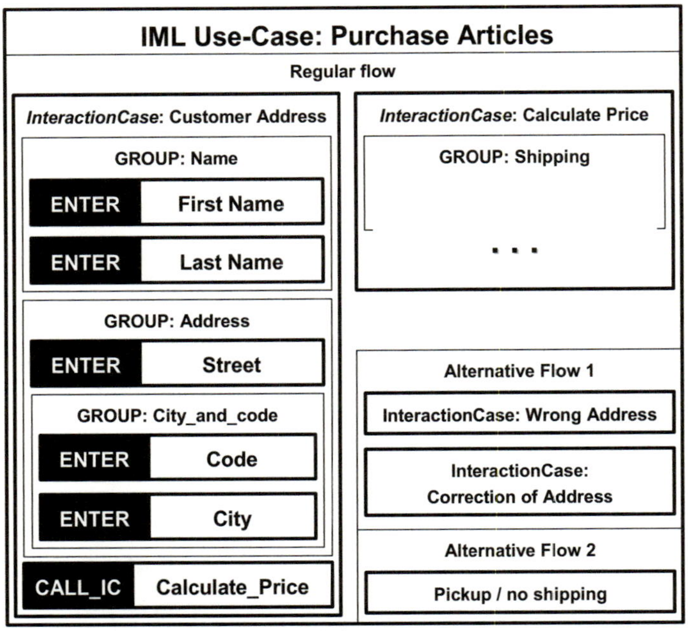

Fig. 7. Sample structure of an IML use case definition.

It becomes easier to define what should be the size of an InteractionCase, if it is considered that the translation of an InteractionCase into a graphical user interface will often be a dialog window or tab.
An InteractionCase covers an entity that has the same topic and contains interrelated information and interaction elements. The amount of interaction steps is similar to a dialog window in a graphical user interface or a dialog sequence in a speech user interface.

3.3 Structuring InteractionCases

InteractionCases are networked with each other by different flow relations, which make it possible to switch to other InteractionCases or even other use cases depending on various conditions. Like modules in software engineering contain classes, which again contain elements, InteractionCases contain different interaction steps like ENTER, SELECT, EDIT and WRITE (see figures 8 to 12). These elements can be used directly or be recursively grouped by semantic group elements structuring the interaction flow. Three of the basic elements are described in the following.

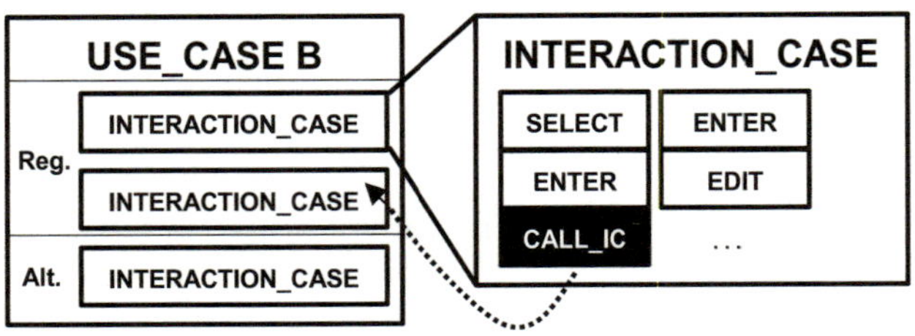

Fig. 8. Structure of use cases and InteractionCases.

ENTER actions define interactions that require the input of new information by the user. Though standard value suggestions may exist, the system holds no representation of the information space the information will come from.

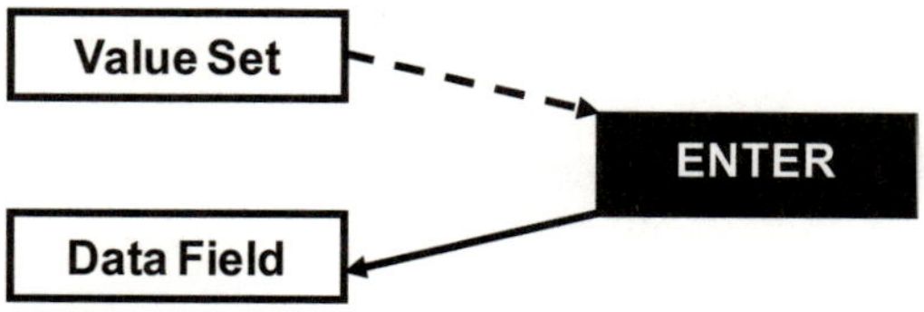

Fig. 9. Concept of the ENTER action.

EDIT actions allow for display and manipulation of information already existing in the system. The user is not required to enter information but may change the existing information if appropriate.

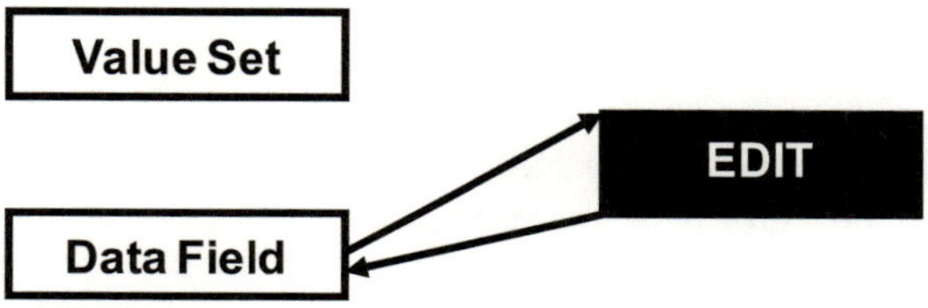

Fig. 10. Concept of the EDIT action.

SELECT actions let the user chose a subset of elements in a pool. While the elements are known, the user needs to select which of them are appropriate in this context.
There also exist hybrid forms like selections with item pools expandable through enter-like actions.

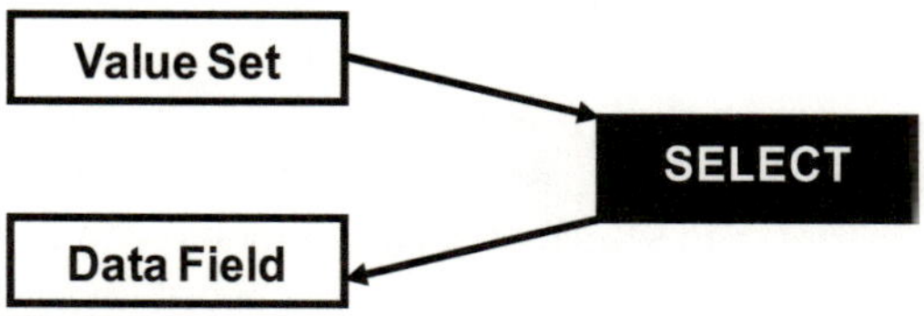

Fig. 11. Concept of the SELECT action.

WRITE is used to describe - mainly textual - system output. Like for the input actions, the sort of output is specified by the type of the content, for example "natural number, range 1 to 31". To be implementation neutral, the selection of display options is accomplished in the TARGET description.

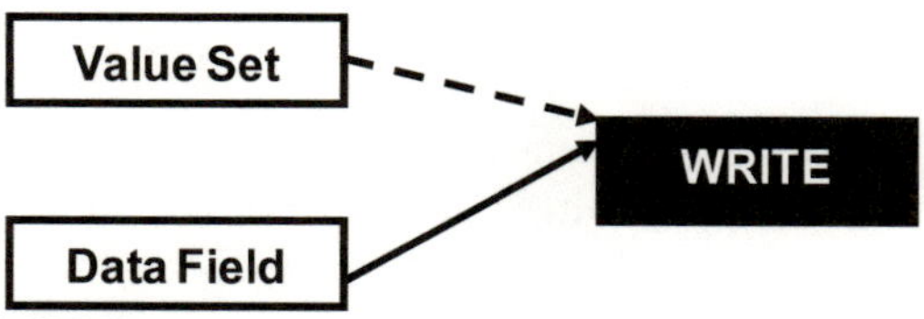

Fig. 12. Concept of the WRITE action.

TARGETs are a sort of interaction entity: All interactions implicitly or explicitly specify their target interface over which the user interacts with the system. Speaking in terms of a graphical user interface, one target could represent a status bar. If no target is indicated, each interaction uses the standard target that is defined with each InteractionCase.

GENERIC Actions: As long as the type of an action is not clarified - like when switching from textual to IML description - it is described with a GENERIC action, which can be easily transformed into or overwritten by any concrete action.

3.3.1 Sub-Structuring with IML Groups

Often a further sub-structuring mechanism is needed to create blocks inside an InteractionCase, which emphasizes the higher coherence of e.g. first name and last name compared to first name and street in an address. The semantic group element allows for a hierarchical structuring of elements as well as groups and provides description mechanisms that help the user interface designer or generator to decide how to transform the grouping meta-information into artifacts and rules for user interaction and UI structures.

Grouping meta-information can be used to prevent separation of elements, to shift elements to a sub-dialog or to arrange elements following the law of proximity. Also calculation of metrics like elements per group or per InteractionCase is facilitated and helps making suggestions for dialog structure improvement on a semantic basis already before dialogs are finally created.

3.3.2 Textual Descriptions

Besides the texts used for direct interaction, each interaction element in IML has attached textual descriptions. Specifying an actor or stakeholder for which the information is intended, like for example designer, developer or user and a representation context like *integrated, online-help, printed* etc. it is possible to differentiate between different target artifacts. This will play an important role in the artifact generation later on. Anytime an online-help or developer documentation is needed, it can be extracted from the model. A profile for each user group will specify which texts (starting from which priority) will be extracted or used for extraction and which language they have to be in.

One of the concept's strengths is the verification capability that comes with such an integrated description: the completion criterion per language. For example, setting the user-related descriptions criterion for "German" to "complete", a tool will be easily capable of checking all descriptions of this type for containing a description in the desired language with the desired state, e.g. "evaluated". Employing this mechanism will lead to fewer problems and lacks in translation to new spoken languages and enforces a complete model-contained documentation.

3.3.3 Actors

InteractionCases usually address only interactions with some of the actors in the complete set of actors referring to the use case, whereas every interaction may again affect only some of these actors. For a consistent model, it is important, that all actors used in an entity are defined on the above level in the model:

actors ⊇ actors(use case) ⊇ actors(InteractionCase) ⊇ actors(interaction)

3.3.4 System Actions

While EDIT, ENTER and SELECT focus on the user perspective of the interaction sequence, PERFORM represents the system actions. This "double-perspective" modeling is necessary to integrate the user and the system view in one model. Though, these actions cannot be viewed mutually independantly: A user action has a coupled request on the systems side, while many system actions will be perceived by the user through the user interface. The next section describes how these concepts can be used for automation.

4. User Interface Generation

Since the early nineties there has been a struggle for developing models and generators for user interface generation. Although some of them have been very promising, none of them has been widely used in practice.

Why did no strong use in practice happen in the last decade? One major answer to this question lies in the fact that often completely new models have been introduced that were not known in practice so far. Analysts and developers would have been forced to learn new modeling techniques and paradigms before seeing a benefit of their efforts. This makes user interface generation a good example for highly developed and specialized approaches that have not found their way into practical software development due to strong requirements, new partial models and missing integration with other aspects of software engineering and user interface design. Although, the results of user interface generator development have had and still have high impact on the research done and might even increase in the dawn of SOA.

The IML approach presented tries to avoid using a completely new model. Textual descriptions of standard use cases can be transferred to IML use cases by creating at least one InteractionCase per use case and transforming every single item or line of the textual description into one generic IML action. Assignment of types, grouping and partition into more InteractionCases can be carried out in a refinement step later on. With the integrative modeling concepts of UML 2 (OMG, 2007; OMG, 2007b) integration into the software engineering landscape will become even easier.

4.1 Prototype Generation from IML Models

The problem of a pure model-based approach and the creation of a prototype based on this model is the long time elapsing between the start of modeling and first user or customer feedback. Our goal was therefore to preserve the advantages of a model-based approach while minimizing the "time to prototype", which leads to the goal of a rapid and integrative model-based user interface prototyping.

IML provides abilities for transformation into an abstract user interface definition directly from an IML-enhanced use case model.

Once a model is completed for a first iteration, concrete interaction elements for abstract definitions must be found (Constantine et al., 2003). To have influence on the final representation, every automated generation process should create an intermediate model or abstract user interface definition, which can be used as basis for decisions or further generation steps, which are necessary in design time UI generation.

A transformer for IML or similar models should work with a transformation description that returns the realizing element type or at least a set of possible realizing element types for a specified interaction and context. The element type is then attached to every abstract component. This makes the generation of the final code the main challenge after the element type has been selected.

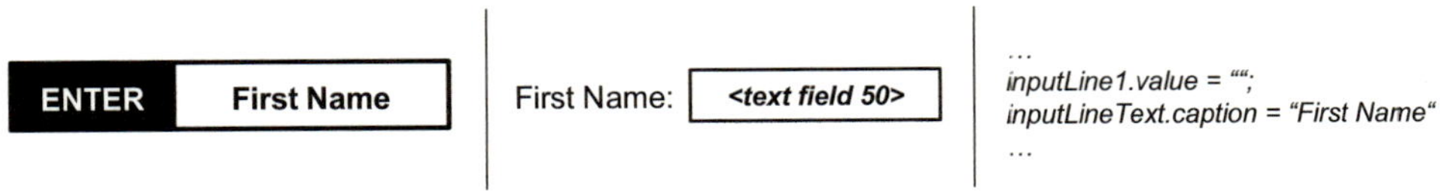

Fig. 13. Transforming specification into a UI prototype.

Layout generation can only be accomplished when element geometry has been selected or is already provided with the transformation description. An overview of layout criteria and rules can be found for example in (Hofmann, 1998).

Stepping over to an object-oriented software design is an alternative to direct prototype generation, especially for large projects and where generation is not available or not applicable.

Using IML it is possible to generate or derive the navigation structure from the model. For example, menus can be synthesized from some use cases that are referenced by the system or basic use case. The interaction flow in a wizard or another structured interaction sequence can also be compiled directly from the interaction specification in an IML model.

4.2 Definition of an Abstract User Interface

Although an IML model sticks close to the user perspective and workflows, it contains enough information to transform the specification into a generic UI model that can serve as a basis not only for dialog design but for user interface prototype code generation. In connection with IML, we have developed a simply structured representation for a generic user interface description - the Dialog Layer Language (DiLL). DiLL is specialized on graphical user interfaces, meaning that for other interaction modes like Voice User Interfaces (VUI) a different and specialized intermediate model will be needed. The Dialog Layer Language is intended for graphical and textual user interfaces only, because it deals with screens, groups and elements related to parallel viewing.

Such an intermediate modeling language is necessary to allow for manual changes in the generated user interface definition without manipulation of code fragments and resource definitions. For such an abstract user interface definition, it is necessary to have a very basic structure with few elements.

DiLL abstracts changes by UI developers from the code layer and provides back-links to the IML model for operations that require IML model information. A DiLL model is created automatically from a valid IML model by the transformer. It contains only SCREENs, GROUPs and ELEMENTs, which all bring types and geometry with them.

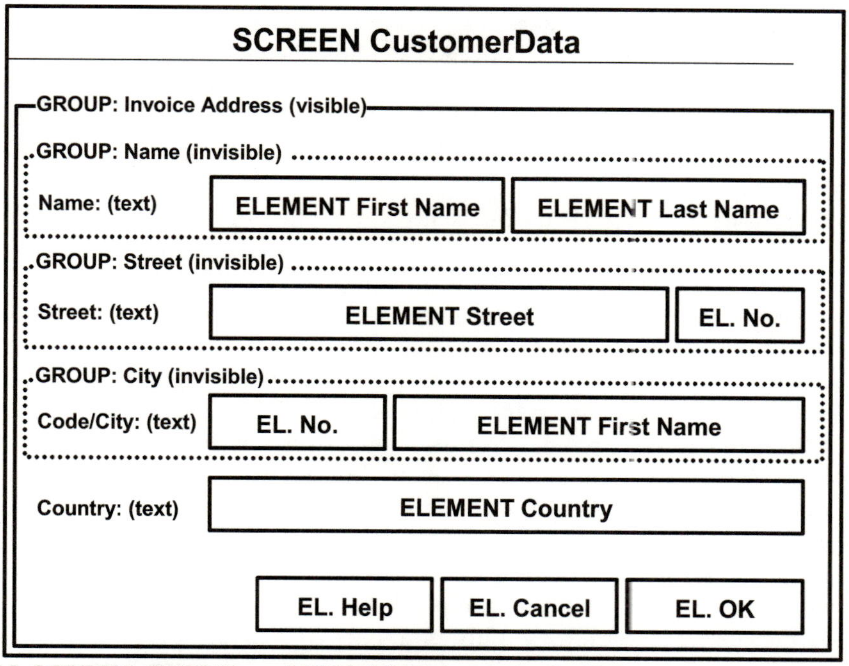

Fig. 14. DiLL SCREEN, GROUPs and ELEMENTs in a sample dialog.

SCREENS provide a sort of empty board like a window or screen, which can be filled with elements. ELEMENTs are parameterized by element type, coordinates etc. Visible and semantic grouping is achieved by the use of the GROUP element.

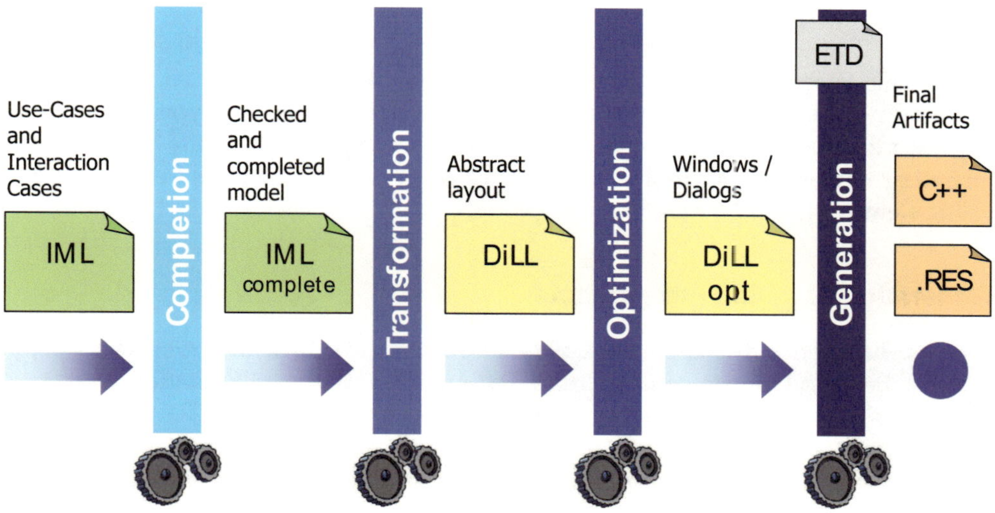

Fig. 15. Transformation Process.

4.3 Prototype Generation Process

The user interface generation process presented here follows a pipeline approach to allow linear transformation and to accomplish the different tasks from model completion to code generation. It is very similar to the visualization pipeline in computer visualization. A transformer prototype for this process has been created covering the following steps:

Completion: Usually, an IML model is not fully completed at generation time due to incremental development. Or it needs completion steps - like generating help IDs - that can be accomplished automatically. Therefore, the completion step checks the IML source model for consistency and completes missing entries as far as possible. If severe problems occur, the transformation process is interrupted.
Transformation: The transformation step interprets the IML model and forms a DiLL model based on the information given in the IML model. The DiLL model contains all interaction elements that are necessary to complete the tasks defined in the IML model: now a generic user interface has been created on the top of the IML specification.
Optimization: Although the DiLL model contains the necessary interaction elements and the overall structure, several optimizations are possible. Balancing dialog elements, separating defined group types from the dialog and the calculation of dialog metrics form only some of the functions that can be applied. Applied design rules can range from simple ones like the "magical number 7 plus or minus 2" (Miller, 1957) of elements on one aggregation layer (like group or window) to complex calculations and conditions depending on field types and their translation to composite elements.
Generation: The optimized DiLL model is the ideal basis for the code generation. For each generation target system a unique Element Transformation Description (ETD) file exists, which describes the DiLL-to-code transformation. This generation target is characterized by the destination platform and the destination programming environment used by the software developers dealing with the results of generation.
The Element Transformation Description (ETD) format is used to describe code insertion into a specific template for a programming project like those of MS Visual Studio. It is an XML-based notation for the code to be generated per specific element type. The generator uses project templates that contain the basic project files together with code insertion marks for the desired platform. Recursive and iterative constructs, counters and conditions form the basic elements in ETD for the insertion process.

5. Generation of other Final Artifacts

So far, we have only discussed the ability to generate the final artifacts[1] user interface prototype, help and documentation from IML models. But a fully staffed IML model provides enough information to allow for generation of artifacts beyond GUI models.

---

[1] We define final artifacts as all artifacts that experience no further transformation and are therefore in their final state - unlike source models or intermediate representations.

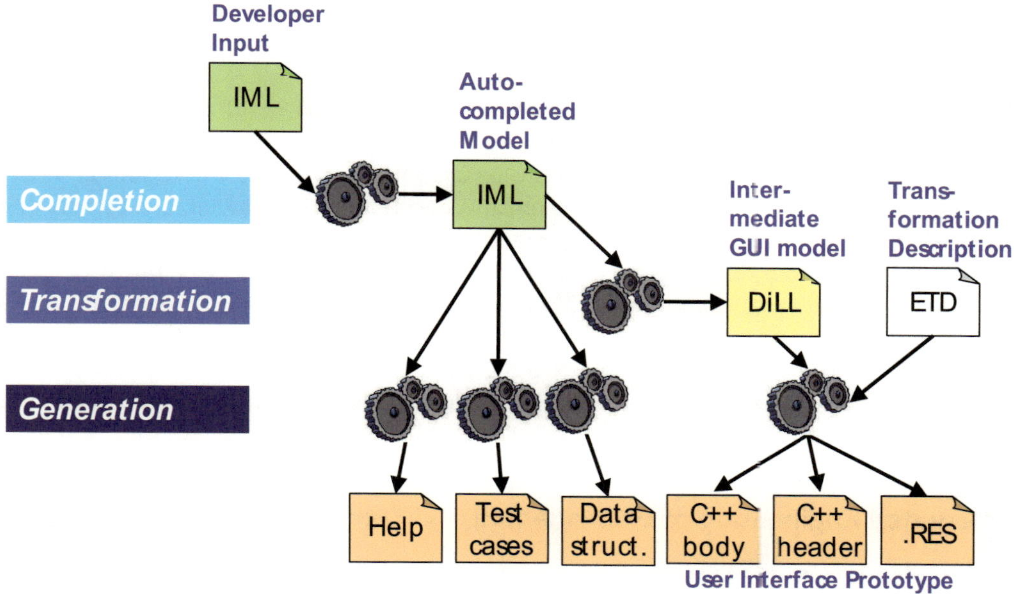

Fig. 16. The generation process also provides final artifacts different from generation results.

Once the IML model has been completed, black box test cases for application testers can be generated from the information given in the interaction flows and attached data definitions. The advantage of these and other generateable artifacts is that changes in the IML model have direct impact on them. Generating artifacts from an IML model, it is not necessary to find and track changes on every artifact but only on the IML model. Using the IML approach for generation of the artifacts as shown in figure 16 will render possible the application of IML as an integrated base model for user-oriented software development processes. Documentation, including user manuals and development status reports can then be generated from appropriate information given in the IML model.

6. Prototyping and Iterations

The main problem with generative models is that they rapidly become incompatible with the software once the first user interface prototype has been generated. This is caused by the fact that developers tend to work on code once the first code artifacts exist, while leaving the source model unchanged. This means that a method for generation must either prevent working on the code before the UI prototype fits the users' needs or must provide mechanisms for relating code changes after generation to the source model parts they were generated from.

While the latter would be better, providing the developer with a model and a prototype depending on each other, it is often not realizable in practice, although a model integration approach provides possibilities for further research on this: Generating prototype code artifacts in the same common model or repository and constructing the links between source (model) and target (code) artifacts, it is possible to update only the affected parts of model and code.

Of course, a straightforward sequence of transformations from model to model can be achieved more easily and complies with the requirements of a waterfall model or a stepwise usage-centered design (Constantine et al., 2003). However, necessary iterations occur in most software development projects because of the ambiguous requirements set: At the beginning of a project, the current state and some major requirements and changes are clear. But a complete set of requirements, which can be used throughout the whole project, is not the usual case. Therefore, model amendments and cycles are nearly inevitable. Supporting iterative development is therefore one major requirement for integrated models.
Methodic and well-founded model creation is crucial for project success. But as human beings make mistakes and cannot write down a complete requirement set at once, the key is to avoid frequent model changes in all steps but to create multiple scenarios in the same cycle and again for the next iteration. Once a model has been agreed upon, a prototype can be generated using a user interface prototype generator. This makes the real iteration very efficient, because a mistake in the model does not lead to cascading changes.

7. Integrated Engineering of User-oriented and Traditional Models

Many problems regarding the integration of user-oriented models and software engineering models result from a stepwise concretization: Implementation neutral models are transformed into specific models making design and implementation decisions. Often, models of different abstraction layers turn out to be incompatible. For this purpose, different methods for manually transferring an initial use case definition to an object-oriented design have already been described (Biddle et al., 2001). To ensure traceability and interconnections between task and object models, many approaches use responsibility as the driving factor.

7.1 Model Integration

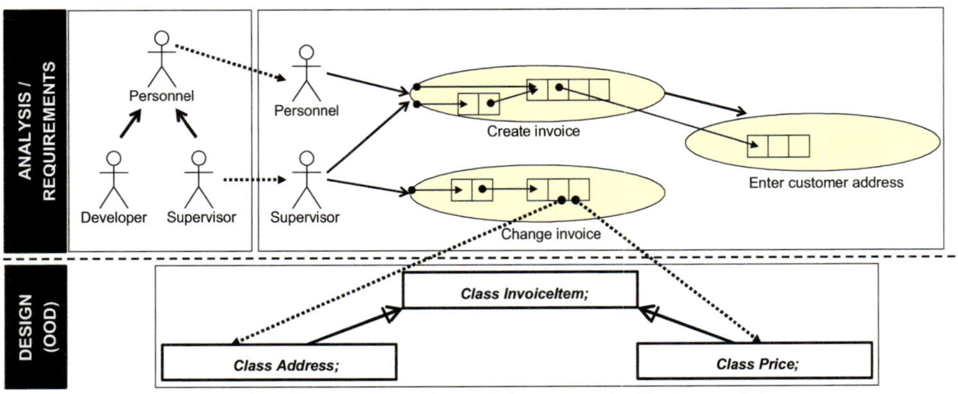

Fig. 17. Interconnection of different partial models in one holistic model.

An alternative is a model integration that interconnects artifacts of different partial models and abstraction layers directly using different forms of associations. In this way, collaborations and responsibilities can be modeled in an integrative way with direct references to the emerging classes created to implement them.

Unfortunately, the essential use cases are often only loosely interconnected with other models that are developed in parallel – e.g. role models – and also in no way have a connection to models of subsequent phases or realization layers.
An InteractionCase or at least a complete Use Case should for example have a link to the implementing dialog classes in the design description, e.g. in the class diagram.

7.2 Generative Models (Deduction)

Another solution to this problem is the integration of requirements specification with interaction models and prototype generation in one close loop. This direct dependency and back-coupling ensures consistency between these three aspects: Requirement models are forced to include information about interaction and can be directly transferred into pure interaction models or even a user interface prototype. On the other hand, the discussion of the generated UI prototype directly reveals shortcomings and necessary changes in the specification.
To achieve this, an integrative model is needed that contains all necessary information but also follows description and perspective of users and customers. Originally, we have used this approach for the user interface generator. It turned out to be applicable when a pure prototyping was done, which allowed us to overwrite the intermediate model and the code prototype with each generation.
Used in iterative and agile development approaches, often changes have already been made in these artifacts. This is where partial code-preserving generation is needed. The effort necessary to join new and old code makes generation inapplicable. A partial generation using an integrated model could solve some of these problems.

7.3 Concurrent Engineering

Concurrent Engineering for usage-centered design processes (Constantine et al., 2003) should be limited to models that have only rare dependencies. While in the usage-centered design process (as proposed in: Constantine et al., 2003) roles and system actors are developed in parallel with only a conjunction over a domain model, a more integrated approach should create a role model that is used in the use case model together with the actors (actors performing one or more roles). It is necessary to distinguish system actors (i.e. systems that play an actor role) from user actors. But as it may not always be clear which interaction comes from systems and which from users, this should not lead to a completely different use case description, if not necessary. As long as users are involved, the description should be quite similar to make them understand the scenario.
Indirect actors that only have impact on the system mediated by other (direct) actors should exist in the role model but in no case be part of a modeled system interaction to avoid confusion in the model.
As an actor may play different roles and sometimes one role may be played by different actors, the current actor's role should always be provided with the USES link or ACTOR in an integrated model. Alternatively, it is possible to create a new actor entity for each actor/role combination.
It is often criticized that user centered designers tend to go too quickly into paper prototyping, whereas in usage-centered design a content model is developed that covers the overall organization of the user interface. The advantage of an integrated model-based

approach in this case is obvious: Mistakes and inconsistencies made in the overall interface architecture can be found using prototypes generated from the model. On the other hand, these findings can again have a direct impact on the model, which unites the advantages of model-based and user centered approaches.

As we can learn from the software engineering process discussion, pure straightforward processes like waterfall can only be used in very specific cases in software development practice. Therefore, one pitfall of straightforward user interface generation approaches often has been the missing back link of the artifacts generated in the process.

This lack of model interconnectivity does not allow corrections in intermediate and final artifacts, because impacts are not visible and a second generation cannot cope with changes made or even overwrites them.

A simple but powerful solution to this problem can be achieved through generating artifacts in a holistic model that contains source model and target artifacts. For a model-internal transformation process it is easy to construct links from a specification artifact to the generated prototype artifact, additionally referencing the transformation used.

Especially for web interfaces such a representation is useful, because it provides very fine-grained and component-based artifacts, which form a complete page when synthesized by a simple export routine. The result of a generation with rules can be any kind of text-based document including ASCII text, source code, HTML or any kind of XML. Once the structure and artifact components are defined, the process is the same.

8. Soft Artifact Engineering

The IML and similar approaches can be extended towards a holistic engineering approach for soft artifacts, which integrates processes, stakeholder perspectives and different model abstraction layers of software and service engineering projects into one model. Such a component- and flow-oriented approach joins the more static perspective of e.g. inheritance and aggregation with the dynamics of interaction, process and artifact flow. Object-oriented paradigms allow for the use of inheritance/classification and template concepts for every artifact type like one of the InteractionCases presented.

To allow for this integration, we propose a slightly different view upon the different models, which we call partial ones. Using one meta-model like MOF (OMG, 2002) for defining each model and one development environment supporting the meta-model and the defined partial models, it is possible to interconnect all partial models, though having all possibilities of the stand-alone models.

This view can be used for all virtual - i.e. "soft" - artifacts, like use cases, dialog designs, software components and services. For this reason and for its ability to provide an approach integrating model and process, we call this approach Soft Artifact Engineering (SAE).

SAE is a holistic and integrative way to allow for the integration of different stakeholders like managers, usability experts, and software developers into development processes for virtual products - i.e. "soft artifacts". The goal is to integrate all models into one component-based and object-oriented meta-model that allows for interconnecting completely different models like interaction specification and business process models. A high degree of freedom for modeling and interconnecting models will be the advantage of these efforts on integration and will lead to an integrated interactive system development approach with abilities for intermediate models and internal user interface prototype generation.

The expansion to other domains like Service Engineering will allow developing services, user interfaces and software in one closely interconnected common model.

9. Summary and Outlook

In this chapter we have provided an overview on how user interface modeling and generation can be approached and how they can be integrated with software engineering. For this purpose, we have presented an approach for better integration with the software engineering models. This is achieved by a process-oriented modeling approach based on (UML) Use Cases. The resulting models have then been used in a pipeline generation process, which supports iterative and integrated development of interactive applications. The process and prototype tool developed offer automated model completion, generation of an intermediate dialog layer language and generation of final artifacts – such as a Visual Studio project containing the interface code and resources as well as help and documentation. The chapter explains the concepts of the model and the generation process, to allow for transfer and application to other model-based user interface generation approaches.

Current developments in software engineering and business IT show a trend towards regarding applications not as fixed and local installations. Instead, a process towards virtualization and decentralization takes place for computing and data as well as business processes and especially services – often referred to as "cloud computing". With dynamically changing services, processes and compositions in decentralized runtime architectures, design-time modeling and generation will not be sufficient anymore.

In the frame of INT-MANUS project (Schlegel & Thiel, 2007) we have been able to prove that processes in production can be executed in a fully decentralized system, generating actions and interactions for each process instance just-in-time locally (Schlegel, 2008). To be able to generate interactions, dedicated semantic models will be needed to derive context and requirements from a classification and interaction model.

First approaches like BPEL4People (IBM et al., 2007) and WS Human Task (IBM et al., 2007b) show the path towards interactive processes and applications deployed and running dynamically in future networked systems. Applying semantic model-based concepts to these environments will offer new possibilities for runtime composition and generation of user interfaces for services in such a cloud and for dynamic and distributed applications in general.

Acknowledgements

The author wishes to thank Dr. Alexander Burst from ETAS GmbH and his former colleagues from the Fraunhofer Institute for Industrial Engineering (IAO) for their kind support of this work. Application and integration of this research has been done in the projects LIKE and KOMPASS funded by the German Ministry of Education and Research (BMBF) as well as INT-MANUS project and I*PROMS Network of Excellence funded by the European Commission under the Sixth Framework Programme.

10. References

Alexander, I. & Robertson, S. (2004). *Understanding Project Sociology by Modeling Stakeholders,* IEEE Software, 21(1), January 2004, pp. 23-27

Ambler, S.W. (2000). *Documenting a use case: What to include, and why,* http://www-106.ibm.com/developerworks/webservices/library/ws-tip-docusecase.html, 2000

Balzert, H.; Hofmann, F; Kruschinski, V. & Niemann, C. (1996). *The JANUS Application Development Environment – Generating More than the User Interface,* In: Computer-Aided Design of User Interfaces, pp. 183-206, Namur University Press

Barclay, P.; Griffiths, T.; McKirdy, J.; Paton, N.W.; Cooper, R. & Kennedy, J. (1999). *The Teallach Tool: Using Models for Flexible User Interface Design.* Proceedings of Computer-Aided Design of User Interfaces II (CADUI'99), pp. 139-158, Kluwer

Beck, K. (1999). *Extreme Programming Explained,* Addison-Wesley

Biddle, R.; Noble, J. & Tempero, E. (2001). *Essential Use Cases and Responsibility in Object-Oriented Development,* Technical Report, CS-TR-01/01

Coad, P. & Yourdon, E. (1991). *Object-Oriented Analysis 2nd Edition,* Yourdon Press, Englewood Cliffs N.J.: Prentice-Hall

Constantine, L.L. & Lockwood, L.A.D. (2002). *Usage-Centered Engineering for Web Applications,* IEEE Software, 19(2), pp. 42-50

Constantine, L.L. (1995). *Essential modeling: use cases for user interfaces.* ACM interactions, Vol. 2, Issue 2, pp. 34-46, New York: ACM Press

Constantine, L.L.; Biddle, R. & Nobel, J. (2003). *Usage-Centered Design and Software Engineering: Models for Integration,* Proceedings of ICSE 2003, pp. 106-113

DeMarco, T. (1979). *Structured Analysis and System Specification,* N.J.: Prentice-Hall, Englewood Cliffs

Erl, T. (2005). *Service-Oriented Architecture – Concepts, Technology, and Design.* Prentice Hall

Firesmith, D.; Henderson-Sellers, B. & Graham, I. (1998). *OPEN Modeling Language (OML) Reference Manual.,* New York: Cambridge University Press, Cambridge

Harel, D. (1987). *Statecharts a visual formalism for complex systems.* In: Science of Computer Programming 1987, pp. 231-274, Elsevier Science Publishers

Henderson-Sellers, B. & Firesmith, D.G. (1999). *Comparing OPEN and UML: the Two Third-generation OO Development Approaches.* Information and Software Technology, Vol. 41, No. 3, pp. 139–156

Hofmann, F. (1998). *Grafische Benutzungsoberflächen: Generierung aus OOA-Modellen.* Spektrum, Akademischer Verlag, Heidelberg, Berlin

IBM et al. (2007). *WS-BPEL Extension for People (BPEL4People),* Version 1.0, June 2007

IBM et al. (2007b). *Web Services Human Task (WS-HumanTask),* Version 1.0, June 2007

ISO (1999). *Human-centred Design Processes for Interactive Systems* (ISO standard 13407: 1999)

Jacobson, I.; Christerson, M.; Jonsson, P. & Övergaard, G. (1992). *Object-Oriented Software Engineering: A Use-Case Driven Approach,* Addision-Wesley

Jacobson, I.; Christerson, M.; Jonsson, P. & Övergaard, G. (1992). *Object-Oriented Software Engineering,* Addison-Wesley, Reading, Mass

Janssen, C.; Weisbecker, A. & Ziegler, J. (1993). *Generating User Interfaces from Data Models and Dialogue Net Specifications.* Proceedings of the SIGCHI Conference on Human Factors in Computing Systems, pp. 418-423, April 24-29, Amsterdam, The Netherlands

Janssen, C.; Weisbecker, A. & Ziegler, J. (1993). *Generating User Interfaces from Data Models and Dialogue Net Specifications,* Proceedings of INTERCHI'93, pp. 418-423, ACM Press

Larson, J.A. (1992). *Interactive Software – Tools for Building Interactive User Interfaces,* Yourdon Press Computing Series, Prentice-Hall

Lauesen, S. (2003). *Task Descriptions as Functional Requirements,* IEEE Software, 20(2), pp. 58-65

Lonczewski, F. & Schreiber, S. (1996). *The FUSE-System: an Integrated User Interface Design Environment,* Proceedings CADUI'96, Namur University Press

Martin, J. & Odell, J. (1992). *Object-Oriented Analysis and Design,* N.J.: Prentice-Hall, Englewood Cliffs

Metzker, E. & Seffah, A. (2003). *User-Centered Design in the Software Engineering Lifecycle: Organizational, Cultural and Educational Obstacles to a Successful Integration,* Proceedings of HCI International 2003, Human-Computer Interaction, Theory and Practice (Part I), pp. 173-177

Miller, G.A. (1957). *The Magical Number 7 Plus or Minus Two: Some Limits in Our Capacity for Processing Information.* Psychological Review, Vol. 101, No. 2 , pp. 343-352

OASIS (2007): *Web Services Business Process Execution Language Version 2.0,* OASIS Standard, 11 April 2007, http://docs.oasis-open.org/wsbpel/2.0/OS/wsbpel-v2.0-OS.pdf

OMG (2002). *Meta Object Facility (MOF) Specification, OMG-Meta Object Facility,* v1.4, http://www.omg.org/cgi-bin/doc?formal/2002-04-03

OMG (2007). *Unified Modeling Language (UML) Infrastructure Version 2.1.1. formal/07-02-06, 2007,* http://www.omg.org/cgi-bin/apps/doc?formal/07-02-06.pdf, 28.3.2007

OMG (2007). *Unified Modeling Language (UML) Superstructure Version 2.1.1. formal/07-02-05, 2007,* http://www.omg.org/cgi-bin/apps/doc?formal/07-02-05.pdf, 28.3.2007

OMG. (2003). *UML 2.0 Superstructure Specification, OMG Final Adopted Specification,* http://www.omg.org/cgi-bin/apps/doc?ptc/03-08-02.pdf

Parnas, D.L. (1972). *On the Criteria To Be Used in Decomposing Systems into Modules.* In: Communications of the ACM, Vol. 15, No. 12, December 1972, pp. 1053–1058

Paulk, M.C.; Curtis, B.; Chrissis, M.B. & Weber, C.V. (1993). *Capability Maturity Model, Version* 1.1, IEEE Software, 10(4), pp. 18-27

Pinheiro da Silva, P. (2000). *UMLi: Integrating User Interface and Application Design.* UML2000 Workshop on Towards a UML Profile for Interactive Systems Development (TUPIS2000), York, United Kingdom

Pinheiro da Silva, P.; Griffiths, T. & Paton, N.W. (2000). *Generating User Interface Code in a Model Based User Interface Development Environment,* Proceedings of the International Working Conference on Advanced Visual Interfaces (AVI2000), pp. 155-160, ACM Press

Pressman, R.S. (1997). *Software Engineering – a Practitioners's Approach, European Adaptation,* Fourth Edition. New York: McGraw Hill

Reisig, W. (1986). *Petrinetze – Eine Einführung,* Berlin, Heidelberg, Springer-Verlag

Rubin, K.S. & Goldberg, A. (1992). *Object behaviour analysis.* Communications of the ACM, Vol. 35, No. 9, pp. 48-62

Rumbaugh, J.; Blaha, M.; Premerlani, W.; Eddy, F. & Lorensen, W. (1991). *Object-Oriented Modeling and Design.* Englewood Cliffs N.J.: Prentice-Hall

Rumbaugh, J.; Jacobson, I. & Booch, G. (1999). *The Unified Modeling Language Reference Manual,* Addison-Wesley

Scheer, A.W. (1994). *Business Process Engineering. Reference Models for Industrial Enterprises,* Berlin: Springer

Schlegel, T. & Thiel, S. (2007). *Semantic Models and Processes for Information Gathering and Interactive Workflow Execution in Decentralized Production Environments.* In: Intelligent Production Machines and Systems - 3rd I*PROMS Virtual International Conference, 2007

Schlegel, T. (2008). *Interactive Processes and Semantic Models in Production Systems,* Proceedings of the First International Conference on Business Sustainability (BS08), Ofir, Portugal

Schlegel, T.; Burst, A. & Ertl, T. (2004). *A Flow Centric Interaction Model for Requirements Specification and User Interface Generation,* Proceedings of the 7th International Conference on WWCS, Bridging Diversity at Work, Damai Sciences, Kuala Lumpur

Schlungbaum, E. & Elwert, T. (1995). *Modellierung von Graphischen Benutzungsoberflächen im Rahmen des TADEUS-Ansatzes,* In: Software-Ergonomie '95, Böcker, H.-D., pp. 331-348, Teubner, Stuttgart

Scott, K. (2004). *Fast Track UML 2.0,* Apress

Szekely, P.; Sukaviriya, P.; Castells, P.; Muthukumarasamy, J. & Salcher, E. (1995). *Declarative Interface Models for User Interface Construction Tools: the MASTERMIND Approach,* Proceedings of the EHCI'95, pp. 120-150, Chapman & Hall, London

Vredenburg, K.; Isensee, S. & Righi, C. (2002). *User-Centered Design: An Integrated Approach,* Prentice Hall

Wiecha, C.; Bennet, W.; Boises, S.; Gould, J. & Green, S. (1990). *ITS: A Tool for Rapidly Developing Interactive Applications.*ACM Transactions on Information Systems, Vol. 8, No. 3, pp. 204-236

World Wide Web Consortium, W3C (2004). *Resource Description Framework (RDF),* http://www.w3.org/RDF/

Contrasting Scenarios: Embracing Speech Recognition

Ben Kraal
Queensland University of Technology
Australia

1. Introduction

The purpose of this chapter is to describe the use of caricatured contrasting scenarios (Bødker, 2000) and how they can be used to consider potential designs for disruptive technologies. The disruptive technology in this case is Automatic Speech Recognition (ASR) software in workplace settings. The particular workplace is the Magistrates Court of the Australian Capital Territory.

Caricatured contrasting scenarios are ideally suited to exploring how ASR might be implemented in a particular setting because they allow potential implementations to be "sketched" quickly and with little effort. This sketching of potential interactions and the emphasis of both positive and negative outcomes allows the benefits and pitfalls of design decisions to become apparent.

A brief description of the Court is given, describing the reasons for choosing the Court for this case study. The work of the Court is framed as taking place in two modes: Front of house, where the courtroom itself is, and backstage, where documents are processed and the business of the court is recorded and encoded into various systems.

Caricatured contrasting scenarios describing the introduction of ASR to the front of house are presented and then analysed. These scenarios show that the introduction of ASR to the court would be highly problematic.

The final section describes how ASR could be re-imagined in order to make it useful for the court. A final scenario is presented that describes how this re-imagined ASR could be integrated into both the front of house and backstage of the court in a way that could strengthen both processes.

1.1 Speech Recognition

Speech recognition, specifically, large vocabulary desktop-based speech recognition, or dictation software, hereafter referred to as automatic speech recognition (ASR), is a disruptive technology because it requires the adoption of new ways of working in order to be useful. For example, as (Kraal, 2008) showed, speech recognition cannot be adopted without also making changes to the work that a person does. Some ways of working, and some kinds of work, are not compatible with the ways that speech recognition must be used.

Understanding how adopting speech recognition will change a particular situation is difficult because the implications are not just limited to one person or one interaction. Adopting speech recognition has wide-ranging implications not just for one person but potentially for whole organisations.

1.2 Field Work with Speech Recognition Users

In order to understand how a disruptive technology, in this instance ASR, affects how people work, field work was done with ASR users. The people studied all worked in the Federal Public Service in Canberra, the national capital of Australia. There were two groups of ASR users who were studied. One group of users had occupational over-use injuries, often called Repetitive Strain Injury (RSI), though RSI is a form of occupational over-use injury. The occupational over-use injury group were unable to type on a standard computer keyboard without pain.

The second group of users did not have an occupational over-use injury and worked for the Parliamentary Reporting Service in Parliament House. Their job was to create the document known as Hansard which is the record of what is said in Parliament's upper and lower houses and various committees. The Hansard group of users used ASR as a way to rapidly moved from audio recordings of what was said in the houses of parliament to a text representation. The Hansard users workflow did not involve feeding the audio record into a speech recognition system as that process is not yet accurate enough. Instead, the Hansard users listened to the audio recordings and re-spoke them. This was significantly more accurate which lead to significantly faster turnaround. Fast turnaround is important for the Hansard users as they have a 24 hour turnaround time on the Hansard document – what is said in parliament needs to be available the next day.

The field work research of speech recognition users showed that using speech recognition systems in a workplace required the user to maintain a delicate socio-technical system of software, hardware and office politics. If any one element of the socio-technical system should fail, the whole assemblage fails, resulting in their inability to use speech recognition for work. Often, users of speech recognition found themselves adapting their ways of working to suit the ASR system, rather than the system adapting to them.

2. The Magistrates Court

A team of researchers I was studying with were approached by the Chief Magistrate of the ACT Magistrates Court to investigate the introduction of ASR technology to the courtroom for use by him in the process of communicating an outcome.

In meetings with the Chief Magistrate we learned that communicating an outcome is a highly charged moment in the Court when the magistrate speaks an outcome for the case that he or she is hearing. An outcome may be a sentence, for example a fine or jail term, or it may be the decision to set a case over until another time to allow all the parties to the case to gather relevant information. An outcome may also be a procedural decision specific to the Court such as a request by the magistrate for any number of specialised reports that are used to inform the actual sentence when it is finally delivered. Calling these varied events "outcomes" allowed us to define them as end points in a courtroom process. The Chief Magistrate would not have referred to these acts formally as outcomes, however this terminology is useful in the context of designing a system to support such actions.

At the time this study was conducted, the magistrate speaking his decision on an outcome aloud to the court. The decision also had to be written down on the "bench sheet" and incorporated into the "defendant's folder". The bench sheet was a piece of paper used by the sitting magistrate for note-taking during a hearing. The bench sheet was also the place where the magistrate would record his or her decision on an outcome. Because many decisions made by the magistrate were repetitive and procedural in nature, a set of large rubber stamps were available for the magistrate's use. The stamps were templates of boilerplate text allowing the magistrate to tick boxes or fill in only limited details in order to record an outcome on the bench sheet. The defendant's folder was a collection of bench sheets and associated documents passed to the magistrate by the prosecution and defence during the series of court appearances that typically make up any particular case.

The Chief Magistrate asked for an ASR system that could replace his existing manual system of handwriting and rubber stamps. The Chief Magistrate thought that, since he was speaking the sentence, an ASR system could be employed to record what he had said and remove the need for him to record sentences on paper. His main reason for wanting an ASR system was so that he could save time. Writing outcomes down is time consuming, particularly as one defendant may be appearing on many charges, each of which will require a decision from the magistrate. A magistrate will often decide to waive many of the individual charges and sentence a defendant on a small selection of the total number. The waived charges still require a stamp and some writing and so still take up some of the magistrate's time that could otherwise be used to hear cases.

After some preliminary ethnographic work at the Court it emerged that the magistrate's act of speaking an outcome was not an event that was self contained but was the beginning of a process distributed in space and time throughout the Court and led to the recording of an outcome in many different places and for many different purposes. A great deal of "back room" work was initiated from one spoken outcome in the courtroom. This contrasted with the Chief Magistrate's view of the process as one that was enacted by him and contained within the courtroom (Dugdale & Kraal, 2006).

The courtroom and the "back room" of the Magistrates Court can be considered as front of house and backstage, much as in a theatre. The front of house refers the courtroom itself and the activity that takes place there. The backstage contains all the unseen workers who perform the mundane "bulk work" of the Court, processing documents and ensuring that the activities on the front of house can take place. The distinction between front of house and backstage is useful because it aligns with the aspects of the court that are more fixed and the aspects that are more able to be changed to suit ASR. Aspects of the Court that are

front of house are typically resistant to change and aspects that are backstage are less resistant.
The elements in the heterogeneous assemblage of the court that are resistant to change are:

- The social world of the Court;
- The Court room layout, as it influences the social world of the Court;
- The work process in the courtroom and all public-facing areas of the Court; and,
- The requirement to record decisions on outcomes made by the magistrate during court

The elements that are more easily able to be changed are:

- The detail of the work process of the "back room", particularly the after-court section; and,
- Details of the defendant's folder but not its use or existence.

These fixed front of house and less fixed backstage aspects of the Court are described in the following subsections.

2.1 Front of House

On entering the courtroom, it is apparent that the physical layout of the Court is something that cannot be significantly changed to accommodate the needs of ASR.

In the courtroom, the magistrate sits at the bench which is raised above the main floor level. The magistrate's associate sits to one end of the bench and below it. The lawyers sit facing the magistrate. The defendant sits next to his or her lawyer. The witness box is toward the other end of the bench with the witness facing the lawyers. A public gallery of varying size sits behind a barrier behind the lawyers. In the Magistrates Court, because of the relatively fast pace, there are often other defendants waiting in the court. Some of these waiting defendants are in the public gallery and some are queued up in front of the barrier, but still behind the lawyers, having been brought up from the lock-up by bailiffs.

The social world of the Court is necessarily bound up in the spatial layout of the participants. The magistrate's authority is symbolised by their elevated position at the bench. The interaction of associate and magistrate is enabled and constrained by the associate's position to the side and below the magistrate. To have a discussion with the associate the magistrate must slide his or her chair over to the associate's side of the bench. Being able to move along the length of the bench requires that the magistrate not be tethered by any cords to microphones that may be required for ASR. This is just one example of how the physical and social aspects of the courtroom have the potential to influence the design of an ASR system for the court.

Slightly less fixed in theory is the architecture of the courtroom. In practice, though, the architecture of the Court is fixed as it is expensive to make significant changes. Court Room One in the Magistrates Court of the Australian Capital Territory is a modern design with pale wood in place of the more traditional dark wood paneling. The ceiling is stepped and indented in various places which leads to areas in the public gallery with very poor acoustics. The design of the Court does not seem to affect the ability of the active players in the Court's process to hear each other.

Various technologies are employed in the courtroom. Microphones are placed in front of the magistrate, the lawyers and the witness box, not to broadcast the speech of the players to the gallery but to allow it to be recorded. The microphones currently used are basically of "lectern" style with a small bud at the end of a semi-flexible stalk. The players in the court do not interact with the microphones due to their unobtrusive placement and because they do not hear any "foldbac (That is, they cannot hear what they sound like through the microphone, as one can when the amplified output of the microphone is broadcast to the room in which one is talking) from the microphones which might inform them that their speech is not being fully captured. The use of microphones in the Court is therefore not a part of the work in the Court nor is it part of the embodied social world of the court, leaving the use and placement of microphones open to change and re-enrollment in a new network that will use ASR.

In communicating a decision, the magistrate's speech must be captured and the lawyers', defendant's and witnesses' speech is of no importance. This means that a method of communicating sentence need not be concerned with the microphones in front of anyone save the magistrate. By extension, the lawyers, defendant and witnesses do not need to be enrolled in a new network.

Depending on the design of the ASR system proposed for the Court, magistrates and associates may have to be enrolled in the new actor-network. From my examination of the work process of the Court, and particularly the work done during court sessions, the associate has a lot of work to do and it would not be possible to add to the workload of the associate without taking some parts away. Because much of the associate's work in court has to do with helping the magistrate manage the work process of the court, it is not desirable for the associate to perform work extraneous to that management. Similarly, the magistrate is concerned, while court is in session, with managing the process of the court and imposing new work on the magistrate, particularly when that work could involve errorful ASR, is extremely undesirable.

As has already been said, the social world of the court is embodied, at least in part, in the spatial layout of the courtroom. This is also true of the work process of the Court as a whole if that work process is seen as the administration of cases that appear before the magistrate. Defendants enter and leave with their lawyers and only those called to appear at any one time can interact with the magistrate and the public prosecutor. Other defendants and lawyers must wait in the spaces assigned to them. Similarly, witnesses may only interact with the Court, the lawyers and the magistrate when called and must otherwise wait. The spaces for waiting are important to the Court's work process as a whole but do not need to be enrolled in a ASR system for communicating decisions.

2.2 Backstage

In backstage of the Court documents are paramount. The most important document for the Court is the Defendant's Folder, which is really a collection of documents. The Defendant's

Folder is made up of many documents. Reports from external agencies are used to inform decisions. Bench sheets with notes from a defendant's previous appearances remind magistrates about their previous decisions.

In much the same way as Air-Traffic Controllers' work is embodied in paper strips (Hughes, Randall, & Shapiro, 1992) the work of the Court is embodied in the defendant's folder. As the folder moves through time in the Court, it is used at various stations to reconstruct what occurred when the defendant it describes appeared before a magistrate. Staff in the back room use the folder as part of their work in recording magistrates' decisions in the Court's computer system. They also insert documents that they generate into the folder for future reference. Magistrate's associates use the folders to prepare for court sessions and will re-order the documents in the folders to assist the magistrate to work more efficiently during court. Magistrates refer to bench sheets and reports in a particular defendant's folder during court to reacquaint themselves with their previous decisions. Because the bench sheet and folder embodies the work of the Court it is quite obdurate in the existing work process, and therefore in the existing actor-network of the court. It would be very difficult to replace it or significantly change it to accommodate a ASR system.

A tension exists within the use of the defendant's folder. The Chief Magistrate wanted to do away with the time-consuming act of writing down decisions but, as is apparent from the descriptions above of the activity in the courtroom, writing down decisions is important for the future reference of the magistrate. Finding a solution to this tension is the main task of designing a ASR system for the Court. Doing away with the act of writing down decisions on outcomes may actually make the work of a future magistrate harder as there will be no record of the past.

The diverse actors who make up the parts of the Court's work process for communicating decisions that take place outside the courtroom will also need to be interested and enrolled in the new ASR actor-network. From a system design point-of-view, the easier it is to enroll the "back room" actors, the easier it will be to introduce the new system. The human actors in the back room are the monitor, the after-court person and the list clerk, all of whom have an interest in what the magistrate says and how decisions are communicated.

The monitor uses a computer system to annotate and mark-up the recording of what is said by everyone in court. Making the monitor part of the new design would be desirable because they already deal with the magistrate's speech. Enrolling the monitor's computer system and the audio feed it relies on may also be necessary.

The after-court person is someone who relies almost totally on the defendant's folder to perform their job. Any change to the folder changes the work of the after-court person because of their reliance on being able to reconstruct the decisions made in court. The work of the after-court person depends on the work of the Court being embodied in the defendant's folder.

2.3 Summary

In Actor-Network Theory, a "point of passage" (Callon, 1986) is an actor who directs, or tries to direct, the network to their interests. In the case of the new network at the ACT Magistrates Court, the "point of passage" whose interest is of importance to a technologist is ASR itself. Other actors in the new network may attempt to assert their power as points of passage but the power of the Chief Magistrate in the Court would seem to be so much greater than that held by the other individuals in the Court's work process that any objections by them would be ignored or cast aside by the Chief Magistrate who is seemingly in favour of the ASR system.

A "trial of strength" is when all the heterogeneous elements of an actor-network must perform their roles. Discussing the trial of strength of an imaginary system is largely moot, but by speculating about such an event points of weakness can be identified and later strengthened. The most obvious point of technical failure is the ASR system itself, not just within the recognition software but the wider system of vocabulary-models, acoustic models, microphones, cabling, user-interfaces and so on. Careful system design involving the users of the system in a user-centred process would lessen the severity of this point of failure, particularly if an iterative user-centred software development process was followed.

The non-technical points of possible failure are more difficult to "design out" of concern because they are less predictable. The best way to "design out" the non-technical points of possible failure is to "design them in" by respecting and valuing the existing work of the human actors in the system and using a new design to aid them in their skilled work. This "designing in" (ideally) takes place when the system is being designed and is necessarily a process of negotiation.

3. Caricatured Scenarios for the Magistrates Court

In order consider the implications of designing an ASR system for the Magisrates Court, I needed to create rough prototypes of the system, both for considering various implications of such a system and for communicating aspects of any potential future system with the Magistrate himself and the Magistrates Court organisation.

Creating even a simple speech recognition system requires creating software which is "heavyweight". Instead, scenarios (Carroll, 1995) were used as a lightweight way to consider different potential implementations of ASR for the Magistrates Court. Technical constraints are incorporated into the scenarios by basing them on pre-existing technical research.

The scenarios used for the description of potential implementations are inspired by those described by Bødker (2000) who suggested paired positive and negative scenarios that were caricatures of action. The positive and negative scenarios are caricatures because they are "over the top". The positive scenarios are wildly optimistic, the negative scenarios pessimistic. Instead of a single scenario that describes imagined future action, these paired scenarios allow description of action as well as showing the imagined positive and negative effects of the design upon the situation. These paired scenarios stimulate ideas and make clear the potentials and problems of ASR in the Court (Kraal, et al., 2006). They serve as "sketches" of potential implementations of a user interface that has no physical representation.

ASR presents unique challenges when producing prototype designs, particularly early prototypes that are intended to stimulate further design thinking rather than be seen as design proposals. A graphical user interface (GUI) can be prototyped using various low-fidelity methods, even to the extent of prototyping in paper (Snyder, 2003), however in ASR interfaces, much of the interaction is invisible and impermanent and therefore difficult to represent on paper using methods derived from GUI design. Other aspects of the speech user interface, for example vocabulary and grammar, are too detailed to specify at the early prototyping stage.

The detailed, caricatured, scenarios that follow describe the use of an ASR system for the Magistrates Court. The scenarios describe a potential implementation that is entirely front of house and is a near-direct replacement for the magistrate writing outcome decisions on a bench sheet. Technical constraints are incorporated into the scenarios by considering pre-existing technical data and fieldwork with users of contemporary ASR software (Kraal, 2008).

3.1 Utopian Scenario

It's 9.30am on a Tuesday as Rob, Chief Magistrate of the ACT, enters the courtroom. He sits down at the bench and court begins. On the bench are several objects: Rob's favourite coffee-mug, a carafe of water and a glass, a few pens, an array of tiny microphones embedded into the small shelf above the surface of the bench and a touch-screen that's about as big as a hand-held computer game. The microphones work together, canceling noises from the Court and capturing Rob's speech when necessary and the touch-screen allows Rob to trigger various modes and actions of the ASR system.

The first few cases that appear are dealt with very perfunctorily and are all set over to another date. Rob does this in concert with the List Clerk who advises him when the next available dates are for the particular sort of cases that appear. Rob's Associate, Claire, organises the cases in this way as it suits Rob's way of working. Once Rob and the List Clerk have found a suitable date, Rob uses the touch-screen to trigger a recognition event that allows him to speak the date for the next part of the case to the Court. Speaking the outcome records it.

The next cases involve people who have been in the lock-up overnight. Rob usually makes a judgment on these cases, often just a bail arrangement but if someone pleads guilty he will sentence them on their first appearance if the sentence is simple and not severe.

The first difficult appearance today is a Mr Tailor who was in a street brawl last night and has been in the lock-up since about 2am. The public prosecutor hands Claire a police report on the incident that Claire hands to Rob for him to read. Mr Tailor's lawyer says that the fight was uncharacteristic and that Mr Tailor is a member of society in good standing who has been employed as a carpenter since he left school at 16. Rob says that the report indicates that Mr Tailor hit three people, including a woman, and that he swore at a police officer. Rob says that these are fairly serious charges and that he will have to sentence Mr Tailor.

Mr Tailor's lawyer and Rob have an exchange that results in Rob postponing sentencing to a date in three week's time. To make this decision official, Rob touches a button on a small touch-screen mounted on the bench. The button is labeled speak decision. The button changes colour from grey to green, showing Rob that the system is ready. Rob says, "Decision in case 54897," and then says the words of the bail agreement, "the defendant is released on bail, recognisance self in the amount of $1000 to reappear three weeks hence" . An indicator next to the button turns yellow and then green, indicating that the decision has been recognised. Rob taps another button labeled print decision. A small laser printer in the bench produces a piece of paper with the decision printed on it. Rob checks that he is happy with the wording, signs it and places it in the bench sheet folder. He taps the next button in the touch-screen, confirm decision. Next to Claire, a laser printer comes to life and produces three identical pages. Claire hands one to each lawyer and one to Mr Tailor. These pages contain the text of the decision and the date of Mr Tailor's next court date. Pressing the confirm decision button has also added the decision to the Court s computer system. The touch screen goes back to its initial state, ready for the next case, as Claire calls for the next defendant.

3.2 Dystopian Scenario

It's 9.32am on a Monday as Rob, Chief Magistrate of the ACT, enters the courtroom. He sits down at the bench and court begins. As Claire, Rob's Associate is calling the first case, Rob plugs himself in to the speech recognition system. A lapel microphone is sewn into the black gown that Rob wears and it needs to be connected to the system.

The first case today is a Mr Jones who caused a car accident last night while he was drunk and has been in the lock-up since about 2am. Mr Jones is pleading guilty on all charges. The public prosecutor hands Claire a police report on the incident. Claire hands the report to Rob. Mr Jones's lawyer says that the drunkenness and accident were uncharacteristic and that Mr Jones is normally home looking after his four children by 9pm. Last night Mr Jones had attended a party at a local club and made a mistake in driving home intoxicated. Rob says that the report indicates that Mr Jones hit two cars and resisted arrest and that these are fairly serious charges, so he will have to sentence Mr Jones.

The defence counsel assents to Rob passing sentence immediately. To make the sentence official, Rob touches a button an a small touch-screen mounted on the bench. The button is labelled speak decision. Nothing happens. Rob taps the touch-screen again and this time it changes colour from grey to green, indicating that the system is ready. Rob says, "Sentence in case 86572," and then says the words of the sentence, "the defendant is found guilty on all charges and is sentenced to three months imprisonment to be suspended forthwith and is released on a good behaviour bond of $1000" . An indicator next to the button turns yellow… and stays yellow, indicating that the decision parser has not been able to correctly determine the sentence. This usually means that the recognition engine has misrecognised a word so that the spoken sentence is not in a form that makes legal sense. Rob hates repeating sentences when the system gets them wrong because he thinks it makes him look foolish. Rob taps the yellow speak decision button again and repeats the sentence. Just as he's finishing, someone in court sneezes! At least half the time, a sneeze or cough from the gallery will ruin the speech recognition of the decision. This time, though, the button turns green so Rob taps the print decision button.

A small laser printer in the bench produces a piece of paper with the decision printed on it. Rob checks the wording, but the system has misrecognised the length of the sentence and the amount of the bond. Why the decision parser can't check these things, Rob doesn't know. He supposes that different amounts are equally legal, even if they are wrong in this instance. It's often the case that when Rob gets a yellow from the speak decision button that the system has also got something else wrong. Rob slides his chair closer to Claire's desk to ask her to try to fix what's gone wrong but he feels the microphone cord tension as he reaches its full length, still not quite close enough to have a quiet word with Claire. So instead he glances down at Claire and lifts his eyebrows significantly. Claire taps a few keys, giving her access to the transcript of what Rob's just said, and begins editing the transcript. The system allows Claire to edit the transcript of the spoken sentence only after it's been parsed correctly.

When Claire's done she nods at Rob and he taps the print decision button again. The decision comes out of the printer and Rob signs it and places it in the bench sheet folder. He taps the next button in the touch-screen labelled confirm decision. Next to Claire, a laser printer comes to life but produces no output. Claire leans over it and sighs. Paper jam. She flips covers and latches and pulls out a mangled piece of paper. She gives Rob a small nod again and he taps the confirm decision button. This time the printer produces three identical pages. Identically faulty. The toner cartridge in the laser printer has run out.

Claire whispers to Rob that they have a problem and Rob says to the court at large, "let's have a ten minute recess while we get someone up here to deal with some small problems we're having". Most people in the court sigh – it's clearly going to be a long day.

3.3 Summary

The scenarios above show how the same technology, implemented in basically the same way, can have radically different outcomes in use. In the utopian scenario, everything is perfect, the interaction is virtually seamlessly integrated into the business of the court. In the dystopian scenario everything breaks down, including the magistrate's sense of control and prestige in the court.

Contrasting the scenarios shows that the introduction of ASR to the court in a near-direct replacement for the magistrate writing on a bench sheet does not just require a computer, but a microphone or system of microphones, a printer, a means to engage the ASR system when necessary and contingency plans when some or all of the interconnected technologies fail. Where the utopian scenario shows how simple the system could be, the dystopian scenario shows that the same technologies could be tremendously disruptive not just to the large-scale running of the courtroom but also the small-scale interpersonal interactions between the magistrate and the associate, as illustrated when the too-short microphone cord prevents Rob from having a private word with Claire, reducing him to facial gestures.

Aspects of the use of ASR in the court are also problematic because of the properties of the court itself. These properties are related to the established work process of the court, the physical arrangement of the space, how the required technologies relate (or do not relate) to one another and so on.

Neither the specifically technical nor the specifically non-technical aspects of introducing an ASR system to the court are responsible for the difficulties involved in such an introduction. Solving the problems in the technical sphere but ignoring the non-technical problems does not make a future system useful or usable. Both the technical and non-technical must be considered together in order for the design of a future ASR system to take into account the complex environment of the court.

4. Re-imagining Speech Recognition for the Magistrates Court

To use ASR in the Magistrates Court necessitates that ASR, as a technology, be re-imagined. Often, ASR applications are seen as a way to replace the act of typing by one user, that is, the dictation paradigm. In the dictation paradigm, an ASR application is used to replace a secretary who takes dictation as the user speaks. However, this is not the only paradigm for the use of ASR.

One possible re-imagined form of ASR that might work for the Court is a model where the users and computers are distributed in space and time, just as the work process of the Court is distributed in space and time. Inherent in this distributed model is the fact that the person whose speech is recognised, the magistrate, is not necessarily the person working with the transcript generated by the ASR system, a back room worker. Distributing the computers involved allows separation of work tasks and recognition tasks as well as allowing multi-pass ASR (Whittaker et al., 2002) which can improve the accuracy of hard-to-recognise speech by allowing a recognition engine to refine a transcription.

As stated previoisly, the elements of the Court that are most plastic, and therefore easiest to change, are:

- The detail of the work process of the "back room", particularly the after-court section; and,
- Details of the defendant's folder but not its use or existence.

This is not to say that these elements will be easy to change, just that they are easier to change than, say, the physical layout of the courtroom. Analysing the work of the Court has shown that these elements are the most flexible to change.

Re-imagined ASR for the Court incorporates a model of the Court's workflow. In the existing work process the magistrate speaks a decision and writes it down and other people perform the coding of that decision into something that allows the machinery of the Court to keep working. A dictation paradigm of ASR can't perform that task because the translation of the magistrate's decision into codes is too nuanced, too detailed, too specialized and too reliant on intelligence and experience. The goal of a re-imagined ASR is to make it easier for the back-room workers to do the parts of their job where intelligence is required and minimise the parts of their jobs that are repetitive.

The Chief Magistrate's request was that any new system remove the need for him to write down every decision. It is quite simple, technically, to record the speech of the Chief Magistrate when he makes a decision. In fact, it is done already and annotated by the monitor. However, using those recordings as a resource to replace or augment the bench sheet is considerably more problematic. Adding to the possible problems of moving to a speech record are the stamps which are currently used and which may act as a prompt to the magistrate would no longer be available. Minimising the amount of writing on a bench sheet by a magistrate requires that the information previously contained on the bench sheet is available elsewhere. Given that the magistrate's speech is recorded it is reasonable to attempt to provide access to that recorded speech.

The problem with accessing speech recordings for the Court, and the back room in particular, is that using the bench sheets and the entire folder is a fact finding exercise where users scan and browse the documents in the folder looking for the specific information that the case-management software requires. Replacing the bench sheet, which at least in part embodies the process of communicating decisions, with an ASR system is a similar problem to that faced by the designers of the air traffic control system described by Hughes, et al. (1992) where a design for replacing paper that was an embodiment of work was proposed. As with the air traffic control work by Hughes et al. (1992) the proposed design for an ASR system for the Court attempts to retain the communicative aspects of the embodied work while introducing new possibilities for interaction to the process.

Using a speech record instead of paper to communicate decisions necessitates scanning and browsing a recording of the magistrate's speech in court. Scanning and browsing a recording of speech is time consuming because speech is one-dimensional and ephemeral. One way of making speech persistent and two-dimensional to support scanning and browsing behaviours is to turn speech into text. A group at AT&T Research looked at voicemail and speech in general and developed the Spoken Content-based Audio Navigation (SCAN) interface. SCAN was developed to be used as a way to access transcripts of broadcast news (Whittaker et al., 1999) and later voicemail (Whittaker et al., 2002). The AT&T researchers had no illusions about the errorful nature of ASR, however they showed that the errorful transcripts allowed users to obtain an overview of audio recordings that was previously impossible. The errorful transcripts turned unusable speech recordings into something useful.

It is important to note that the interface described in the scenario below is not a proposed solution, but is a way of exploring and building on the ideas presented until this point in this thesis. A solution would need extensive testing with proposed users and would have to undergo several iterations before it would be ready to be used "live". The design for the interface is speculative and arises from the fieldwork described elsewhere in this thesis. Presenting this design here is not an attempt to say "here is an ideal design for ASR in the

Court" but rather a way to show how the fieldwork and contrasting caricatured scenarios have led to a potential outcome.

The interface described in the next section has some similarities and some differences with the SCAN interface (Whittaker et al., 2002; Whittaker et al., 1999). SCAN was the implementation of a new paradigm in accessing speech records, What You See Is (Almost) What You Hear or WYSIAWYH. The primary goal of WYSIAWYH was to present a visual analogue to recordings of speech. SCAN used transcripts of speech generated by ASR software to facilitate the visual analogue. To create the transcripts the speech was broken into "paratones" and then passed through an ASR engine several times, allowing the recogniser to improve on the transcript. The results of the transcription for each paratone was then combined into the errorful transcript of the particular audio recording. The terms in the transcripts were then indexed for later retrieval. Users could enter natural language queries into the SCAN interface and the system would return ranked transcripts that the user could select to view and, if required, listen.

SCAN had an "overview" feature that displayed the incidence of keywords in the paratones of the transcript and the transcript itself. By providing a visual overview of the keywords in various paratones, SCAN allowed the user to skim the document more quickly than if they had to scan the entire transcript, which could be the textual representation of 25 minutes of speech. After using the overview section to jump to a potentially relevant paratone, the user could read the (errorful) transcript. If the transcript contained too many errors to be sensible the user could click the paragraph to play the audio it represented.

The SCAN interface was empirically tested and found to be more effective than just listening to the recordings in fact-finding tasks. Additionally, subjects in the experiments found the SCAN interface easier to use than just listening to the audio and listened to a shorter amount of audio to complete the tasks set them. The researchers found that increases in transcript accuracy had an influence on the perception of the difficulty of the task and on the actual quality of the answers the subjects gave. The mean accuracy of the transcripts in the tests was 67% with a maximum of 88% and a minimum of 35%. SCAN was found to be particularly useful for fact-finding tasks using the broadcast news corpus.

The researchers noted that there are disadvantages to the SCAN approach. The chief disadvantage is over-reliance by users on transcripts. Because the transcripts are inherently errorful relying on them can introduce errors into information extracted from the transcripts. They suggest introducing a representation of the ASR confidence measure, that is word probability, to the transcript. Words that the system was more confident about could be presented in darker type and words that had a lower confidence could be presented in a lighter type allowing the user to judge for themselves the accuracy of the text. Some users in the studies of the SCANMail interface suggested that the transcripts could be editable to allow for correction of errors should they be found. (Whittaker & Amento, 2004) built and tested an editable version of the SCANMail interface and found it to be usable and useful.

For clarity, it must be said that the interface described here has no relationship to the caricatured interfaces described in previous sections. Where caricatured scenarios are useful for sketching ideas and making clear benefits and traps of an implementation, a single scenario is still best for communicating a final solution.

I will refer to the interface described in this section as the Interface for Court Audio Access (ICAA). The main difference between SCAN and ICAA is that SCAN was intended to provide open-ended search capabilities over a large corpus of speech, either broadcast news (Whittaker et al., 1999) or voicemail (Whittaker et al., 2002) where ICAA would not require the ability to search over all speech recorded by the system but would instead be directed at searches of a single transcript or group of transcripts relevant to a particular case. ICAA would replace bench sheets or augment a greatly simplified version of the existing bench sheets, allowing the magistrates freedom from writing large amounts by hand while still allowing workers in the back room access to the information they require to perform their work.

4.1 The ICAA Scenario

The Interface for Court Audio Access (ICAA) scenario is partly inspired by the work of (Kraal, et al. (2002). In keeping with previous work that has used ethnographic methods (Hughes et al., 1992) and scenarios (Satchell, 2003) to describe future designs, the technical details of the scenario that follows are not described. The purpose of the scenario is to describe the system in use. The system does not exist - the scenario is an example only. The scenario has two parts, front of house (section 4.1.1) and back of house (section 4.1.2).

4.1.1 Front of House

It's Monday morning, always the busiest time for the A-list with all of the weekend arrests to deal with, and Court has just resumed at 11.07am, Magistrate Rob Cowley presiding. They're up to the drink-driving charges. First up, Henry Webb, representing himself. Claire hands up Mr Webb's folder. As it crosses the boundary from Claire's desk to the Bench, the touch-screen on the bench shows the charge numbers for the case in the folder---Mr Webb's driving under the influence charge---there's only one number. Mr Webb pleads guilty but states that this is his first charge for driving under the influence in 38 years of driving and indeed his first criminal charge ever.

Rob asks the public prosecutor what Mr Webb's blood-alcohol content was. "Zero point zero six, your worship". Barely over the legal limit and fairly obviously a lapse of judgment on Mr Webb's part. Rob notes it down on a blank sheet of paper in the folder in front of him. He's obviously contrite and just appearing in court seems to have scared him so much he'll be catching cabs from now on. Rob decides to give Mr Webb a good behaviour bond and a stern lecture.

Use of ICAA begins in the courtroom when no actual "interface" is visible. ICAA's intrusion into the courtroom itself is limited to a microphone, a few RFID sensors, a small touch screen on the bench and a small, fast printer on the associate's desk.

As court progresses, ICAA makes no intrusion into proceedings until a case comes to a point where the magistrate would previously have written a decision on the bench sheet.

The microphone and touch-screen are directly related to ASR. The magistrate uses the touch-screen as a way to start and stop the speech recognition when he's speaking a decision.

The printer on the associate's desk produces dockets that show a decision, or series of decisions, have been made relating to the case at hand. The RFID sensors sense RFID tags embedded in the folder. As the folder is passed between associate and magistrate sensors in the bench record the passing, allowing the system to dip into a database for pertinent information, for example charge numbers and various details relating to the defendant, if known, such as address and employer. The touch screen can then display these details.

Stern lecture over, it's time to sentence Mr Webb to good behaviour. Rob taps the touch-screen to start the decision-recording process. The gesture is so subtle that no-one in court really notices it. The screen shows "ready for decision" and still shows the charge numbers.

An audio recording has been going on since Rob sat down and court began. When Rob taps the screen to tell it he is about to speak a decision, the system tags the recording, allowing a future listener, or the ASR system, to jump to the sentence.

"In the matter of charge number HW39674, Henry Webb is hereby released on recognisance self in the amount of $1000 on the condition that he be of good behaviour for twelve months."

Rob taps the screen again, ending the recording. The screen shows "recording finished". Rob hands Mr Webb's folder back to Claire and as it crosses the boundary from the bench to her desk the touch screen shows "next case". At the same time, a small printer on Claire's desk produces a docket with a ten-digit number and a few details relating to the case. She puts it in the folder and puts the folder on her "done" pile.

Mr Webb's day in court is over and he's free to go.

So far, most aspects of the court's work process are much the same as they are currently. Handwritten decisions have been done away with, as was the purpose of this design, and replaced with what is from the magistrate and associate's perspective technology that is unobtrusive. The technology introduced into the court is strong and simple, in keeping with the findings that the ASR system introduced to the Court and does not significantly disrupt the work process in the courtroom or impinge on the theatre of the court.

While Mr Webb has been getting his lecture, and indeed since court has started, Molly has been in the monitor's booth watching and listening to everything. Molly has a computer in front of her with special software that can annotate the audio recording of what's going on in court. Since this is the A-list, Molly's job is just to record which lawyers are appearing when. Molly also has a paper master charge sheet listing every charge that's appearing in court today. She uses the charge sheet to record which charge numbers are dismissed and which charge numbers the magistrate decides to deal with. In theory, with the ASR system in place, the monitor's job is unnecessary, however, ICAA keeps the monitor's job and makes the annotations work as part of the ASR system.

The monitor still uses the paper charge sheet to cross off dismissed charges so that the ASR system has a backup in case something goes very wrong. The charge sheet also helps the person doing the after-court processing, the process of which is described later in this scenario.

4.1.2 Backstage

The defendants' folders and the monitor's master charge sheet make their way to the back room and become the responsibility of Julie. Julie works in the after court section, processing folders from the day in court and entering details of the magistrates' decisions into the Court's case management software. The ICAA and the case management software (CMS) work together to help Julie do her job.

Julie takes the first folder, which belongs to a Mr Smith, from the big pile next to her desk, opens it and types the code on the docket at the top of the documents in the file into the ICAA. This works much better than the way things were about a month ago when they installed sensors in Julie's desk to automatically detect which folder Julie had selected. The sensors worked fine but they meant that Julie couldn't place the folders on her desk the way that she used to. Julie had the I.T. guys remove the sensors - she's happy to type a number if it means she can put the folder she's working on wherever she likes.

The folders and the RFID sensors work in the courtroom because there is a very clear demarcation between the bench, where the folders are "in play" and the associate's desk where the folders are "waiting". On Julie's desk the distance between the "in play" area and the "waiting" area is too fine and too variable for the sensors to work reliably.

Julie had the ICAA thrust upon her by the court. The ICAA is intended to help the magistrates in court and allow them to not write down decisions on outcomes but it still needs to communicate those outcomes to the people who need to know them. Julie's uses the ICAA because it is her job to process what is said in court. The ICAA is designed to make it as easy as possible for Julie to work with the audio and the transcript that is generated from it using ASR. Julie's previous experience with her job before the ICAA was introduced allows her to work with the transcript. Finally, Julie understands that the transcript is pretty close to the old handwritten bench sheet. She could either fight the new system or see it as a different skill to learn.

After entering the code from the docket, the ICAA case window appears with the most recent transcript from Mr Smith's trial already open in the transcript pane. If there were other transcripts from previous appearances, they'd be in the archive pane, but this is Mr Smith's first time in court. By scanning the transcript, Julie is able to assess what has happened in court and what decisions the magistrate has made. In this case, Mr Cowley has dismissed a bunch of charges and set aside hearing the remaining charges for a later date.

Clearly this person has pleaded not guilty. The ICAA is really good at recognising spoken charge numbers so Julie quickly scans the transcript to make sure that nothing is really wrong and tells the ICAA to tell the CMS to record that the charges were dismissed. All this takes is a few mouse clicks.

The ICAA is so good at recognising charge numbers because the touch-screen shows the magistrate the charge numbers for the case at hand. This serves two purposes. It prompts the magistrate so that the charge numbers are easy to view and it primes the ASR software so that when it "hears" a charge number it will only recognise it if the number is from the list of charges in the case at hand. The RFID tags in the folder allow the ASR system to narrow the possibilities of what charge numbers the magistrate could say, leading to better recognition accuracy.

After taking care of the dismissed charges, Julie is able to get the longer part of Mr Cowley's decision where the case is set over for a date in three weeks time. The system has jumped through the transcript to the next part of the decision. Mr Cowley said that he'll hear the case on the 23rd of this month. The system understood that really well as it's in black text. He gave a few other orders that the system isn't that confident it's understood---they're in varying shades of gray---though they make enough sense as Julie reads through the transcript.

Using different shades to display the confidence of a recognised word or phrase has been used successfully in other transcript-based interfaces to underlying audio (Whittaker & Amento, 2004).

Julie is able to select the part of the transcript that has the date in it and drag it to the field in the CMS that accepts dates. The ICAA knows enough about spoken dates to convert the spoken "23rd of January, 2006" to 23/01/06. Julie makes sure the conversion is correct. Now she switches her attention to the CMS pane and fills in the rest of the required information. Mr Cowley has neglected to say which charges he'll be hearing on the 23rd, which isn't a problem in court as it's fairly obvious when he's dismissed a lot of charges, but the CMS needs to know exactly which ones he'll be hearing. The CMS assumes that unless charges are dismissed they're still current, so Julie confirms that with the CMS and checks quickly with the master charge sheet from the monitor. Before this folder is done, Julie has to print the CMS's summary of the outcomes so far and some letters to send to the various parties involved in the case. These letters are just proforma and are generated by the CMS. A letter for the public prosecutor's office; one for Mr Smith; one for Mr Smith's lawyer. They're printed in duplicate; one copy for the folder and one copy for Julie's outbox. While the printer takes its time, Julie pulls out the next folder, Ms Barker.

4.1.3 Summary

The front of house scenario above shows how ASR can be incorporated into the work process of the Court without disrupting the theatre of the courtroom. The back stage scenario shows how ASR could work with the back room workers, relieving them of some of the more repetitive aspects of their work and leveraging their expertise in interpreting and working with magistrates decisions.

The caricatured scenarios contributed to these final scenarios by making clear where the weak points in ASR for the court lay. These new scenarios aim to overcome those weak points by working with the strengths of each of the actors, human and non-human, in the entire Court work process and by also working with the strengths of ASR to produce a fast, if errorful, good enough transcript of a magistrates spoken decision.

5. Conclusion

This chapter has shown how caricatured scenarios (Bødker, 2000) can be used to "sketch" interactions that have no real physical or graphical manifestation by examining a potential use of speech recognition software (ASR) in the Magistrates Court of the Australian Capital Territory. The caricatures scenarios are used to show the benefits and limitations of potential implementations of ASR, allowing the potentials and pitfalls to be readily apparent. Of course, caricatured scenarios are of use in areas other than ASR and could be of great use in fields where it is difficult to create a manifestation of an interface, for example ubiquitous computing. Caricatured scenarios could also be used to "sketch" interactions where a combination of products mediate interaction with a service, for example in the way that the iPod and iTunes desktop software work together as an interface to the iTunes store.

This chapter has also shown how ASR can be re-considered as a productive technology that has benefits and limitations. Methods to mitigate the limitations are presented which can be of benefit to ASR designers. Productive use of ASR requires bringing together many aspects of a situation including technology, work process, spatial layout and acoustic considerations. Using caricatured scenarios allows initial ideas for ASR systems to be tested conceptually before committing to implementation and can also be used to direct further fieldwork which can be used to obtain a deeper understanding of a particular situation.

Caricatured scenarios are a tool that designers and researchers can use to explore the use of disruptive technologies and communicate the implications of introducing disruptive technologies to existing work practices.

6. References

Bødker, S. (2000). Scenarios in user-centred design - setting the stage for reflection and action. Interacting with Computers, 13, 61-75.

Callon, M. (1986). Some elements of a sociology of translation: domestication of the scallopes and the fishermen of St Brieuc Bay. In J. Law (Ed.), Power, Action and Belief (pp. 196--233). London, Boston and Henley: Routledge & Kegan Paul.

Carroll, J. M. (Ed.). (1995). Scenario-based design. Envisioning work and technology in System Development. New York: Wiley.

Dugdale, A., & Kraal, B. (2006). Magistrates and voice recognition: reconceptualising agency. Paper presented at the OZCHI 2006, Sydney, Australia.

Hughes, J., Randall, D., & Shapiro, D. (1992). Designing with Ethnography: Making work visible. Interacting with Computers, 5(2).

Hughes, J. A., Randall, D., & Shapiro, D. (1992). Faltering from ethnography to design. Paper presented at the CSCW '92: Proceedings of the 1992 ACM conference on Computer-supported cooperative work.

Kraal, B. (2008). Considering use and design of speech recognition systems : investigating users of complex socio-technical systems. : Verlag, VDM.

Kraal, B., Dugdale, A., & Collings, P. (2006). Scenarios for Embracing Errorful Automatic Speech Recognition. Paper presented at the OZCHI 2006, Sydney, Australia.

Kraal, B., Wagner, M., & Collings, P. (2002, November). Improving the design of dictation software. Paper presented at the Australian Speech Science and Technology Conference, University of Melbourne, Victoria, Australia.

Read, J. C., MacFarlane, S., & Casey, C. (2002). Oops! Silly me! Errors in a handwriting recognition-based text entry interface for children. Paper presented at the NordiCHI '02: Proceedings of the second Nordic conference on Human-computer interaction, New York, NY, USA.

Satchell, C. (2003, November 26-28). The Swarm: Facilitating fluidity and control in young people's use of mobile phones. Paper presented at the OZCHI 2003, Brisbane, Australia.

Snape, L., Casey, C., MacFarlane, S. J., & Robertson, L. (1997). Using Speech in Multimedia Applications. Paper presented at the TCS Conference, Bangor, Wales.

Snyder, C. (2003). Paper prototyping : the fast and easy way to design and refine user interfaces. San Francisco, Calif.: Morgan Kaufmann.

Whittaker, S., & Amento, B. (2004). Semantic speech editing. Paper presented at the CHI 2004: SIGCHI conference on Human factors in computing systems, New York, NY, USA.

Whittaker, S., Hirschberg, J., Amento, B., Stark, L., Bacchiani, M., Isenhour, P., et al. (2002). SCANMail: a voicemail interface that makes speech browsable, readable and searchable. Paper presented at the CHI '02: SIGCHI conference on Human factors in computing systems.

Whittaker, S., Hirschberg, J., Choi, J., Hindle, D., Pereira, F., & Singhal, A. (1999). SCAN: designing and evaluating user interfaces to support retrieval from speech archives. Paper presented at the SIGIR '99: 22nd annual international ACM SIGIR conference on Research and development in information retrieval.

Evaluation of the interface prototypes using DGAIU abstract representation models

Susana Gómez-Carnero and Javier Rodeiro Iglesias
University of Vigo
Spain

1. Introduction

The user interface is determinant for the success or failure of a software application. Its development is demanding as referring to time and costs of production. Myers and Rosson (Myers & Rosson, 1992) determine—according to inquiries on developers—that the efforts employed in building the interface of an interactive software rate around the 48%, whereas Garthner Group (Garthner Group, 1994) situate them around the 70%. Hence, optimizing the quality of the user interface by means of an effective design becomes vital so as to obtain its maximum acceptability.

The acceptability of a user interface is measured according to three main points:

1. **¿Is the user interface kind to the user view?** In this case, the acceptability would be linked to the aesthetical properties of the interface. The load memory of the user or its functional correctness is not considered. The main point so far is that the user interface remains friendly and kind to the user's view.
2. **¿Does the user interface do what it has to do?** Testing whereas the user interface remains useful to accomplish successfully the tasks it was created for, both in the sense of its capacity to do what the user wants, and with respect to the user's capacity to do what the interface wants. This second point is closely related to the tasks that a user will have to perform over the user interface.
3. **¿Is the use of the user interface easy for the user?** Here, the usability term is introduced (Shackel, 1986) (Eason, 1988) (ISO, 1992) (ISO, 1993) (Nielsen, 1993) (IBM, 1993). If a user considers that the use of the user interface is too complicated, the user may not accept this user interface even though it may still remain efficient or aesthetically kind to the user.

The assessment of the functionality of these criteria, then, is really complicated. This remains so because of the means whereby the assessment has generally being carried out, mainly drawing on subjective appreciations through polls or inquiries on experts' opinions or questionnaires made to the users (Molich & Nielsen, 1990) (Preece & Rogers, 1994) (Nielsen, 1993) (Wharton, 1994). Therefore, and given the subjectivity of the user interface assessment in user interface qualitative evaluation techniques, it would be interesting to reach a more direct and discrete method of assessment in order to avoid the 'inaccuracy' of subjective perception. A possible solution for this would be that the user got to interact with a prototype of the user interface generated from a specification model obtained in a previous phase of analysis of its requirements. Hence, the user could obtain a more rigorous view of the user interface, while helping the early identification of possible problems before time and money are ineffectually spent for the industry. Most of the evaluation methods are conceived after the creation of the software. Due to the costs of software development, then, it seems reasonable to suggest as necessary doing the evaluations previously to any software implementations.

There exists a great amount of research on the above mentioned criteria, but most of it is in theoretical state and isn't yet available for implementation. In fact, after the examination of different representation techniques in order to study whether these criteria can apply to complex interfaces—and thus derive an objective manner for their assessment—the conclusion is that these criteria remain somewhat unpractical and incomplete. Therefore, we present here an alternative notation that allows representing the user interface in an abstract manner while paying attention to its components, to its visual presentation (in graphic terms) and to its interaction with the user.

In this chapter, we present the part of the notation which represents the functionality of the user interface, so that the outcome will be a user interface that allows us to do semiautomatic assessments minimizing the developmental and evaluative costs. In section 2, we introduce the part of the notation corresponding to user interface behaviour representation. Section 3, then, proceeds to the notation that has to be used for test evaluation. In section 4 the EAU tool is introduced, which will allow users a dynamic assessment of the functionality of the user interface through an interactive simulation. And finally, in section 5, we expose the conclusions drawn out of this chapter's research.

2. DGAUI Representation

There is literature on user interface representation models. Reviewing research on different models for user interfaces, and focusing on those that proposed the visual representation mode (Gómez-Carnero, 2008), we here consider that the nature of the problems deriving from these models makes it necessary to come across an alternative solution. The proposed DGAUI representation is premised over the fact that the visual user interface is not a continuous structure. In fact, it argues that the visual user interface is made of discrete finite elements known as user interface components that define the interface as a composition of individual elements. These user interface components follow a topological hierarchy, so that one component may be contained within another (Rodeiro, 2001).

The notation for the definition of the visual user interface allows:

- To define the visual user interface components, with standard graphical primitives if the component has visual representation in the user interface; or else to determine properties if the component is for input information or simply a container of other user interface components.
- To determine the topological composition of visual user interface components so as to create the visual user interface with which the user interacts in a given moment.
- To represent the dialogue between the different components within the user interface, signalling the events to which a component reacts to and the manner in which the other visual user interface components respond to this.

The best choice in structuring the notation is XML. This will allow creating a DTD that will ease the parsing of notation structures.

Paying attention to the semantics of the notation, the first part conveys the initial representation of the visual user interface, while the second communicates the representation of the structure of any of the states that the user interface experienced derived of the interaction of its components—including as well the transitions between states. Given that the nature of the two parts in the notation is so discordant, we divide the notation in two DTD. The first (called **DGAUI-DEF**) consists of a detailed definition of each of the user interface components that constitute an interface. This separation is effective for the reusability of component definitions in other visual user interface representations. The second DTD (called **DGAUI-INT**) depends on the first, for this second notation is calculated from the first. The DGAUI-DEF contains all the states that a visual user interface can reach. This set of states can be calculated from the initial representation of the user interface. The initial state is made of the properties introduced into the user interface components' definition. After the onset state, a series of possible individual events that may take place over a user interface component or over the components in a state are simulated, and the changes produced on the components will determine a new state (one that already exists or one that is identified as new) and a transition between the actual state and the new state. This is the application of the concept the state diagrams for a user interface but generates from interaction on individual user interface components. This notation is oriented to the state of the visual user interface components instead of being oriented to the state of the whole visual user interface. An overall state of the visual user interface would be obtained from the combined states of the different components in a visual user interface.

Thus, the notation conveys the separation between the presentation and the behaviour of the user interface. The presentation is located in the representation definition while the functionality is located on the states and the transitions between states. These transitions between states are calculated using hypothetical user actions (events) on the visual user interface components and using also events of the system.

By **interface state** we understand any of the conjunctions of the visual user interface components that, according to the value of its properties, can be reached through the interaction with a user in a given moment.

For the definition of the notation we consider that:

- The user actions are not arbitrary.
- The set of visual user interface states are finite and can be described and evaluated.
- A visual user interface state depends on the components that form it and their properties.
- A state is a moment in the visual user interface in which the visual user interface is waiting for a user's action, and where the visual user interface does not change while the user is not interacting with it.

Thus, each state is characterized by the value that the components of an interface acquire according to the following four properties:

- *Visible*: Indicating the visibility of the component. Visible (T) or not Visible (F) on screen.
- ***Active***: Indicates if the component responds to a user's actions (T) or not (F). If the component has Activo (F) in a state it doesn't exist transition to other state caused by this component.

- *InfI*: This property activates the input of data associated to the component. If the component property has the value of True it will accept data given by the user.
- *InfO*: The output of data associated to the component is activated. If this property has value True the component will show the data sent from the "core" of the application to the user.

Events are user's actions over input hardware devices on the system. These are detected by the system which will respond to them according to the behavioural patterns set for the system to follow. An event is a single user action; for example, drag and drop is the combination of three single actions or events: click, move and release. Similarly, we can define **pre-conditions** and **post-conditions** for the events. If an event is defined using the notation of a visual user interface component and it has no pre-condition, the changes in other components can take place only if the event over this component is produced. For example, in the event RightClick over ComponentTwo the condition is "ComponentOne:Activo(T)" (the property Activo of componentOne has value True); here, the user action over ComponentTwo will not be performed if the value of ComponentOne in property Activo is F. For post-conditions, though, we need to define the values of the properties that must be satisfied in order to reach the next state, that is, we need to define the values of the transitions.

The notation does not limit the events that can be defined for interaction. The HCI engineer can define the events that she/he considers necessary and communicate their meaning to the workgroup. Some examples of basic events that we use are:

- *LeftClick:* click over left Mouse button.
- *RightClick*: click over right Mouse button.
- *ReLeClick*: Release left Mouse button.
- *ReRiClick*: Release right Mouse button.
- *MouseOn*: Mouse pointer over a component.
- *Key(key of keyboard)*: keyboard keys combination.

It is possible to calculate the events from the states with DGAUI from the events of the components in the visual user interface. Thus, if we know that a component is affected by an event, we can build an oriented labelled state graphic of the user interface and establish which will be its following state. The vertexes are the states of the visual user interface and the labelled arcs are the transitions between states. There are two particularly important states for the functionality of the interface:

- *Initial state*: a vertex in which all the associated arcs are exit arcs and in which there are no entrance arcs which may possibly be reached without passing through the initial state.
- *Final State*: a vertex in which all the associated arcs are input arcs and where there is none of exit. The existence of two or more vertexes that only have input arcs is symptomatic of an anomaly in the visual user interface, for it will correspond to two different Final States.

A set of possible derivative states may be obtained from the initial state if a user's action is performed over it. This is done by applying the events over the visual user components with property Activo(T) and by making the associate changes of interaction on the other visual user components. The rest of the states can be obtained from this first set of derivative states

by applying the same processes to each one of the states, until reaching a final state where any visual user component has value True in the properties Active and Visible.
It is possible to identify transitions or arcs, labelled with a component and the event that is applied in order to trigger the state, from previously identified states, during the obtaining stage in the process of state creation in the user interface.
Two states are equal, and therefore, the same state, if all their visual user interface components have the same values in properties Active, Visible, InfI and InfO. The components that belong within a state are the ones that have some function within the state. A visual user interface component belongs to a state if it has some functionality. This functionality may derive from a visual appearance that conveys relevant information about the interface to the user (in this case the component property Active has value True). Or else, the functionality may derive from the fact that the visual user interface component causes changes on the properties of other components when an event is triggered. In any case, one of the advantages of this notation system is that it allows the modification of the visual properties of a component without causing any variations in its behaviour (the user cannot see the component but its behaviour is maintained along intermediate states).
If the modification of the appearance of a visual user interface component is so that it changes the functionality of the component, this would result in the configuration of a different visual user interface component. The interpretation of the appearance of the component in a visual user interface by the user must be unique for each visual user interface component and must also help to identify and clarify its functionality to the user. Otherwise, the component will remain ambiguous and the visual user interface design will be wrong.
This situation is common in interactive models that use interactors for the specification of components. The specification of the interactor is given or defined to specify the different states that may be reached by a component through its interaction with a user. According to the traditional specification of interactors, there is a definite functionality and a unique appearance for each state interactor. There is no model considering multiple renderings or visualizing options for a unique given interactor state. This is so because the specification centres on the dialogue of the interactor instead of on its visual appearance.
In the DGAUI proposal, there exists the possibility of different appearances for the components in the visual user interface—counting on their being triggered by a user's actions by means of visual operations—but the behaviour of the visual user interface component is always the same. Visual operations are, for example, resizing or changes on the size of visual user interface components. By resorting to the DGAUI, the consistence of the visual interface is implicitly maintained, for two visual user interface components created with the same appearance should follow the same behavioural pattern. And even if the appearance of the visual user interface component is altered or modified as the result of a personal choice made by the user, this modification will not affect the behaviour of the visual user interface component.
The DGAUI proposal does not consider the representation of abstract information in the application because this work is oriented to the early stages in the prototyping of the application. The participation of visual user interface components as elements that may allow the user to choose the input and output of information on the user interface is defined including in version 3.04 the domain definition of data or the mask for text input. If a user's action changes dramatically the appearance of a visual user interface component, then this

new appearance would be a new visual user interface component, and hence, a different visual user interface state.
If the visual user interface is correct there should only exist a state in which all the visual user interface components would have the properties Active and Visible with value False (in the final state). Likewise, the initial state of the user interface can be unequivocally identified from the representation of the visual user interface components in the DGAUI-DEF, through an examination of their properties.
In order to simplify its comprehension, here follows a description of the DTD DGAUI-DEF.

Item	Description
<!ELEMENT Composicion (Componente+)>	The composition indicates the topologic relation among the components contained within a containing component.
<!ELEMENT Componente (Alineado?, Equiespaciado?, Subcomponentes)> <!ATTLIST Componente Nombre CDATA #REQUIRED >	Each component is identified by a name and contains a group of subcomponents which facilitates the identification of the alignment characteristics and the equidistant spacing for each subcomponent.
<!ELEMENT Alineado (#PCDATA)> <!ATTLIST Alineado opcion (iz | de | su | in) #REQUIRED >	It signals that the contained components are aligned. There are various possibilities: right or left alignment, or else top or bottom alignment, all of which occur at a given distance in pixels.
<!ELEMENT Equiespaciado (Nombre+)> <!ELEMENT Nombre (#PCDATA)>	It highlights that the contained components are equidistant from one another and from the borders of the containing component.
<!ELEMENT Subcomponentes (Cont+)>	Grouping of the subcomponents in the containing component.
<!ELEMENT Cont (#PCDATA)> <!ATTLIST Cont InfI CDATA #IMPLIED InfO CDATA #IMPLIED >	The component introduces information given by the user (InfI). The component shows information from the application (InfO).

<table>
<tr><td><!ELEMENT Descripcion (Grafico* | Texto* | Enumeracion*)*></td><td>The description of each component in the interface signals that it can be a graphic, a textual component, or a graphic defined by enumeration.</td></tr>
<tr><td><!ELEMENT Grafico ((Rectangulo | Linea | Circulo | Elipse | Poligono), EstiloLinea?, AnchoLinea?, ColorLinea?, ColorRelleno?, Posición?, Tamano?, Datos?)>

<!ATTLIST Grafico
Nombre CDATA #REQUIRED
Visible (t | f) #REQUIRED
Activo (t | f) #REQUIRED
InfI (t | f) #IMPLIED
InfO (t | f) #IMPLIED
></td><td>The graphic component is defined by its name, a primitive, the style, wideness and color of its line, its filling color, its position and size, as well as the type of data that may get into the system or out of the system through such a component.</td></tr>
<tr><td><!ELEMENT Rectangulo (Coordenada, Coordenada)></td><td>The rectangle derives from two coordinates that determine their diagonal.</td></tr>
<tr><td><!ELEMENT Linea (Coordenada, Coordenada)></td><td>The line derives from two coordinates that determine its ends.</td></tr>
<tr><td><!ELEMENT Circulo (Coordenada, Radio)>
<!ELEMENT Radio (#PCDATA)></td><td>The circle derives from a coordinate that determines the circle's centre and from a number that indicates its radio.</td></tr>
<tr><td><!ELEMENT Elipse (Coordenada, Coordenada, AnguloInicio, AnguloFin)>
<!ELEMENT AnguloInicio (#PCDATA)>
<!ELEMENT AnguloFin (#PCDATA)></td><td>The ellipsis derives from the main rectangle within the ellipsis and from two angles: an onset angle and an ending angle.</td></tr>
<tr><td><!ELEMENT Poligono (Coordenada, Coordenada, Coordenada+)></td><td>The polygon derives from the coordinates which determine its vertexes.</td></tr>
<tr><td><!ELEMENT Coordenada (Px, Py)>
<!ELEMENT Px (#PCDATA)>
<!ELEMENT Py (#PCDATA)></td><td>Every coordinate derives from a given position for the X axis and another for the Y axis.</td></tr>
</table>

<table>
<tr><td><!ELEMENT EstiloLinea EMPTY>

<!ATTLIST EstiloLinea
Estilo (continua | discontinua)
#REQUIRED
></td><td>The study of the line admits two values: continuous and discontinuous.</td></tr>
<tr><td><!ELEMENT AnchoLinea (#PCDATA)></td><td>Pixel size of the primitive line.</td></tr>
<tr><td><!ELEMENT ColorLinea (#PCDATA)></td><td>Line color in format RGB XXXXXX</td></tr>
<tr><td><!ELEMENT ColorRelleno (#PCDATA)></td><td>Filling color in format RGB XXXXXX</td></tr>
<tr><td><!ELEMENT Posicion (Fija | Relativa)>
<!ELEMENT Fija (Coordenada)>
<!ELEMENT Relativa (OpCRel?, Coordenada)>
<!ELEMENT OpCRel (Centrado | (Justificado, Justificado?))>

<!ELEMENT Centrado EMPTY>

<!ATTLIST Centrado
Tipo (h | v | a) #REQUIRED
>

<!ELEMENT Justificado (#PCDATA)>

<!ATTLIST Justificado
Tipo (de | iz | su | in) #REQUIRED
></td><td>The position of a component determines its location within a containing component or within the device. This position may be fixed or relative, signalled by topologic restrictions in the area OpCRel; in any case, this position derives from a coordinate that signals its left top position (with respect to its containing component or else to the visualizing device)

The component is centered according to its containing component. The centering may be horizontal, vertical or both.

Alignment of the component on the right, left, top or bottom sides of a containing component according to a given number of pixels.</td></tr>
</table>

<!ELEMENT Tamano (Valorx, Valory)> <!ATTLIST Tamano Tipo (fijo | relativo) #REQUIRED > <!ELEMENT Valorx (#PCDATA)> <!ELEMENT Valory (#PCDATA)>	Size of the component within the containing component or within the visualizing device.
<!ELEMENT Datos (Tipo?)> <!ELEMENT Tipo (#PCDATA)> <!ATTLIST Tipo Longitud CDATA #IMPLIED RangoInf CDATA #IMPLIED RangoSup CDATA #IMPLIED Decimales CDATA #IMPLIED >	Conditions to be met by the input and output of data in the interface; attributes may vary depending on the type of data.
<!ELEMENT Texto (Txt, Fuente, TamanoFuente, ColorFuente, EstiloFuente, Posicion, Tamano)> <!ATTLIST Texto Nombre CDATA #REQUIRED Visible (t | f) #REQUIRED Activo (t | f) #REQUIRED > <!ELEMENT Txt (#PCDATA)> <!ELEMENT Fuente (#PCDATA)> <!ELEMENT TamanoFuente (#PCDATA)> <!ELEMENT ColorFuente (#PCDATA)> <!ELEMENT EstiloFuente (#PCDATA)>	The textual component is defined by the text that it presents, its type, size and font color; besides, it also conveys the characteristics of size and position. The size can be fixed or relative.
<!ELEMENT Enumeracion (Fichero, Posicion, Tamano)> <!ATTLIST Enumeracion Nombre CDATA #REQUIRED Visible (t | f) #REQUIRED Activo (t | f) #REQUIRED > <!ELEMENT Fichero (#PCDATA)>	The graphic components by enumeration contain the folder's route that contains the corresponding graphic's image.

<table>
<tr><td><!ELEMENT Dialogo (ItemDialogo*)></td><td>The dialogue about the components in the interface is formed by.</td></tr>
<tr><td><!ELEMENT ItemDialogo (Precondiciones?, Respuesta)>

<!ATTLIST ItemDialogo
Elemento CDATA #IMPLIED
Evento CDATA #REQUIRED
></td><td>Each ItemDialogo is made of the component from which the dialogue derives (Element), the event that triggers it, the preconditions that must be met, and the answer that such event triggers on the component.</td></tr>
<tr><td><!ELEMENT Precondiciones (Precondicion+)>
<!ELEMENT Precondicion (#PCDATA)>

<!ATTLIST Precondicion
Visible (t | f) #IMPLIED
Activo (t | f) #IMPLIED
InfI (t | f) #IMPLIED
InfO (t | f) #IMPLIED></td><td>The preconditions indicate the condition/s that must be met for the dialogue to be produced.</td></tr>
<tr><td><!ELEMENT Respuesta (Cambio+)>
<!ELEMENT Cambio (#PCDATA)>

<!ATTLIST Cambio
Visible (t | f) #IMPLIED
Activo (t | f) #IMPLIED
InfI (t | f) #IMPLIED
InfO (t | f) #IMPLIED
ProcID CDATA #IMPLIED
></td><td>The answer indicates the changes occurred in the properties of other components.</td></tr>
</table>

Table 1. DTD DGAIU-DEF

The visual user interface component definition, the topological composition, and the dialogue between components are constants for a visual user interface. The information that is introduced for each state of the visual interface refers to the values of the properties in the visual user interface components.

Once the states which a visual user interface goes through are obtained we use a state graph (multidigraph) to represent the whole set of transitions between states. In the state graph, the vertexes correspond to the visual user interface states and the arcs represent the transitions from one state to another. The arcs are labelled with the name of the visual user interface component and the event that causes the transition.

The XML document (DGAUI-INT) contains the following information:

- *The Topological Composition* of the visual user interface components contained in other visual user interface components.
- *The Information about the evolution of the visual user interface.* All the visual user interface states are defined by the description and properties of its components.

The initial state is obtained from the description of the components in the visual user interface and the rest of other possible states are obtained as part of an automatic process.

- *Set of transitions between states.* This is obtained during the automatic process of states identification.

Thus following, the detailed description of the DTD DGAUI-INT is given:

<table>
<tr><th>Item</th><th>Description</th></tr>
<tr><td><!ELEMENT Composicion (Componente+)></td><td>The composition is the same as the one noted in DTD DGAUI-DEF .</td></tr>
<tr><td>< !ELEMENT Estados (Estado+)*></td><td></td></tr>
<tr><td><!ELEMENT Estado (Descripcion?)>
<!ATTLIST Estado
Numero CDATA #REQUIRED
></td><td>Each state is formed by a state number and the description of the components that make that state; that is, those components that are visible or active or those components with any of the properties of InfI o InfO valued as T.</td></tr>
<tr><td><!ELEMENT Descripcion (Grafico* | Texto* | Enumeracion*)*></td><td>The description of each component in the interface indicates that it can be a graphic, a textual component, or a graphic defined by enumeration.</td></tr>
<tr><td><!ELEMENT Grafico ((Rectangulo | Linea | Circulo | Elipse | Poligono), EstiloLinea?, AnchoLinea?, ColorLinea?, ColorRelleno?, Posición?, Tamano?, Datos?)>
<!ATTLIST Grafico
Nombre CDATA #REQUIRED
Visible (t | f) #REQUIRED
Activo (t | f) #REQUIRED
InfI (t | f) #IMPLIED
InfO (t | f) #IMPLIED
></td><td>The graphic component is defined by its name, its primitive, the style, wideness and color of the line, its filling color, its position and size, and the kind of data that can get into the system out of the system through it.</td></tr>
<tr><td><!ELEMENT Rectangulo (Coordenada, Coordenada)></td><td>The rectangle derives from the coordinates that determine its diagonal.</td></tr>
</table>

<!ELEMENT Linea (Coordenada, Coordenada)>	The line derives from two coordinates that determine its ends.
<!ELEMENT Circulo (Coordenada, Radio)> <!ELEMENT Radio (#PCDATA)>	The circle derives from a coordinate that determines its centre and a number that indicates its radio.
<!ELEMENT Elipse (Coordenada, Coordenada, AnguloInicio, AnguloFin)> <!ELEMENT AnguloInicio (#PCDATA)> <!ELEMENT AnguloFin (#PCDATA)>	The ellipsis derives from the main rectangle within the ellipsis and two angles: an onset angle and an ending angle.
<!ELEMENT Poligono (Coordenada, Coordenada, Coordenada+)>	The polygon derives of the coordinate, which determines its vertexes.
<!ELEMENT Coordenada (Px, Py)> <!ELEMENT Px (#PCDATA)> <!ELEMENT Py (#PCDATA)>	Each coordinate derives from a position in the *X* axis and another in the *Y* axis.
<!ELEMENT EstiloLinea EMPTY> <!ATTLIST EstiloLinea Estilo (continua | discontinua) #REQUIRED >	The style of line admits two values: continuous and discontinuous.
<!ELEMENT AnchoLinea (#PCDATA)>	Size in pixels of the primitive line.
<!ELEMENT ColorLinea (#PCDATA)>	Line color in format RGB XXXXXX
<!ELEMENT ColorRelleno (#PCDATA)>	Filling color in format RGB XXXXXX
<!ELEMENT Posicion (Fija | Relativa)> <!ELEMENT Fija (Coordenada)> <!ELEMENT Relativa (OpCRel?, Coordenada)> <!ELEMENT OpCRel (Centrado | (Justificado, Justificado?))>	The position of a component determines its location within a containing component or within the device. This position may be fixed or relative, signalled by topologic restrictions in the area OpCRel; in any case, this position derives from a coordinate that signals its left top position (with respect to its containing component or else with respect to the visualizing device)

<table>
<tr><td><!ELEMENT Centrado EMPTY>
<!ATTLIST Centrado
Tipo (h | v | a) #REQUIRED
>

<!ELEMENT Justificado (#PCDATA)>
<!ATTLIST Justificado
Tipo (de | iz | su | in)
#REQUIRED
></td><td>The component is centered with respect to its containing component. The centring can be horizontal, vertical or both.

Alignment of the component on the right, left, top or bottom side of its containing component a given number of pixels.</td></tr>
<tr><td><!ELEMENT Tamano (Valorx, Valory)>
<!ATTLIST Tamano
Tipo (fijo | relativo) #REQUIRED
>
<!ELEMENT Valorx (#PCDATA)>
<!ELEMENT Valory (#PCDATA)></td><td>Size of the component within the containing component or within the visualizing device.</td></tr>
<tr><td><!ELEMENT Datos (Tipo?)>
<!ELEMENT Tipo (#PCDATA)>
<!ATTLIST Tipo
Longitud CDATA #IMPLIED
RangoInf CDATA #IMPLIED
RangoSup CDATA #IMPLIED
Decimales CDATA #IMPLIED
></td><td>The conditions to be met by the input and output data in the interface; attributes may vary depending on the type of data.</td></tr>
<tr><td><!ELEMENT Texto (Txt, Fuente, TamanoFuente, ColorFuente, EstiloFuente, Posicion, Tamano)>
<!ATTLIST Texto
Nombre CDATA #REQUIRED
Visible (t | f) #REQUIRED
Activo (t | f) #REQUIRED
>
<!ELEMENT Txt (#PCDATA)>
<!ELEMENT Fuente (#PCDATA)>
<!ELEMENT TamanoFuente (#PCDATA)>
<!ELEMENT ColorFuente (#PCDATA)>
<!ELEMENT EstiloFuente (#PCDATA)></td><td>The textual component is defined by the text that it presents, its kind, size and font colour; besides, it also conveys the characteristics of size and position. The size can be fixed or relative.</td></tr>
</table>

<!ELEMENT Enumeracion (Fichero, Posicion, Tamano)> <!ATTLIST Enumeracion Nombre CDATA #REQUIRED Visible (t | f) #REQUIRED Activo (t | f) #REQUIRED > <!ELEMENT Fichero (#PCDATA)>	The graphic components by enumeration contain the folder's route that contains the corresponding graphic's image.
<!ELEMENT Transiciones (Transicion*)>	
<!ELEMENT Transicion (Precondiciones?)> <!ATTLIST Transicion EstadoInicial CDATA #REQUIRED Elemento CDATA #IMPLIED Evento CDATA #REQUIRED EstadoFinal CDATA #REQUIRED Alcanzable (t | f) #IMPLIED >	Each transition is made of an original transition state, the component (element) over which the event takes place, the event which triggers the transition, and the indicator that signals whether the transition is feasible.
<!ELEMENT Precondiciones (Precondicion+)> <!ELEMENT Precondicion (#PCDATA)> <!ATTLIST Precondicion Visible (t | f) #IMPLIED Activo (t | f) #IMPLIED InfI (t | f) #IMPLIED InfO (t | f) #IMPLIED >	The preconditions indicate the condition/s that must be met for the transition from one state to another to occur.

Table 2. DTD DGAIU-INT

3. Definition of the User Tests

Once the visual user interface is defined, we can proceed to create a notation that will define the tests that must be carried out on a given visual user interface to test its liability. The aim is to record as many parameters and actions as possible and necessary during a user's interaction with a user interface prototype. The DGAUI provides a description of the appearance of the components and the states that may be obtained from a standard rendering device. It also provides renderings of the user tasks and the states that a user can derive by deploying the visual user interface. The first step, then, in automating the evaluation of the visual user interface, and as signalled above, will be to define a notation that may allow us to describe the atomic parts of the evaluation.

As occurred in the case of the DGAUI-DEF, we will use XML in structuring the notation. With this, we will create a DTD that will allow us an easy parsing of notation structures. It is possible to define as many evaluations as it is desired. Each evaluation is formed by a set of user tasks that have to be performed, and the following information should be provided for each of the user tasks:

- A description. (A textual description of the user task for documentation)
- The parameters that have to be assessed and recorded during the evaluation process. These may be *Time Parameters*, for instance, the total amount of time used by the user in accomplishing the task; the time elapsed until the user starts interacting with the task; average time in between events; time elapsed until the first mistake by the user takes place, etc. Other parameters may be *counter parameters*, that is, the number of user events; the number of user mistakes during the evaluation task; the number of times that an error takes place; etc. A final possible parameter to quantify may be the *error parameter*, identifying and controlling types of user mistakes/errors; for example, which is the most frequent user mistake or which is the most frequent mistake or error in a state.
- The different states that a visual user interface will go through during the accomplishment of a task, including a description of the transitions that are generated between states, highlighting the event that must be carried over a given component for the transition to take place. In the prototype that the user will manipulate it will be clearly defined which are the possible states and the resulting transitions.

The description in full of the DTD is as follows:

Item	Description
<!ELEMENT DPU (Prueba)>	Interface test description
<!ELEMENT Prueba (Descripcion,Interfaz,Tareas)> <!ELEMENT Descripcion (#PCDATA)> <!ELEMENT Interfaz (#PCDATA)>	The test is defined departing from a description of the very test, of the identification of the interface over which the test is done and the limitation of the activities that the user will have to perform over it.
<!ELEMENT Tareas (Tarea+)> <!ELEMENT Tarea (Descripcion, Parametros, Estados)>	Each task that the user has to perform as part of the test includes its own descriptions, the parameters that will be measured for the fulfilment of the test and the states to be measured by these parameters.

<table>
<tr><td><!ELEMENT Parametros (Parametro*)>
<!ELEMENT Parametro (Nombre, Tipo, Estado_Inicial, Estado_Final)></td><td>The parameters are identified by a name and belong to a type.</td></tr>
<tr><td><!ELEMENT Nombre (#PCDATA)></td><td>Name of the parameter</td></tr>
<tr><td><!ELEMENT Tipo
(Tiempo | Contador | Error)>

<!ELEMENT Tiempo EMPTY>
<!ATTLIST Tiempo
Caracteristica (TTotal | TPrimerEvento | TMedioEntreEventos | TMedioReaccion | TPrimerError) #REQUIRED
>

<!ELEMENT Contador EMPTY>
<!ATTLIST Contador
Caracteristica (NumEventos | NumErrores | NumOcuError) #REQUIRED
>

<!ELEMENT Error (Descripcion?, ID_Estado?, Evento?, Componente?)>
<!ATTLIST Error
Caracteristica (IdError | EstadoError | ErrorMasFrec) #REQUIRED
>
<!ELEMENT ID_Estado (#PCDATA)></td><td>The parameters can be of three different types:

Time: referring to temporal aspects.

Counter: referring to quantitative values related to the user's actions.

Error: referring to failures occurred during the task's performance.</td></tr>
<tr><td><!ELEMENT Estado_Inicial (#PCDATA)></td><td>State in which the assessment of the parameter begins</td></tr>
<tr><td><!ELEMENT Estado_Final (#PCDATA)></td><td>State in which the assessment of the parameter ends.</td></tr>
<tr><td><!ELEMENT Estados (Estado*)>
<!ELEMENT Estado (Parametros?, Transicion)></td><td></td></tr>
<tr><td><!ELEMENT Transicion (Estado_Inicial, Estado_Final, Componente, Evento)>

<!ELEMENT Componente (#PCDATA)>

<!ELEMENT Evento (#PCDATA)></td><td>The transition is identified by the onset state, the component over which the event must be produced, the event that has to take place and the final state derived from its production</td></tr>
</table>

Table 3. DTD DPU

In the following lines, we provide a detailed description of each ot the parameters that can be assessed:

Time

- Total time (TTotal): time that the user devotes in implementing the task.
- Time Firs Event (TPrimerEvento): Time that the user devotes in accomplishing an event the first time that she/he has contact with the interface.
- Average time between events (TMedioEntreEventos): Time that the user spends in between two successive events.
- Average time of reaction (TMedioReacción): Time that the user takes in accomplishing a new event after making a mistake.

Counter

- Number of events (NumEventos): number of successful and failed events that the user needs to accomplish the task.
- Number of mistakes (NumErrores): total number of mistakes that were generated during the task.
- Number of appearance of the same mistake (NumOcuError): number of times that each mistake has taken place.

Error

- Error identifier(IdError): textual identification of the error.
- Error State(EstadoError): state in which the error has taken place.
- Most frequent error (ErrorMasFrec): the most frequent error in the test.

4. Evaluator for the user's actions (EUA)

The EAU tool allows the user to dynamically evaluate the visual user interface usability. This evaluation is carried out trough an interactive simulation of the interface. From the abstract notation of DGAUI (DGAUI-INT) we can build the visual appearance of the states in the interface and simulate possible user actions over the components. With de EAU notation it becomes possible to define the user tasks that a user can try. The simulation reproduces the visual appearance of the interface following the user tasks described in section 3.

Through the interaction of the user with the simulator, a great amount of information is recorded according to the parameters set forth in section 3. This information is stored in a data base for its future study and analysis. Hence, this tool allows the HCI engineer to define as many assessments as may be thought necessary, obtaining quantitative information about the actual impact of a user on the visual user interface. Normally, the HCI engineer explains to the user which are the aims to be reached while evaluating the visual user interface by means of the prototype. Then, with the information obtained, the HCI engineer can determine if the interface has any problems before starting its coding.

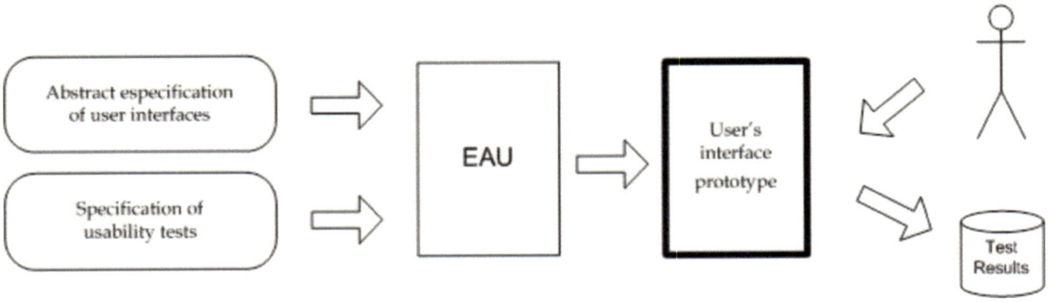

Fig. 1. Schema for the functioning of the EAU tool.

The EAU tool shows a simple interface with two basic functionalities:

- Load Interface: which allows the selection of an XML file that contains the visual user interface description (DGAUI-DEF and GDAUI-INT) and which generates the visual appearance of the states in the user interface.
- Test Interface: necessary in order to evaluate the visual user interface, by selecting the individual user task definitions that complete the evaluation (AEU XML file). By means of these definitions, and through the configuration of the parameters in order to have access to the data base, the simulation is executed. The information about each user's interaction with the prototype is stored in the data base for study.

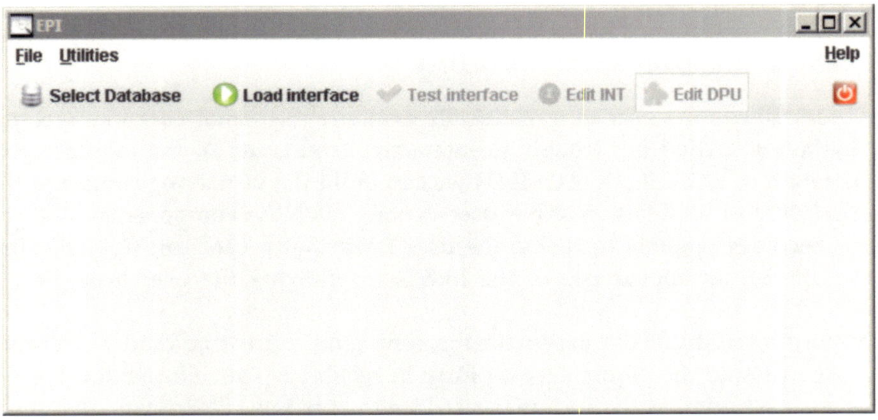

Fig. 2. Main window for the application.

Figure 3 Shows a visual user interface state generated by the EAU tool from a DGAUI description. The interface example corresponds to an average text processor.

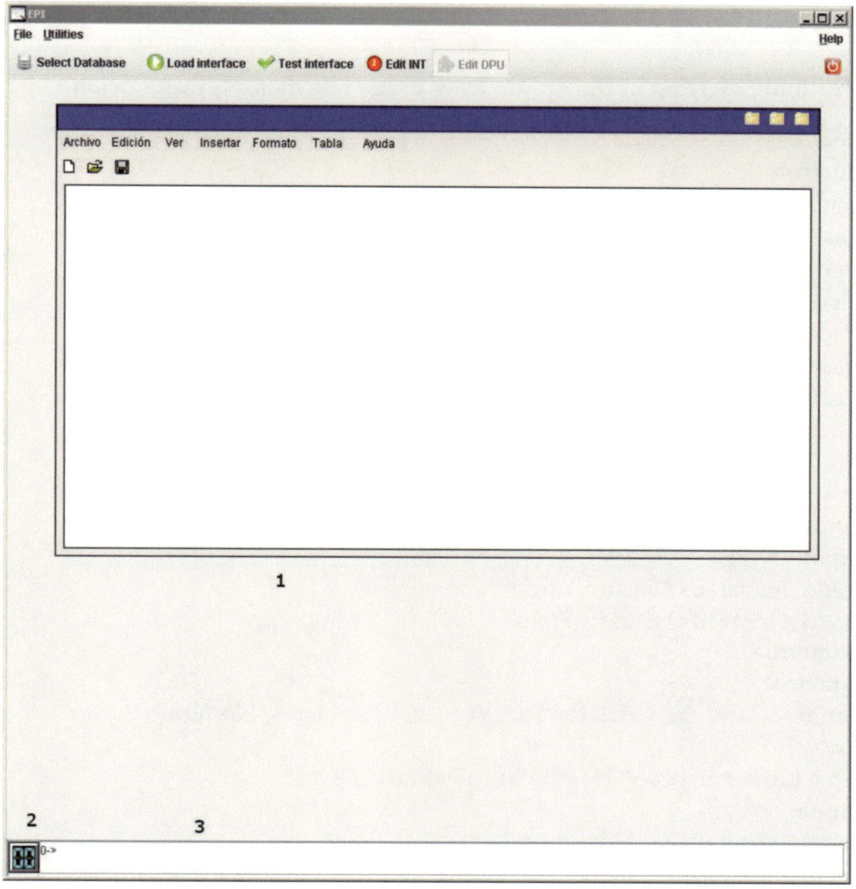

Fig. 3. Text processor prototype.

Zone 1: Shows the interface.
Zone 2: Shows the state that the interface is in.
Zone 3: Shows the record of states that the interface has gone through.

We will here take as an example the definition of a test that will assess the accomplishment of a task consisting on the selection of the option New in the File menu. We will evaluate the following parameters: Total time devoted for the execution of the task; number of events; time in which the first event takes place; average time in between events and total number of errors produced throughout the task.

The defining code is as follows:

```
<?xml version="1.0" encoding="ISO-8859-1"?>
<!DOCTYPE DPU SYSTEM "DPU.dtd">
<DPU>
<Prueba>
 <Descripcion>Prueba1</Descripcion>
 <Interfaz>Editor</Interfaz>
```

```
<Tareas>
 <Tarea>
  <Descripcion>Selection of the option New in the File menu</Descripcion>

  <Parametros>
  <Parametro>
    <Nombre> Total time devoted for the execution of the task </Nombre>
    <Tipo>
     <Tiempo Caracteristica="TTotal"/>
    </Tipo>
    <Estado_Inicial>0</Estado_Inicial>
    <Estado_Final>10</Estado_Final>
   </Parametro>
   <Parametro>
    <Nombre> Number of events </Nombre>
    <Tipo>
     <Contador Caracteristica="NumEventos"/>
    </Tipo>
    <Estado_Inicial>0</Estado_Inicial>
    <Estado_Final>10</Estado_Final>
   </Parametro>
   <Parametro>
    <Nombre> Time in which the first event takes place </Nombre>
    <Tipo>
     <Time Caracteristica=" TMedioEntreEventos "/>
    </Tipo>
    <Estado_Inicial>0</Estado_Inicial>
    <Estado_Final>10</Estado_Final>
   </Parametro>
   <Parametro>
    <Nombre> Average time in between events </Nombre>
    <Tipo>
     <Time Caracteristica=" TMedioEntreEventos "/>
    </Tipo>
    <Estado_Inicial>0</Estado_Inicial>
    <Estado_Final>10</Estado_Final>
   </Parametro>
   <Parametro>
    <Nombre> Total number of errors produced throughout the task </Nombre>
    <Tipo>
     <Contador Caracteristica="NumErrores"/>
    </Tipo>
    <Estado_Inicial>0</Estado_Inicial>
    <Estado_Final>10</Estado_Final>
   </Parametro>
  </Parametros>
```

```
  <Estados>
   <Estado>
    <Transicion>
     <Estado_Inicial>0</Estado_Inicial>
     <Estado_Final>2</Estado_Final>
     <Componente>Marc_Archivo</Componente>
     <Evento>MouseOn</Evento>
    </Transicion>
   </Estado>
   <Estado>
    <Transicion>
     <Estado_Inicial>2</Estado_Inicial>
     <Estado_Final>9</Estado_Final>
     <Componente>Marc_Archivo_Selec</Componente>
     <Evento>LeftClick</Evento>
    </Transicion>
   </Estado>
   <Estado>
    <Transicion>
     <Estado_Inicial>9</Estado_Inicial>
     <Estado_Final>10</Estado_Final>
     <Componente>Menu_Archivo_op_nuevo</Componente>
     <Evento>MouseOn</Evento>
    </Transicion>
   </Estado>
  </Estados>
 </Tarea>
</Tareas>
</Prueba>
</DPU>
```

Once the test is finished, the results would appear on the screen.

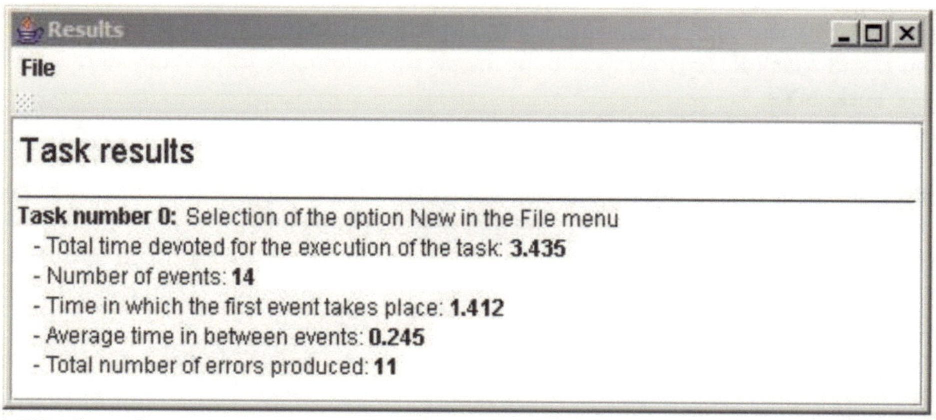

Fig. 4. Window showing the results of the test in EAU

5. Conclusions

In this chapter we have presented an abstract representation of user interfaces particularly designed for visual interactive systems. The focus of this representation has been the visual aspect of the user interface because, for the user, it remains the most important part. It is through the interaction with the appearance of a user interface that the user obtains information from the user interface, and reacts to it.
Another aspect explored in this essay is the relevance of the appearance of the behaviours in the visual user interface components (with varying sizes and positions). Such variations allow for the same state of a component to render different functions.
We have proved that it is possible to describe a set of interface user tasks in a notation; similarly, we have shown how to automatically generate a prototype with which to assess the user interface behaviour with its users and its acceptability by them in a quantitative manner.

6. References

Eason, K. (1988). Information Technology and Organizational Change. Taylor and Francis, London.

Gartner Group (1994). Annual Symposium on the Future of Information Technology, Cannes 7-10 November 1994.

Gómez Carnero, S. (2008). Sistematización de la validación de interacción del usuario sobre la visualización en interfaces de usuario usando especificación abstracta. PhD Thesis. Universidad de Vigo. March 2008.

IBM (1993). IBM Dictionary of Computing. McGraw-Hill.

ISO (1992). Software product evaluation quality characteristics and guidelines for their use.

ISO (1993). Ergonomics Requirements for Office Work with Visual Displays Terminals: Guidance and Usability.

Molich R. y Nielsen J. (1990). Heuristic evaluation of user interfaces. Proceedings of ACM CHI 1990. Seattle, WA, April 1990, Pág. 249-256, 1990.

Myers B. A. y Rosson M. B.(1992). Survey on user interface programming. CHI'92 Conference Proceedings on Human Factors in Computing Systems (Bauersfeld P.,Bennett J. y LYNCH G. eds.), page. 195-202. ACM Press, Nueva York, NY.

Nielsen, J. (1993). Usability Engineering. Academic Press, London.

Nielsen J. and Mack R. L. (1994). Usability Inspection Methods. John Wiley and Sons, New York, NY.

Preece, J., Rogers, Y., Sharp, H., Benyon, D., Holland, S. And Carey Tom. (1994). Human-Computer Interaction. Addison-Wesley Publishing, Reading, Mass.

Rodeiro Iglesias, J. (2001). Representación y análisis de la componente visual de la interfaz de usuarios. PhD Thesis. Universidad de Vigo. September 2001.

Shackel, B. (1986). Ergonomics in designing for usability. In M. D. Harrison and A. Monk, editors. People and Computers: Designing for Usability. Cambridge University Press.

Wharton C. (1994). The cognitive walkthrough method: a practitioner's guide. Usability Inspection Methods (NIELSEN J. y MACK R. L. eds.). John Wiley & Sons, New York, NY, Page. 105-140, 1994.

30

Narration Board as a Design Tool for Visualising Design Concepts for Interface Designers

Chui Yin Wong[1] and Chee Weng Khong[2]
Interface Design Department, Faculty of Creative Multimedia, Multimedia University, 63100 Cyberjaya, Malaysia
{cywong[1]; cwkhong[2]}@mmu.edu.my

1. Introduction

In recent years, user studies have been highly advocated by human-computer interaction (HCI) researchers and practitioners to elicit user requirements for future products and services. In doing so, it is imperative for HCI and design communities to delve into user problems, and gain in-depth understanding of users' behaviour. To translate the data gathered from user studies throughout the design process, scenarios are usually presented as text-based descriptions that depict personas within social contexts. However, scenarios that are depicted in text form have limited communicative values. Text-based scenarios pose problems to the design team as they find it complicated to grasp the gist of ideas and share a common ground across a multi-disciplinary team. A scenario described in text is limited to the fluency and vocabulary of the author, and the subsequent interpretation by its readers.

Having a coherent design vision across a multi-disciplinary team is crucial to streamline the design process. Usually, a multi-disciplinary team is comprised of various backgrounds, such as a project manager, interface designers, graphic artists, human factors specialists, user researchers, technical writers, software developers, engineers and marketing personnel. Moreover, text-based scenarios may not be well comprehended to achieve the high-level product conceptualisation process required for the design team.

To conceptualise user scenarios into visual and textual presentation, the narration board is a powerful design tool to help translate user observation studies into a storytelling format. It also helps to communicate design values and ideas among the design team via visualising user scenarios in its proper context during the early design stages. Hence, an interface designer plays an imperative role in conceptualising ideas and presenting a shared goal in a visualised form, rather than a limited text-based description. As a result, the objectives of this chapter are twofold. The first section discusses the rationale and the context of narration boards. We will highlight how a narration board is a useful design tool to conceptualise and visualise user scenarios for future design concepts in a multi-disciplinary design team. Secondly, this chapter attempts to examine the effectiveness of the narration board by quantifying its narrative components in relation to the attributes of the final design concepts. This is important as we later exhibit the values of the narration board towards communication and sharing of ideas, design principles, and intended lifestyles.

2. Role of Narration or Storytelling

2.1 Rationale of Narration

According to the National Storytelling Network, storytelling is defined as *an ancient art form and a valuable form of human expression.* Storytelling or narration is used interchangeably in this text, which delineates a story that is created in a constructive form (written, spoken, poetry, prose, images, song, theatre or dance) describing a sequence of fictional or non-fictional events. It is an interactive art of using words and actions to reveal the elements and images of a story while encouraging the listener's imagination (National Storytelling Network, n.d.). Basically, storytelling is perceived as an acceptable channel to share similar beliefs and thoughts among a community. In general, stories are easily remembered by society rather than design principles, facts and figures.

There are several reasons why stories are good communication catalysts for a multi-disciplinary design team [Erickson, 1995; Specialist Library Knowledge Management; National Storytelling Network, Society for Storytelling]:

- *Stories communicate ideas holistically, conveying rich yet clear messages.* Thus, they are an excellent way of communicating intricate ideas and concepts in an easy-to-understand format. Therefore, stories allow people to convey tacit knowledge that might otherwise be difficult to articulate.

- *Stories are easily remembered* by people because they are circulated with human passion and emotions. Storytelling looks at objects and events from human perspective, making it easier for people to relate to them.

- *Stories aid in team-building* as it becomes a communication tool to share similar user-activities events and information that help in constructing vision. It eases the communication flow by nurturing a sense of community and help to build relationships, especially in a multi-disciplinary design team.

- *Storytelling provides the context* in which knowledge arises as well as the knowledge itself, and hence it can increase the likelihood of accurate and meaningful transfer of knowledge.

- *Storytelling is interactive.* Storytelling involves a two-way interaction between a storyteller and one or more listeners. The responses of the listeners influence the telling of the story. In fact, storytelling emerges from the interaction and cooperative, coordinated efforts of teller and audience. It is known that different culture and situation creates different expectations for the exact roles of storytellers and listeners, who speak how often and when, for instance, that create different forms of interaction. The interactive nature of storytelling partially accounts for its immediacy and impact, where it directly connect to the teller and audience.

- *Storytelling presents a story.* Storytelling involves the presentation of a story in a narrative form. Stories from a specific culture can be used to provide an insight into that culture. Thus, storytelling develops awareness of historical and global cultures, the need for inter-generational exchange and its rewards. Thus, a storyteller can widen the range of people's emotional, cultural and moral responses.

- *Storytelling is universal.* Stories and storytelling are universal aspects of human communication that connect people through time and across cultures. It works for all age groups from children to adults.

2.2 Narration Board as a Communication Tool

Storytelling has been previously applied in different disciplines such as film, entertainment, education, faith and religion, heath and therapy, library, museum and heritage, knowledge management, business and organisations (Glassner, 2004; Crawford, 2004; Cox and Albert, 2003; Morris, 2003; Booth, 2001; Irving, 2004; Sawin, 2004; Schneider, 2002; Sima and Cordi, 2003; Snowden, 2002; Wacker and Silverman, 2003; Walsh, 2003). Having said this, storytelling has also been adopted in HCI and design communities in a different manner.

HCI researchers and design practitioners recognise the importance of gaining user insight from fieldwork studies. In many ways, user researchers or ethnographers conduct user studies to elicit user requirements during the early stages of the design process. This is meant to have a closer understanding of how users behave and interact with artefacts within the real environment. Such studies will highlight social activities, trends and values, which are then analysed and incorporated in the scenario-building process to depict user personas in the context of use. However, it is rather difficult to communicate user problems and translate user scenarios in its context among a multi-disciplinary design team. Thus, having a unified vision and shared value among a multi-disciplinary team is crucial in making a design project successful. User researchers and interface designers can work collaboratively to transform user stories and formulate user scenarios into visual presentation form. As a result, narration (or story) board is a powerful design tool to translate the user insight in a cross-multidisciplinary team.

At the Interface Design (ID) Department, we worked closely with Telenor Research and Innovation Asia Pacific (TRICAP) for a design project with the theme *"Digital Communities"* in 2006-2007. Thirty-six (36) design projects were successfully completed. During the panel judgement session, narration boards were used as one of the persuasive design tools to present user scenarios, and also to highlight possible design solutions to solve the exhibited user problems (see Figure 1 and 2). Out of the 36 design projects, five (5) best design projects were shortlisted for presentation among the TRICAP staff and management team (see Figure 3, 4 and 5). Narration boards were used as a communication tool for pitching ideas to convince the management team about the novelty of the design project's solutions. All narration boards were illustrated with user scenarios in context.

Fig. 1. Narration board being used as a communication tool to highlight user problems and user scenarios during a design judging panel session (courtesy of ID/FCM, 2009).

Fig. 2. An Interface designer presenting user scenarios with the aid of narration boards (courtesy of ID/FCM, 2009).

Fig. 3. A team of interface designers pitching their design ideas using narration boards to the TRICAP management team (courtesy of ID/FCM, 2009).

Fig. 4. Narration boards are used to communicate the ideas across the management team during a design presentation (courtesy of ID/FCM, 2009).

Fig. 5. The audience were engaged with user stories illustrated in the narration boards (courtesy of ID/FCM, 2009).

3. Narration in the Design Context

3.1 Narration in the Design Process

Narration has been used and applied in different stages of the design process. van der Lelie (2006) described the value of storyboards in the product design process. The term "storyboard" is used instead of narration board. In each phase of the design process, the form of storyboards has its own style of exploring, developing, discussing or presenting the product-user interactions. The design process ranges from *analysis, synthesis, simulation, evaluation* to *decision* phase. The consideration of visualisation style is illustrated differently in relation to design activities, purpose/goals, and its representation form in each phase of design process (van der Lelie, 2006).

Despite that, there is a fascinating interest in exploring the context of use via ethnographic studies. There is also a noticeable lack of ability in articulating the problem-user concept, and how the information shown by the narration board can be used in the design process (Pedell and Vetere, 2005). At ID Department, we adopt a User Interface Design (UID) Process (Figure 6) across all the design projects (Wong, Khong and Thwaites, 2008). Here, we focus and discuss how narration boards are used in the interface design process at the early stages of concept design for ideation purposes instead of following through the whole UID process. Figure 7 shows the brief requirements in the conceptual design phase for interface designers.

There are two types of narration boards being adopted, which are the Narration Board (pre-ideation) and Narration Board (post-ideation) (Wong and Khong, 2007). For the Narration Board (pre-ideation), interface designers are required to translate the results of observation studies, lifestyles, moods and market research into problem scenarios highlighting the problems or any issues that users face in the real environment. Different design aids such as mood boards, product design specifications, and product positioning are also developed in assisting designers to achieve a holistic grasp on the concept designs being developed. The interface designers will then be required to produce another Narration Board (post-ideation) to project how their concept designs will be used in future scenarios.

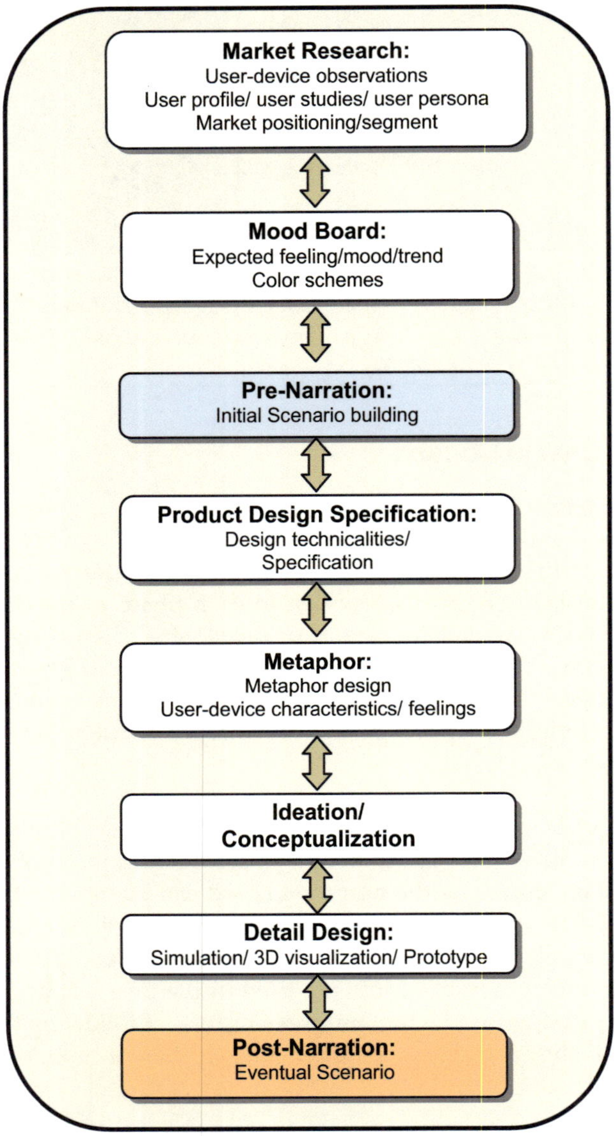

Fig. 6. A simplified User Interface Design Process (UID) Model diagram showing the design tools and human factors techniques applied across the design process (Wong, Khong and Thwaites, 2008).

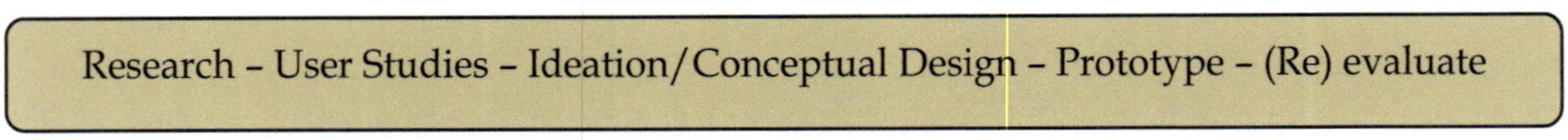

Fig. 7. Brief Conceptual Design Phase (Wong and Khong, 2007).

In the realm of interface design, communication between designers and other team members are important for a successful design project. Narration board is a valuable design tool to the design team as it provides a common visual-based medium to share the common understanding of future design developments.

Conventionally, scenarios are illustrated in textual descriptions to portray user-interaction scenarios (Rosson and Carroll, 2002). For designers, visual-based mediums are important to assist them in 'visualising' and developing ideations for future design solutions. In such circumstances, scenarios described in visual forms accompanied by text explanations serve the communication purpose within the design team. Nonetheless, visual-based narrative is a valuable aid in provoking the thinking process, evoking ideations and to spur creativity to higher levels for interface designers. Van der Lelie (2006) highlighted the value of storyboards in product design process, particularly for product designers in understanding the product-user interaction in context. She mentioned that a product design storyboard is powerful means to the designer, simply because it enables the reader access to the expressed ideas on two levels:

(i) The reader can *experience* the visualised interactions by empathising with the user or the situation. This help(s) to establish a common ground, which supports communication within the design team about each member's thoughts. These thoughts could be difficult to communicate in the abstract form due to individual's different disciplines.
(ii) The reader can *reflect* on the visualised interactions from his or her own expertise, by withdrawing the experience and looking at the unfolding event. It was highlighted that storyboard represents many of the important aspects of the contexts in visual form, and to supports analysis and elicit discussions, and inform the team members in picking up certain aspects of interaction by referring to the issues or areas of concentration in visual form.

3.2 Adoption of Narration or Storytelling into User Scenarios

As described in earlier section, storytelling has been widely adopted in different disciplines, particularly in film, animation, education, design and business. For instance, Walt Disney uses storyboards for creating motion pictures and animation characters in their film production process. In the real business world, multi-national companies like IBM's Knowledge Socialisation Project use storytelling to share business visions within the organizations. Instructional designers may use storyboards to create learning objects for courseware design whilst developing educational systems.

In design practice, storytelling has been used by designers to share the conceptual design prototypes and design solutions across the design team. Stories and event scenarios are collected from observational fieldwork studies to share user behaviour, cultural belief, and insight to the whole design team for design strategy. Stories are concrete accounts of particular people and events, in particular situations; scenarios are often more abstract and they are scripts of events that may leave out details of history, motivation, and personality (Erickson, 1995). Despite the differences, storytelling and scenarios are intertwined and both are difficult to be distinguished as design stories or user-interaction scenarios.

In the user requirement stage, user researchers collect user stories and observational information from fieldwork studies. Observational data is then translated and analysed into various themes and consumer insights. This helps to create realistic example and build scenarios as shared stories in the design team. User profiles, characters and goals form personas in scenario-building process. Cooper (1999) first proposed the concept of persona and it has widely applied in academic and industrial practice and the concept has been integrated in various design projects. In essence, persona is an archetype person representing a user profile whereas scenarios inherently describe how a person interacts with the product in the context of use.

As mentioned in 2.1 section, stories are easily memorized by people, the medium of presenting storytelling are crucial in making the stories memorable and the shared visions are inherently comprehended within the design team. Rosson and Carroll (2002) described user-interaction scenarios are setting, actors, task goals, plans, evaluation, actions and events. However, the design scenario activities are illustrated in conventional text-based description, embedding characteristic elements of user interaction scenarios. We are particularly interested to translate user stories into narration boards to assist interface designers in conceptualising final design concepts. It is always a challenge for designers to grasp the user problems and brainstorm ideas in order to produce design solutions. Thus, next section describes how narrative scenarios are illustrated in pictorial form to conceptualise high-level of user-interaction scenarios.

3.3 Types of Narration Boards

Several types of medium have been used to illustrate narration or storytelling in either analogue or digital format such as hand drawing, sketching, photography and video (Cheng, 2006; van der Lelie, 2006). There are some software tools developed for storytelling such as DEMAIS (Bailey, Konstan and Carlis, 2001), and Comic Book Creator™. In developing narration boards, the interface designers are required to consider the characteristics of user personas, scenarios and context of use. They are able to select any medium of communication to illustrate the narrative scenarios. Due to time and cost considerations, hand sketching, marker rendering and drawing on layout pads are the most cost-effective way. The designers then scan their narrative scenarios into digital formats, which can then be posted online for sharing purposes. Alternatively, the interface designers can transfer the photographs they have captured during their observation studies using graphical software such as Adobe Flash™, Adobe Photoshop™ or Comic Book Creator™.

Narration boards also play an important role in bridging the communication gap between the design team and other corporate departments such as top management, manufacturing department and the clients themselves. Pedell and Vetere (2005) also illustrated how picture scenarios were used to represent context in design process. Generally, there are two types of narration boards, which are Narration Board (pre-ideation) and Narration Board (post-ideation).

(i) *Narration Board (pre-ideation)*: For top management and the clients, they usually do not have ample time to go through the detailed design levels. Hence, narration board assists in projecting the problem scenarios of the user experience, particularly at the user requirement stage. This is illustrated in the Narration Board (pre-ideation) (Figure 8). An example of the E-Hovx project depicts a scenario faced by a primary school pupil encountering danger as he is robbed on his way home from school.

(ii) *Narration Board (post-ideation)*: On the other hand, top management and clients will be able to grasp the design solutions from the illustration of how the intended users interacting with the new product design concepts or design solutions in the future scenarios as demonstrated in Narration Board (post-ideation) (Figure 9). Figure 9 shows how the concept of the E-Hovx device assisting in the scenario by producing an alarm to alert the pupil and to ward off any potential harm.

Fig. 8. An example of a Narration Board (pre-ideation) is depicting a scenario of a primary school pupil who is robbed on the way to home from school (courtesy of ID/FCM, 2009).

Fig. 9. An example of Narration Board (post-ideation) illustrating a scenario of how E-Hovx plays as a role in protecting the primary pupil from a potential robbery (courtesy of ID/FCM, 2009).

4. Evaluating Narration Board for Visualising Final Design Concept

4.1 Method

In order to evaluate how narration boards (pre-ideation) are effective design tools in assisting interface designers for generating ideations and visualizing final design concepts, an empirical study was conducted. The study examines the relation between the two variables of narration boards and final design concepts. The study considered twenty (20) different design projects developed by interface designers as test subjects (sample size N=20) at the Interface Design Department (Wong and Khong, 2007). Based on the above description, the null hypothesis (Ho) is "there is no relation between narration board and final design concept". The alternative hypothesis (H1) is where 'there is a positive association between the narration boards (pre-ideation) with final design concept for a design project.'

To produce a successful narration board, there are certain elements to be highlighted by the designers. Truong, Hayes and Abowd (2006) highlighted that there are five significant elements for a narration board to convey its narrative across to the design team. The five elements of Narration Board are described as follows:

(i) *Level of detail:* the level of detail presents in a storyboard must take into account how many objects and actors might be present in a particular frame, the level of photorealism incorporated by the designer, and the designer's choice to display the entire scene or only details of the interface.

(ii) *Inclusion of text:* designers can include text either through tagline narrations for each pane or within individual frames as speech, thought bubbles, or labels and signs that would be present in the real life environment depicted in the storyboard. Alternately, designers can choose to depict the story entirely using visual elements with no text.

(iii) *Inclusion of people and emotions:* storyboards can include renditions of human users demonstrating interactions with an interface. Designers can also use these characters to build empathy for potential users, display motivation, or convey other intangible elements, such as how the application affects the user. Alternatively, designers can also build empathy by removing people entirely and drawing the interaction as though the reader is the actor.

(iv) *Number of frames:* the number of different panels present in a single storyboard can vary anywhere between 1 and more than 20 frames, although the majority of storyboards we collected included between 3 and 6 frames, noted by experts to be the optimal size for conveying a single feature or activity. Multiple features and activities were usually depicted in multiple storyboards.

(v) *Portrayal of time:* designers can explicitly indicate time passing within a storyboard or use transitions that convey changes over time, and may include indicators of a known event, festival, age, or season.

On the other hand, there are also 5 attributes that determine how usable and functional the final design concepts are deriving from the input of the narration board. These 5 attributes of generating Final Design Concept in the later conceptual design stage are:

(i) *Form and functionality:* shape and structure of an object; physical, functional, and performance characteristics or specifications that uniquely identify a component or device and determine its interchange-ability in a product or system. The belief is that the shape of an artefact or interface should have an intrinsic relationship to its intended function or purpose. Especially in interface design, the design of an artefact or interface is more often than not intended to achieve a purpose, task or usage.

(ii) *Usability (ease of use):* usability is defined as the 'effectiveness, efficiency, and satisfaction with which a specified set of users can achieve a specified set of tasks in a particular environment (International Organisation for Standardization (ISO), 1998). The final design concept is examined based on how usable is the design for its targeted users to achieve the product's goal and tasks.

(iii) User-artefact illustration: the final design solution is usually illustrated in visual form either in two- or three-dimension (2D or 3D). It is essential to portray and depict how the intended user may interact with the final design concept. For this, designers adopt and apply the sketch analysis technique to illustrate user-artefact interactions. Basically,

sketch analysis (Stolpmann and Roller 1993; Arnheim 1996) is a technique of applying skills and experience in sketching human forms so as to study and visualise human-device interaction. It allows designers to utilise their drawing skills in visualising body positions, form and pose especially on parts of the body that humans utilise to interact with their environment. This method elicits visual analysis and design feedback of users with the future product.

(iv) *Product semantics:* Krippendorff and Butter (1989) defines product semantics as a systematic inquiry into how people attribute meanings to artefacts and interact with them accordingly and as a vocabulary and methodology for designing artefacts in view of the meanings they could acquire for their users and the communities of their stakeholders. Users generally understand artefacts by their interfaces, and sometimes how the artefact presents to the user may indicate its affordance. In this case, the meaning of an artefact used highlights the range of imaginable senses and actions that users can expect. Interfaces need to be designed in the way of producing 'an intrinsically motivating interaction between human actors and their artefacts (Krippendorff and Butter, 1989; Krippendorff, 2006).'

(v) *Design appeal (emotional and mood):* an emotion is a mental and physiological state associated with a wide variety of feelings, thoughts, and behaviour. Scherer (2003) defined emotion as episodes of massive, synchronized recruitment of mental and somatic resources allowing to adapt to or cope with a stimulus event subjectively appraised as being highly pertinent to the needs, goals, and values of the individuals. Design appeal indicates emotions that always imply and involve a relation between the person experiencing them and a particular object whether s/he is afraid or proud of something (Desmet, 2003). The attribute of design appeal is to facilitate the relationships between the final design concepts (products) and user responses with regards to emotion or mood.

This study looks at 20 design projects (DP) developed by interface designers addressing a design theme titled *i-Companion* (Wong and Khong, 2007). The DPs were selected based on the inclusion of the Narration Board (pre-ideation) and final design concepts from the design process. To quantify the effectiveness of the narration board, the usability specialists justified the scores based on a 1-5 point Likert scale (1 is the least, 5 is the most applicable of applying the elements) on the elements of the narration board. The elements look at level of detail, inclusion of text, inclusion of people and emotions, number of frames, and portrayal of time. Subsequently, a final score was given on the 20 DPs respectively based on the sum of the 5 narration board elements. On the other hand, to evaluate the output of final design concepts, the final design concept scores were calculated with the total sum of the 5 attributes, that is form and functionality, usability, user-artefact illustration, product semantics, and design appeal (emotional and mood) on the 20 DPs respectively.

4.2 Results of Pre-Narration Boards and Final Design Concepts

The table below (table 1) shows the summary of the final scores of narration board and final design concepts for the 20 DPs.

Design Project (DP)	Narration Board Scores (N)	Final Design Concept Scores (C)
DP 1	16	13
DP 2	17	18
DP 3	12	12
DP 4	10	9
DP 5	12	7
DP 6	8	7
DP 7	19	12
DP 8	13	7
DP 9	10	10
DP 10	12	13
DP 11	18	21
DP 12	12	8
DP 13	9	5
DP 14	5	5
DP 15	12	15
DP 16	12	11
DP 17	15	15
DP 18	14	16
DP 19	17	16
DP 20	16	17

Table 1. A summary of the final scores on Narration Board and Final Design Concepts for 20 Design Projects.

Table 2 below shows a random selection of the Narration Boards (pre-ideation) and Final Design Concept for the *'i-Companion'* design project:

<table>
<tr><th>Design Projects</th><th>Final Design Concepts</th></tr>
<tr><td>

<u>Design Project (DP) 1:</u>

</td><td>

</td></tr>
</table>

Design Project (DP) 5:

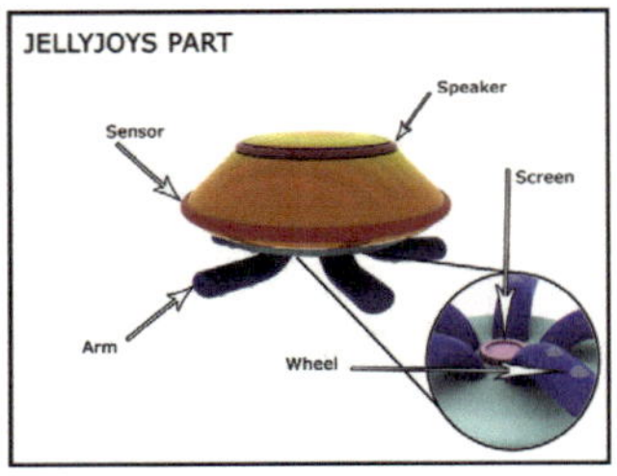

Design Project (DP) 11:

Design Project (DP) 15:

Design Project (DP) 17:

Design Project (DP) 18:

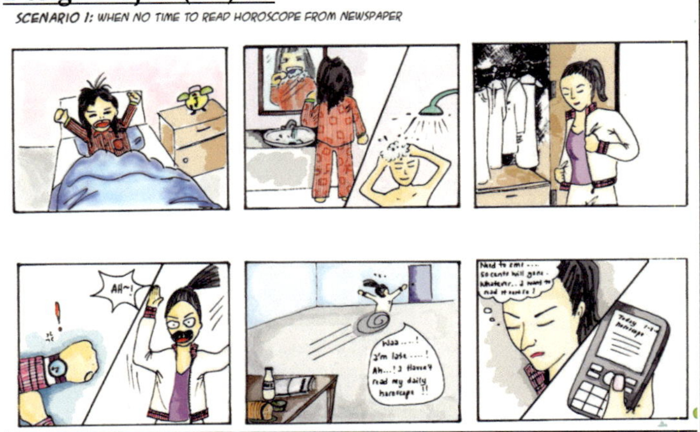

Design Project (DP) 20:

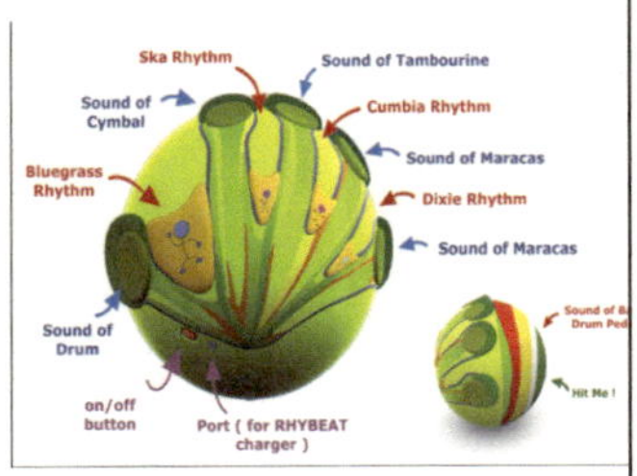

Table 2. Some examples of Narration Boards (pre-ideation) and Final Design Concepts for *'i-Companion'* Design Project (courtesy of ID/FCM, 2009).

5. Data Analysis and Discussions

To examine the association of both the variables narration board and final design concept, non-parametric Spearman's Rho test was carried out to study the correlation coefficient for the sample size (N) of 20. The diagram below (table 3) shows the correlation matrix of the two variables (scores of narration board and final design concept). From the diagram, there is a statistically significant positive correlation between narration board and final design concept scores (rho=0.78, df = 18, p<0.001). Thus, those with higher scores in terms of the narration board components tend to produce better final design concepts, and vice versa.

Correlations

			Narration Scores	Concept Scores
Spearman's rho	Narration Scores	Correlation Coefficient	1.000	.775**
		Sig. (2-tailed)	.	.000
		N	20	20
	Concept Scores	Correlation Coefficient	.775**	1.000
		Sig. (2-tailed)	.000	.
		N	20	20

**. Correlation is significant at the 0.01 level (2-tailed).

Table 3. Spearman's correlation produced by Correlate for the two variables (narration board and final design concept).

In order to examine whether there is a curvilinear relationship or any outliers on a correlation, the final scores of two variables (narration board scores and final design concept scores) were reported in a scatterplot diagram (Figure 10). From the diagram, there was no evidence of a curvilinear relationship or the undue influence of outliers.

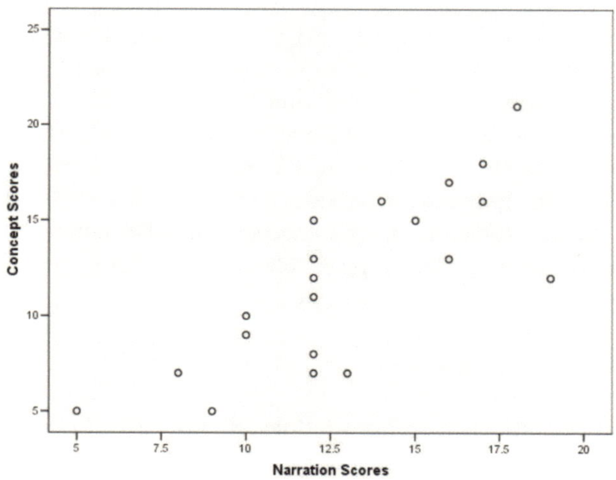

Fig. 10. A scatterplot diagram showing the relation of narration board scores and final design concept scores for 20 design projects.

Apparently, the result shows that there is statistically significant positive relation between the two variables of narration board and final design concept. In other words, the higher scores of narration board would have the tendency of producing higher scores for the final design concepts as well. This is proven true where an interface designer, who is proficient in applying his or her design skills whilst possessing high levels of creativity, will usually be articulate enough to generate better design solutions and usable final design concepts. The creation of the narration board by designers requires them to be skilful in several areas such as 2D-3D visualisation, composition (still images and video), presentation techniques (marker rendering, colouring,), photography, compilation, and storytelling. It is really up to the individual designer to select the best method to convey the narrative. As mentioned in the earlier text, the narration can be produced in digital or analogue formats. Nevertheless, it is found that skilful designers tend to select the mediums and methods of conveying storytelling in reflection of their personal maturity in the design sense, thus seemingly creating a correlation to their final design output.

However, there are some instances such as that exhibited by DP 5 and DP 8 indicating higher scores in the narration board while achieving lower scores in the final design concept. The reason for this is mainly due to time constraints faced by the interface designers having spent too much time and effort in producing the narration board (pre-ideation) and other design tools, resulting in lesser time to formulate complete ideations at the final design stage. As good as the narration gets, designers sometimes tend to get too involved in the process and misjudge the required timeline in producing the overall final design proposals. This is the case for designers of DP5 and DP8.

DP13 and DP14 scored the lowest for Narration Board, and noticeably similar low scores for their respective final design concept scores. Although DP13 applied photography in the pre- and post-ideation Narration Boards, the storytelling largely lacks the level of detail and a very poor treatment of highlighting the problems faced by the user. The final design was poorly developed and does not highlight enough details, such as in its form, functionality, overall design appeal, usability and selection of colour, in answering the user problems displayed by the pre-ideation Narration Board. On the whole, the solution provided by the final design concept was not coherent with the design theme of *i-Companion*. DP14, on the other hand, provided a very poor presentation of the pre- and post-ideation Narration Boards. The designer did not attempt to provide the detail and effort in storytelling the user problems in a concise manner. In addition, the designer's treatment on the boards was mostly using a soft pencil and colour pencils, and lacked the rigour in storytelling. In a somewhat similar fashion, the final design concept was also not well conceived and was poor in its selection of form, design appeal, selection of colour, overall visualisation, and detailing.

Two high scoring Narration Board design projects are DP7 and DP11 respectively. Although DP7 provided a storytelling more in textual form, its Narration Board communicated poorly in visual means lacking the way of projecting emotion and humanistic values into its storytelling. The designer was careful in the textual description, but it was obvious that that was still somewhat inadequate to portray the overall user problem. The final concept design output from DP7 also lacked design appeal and treatment as compared to DP11. On the other hand, DP11 provided a very rich and balanced storytelling. The level of visual detail, emotions and humanistic considerations seems to carry forward into the formulation of the final design consideration.

The general observations gathered from this study tend to imply that the more elements of the Narration Board are applied, the higher the impact and the better the design solutions will be formulated by the interface designers. For instance, the pre-ideation narration board in Figure 8 reveals that there were certain level of details applied in narration board such as richness in colour, 8 narrated frames in sequence with number order, appropriate text inclusion in dialogues, portrayal of time and location, facial expression of users in the scenarios, issues highlighted in the user-scenario context revealing user requirements for problem-solving solutions. As a result, a device called *E-Hovx* was produced as the final design concept to help solve the pre-scenarios as shown in Figure 9. The *E-Hovx* device was also produced in high resolution 3D modelling and final prototype using Rapid Prototyping machine for detailed visualization and testing purpose.

6. Conclusion

In general, narration boards provide a visual reference for interface designers in terms of illustrating user problems via scenarios and a medium to promote future user-interaction scenarios. In many ways, its approach is visually tacit. When applied in a holistic manner, narration boards are powerful visual communication aids that can provide input towards design strategies. Its use not only benefits the design team but also helps to convey ideations to top management and to clients. It is proven that designers are more panache and creative in employing mixed mediums for producing narration boards. In a nutshell, a narration board with the required components of level of detailing, inclusion of text, inclusion of people and emotions, appropriate number of frames and portrayal of time will greatly help in visualising and generating final design concepts for interface designers.

Having said this, future studies will examine the relation of each component of the narration board with the attributes of the final design concepts. The future study will also cover which components will affect and result in the most usable and effective final design concept output. Apart from this, various expert opinions from multi-disciplinary team will be gathered to examine the uptake of narration board in visualising final design solutions in practice.

7. Acknowledgements

The authors would like to express gratitude to the staff and ID students involved in the *i-Companion* design projects at the Interface Design Department (ID), Faculty of Creative Multimedia (FCM) at Multimedia University (MMU) Malaysia. We also wish to thank our industrial collaborator, Telenor Research and Innovation Asia Pacific (TRICAP) for supporting our design efforts as mentioned in the paper.

8. Disclaimer

The authors wish to emphasize that the names and images shown in this paper are only for training and educational purposes, and does not intentionally infringe the rights of individuals or organisations. Any company names, registered trademarks or commercial names mentioned or shown in the text solely belong to their respective owners, organisations and institutions.

9. References

Arhnheim, R. (1996). Sketching and the psychology of design. In: Margolin, V and Buchanan, R (eds). *The idea of design: a Design Issues reader*, pp. 70-74, MIT Press, Cambridge, Mass.

Bailey, B., Konstan, J., and Carlis, J. (2001). DEMAIS: Designing Multimedia Applications with Interactive Storyboards. In *MM01*, pp. 241-250, Ottawa, Canada, Sept. 30 - Oct 5, 2001, ACM, New York.

Booth, E. (2001). *The Everyday Work of Art: Awakening the Extraordinary in Your Daily Life*, iUniverse.com, Inc., ISBN 0-595-19380-3, Lincoln, NE

Cheng, K. (2006). *Storytelling Techniques Workshop*. Available online at http://www.ok-cancel.com/archives/article/2006/02/storytelling-techniques-workshop.html

Comic Book Creator. Available online at http://www.planetwidegames.com

Cooper, A. (1999). *The Inmates are running the asylum*. SAMS, Indiana

Cox, A. M. and Albert, D. H. (eds.) (2003). *The Healing Heart – Families: Storytelling to Encourage Caring and Healthy Families and The Healing Heart – Communities: Storytelling to Build Strong and Healthy Communities*, New Society Publishers, ISBN 0-86571-466-5 and 0-86571-468-1.

Crawford, C. (2004). *Chris Crawford on interactive storytelling*, New Riders Games, ISBN 0321278909

Desmet, P.M.A. (2003). A multilayered model of product emotions. *The Design Journal*, vol. 6, no. 2, pp.4-13

Erickson, T. (1995). *Notes on Design Practice: Stories and Prototypes as Catalysts for Communication*. Available online at http://www.pliant.org/personal/Tom_Erickson/Stories.html

Glassner, A. (2004). *Interactive Storytelling: Techniques for 21st Century Fiction*, AK Peters, ISBN 1568812213

IBM Knowledge Socialization Project. Available online at http://www.research.ibm.com/knowsoc/

Irving, J. (2004). *Stories Never Ending: A Program Guide for Schools and Libraries*, Libraries Unlimited, ISBN 1-56308-997-1, Westport, CT

International Organization for Standardization (ISO) (1998). *Ergonomic requirements for office work with visual display terminals (VDTs) - Part 11: Guidance on Usability (ISO 9241-11:1998)*, Geneva.

Khong, C.W. (2000). A Review of Applied Ergonomics Techniques Adopted by Product Designers. In: Lim, K.Y. et. al. (ed.): *Proceedings of 4th APCHI and 6th ASEAN Ergonomics 2000 (APCHI/SEAES 2000)*, pp. 317-322, Elsevier, Singapore.

Krippendorff, K. (2006). *The Semantic Turn.* CRC Press, ISBN 0-415-32220-0, Boca Raton, Florida

Krippendorff, K. and Butter, R. (Eds.) (1989). Product Semantics. *Design issues,* vol. 5, no. 2, pp. 83

Morris, D. (2003). *Marketing Strategy: A Storytelling Approach,* University of New Haven Press, ISBN 0-936285-29-x, West Haven, CT

National Storytelling Network (n.d.) *What is storytelling?* Available at http://www.storynet.org/resources/knowledgebank/whatisstorytelling.html (access on February 2009)

Pedell, S. and Vetere, F. (2005). Visualizing use context with picture scenarios in the design process. In *Proceedings of the 7th International Conference on Human-computer Interaction with mobile device & services (Mobile HCI 2005),* pp. 271-274, Salzburg, Austria

Rosson, M. and Carroll, J. (2002). *Usability Engineering: Scenario-based Development of Human-computer Interaction,* Morgan Kauffman Publishers, San Francisco

Sawin, P. (2004) *Listening for a Life: A Dialogic Ethnography of Bessie Eldreth through Her Songs and Stories,* Utah State University Press, ISBN 0-87421-582-X, Logan, UT

Scherer, K R. (2003). Introduction: Cognitive components of emotion. In R. J. Davidson, H. Goldsmith, K. R. Scherer (Eds.). *Handbook of the Affective Sciences,* pp. 563-571, Oxford University Press, New York and Oxford

Schneider, W. (2002). *So They Understand: Cultural Issues in Oral History,* Utah State University Press, ISBN 0-87421-550-1, Logan, UT

Sima, J. and Cordi, K. (2003). *Raising Voices: Creating Youth Storytelling Groups and Troupes,* Libraries Unlimited, ISBN 1-56308-919-X, Westport, CT

Society for Storytelling. Using storytelling in Museums: why tell stories in museums. Available at http://sfs.org.uk/special_interest_groups/museums_and_heritage/using_storytellers_in_museums/ (access at February 2009)

Stolpmann, M and Roller, D. (1993). Sketching editor for engineering design. Advances in Human Factors. Special issue on HCI: Software and Hardware from the *Proceedings of the 5th International Conference Interaction,* pp.609-614, 8-13th August, 1993, Orlando, Florida.

Snowden, D. (2002). Narrative Patterns: uses of story in the third age of knowledge management. *Journal of Information and Knowledge Management,* vol. 1, no. 1, pp.1-6

Specialist Library Knowledge Management. *Storytelling.* Available at http://www.nelh.nhs.uk/knowledge_management/km2/storytelling_toolkit.asp

Truong, K.N., Hayes, G. R. and Abowd, G. D. (2006). Storyboarding: An Empirical Determination of Best Practices and Effective Guidelines. In: Carroll, J. (ed): *Proceedings of the 6th ACM conference on Designing Interactive Systems,* pp. 12-21, ACM Press, University Park, PA, USA

van der Lelie, C. (2006). The value of storyboards in the product design process. *Personal and Ubiquitous Computing,* Vol. 10, Issue 2, (Jan 2006) 159-162

Wacker, M. B. and Silverman, L. L. (2003). *Stories Trainers Tell: 55 Ready-to-Use Stories to Make Training Stick,* Jossey-Bass, ISBN 0-7879-6436-0, Pfeiffer

Walsh, J. (2003). *The Art of Storytelling: Easy Steps to Presenting an Unforgettable Story,* Moody Publishers, ISBN 0-8024-3306-5, Chicago

Wong, C.Y. and Khong, C.W. (2007). Quantifying the Narration Board for Visualising Final Design Concepts by Interface Designers, In: Julie Jacko (ed.), *Proceedings of Human-computer Interaction: 12th International Conference, HCI International 2007, LNCS 4550*, pp.1240-1249, ISBN 978-3-540-73104-7, Beijing, China, July 22-27, Springer, Berlin, Heidelberg

Wong, C.Y., Khong, C.W. and Thwaites, H. (2008). Applying User Interface Design Process Model for a Mobile Community Project for the Deaf. International Journal of Interactive Mobile Technologies (iJIM), vol. 2, no. 4, October 2008, pp. 30-37, ISSN: 1865-7923